Paulina Mayo

Empezando a redactar

CECILIA BEUCHAT
CLEMENTINA MALDONADO

Editorial Andrés Bello
Barcelona • Buenos Aires • México D.F. • Santiago de Chile

Este texto ha sido aprobado como Material Didáctico Complementario y de Consulta de la Educación Chilena, para la enseñanza del Castellano, a nivel de 3° y 4° Año Básico, por orden N° 0134, de la Dirección de Educación del Ministerio de Educación.

Primera edición, 1982
Segunda edición, 1983
Tercera edición, 1987
Cuarta edición, 1988
Quinta edición, 1990
Sexta edición, 1991
Séptima edición, 1992
Octava edición, 1992
Novena edición, 1993
Décima edición, 1994
Undécima edición, 1995
Duodécima edición, 1996
Decimotercera edición, 1998

Av. Ricardo Lyon 946, Santiago de Chile

Inscripción N° 55.005

Se terminó de imprimir esta decimotercera edición de 5.000 ejemplares en el mes de febrero de 1998

Ilustraciones de Marta Carrasco

IMPRESORES: Impreandes Presencia S. A.

IMPRESO EN COLOMBIA / PRINTED IN COLOMBIA

ISBN: 956-13-0361-2

Para nuestros hijos Fernando, Claudia y Pablo, y para todos aquellos niños que desean y sienten la necesidad de expresar sus pensamientos y sentimientos por escrito.
Para los profesores que tienen la misión de ayudar en esta tarea.

ÍNDICE

Este libro pertenece a

....

¡Hola! ¿Qué tal?

Este libro es para ti. Esperamos que resulte muy entretenido.

Te vamos a presentar a unos personajes que van a aparecer de vez en cuando. Ellos quieren acompañarte a través de estas páginas, y ayudarte si es necesario.

MIGUEL Y EL MARCIANO

Miguel estaba un día en su pieza muy, pero muy aburrido. Ya había hecho todas sus tareas. Los niños del barrio no estaban, y había que esperar el cumpleaños para recibir ese hermoso libro que mamá le prometiera.

Estaba tendido sobre su cama cuando, de pronto, vio algo que lo dejó asombrado. En la ventana había...

¡¡¡UN MARCIANO!!!

Tal cual como lo lees... ¿Te imaginas? Uno igual a esos que salen en la televisión y en algunos libros.

Miguel abrió la ventana y se encontró con este marciano que, por lo demás, tenía cara de ser muy amistoso.

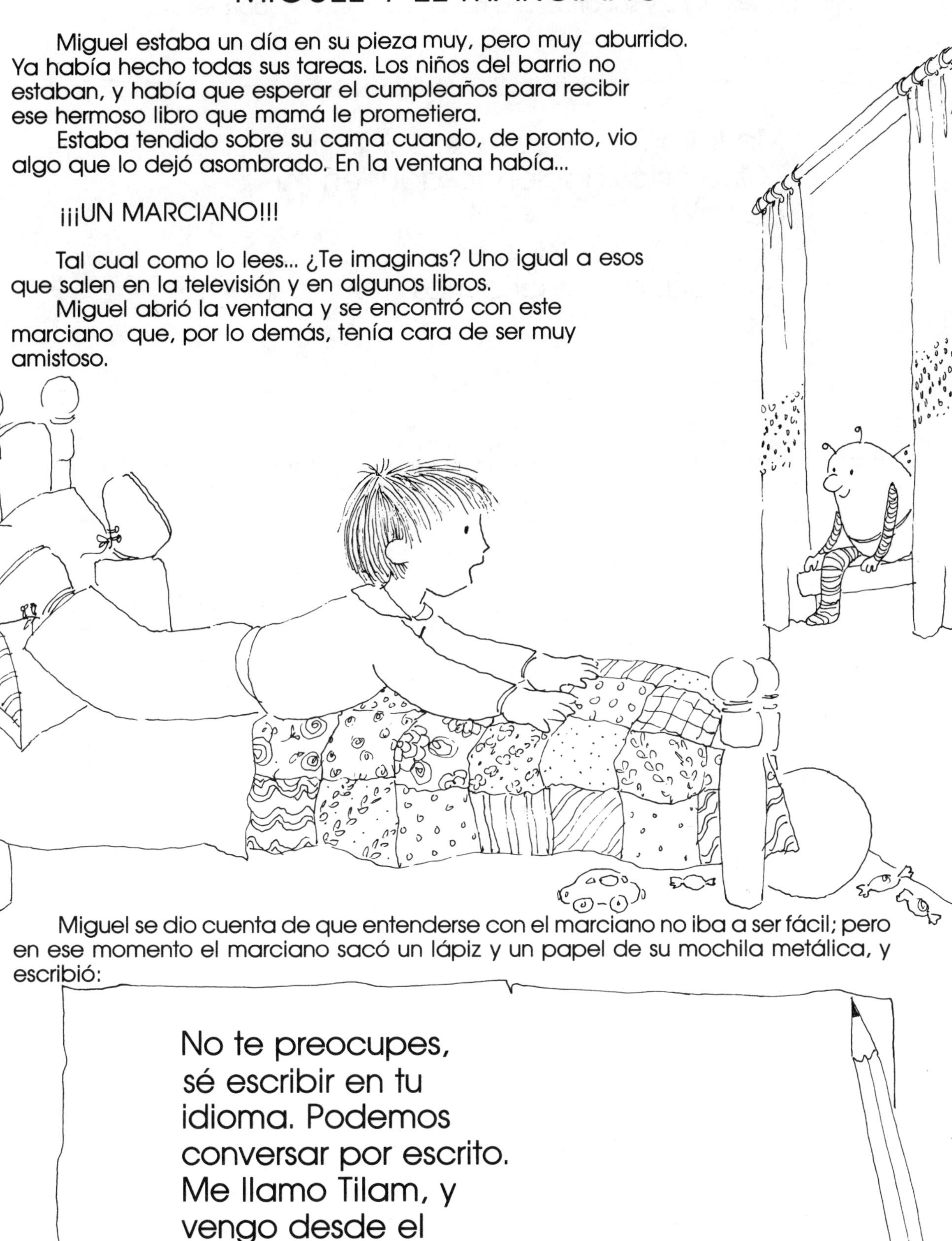

Miguel se dio cuenta de que entenderse con el marciano no iba a ser fácil; pero en ese momento el marciano sacó un lápiz y un papel de su mochila metálica, y escribió:

No te preocupes, sé escribir en tu idioma. Podemos conversar por escrito. Me llamo Tilam, y vengo desde el planeta Marte.

Miguel no podía creerlo. ¡Ah, no! Esto no sucedía todos los días. Corrió a su escritorio y sacando una hoja de papel y un lápiz, escribió:

> Me llamo ....
> ¿Qué estás haciendo aquí en mi pieza?
> Te invito a sentarte en mi ....
> Así podemos escribirnos mejor.

(Fíjate que Miguel se apuró demasiado y faltan algunas palabras. Escríbelas tú.)

Así fue como esa tarde Miguel se entretuvo con su nuevo amigo, el cual prometió venir nuevamente.

Al día siguiente apareció Tilam.

Traía en una .... una ....

y en la otra .... un .... que decía:

> Amigo Miguel:
> Encontré esto. Quiero saber qué es, y para qué sirve.

Miguel le contestó:

¡Mmmm! Me encanta lo que
traes. Es una ...., y se
....
La ◯ .... es una
....
muy sabrosa. Pero, ¡ten cuidado!
A veces salen ...., y
otras veces son tan ....
como el azúcar.
Te pillé, Tilam. La sacaste
del .... que hay en mi ....
Toma un .... y
pélala. Te va a gustar.

UN CUENTO

Un día de lluvia, en que hacía mucho frío, el abuelo se sentó al lado del fuego. Los niños le pidieron que les leyera un cuento.

Este es el cuento, pero está algo incompleto. Mientras vayas leyendo, completa lo que falta.

"RICITOS DE ORO"

En una  .... solitaria del ....

vivía una familia de osos.

Un día, antes de ir a pasear, la mamá preparó la comida y la repartió en

tres ....

Mientras los ....paseaban, una ....

llamada "Ricitos de Oro" pasó por la...............de los tres .... y miró por

la ....

Al ver los.................... con comida sobre la..................., abrió la

.... y entró muy despacito.

Se sentó en una .... , pero le quedó grande. Se

sentó en otra ...., pero también le quedó grande. Por fin,

se sentó en la .... del ...., y allí quedó muy bien.

Luego se comió toda la .... del osito, y se fue al dormitorio.

Se acostó en la.. más pequeña, y allí se durmió.

Cuando los..................................llegaron, se dieron cuenta de que alguien

había entrado en su.................. . Buscaron y encontraron a ....

durmiendo. Al oír las voces de los osos, ella despertó. Se asustó mucho, y salió

corriendo hacia el..................................... , y los osos no la vieron nunca más.

¿Te gustó? Es hermoso, ¿verdad?
Cuéntaselo a alguien que tú quieras.
Aquí puedes dibujar lo que más te gustó.

UNA DIABLURA DE ESCOBINA

¿Les cuento? Acabo de hacer una diablura, y nadie sabe que fui yo.

Mientras estaban imprimiendo este libro, me metí en él, y con la escoba barrí la mitad de todas estas páginas ¡Ja! ¡Ja! ¡Ja! Miren cómo quedó...
Pero ahora... ¡Uf! Estoy muy arrepentida...
¿Ustedes me ayudarían a completar? Se los voy a agradecer.

El niño abraza a su perro.

El pajarito está ....

El loro come ....

Las mariposas ....

El gato ....

¿Qué observas aquí?

El perro quiere ....

....

El gato huye porque ....

....

Los patitos nadan ....

....

MIRANDO CARAS

Una mañana Toño encontró al abuelo con una cara muy sonriente, y le preguntó si estaba contento.

– Sí –contestó el abuelo–..¿Cómo lo sabes?

– Se te nota en la cara –le respondió Toño.

– Es cierto –repuso el abuelo–. Generalmente las personas expresamos lo que sentimos y pensamos a través de nuestro rostro. Fíjate, por ejemplo, en esta lámina.

– ¿Por qué crees que se ríen esos niños?

– ... el payaso –respondió Toño.

– Epa, epa... ésa no es forma de contestar, amiguito. Todos te entenderemos mejor si respondes con oraciones completas.

Entonces Toño dijo:

....

¿Por qué el rostro de este señor expresa susto?

....

....

¿Qué piensas de esta cara? A este señor parece que le sucedió algo poco agradable. ¿Qué sería?

....

....

¿De qué se reirá este señor?

....

....

¿Por qué crees que este niño tiene esa cara?

....

....

Ahora mira este rostro. ¿Por qué estará llorando?

....

....

Busca en alguna revista una cara que te llame la atención, o dibuja un rostro como tú quieras. Luego escribe algo sobre él.

....

....

....

....

....

EXCLAMANDO Y PREGUNTANDO

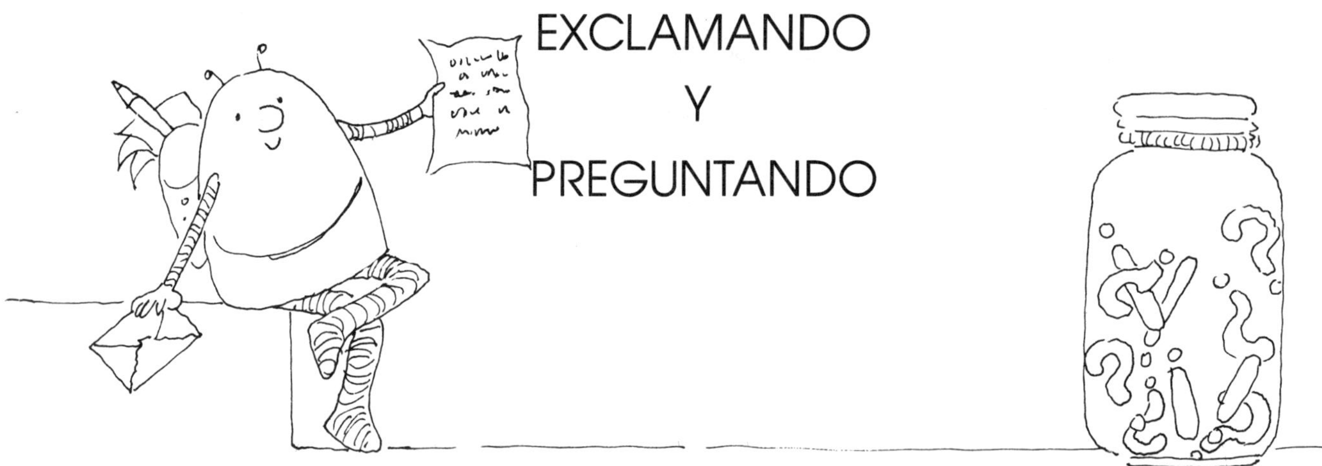

¡Hola, amiguitos!

Estoy un poco apenado. ¿Les cuento? He leído algunas cartas de mis amiguitos terrícolas, pero... ¡uf!. A veces me resulta muy difícil entender por qué a ellos se les olvida colocar los signos de exclamación e interrogación. Yo a veces no sé si me están preguntando algo o me lo están contando.

Tal vez a algunos de ustedes les pase lo mismo. Por si así fuera, los invito a repasar, para que puedan usarlos bien en este libro.

Tilam

¡Auxilio!

¡Mmmm! ¡Qué rico!

¡Salgan de aquí inmediatamente!

AHORA TE TOCA A TI

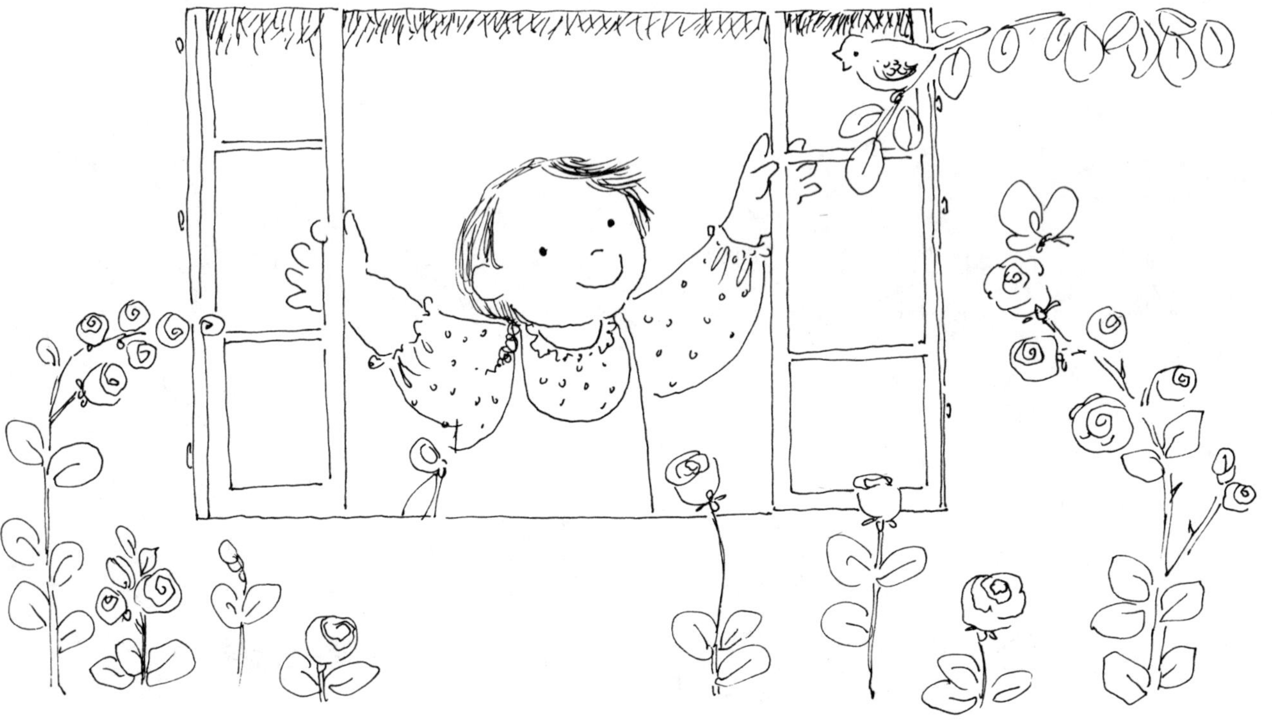

VEAMOS AHORA ESTO OTRO:

¿Puedo abrir este paquete?

¿De qué te ríes?

COMPLETA TÚ AHORA:

¿...?

¿...?

A Rosita le encanta el cuento "El Príncipe Feliz". ¿Lo conoces tú? Lo escribió Oscar Wilde, escritor inglés, quién también tiene otros cuentos muy entretenidos.

No te lo vamos a contar, pero te diremos que se trata de la estatua de un príncipe que estaba colocada en la plaza de la ciudad. Se sentía muy triste y sola.

Un día llega una golondrina y...
Si quieres saber cómo sigue, pide a tu profesor o a tus padres que te digan dónde lo puedes encontrar y lo lees.

Aquí hemos escrito algunas partes del cuento para que tú coloques los signos de interrogación o de exclamación, según corresponda.

a) – De qué sirve una estatua si ni siquiera la protege a una de la lluvia –preguntó la golondrina.

b) – Esto sí que es curioso. No hay en el cielo ni una sola nube, las estrellas brillan, y sin embargo, llueve.

c) La golondrina miró hacia arriba, y vio... Qué fue lo que vio.

ch) – Me voy a Egipto. Adiós. –Y la golondrina se echó a volar.

d) – Dónde encontraré un lugar para cobijarme.

e) – Quién eres –preguntó la golondrina.

–Soy el Príncipe Feliz.

–Y entonces, por qué lloras Casi me has empapado por completo con tus lágrimas.

f) – Qué hermosas son las estrellas –exclamó el Príncipe Feliz.

g) – Ay de mí. No tengo más rubíes en mi espada –dijo tristemente el Príncipe Feliz.

COLOCANDO COMAS

Un día, el abuelo Pancho encontró a uno de sus nietos muy afligido.

–¿Por qué te noto preocupado, Julito?

–¡Ay, abuelo! ¿Cómo no voy a estar preocupado? Mañana tendré prueba de redacción y nunca sé cuándo tengo que usar las comas. Estoy seguro de que me va a ir muy mal.

–¡Cálmate! Trataré de ayudarte. Justamente aquí tengo un libro que nos puede servir. Veamos.

Platero es pequeño, peludo, suave.
El gigante cruzó ríos, cerros, montañas.
En mi quinta hay cien árboles bellos:
ciruelos redondos,
limoneros rectos,
y naranjos de brotes lustrosos.

AHORA VUELVE A LEER:

Platero es pequeño peludo suave.
El gigante cruzó ríos cerros montañas.
En mi quinta hay cien árboles bellos: ciruelos redondos limoneros rectos y naranjos de brotes lustrosos.

–¿Qué diferencia has notado?

Seguramente te diste cuenta de que en lo que está escrito dentro del rectángulo no hay comas.
Colócalas tú.

–¡Ah!, ya entendí...
Cada vez que nombro varias cosas tengo que colocar comas.

En el cuento que leyó el abuelo Pancho el otro día, aparecen los siguientes personajes:

Un dragón , ... , ... y ....

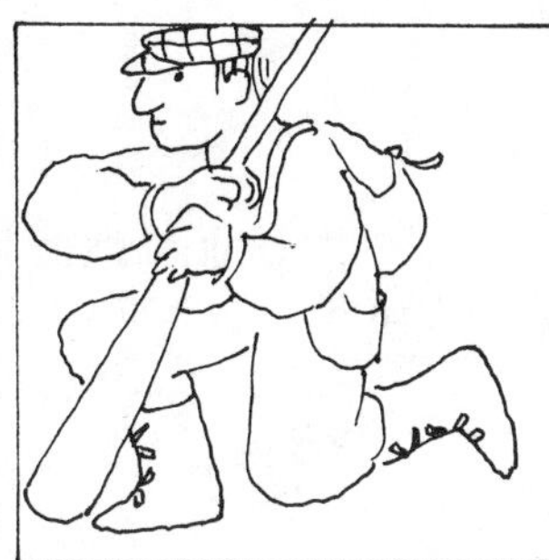

Los personajes del cuento "Caperucita Roja" son:

....

....

....

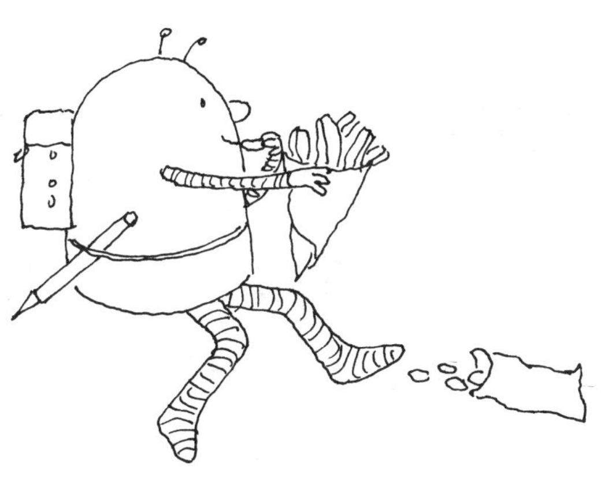

A Tilam le encanta comer alimentos terrícolas. Sus preferidos son: helados de frutilla, plátanos con miel, las papas fritas y el maní tostado.

Y, a ti, ¿qué te gusta más?

A mí me gusta ....

....

....

....

(¡Acuérdate de colocar las comas!)

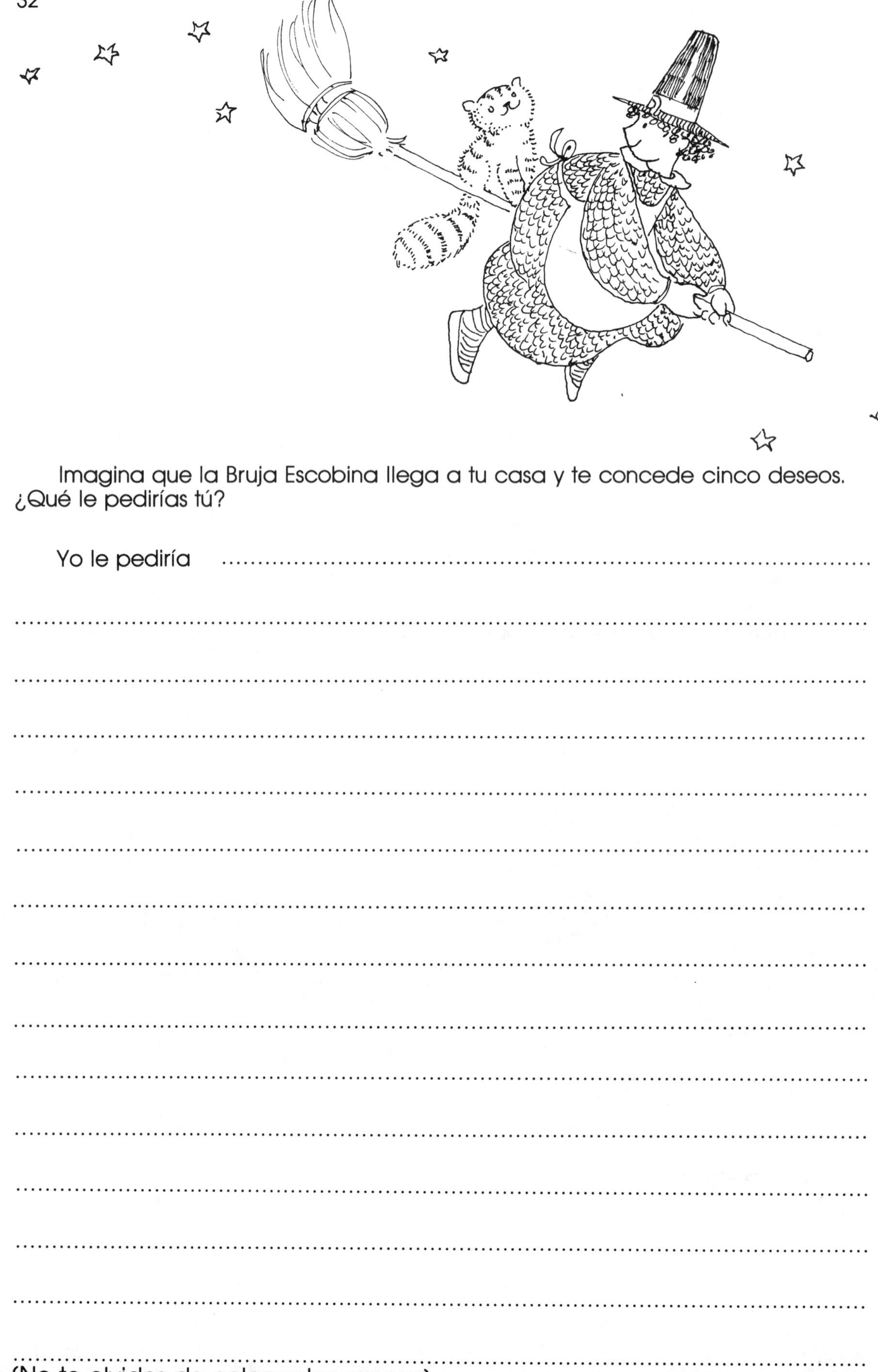

Imagina que la Bruja Escobina llega a tu casa y te concede cinco deseos. ¿Qué le pedirías tú?

Yo le pediría ....

....

....

....

....

....

....

....

....

....

....

....

....

....

....

(No te olvides de colocar las comas.)

HISTORIA DE UN ÁRBOL

Me gusta contemplar los árboles en otoño. ¿Alguna vez los has observado bien? Te contaré que nosotros podemos hacer que los árboles piensen y hablen. Sólo necesitamos un poco de imaginación. ¿Qué te parece? ¿Lo intentamos? (Para que te quede bien, no te olvides de empezar con mayúscula, utilizar puntos, comas y otros signos que sean necesarios.)

¡Ay! Ya empiezan a amarillar mis hojas; luego el viento las arrastrará y cubrirán el suelo. ¿Qué sucederá con estos pájaros que anidan entre mis ramas?

Uno de los pajaritos que vive entre las ramas del álamo piensa:

....

....

....

…gunos .... no se deshojan en .... ; se ven siempre verdes.
¿Qué pensará este pino que durante todo el año conserva sus hojas?

....

....

....

....

¿Qué conversará el pino con el pobre álamo que se está deshojando?

....

....

....

....

....

....

....

....

....

....

....

Y LLEGA EL INVIERNO

Al terminar el .... llega el ....

Ahora sí que hace bastante frío.

El .... sopla fuerte y arrastra las ....

oscuras; el cielo está gris.

Cae la .... y el paisaje se ve triste; todo se moja y se forma barro, mucho barro.

El pobre álamo que había empezado a deshojarse en otoño, ha quedado con sus .... desnudas y exclama:

....

....

....

....

....

....

....

....

....

....

El invierno siente pena al ver al álamo deshojado, sin nidos y tiritando cuando el viento lo toca. Decide conversar con él para consolarlo.

–¡Querido álamo, no te aflijas tanto! Haz cuenta que estás dormido y la lluvia que te entrego riega tus raíces y te alimenta. Cuando llegue el calor tendrás hermosas hojas nuevas y los pájaros anidarán nuevamente entre tus ramas.

El álamo, que había vivido muchos inviernos, sabía que todo eso sucedería.

¿Qué crees tú que le contestó el álamo al invierno?

....

....

....

....

....

....

....

¡AL FIN LLEGA LA PRIMAVERA!

¡Qué contento se siente nuestro amigo, el ....!

Se acabó su tristeza, pues cada día descubre

.... nuevas en sus ramas.

Pasan las semanas y se ha vuelto a convertir en un

.... hermoso. Los .... pían y vuelan

llevando ramitas secas para hacer sus ....

Este pajarillo le dice al álamo:

....

....

....

....

....

La primavera se hace presente en todas partes. A la orilla del camino brotan florecillas silvestres. El viento frío invernal se ha transformado en una .... fresca, suave y perfumada.

El .... brilla y da calor.

El .... está azul y con algunas ....

blancas como el algodón.

Claudia y Pablo se cansaron de jugar y se han sentado cerca de sus padres, a la sombra del hermoso ....

El pobre álamo, que estuvo tan solo en los meses invernales, ¿qué pensará ahora que se siente acompañado?

....

....

....

....

....

....

....

....

....

TOÑO Y LA LAGARTIJA

Toño sale al patio. Hay un hermoso día de sol. Sopla la brisa fresca. La ropa que está tendida en el alambre parece que se fuera a volar. Las mariposas blancas y amarillas se detienen golosas sobre las flores. Con sus ojotas, Toño levanta tierra al caminar, tierra suelta que hay bajo el largo parrón.

De repente, ¡oh, sorpresa!, una lagartija corre por el muro y se detiene. Los ojos de Toño también se detienen y esperan. ¡Qué lindos colores tiene esta lagartija! ¿Las lagartijas serán hijas de los lagartos? ¿O no será que las lagartijas cuando crecen se convierten en lagartos?

Toño se acerca de puntillas; trata de no respirar. Sus ojos negros, grandes, no se mueven de la lagartija y sus manos están listas para cogerla. La guardará en un frasco; después le amarrará una pitilla al cuello y caminará con ella por el patio como lo hacía con su perro "Valiente". Ya va a cogerla; falta poco; parece que la lagartija estuviera pegada al muro. Ya: un, dos, tres, ¡zas!. La mano de Toño pega en la pared: el niño siente dolor y ...¡cataplum!, resbala, y cae sobre unos rosales.

La lagartija sube rapidísimo al borde de la pared y desde allí da vuelta la cabeza. Parece burlarse de Toño, y en cuanto éste trata de levantarse ella ya ha desaparecido en la casa vecina.

Este amiguito es ....

Los ojos de ....

son de color..

Toño no usa zapatos, usa ....

En el muro, el niño encontró una ....

....

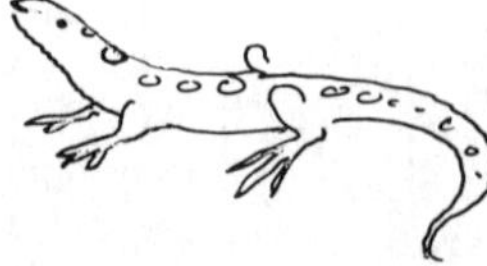

¿Qué le sucedió a Toño?
Ordena estas palabras y sabrás qué le sucedió.

los Toño rosales aplastó

....

resbaló se y Toño cayó

....

Toño vio a la lagartija y pensó:

....

....

¿Qué pensaría la lagartija?

....

....

....

¿Qué conversarán Toño y la lagartija?
Imagínate este milagro.

....

....

....

....

....

....

....

....

....

LAS AVENTURAS DE TOÑO

Toño estaba en cama resfriado. Como no tenía fiebre, su madre le pasó varias revistas y libros para que se entretuviera. Hojeando un libro de animales, Toño leyó:

"El cóndor es el ave más grande del mundo. Con sus alas desplegadas mide 3 metros y 25 centímetros. Puede remontarse hasta los picachos más altos de la cordillera de los Andes".

A Toño le fascinó el cóndor. Cerró los ojos y se imaginó montado en él. Recordaba que una vez le habían contado la historia de un niño sueco que recorrió su país montado en un pato. ¿Cómo podría compararse un pato con un cóndor?...

Y Toño se sentía elevado por los aires; sus piernas rodeaban el cuerpo del ave, y sus manos, el cuello. Las poderosas y enormes alas parecían las de un avión. ¡Qué maravilla! ¿A dónde lo llevaría?

De repente, escuchó una voz:

–¿A dónde quieres ir?

¿El cóndor hablaba? ¡Esto era el colmo!

–Llévame lejos, muy lejos; quiero conocer el mundo –dijo Toño.
El cóndor voló por sobre una playa,y Toño vio:

....

....

....

El cóndor voló por sobre la cordillera, y Toño vio:

....

....

....

....

Cuando el cóndor siguió su viaje, llegó al campo. Toño quedó encantado.
¿Qué vio?

....

....

....

¿Conoces este lugar? ¿Por dónde irá ahora el cóndor?

....

....

....

Toño estaba cansado de tanto volar y le pidió al cóndor que descendieran un rato.

¿Dónde se escondieron Toño y el cóndor?

....

....

....

....

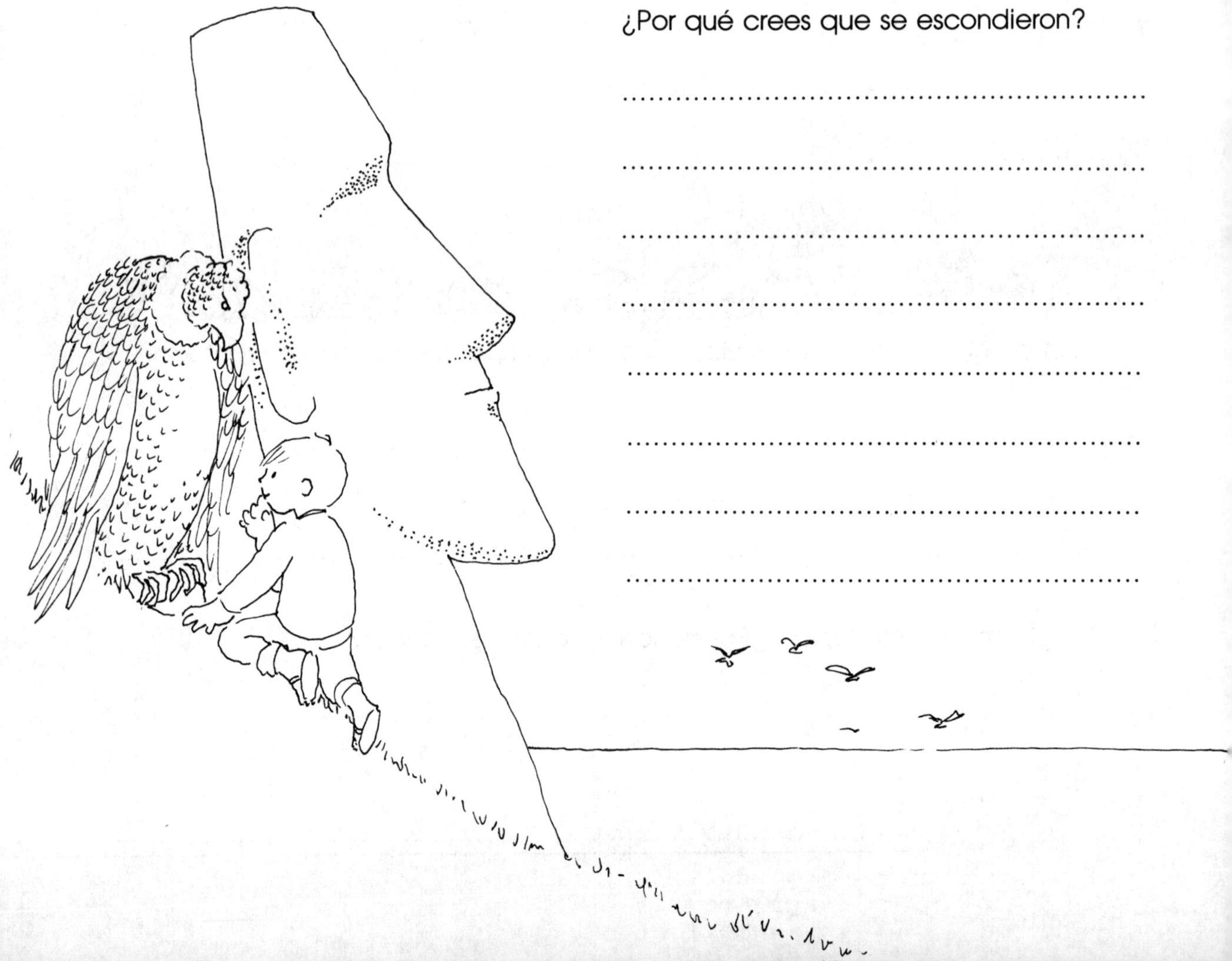

¿Por qué crees que se escondieron?

....

....

....

....

....

....

....

....

Amigo, sigamos volando
Bueno; llévame a otra isla

El cóndor llevó a Toño hacia el lugar donde vivió Robinson Crusoe. Toño

conocerá la isla ....

Cuando descendieron, el cóndor aprovechó para descansar y Toño se acercó a un embarcadero.

Allí se quedó con la boca abierta. Nunca había visto este animal. Un pescador que sujetaba el animal le conversó. Escribe lo que Toño le contestó:

¿Qué miras con cara de susto?

....

....

....

Estas son langostas. Su carne es muy sabrosa.

....

....

....

¡Te regalo esta langosta! Dile a tu mamá que la ponga a cocer, y se la comen.

....

....

....

Toño, muy contento, se puso a gritar:

– ¡Mamá, mamá, me regalaron una langosta! Hay que cocerla. ¡Es una langosta.... se llama langosta...!

– ¡Ay Toño!, cada vez que te pones a leer te quedas dormido. ¿Qué gritos son esos acerca de una langosta? Tu libro está abierto en la lámina del cóndor, y el cóndor no tiene nada que ver con la langosta.

– Mamá, estaba soñando... ¡Quiero contarte el sueño!

– Encantada, Toño querido, pero mientras te preparo la comida, escríbemelo. Cuando tu padre llegue más tarde, se lo leeré y él se divertirá con ese sueño que tanto te ha gustado, ¿qué te parece?

Y así empezó Toño:

Soñé que viajaba montado ....

....

....

....

....

....

....

....

....

....

....

....

....

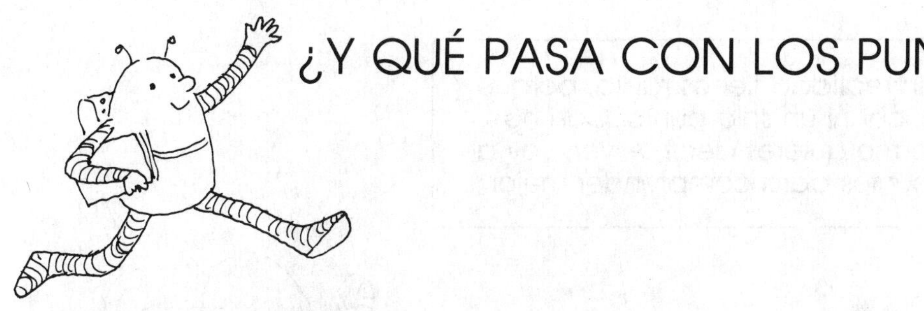

¿Y QUÉ PASA CON LOS PUNTOS?

Hoy día Toño anda de mal humor. Tenía deseos de ir al cine, pero nadie lo podía acompañar. En eso aparece Tilam.

¡Hola, Toño! ¿Cómo estás?
Te noto algo triste.
¿Por qué no me cuentas qué te pasa?

Toño toma un papel, y un lápiz y escribe:

No estoy triste no me pasa nada tengo rabia porque quería ir al cine nadie me quiere acompañar tendré que buscar la manera de entretenerme en algo.

Parece que en realidad tienes rabia, porque has escrito sin colocar ni un solo punto. Casi no te entiendo lo que me quieres decir. A ver, voy a colocar algunos puntos para comprender mejor.

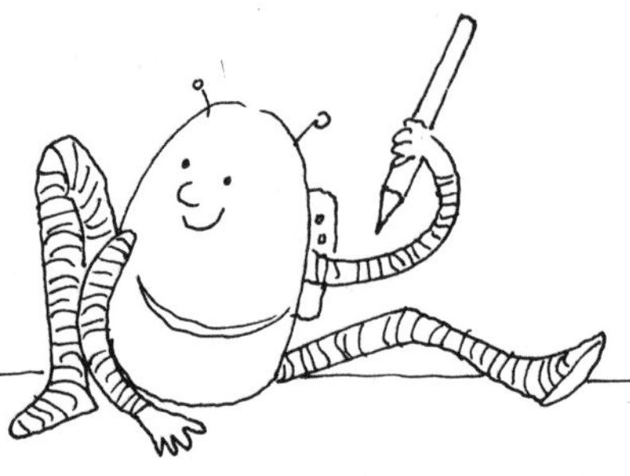

No estoy triste. No me pasa nada. Tengo rabia, porque quería ir al cine. Nadie me quiere acompañar. Tendré que buscar la manera de entretenerme en algo.

En eso, entró el abuelo a la habitación.

–¿Qué están haciendo? –preguntó sentándose junto a ellos.

–¡Ay, abuelo! Parece que cuando escribo, no coloco punto seguido. Tilam dice que no me entiende nada, y me corrige.

Tilam tiene razón. Para poder entender con claridad lo que alguien escribe, es preciso colocar punto seguido, y también punto aparte.

Revisando mis libros encontré algunas cosas hermosas.

Algunos escritores escriben en forma bonita sobre cosas tan simples y corrientes, como por ejemplo, sobre el mar.

"En estos días tranquilos, suaves, templados, se puede pasar horas contemplando el mar. Las grandes olas verdosas se persiguen hasta morir en la playa. El sol brilla sobre la espuma. Al anochecer, algún delfín destaca su cuerpo y sus aletas negras en el agua".

Pío Baroja
español

–¡Qué hermoso! –repuso Toño. Se me está olvidando mi rabia. ¿Por qué no lees otro trozo, abuelo?

–¡Desde luego! –contestó el abuelo–. Pero recuerda que estamos hablando de la necesidad de usar punto seguido. En el trozo donde se habla del mar te habrás dado cuenta de las veces que se baja la voz y se hace una corta pausa, ¿verdad?

–Sí, ya entendí. Cuando uno ha expresado una idea coloca punto seguido, y al leerlo se hace una pausa.

Yo también descubrí cuándo se usa punto seguido.

Vamos a ver si es cierto. Aquí hay unos trozos donde faltan los puntos seguidos. Colóquenlos ustedes. (Y tú, amiguito, también.)

Me enojé con mi amigo Pedro me había dicho una palabra grosera no lo invitaré a la fiesta de mi cumpleaños.

La escuela donde estudio es pequeña me agrada mucho porque tiene un patio hermoso hay un ciruelo y un damasco en primavera se cubren de flores.

Ayer fuimos al zoológico vimos el oso polar y el elefante hay muchos animales curiosos no pude ver el tigre de Bengala el cuidador dijo que estaba durmiendo siesta.

¡Cuidado, amigos! Tengo que meterme en esto, a pesar de que no me han llamado. En estos trozos hay una "trampita". Te voy a recordar algo. Después de colocar el punto, no olvides usar mayúscula.

Comparemos para ver si está bien.
¿Cuántos puntos pusieron ustedes? Lean los trozos con su puntuación correcta.

Me enojé con mi amigo Pedro. Me había dicho una palabra grosera. No lo invitaré a la fiesta de mi cumpleaños.

La escuela donde estudio es pequeña. Me agrada mucho, porque tiene un patio hermoso. Hay un ciruelo y un damasco. En primavera se cubren de flores.

Ayer fuimos al zoológico. Vimos el oso polar y el elefante. Hay muchos animales curiosos. No pude ver el tigre de Bengala. El cuidador dijo que estaba durmiendo siesta.

Abuelo, recuerda que ibas a leerme otro trozo bonito.

Sí, lo recuerdo. Aquí está. Te leeré un hermoso trozo de un escritor chileno: Oscar Castro.

Ustedes, amiguitos, fíjense en los puntos seguidos que hay en él.

"En el huerto de Juanito despliega su rosado velamen el almendro. Despiertan, soñolientos, los primeros lirios azules. La luz anda pisando el color de las rosas. Es primavera, una temprana primavera de cristales y aguas. El jilguero despierta y mira el huerto. Entonces le amanece el corazón y surgen de su garganta limonera los más puros arpegios. El jilguero cuenta el mundo en su lenguaje de maravilla. Trina el jilguero en su idioma que sólo las flores y los niños comprenden. Para traducirlo, será preciso retornar a la infancia del sueño".

Tilam también leyó el hermoso trozo de Oscar Castro, y luego lo escribió en su pizarra.

¿Y qué pasa con el punto aparte? ¿Cuándo se usa?

¡Es muy fácil! Leamos este trozo, y tú solo descubrirás cuándo debes emplearlo.

Una tortuga, disgustada de andar siempre por la tierra, suplicó al águila que la levantase por los aires.

Así lo hizo el águila remontando a la tortuga más allá de las nubes. Al verse en tal altura la tortuga exclamó:

–¡Qué envidia me tendrán ahora los animales que se mueven en el suelo, al verme encumbrada entre las nubes!

Al oír esto, el águila se molestó de tanta vanidad y soltó a la tortuga, dejándola caer sobre unos peñascos. Allí terminó su existencia.

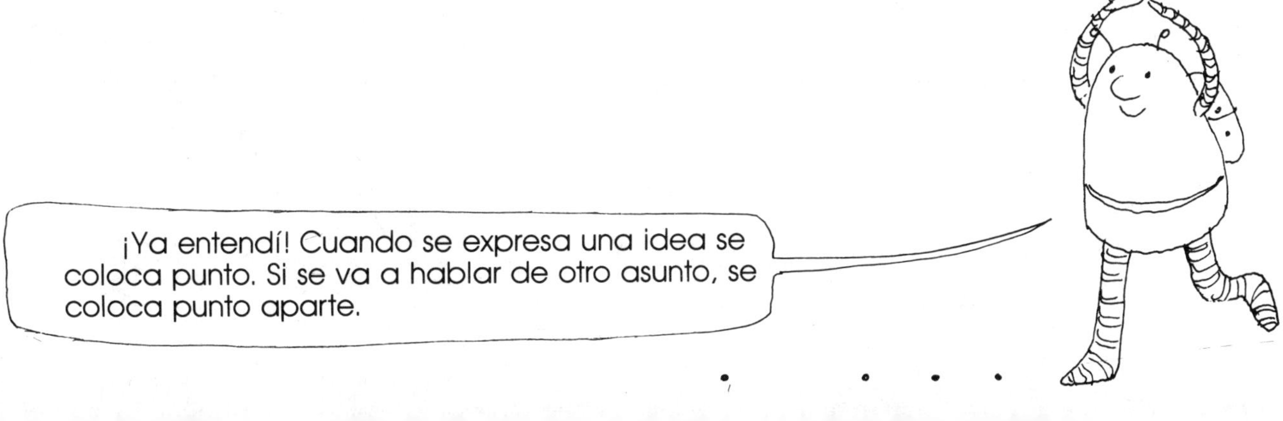

¡Ya entendí! Cuando se expresa una idea se coloca punto. Si se va a hablar de otro asunto, se coloca punto aparte.

El abuelo quiso seguir trabajando, y escribió un trozo sin puntos. Ayúdale a Tilam y a Toño a colocar los puntos.

"Cierto día muy caluroso, una paloma se paró en la rama de un árbol debajo de él corría un riachuelo de pronto, una abejita se acercó a beber, y casi cae al agua la paloma, que estaba mirando, voló hacia ella y la sacó en el pico poco después, un cazador pasó por allí y quiso dispararle a la paloma en ese momento, llegó la abeja y picó al hombre en la mano el dolor hizo que el cazador fallara el tiro, y así se salvó la linda palomita".

Escribe el trozo colocando los puntos seguidos y los puntos apartes

....

....

....

....

....

....

....

....

....

....

....

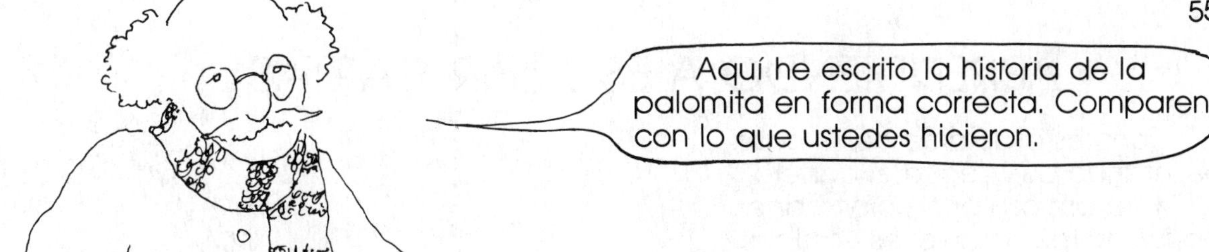

Aquí he escrito la historia de la palomita en forma correcta. Comparen con lo que ustedes hicieron.

"Cierto día muy caluroso, una paloma se paró en la rama de un árbol. Debajo de él corría un riachuelo.

De pronto, una abejita se acercó a beber, y casi cae al agua. La paloma, que estaba mirando, voló hacia ella y la sacó en el pico.

Poco después, un cazador pasó por allí y quiso dispararle a la paloma. En ese momento, llegó la abeja y picó al hombre en la mano.

El dolor hizo que el cazador fallara el tiro, y así se salvó la linda palomita".

APRENDIENDO A ESCRIBIR CARTAS

Toño está delante de su casa esperando que llegue el cartero.
Está ansioso por recibir cartas de los amigos a quienes escribió. Las direcciones las encontró en una revista infantil.

Los amigos a quienes escribió Toño son:

IKITO SAKAMOTO
del Japón

PETER LUND
que vive en
Suiza

NUNO OKARA
de Africa del Sur

Además les escribió a dos niños chilenos:

ROSA PAREDES
que vive en Arica,
la ciudad situada más al
norte de nuestro país.

VICENTE RAMIREZ
que es de Ancud,
Chiloé

Por fin; allí viene don Simón, el cartero, pero... ¡bah!, ¡qué raro! Trae una cara tan preocupada... Extraño, pues don Simón es muy risueño, y siempre anda alegre.

– ¡Hola, don Simón!

– ¡Hola, hijo!

– ¿Me trae alguna carta?

– Sí, Toño, te traigo varias...,pero no sabes lo que me ha pasado... Las tenía juntas para ti, y ayer con la lluvia se me mojó el bolsón, y mira lo que ha sucedido. Las cartas se han abierto y les ha entrado agua. Hay algunas que se les han borrado algunas partes...

Toño, un poco apenado, toma las cartas y dice:

– No se preocupe, don Simón, esto tiene remedio... ¡Muchas gracias!

Toño toma una carta y la abre. Es de Peter. Mírala tú.

Berna, 25 de ( )

Querido ( ) :

Recibí ( ) que me alegró mucho. Estoy contento de tener un amigo ( )
Mi papá estuvo mucho tiempo en Chile y aprendió el castellano.

A mí me gusta coleccionar estampillas y tengo una colección muy linda. Ojalá me pudieras ( ) algunas ( ) .
Yo te envío aquí unas postales de mi ciudad.
Te ( ) con cariño,

tu amigo ( )

¡Qué lástima! Sobre la carta cayeron algunas gotas de agua y las palabras se borraron. ¿Qué habrá escrito Peter en esas partes que ahora no se ven? Escríbelas tú, para que Toño las pueda leer.

Toño está muy contento con la carta de Peter. Luego toma otra. Esta trae estampillas chilenas.

Sr.
Toño Sepúlveda
Los Copihues 33
Santiago de Chile.

La abre ansiosamente, pero ¡otra vez! El agua ha borrado algunas partes de la carta. ¡Pobre, Toño! ¿Quieres ayudarle, por favor?

( ) , ( )

( ) :

No te imaginas lo ( ) que me puse cuando llegó tu ( ).

Me llamo ( ). Estudio en una escuela en Azapa. Todos los días nos juntamos varios compañeros para irnos caminando hasta ella.

Aquí no llueve casi nunca, y hace calor.

Azapa es un valle regado por el río San José.

Se cultivan hermosos claveles de todos colores.

Somos siete hermanos.

Ojalá me envíes una carta pronto.

Toño está feliz con las cartas de sus amigos, y toma ahora otra. Aquí el agua

¿Qué te parece si tú pones lo que borró el agua?

Toño mira el remitente... ¿De quién será esa carta? Adivina y colócalo.

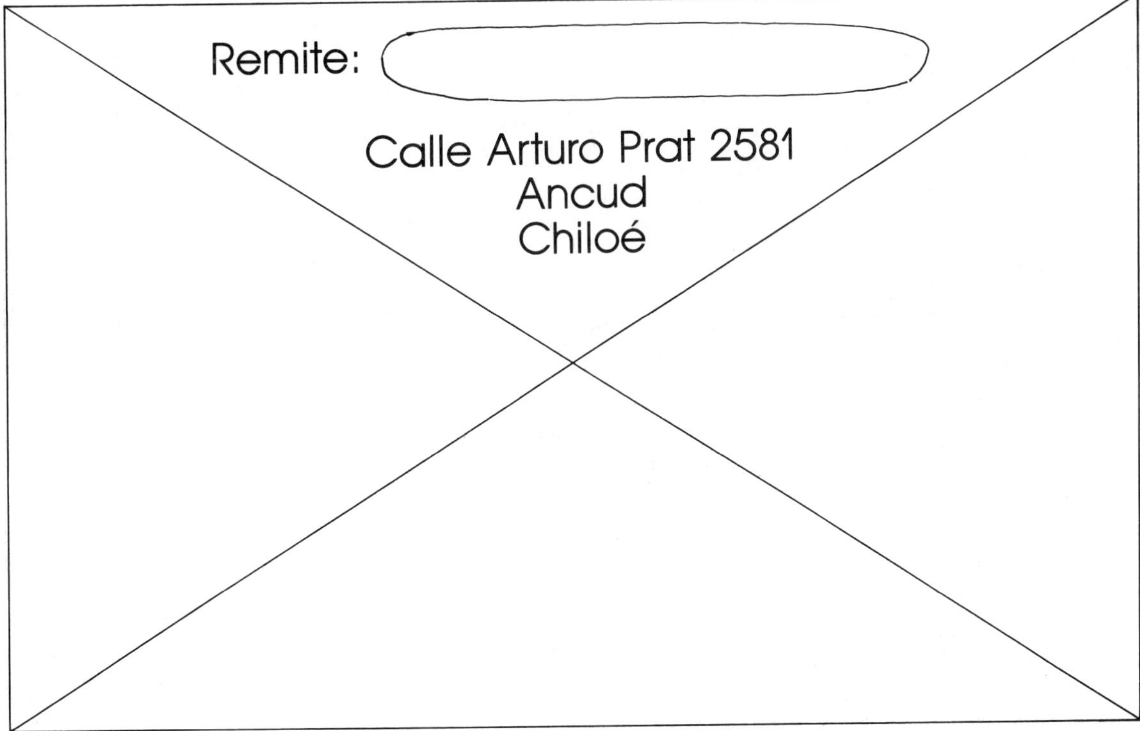

Toño lee sorprendido:

Querido

Mi nombre es y tengo 9 años. Estoy en 4° año, y me gusta mucho ir al colegio.

¿Te cuento? Voy a ir a Santiago en las vacaciones de invierno. A lo mejor tú me puedes mostrar la ciudad. Iremos con mi mamá y mi hermanita.

Te voy a llevar una lancha chilota de regalo. Mi papá las hace talladas. Te van a gustar.

¿Qué más crees tú que le escribió?

Toño mira una y otra vez las cartas, y no escucha que la mamá lo está llamando.

¿Te gustaría a ti tener un amigo en otra parte del mundo? Es muy entretenido, se aprenden muchas cosas.

¿Por qué no escribes una carta? Elige alguno de los amigos de Toño, y le envías una. O si quieres puedes también escribirle a Toño.

No se te olvide hacer el sobre. Tú ya sabes cómo se hace.

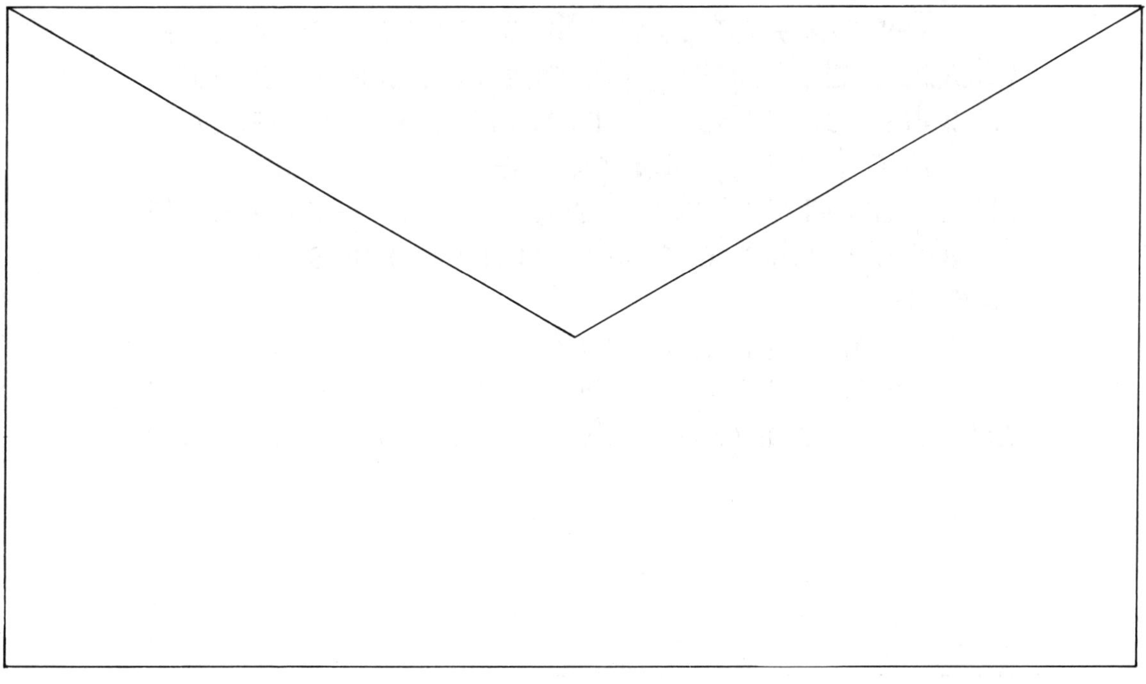

¿Ves qué entretenido es? ¿Quieres recibir tú ahora una carta? Imagínate que Nuno, el niño de Africa, te envió esta carta.

Ciudad del Cabo, 10 de marzo de ....

Querido .... :

Mi nombre es Nuno Okara, y soy africano. Hacía mucho tiempo que deseaba tener un amigo chileno. Cada vez que miro el mapa, me llama la atención lo largo y angosto que es tu país.

Tengo 9 años y asisto a una escuela en Ciudad del Cabo. Mi papá trabaja en un hospital de niños, y mi mamá es profesora.

A mí me gusta leer, especialmente libros de aventuras. Tengo una hermana de 8 años. A ella le gusta leer cuentos de hadas.

¿A ti te gusta leer?

Otra cosa que me gusta hacer es ir a la piscina y bañarme. Aquí hace mucho calor.

¿Qué haces tú en tu tiempo libre?

A mí me gustaría ser médico como papá, en cambio a mi hermana le encantaría ser periodista. Ella tiene muchos amigos a los que les escribe cartas.

Cuéntame de ti, y de cómo es Chile. Te envío una foto de mi familia.

Te saluda
tu amigo
NUNO

P.D. Ojalá me mandaras algunas postales de Chile.
Gracias

¿Te gustaría contestarle? Es fácil, y tu carta no necesita ser tan larga. Escribe todo lo que tú quieras.

La dirección de Nuno es:

Nuno Okara
Cabo Verde 831 - Norte
Ciudad del Cabo
Africa del Sur.

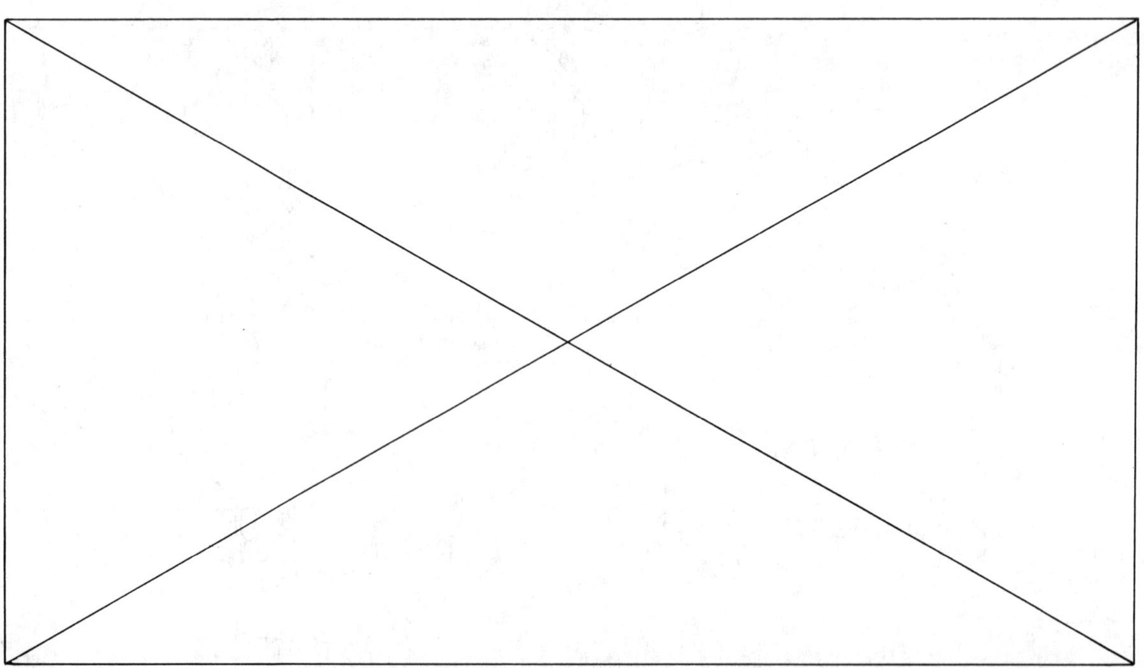

JUGANDO CON LAS PALABRAS

Tilam se ha acostumbrado tanto a entenderse con Toño a través de su pizarra... ¡Qué raro! Fíjate que escribe bien, como tú lo has podido comprobar, pero no se atreve a conversar: dice que las palabras se le enredan en la lengua. En fin, tal vez algún día aprenderá a hablar en nuestro lenguaje.

Ahora se ha puesto de acuerdo con Toño para escribir oraciones cambiando el orden de las palabras. En esta forma:

LOS PESCADORES MADRUGARON PARA IR A PESCAR CORVINAS.

Para ir a pescar corvinas, los pescadores madrugaron.

Madrugaron los pescadores para ir a pescar corvinas.

Los pescadores, para ir a pescar corvinas, madrugaron.

Es entretenido este juego de palabras. Prueba tú.

Los niños jugaban entre los árboles del bosque.

....

....

El campesino trabaja desde el amanecer.

....

....

OTRO JUEGO CON PALABRAS

Consiste en leer las palabras del lado izquierdo y escribir una oración en la cual ellas aparezcan.

Por ejemplo, así:

puente El perrito de Toño no cruza el **puente**,
río pues teme caerse al **río**.

mar
....
barco

nubes
....
cielo

árbol
....
gato

OTRO JUEGO:

¿Coloquemos otro verbo?

En invierno llueve y .... mucho.

Los conejos corren y .... por el campo.

Los caballos trotan y .... por el potrero.

¿Coloquemos otro adjetivo?

El gato .... de Claudia duerme sobre un cojín.

El .... zorzal hizo su nido en el naranjo.

Las .... palomas regresan a su palomar.

AHORA JUGUEMOS A ALARGAR ORACIONES

En el verano...

En el verano hace calor.
En el verano hace calor y los días son largos.
Tenemos vacaciones largas en el verano.

AHORA, SIGUE TU:

Allá lejos...

Allá lejos se ve una casa.

....

....

En la playa...
En la playa juegan los niños.

....

....

Y... ¿QUÉ OTRA COSA PODRÍA SUCEDER?

Llovía torrencialmente y ....

Soplaba un fuerte viento y ....

En la calle se formaban pozas de agua y ....

¿ADIVINEMOS LO QUE PIENSAN NUESTROS AMIGOS?

Yo deseo que ....

....

....

Me parece necesario que ....

....

....

Me parece extraño que ....

....

....

....

¿Creen ustedes que ....

....

....

....

HABLEMOS DE CONCORDANCIA

Fíjate que a Toño le dieron de tarea hacer cinco oraciones. El las hizo, ¡por supuesto!, pero se sintió un poco apenado cuando la profesora le dijo que era necesario corregirlas. ¿Qué errores tendrían?

Estas son las oraciones que hizo Toño:

– El pueblo de los cuales te hablé era bonitos.

– El postre era exquisita.

– El campo estaban floridos.

– Marta y su amiga juega en el jardín.

– Nosotros vendremos ayer de Osorno.

Amiguitos, ayudemos a Toño. Yo corrijo la primera oración y ustedes corrigen las otras.

– El pueblo del cual te hablé era bonito.

....

....

....

....

¡Gracias, Tilam! ¡Gracias, amigos! Pero quiero estar seguro de que aprendí a hacer oraciones. Tilam, por favor, escribe oraciones con errores y yo las corrijo, ¿quieres?

¡Conforme! En mi pizarra las escribiré.

– Mañana viajé de regreso a mi planeta.

– Mañana probé las ricas cereza.

– Las mariposas y la abeja revolotea en el jardín.

Así las corrigió Toño:

– Mañana viajaré de regreso a mi planeta.

– Mañana probaré las ricas cerezas.

– Las mariposas y la abeja revolotean en el jardín.

Dicen que soy "metete", pero no me importa.

Ahora yo escribiré oraciones con errores y tú, amiguito, las corregirás, ¿de acuerdo?

¡Esto es divertido!

– Las escobas de las brujas son voladora.

– Mi escoba es mágico.

– Yo soy "metete" y Tilam es sabia.

– No me gustan las niñas peleadora.

– Ayer la profesora felicitó a Toño por su correcta oraciones.

¿Dónde están los errores que cometió Escobina? Hay cinco. ¡Descúbrelos!

¡Psst, amigo, lee lo que está en mi pizarra y descubrirás los errores!

– Las escobas de las brujas son voladoras.
– Mi escoba es mágica.
– Yo soy "metete", y Tilam es sabio.
– No me gustan las niñas peleadoras.
– Ayer la profesora felicitó a Toño por sus correctas oraciones.

Completa ahora tú.

(hermosa)

Las flores de mi jardín..

....

El gato y el perro ....

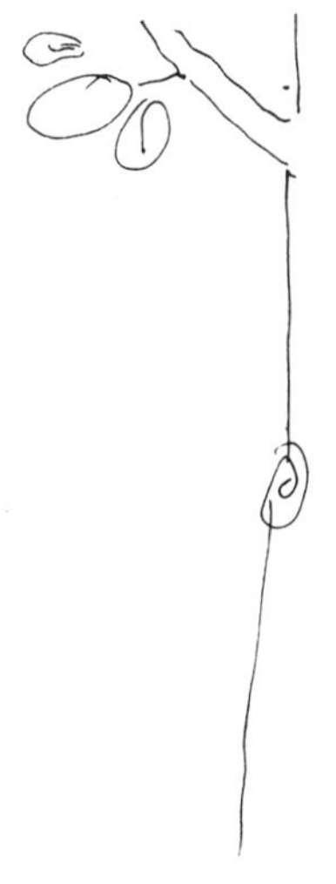

Los pajarillos .... sobre las ramas.

EMPEZANDO A ESCRIBIR HISTORIAS

Lee la historia que inventé
cuando miré estas láminas.

Pablo y Claudia se acercaron a la reja donde estaba "Guardián", y con un palo comenzaron a molestarlo. "Guardián" ladraba furioso. Los niños se fueron riendo y... ¡qué miedo! "Guardián" apareció por detrás de la reja. Pablo y Claudia se llevaron un buen susto. Por suerte pudieron subirse a un árbol.

Observa estos dos cuadros y escribe lo que sucede en cada uno de ellos.

"Cascabel" encontró ....

....

Rápidamente, ...

....

Pablo y Claudia tenían un pajarito...

¿Qué dirías tú de estos niños? Escríbelo.

....

....

....

....

....

....

....

....

....

....

....

....

Este es el cuento de Daniela y su muñeca. Escríbelo, ¿quieres?

Ahora escribe completa la historia de Daniela y su muñeca.

....

....

....

....

....

....

....

....

....

¿Quieres dibujar algo del cuento que tú escribiste?

LA RANA Y SUS AMIGOS

¡Mira qué ocurrencia, escribir palabras sueltas, a tontas y a locas...
¡No, no, no!

Ordénalas, por favor.

amiguitos cuatro rana la tiene

....

pasear con va a ellos

....

agua se la tira rana al

....

nadar no sus amigos saben

....

se sus amigos burlaba rana la de

....

sintieron ellos se ofendidos

....

a pusieron pensar amigos se los

....

fabricaron la amigos un los barco rana de

....

Aquí hay una historia muy entretenida, pero parece que la **bruja** Escobina se anduvo metiendo en ella, y quedaron algunos espacios en blanco, o, tal vez quiere que tú los completes. Te invitamos a llenar lo que falta.

¡Creemos que será divertido!

Había una vez ....

....

....

....

....

....

–¡Cua - ja - ja! ¡Cua - ja - ja! –se reía la rana.

Los amigos de la rana

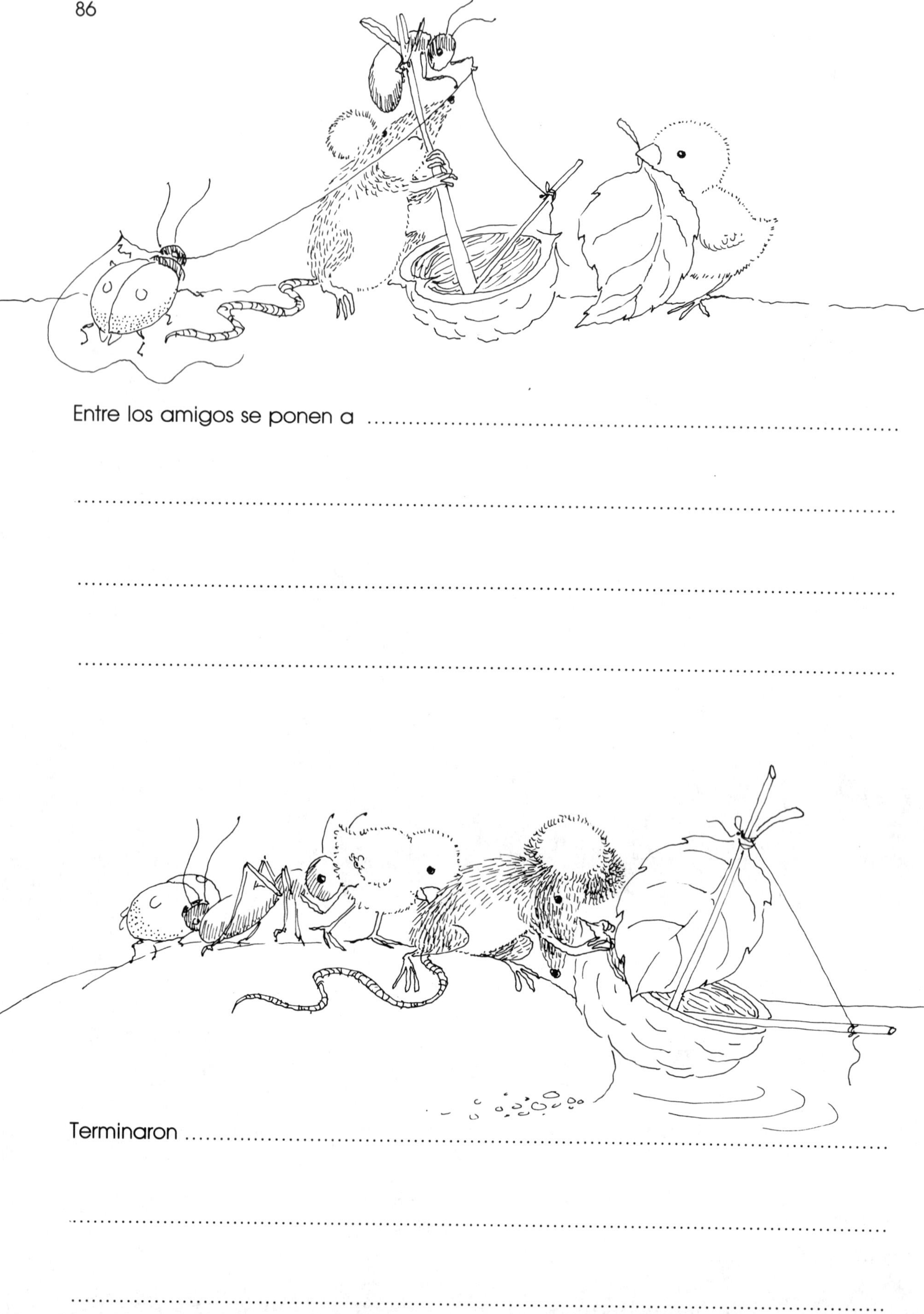

Entre los amigos se ponen a ....

....

....

....

Terminaron ....

....

....

Y así termina esta historia.

....

....

....

....

....

....

....

....

....

MARCELA Y MARCELO CUENTAN CUENTOS

A Marcela le encanta contarle cuentos a su hermano chico. Desgraciadamente, tiene la costumbre de usar "y" a cada momento. Por ejemplo, así contó un día el cuento llamado "El burro cargado".

"Había una vez un burro que llevaba unos sacos con sal. El burro pasó por el río y se cayó y se le mojaron los sacos y se deshizo la sal y el burro no se sentía pesado y se puso muy contento".

(Marca con un círculo rojo todas las "y" que Marcela usó de más en el cuento).

ASÍ HABÍA CONTADO EL CUENTO LA PROFESORA DE MARCELA:

"Había una vez un burro que llevaba unos sacos con sal. Al tratar de cruzar un río, el burro tropezó con una piedra, resbaló y cayó al agua. Naturalmente, los sacos con sal se mojaron y la sal se deshizo. El burro se sintió muy aliviado de su carga y se puso a rebuznar de alegría: ¡ía-ía-ía!

Marcelo también es aficionado a contar cuentos. Él se los cuenta a sus compañeros. Pero tiene la costumbre de usar con mucha frecuencia la palabra "entonces... entonces... entonces..."

Un día, Marcelo y dos de sus compañeros no pudieron asistir a la clase de educación física porque estaban muy resfriados. El profesor los dejó en la sala, y ellos decidieron entretenerse contando cuentos. Marcelo empezó:

"Una vez un ladrón entró en el patio de una casa. Entonces el perro empezó a ladrar; entonces el ladrón le tiró pan para que se quedara callado. Entonces el perro le preguntó que por qué le daba ese pan, y el ladrón le dijo que para alimentarlo. El perro le dijo que no le creía y que después que le robara a su amo, lo dejaría morir de hambre. Entonces el perro le dijo que le convenía ladrar y despertar a su amo; entonces el ladrón se fue.

Subraya con un lápiz de color las palabras "entonces" que Marcelo usó de más.

Ahora escribe tú el cuento. Naturalmente puedes usar la palabra "entonces", pero no repetirla tantas veces como lo hizo Marcelo.

"La historia del ladrón"

....

....

....

....

....

....

....

....

....

....

....

....

....

....

....

Ahora cuéntale tú a Tilam lo que hicieron Toño y Claudia cuando fueron al zoológico. Te ayudaremos con unas fotos que sacamos.

Toño y Claudia fueron al zoológico.

....

....

....

....

....

....

....

LOS PROBLEMAS DE TOÑO

El otro día estaba Toño muy preocupado. El abuelo, cuando lo vio, le preguntó qué le pasaba.

—Mira, abuelo, la señorita siempre me encuentra las composiciones mal hechas. Dice que es muy entretenido lo que yo escribo, pero que soy muy desordenado para exponer mis ideas. Me paso de una cosa a otra, y repito cosas. ¿Cómo se puede hacer, abuelo?

—Hum, sí, hijo. En realidad, eso les pasa a muchos niños como tú. Ustedes se entusiasman escribiendo y no ordenan lo que van a poner. Verás, cuando yo era profesor, les enseñaba a mis alumnos. Veamos qué puedo hacer por ti. ¿Qué has puesto allí?

ESTO ESCRIBIÓ TOÑO :

EL DÍA DE MI CUMPLEAÑOS

Yo cumplí el domingo ocho años. En la noche miré mis regalos y estaba muy contento. Mi papá en la mañana me dio una bicicleta. Vinieron todos mis amigos. Tilam vino y me trajo una nave espacial de juguete. Mi mamá nos dio chocolate y un pedazo de torta. Había globos y serpentinas. Nos disfrazamos con unos trajes viejos.

–¡A ver, a ver! –dijo el abuelo–. Primero que nada hay que ordenar las cosas. Te daré un ejemplo.

ESTO ESCRIBIÓ EL ABUELO:

EL DÍA DE MI CUMPLEAÑOS

El domingo cumplí ocho años. Mi papá me regaló una bicicleta en la mañana. En la tarde vinieron todos mis amigos. Mi mamá nos dio chocolate y un pedazo de torta. Había globos y serpentinas. Nos disfrazamos con unos trajes viejos.

Tilam me trajo una nave espacial de juguete.

En la noche, miré todos mis regalos y estaba muy contento.

–¿Ves que es fácil? Sólo es cuestión de ir pensando y ordenando las ideas. No hay que saltarse de una cosa a otra.

ESCRIBIENDO MÁS HISTORIAS

UNA TARDE EN EL DESVÁN

Esa tarde el abuelo Pancho llamó a los niños y les dijo:

–Hoy vamos a subir al desván de la casa. Quiero abrir un viejo baúl a ver si allí encuentro algunas cosas que ando buscando. ¿Quieren venir conmigo?

–¡Sí, sí! –gritaron todos.

Juntos subieron la escalera que llevaba al techo. Había mucho polvo y telas de araña. En un rincón estaba el baúl. El abuelo sacó una llave del bolsillo y lo abrió.

Cuéntanos qué crees tú que encontraron dentro de él, y qué piensas tú que hicieron los niños y el abuelo esa tarde.

El abuelo Pancho y los niños subieron al desván. Allí...

....

....

....

....

....

....

HISTORIAS SIN TÍTULO

Como tú ya has podido ver, al abuelo Pancho le encanta contar cuentos. Pero al pobre le falla a veces la memoria, y no sabe cómo se llaman. Aquí, por ejemplo, hay tres escenas de tres cuentos distintos. Pero si tú le preguntas cómo se llaman los cuentos, te va a contestar que se le olvidó.

¿Qué títulos les pondrías tú?

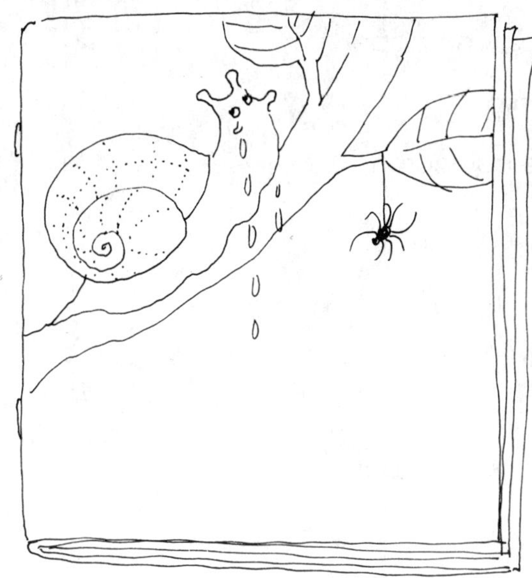

....

....

HISTORIA DE UN VOLANTÍN

Un día Toño y Claudia salieron a encumbrar un volantín. Subieron al Cerro San Cristóbal, y buscaron una parte en que hubiese bastante lugar y corriera viento.

El volantín lo habían fabricado ellos mismos, con papel de seda de distintos colores, palitos y pegamento.

También le pintaron ojos, nariz y boca, y le colocaron una cola hecha con cintas de papel.

–Pareciera que está vivo –comentó Toño.

–A lo mejor está vivo –respondió Claudia.

El volantín se encumbró, y subió y subió.

Los niños gritaron de alegría. Pero, de pronto, no sabes lo que pasó...

¿Quieres que te contemos?

A Toño se le soltó el hilo donde estaba amarrado el volantín, y éste siguió volando solo en el espacio, hasta que se perdió.

Pasaron muchas horas, y gracias a que corría una suave brisa el volantín se mantuvo en el aire.

Pero al llegar la noche ya no pudo mantenerse flotando en el aire, y cayó suavemente sobre el techo de una casa.

¿Cómo crees que se sentiría el volantín? ¿Qué habrá pensado esa noche? ¿Cómo habrá terminado esta historia? Sigue escribiendo tú como quieras esta historia.

....

....

....

....

....

....

....

....

....

....

....

....

....

ESCOBINA Y LOS CUENTOS

La bruja Escobina es muy diabla. Ahora le ha dado por recortar los cuentos del abuelo Pancho, y sólo les deja el final.

¡Imagínate!

Pero nosotros vamos a darle una sorpresa, y escribiremos lo que falta. ¿Qué te parece?

Aquí está el final. Tú piensas un poquito, y te imaginas lo que pasó antes, y lo escribes. ¿De acuerdo? Puedes, si quieres, dibujar algo. No olvides el título.

....

Autor: ....

....

....

....

....

....

A Toño le tuvieron que enyesar el pie, y Claudia lo acompañó toda la tarde para que no se aburriera.

Aquí hay otro final, y un poco del comienzo. ¿Inventemos lo que falta?

....

Autor: ....

Toño y Claudia salieron temprano esa mañana. Se encaminaron hacia los cerros. Era un hermoso día.

....

....

....

....

....

....

....

....

....

....

....

....

....

Muy contentos, Toño y Claudia le dieron las gracias al viejecito y bajaron por la colina hasta llegar a la casa, donde la mamá y el papá los estaban esperando algo preocupados.

OBSERVAR Y DESCRIBIR

Aquí están tus amigos: Tilam, el abuelo Pancho y la bruja Escobina.
Observa y **descríbelos.** Di cómo son, cómo están vestidos, dónde se encuentran, lo que tienen en sus manos.
Anota sólo lo que ves. No agregues nada más.

....

....

....

....

....

....

Tú has hecho la **descripción** de tus amigos.

–¡Mira, qué lindo lo que he encontrado...!, –le escribió un día Tilam a Toño.

–¡Bah!, pero si es sólo una hoja.

–¡Sí, pero fíjate bien –escribió el marciano:

"Es una hermosa hoja de otoño. Parece una estrella, pues tiene varias puntas. Su nervadura, casi seca, la recorre por toda la superficie.

En algunas partes tiene color café, y en otras, un suave color amarillo".

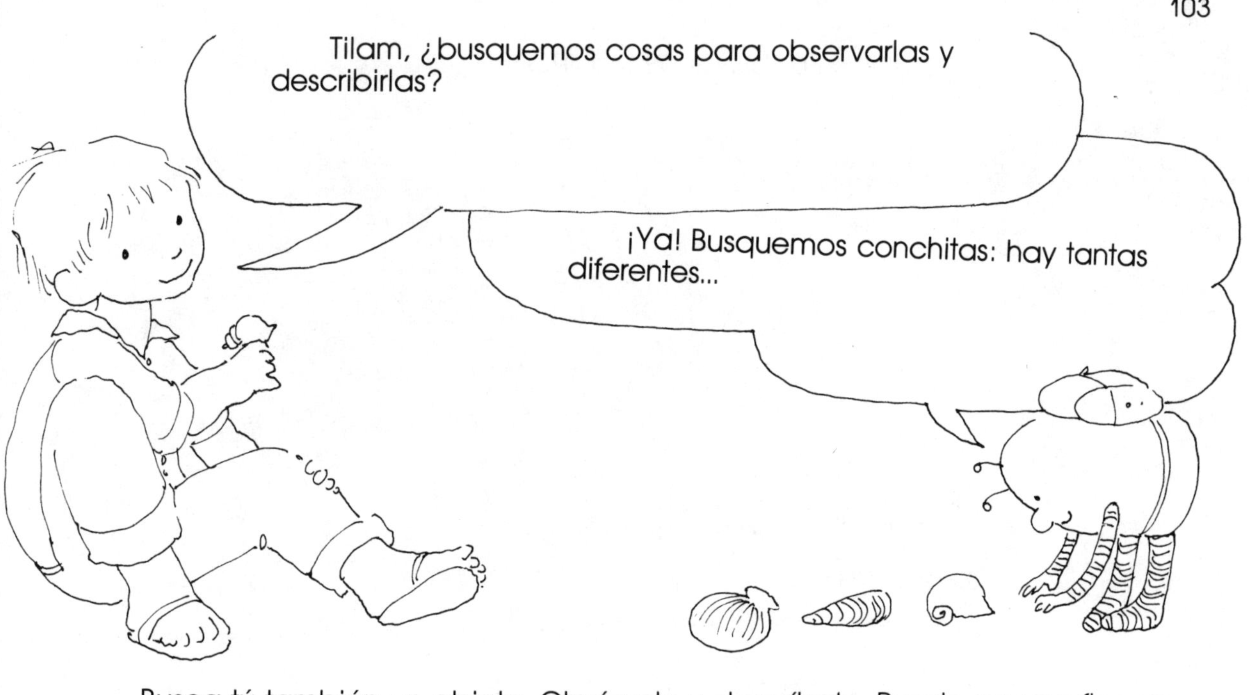

Tilam, ¿busquemos cosas para observarlas y describirlas?
¡Ya! Busquemos conchitas: hay tantas diferentes...

Busca tú también un objeto. Obsérvalo y descríbelo. Puede ser una flor, un juguete, una bolita de cristal, una fruta, o lo que desees.

DIBUJA EL OBJETO QUE ELEGISTE

AHORA, DESCRÍBELO

....

....

....

....

EL SUEÑO DE RONRÓN

HABLEMOS DE LOS SUEÑOS

Tú, tus hermanos, tus padres, tus amigos, el abuelo Pancho, todos soñamos. ¿Crees tú que soñarán Tilam y la bruja Escobina?...

A veces, tenemos sueños agradables. Otras veces, tenemos sueños desagradables y se llaman pesadillas. Éstas más vale no recordarlas. Pero es bonito recordar los sueños agradables.

Mira: el enano Ronrón duerme profundamente y sueña... Escribe lo que está soñando:

EL SUEÑO DE RONRÓN

....

....

....

....

....

....

....

....

....

....

....

....

Dicen que los animales también sueñan...

¿Qué sueña Toqui?
¿Qué sueña Micifuz?

Cuenta algún sueño que te haya resultado agradable o divertido.

Una noche soñé ....

....

....

....

....

....

....

....

....

....

....

....

....

....

....

¡Ah, amiguitos! ¿Ustedes creen que yo no sueño? Todas las brujas soñamos. Les voy a contar que un día anduve volando en mi escoba por hermosos lugares. En la noche soñé con uno de ellos. Les voy a contar cómo era.

EL SUEÑO DE ESCOBINA

Era un lugar muy hermoso. Había una extensa playa de arenas blancas, y el mar estaba muy azul. Al fondo se veían cerros llenos de bosques de pinos. El cielo estaba claro, y sólo se veían algunas nubes. El sol brillaba, llenando todo de luz.

Tilam también sueña. A él, igual que a Escobina, le gustan los paisajes. Una vez le contó a Toño este sueño.

EL SUEÑO DE TILAM

Soñé que subía por una montaña y desde allí se veía el valle. La silueta del río hacía contraste con los verdes prados. Numerosos sauces crecían a la orilla del agua. Más allá, los campesinos trabajaban arando sus tierras. Muchos pajarillos con el pechito rojo revoloteaban; creo que se llaman loicas.

Pídele a un amigo o amiga que te cuente algún sueño y tú lo escribes.

....

....

....

....

....

....

....

....

....

....

....

....

....

....

....

UNA EXCURSIÓN

¡Qué hermosos lugares han descrito nuestros amigos! Dan deseos de ir hasta allá.

¿Podrías describir este paisaje? Te ayudaremos un poco.

Era un .... valle escondido entre .... y cerros.

Un .... de .... corría por él.

¡Era un .... lugar!

Algunas .... muy .... saltaban desde los árboles y se

dejaban alimentar por los ....

Un aire ..,................. movía .... , mientras que .... pajaritos

cantaban sobre ....

....

....

....

....

....

Era la noche de Navidad. En la casa de Toño y Daniela hubo fiesta. Los padres, abuelos y amigos de los niños se habían reunido para recordar esa hermosa noche del 24 de diciembre cuando nació Jesús.

Pasadas las 12 de la noche, el cansancio obligó a Toño y a Daniela a acostarse. Naturalmente, llevaron los juguetes que les habían regalado. Y se durmieron...

Observa el dormitorio y **descríbelo**.

Te podemos ayudar un poco. Por ejemplo:

¿Dónde están acostados los niños?

¿Cómo son el pelo y el rostro de Pablo y Daniela?

¿Qué tienen los niños en sus manos?

¿Qué hay en el suelo de la pieza?

¿Qué hay en las murallas?

RECUERDA: Al **describir** debes anotar lo que ves y cómo son las personas y las cosas que ves.

Puedes empezar así:

Toño y Daniela están durmiendo ....

....

....

....

PANADERÍA
VERDULERÍA
Helados

EL PAÍS DE LOS ANIMALES

¡Mira qué hermosos! Aquí viven muchos animalitos. Observa atentamente.

¿Qué animales ves?
¿Cómo están vestidos?
¿Qué están haciendo?

Describe la lámina.

En este curioso pueblo ....

....

....

....

....

....

....

....

....

....

....

PANADERIA
VERDULERÍA
Helados

Ahora te invito a hacer algo muy entretenido.
Esta lámina ya la conoces, ¿verdad? Tú la **describiste.** Píntala. Mientras la pintas, piensa:

– ¿Por qué un chanchito lleva un bolsón colgando de su hombro?

– ¿Qué crees tú que está haciendo?

– ¿Por qué sus amigos se ven contentos?

Escribe lo que tú te imaginas. **Interpreta** lo que ves.

....

....

....

....

....

....

....

....

....

....

....

....

EN LA COCINA

¡Qué rico!
Anota lo que ves.

En esta cocina ....

HACIENDO UNA FIESTA

Hoy está lloviendo afuera. Los niños han decidido hacer una fiesta ....

ÉRASE UNA VEZ UN GIGANTE

Describe e interpreta esta lámina.

INVENTA UNA HISTORIA

LOS AMIGOS SE DESPIDEN

¡Adiós, amigos! Ha sido maravilloso conocer la Tierra y conocerlos a ustedes. Les prometo que si nos volvemos a encontrar no sólo escribiré, sino que les hablaré en el lenguaje terrícola.

¡Queridos amiguitos! Me he entretenido mucho con ustedes. Espero que ustedes también se hayan entretenido escribiendo.

¡Ojalá que algún día nos volvamos a encontrar!...

Yo no me despediré de ustedes. No me gustan los adioses, ni las despedidas. Volando en mi escoba mágica entraré hasta sus casas y sus escuelas para leer lo que escriban. Ya saben que soy una "metete" incorregible.

POWER GENERATION HANDBOOK

Selection, Applications, Operation, and Maintenance

Philip Kiameh

McGRAW-HILL
New York Chicago San Francisco Lisbon London Madrid
Mexico City Milan New Delhi San Juan Seoul
Singapore Sydney Toronto

The McGraw-Hill Companies

Library of Congress Cataloging-in-Publication Data
Kiameh, Philip.
Power generation handbook : selection, applications, operation, and maintenance / Philip Kiameh.
p. cm.
Includes index.
ISBN 0-07-139604-7
1. Electric power production. I. Title.
TK1001 K52 2002
621.31—dc21 2002026524

6 7 8 9 0 IBT/IBT 0 9

ISBN 0-07-139604-7

The sponsoring editor for this book was Kenneth P. McCombs, the editing supervisor was David E. Fogarty, and the production supervisor was Sherri Souffrance. It was set in the HB1 design in Times Roman by Wayne Palmer and Joanne Morbit of McGraw-Hill Professional's Hightstown, N. J. composition unit.

Printed and bound by IBT Global.

This book was printed on acid-free paper containing a minimum of 50% recycled, de-inked fiber.

To my son, Joseph

CONTENTS

Chapter 4. Turbine Governing Systems 4.1

Chapter 5. Steam Chests and Valves 5.1

Chapter 6. Turbine Protective Devices 6.1

Chapter 7. Turbine Instrumentation 7.1

Chapter 8. Lubrication Systems 8.1

Chapter 9. Gland Sealing System 9.1

Chapter 10. An Overview of Gas Turbines 10.1

Chapter 11. Gas Turbine Compressors 11.1

Chapter 12. Gas Turbine Combustors 12.1

Chapter 13. Axial-Flow Turbines 13.1

Chapter 14. Gas Turbine Materials 14.1

PREFACE

Power Generation Handbook provides a thorough understanding of gas turbines, steam power plants, cogeneration, and combined-cycle power plants (gas turbines operating in conjunction with steam power plants). Each of the components, such as compressors, gas and steam turbines, combustors, heat recovery steam generators, governing systems, deaerators, condensers, feedwater heaters, pumps, lubricating systems, transformers, and generators, are covered in detail. The selection considerations, operation, maintenance, economics, emission limits, instrumentation, and control systems are also covered thoroughly. All the significant improvements and power enhancement techniques that were made to these plants during the past two decades are explained. The reader will gain an in-depth understanding of these plants and their numerous advantages.

The book was written for all technical individuals including engineers of all disciplines, managers, technicians, operators, and maintenance personnel. All the concepts are presented in a simple and practical manner that allows the reader to understand them without relying on advanced mathematical equations. This book is a must for any individual who has an interest in power generation.

Deregulation of electricity markets is sweeping across the world. There will be increasing opportunities for highly efficient power generating plants, such as combined-cycle and cogeneration plants, to compete against the older plants of established utilities. These new plants are environmentally friendly and more than twice as efficient as the older fossil and nuclear generating plants. Independent power producers and utilities are planning to construct additional combined-cycle and cogeneration plants due to their short construction lead-time and low capital investment.

Combined-cycle plants have a 4- to 5-year payback period due to low staffing requirements and low operating and maintenance costs. They also have the advantage of long-term fuel price stability, fuel flexibility, and low emissions. These plants can be located close to the power-user, reducing transmission costs and increasing reliability. Studies have identified combined-cycle plants to be the most economic of available power generating methods. A shakeup in the electricity market is forecasted, and the competitive edge of combined-cycle plants provides them with a promising future.

I sincerely hope that this book will be as interesting to read as it was for me to write and that it will be a useful reference to anyone interested in power generation.

Philip Kiameh

ACKNOWLEDGMENTS

Reprinted from M. M. El-Wakil, *Power Plant Technology*, McGraw-Hill, New York, 1984, with permission from McGraw-Hill: Figs. 1.1 to 1.8, Tables 1.1 to 1.3, Figs. 2.1 to 2.14, Tables 2.1 and 2.2, Figs. 10.4, 21.1, 21.2, 21.4 to 21.7, and 21.9 to 21.12.

Reprinted from J. G. Van Wylen, *Fundamentals of Classical Thermodynamics*, 2d ed., John Wiley & Sons, New York, 1976, with permission from John Wiley & Sons, Inc.: Figs. 1.3 to 1.5 and Table 1.4.

Reprinted from G. Willis, *Lubrication Fundamentals*, Mobile Oil Corporation, Marcel Dekker, New York, 1980, with permission from Marcel Dekker: Figs. 3.1 to 3.11.

Reprinted from British Electricity International, *Modern Power Station Practice*, 3d ed., Pergamon Press, Oxford, United Kingdom, 1991, with permission from Elsevier Science: Figs. 4.1 to 4.18, 5.1 to 5.3, 6.1, 6.2, 8.1 to 8.17, Table 8.1, Figs 9.1 to 9.6, 32.1 to 32.34, and 32.36 to 32.46.

Reprinted from Meheran P. Boyce, *Gas Turbine Engineering Handbook*, Gulf Publishing Company, Houston, Tex, 1995, with permission from Butterworth-Heinemann: Figs. 10.2, 10.3, 10.13, 12.1, 12.2, 12.4 to 12.6, 12.18, 13.1 to 13.17, 14.1 to 14.3, Tables 14.1 and 14.2, Tables 15.1 and 15.2, Figs. 16.1 to 16.20, 17.1 to 17.10, Tables 17.1 to 17.4 and 17.5.

Reprinted with permission from VA Tech Ferranti-Packard Transformers Ltd.: Figs. 29.2, 29.4, and Fig 29.5.

Reprinted from S. D. Myers, and J. J. Kelly, *Transformer Maintenance Guide,* Transformer Maintenance Institute, Division of S. D. Myers, Inc., Cuyahoga Falls, Ohio, with permission from S.D. Myers, Inc.: Figs. 29.9 to 29.12 and Tables 29.2 to 29.4.

Reprinted with permission from Rolls-Royce: Figs. 10.6a, 10.8, 10.16, 10.17, 12.3, 12.8, 12.11, 12.12, 12.19, and 12.20.

Reprinted with permission from General Electric: Figs. 10.6b, 10.15, 12.7, 12.10, 12.17, 14.4, 18.2 to 18.4, 21.3, 25.1 to 25.3, Table 25.1, and Figs. 31.1 (b) and (c) and 31.6.

Reprinted from H. Cohen, G. F. C. Rogers, and H. I. H. Saravanamuttoo, *Gas Turbine Theory*, 2d ed., Longman Group Limited, 1972, with permission from Pearson Education: Figs. 11.1 to 11.9.

Reprinted with permission from Solar Turbines: Fig. 18.1.

Reprinted with permission from Environment Canada: Figs. 20.1, Tables 20.1 and 20.2, and Fig 20.2.

Reprinted from D. Halliday and R. Resnick, *Physics, Part Two*, 3d ed., John Wiley & Sons, 1978, with permission from John Wiley & Sons, Inc.: Figs. 26.1 to 26.21 and Tables 26.1 and 26.2.

Reprinted from S. J. Chapman, *Electric Machinery Fundamentals*, 2d ed., McGraw-Hill, New York, 1991, with permission from McGraw-Hill: Figs. 27.1, 27.6, 28.1 to 28.3, 28.6 to 28.10, Example 28.1, Figs. 30.1 to 30.9, 31.2 to 31.5, 31.7 to 31.20, 31.22 to 31.34.

POWER GENERATION HANDBOOK

CHAPTER 1
REVIEW OF THERMODYNAMIC PRINCIPLES

The design, operation, and performance of electricity-generating power plants are based on thermodynamic principles.[1,2]

THE FIRST LAW OF THERMODYNAMICS

The first law of thermodynamics is the law of conservation of energy. It states that energy can be neither created nor destroyed. The energy of a system undergoing change (process) can vary by exchange with the surroundings. However, energy can be converted from one form to another within that system.

A *system* is a specified region, not necessarily of constant volume or fixed boundaries, where transfer and conversions of energy and mass are taking place. An *open system* is one where energy and mass cross the boundaries of the system. A *steady-state open system,* also called the *steady-state, steady-flow* (SSSF) *system,* is a system where mass and energy flows across its boundaries do not vary with time, and the mass within the system remains constant.

An SSSF system is shown in Fig. 1.1.

The first-law equation for that system is

$$\mathrm{PE}_1 + \mathrm{KE}_1 + \mathrm{IE}_1 + \mathrm{FE}_1 + \Delta Q = \mathrm{PE}_2 + \mathrm{KE}_2 + \mathrm{IE}_2 + \mathrm{FE}_2 + \Delta W_{\mathrm{sf}} \qquad (1.1)$$

where PE = potential energy [$= mzg/g_c$, where m = mass of quantity of fluid entering and leaving the system, z = elevation of station 1 or 2 above a datum, g = gravitational acceleration, and g_c = gravitational conversion factor (32.2 $\mathrm{lb}_m \cdot \mathrm{ft}/(\mathrm{lb}_f \cdot \mathrm{s}^2)$ or 1.0 $\mathrm{kg} \cdot \mathrm{m}/(\mathrm{N} \cdot \mathrm{s}^2)$].

KE = kinetic energy ($= mV_s^2/2g_c$), where V_s = velocity of the mass.

IE = internal energy ($= U$). The internal energy is a sole function of temperature for perfect gases and a strong function of temperature and weak function of pressure for nonperfect gases, vapors, and liquids. It is a measure of the internal (molecular) activity and interaction of the fluid.

FE = flow energy ($= PV = Pmv$). The flow energy or flow work is the work done by the flowing fluid to push a mass m into or out of the system.

ΔQ = net heat added [$= Q_A - |Q_r|$, where Q_A = heat added and Q_r = heat rejected across system boundaries; $\Delta Q = mc_n(T_2 - T_1)$, where c_n = specific heat that depends upon the process taking place between 1 and 2. Values of c_n vary with the process (refer to Table 1.1)].

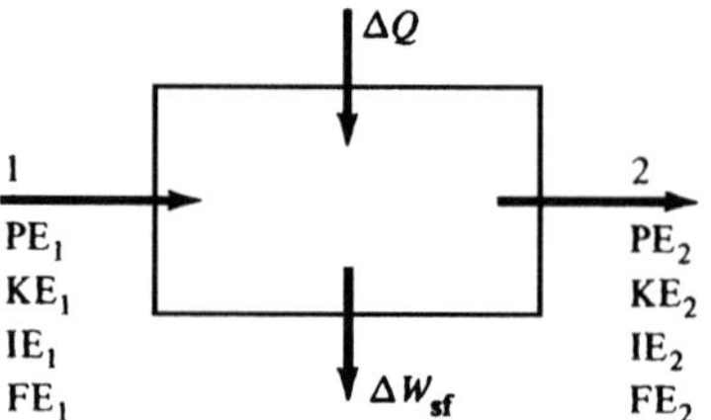

FIGURE 1.1 Schematic of a steady-state, steady-flow (SSSF) system with one inlet and one outlet.

TABLE 1.1 Values of c_n and n for Various Processes

Process	c_n	n
Constant pressure	c_p	0
Constant temperature	∞	1
Adiabatic reversible	0	$k = \frac{c_p}{c_v}$
Constant volume	c_v	∞
Polytropic	$c_v \frac{k-n}{1-n}$	$0 - \infty$

ΔW_{sf} = net steady-flow mechanical work done by the system [$= W_{by} - |W_{on}|$, where W_{by} = work done by system (positive) and W_{on} = work done on system (negative)] .

$$\Delta W_{sf} = -\int_1^2 V \cdot dP \tag{1.2}$$

A relationship between P and V is required. The most general relationship is given by

$$PV^n = \text{constant} \tag{1.3}$$

where n is called the polytropic exponent. It varies between zero and infinity. Its value for certain processes is given in Table 1.1. The first-law equation becomes

$$\frac{z_1 g}{g_c} + \frac{V_{s1}^2}{2g_c} + u_1 + P_1 v_1 + \Delta q = \frac{z_2 g}{g_c} + \frac{V_{s2}^2}{2g_c} + u_2 + P_2 v_2 + \Delta W_{sf} \tag{1.4}$$

where $u = U/m$ (specific internal energy), and $v = V/m$ (specific volume). A list of common thermodynamic symbols is presented in Table 1.2.

ENTHALPY

Enthalpy is defined as

$$H = U + PV \quad \text{or} \quad h = u + Pv$$

and the first law becomes

TABLE 1.2 Some Common Thermodynamic Symbols

c_p	=	specific heat at constant pressure, Btu/(lb$_m$ · °F) [J/(kg · K)]
c_v	=	specific heat at constant volume, Btu/(lb$_m$ · °F) [J/(kg · K)]
h	=	specific enthalpy, Btu/lb$_m$ (J/kg)
H	=	total enthalpy, Btu (J)
J	=	energy conversion factor = 778.16 ft · lb$_f$/Btu (1.0 N m/J)
M	=	molecular mass, lb$_m$/lb · mol or kg/kg · mol
n	=	polytropic exponent, dimensionless
P	=	absolute pressure (gauge pressure + barometric pressure), lb$_f$/ft^2; unit may be lb$_f$/in^2 (commonly written psia, or Pa)
Q	=	heat transferred to or from system, Btu or J, or Btu/cycle or J/cycle
R	=	gas constant, lb$_f$ · ft/(lb$_m$ · °R) or J/(kg · K) = $\overline{R}/M$
$\overline{R}$	=	universal gas constant = 1.545.33, lb$_f$ · ft/(lb · mol · °R) or 8.31434 × 10^3 J/(kg · mol · K)
s	=	specific entropy, Btu/(lb$_m$ · °R) or J/(kg · K)
S	=	total entropy, Btu/°R or J/kg
t	=	temperature, °F or °C
T	=	temperature on absolute scale, °R or K
u	=	specific internal energy, Btu/lb$_m$ or J/kg
U	=	total internal energy, Btu or J
v	=	specific volume, ft^3/lb$_m$ or m^3/kg
V	=	total volume, ft^3 or m^3
W	=	work done by or on system, lb$_f$ · ft or J, or Btu/cycle or J/cycle
x	=	quality of a two-phase mixture = mass of vapor divided by total mass, dimensionless
k	=	ratio of specific heats, c_p/c_v, dimensionless
η	=	efficiency, as dimensionless fraction or percent

Subscripts used in vapor tables

f	refers to saturated liquid
g	refers to saturated vapor
fg	refers to change in property because of change from saturated liquid to saturated vapor

$$\frac{mz_1g}{g_c} + \frac{mV_{s1}^2}{2g_c} + H_1 + \Delta Q = \frac{mz_2g}{g_c} + \frac{mV_{s2}^2}{2g_c} + H_2 + \Delta W_{sf} \tag{1.5}$$

Enthalpies and internal energies are properties of the fluid. This means that each would have a single value at any given state of the fluid. The specific heat at constant volume is

$$c_v = \left(\frac{\partial u}{\partial T}\right)_v \tag{1.6}$$

The specific heat at constant pressure is

$$c_p = \left(\frac{\partial h}{\partial T}\right)_p \tag{1.7}$$

$$c_p - c_v = R$$

where R is the gas constant.

For ideal gases:

$$du = c_v dT \tag{1.8}$$

$$dh = c_p dT$$

where c_v and c_p are constants. They are independent of temperature for monatomic gases such as He. They increase with temperature for diatomic gases such as air and more so for triatomic gases such as CO_2 and so forth. Therefore, for constant specific heats or for small changes in temperature:

$$\Delta u = c_v \Delta T \tag{1.9}$$

$$\Delta h = c_p \Delta T$$

Following are some examples:

- For a steam generator, $\Delta W_{sf} = 0$, $PE_2 - PE_1$ is negligible, $KE_2 - KE_1$ is negligible, $\Delta Q = H_2 - H_1$, and $\Delta q = h_2 - h_1$.
- For gas or steam turbine, ΔQ = negligible, $PE_2 - PE_1$ is negligible, $KE_2 - KE_1$ is negligible, and $\Delta W_{sf} = H_1 - H_2$.
- For water (or incompressible fluid) pump, ΔQ is negligible, $PE_2 - PE_1$ is negligible, $KE_2 - KE_1$ is negligible, $U_2 = U_1$, $V_2 = V_1 = V$ (incompressible fluid), and $\Delta W_{sf} = FE_1 - FE_2 = V(P_1 - P_2)$.

CLOSED SYSTEM

In the open system, mass crosses the boundaries. In the *closed system,* only energy crosses the boundaries. The first law for the closed system becomes

$$\Delta Q = \Delta U + \Delta W_{nf} \quad \text{(change with time, before and after the process has taken place)} \tag{1.10}$$

ΔW_{nf} is called the no-flow work. It is given by

$$\Delta W_{nf} = \int_1^2 P dV \tag{1.11}$$

THE CYCLE

To convert energy from heat to work on a continuous basis, one needs to operate a cycle. A *cycle* is a series of processes that begins and ends at the same state and can be repeated indefinitely. Figure 1.2 illustrates an ideal diesel cycle.

Process 1 to 2. Ideal and adiabatic (no heat exchanged) compression

Process 2 to 3. Heat adidtion at constant pressure

Process 3 to 4. Ideal and adiabatic expansion process

Process 4 to 1. Constant-volume heat rejection

The first law becomes

$$\Delta Q_{net} = Q_A - |Q_R| = \Delta W_{net} \tag{1.12}$$

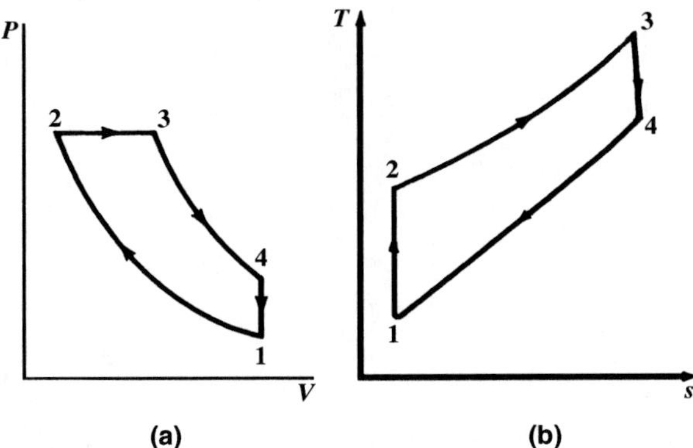

FIGURE 1.2 Pressure-volume (*a*) and temperature-entropy (*b*) diagrams of an ideal diesel cycle.

PROPERTY RELATIONSHIPS

Perfect Gases

Property relationships for perfect gases for different processes are given in Table 1.3 A *perfect* (or *ideal*) *gas* is one that, at any state, obeys the equation of state for perfect gases:

$$Pv = RT \tag{1.13}$$

Imperfect Gases

A *nonperfect gas* is one in which the molecules are close enough to exert forces on each other as when a perfect gas is highly compressed and/or highly cooled with respect to its critical conditions. The behavior of imperfect gases is given by

$$Pv = ZRT \tag{1.14}$$

where Z is the compressibility factor that depends on P, T, and the gas itself.

VAPOR-LIQUID PHASE EQUILIBRIUM IN A PURE SUBSTANCE

Consider a piston-cylinder arrangement containing 1 kg of water (refer to Fig. 1.3). Suppose the initial pressure and temperature inside the cylinder are 0.1 MPa and 20°C. As heat is transferred to the water, the temperature increases while the pressure remains constant. When the temperature reaches 99.6°C, additional heat transfer results in a change of phase, as indicated in Fig. 1.3 (*b*). Some of the liquid becomes vapor. However, during this process, both temperature and pressure remain constant, but the specific volume increases considerably. When

TABLE 1.3 Perfect-Gas Relationships (Constant Specific Heats)

Process	P, v, T relationships	$u_2 - u_1$	$h_2 - h_1$	$s_2 - s_1$	w (nonflow)	w (flow)	Q
Isothermal	T = constant $P_1/P_2 = v_2/v_1$	0	0	$(R/J)\ln(v_2/v_1)$	$(P_1v_1/J)\ln(v_2/v_1)$	$(P_1v_1/J)\ln(v_2/v_1)$	$(P_1v_1/J)\ln(v_2/v_1)$
Constant pressure	P = constant $T_2/T_1 = v_2/v_1$	$c_v(T_2 - T_1)$	$c_p(T_2 - T_1)$	$c_p\ln(T_2/T_1)$	$P(v_2 - v_1)/J$	0	$c_p(T_2 - T_1)$
Constant volume	v = constant $T_2/T_1 = P_2/P_1$	$c_v(T_2 - T_1)$	$c_p(T_2 - T_1)$	$c_v\ln(T_2/T_1)$	0	$v(P_1 - P_2)/J$	$c_v(T_2 - T_1)$
Isentropic (Adiabatic reversible)	s = constant $P_1v_1^k = P_2v_2^k$ $T_2/T_1 = (v_1/v_2)^k - 1$ $T_2/T_1 = (P_2/P_1)^{(k-1)/k}$	$c_v(T_2 - T_1)$	$c_p(T_2 - T_1)$	0	$\dfrac{(P_2v_2 - P_1v_1)}{J(1 - k)}$	$\dfrac{k(P_2v_2 - P_1v_1)}{J(1 - k)}$	0
Throttling	h = constant T = constant $P_1/P_2 = v_2/v_1$	0	0	$(R/J)\ln(v_2/v_1)$	0	0	0
Polytropic $T_2/T_1 = (P_2/P_1)^{(n-1)/n}$	$P_1v_1^n = P_2v_2^n$ $T_2/T_1 = (v_1/v_2)^{n-1}$	$c_v(T_2 - T_1)$	$c_p(T_2 - T_1)$	$c_v\ln(P_2/P_1)$ $+ c_p\ln(v_2/v_1)$	$\dfrac{(P_2v_2 - P_1v_1)}{J(1 - n)}$	$\dfrac{n(P_2v_2 - P_1v_1)}{J(1 - n)}$	$c_v\left(\dfrac{k - n}{1 - n}\right)(T_2 - T_1)$

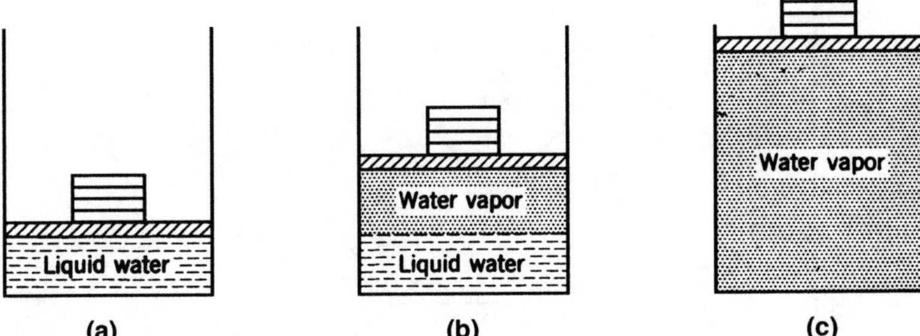

FIGURE 1.3 Constant-pressure change from liquid to vapor phase for a pure substance. (*a*) Liquid water, (*b*) liquid water–water vapor, (*c*) water vapor.

all the liquid has vaporized, additional heat transfer results in increase in both temperature and specific volume of the vapor.

The *saturation temperature* is the temperature at which vaporization occurs at a given pressure. This pressure is called the *saturation pressure* for the given temperature. For example, for water at 0.1 MPa, the saturation temperature is 99.6°C.

For a pure substance, there is a relationship between the saturation temperature and the saturation pressure. Figure 1.4 illustrates this relationship. The curve is called the *vapor-pressure curve.*

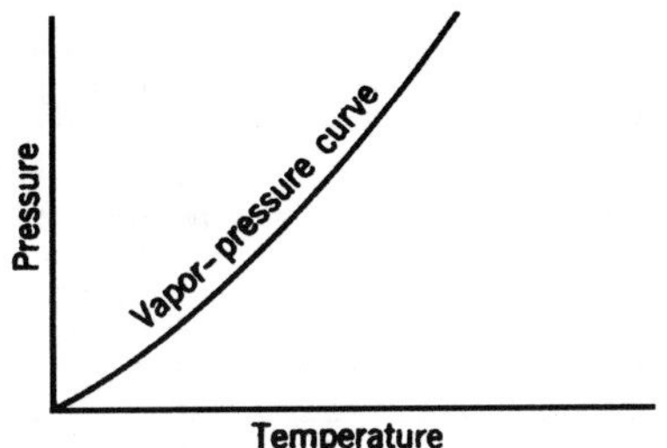

FIGURE 1.4 Vapor-pressure curve of a pure substance.

If a substance exists as liquid at the saturation temperature and pressure, it is called *saturated liquid.* If the temperature of the liquid is lower than the saturation temperature for the existing pressure, it is called *subcooled liquid* (or *compressed liquid,* implying that the pressure is greater than the saturation pressure for the given temperature).

When a substance exists as part liquid and part vapor at the saturation temperature and pressure, its quality (x) is defined as the ratio of the vapor mass to the total mass.

If the substance exists as vapor at the saturation temperature, it is called *saturated vapor.* When the vapor is at a temperature greater than the saturation temperature (for the existing pressure), it is called *superheated vapor.* The temperature of a superheated vapor may increase while the pressure remains constant.

Figure 1.5 illustrates a temperature-volume diagram for water showing liquid and vapor phases. Note that when the pressure is 1 MPa, vaporization (saturation temperature) begins at 179.9°C. Point *G* is the saturated-vapor state, and line *GH* represents the constant-pressure process in which the steam is superheated. A constant pressure of 10 MPa is represented by line *IJKL.* The saturation temperature is 311.1°C. Line *NJFB* represents the saturated-liquid line, and line *NKGC* represents the saturated-vapor line.

At a pressure 22.09 MPa, represented by line *MNO,* we find, however, that there is no constant-temperature vaporization process. Instead, there is one point, *N,* where the curve has a zero slope. This point is called the *critical point.* At this point, the saturated-liquid and saturated-vapor states are identical.

The temperature, pressure, and specific volume at the critical point are called the *critical temperature, critical pressure,* and *critical volume.* The critical-point data for some substances are presented in Table 1.4.

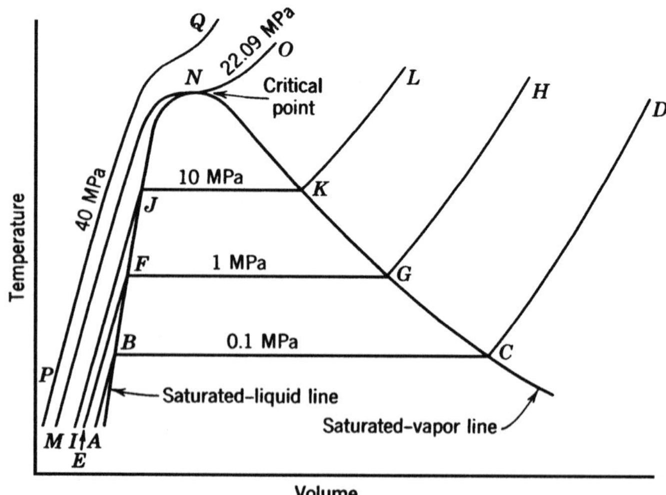

FIGURE 1.5 Temperature-volume diagram for water showing liquid and vapor phases (not to scale).

TABLE 1.4 Constants for Some Fluids*

Fluid	M	R, ft · lb_f/(lb_m · °R)	P_c		T_c	
			psia	bar	°R	K
Air	28.967	53.34	547.43	37.744	557.1	309.50
Ammonia	17.032	90.77	1635.67	112.803	238.34	132.41
Carbon dioxide	44.011	35.12	1071.34	73.884	547.56	304.20
Carbon monoxide	28.011	55.19	507.44	34.995	239.24	132.91
Freon-12	120.925	12.78	596.66	41.148	693.29	385.16
Helium	4.003	386.33	33.22	2.291	9.34	5.19
Hydrogen	2.016	766.53	188.07	12.970	59.83	33.24
Methane	16.043	96.40	67.31	46.418	343.26	190.70
Nitrogen	28.016	55.15	492.91	33.993	227.16	126.20
Octane	114.232	13.54	362.11	24.973	1024.92	569.40
Oxygen	32.000	48.29	736.86	50.817	278.60	154.78
Sulfur dioxide	64.066	24.12	1143.34	78.850	775.26	430.70
Water	18.016	85.80	3206.18	221.112	1165.09	647.27

*Multiply values of R by 5.343 to convert to J/(kg · K).

A constant-pressure process at a pressure greater than the critical pressure is represented by line PQ. If water at a pressure of 40 MPa and 20°C is heated in a constant-pressure process, there will never be two phases present. However, there will be a continuous change of density.

THE SECOND LAW OF THERMODYNAMICS

The second law puts a limitation on the conversion of heat to work. Work can always be converted to heat; however, heat cannot always be converted to work.

The portion of heat that cannot be converted to work is called *unavailable energy.* It must be rejected as low-grade heat after work is generated.

The second law states that the thermal efficiency of converting heat to work, in a power plant, must be less than 100 percent. The Carnot cycle represents an ideal heat engine that gives the maximum-value of that efficiency between any two temperature limits. In a steam or gas power plant, heat is received from a high-temperature reservoir (a *reservoir* is a source of heat or heat sink large enough that it does not undergo a change in temperature when heat is added or subtracted from it), such as steam generators or combustors.

Heat is also rejected in a steam or gas power plant to a low-temperature reservoir, such as condensers or the environment. The work produced in the steam or gas power plant is the difference between the heat received from the high-temperature reservoir and the heat rejected to the low-temperature reservoir.

THE CONCEPT OF REVERSIBILITY

Sadi Carnot introduced the concept of reversibility and laid the foundations of the second law. A *reversible process,* also called an *ideal process,* can reverse itself exactly by following the same path it took in the first place. Thus, it restores to the system or the surroundings the same heat and work previously exchanged.

In reality, there are no ideal (reversible) processes. Real processes are irreversible. However, the degree of irreversibility varies between processes.

There are many sources of irreversibility in nature. The most important ones are friction, heat transfer, throttling, and mixing. Mechanical friction is one in which mechanical work is dissipated into a heating effect. One example would be a shaft rotating in a bearing. It is not possible to add the same heat to the bearing to cause rotation of the shaft.

An example of fluid friction is when the fluid expands through the turbine, undergoing internal friction. This friction results in the dissipation of part of its energy into heating itself at the expense of useful work. The fluid then does less work and exhausts at a higher temperature. The more irreversible the process, the more heating effect and the less the work.

Heat transfer in any form cannot reverse itself. Heat transfer causes a loss of availability because no work is done between the high- and low-temperature bodies.

EXTERNAL AND INTERNAL IRREVERSIBILITIES

External irreversibilities are those that occur across the boundaries of the system. The primary source of external irreversibility in power systems is heat transfer both at the high- and low-temperature ends.

Internal irreversibilities are those that occur within the boundaries of the system. The primary source of internal irreversibilities in power systems is fluid friction in rotary machines, such as turbines, compressors, and pumps.

THE CONCEPT OF ENTROPY

Entropy is a property (e.g., pressure, temperature, and enthalpy). Entropy is given by the equation

$$\Delta Q = \int_1^2 TdS \qquad \text{(reversible process only)} \tag{1.15}$$

For a reversible, adiabatic process, $\Delta Q = 0$. Therefore,

$$\left(\int_1^2 TdS = 0\right) \rightarrow (dS = 0) \rightarrow (S = \text{constant}) \tag{1.16}$$

Figure 1.6 illustrates a few processes on the temperature-entropy diagram. A reversible adiabatic process is shown as 1-2_s in Fig. 1.6. Assume that the expanding fluid is a perfect gas (the same conclusion can be drawn for vapor or a mixture of liquid and vapor). Lines P_1 and P_2 in Fig. 1.6 are constant-pressure lines ($P_1 > P_2$). Process 1-2 in Fig. 1.6 illustrates an adiabatic but irreversible process. Irreversibility has manifested itself in an increase in temperature of the gas at P_2 ($T_2 > T_{2s}$).

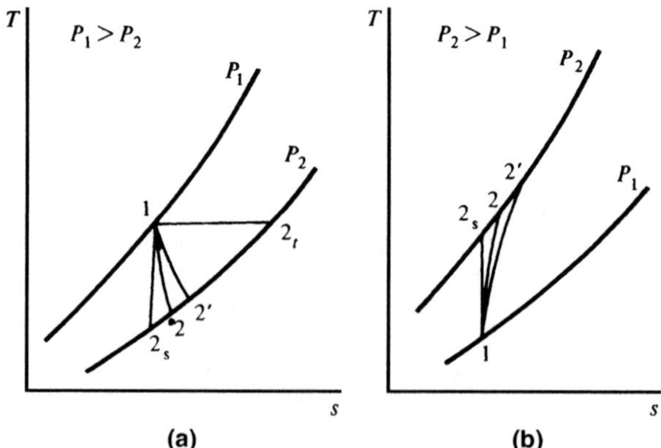

FIGURE 1.6 Expansion (*a*) and compression (*b*) of a gas from P_1 to P_2 on the *T-S* diagram. Process 1-2_s is adiabatic reversible; process 1-2 is adiabatic irreversible; and process 1-2_t is throttling.

More irreversible expansion results in greater self-heating of the gas, as shown in process 1-2. Therefore, when irreversibility increases in an adiabatic process, the entropy increases as well. The work produced decreases with an increase in irreversibility.

Process 1-2_t is a constant-temperature process (for a gas, it is a constant enthalpy as well). This is a throttling process, where ΔH is zero and all the energy is dissipated in fluid friction. This is the most irreversible process. It creates the most increase in entropy.

The degree of irreversibility for an expansion in a turbine is given by the *polytropic turbine efficiency,* η_T (sometimes called the *isentropic* or *adiabatic turbine efficiency*). It is equal to the ratio of actual work to ideal work.

The polytropic turbine efficiency is given by

$$\eta_T = \frac{H_1 - H_2}{H_1 - H_{2s}} = \frac{h_1 - h_2}{h_1 - h_{2s}} \tag{1.17}$$

For constant specific heats

$$\eta_T = \frac{T_1 - T_2}{T_1 - T_{2s}} \tag{1.18}$$

If the fluid is being compressed [Fig. 1.6 (*b*)], an adiabatic, reversible compression follows the constant entropy path $1\text{-}2_s$. If the process changes to adiabatic irreversible compression, the gas leaves at higher temperature T_2.

The fluid in this process absorbs some work input, which is dissipated in fluid friction. The greater the irreversibility, the greater the exit temperature ($T_{2'} > T_2' > T_{2s}$) and the greater the increase in entropy.

Since $dh = c_p dT$ for gases, then,

$$H_{2'} > H_2 > H_{2s} \tag{1.19}$$

and the work absorbed in compression $|W_c|$ increases with irreversibility.

The degree of irreversibility is given by the compressor efficiency. It is called the *polytropic compressor efficiency,* η_c (sometimes it is called the *isentropic* or *adiabatic compressor efficiency*). It is equal to the ratio of ideal work to actual work (the reverse of that of the expansion) and is given by

$$\eta_c = \frac{H_{2s} - H_1}{H_2 - H_1} = \frac{h_{2s} - h_1}{h_2 - h_1} \tag{1.20}$$

For constant specific heats

$$\eta_c = \frac{T_{2s} - T_1}{T_2 - T_1} \tag{1.21}$$

We can conclude that the change of entropy is a measure of the unavailable energy. Therefore, entropy is a measure of irreversibility. This implies that entropy is a measure of disorder. Entropy of the universe is continually increasing and available energy is continually decreasing.

Figure 1.7 illustrates vapor expanding from pressure P_1 to pressure P_2, where P_2 is in the two-phase region. Even if the exit temperature of the adiabatic reversible and adiabatic

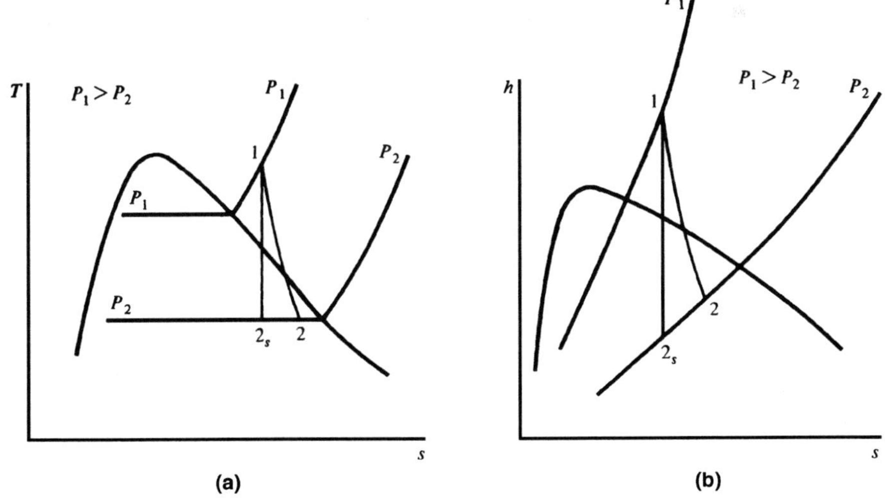

FIGURE 1.7 Expansion fo a vapor from P_1 to P_2 on the (*a*) *T-s* and (*b*) Mollier (*h-s*) diagrams. Process $1\text{-}2_s$ is adiabatic reversible, and process 1-2 is adiabatic irreversible.

irreversible processes is the same, the exit enthalpy is greater in the case of the irreversible process ($h_2 > h_{2s}$) and the work is less:

$$h_1 - h_2 < h_1 - h_{2s} \tag{1.22}$$

The degree of irreversibility is given by the turbine efficiency.

THE CARNOT CYCLE

Sadi Carnot introduced the principles of the second law of thermodynamics, the concepts of reversibility and cycle. He also proved that the thermal efficiency of a reversible cycle is determined by the temperatures of the heat source and heat sink.

The Carnot cycle is shown in Fig. 1.8 on the *P-V* and *T-S* diagrams. It is composed of four processes:

1. *Process 1-2.* Reversible adiabatic compression
2. *Process 2-3.* Reversible constant-temperature heat addition
3. *Process 3-4.* Reversible adiabatic expansion
4. *Process 4-1.* Reversible constant-temperature heat rejection

$$\text{Heat addition:} \quad Q_A = T_H (S_3 - S_2) \tag{1.23}$$

$$\text{Heat rejection:} \quad Q_R = T_L (S_1 - S_4) \tag{1.24}$$

$$\text{Net work:} \quad \Delta W_{\text{net}} = Q_A - |Q_R| \tag{1.25}$$

$$\text{Thermal efficiency:} \quad \eta_{\text{th}} = \frac{\Delta W_{\text{net}}}{Q_A} \tag{1.26}$$

Thus, the thermal efficiency of the Carnot cycle η_c is given by

$$\eta_c = \frac{T_H - T_L}{T_H} \tag{1.27}$$

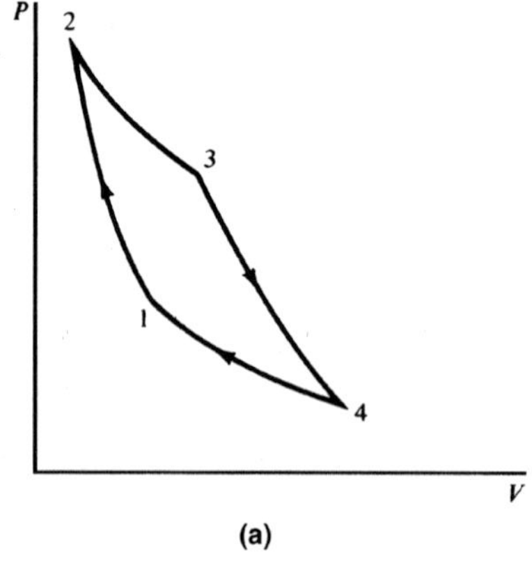

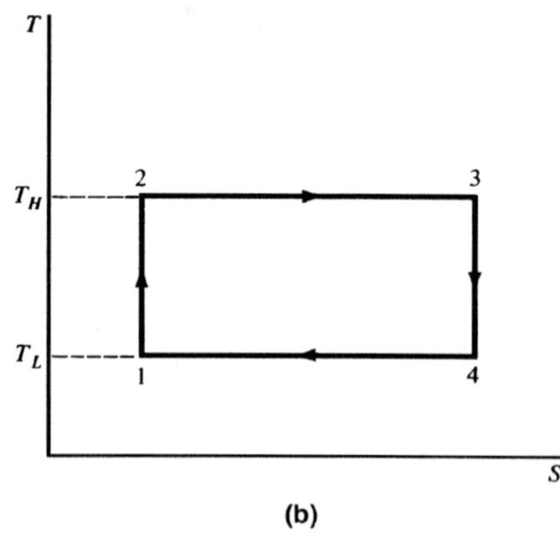

FIGURE 1.8 Carnot cycle on the (*a*) *P-V* and (*b*) *T-S* diagrams.

The thermal efficiency of the Carnot cycle is dependent on the heat source and heat sink temperatures. It is independent of the working fluid.

Since the Carnot cycle is reversible, it produces the maximum amount of work between two given temperature limits, T_H and T_L. Therefore, a reversible cycle operating between given temperature limits has the highest possible thermal efficiency of all cycles operating between these same temperature limits. The Carnot cycle efficiency is to be considered an upper efficiency limit that cannot be exceeded in reality.

REFERENCES

1. El-Wakil, M. M., *Power Plant Technology,* McGraw-Hill, New York, 1984.
2. Van Wylen, J. G., *Fundamentals of Classical Thermodynamics,* John Wiley & Sons, New York, 1976.

CHAPTER 2
STEAM POWER PLANTS

THE RANKINE CYCLE

The Rankine cycle is the most widely used cycle for electric power generation. Figure 2.1 illustrates a simplified flow diagram of a Rankine cycle. Figure 2.2(*a, b*) shows the ideal Rankine cycle on *P-v* and *T-s* diagrams. Cycle 1-2-3-4-*B*-1 is a saturated Rankine cycle (saturated vapor enters the turbine). Cycle 1′-2′-3-4-*B*-1′ is a superheated Rankine cycle.

The cycles shown are internally reversible. The processes through the turbine and pump are adiabatic reversible. Hence, vertical on the *T-s* diagram. There are no pressure losses in the piping. Line 4-*B*-1-1′ is a constant-pressure line.

The reversible Rankine cycle has the following processes:

Line 1-2 or 1′-2′. Adiabatic reversible expansion through the *turbine.* The exhaust vapor at point 2 or point 2′ is usually in the two-phase region.

Line 2-3 or 2′-3. Constant-temperature and, being a two-phase mixture process, constant-pressure heat rejection in the condenser.

Line 3-4. Adiabatic reversible compression by the *pump* of saturated liquid at the condenser pressure, point 3, to subcooled liquid at the steam generator pressure, point 4. Line 3-4 is vertical on both the *P-v* and *T-s* diagrams because the liquid is essentially incompressible and the pump is adiabatic reversible.

Line 4-1 or 4-1′. Constant-pressure heat addition in the *steam generator.* Line 4-*B*-1-1′ is a constant-pressure line on both diagrams. Portion 4-*B* represents bringing the subcooled liquid, point 4, to saturated liquid at point *B*. Section 4-*B* in the steam generator is called an *economizer.* Portion *B*-1 represents heating the saturated liquid to saturated vapor at constant pressure and temperature (being a two-phase mixture), and section *B*-1 in the steam generator is called the *boiler* or *evaporator.* Portion 1-1′, in the superheat cycle, represents heating the saturated vapor at point 1 to point 1′. Section 1-1′ in the steam generator is called a *superheater.*

Following is the thermodynamic analysis based on a unit mass of vapor in the cycle:

Heat added

$$q_A = h_1 - h_4 \quad \text{Btu/lb}_m \text{ (or J/kg)} \tag{2.1}$$

Turbine work

$$w_T = h_1 - h_2 \quad \text{Btu/lb}_m \text{ (or J/kg)} \tag{2.2}$$

Heat rejected

$$|q_R| = h_2 - h_3 \quad \text{Btu/lb}_m \text{ (or J/kg)} \tag{2.3}$$

Pump work

$$|w_p| = h_4 - h_3 \tag{2.4}$$

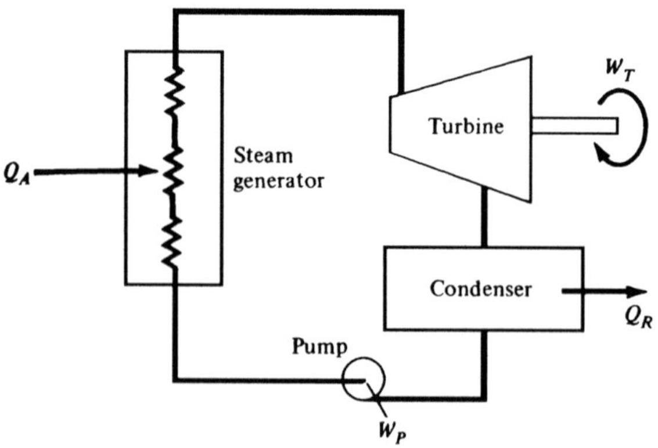

FIGURE 2.1 Schematic flow diagram of a Rankine cycle.

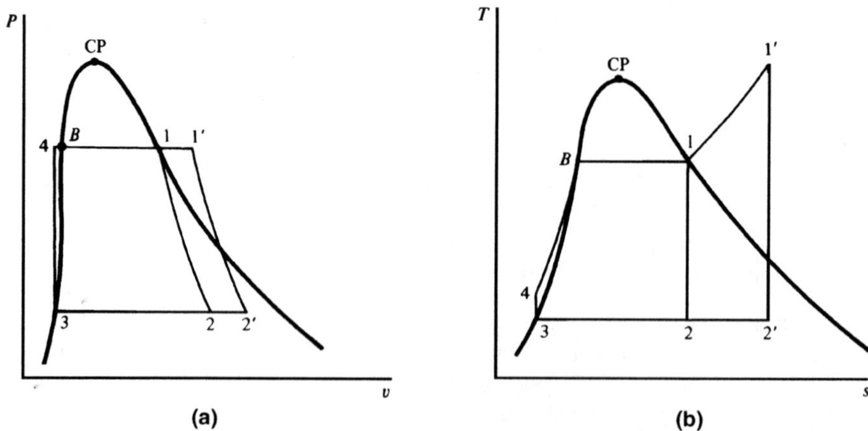

FIGURE 2.2 Ideal Rankine cycles of the (*a*) *P-V* and (*b*) *T-s* diagrams. Line 1-2-3-4-*B*-1 = saturated cycle. Line 1′-2′-3-4-*B*-1′ = superheated cycle. CP = critical point.

Net work

$$\Delta w_{net} = (h_1 - h_2) - (h_4 - h_3) \quad \text{Btu/lb}_m \text{ (or J/kg)} \quad (2.5)$$

Thermal efficiency

$$\eta_{th} = \frac{\Delta w_{net}}{q_A} = \frac{(h_1 - h_2) - (h_4 - h_3)}{(h_1 - h_4)} \quad (2.6)$$

For small units where P_4 is not much larger than P_3,

$$h_3 \approx h_4 \quad (2.7)$$

The pump work is negligible compared with the turbine work, the thermal efficiency (with little error) is

$$\eta_{th} = \frac{h_1 - h_2}{h_1 - h_3} \tag{2.8}$$

This assumption is not true for modern power plants, where P_4 is 1000 psi (70 bar) or higher, while P_3 is about 1 psi (0.07 bar). In this case, the pump work may be obtained by finding h_3 as the saturated enthalpy of liquid at P_3 from the steam tables. One can find h_4 from the subcooled liquid tables at T_4 and P_4 (assuming that $T_3 = T_4$).

An approximation for the pump work may be obtained from the change in flow work:

$$w_p = v_3 (P_4 - P_3) \tag{2.9}$$

REHEAT

Reheat improves the cycle efficiency. Figures 2.3 and 2.4 illustrate the flow and *T-s* diagrams of an internally reversible Rankine cycle (i.e., the process through the turbine and pump is adiabatic and reversible. Also, there is no pressure drop in the cycle). The cycle superheats and reheats the vapor. The vapor in the reheat cycle at point 1 is expanded in the high-pressure turbine to point 2.

Note: Line *ab* represents the primary coolant in a counterflow steam generator (the primary heat source is the combustion gases from the steam generator furnace).

The vapor is returned back to the steam generator where it is reheated at constant pressure (ideally) to a temperature near that at point 1. The reheated steam now enters the low-pressure turbine where it expands to the condenser pressure.

In a reheat cycle, heat is added twice: from point 6 to point 1 and from point 2 to point 3. It keeps the boiler-superheat-reheat portion from point 7 to point 3 close to the primary fluid line *ae*. This increases the cycle efficiency.

Reheat also produces drier steam at the turbine exhaust (point 4 instead of point 4′). Modern fossil-fueled power plants have at least one stage of reheat. If more than two stages of reheat are used, cycle complication occurs and the improvement in efficiency does not justify the increase in capital cost.

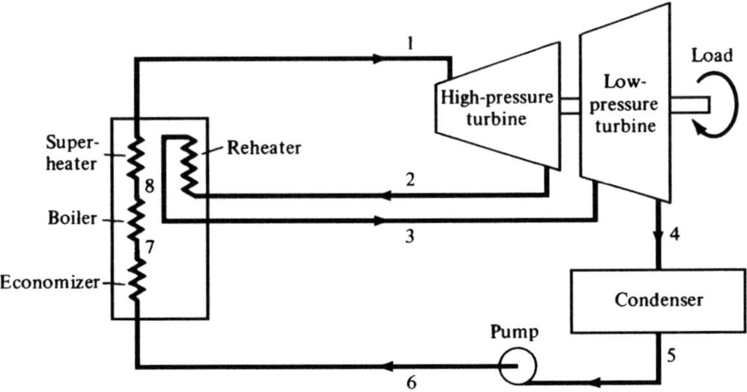

FIGURE 2.3 Schematic of a Rankine cycle with superheat and reheat.

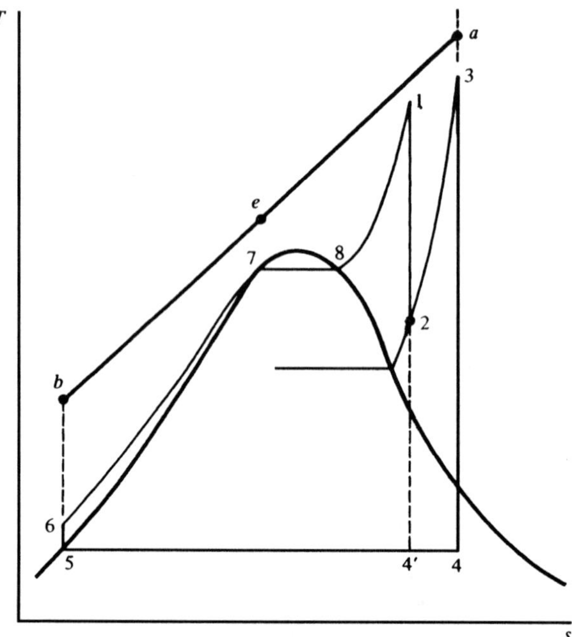

FIGURE 2.4 *T-s* diagram of Rankine cycle of Fig. 2.3.

In some plants, the steam is not reheated in the steam generator. It is reheated in a separate heat exchanger *reheater.* A portion of the steam at point 1 is used to reheat the steam at point 2. This flow condenses and is sent to the feed water heaters. The reheat cycle involves two turbine work terms and two heat addition terms. (Refer to Fig. 2.4.)

$$W_T = (h_1 - h_2) + (h_3 - h_4) \tag{2.10}$$

$$|W_p| = h_6 - h_5 \tag{2.11}$$

$$\Delta W_{\text{net}} = (h_1 - h_2) + (h_3 - h_4) - (h_6 - h_5) \tag{2.12}$$

$$q_A = (h_1 - h_6) + (h_3 - h_2) \tag{2.13}$$

$$\eta_{\text{th}} = \frac{\Delta W_{\text{net}}}{q_A} \tag{2.14}$$

The reheat pressure P_2 affects the cycle efficiency. Figure 2.5 illustrates the variation in cycle efficiency as a function of the ratio of reheat pressure to initial pressure P_2/P_1. P_1 = 2500 psia, T_1 = 1000°F, and T_3 = 1000°F. If the reheat pressure is too close to the initial pressure, the increase in cycle efficiency is minimal because only a small portion of heat is added at high temperature.

The optimum reheat efficiency is reached when P_2/P_1 is between 20 and 25 percent. Lowering the reheat pressure, P_2 further causes the efficiency to decrease again (area 2-3-4-4′ decreases if P_2 drops below 0.2).

Exhaust steam is drier in a reheat cycle. A superheat-reheat power plant is designated $P_1/T_1/T_3$ (e.g., 2500 psi/1000°F/1000°F). Table 2.1 compares the performance of five plants. Note the increase in efficiency due to reheating and the significant drop in efficiency caused by using nonideal fluids.

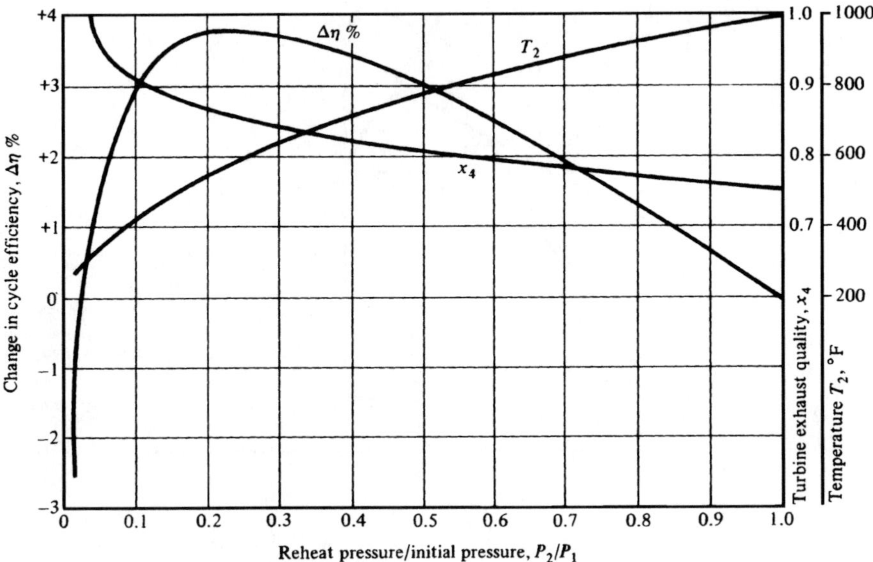

FIGURE 2.5 Effect of reheat-to-initial-pressure ratio on efficiency, high-pressure turbine exit temperature, and low-pressure turbine exit quality. Data for cycle of Fig. 2.7 with initial steam at 2500 psia and 1000°F, and steam reheat to 1000°F (2500/1000/1000).

TABLE 2.1 Steam Power Plant Performance Comparison

	Cycle				
Data	A Superheat 2500/1000	B 2500 saturated	C Superheat 1000/668.11	D 2500/ 1000/1000	E 2500/1000 nonideal
Turbine inlet pressure, psia	2500	2500	1000	2500	2500
Turbine inlet temperature, °F	1000	668.11	668.11	1000	1000
Condenser pressure, psia	1	1	1	1	1
Inlet steam enthalpy, Btu/lb$_m$	1457.5	1093.3	1303.1	1457.5	1457.5
Exhaust steam enthalpy, Btu/lb$_m$	852.52	688.36	834.44	970.5	913.02
Turbine work, Btu/lb$_m$	604.98	404.94	468.66	741.8	544.48
Pump work, Btu/lb$_m$	7.46	7.46	2.98	7.46	11.52
Net work, Btu/lb$_m$	597.52	397.48	465.68	734.34	532.96
Heat added, Btu/lb$_m$	1380.31	1016.11	1230.39	1635.10	1376.25
Exhaust steam quality	0.7555	0.5971	0.7381	0.8694	0.8139
Cycle efficiency, %	43.29	39.12	37.85	44.91	38.73

REGENERATION

External irreversibility is caused by the temperature differences between the primary heat source (combustion gases or primary coolant) and the working fluid. Temperature differences between condensing working fluid and the heat sink fluid (condenser cooling water or cooling air) also cause external irreversibility.

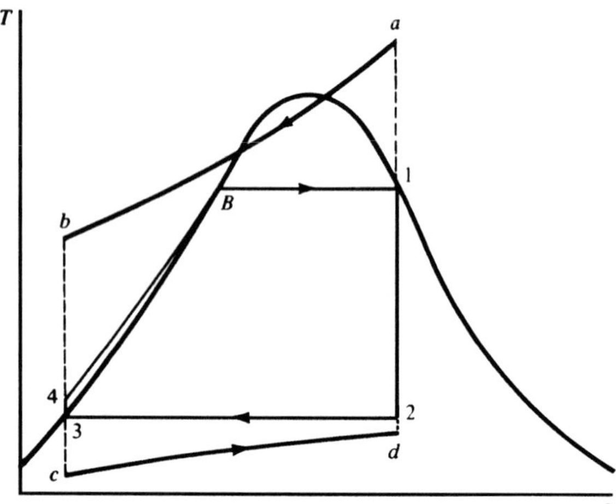

FIGURE 2.6 External irreversibility with Rankine cycle.

Figure 2.6 illustrates the working fluid (line 4-*B*-1-2-3-4) in a Rankine cycle. Line *a*-*b* represents the primary coolant in a counterflow steam generator, and line *c*-*d* represents the heat sink fluid in a counterflow heat exchanger. If line *a*-*b* is too close to line 4-*B*-1, the temperature differences between the primary coolant and the working fluid would be small. Therefore, the irreversibilities (caused by heat loss from the primary coolant) are small, but the steam generator is large and costly.

If line *a*-*b* is much higher than line 4*B*-1 (significant temperature differences between the primary coolant and the working fluid), the steam generator would be small and inexpensive, but the overall temperature differences and irreversibilities would be large. Hence, the plant efficiency would be reduced.

An examination of Fig. 2.6 reveals that a great deal of irreversibilities occur prior to the point of boiling (i.e., in the economizer section of the steam generator where the temperature differences between line *b*-*a* and line 4-*B* are the greatest of all during the entire heat addition process).

The thermal efficiencies of all types of power plants suffer from this irreversibility, which can be eliminated if the liquid is added to the steam generator at point *B* instead of point 4. The process of *regeneration* achieves this objective by exchanging heat between the expanding fluid in the turbine and the compressed fluid before heat addition.

FEEDWATER HEATING

Feedwater heating is accomplished by heating the compressed liquid at point 4 in a number of finite steps in heat exchangers ("feedheaters") by steam that is bled from the turbine at selected stages. (See Fig. 2.6.) Modern steam power plants use between five and eight feedwater heating stages. None is built without feedwater heating.

In a regenerative cycle, the liquid enters the steam generator at a point below point *B* (Fig. 2.6). An economizer section (this is the part of the steam generator that heats the incoming fluid between points 4 and B) is still needed. However, it is much smaller than the one that is needed for nonregenerative cycles. The efficiency of a well-designed Rankine cycle is the closest to the efficiency of a Carnot cycle.

The three types of feedwater heaters include:

1. Open or direct-contact type
2. Closed type with drains cascaded backward
3. Closed type with drains pumped forward

THE INTERNALLY IRREVERSIBLE RANKINE CYCLE

Internal irreversibility is primarily the result of fluid friction, throttling, and mixing. The most important irreversibilities in a cycle occur in turbines and pumps, and pressure losses occur in heat exchangers, pipes, bends, valves, and so on. In turbines and pumps, the assumption of adiabatic flow is still valid (the heat losses per unit mass is negligible). However, the flow is not reversible. The entropy in both processes increases. This is illustrated in Fig. 2.7.

The *turbine polytropic efficiency* η_T (sometimes called *adiabatic* or *isentropic efficiency*) is given by

$$\eta_T = \frac{h_1 - h_2}{h_1 - h_{2s}} \tag{2.15}$$

Note: η_T is different from the cycle thermal efficiency.

Well-designed turbines have high polytropic efficiencies. They are usually in the order of 90 percent. The presence of moisture in the steam reduces η_T.

Process 2-3 (Fig. 2.7) in the condenser occurs at constant pressure and constant temperature (a two-phase condensation process). The pump process is also adiabatic and irreversible. The entropy in this process increases. It is a liquid (single-phase) process (3-4). The temperature and enthalpy process (3-4) increases more than does the adiabatic and reversible process (3-4_s). Therefore, the pump absorbs more work in an irreversible process.

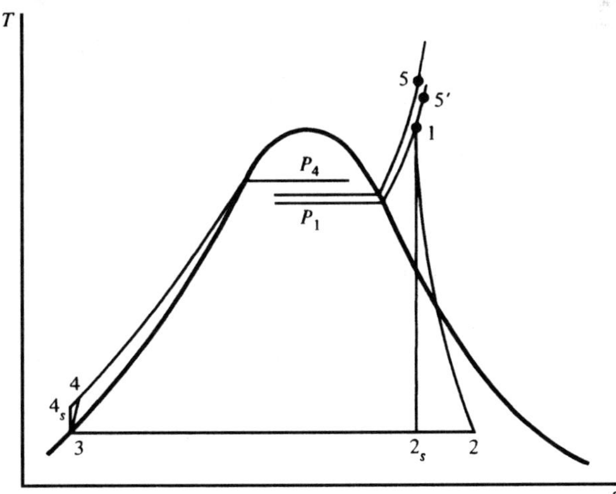

FIGURE 2.7 A *T-s* diagram of an internally irreversible superheat Rankine cycle.

The *pump polytropic efficiency* η_p (sometimes called *adiabatic* or *isentropic efficiency*) is given by

$$\eta_p = \frac{h_{4s} - h_3}{h_4 - h_3} = \frac{\text{(ideal work)}}{\text{(actual work)}} \tag{2.16}$$

η_p is the reverse of η_T.

The actual pump work is given by

$$W_p = \frac{h_{4s} - h_3}{\eta_p} \approx \frac{v_3 (P_4 - P_3)}{\eta_p} \tag{2.17}$$

The liquid leaving the pump is at a higher pressure than the turbine inlet (due to friction throughout the system). The steam leaving the steam generator at point 5 enters the turbine at point 1. (See Fig. 2.7.) The pressure drop between points 5 and 1 is the result of the combined effects of friction and heat losses. Point 5′ represents the frictional effects in the pipe connecting the steam generator and turbine, including the turbine throttle valve. Heat losses from that pipe reduce the entropy to 1.

OPEN OR DIRECT-CONTACT FEEDWATER HEATERS

The extraction steam is mixed directly with the incoming subcooled feedwater in the open or direct-contact feedwater heater. The mixture becomes saturated water at the extraction steam pressure.

Figure 2.8 (*a, b*) shows the flow diagram and corresponding *T-s* diagram for a Rankine cycle using two feedwater heaters—one a low-pressure feedwater heater and the other a high-pressure feedwater heater. (The low-pressure feedwater heater is upstream of the high-pressure feedwater heater.) Normally, modern power plants use one open-type feedwater heater and between four and seven other heaters.

A typical feedwater heater is shown in Fig. 2.9. The condensate "saturated water" leaves the condenser at point 5. It is pumped to point 6 to the same pressure as extraction steam at point 3. The subcooled water at point 6 and wet steam at point 3 mix in the low-pressure feedwater heater to produce saturated water at point 7.

The amount $\dot{m}_3$ is sufficient to saturate the subcooled water at point 6. If the extraction steam at point 3 were $\dot{m}_3'$ (where $\dot{m}_3' > \dot{m}_3$), the flow at point 7 would be a two-phase mixture that would be difficult to pump. The pressure at line 6-7 (constant) cannot be higher than the extraction steam at point 3. Otherwise, reverse flow of condensate water would enter the turbine at point 3.

A second pump is needed to pressurize the saturated water from point 7 to a subcooled condition at point 8, which is the pressure of extraction steam at point 2. The steam at point 10 enters the steam generator at its pressure. A deaerator is usually added to the open-type feedwater heaters. The mixing process increases the surface area and liberates noncondensable gases (e.g., N_2, O_2, and CO_2). These gases can be vented to atmosphere. Hence, the arrangement is called *deaerating heaters* or *DA*.

The mass balance is as follows:

Mass flow between points 1 and 2 = 1.

Mass flow between points 2 and 9 = $\dot{m}_2$.

Mass flow between points 2 and 3 = $1 - \dot{m}_2$.

Mass flow between points 3 and 7 = $\dot{m}_3$.

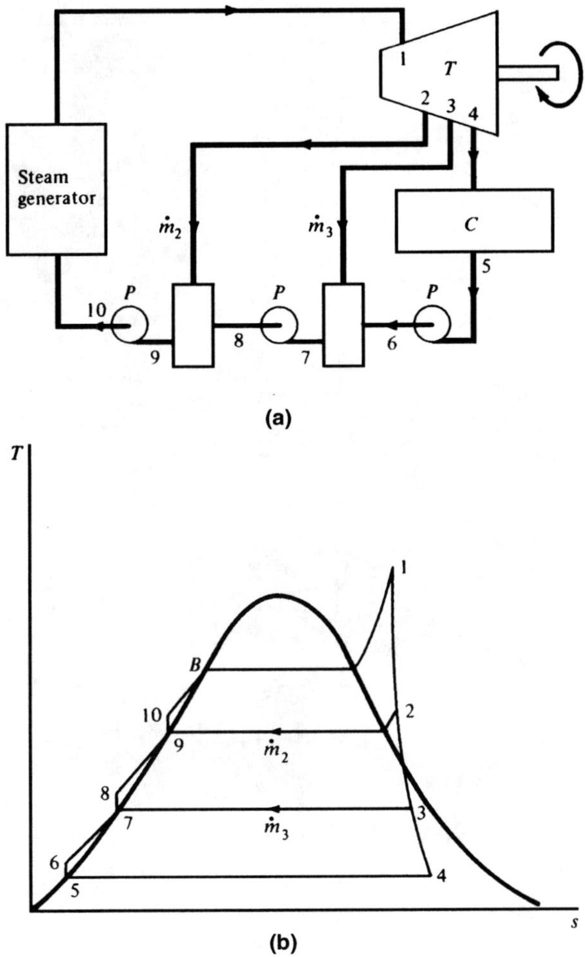

FIGURE 2.8 (*a*) Schematic flow and (*b*) *T-s* diagrams of a nonideal superheat Rankine cycle with two open-type feedwater heaters.

Mass flow between points 3 and 7 $= 1 - \dot{m}_2 - \dot{m}_3$.
Mass flow between points 7 and 9 $= 1 - \dot{m}_2$.
Mass flow between points 9 and 1 $= 1$.

The energy balances for the high- and low-pressure feedwater heaters, respectively, are as follows:

$$\dot{m}_2 (h_2 - h_9) = (1 - \dot{m}_2)(h_9 - h_8) \tag{2.18}$$

$$\dot{m}_3 (h_3 - h_7) = (1 - \dot{m}_2 - \dot{m}_3)(h_7 - h_6) \tag{2.19}$$

Heat added

$$q_A = (h_1 - h_{10}) \tag{2.20}$$

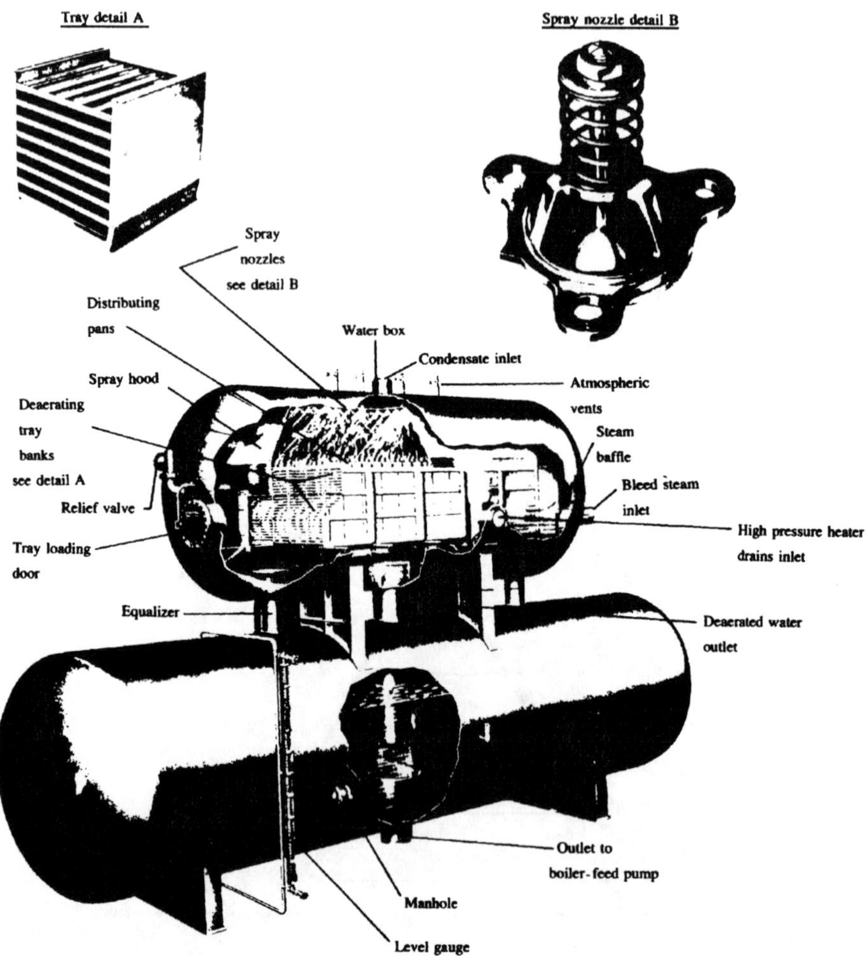

FIGURE 2.9 A typical combination open-type deaerating feedwater heater. (*Courtesy Chicago Heater, Inc.*)

Turbine work

$$w_T = (h_1 - h_2) + (1 - \dot{m}_2)(h_2 - h_3) + (1 - \dot{m}_2 - \dot{m}_3)(h_3 - h_4) \tag{2.21}$$

Pump work

$$\begin{aligned} |\Sigma w_p| &= (1 - \dot{m}_2 - \dot{m}_3)(h_6 - h_5) + (1 - \dot{m}_2)(h_8 - h_7) \\ &+ (h_{10} - h_9) \approx (1 - \dot{m}_2 - \dot{m}_3)\frac{v_5 (P_6 - P_5)}{\eta_p J} \\ &+ (1 - \dot{m}_2)\frac{v_7 (P_8 - P_7)}{\eta_p J} + \frac{v_9 (P_{10} - P_9)}{\eta_p J} \end{aligned} \tag{2.22}$$

Heat rejected

$$|q_R| = (1 - \dot{m}_2 - \dot{m}_3)(h_4 - h_5) \tag{2.23}$$

Net cycle work

$$\Delta w_{\text{net}} = w_T - |w_p| \tag{2.24}$$

Cycle thermal efficiency

$$\eta_{\text{th}} = \frac{\Delta w_{\text{net}}}{q_A} \tag{2.25}$$

Work ratio

$$WR = \frac{w_{\text{net}}}{w_T} \tag{2.26}$$

where η_p is the pump efficiency and $J = 778.16 \text{ ft} \cdot \text{lb}_f/\text{Btu}$.

Note that the turbine work has decreased for the same mass-flow rate because of reduced turbine mass-flow rate after bleeding. The pump work has also increased.

Note also the decrease in heat added which makes up more than the loss on net work. This results in significant improvement in cycle efficiency. The improvement in efficiency increases with the number of feedwater heaters. The maximum number of feedwater heaters used is eight. Any increase beyond eight causes little increase in efficiency and adds complications to the system. The increase in capital cost would not justify the increase in efficiency.

CLOSED-TYPE FEEDWATER HEATER WITH DRAINS CASCADED BACKWARD

This is the most commonly used type of feedwater heaters in power plants. It is a shell-and-tube heat exchanger. The feedwater passes through the tubes. On the shell side, the bled steam transfers energy to the feedwater as it condenses. Feedwater heaters are very similar to condensers, but they operate at higher pressures.

A boiler feedpump is usually placed after the deaerater. Figure 2.10 illustrates the flow diagram and the corresponding *T-s* diagram of a nonideal superheat Rankine cycle.

The cycle has two feedwater heaters of this type. Only one pump is needed. The bled steam condenses in each feedwater heater. Then, it is fed back to the next lower-pressure feedwater heater (it cascades from higher-pressure to lower-pressure heaters). Wet steam at point 3 is admitted and transfers its energy to high-pressure subcooled water at point 6.

Figure 2.11 illustrates the temperature-length diagram of this heater. The temperature of the water at point 7 cannot reach the inlet bled steam temperature at point 3. A difference called the *terminal temperature difference* (TTD, sometimes simply TD) is defined for all closed feedwater heaters as

$$\text{TTD} = \text{saturation temperature of bled steam} - \text{exit water temperature} \tag{2.27}$$

Usually, the TTD is in the order of 2.78°C (5°F).

A closed feedwater heater that receives saturated or wet steam can have a drain cooler. Thus, it is composed of a condensing section and a drain cooler section (Fig. 2.11).

Table 2.2 shows the results of example calculations for ideal Rankine cycles. By comparing cycles C and B, note the reduction of work but the improvement of η_{th} in cycle C due to feedwater heating. In general, comparison between the various cycles shows large increases in efficiencies as a result of superheat, reheat, and the use of one feedwater heater.

Figure 2.12 shows a flow diagram of an actual 512-MW power plant with superheat, reheat, and seven feedwater heaters.

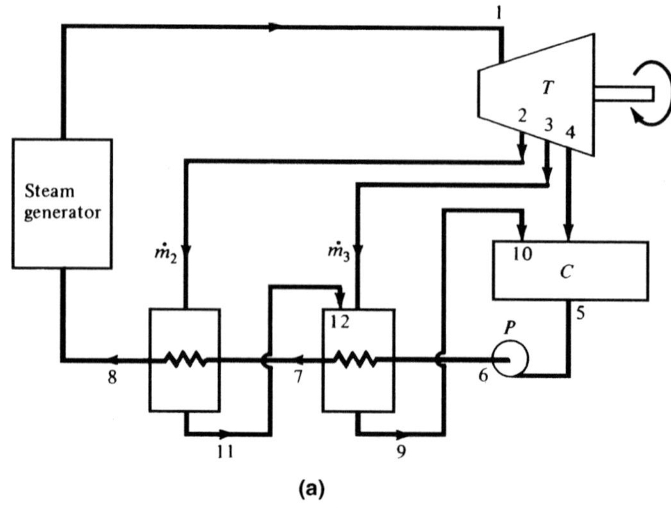

(a)

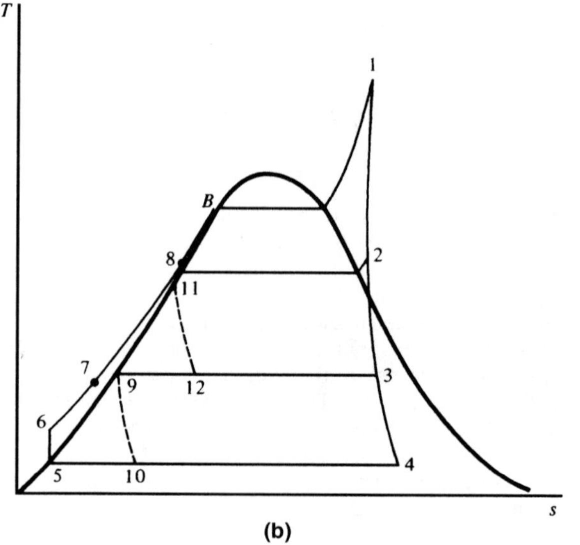

(b)

FIGURE 2.10 (*a*) Schematic flow and (*b*) *T-s* diagrams of a nonideal superheat Rankine cycle with two closed-type feedwater heaters with drains cascaded backward.

EFFICIENCY AND HEAT RATE

The actual thermal efficiency of power plants is less than those computed earlier because the analysis did not include the various auxiliaries used in a power plant and the various irreversibilities associated with them.

The *gross efficiency* is calculated using the gross power of the turbine generator. This is the power [in megawatts (MW)] that is produced before supplying the internal

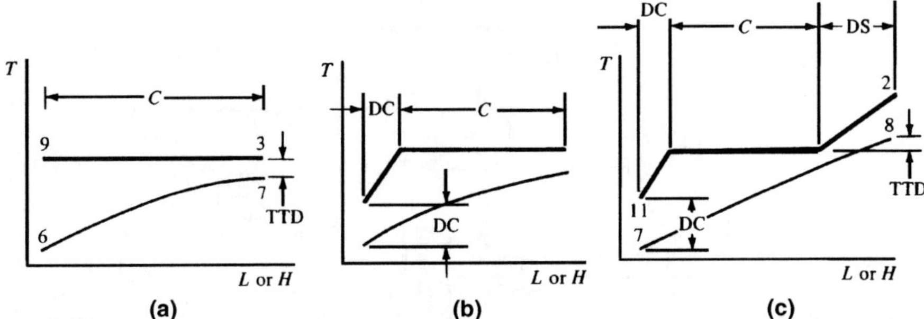

FIGURE 2.11 Temperature-enthalpy diagrams of (*a, b*) low-pressure and (*c*) high-pressure feedwater heaters of Fig. 2.15. C = condenser, DC = drain cooler, DS = desuperheater, TTD = terminal temperature difference.

TABLE 2.2 Results of Example Calculations for Ideal Rankine Cycles*

Cycle	Particulars	Δw_{net}	q_A	η%	$\lvert q_R \rvert$	WR
A	No superheat; no fwh†	413.72	1120.19	36.93	706.49	0.9928
B	Superheat; no fwh	579.11	1432.69	40.42	853.58	0.9949
C	Superheat; one open fwh	519.3	1203.95	43.13	685.25	0.9939
D	Superheat; one closed fwh; drains cascaded; DC†	520.31	1212.04	42.93	691.68	0.9943
E	Superheat; one closed fwh; drains pumped; DC	529.85	1245.63	42.54	715.73	0.9945
F	Superheat; one closed fwh; drains pumped; no DC	520.59	1210.48	43.01	689.95	0.9943
G	Superheat; reheat; one open fwh	641.59	1447.44	44.33	805.83	0.9951
H	Superheat; reheat; two closed fwh; drains cascaded	609.83	1351.0	45.14	727.62	0.9952
I	Supercritical; double reheat; no fwh; 3500/1000/1025/1050	861.95	1831.92	47.05	969.97	0.9880

*All values in Btu/lb_m; all examples, except for cycle A (which is saturated), and cycle I, are at 1000 psia/1000°F. All are at 1 psia condenser pressure.

†DC = drain cooler, fwh = feedwater heater.

equipment of the power plant (e.g., pumps, compressors, fuel-handling equipment, computers, etc.).

The *net efficiency* is calculated based on the net power of the plant (the gross power minus the power needed for the internal equipment of the plant).

SUPERCRITICAL PLANTS

Figure 2.13 illustrates the *T-s* diagram of an ideal supercritical, double-reheat 3500 psi/1000°F/1025°F/1050°F power plant. They usually have higher thermal efficiencies than subcritical plants. Their capital cost is higher than subcritical plants due to the need for suitable material and sealing devices that can withstand high temperature and pressure for long periods of time.

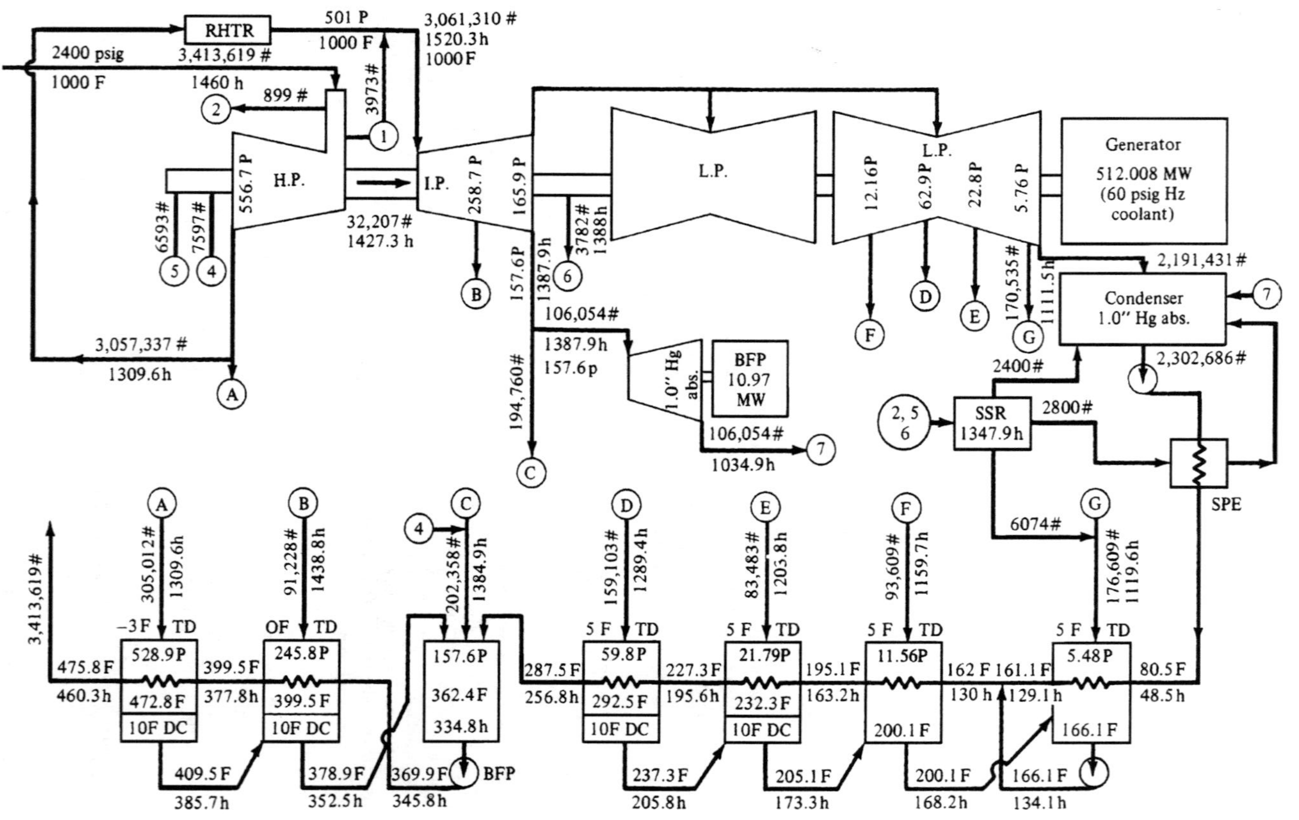
RHTR
2400 psig
1000 F
3,413,619 #
501 P
1000 F
3,061,310 #
1520.3h
1000F
1460 h
899 #
3973#
H.P.
556.7 P
6593#
7597#
32,207#
1427.3 h
3,057,337 #
1309.6h
I.P.
258.7 P
165.9 P
157.6P
1387.9h
3782#
1388h
L.P.
L.P.
12.16P
62.9P
22.8P
5.76 P
170,535#
1111.5h
Generator
512.008 MW
(60 psig Hz
coolant)
2,191,431#
Condenser
1.0" Hg abs.
2,302,686#
106,054#
1387.9h
157.6p
194,760#
1.0" Hg
abs.
BFP
10.97
MW
106,054#
1034.9h
2400#
SSR
1347.9h
2800#
6074#
SPE
3,413,619#
305,012#
1309.6h
-3F
TD
528.9P
472.8F
10F DC
475.8F
460.3h
399.5F
377.8h
409.5F
385.7h
91,228#
1438.8h
OF
TD
245.8P
399.5F
10F DC
378.9F
352.5h
202,358#
1384.9h
157.6P
362.4F
334.8h
369.9F
345.8h
BFP
287.5F
256.8h
159,103#
1289.4h
5 F
TD
59.8P
292.5F
10F DC
227.3F
195.6h
237.3F
205.8h
83,483#
1203.8h
5 F
TD
21.79P
232.3F
10F DC
195.1F
163.2h
205.1F
173.3h
93,609#
1159.7h
5 F
TD
11.56P
200.1F
162 F
130 h
200.1F
168.2h
161.1F
129.1h
176,609#
1119.6h
5 F
TD
5.48P
166.1F
166.1F
134.1h
80.5F
48.5h

FIGURE 2.12 Flow diagram of an actual 512-MW, 2400 psig/1000°F/1000°F reheat power plant with seven feedwater heaters. The standard notations in this diagram are as follows:

AE	available energy or isentropic enthalpy difference, Btu/lb_m
BFP	boiler feedpump
DC	drain cooler terminal temperature difference [see Fig. 2.11 (*b, c*)], °F
EL	exhaust loss, Btu/lb_m
ELEP	expansion line endpoint enthalpy, Btu/lb_m
h	enthalpy, Btu/lb_m
P	pressure, psia
RHTR	reheater
SGFP	steam generator feedpump
SJAE	steam-jet air ejector condenser
SPE	steam packing exhaust condenser
SSR	steam seal regulator
TD or TTD	terminal temperature difference (see Fig. 2.11), °F
UEEP	used-energy endpoint, Btu/lb_m
#	mass-flow rate, lb_m/h

(Courtesy Wisconsin Power & Light Co.)

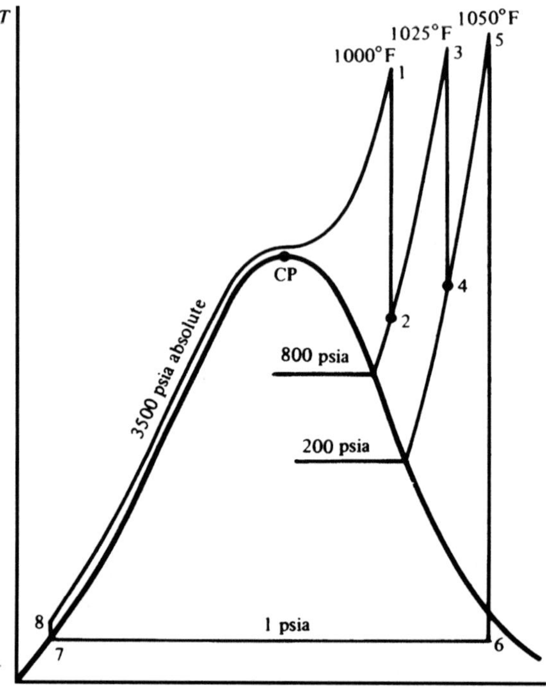

FIGURE 2.13 *T-s* diagram of an ideal supercritical, double-reheat 3500/1000/1025/1050 steam cycle.

COGENERATION

Cogeneration is the simultaneous generation of electricity and steam (or heat) in a power plant. Cogeneration is recommended for industries and municipalities because it can produce electricity more cheaply and/or more conveniently than a utility. Also, it provides the total energy needs (heat and electricity) for the industry or municipality.

Cogeneration is beneficial if it saves energy when compared with separate generation of electricity and steam (or heat). The cogeneration plant efficiency η_{co} is given by

$$\eta_{co} = \frac{E + \Delta H_s}{Q_A} \tag{2.28}$$

where E = electric energy generated
ΔH_s = heat energy, or heat energy in process steam
= (enthalpy of steam entering the process) − (enthalpy of process condensate returning to plant)
Q_A = heat added to plant (in coal, nuclear fuel, etc.)

For separate generation of electricity and steam, the heat added per unit of *total* energy output is

$$\frac{e}{\eta_e} + \frac{(1 - e)}{\eta_h} \tag{2.29}$$

where e = electrical fraction of total energy output = $[E/(E+\Delta H_s)]$
η_e = electric plant efficiency
η_h = steam (or heat) generator efficiency

The *combined efficiency* η_c *for separate generation* is therefore given by

$$\eta_c = \frac{1}{(e/\eta_e) + [(1 - e)/\eta_h]} \tag{2.30}$$

Cogeneration is beneficial if the efficiency of the cogeneration plant [Eq. (2.28)] is greater than that of separate generation [Eq. (2.30)].

Types of Cogeneration

The two main categories of cogeneration are (1) the topping cycle and (2) the bottoming cycle.

The Topping Cycle. In this cycle, the primary heat source is used to generate high-enthalpy steam and electricity. Depending on process requirements, process steam at low enthalpy is taken from any of the following:

- Extracted from the turbine at an intermediate stage (like feedwater heating).
- Taken from the turbine exhaust. The turbine in this case is called a *back-pressure turbine.*

Process steam requirements vary widely, between 0.5 and 40 bar.

The Bottoming Cycle. In this cycle, the primary heat (high enthalpy) is used directly for process requirements [e.g., for a high-temperature cement kiln (furnace)]. The low-enthalpy waste heat is then used to generate electricity at low efficiency.

This cycle has lower combined efficiency than the topping cycle. Thus, it is not very common. Only the topping cycle can provide true savings in primary energy.

Arrangements of Cogeneration Plants

The various arrangements for cogeneration in a topping cycle are as follows:

- Steam-electric power plant with a back-pressure turbine.
- Steam-electric power plant with steam extraction from a condensing turbine (Fig. 2.14).
- Gas turbine power plant with a heat recovery boiler (using the gas turbine exhaust to generate steam).
- Combined steam-gas-turbine cycle power plant. The steam turbine is either of the back-pressure type or of the extraction-condensing type.

Economics of Cogeneration

Cogeneration is recommended if the cost of electricity is less than the utility. If a utility is not available, cogeneration becomes necessary, regardless of economics.

The two types of power plant costs are (1) capital costs and (2) production costs. *Capital costs* are given in total dollars or as unit capital costs in dollars per kilowatt net. Capital

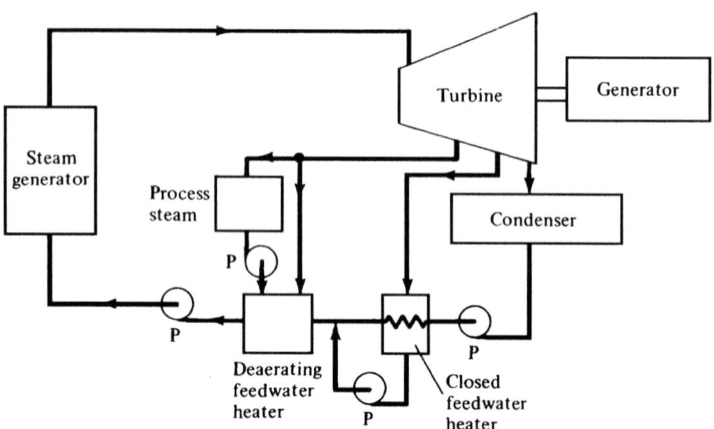

FIGURE 2.14 Schematic of basic cogeneration plant with extraction-condensing turbine.

costs determine if a plant is good enough to obtain financing. Thus, it is able to pay the fixed charges against capital costs.

Production costs are calculated annually, and they are given in mills per kilowatt hour (a *mill* is U.S.$0.001). Production costs are the real measure of the cost of power generated. They are composed of the following:

- Fixed charges against the capital costs
- Fuel costs
- Operation and maintenance costs

All the costs are in mills per kilowatt hour. They are given by

$$\text{Production costs} = \frac{\text{total } (a + b + c) \text{ \$ spent per period} \times 10^3}{\text{KWh (net) generated during the same period}} \tag{2.31}$$

where the period is usually taken as one year.

The plant operating factor (POF) is defined for all plants as

$$\text{POF} = \frac{\text{total net energy generated by plant during a period of time}}{\text{rated net energy capacity of plant during the same period}} \tag{2.32}$$

CHAPTER 3
STEAM TURBINES AND AUXILIARIES

In a steam turbine, high-enthalpy (high pressure and temperature) steam is expanded in the nozzles (stationary blades) where the kinetic energy is increased at the expense of pressure energy (increase in velocity due to decrease in pressure). The kinetic energy (high velocity) is converted into mechanical energy (rotation of a shaft – increase of torque or speed) by impulse and reaction principles. The impulse principle consists of changing the momentum ($m\mathbf{V}$) of the flow, which is directed to the moving blades by the stationary blades. The jet's impulse force pushes the moving blades forward. The reaction principle consists of a reaction force on the moving blades due to acceleration of the flow as a result of decreasing cross-sectional area.

Figure 3.1 illustrates a turbine with impulse blading. It has one velocity-compounded stage (the velocity is absorbed in stages) and four pressure-compounded stages. The velocity is reduced in two steps through the first two rows of moving blades. In the moving blades, velocity decreases while the pressure remains constant.

Figure 3.2 illustrates a reaction turbine. The reaction stages are preceded by an initial velocity-compounded impulse stage where a large pressure drop occurs. This results in a shorter, less expensive turbine. Figure 3.3 illustrates the arrangement of components in a steam power plant.

TURBINE TYPES

Steam turbines up to between 40 and 60 MW rating are usually single-cylinder machines. Larger units use multiple cylinders to extract the energy from the steam.

Single-Cylinder Turbines

The two types of steam turbines are *condensing* and *back-pressure* (noncondensing). Figure 3.4 illustrates these types and some of their subclassifications. Back-pressure turbines exhaust the steam at the pressure required by the process. Automatic extraction turbines allow part of the steam to be withdrawn at an intermediate stage (or stages) while the remainder of the steam is exhausted to a condenser. These turbines require special governors and valves to maintain constant pressure of the extraction steam while the turbine load and extraction demand are varying. Uncontrolled extraction turbines are used to supply steam to feedwater heaters, since the pressure at the extraction points varies with the turbine load.

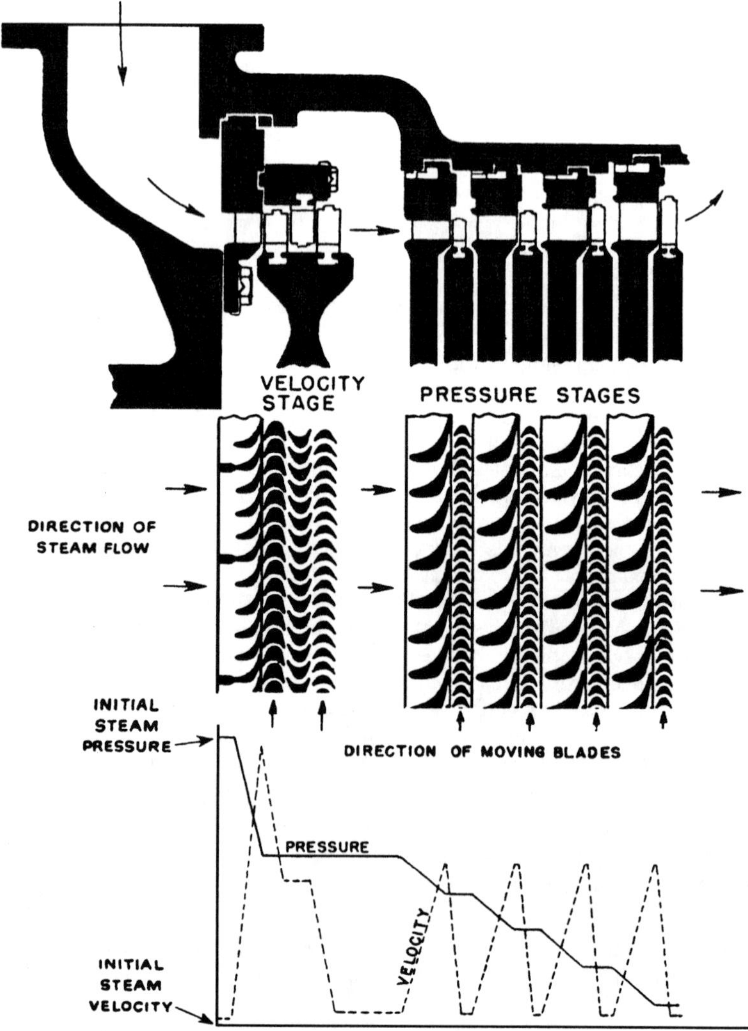

FIGURE 3.1 Turbine with impulse blading. Velocity compounding is accomplished in the first two stages by two rows of moving blades between which is placed a row of stationary blades that reverses the direction of steam flow as it passes from the first to the second row of moving blades. Other ways of accomplishing velocity compounding involve redirecting the steam jets so that they strike the same row of blades several times with progressively decreasing velocity.

Many moderate-pressure plants have added high-pressure noncondensing turbines to increase capacity and improve efficiency. High-pressure boilers are added to supply steam to the noncondensing turbines, which are designed to supply the steam to the original turbines. These high-pressure turbines are called *superposed,* or *topping,* units. Mixed-pressure turbines are designed to admit steam at low pressure and expand it to a condenser. These units are used mainly in cogeneration plants.

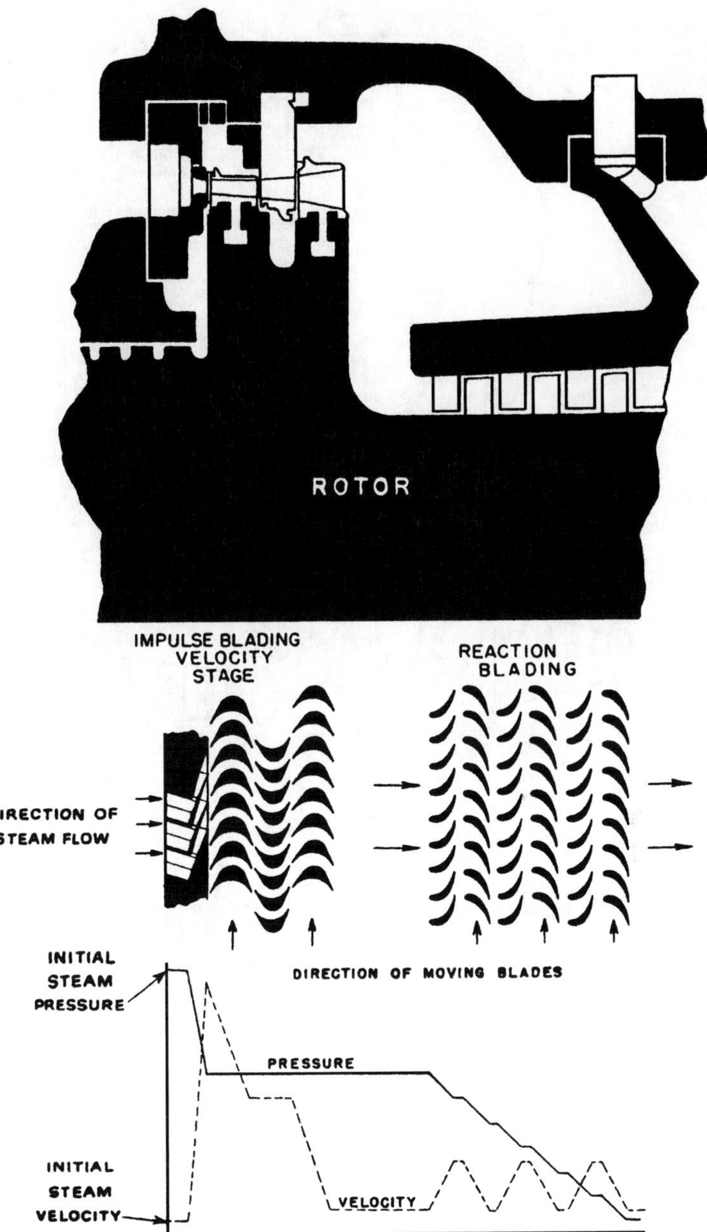

FIGURE 3.2 Reaction turbine with one velocity–compounded impulse stage. The first stage of this turbine is similar to the first velocity-compounded stage of Fig. 3.1. However, in the reaction blading of this turbine, both pressure and velocity decrease as the steam flows through the blades. The graph at the bottom shows the changes in pressure and velocity through the various stages.

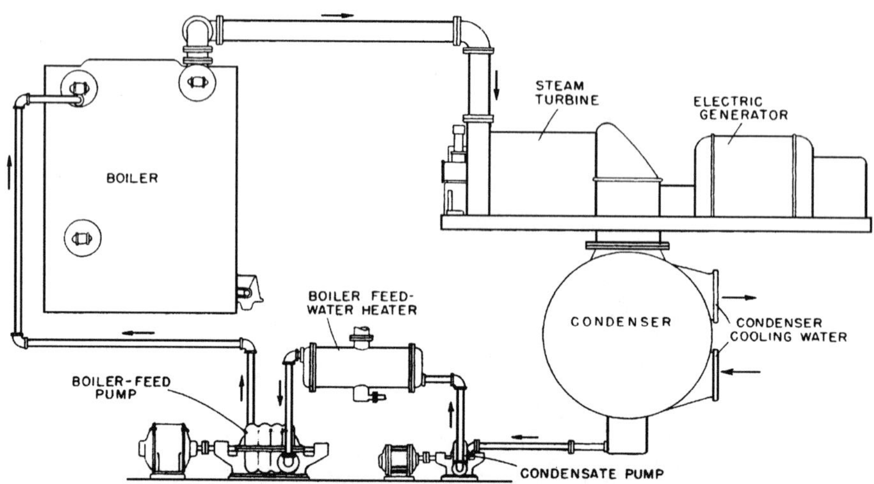

FIGURE 3.3 Simple power plant cycle. This diagram shows that the working fluid, steam and water, travels a closed loop in the typical power plant cycle.

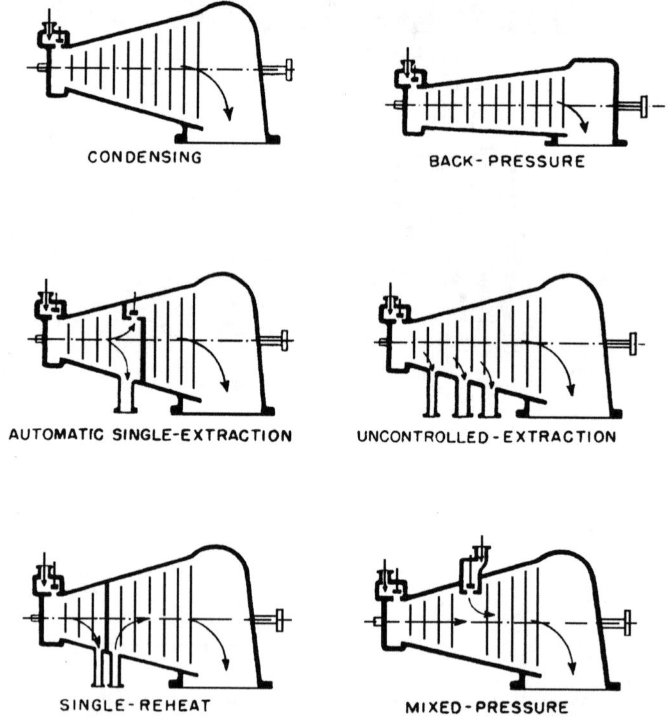

FIGURE 3.4 Single-cylinder turbine types. Typical types of single-cylinder turbines are illustrated. As shown, condensing turbines, as compared to back-pressure turbines, must increase more in size toward the exhaust end to handle the larger volume of low-pressure steam.

Compound Turbines

Compound turbines have more than one cylinder: a high-pressure and a low-pressure turbine. The low-pressure cylinder is usually of the double-flow type to handle large volumes of low-pressure steam (due to limitations on the length of the blades). Large plants may have an intermediate pressure cylinder and up to four low-pressure cylinders. The cylinders can be mounted along a single shaft (tandem-compound), or in parallel groups with two or more shafts (cross-compound). Reheating is usually done between the high- and intermediate-pressure turbines. Figure 3.5 illustrates some of these arrangements.

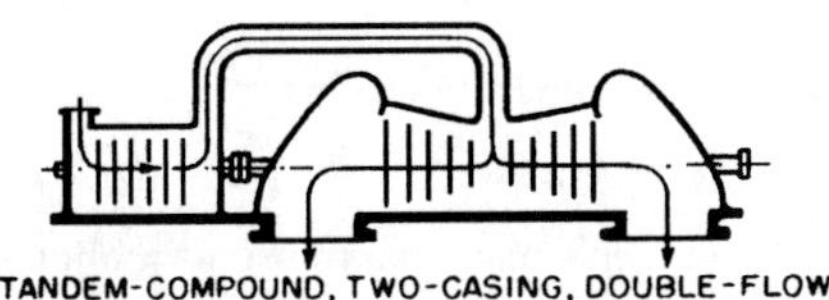

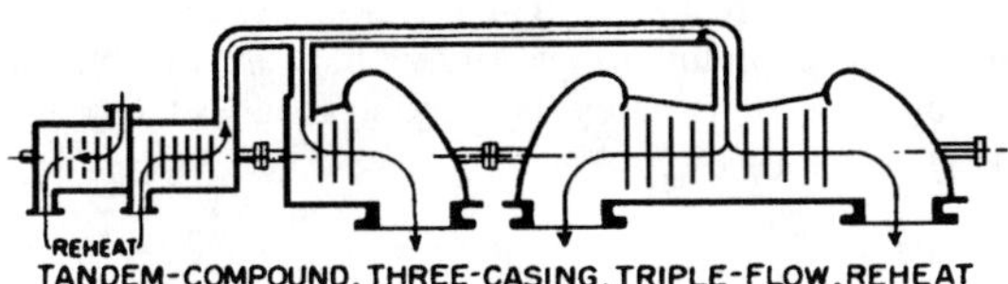

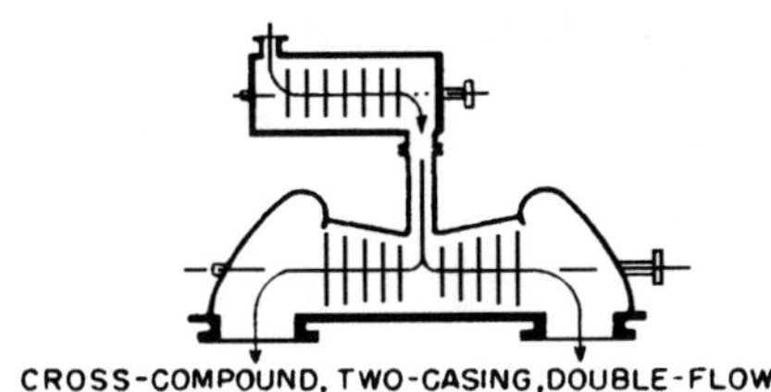

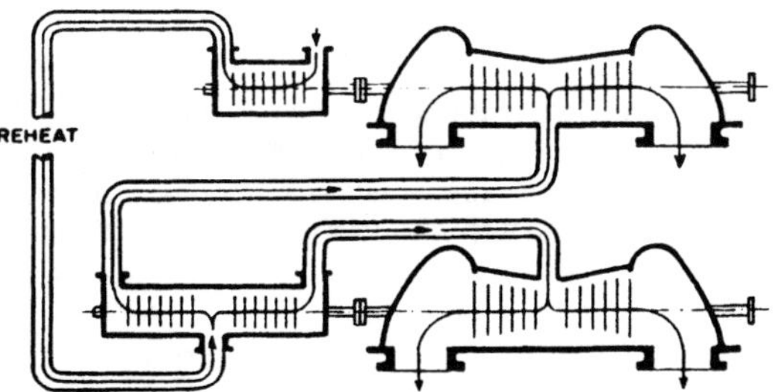

FIGURE 3.5 Some arrangements of compound turbines. While many arrangements are used, these diagrams illustrate some of the more common ones.

TURBINE CONTROL SYSTEMS

All steam turbines have at least two independent governors that control the flow of steam. The first shuts off the steam supply if the turbine speed exceeds a predetermined maximum. It is often called an *emergency trip*. The second, or main, governor throttles the flow of steam to maintain constant speed (in units not synchronized to a grid) or to vary the load (in units synchronized to a grid). The governors of extraction, mixed-pressure, and back-pressure turbines control the steam flow while the speed and pressures are varying. These governors are usually extremely complex.

Speed Governors

Speed governor systems consist of the following:

- Speed-sensitive element
- Linkage or force-amplifying mechanism that transmits motion from the governor to the steam control valves
- Steam control valves (governing valves)

Figure 3.6 illustrates a centrifugal, or flyball, governor. The weights, mounted on opposite sides of the spindle and revolving with it, move outward by centrifugal force against a spring when the turbine speed increases. This action actuates the steam admission valve by one of the following:

- Mechanical linkage
- Operation of the pilot valve of a hydraulic system, which admits or releases oil to opposite sides of a power piston, or to one side of a spring-loaded piston (movement of the power piston opens or closes the steam valves)

Moderate and large units are equipped with a double-relay hydraulic system to boost the force of a centrifugal governor and to reduce the response time of the system. Intercept valves are installed upstream of the intermediate-pressure turbine. They are closed by the governor system upon a load rejection (opening of the circuit breaker as a result of a disturbance in transmission) or a sudden load reduction. The intercept valves interrupt the flow of steam from the high-pressure turbine, the reheater, and the piping to the intermediate-pressure turbine, thus preventing overspeeding of the turbine.

Pressure Governors

The governors of back-pressure and automatic extraction turbines are designed to maintain constant extraction or exhaust pressure, regardless of the load. The signal from a pressure transducer is communicated to the steam extraction control valves and the speed governor, which controls the steam flow to the turbine. On automatic extraction turbines, the governor coordinates the signals from the pressure and speed transducer to maintain constant speed.

LUBRICATION REQUIREMENTS

The parts requiring lubrication include journal and thrust bearings, hydraulic control system, oil shaft seals, gears, flexible couplings, and turning gears.[1]

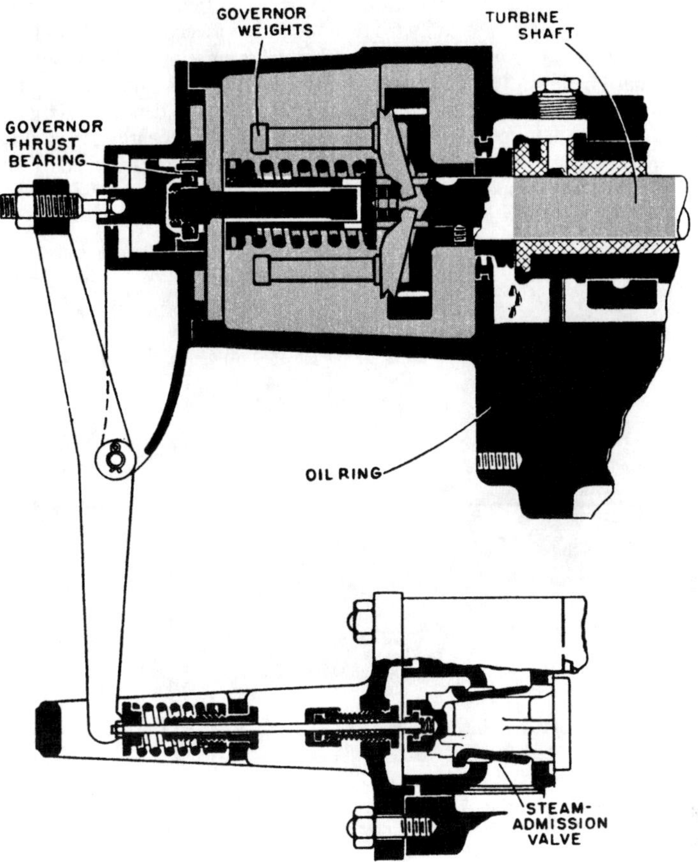

FIGURE 3.6 Mechanical speed governor. A simple arrangement such as this using a flyball governor is suitable for many small turbines.

JOURNAL BEARINGS

Hydrodynamic journal bearings are used to support steam turbines and generators. Due to the extremely tight clearances between the moving blades and the casing, these bearings must be accurately aligned and must operate without any appreciable wear to maintain the shaft in its original position and avoid damage to the blades. The bearings are usually of the horizontally split shell and they are lined with tin-base babbitt (soft metal).

The passages and grooves inside the turbine bearings are designed to allow more oil than required for lubrication only. The additional oil is required to remove frictional heat and heat conducted to the bearings along the shaft from the hot sections of the turbine. The oil flow must maintain the bearings at proper operating temperature. In most applications, the oil leaving the bearings is around 160°F (71°C). An *oil-lift* system (jacking oil) is needed for most large turbines to lift the turbine and reduce the possibility of damage during start-up and shutdown. The jacking oil system is also needed to reduce the starting load on the turning gear. A positive-displacement pump delivers high-pressure oil to openings in the bottom of the bearings. The high-pressure oil lifts the shaft and floats it on an oil film until the shaft speed is high enough to create a hydrodynamic film between the shaft and the babbitt.

A phenomenon known as *oil whip* or *oil whirl* occurs in relatively lightly loaded, high-speed journal bearings. The center of the journal (portion of the shaft inside the bearing) assumes an eccentric position in the bearing. This position is determined by load, speed, and oil viscosity. Since the stable position is near the center of the bearing, the journal center starts to move in a circular path about the stable position. The vibrations created by this motion have a frequency of less than one-half the shaft speed. Pressure-pad (Fig. 3.7), three-lobe (Fig. 3.8),

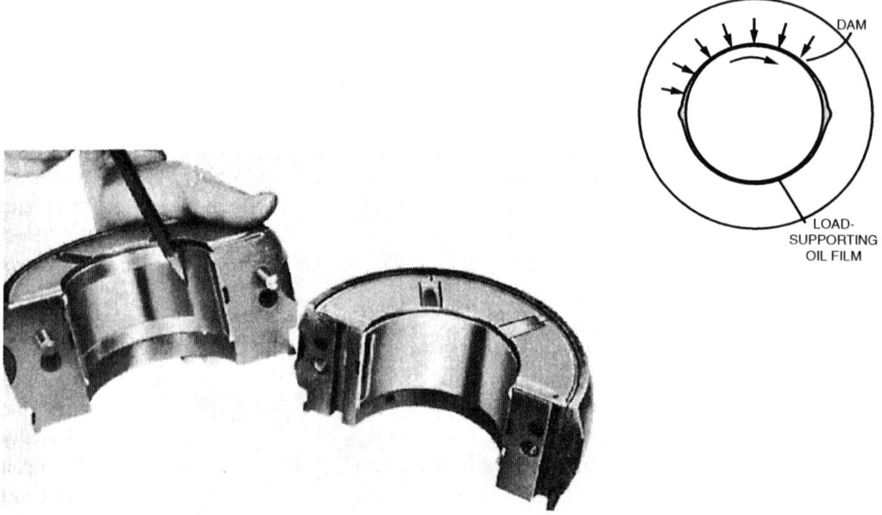

FIGURE 3.7 Pressure bearing. The wide groove in the upper half ends in a sharp dam at the point indicated. As shown in the insert, this causes a downward pressure that forces the journal into a more eccentric position that is more resistant to oil whirl.

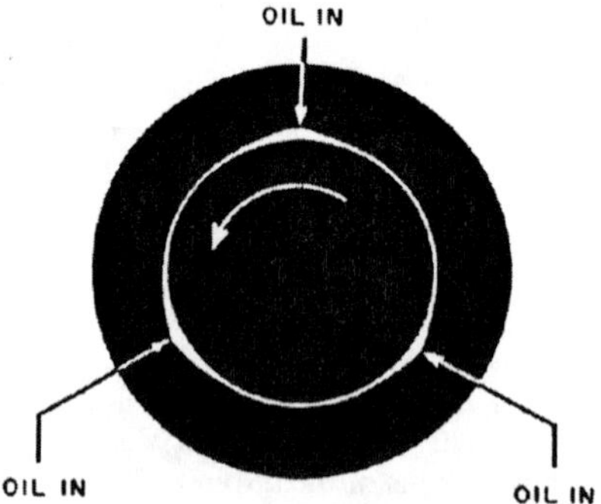

FIGURE 3.8 Three-lobe bearing. The shape of the bearing is formed by three arcs of radius somewhat greater than the radius of the journal. This has the effect of creating a separate hydrodynamic film in each lobe, and the pressures in these films tend to keep the journal in a stable position.

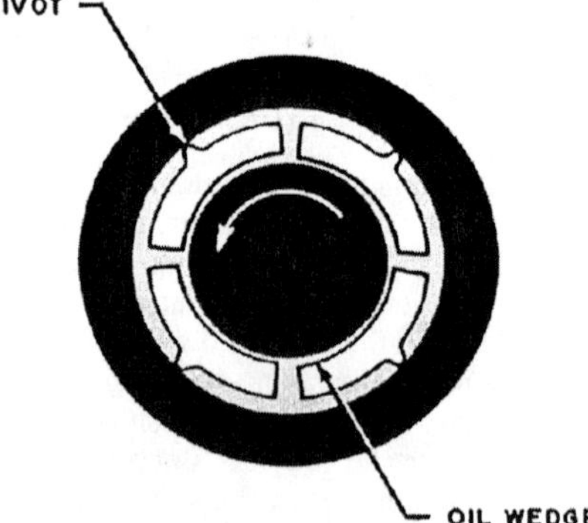

FIGURE 3.9 Tilting-pad antiwhip bearing. As in the three-lobe bearing, the multiple oil films formed tend to keep the journal in a stable position.

and tilting-pad (Fig. 3.9) bearings are designed to suppress oil whip. The pressure-pad bearing suppresses oil whip by having a wide groove that ends in a sharp dam, which causes downward pressure that forces the journal into a more eccentric position to resist oil whirl. The other types rely on the formation of multiple oil films to preload the journal and prevent oil whip.

THRUST BEARINGS

Axial thrust is caused by the difference in pressure across each row of moving blades. Rotors that are stepped up in diameter also create axial thrust. This thrust is counteracted by axial thrust bearings, which maintain the rotor in correct axial position.

Small turbines use babbitt-faced ends on the journal bearings, or rolling-element thrust bearings. Medium and large turbines use tilting-pad tapered-land thrust bearings as shown in Fig. 3.10 and 3.11, respectively.

HYDRAULIC CONTROL SYSTEMS

Medium and large turbines use hydraulic control systems to transmit the signals from speed or pressure transducers to the steam control valves. Modern turbines use electrohydraulic control systems that operate at high pressure [1500 to 2000 psi (10.3 to 13.8 MPa)] to provide the rapid response needed to control these units. These systems include an independent reservoir and two separate and independent pumping systems. Gas-charged accumulators are also used to provide the large fluid flow required instantaneously upon sudden changes in load. The quality of the hydraulic fluid used must be maintained within tight tolerance due to the critical nature of these systems (disasters have occurred in the past due to slow response of the governing system). The fluid must be filtered and particulate contamination must be maintained within strict limits. Heaters

FIGURE 3.10 Combined journal and tilting-pad thrust bearing. A rigid collar on the shaft is held centered between the stationary thrust ring and a second stationary thrust ring (not shown) by two rows of tilting pads.

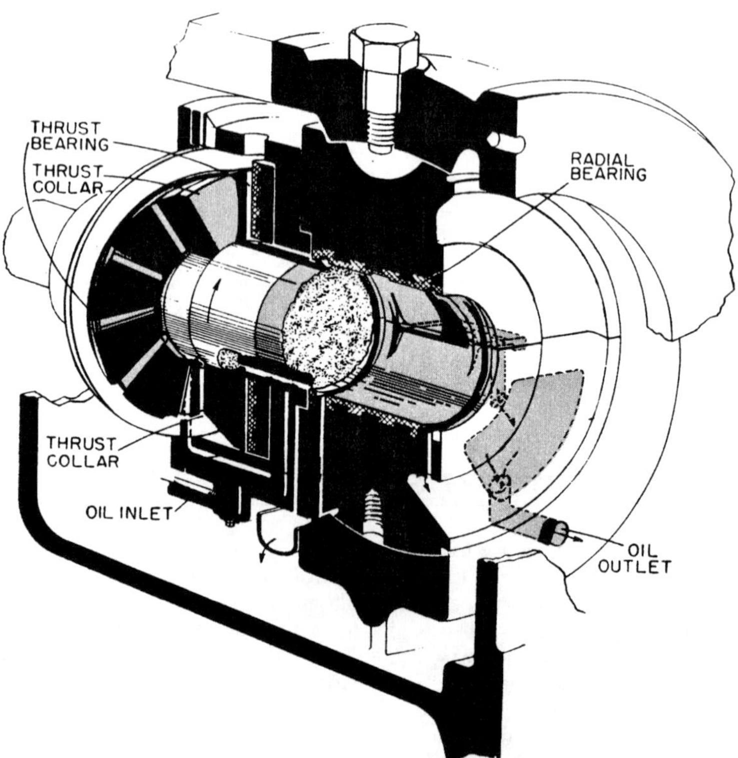

FIGURE 3.11 Tapered-land thrust bearing and plain journal bearing. The thrust bearing consists of a collar on the shaft, two stationary bearing rings, one on each side of the collar. The babbitted thrust faces of the bearing rings are cut into sectors by radial grooves. About 80 percent of each sector is beveled to the leading radial groove, to permit the formation of wedge oil films. The unbeveled portions of the sectors absorb the thrust load when speed is too low to form hydrodynamic films.

and coolers are used to maintain the temperature and, thus, viscosity in a narrow range. Fire-retardant fluids (FRFs) are used in these systems to prevent a fire from occurring upon a leak, which would spray hydraulic fluid on hot-steam piping and valves due to high pressure.

GEAR DRIVES

Efficient turbine speed is sometimes different from the operating speed of the equipment being driven. In these applications, the turbine is connected to the driven equipment by reduction gears. A separate oil-tight casing is usually used to enclose the gears that are connected to the turbine and driven equipment through flexible couplings. The oil circulation system for the gears may be entirely separate from the turbine system or may be supplied from it. A separate pump is used in the latter case.

TURNING GEAR

During start-up and shutdown, the rotor should be rotated slowly to avoid uneven heating or cooling, which could distort or bow the shaft. A barring mechanism or a turning gear is used for this purpose. The turning gear consists of a motor that is temporarily coupled to the turbine by reduction gears. The turning gear speed is usually below 100 rpm. A separate auxiliary oil pump is used to provide adequate flow to the bearings during the low-speed operation. The service water flow in the oil coolers is maximized to increase the viscosity of the oil and assist in maintaining the oil film in the bearings. The jacking oil system is operated while the turning gear is operating.

FACTORS AFFECTING LUBRICATION

Circulation and Heating in the Presence of Air

Heat is generated within the bearings by friction and heat conduction along the shaft. Oil is broken into droplets while it is flowing. This allows greater exposure to air. During operation, oxidation (combination of the oil molecules with oxygen) occurs. Fine metal particles resulting from wear or contamination and water act as a catalyst (enhance the rate) to oxidation. The viscosity of oil increases with oxidation. Insoluble oxidation products such as varnish and sludge may settle out on governor components, in bearings, heat exchangers, and strainers. Their accumulation will interfere with governor operation and oil flow to the bearings.

Contamination

Water is the most prevalent contamination in turbine lubrication systems. Three common sources of water include:

1. Leaking turbine and pump seals
2. Condensation of humid air
3. Water leaks in heat exchangers

Emulsion will form when the oil is mixed with water. The emulsion will separate quickly when the oil is new and clean. The water will settle in the reservoir where it can be removed by purification equipment. Oxidation or contamination of the oil will increase the tendency of the oil to emulsify. Emulsions can mix with insoluble oxidation products and dirt to form sludges. Water can combine with air to form red and black rust, which is similar in appearance to pipe scale. Particles of rust have the following effects:

- Act as catalysts that increase the rate of oil oxidation.
- Scratch the journals and cause excessive wear.
- Get entrained into the small clearances of the governing system. This will cause sluggish operation and, in extreme cases, disasters (due to slow operation of the governing valve).

Oil can become contaminated by air to form "bubbly" oil. This oil is compressible and can cause sponginess in hydraulic controls. It may reduce the load-carrying capability of oil films. Entrained air increases the rate of oxidation. An excessive amount of air can generate foaming in the reservoir or bearing housings.

LUBRICATING OIL CHARACTERISTICS

The steam turbine oil should have (1) the proper viscosity at operating temperatures to provide the lubricating films, and (2) adequate load-carrying ability to reduce wear.

Viscosity

The journal and thrust bearings of steam turbines require lubrication. Oils having higher viscosity provide a greater margin of safety in the bearings. However, its friction losses are high. In high-speed turbines, the heat generation becomes significant. Most oils used in this service have International Organization for Standardization (ISO) viscosity grade 32 [28.8 to 35.2 centistokes (cSt) at 40°C]. Higher viscosity is used in some applications, ISO viscosity grade 46 (41.4 to 50.6 cSt at 40°C).

Higher-viscosity oils are used for geared turbines to provide adequate lubrication for the gears. Most of these systems use oils of ISO viscosity grade 68 (61.2 to 74.8 cSt at 40°C). Some geared turbines cool the oil in a heat exchanger before delivering it to the gears. The increase in viscosity provides better protection for the gears.

Load-Carrying Ability

Steam turbines normally use mineral oils. Boundary lubrication conditions occur in turbines not equipped with lifts. Wear will occur under these conditions unless lubricants with enhanced film strength are used. The higher viscosity of cool oil provides the increase in load-carrying ability of the oil films needed during start-up. Additives are also frequently used in turbine oil to improve the film strength.

Oxidation Stability

The ability to resist oxidation is the most important characteristic of turbine oils. This property is important from the standpoint of retention of viscosity (resistance to the formation of sludges, deposits, and corrosive oil oxyacids) and retention of the ability to separate water, resist foam, and release entrained air.

Protection Against Rusting

Rust inhibitors are required from turbine oils to improve their ability to protect against rusting of ferrous surfaces. These inhibitors "plate out" on metal surfaces to resist the penetration of water.

Water-Separating Ability

New mineral oils usually resist emulsification when there is water ingress. Any emulsion formed breaks quickly. Some additives such as rust inhibitors increase the tendency of an oil to emulsify. Thus, additives should be selected carefully to ensure that the oil has good water-separating ability.

Foam Resistance

Turbine oils usually contain defoamants to reduce the foaming tendency. Since oxidation increases the tendency to foam, good oxidation stability is essential to maintain good resistance to foaming.

Entrained-Air Release

Entrained air can cause sponginess and delayed or erratic response. Some additives are known to degrade the ability of the oil to release entrained air. Thus, the additives selected for turbine oil should not reduce its ability to release air.

Fire Resistance

Fire-resistant fluids (FRFs) are normally used in electrohydraulic governor control systems due to high pressures (up to 3000 psi). Phosphate esters or blends of phosphate esters and chlorinated hydrocarbons are normally used. These systems are extremely sensitive to the presence of solid contaminants. Considerable attention should be paid to the filtration of the oil.

REFERENCE

1. Wills, G., *Lubrication Fundamentals*, Marcel Dekker, New York, 1980.

CHAPTER 4
TURBINE GOVERNING SYSTEMS

The four main functions of the governing system[1] are as follows:

1. To limit the speed rise to an acceptable limit upon a load rejection (when the unit is suddenly disconnected from the load)
2. To control the power that is generated by controlling the position of the steam governing valve (or fuel valve in gas turbines)
3. To control the speed of the turbogenerator during initial run-up and synchronization
4. To match the power that is generated to the power that is required by the load by responding to frequency changes [only when the generator is operating in islanding mode (i.e., alone), independently from the grid]

The first function is critical to the safety and availability of the plant. If the breaker connecting the generator to the grid opens during normal operation, the shaft speed will increase significantly due to the elimination of the countertorque produced by the generator. The steam flow must be reduced instantly to limit the speed rise. Most machines have a separate overspeed trip to ensure safety of the plant and personnel upon failure of the governing system. It consists of overspeed bolts that protrude out of the shaft. They trip a lever when their overspeed setpoint is reached. This results in depressurization of the hydraulic oil of the governing system leading to closure of the governing valve. Another trip on high acceleration is also included in some plants. Upon a load rejection (opening of the breaker connecting the generator to the grid), acceleration sensors trip the steam valves on high acceleration.

Following a load rejection, the governor must maintain the unit at the running speed. This is done for two reasons:

1. To ensure continuity of the unit power supplies from its own generator through the unit service transformer (UST).
2. Providing resynchronization capability to the unit upon termination of the fault.

Note: Many problems occurring on the grid are short-lived (lasting less than 1 hour).

The initial transient overspeed (normally limited to less than 8 percent) that occurs after a load rejection is caused by the following two reasons:

1. The response time of the governing valve (GV) or the emergency stop valve (ESV) to close
2. The stored energy of the steam within the turbines and their associated pipework

Figure 4.1 illustrates a typical electrical governing system used in a plant having multiple steam turbines. It includes at least one closed-loop control system. The main feedback is the speed of the turbine shaft. A triplicated circuit using magnetic pickup sensors measures the shaft speed at a toothed wheel located at the high-pressure (HP) end of the shaft. A modular electronic system processes the signal. The electronic system is often located in a cubicle that is remote from the turbine. The output signal from the electronic system is directed to each steam valve on the turbines.

The processing varies with each application. However, it generally includes the following:

- Speed versus load characteristic of the turbine generator when the machine is synchronized
- Predetermined relationship between the governing valve position and the intercept valve position
- Features that limit the maximum speed of the turbogenerator
- Features that limit the power output
- Features that allow testing of the system

Each steam valve has a relay that converts the low-power electrical signal generated by the processing equipment into movement of the valve stem. Several stages of hydraulic amplification are used due to the substantial mechanical forces [150 kilonewtons (kN)] and short stroking time [<200 milliseconds (ms) upon a load rejection]. The governing system

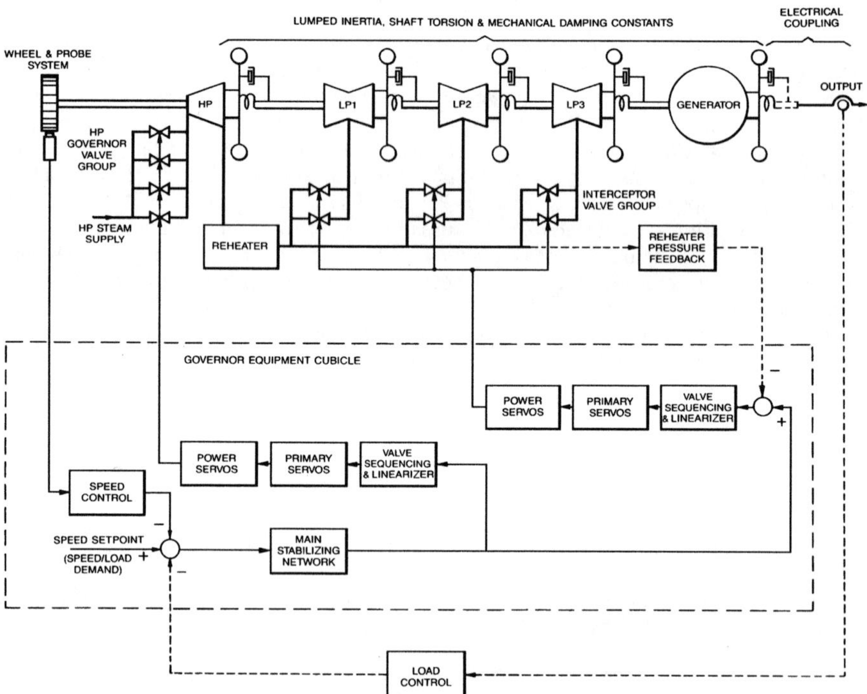

FIGURE 4.1 Electrical governing system applied to a wet-steam turbine.

must be able to provide fine control over load (or speed when the machine is not synchronized). A typical dead band of modern governing systems is less than ±36 millihertz (mHz). Its sensitivity in positioning the valve is within 0.2 percent of the required position. Hydraulic equipment having high precision and fine clearances are used to achieve high resolution and amplification of small electric signals.

Earlier mechanical/hydraulic governing systems shared the lubricating oil supply with the turbine. However, modern governing systems use a separate high-quality fluid to improve the reliability and accuracy of the system. Modern governing systems also have a much higher hydraulic pressure in their actuators than earlier governing systems (1500 psi versus 200 psi). This increase in the hydraulic pressure was done to reduce the size of the actuator and the response time of the valve. However, the high hydraulic pressure created a fire hazard in the plant. Any small leak from the high-pressure hydraulic system would generate an oil mist that settles on hot turbine bearings and pipes. These oil leaks can easily generate a fire in the plant. Modern governing systems use a special oil called *fire-retardant fluid* (FRF). This fluid is commonly known as phosphate ester. It does not ignite when it settles on hot bearings and pipes.

GOVERNOR CHARACTERISTICS

All electrical systems experience faults. Safety is maintained in these situations by protective equipment that opens circuit breakers to isolate the fault. The governing system of a turbine generator must be able to handle a full-load rejection safely and provide appropriate contributions to the regulation of system frequency. The relationship between the generated load of a unit and speed is the main characteristic of a governing system. Figure 4.2 illustrates the *frequency regulation characteristic,* also known as the *speed-droop characteristic,* of the governor.

The steady-state overall frequency regulation is defined as

$$\frac{N_0 - N_{PR}}{N_R} \times 100\% \tag{4.1}$$

where N_R = rated speed
N_{PR} = speed at full-load
N_0 = speed at no load

This characteristic allows a machine to share load with other machines and permit the operator to adjust the load generated by the machine. Figure 4.3 illustrates how variations of the speed setpoint affect the generated load. If the machine is not synchronized and the no-load speed setpoint is raised from a_1 to a_3, the frequency will increase from a_1 to a_3. However, if the machine is synchronized to a grid operating at constant frequency a_1, an increase in no-load speed setpoint from a_1 to a_2 and then a_3 will increase the load to b_2 and then b_3. The linear characteristic shown in Figure 4.3 is for an ideal case. In reality, the characteristic may be nonlinear. The no-load speed setpoint is adjusted between a_1 at no-load and a_3 at full-load. This range of operation is normally between 4 and 6 percent.

Figure 4.3 illustrates also the phenomenon of *overwound* speed setpoint. If the operator has adjusted the speed setpoint to give characteristic a_3b_3 (the unit is running at full-load at a frequency f), a decrease in the grid frequency by an amount Δf will give an indication that the load will increase to c_3. However, since the load is determined by the turbine, which is already operating at full power, the load will not increase beyond b_3. The speed setpoint is

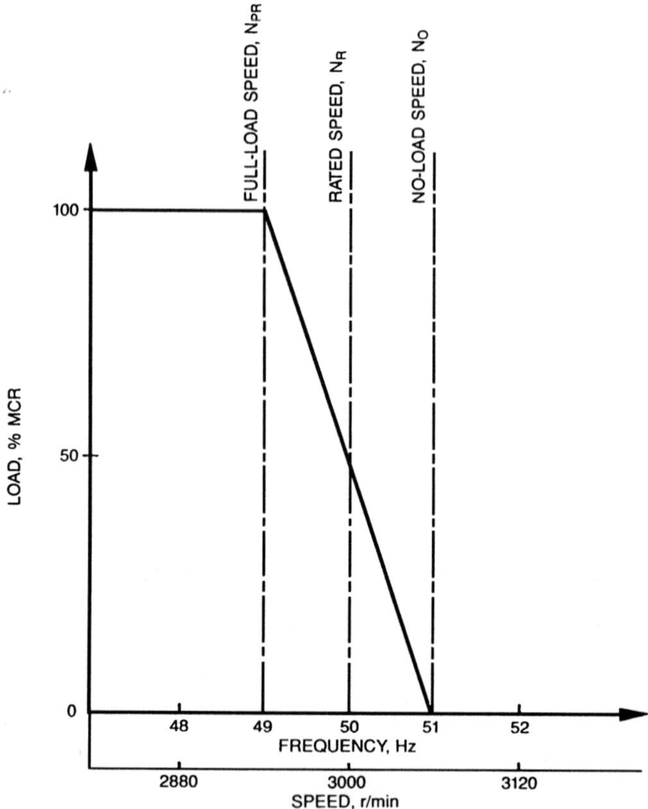

FIGURE 4.2 Governor frequency regulation characteristic.

called in this case *overwound.* The disadvantage of this situation is that if the operator is asked to reduce the load on the unit, he or she is unable to do so immediately. The load can only be reduced when the speed setpoint is lowered to the line given by c_2a_2. Normally, an alarm is annunciated to inform the operator of the overwound condition, or the setpoint is reduced automatically so an immediate response is possible when required.

Most units have the ability to adjust the droop. A typical high value of 25 percent droop is beneficial to reduce transient steam pressure variations if the system frequency fluctuates. On-load droop adjustment normally implies a change in load. Most governors have the ability to change the droop in a "bumpless" manner.

Figure 4.4 illustrates the characteristics of additional overspeed-limiting facilities that are incorporated into the design to limit the overspeed upon a load rejection. This is done to limit the overspeed below the overspeed trip setpoint when the governor has high droop. If the governor has low droop (e.g., 4 percent or less), there is no need for overspeed-limiting facilities because the overspeed is limited by the normal droop characteristic. In all cases, the turbine valves must close within a fraction of a second to limit the overspeed below the trip setpoint.

On units that have reheaters (e.g., Fig. 4.1), the intercept governing valves must also be closed rapidly upon a load rejection. If only the HP governing valves were closed, the

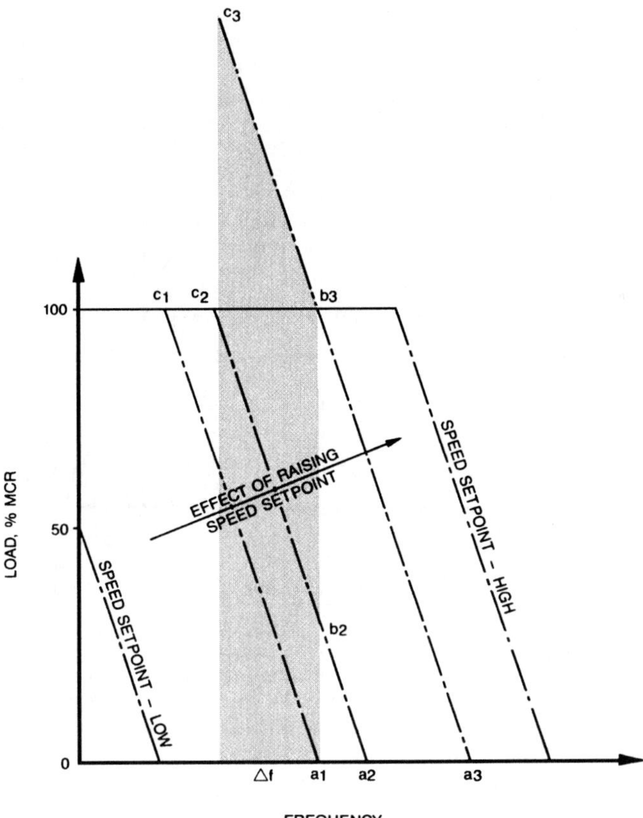

FIGURE 4.3 Effect of variation of speed setpoint.

stored steam energy in the reheater and associated pipe work is sufficient to destroy the machine due to excessive overspeed.

The thermal efficiency will be reduced if the intercept valves are used for throttling the steam. Therefore, these valves are normally fully open over the normal load range of the machine. This operating regime is called *HP governing.* It is achieved by adding a fixed bias to the signal that controls the intercept valves. This gives them the same speed-versus-load characteristic as the HP governor valves, but they are more open by a fixed amount of the bias (typically, 50 percent).

Another mode of operation (often provided as a switched option) uses the intercept valves to throttle the steam flow. The *spinning spare capability* (the capability of the unit to increase load rapidly in response to a reduction in the grid frequency or a demand for increased load) of the unit is enhanced. However, the thermal efficiency is reduced. This may be important for grids that experience large fluctuations in frequency or where there are insufficient machines having good regulating characteristics. This mode of operation is called *HP plus IP governing* or *parallel governing.* The reheater pressure is normally proportional to the load in the HP governing mode. However, the reheater pressure is constant over the load range from 50 to 100 percent in the HP-plus-IP governing mode. This means that at 50 percent load, the reheater pressure will be the full-load value of, for instance, 40 bar instead of 20 bar. The spinning spare

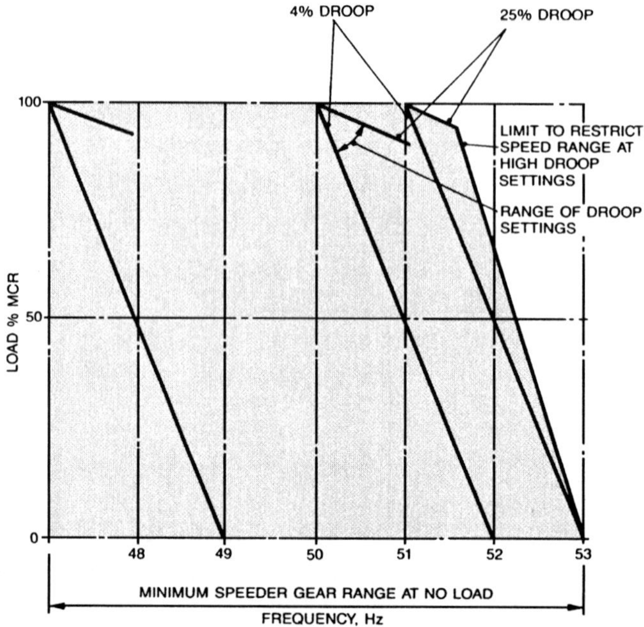

FIGURE 4.4 Turbine speed governor characteristics. *Note:* The required range of operation is indicated by the shaded area. Governor characteristics may extend outside this area provided this does not impair the safety of the system or cause the set to trip on overspeed or loss of full load.

capability will be improved by the additional thermal energy available due to having the reheater at full-load pressure. Therefore, the intermediate-pressure (IP) and low-pressure (LP) turbines will be able to provide their full-load torque almost immediately.

SUBSIDIARY FUNCTIONS

This section describes additional functions of the governing system. These functions are not included in all governing systems. In some cases, they may not be essential to the unit being controlled.

Acceleration Feedback

Acceleration feedback is used for two reasons:

1. To improve the damping of the governor by providing a secondary stabilizing term
2. To prevent overspeed upon a load rejection

If the governing system does not have acceleration feedback, its response would be controlled by the speed error (speed setpoint − measured speed). If the speed droop is set to 4 percent, no action would be taken by the governing system upon a load rejection until the measured speed exceeds 104 percent. Additional delays occur in the hydraulic system. This system may not be able to limit the overspeed to 10 percent.

A governor using acceleration feedback will be able to send a signal to close the steam valves as soon as acceleration is detected. The valves will be instructed to close within 30 ms of a load rejection. The valves should be fully closed 100 ms later. A typical response to a load rejection is shown in Fig. 4.5. The permanent overspeed has the same value as the speed droop. Most governors initiate a turbine runback to lower the no-load speed setpoint to eliminate the permanent overspeed.

A threshold is preset into the detection system to ensure that the acceleration feedback is activated during a significant load rejection only. The acceleration feedback is also only activated when the acceleration signal is present for a predetermined time.

Unloading Gear

The unloading gear is usually complementary to a protective function that would normally cause a turbine trip. It involves early detection of the condition that will likely cause a trip and decreasing the turbine load to reduce the probability of tripping. If the trip does occur eventually, the transient effect on the plant would be reduced because the trip occurred at a lower load.

An unloading is normally provided for the condenser shell pressure. The pressure is normally measured at tapping points on the condenser. During normal operation, the unloader has no effect. The condenser shell side pressure is around 5 kilopascals (kPa) absolute [-96 kPa (g), or 96 kPa vacuum]. If the condenser shell side pressure starts to increase due to system fault (e.g., air ingress into the shell side of the condenser or fouling of the condenser tubes, etc.), the turbine starts to unload progressively. Above a threshold of 120 millibars (mbar) (12 kPa), the degree of unloading is linearly proportional to the condenser shell side pressure. Figure 4.6 illustrates a typical unloading characteristic. The degree of unloading is normally limited to around 20 percent load. This is done to avoid motoring the unit or overheating the turbine due to reduced steam flow.

If the cause of unloading is eliminated and the condenser shell side pressure drops to its normal value, the turbine remains unloaded until the operator or a separate automatic control feature restores the load. The operation of the loading gear is prevented (veto) during initial start-up and loading until the exhaust pressure is reduced to a value that will not restrict increased loading up to full load.

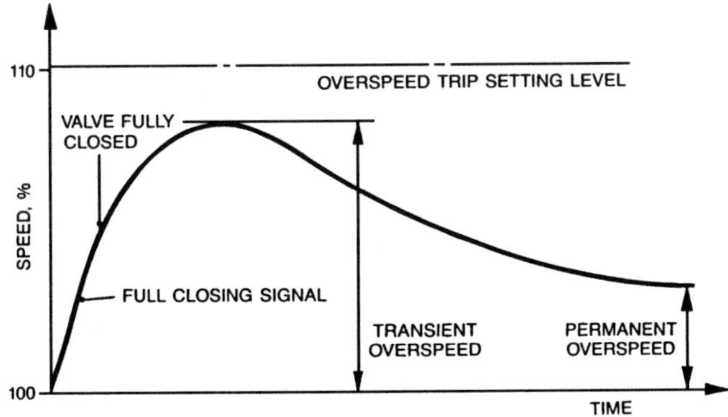

FIGURE 4.5 Turbine response to load rejection.

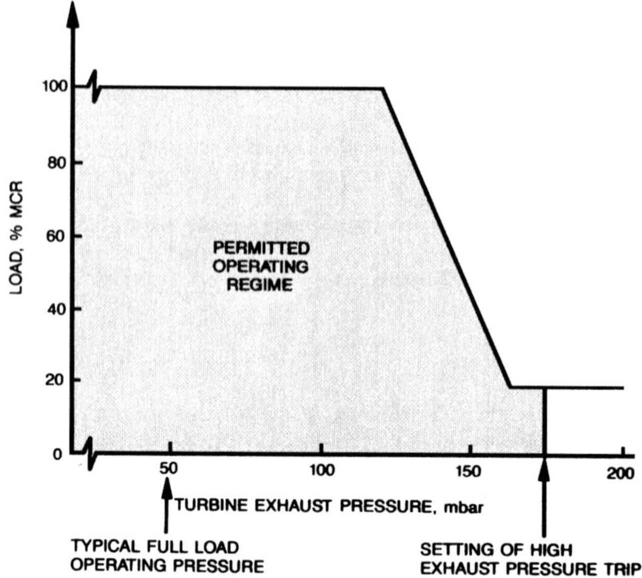

FIGURE 4.6 Turbine exhaust pressure unloading characteristic.

The operator normally removes the veto when the unit is unloaded. However, if forgotten, the veto will be removed automatically when the condenser shell side pressure reaches the value that permits full load (around 120 mbar, as shown in Fig. 4.6).

Governor Speed Reference

The governor speed reference is the main input used to control the turbine. This speed control can either be done by the operator or automatically. Before synchronization, the range of the speed reference is from 3 percent (minimum controllable speed) to 104 percent (highest speed at which the turbine generator is capable of synchronizing). Once the machine is synchronized, the range of the speed reference will be limited to between 94 and 106 percent.

Prior to synchronization, the speed reference's rate of increase can be selected by the operator. The rate of decrease in the speed reference is normally constant.

When the turbine generator approaches the synchronization speed, the rate of increase of the speed reference will change. The new rate of increase of the speed reference must be compatible with the autosynchronizing unit. It is usually selected to provide fast and certain synchronization. After synchronization, the rate of increase of the speed reference is normally set to travel the range from 0 to 6 percent in 1 minute. The governor speed reference is used now to load the machine.

Closed-Loop Control of the Turbine Electrical Load

Closed-loop control of the turbine electrical load is added to the basic governing system to improve the accuracy of the load-droop characteristics. It also facilitates the variations of the droop setting. The trimming signal of the speed-droop system in the basic governor is derived from the steam valve position. Since the relationship between the steam flow and the valve position is nonlinear, the basic speed governor uses an inverse function to linearize the steam flow relationship with the valve position at one nominal set of steam conditions. However, when the conditions vary, imperfections will occur due to significant nonlinearities. The closed-loop load control overcomes these imperfections by superimposing a trimming signal on the governor speed reference. Figure 4.7 illustrates a block diagram of the load loop. Figure 4.8 illustrates its characteristic.

The load loop operates over a limited range of frequency. The unit will respond to any large errors in frequency in a manner similar to a unit having 4 percent droop characteristics, even when the load loop droop is set to higher or infinite values.

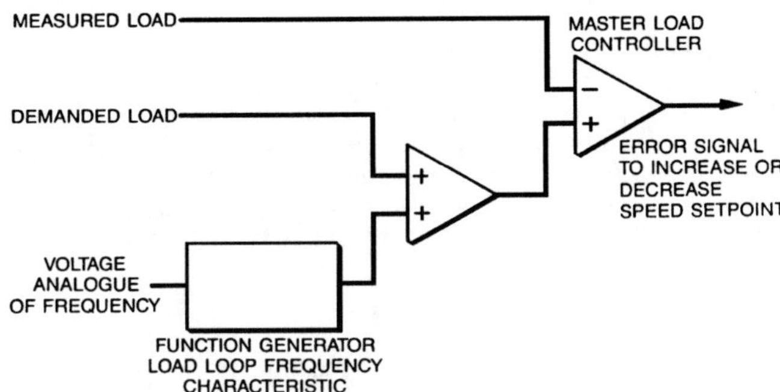

FIGURE 4.7 Block diagram of load loop.

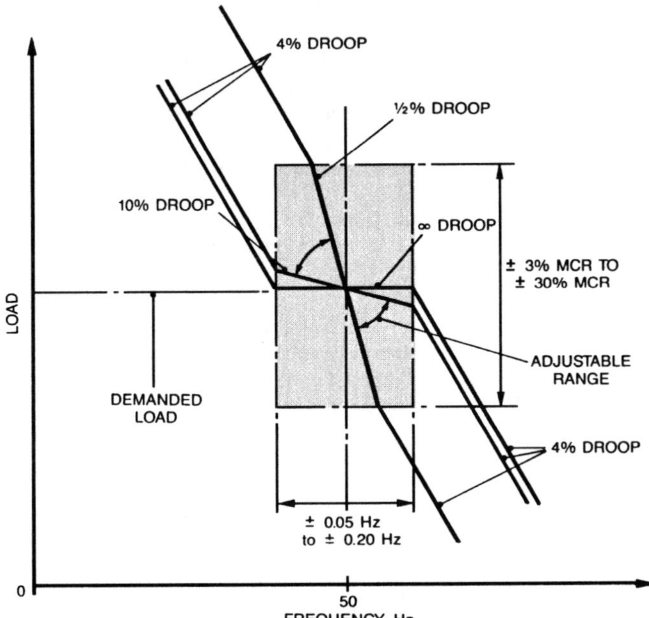

FIGURE 4.8 Load loop frequency "box" characteristic.

The effect of sudden load changes on the boilers is limited, even if the unit has low speed droop, by limiting the range of the load over which the load loop operates. The variable droop is permitted over a narrow range of speed and load. This range is called the *box characteristics*.

When the grid frequency drops, all units increase their load because the load loop (acting through the governor speed reference) is slow-acting. Then, the units having high or infinite load loop droops will slowly reduce their load. They return to a value near the original load. This allows the machines having low droop to pick up load at a rate compatible with their boilers. The advantage of this arrangement is that some units can be designated to pick up the load rapidly while those unable to accommodate such a transient can still provide a useful contribution to the control of the falling frequency.

Overspeed Testing

The overspeed testing is performed to prove the actual value of the overspeed protection trip setpoint. The test is performed when the unit is unsynchronized. The operator has to operate a key-locked test switch before the test. This permits a governor speed range up to 13 percent rather than 6 percent. The governor no-load speed setpoint is increased to the trip setpoint.

Automatic Run-Up and Loading Systems

The two main reasons for automatic run-up and loading systems are

1. To assist the operator in performing the complex sequence of checks required prior to and during start-up
2. To run up and load the machine in a safe and consistent manner

Figure 4.9 illustrates a sophisticated automatic run-up and loading system. The scope of this system assumes that separate operator actions were taken to bring all the auxiliary systems needed for the safe operation of the turbine to a satisfactory state of readiness. Thus, lubricating oil, main and auxiliary cooling water systems, and so on, will have been brought into service. A digital-state signal will indicate when each of these conditions or prestart interlocks is satisfied.

Sufficient redundancy is provided due to the large number of plant-mounted transducers. This is done to permit automatic run-up and loading with high availability. Failed transducers are identified to the operator.

Automatic control may be restricted if several minor input signals are lost or one of a duplicate pair of major signals. Only manual control may be possible if further signals fail.

The operator must then decide if there are sufficient indications to permit continued run-up or loading. Otherwise, the operator must hold the unit in a safe condition while repairs are in progress, or shut down the turbine.

The main function of the automatic run-up and loading system is to limit the thermal stresses within the turbine rotor and valve chests while the speed and load are changing. The stress is measured directly by thermocouples. They measure the difference between the inner and midwall metal temperatures at suitable points. The stress measurement is used to control the run-up or load changes to the best values. The control is a closed-loop type. It acts on the governor to maintain the stress constant at the reference value during run-up.

There is an exception to this strategy during the critical-speed bands (these bands could stretch for a few hundred revolutions per minute depending on rotor dynamics). A large stress margin is established before entering the critical-speed band. Rapid acceleration is

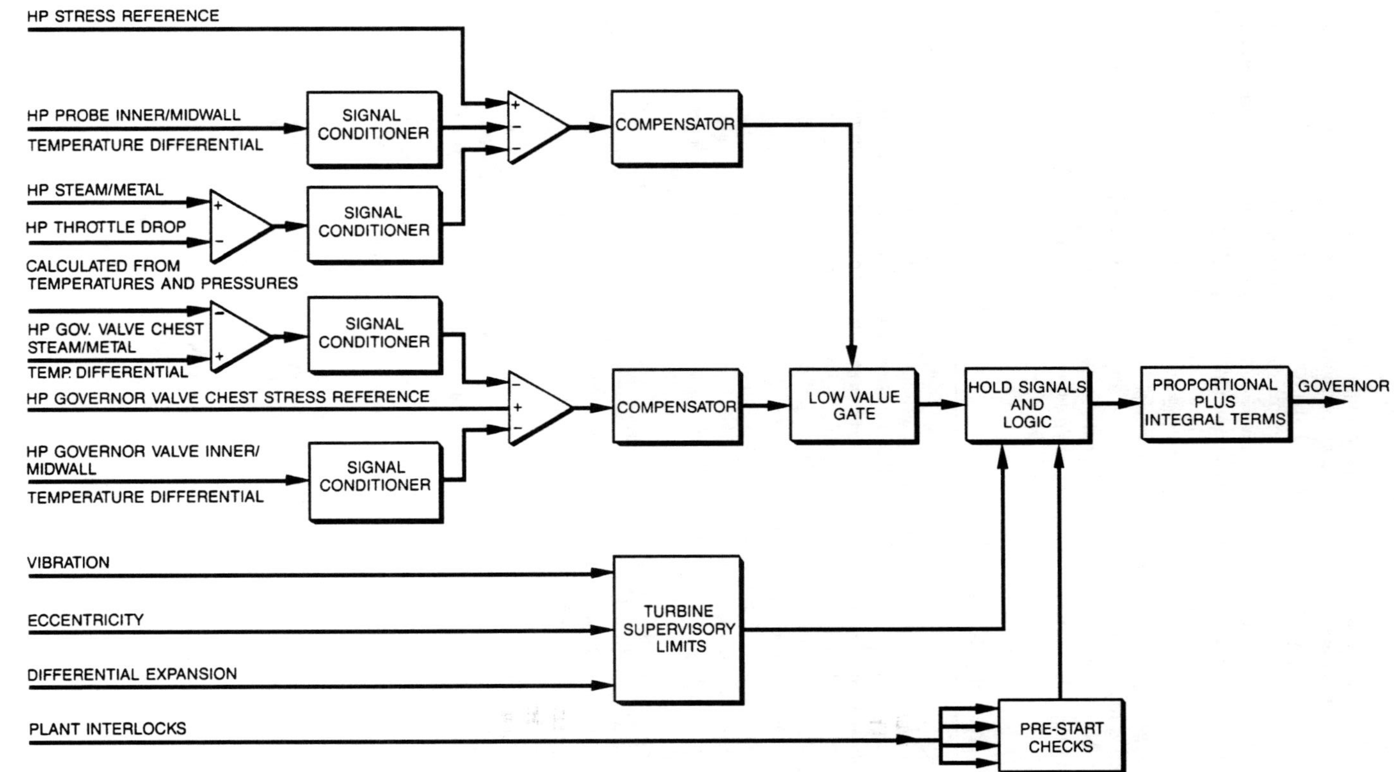

FIGURE 4.9 Automatic run-up and loading equipment.

provided throughout the band to avoid resonance. All "hold" signals from the operator or any other source are rejected while the speed is within the band.

The *turbine supervisory equipment* (TSE) receives signals indicating vibration, eccentricity, and differential expansion (between the rotor and the stator). It sends "hold" signals during run-up and loading when any of these signals reach its limit. If the magnitude of the signal does not decrease, it sends a signal to reduce the speed or power. The signal from the TSE is rejected (vetoed) when the speed is within the critical-speed bands. If the controlling parameter is reduced to 80 percent of the limit, the "hold" will be released. If a second limit is reached, the operator is advised to trip the unit.

A block load of about 5 percent is applied after the unit is synchronized. This is done to prevent motoring the generator due to changes in grid frequency. Figure 4.10 illustrates all the described functions of the most complex governing system.

ELECTRONIC GOVERNING

Figure 4.11 illustrates a detailed block diagram of a typical single-channel governing system. A three-channel system (Fig. 4.12) is normally used to satisfy the reliability requirements of governing systems. It works on the principle of "majority voting circuits." These circuits are extremely simple and reliable. They work on the principle that for small changes in the input signals, the output signal produced is the average of the inputs. For large changes, the median signal is selected.

The error of the governing system is defined as the difference between the required speed (speed setpoint) and the measured speed (feedback). The gain of the governor is the change in valve position (e.g., 10 percent) achieved for 1 percent change in turbine speed error. The gain is maintained low to provide a large stability margin for the governing system.

During run-up, the steam flow required is very low compared with the steam flow required during full-load operation (2 to 3 percent of full load). This is the flow required to overcome the friction at the bearings and the windage losses (rubbing of air or hydrogen on the generator rotor). The speed-sensing device is installed in the proximity of a toothed wheel coupled to the main turbine shaft.

For constant steam inlet conditions, the output power from the turbine varies linearly with the steam flow passing through it. Figure 4.13 (*a*) illustrates this characteristic. It is known as the *Willans line*. In a conventional condensing-steam turbine, the flow is also directly proportional to the pressure drop across it.

The desired characteristic is therefore that the steam demand input to the valve position controller should vary linearly with steam flow (i.e., with load). However, the inherent features of the valve design are nonlinear. A valve linearization function is introduced into the governor to restore the required linearity. In particular, the relationship between the valve area versus the steam flow is nonlinear [Fig. 4.13 (*b*)]. The valve lift varies in a nonlinear fashion with the valve area [Fig. 4.13 (*c*)]. The two effects are linearized by using linearizing circuits to give the steam demand the characteristic shown in Fig. 4.13 (*d*).

Three-channel valve steam demand signals are fed to each individual valve controller. The controller takes a majority vote of these signals to form a signal demand. The feedback to the controller is the signal derived from a valve position transducer.

REHEATER RELIEF VALVES

The reheater relief valves are used on all machines. They prevent overpressurization of the reheater and are spring-loaded, set to open at a predetermined pressure.

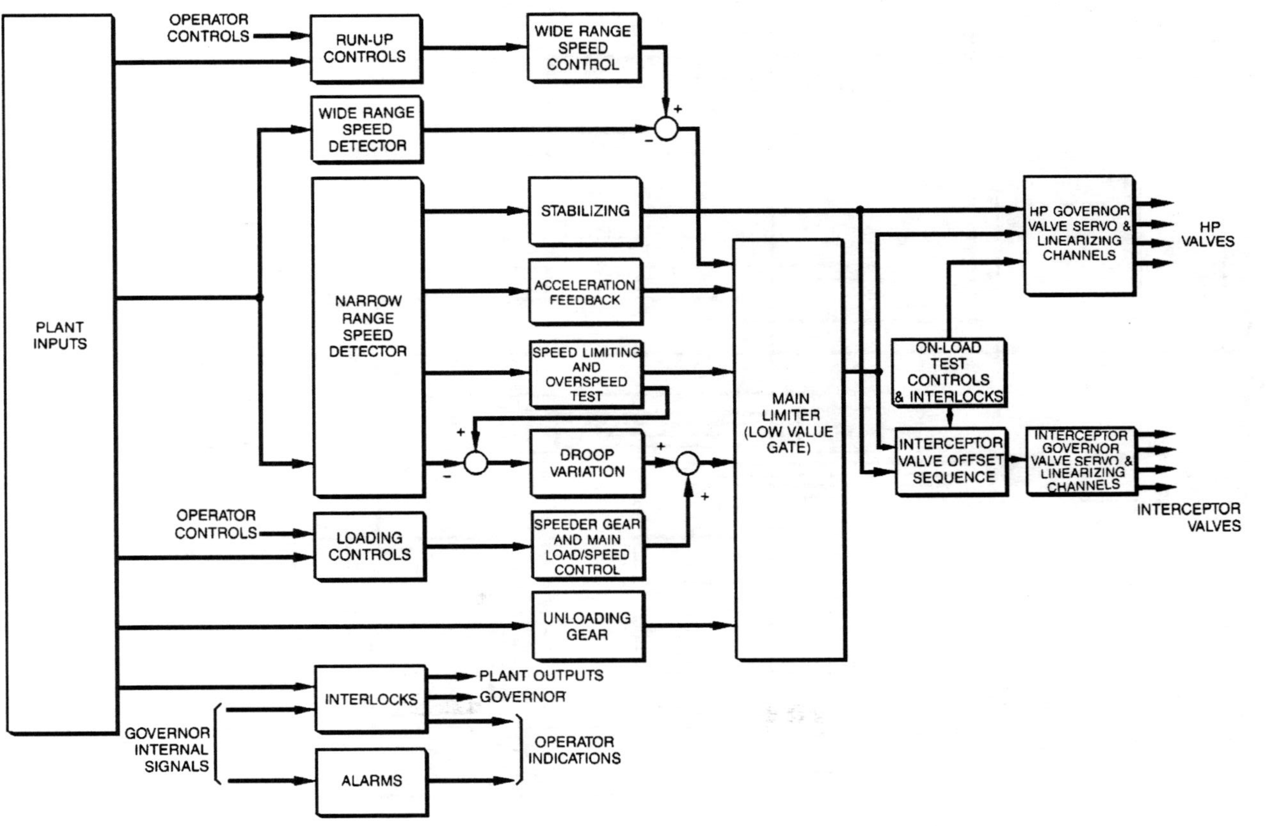

FIGURE 4.10 Governor overall block diagram.

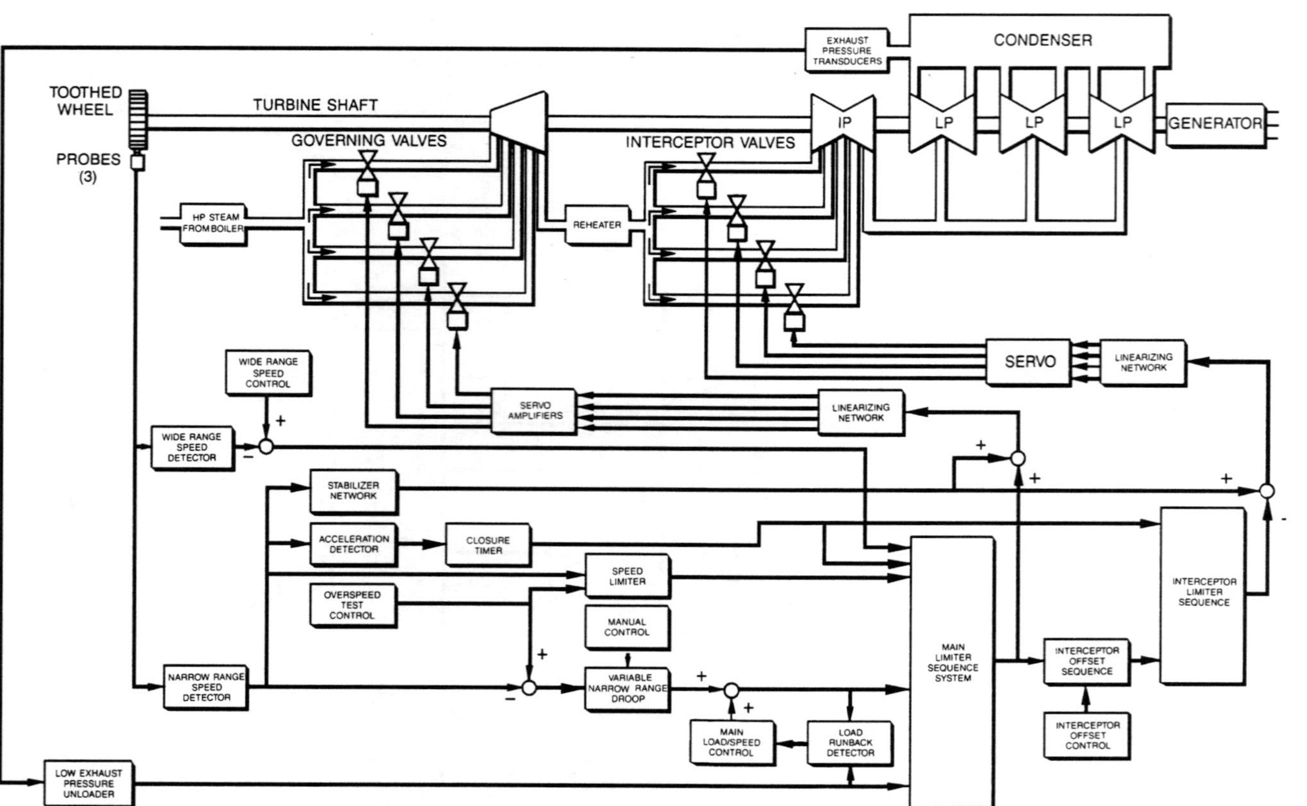

FIGURE 4.11 Detailed block diagram of a single-channel governing system.

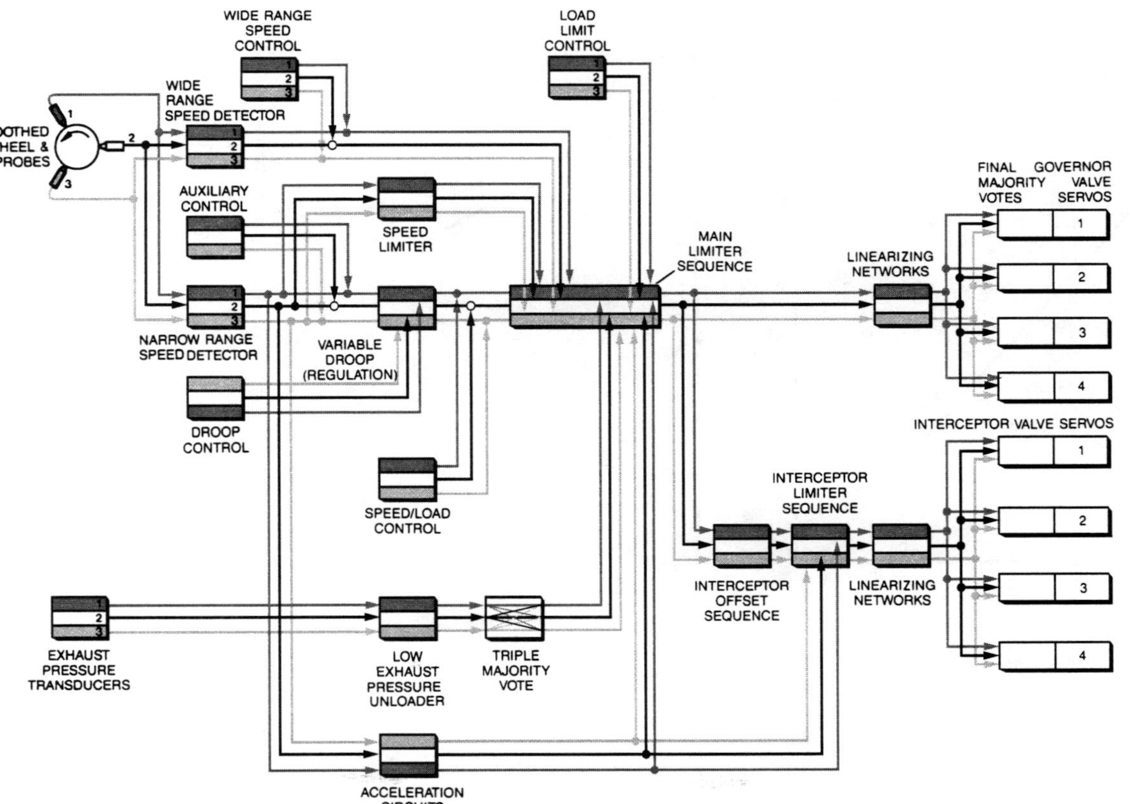

FIGURE 4.12 Block diagram of a three-channel governing system.

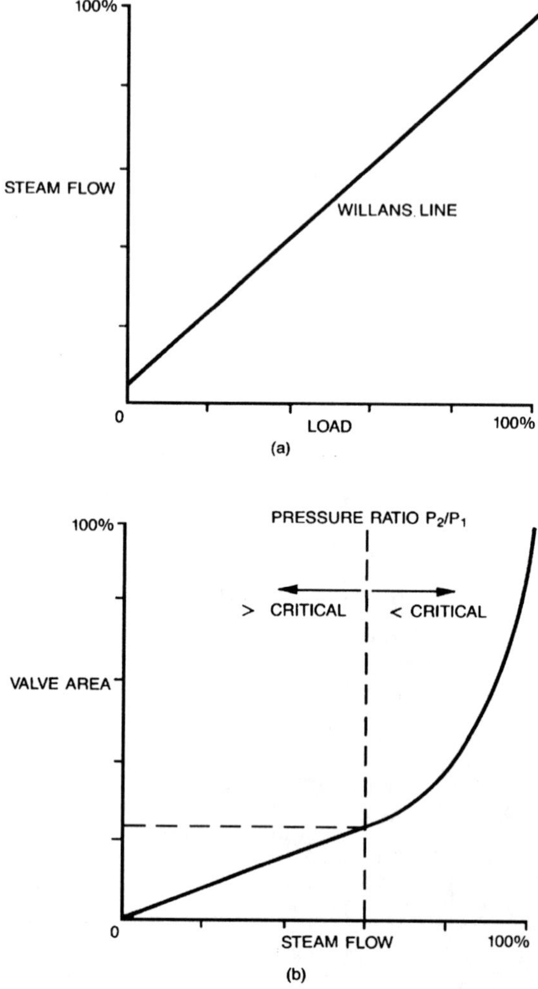

FIGURE 4.13 Typical steam load/valve characteristics. (*a*) Variation of steam flow with the load; (*b*) Variation of valve area with steam flow.

In addition, on some units, relatively small release valves are used to release steam in the reheater system to the atmosphere or to the condenser when the governor valves and interceptor valves close suddenly during an emergency. Although the steam may not be at a sufficiently high pressure to open the relief valves, any residual steam trapped in the HP turbine and reheater could lead to overheating of the blades in the HP turbine due to churning of relatively high-density steam. The release valves are located in the connecting steam piping between the reheater and the interceptor valves. They are signaled to open under certain conditions to prevent overheating of the blades.

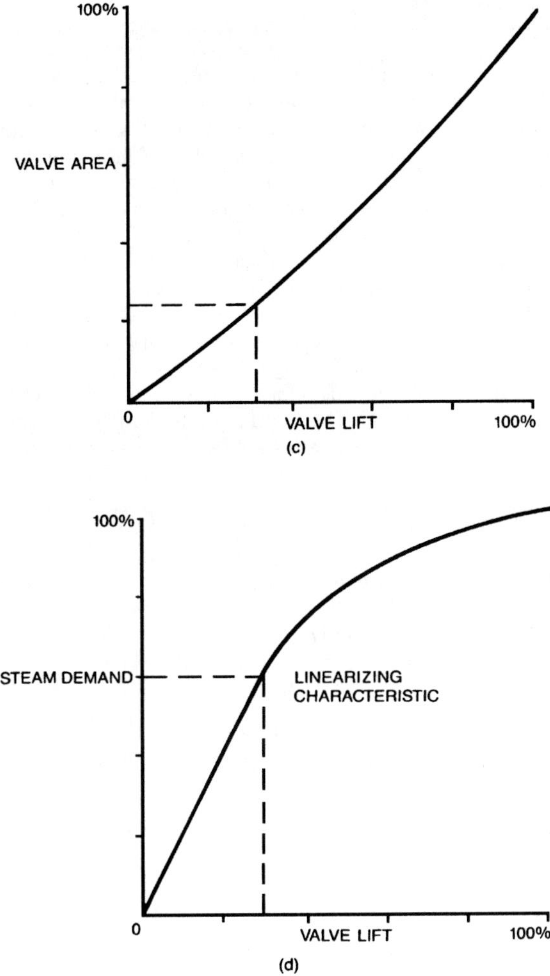

FIGURE 4.13 *Continued* Typical steam load/valve characteristics. (*c*) Variation of valve area with valve lift; (*d*) Variation of steam demand with valve lift (known as linearizing characteristic).

The release valves are actuated hydraulically or pneumatically. If an electronic governor is installed, the release valves open by energizing solenoid valves. They are signaled to open under the following three conditions:

1. Loss of tripping pressure
2. High shaft acceleration
3. Closure of all interceptor steam relays

These conditions include circumstances of turbine trips or turbine load rejection without tripping. Churning of the steam could occur either during turbine rundown following a trip or during the period of interceptor valve closure upon a load rejection.

HYDRAULIC FLUID SYSTEM

Large turbine generators use high-pressure hydraulic fluid to provide the large opening forces and rapid stroking times for the valves. The hydraulic fluid must be able to flow through small-clearance components in the valve relays. The system pressure is selected to allow the use of an economically sized relay capable of providing the required opening forces. For small turbines (<500 MW), the hydraulic pressure is around 35 bar or less. For larger turbines, system pressures of between 70 and 150 bar are needed.

These high hydraulic pressures create a significant fire hazard. A small leakage can result in a jet of oil being sprayed over a considerable distance. This oil will fall on hot (typically, 565°C in coal-fire plants) steam pipes located in the vicinity of the leak. This necessitates the use of double enclosure of the pipework and components or the use of a fire-resistant fluid (FRF). Most plants use FRFs made of phosphate ester. These systems are completely separate from the lubricating oil systems.

Phosphate ester fluids have the advantage of having similar viscosity and lubricating characteristics to the lubricating oil. Thus, earlier units using high-pressure oil can be converted to phosphate ester. These fluids also have the fire resistance required and a long service life. They can be maintained in adequate condition for a long period without the need for replacement.

The fluid condition should be monitored regularly. Any deviation outside the limiting values of the parameters should be investigated promptly. Otherwise, a serious accident could occur. A few decades ago, a plant in Great Britain experienced an increase in the viscosity of the governing system fluid. The steam valves were sluggish upon a load rejection. This led to overspeed of the turbine and failure of the generator hydrogen seals. The hydrogen leak created an explosion that killed some workers and damaged the plant extensively.

The fluid supply system includes a reservoir and a high-pressure pump (Fig. 4.14). The reliability of the system is increased by installing two pumping lines.

Axial-piston or screw-type pumps (Fig. 4.15) are normally used for this application. Adequate suction pressure is required. Otherwise, cavitation and erosion will occur in the

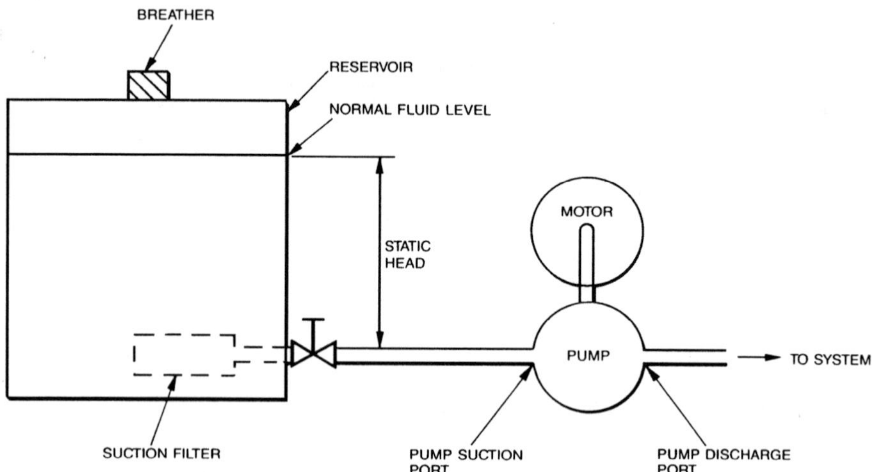

FIGURE 4.14 Pump suction arrangement for a separately mounted pump.

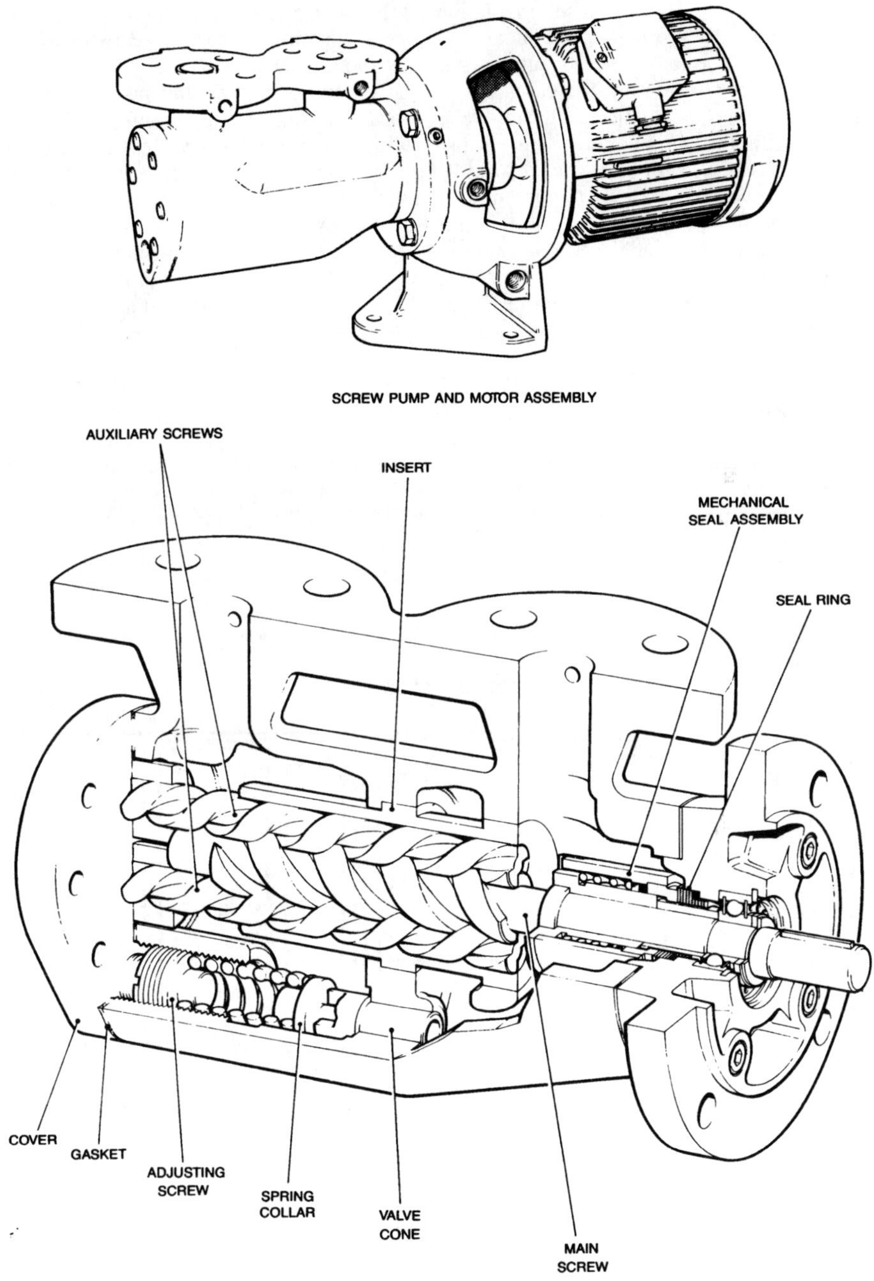

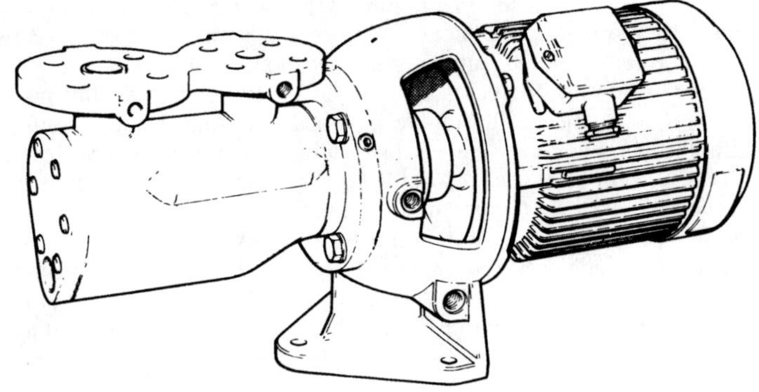

SCREW PUMP AND MOTOR ASSEMBLY

AUXILIARY SCREWS
INSERT
MECHANICAL SEAL ASSEMBLY
SEAL RING
COVER
GASKET
ADJUSTING SCREW
SPRING COLLAR
VALVE CONE
MAIN SCREW

FIGURE 4.15 Typical screw pump and motor assembly.

pumping system. This will result in a failure of the system and a lengthy outage. A coarse filter is normally installed at the suction of the screw pump. A separate centrifugal boost pump is also normally used. Its outlet pressure is about 7 bar.

The fluid temperature increases due to the pumping process and being circulated through valve relays adjacent to hot steam pipes. The fluid has optimum conditions at 40°C. At higher temperatures, the viscosity will decrease. Excessive leakage from the pump and the system may occur. At still higher temperatures, the fluid starts to break down. Conversely, at lower temperatures, the viscosity of the fluid increases. It becomes difficult to pump. The pressure drop in the system also becomes excessive. The required flow rate may not be achieved. For these reasons, heat exchangers are installed in all systems. If cold starting is essential, heaters may also be required. The fluid temperature is maintained at 40°C at the main pump. Figure 4.16 illustrates a schematic diagram of a typical pumping system.

Filtration

Filtration is required for any fluid supply system. The standards are determined by the smallest clearances in the system. The purpose of the filters is to remove impurities from the system. Impurities are generated continuously within the system from wear inside the pump and other moving components. Some impurities are introduced by the air entering

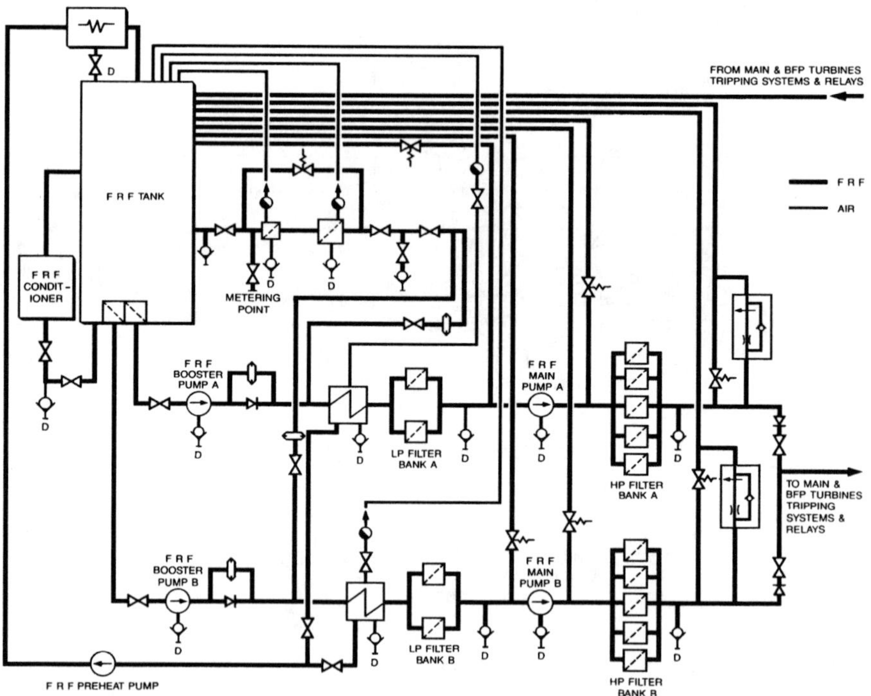

FIGURE 4.16 Fire-resistant fluid pumping system.

through the reservoir breather or in the valve relays. Impurities are small particles suspended in the fluid. They have irregular size, shape, and chemical composition.

Water should never be introduced into the system during operation and maintenance. The system should also never be cleaned using chlorinated solvents. Nevertheless, water still enters the system due to contact of the fluid with air in the reservoir and in the valve relays and drain lines. A vacuum dehydration unit (Fig. 4.17) is normally used to maintain the water concentration below 2000 parts per million (ppm). The unit takes the fluid from the reservoir and then returns the conditioned fluid to the reservoir. The fluid is pumped from the main reservoir into the conditioner reservoir. It is heated to 80°C. Then, it is passed into a vacuum chamber where the water is extracted. The processed fluid is then passed through a Fuller's earth filter, which reduces the water content further, and also

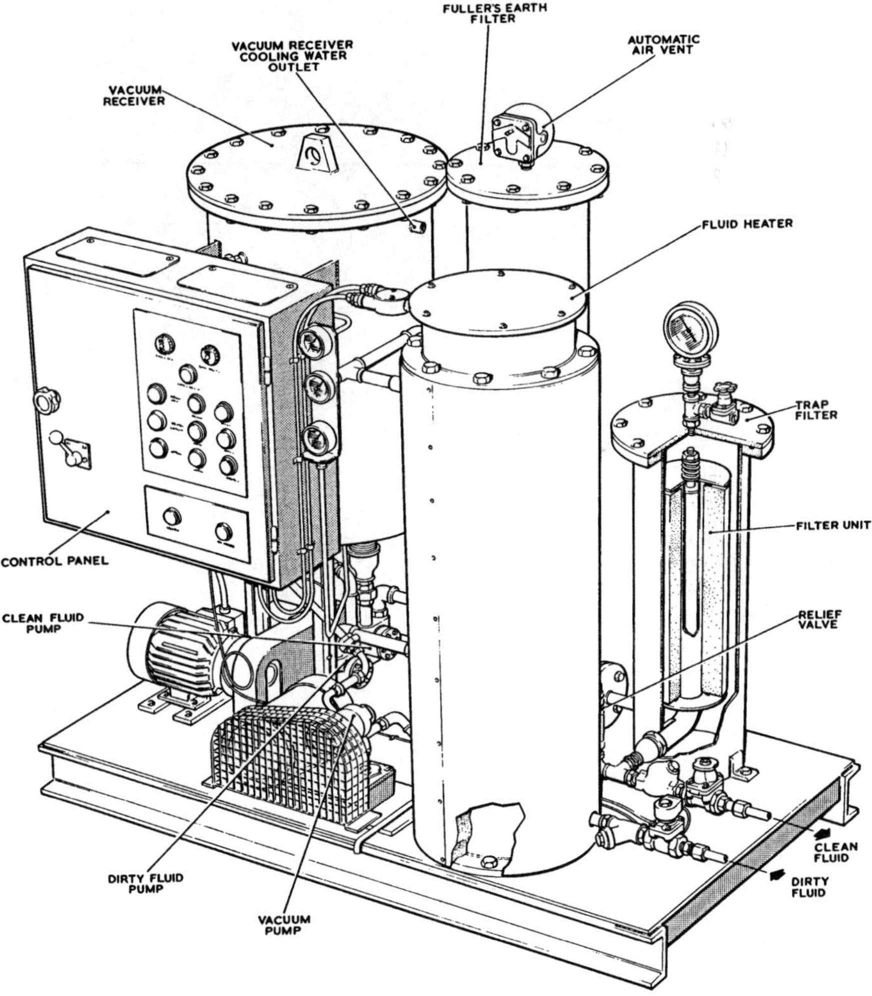

FIGURE 4.17 Fire-resistant fluid conditioner.

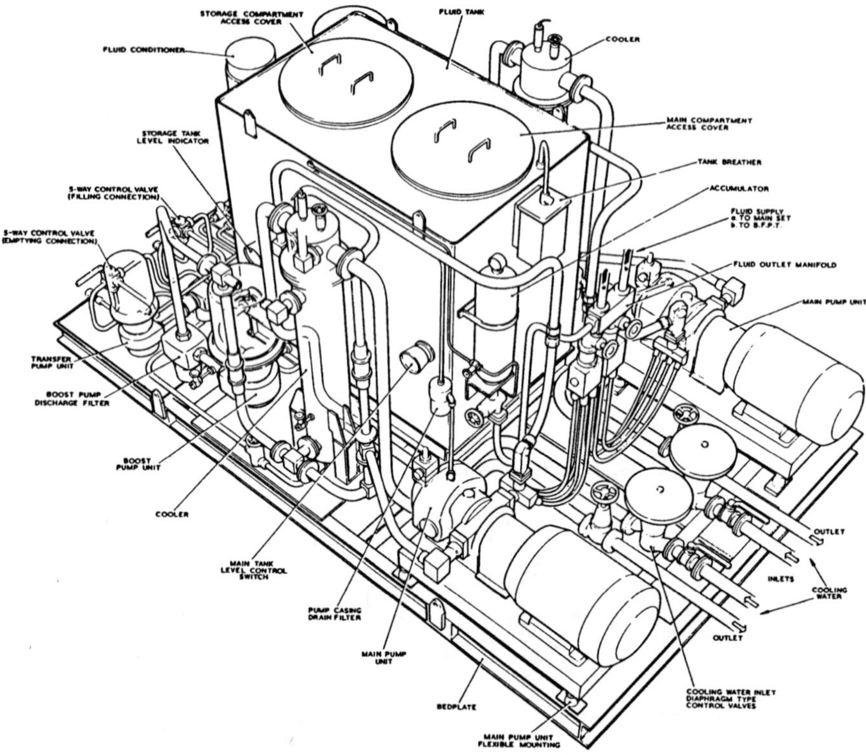

FIGURE 4.18 Fire-resistant fluid packaged unit.

reduces acidity. A trap filter is normally installed after the earth filter. Its main purpose is to capture the earth if the earth filter ruptured accidentally.

Figure 4.18 illustrates an FRF-packaged unit. The joints in the pipework are kept to a minimum. They are welded wherever possible. All pipework is made from stainless steel to avoid corrosion. Interlocks are included to shut down the pumping line if the pump suction pressure or outlet temperature is low.

REFERENCE

1. British Electricity International, *Modern Power Station Practice*, 3d ed., Pergamon Press, Oxford, United Kingdom, 1991.

CHAPTER 5
STEAM CHESTS AND VALVES

STEAM CHEST ARRANGEMENTS AND CONSTRUCTION

The steam leaving the superheater goes through the emergency stop valves (ESVs) and associated governing valves (GVs) before entering the high-pressure (HP) turbine.[1] The ESVs and GVs are housed in steam chests. These steam chests are manufactured from closed-die alloy-steel forgings welded together, or from alloy-steel castings. They also have simple shapes. This is done to reduce the thermal stresses and hence the possibility of thermal fatigue.

Similar steam chests house the reheat emergency stop valves (RESVs) and interceptor valves (IVs). These steam chests are located between the reheater and the intermediate–pressure (IP) turbines. They are manufactured from alloy-steel castings. They are thinner but larger than the HP steam chests due to lower steam pressures.

The steam chests are normally mounted alongside the turbine. The four steam mains, together with four ESVs and four GVs, are normally arranged two on each side of the turbine.

Figure. 5.1 illustrates a typical steam chest arrangement of a 660-MW unit. There is a steam chest on each side of the machine. It has an ESV on each end and the two GVs are connected to the common chamber between the ESVs.

STEAM CHEST MATERIAL

The chests are manufactured from alloy steel. On 660-MW units operating at 565°C, the material is usually 0.5 CrMoV steel. In some recent units operating at 538°C, the chest material is 2.25 Cr steel. Higher-chrome ferrite steels with improved creep resistance are also used on larger units operating at 565°C.

The seats of the valves are of the removable-plate type. These seats are normally screwed in place. The mating faces of the valves and their seats are made of *Stellite*™. This is done to resist wear caused by steam erosion. The wear will occur mainly when the valve is cracked open. A jet is propelled at high velocity due to the large pressure differential across the narrow port opening. The Stellite facing also provides protection against impact damage, which occurs during normal valve closure. It also occurs during frequent high-speed test closures. This damage is alleviated normally using cushioning devices in the relay system or slow-motion testing. Specially treated alloy-steel sleeves in the valve covers support and guide the valve spindles.

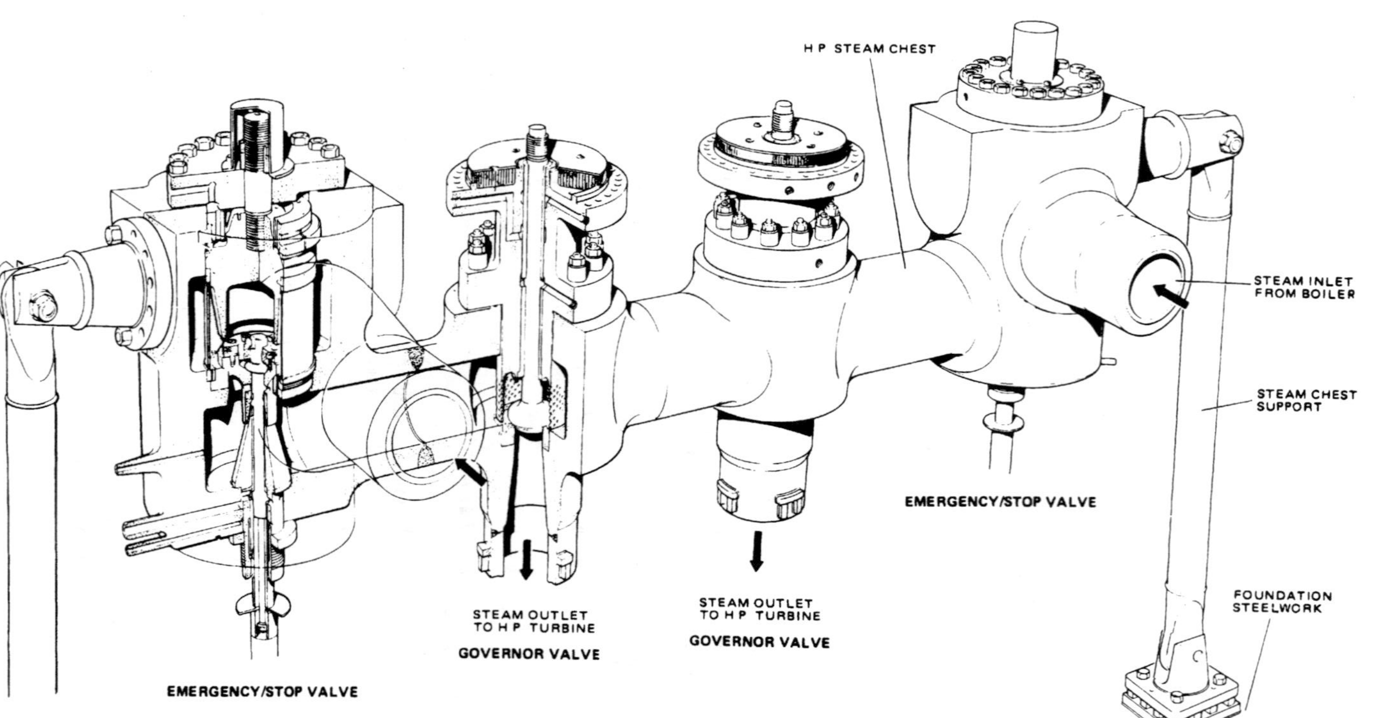

FIGURE 5.1 Typical steam chest arrangements.

STEAM STRAINERS

Each ESV is surrounded by a cylindrical strainer. The strainer has many 2- to 5-mm-diameter holes. It prevents solid particles of foreign matter from getting entrained with the steam entering the turbine. These particles could cause serious damage to the turbine blading if they enter the turbine. It is essential to have a thorough steam blow of all pipework before commissioning a plant.

EMERGENCY STOP VALVES

The two purposes of the ESVs (also known as *stop valves*) are:

1. To interrupt the steam flow promptly during an emergency trip
2. To cut off the steam supply when the unit is shut down

The valves are tested on-power regularly (at least once a month) to ensure they will close during an emergency. The load is reduced during this testing. The valves are tested in sequence, one at a time, during the on-load testing.

The ESV is normally a single-seated unbalanced plug-type valve. It has an internal small pilot valve that opens first. The pilot valve can be opened against main steam pressure. It is also used during run-up because the steam flow is from 1 to 2 percent of the full-load steam flow. It also reduces the force required to actuate the valve. When the machine reaches operating speed, the GVs, which have been open, close in. At this stage, it is possible to open the ESVs because the upstream and downstream pressure of the valve have been equalized. Figure 5.2 illustrates a typical ESV. Flap valves are used as reheat emergency stop valves (RESVs) for some 500 and 660 MW units. The steam in these valves has moderate pressure and large specific volume.

GOVERNOR VALVES

The governor valves control the steam flow entering the turbine. Since the generator converts mechanical energy to electrical energy, the governor valves control the generator load when the machine is synchronized to the grid.

Modern power plants use the governor valves to throttle the steam flow during turbine run-up to speed. However, earlier machines use pilot valves in the ESV in conjunction with the governor valves during run-up (the steam flow during run-up is less than 2 percent of the steam flow required during full-load operation). Figure 5.3 illustrates a typical governor valve.

REFERENCE

1. British Electricity International, *Modern Power Station Practice,* 3d ed., Pergamon Press, Oxford, United Kingdom, 1991.

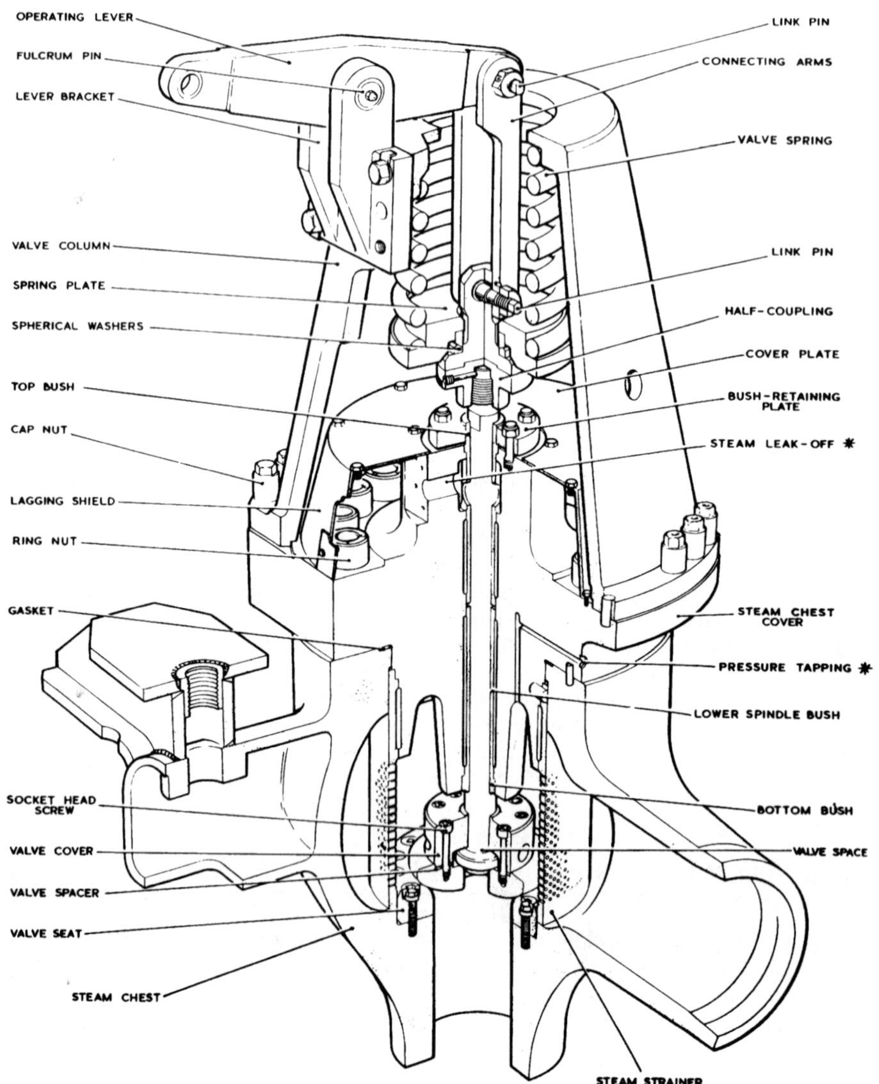

FIGURE 5.2 Typical emergency stop valve. (*, shown out of position.)

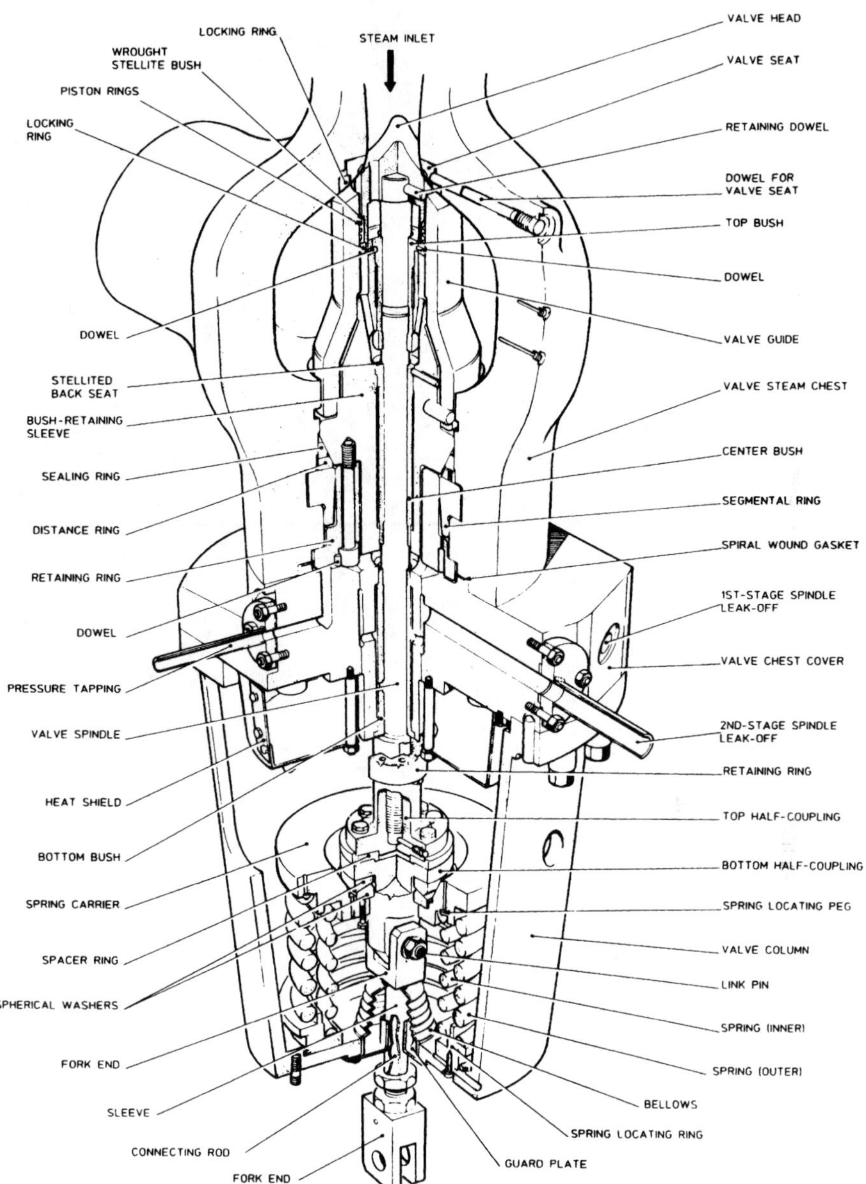

FIGURE 5.3 Governor valve.

CHAPTER 6
TURBINE PROTECTIVE DEVICES

POSSIBLE HAZARDS

Abnormal turbine operating conditions will cause damage to the plant and possibly to personnel if allowed to persist.[1] The possible dangers include the following:

- Overspeeding
- Lubricating oil failure
- High turbine exhaust pressure (low condenser vacuum)
- Governor failure
- Water ingress to blading
- Thrust bearing failure
- Excessive vibration
- Excessive temperature differentials
- Excessive eccentricity

Supervisory equipment normally monitors the last four items. The remaining dangers have more immediate effects on the plant. They are detected by systems that depressurize the hydraulic pressure of the governing system. This results in shutting the steam valves and disconnecting of the generator.

The preceding list includes dangers that only affect the turbine. Other hazards specific to the boilers, generator, transformers, and high-voltage connections can also initiate a turbine generator trip.

The consequences of overspeed are very serious for the plant and personnel. Therefore, the protective systems have been designed to prevent overspeed. The turbine governing system protects the unit from overspeed. However, if it malfunctions, a separate overspeed tripping system will become activated. When the generator is connected to the grid, the turbine cannot overspeed (the generator is coupled magnetically with the grid). The possibility of overspeed occurs during run-up and when the unit is disconnected suddenly from the load (during a load rejection). The unit is normally disconnected from the grid due to an internal problem such as a loss of lubricating oil. The possibility of overspeed is normally reduced by coordinating the opening of the circuit breaker and the closure of the steam valves. The turbine will overspeed when the torque generated by the steam flow exceeds the countertorque generated by the load. Thus, whenever possible, the steam valves should close while the unit is still connected to the grid.

When the steam flow drops below the one required to overcome friction losses [bearings and windage (rubbing of air or hydrogen against the generator rotor)], the generator starts to act as a motor. It starts to pull current from the grid to continue running at the operating speed. The circuit breaker now opens on reverse power. This sequence of activities prevents the chance of overspeed. This type of a trip is known as *category B trip*. If the steam valves fail to close and the generator gets disconnected from the grid, the unit will suffer disastrous consequences. However, if the generator remains connected to the grid when the steam valves fail to close, the turbine will not overspeed. The unit can be shut down safely by closing the boiler stop valves. All tripping conditions that follow this sequence of events are known as category B trips. They include the following:

- Governor failure
- Lubricating oil failure
- Overspeed
- Water ingress
- Manual emergency stop

Other trips, such as turbine high–exhaust pressure trips and some electrical trips, require immediate disconnection of the generator from the grid. These trips are known as *category A trips*. If the turbine exhaust pressure is high, the last stage of the blades in the low-pressure (LP) turbine will become overheated and damaged. The turbine unloading gear (included in the governing system) reduces the turbine load to avoid tripping. Some units use LP exhaust temperature sprays. They are activated when high temperature is detected. They are also used when the turbine load drops below a predetermined value. The possibility of heating the turbine blading at low load is high. This is due to the low flow that is unable to remove the heat generated. The LP turbine also has bursting diaphragms fitted in the casing. They operate at a pressure slightly higher than atmospheric.

Alternating-current (AC) and standby direct-current (DC) pumps ensure continuous supply of lubricating oil to the bearings. However, in case of a pipe fracture, the turbine is tripped on low lubricating oil pressure. If the governing system fails (e.g., due to failure of more than one channel), a tripping signal is sent to the protection scheme.

Water can enter the turbine due to malfunction of the boiler or feed controls. This event has a higher probability of occurrence during load variations. Wet steam or even slugs of water could enter the high-pressure (HP) steam line. The protection required varies with the boiler type and the degree of hazard. If superheated steam is supplied from a steam drum, turbine protection may not be required if the loss of boiler firing can be adequately detected and alarmed. In this case, the operator can take the necessary corrective action.

If superheated steam is supplied from a once-through boiler, the turbine should be tripped on low steam temperature before saturated steam reaches the turbine. If the turbine is not tripped in this case, the turbine blades could become fractured. The sudden ingress of wet steam could generate significant axial (thrust) loads on the turbine blading. Thus, the plant must be designed to accept this condition or be protected against it. Water can also enter the turbine from the feedheaters (backflow). This can occur upon a load rejection. In this case, the pressure inside the turbines drops to a lower value than the one in the feedheaters. Check valves are installed on the extraction lines to the feedheaters to prevent this reverse flow.

PROTECTION SCHEME

There are two types of trip-initiating devices:

1. Devices that are operated by an electrical changeover contact

2. Devices that are capable of tripping the hydraulic fluid system directly

A trip closes the turbine steam valves and opens the generator circuit breaker. As explained earlier, the trips are divided into categories A and B. Redundancy is built into the tripping system. The failure of one element in the system does not prevent tripping. The system includes features to avoid spurious tripping as much as possible. Figure 6.1 illustrates the main functions of the hydraulic tripping system.

The interfaces with the electrical tripping system and the relays of the emergency stop valves (ESVs) and governing valves (GVs) are also shown. The redundancy of the electrical tripping system is not shown.

The unit has two sets of emergency trip valves and trip plungers. Each set is associated with a set of overspeed trip bolts mounted in the turbine shaft. High-pressure fluid is supplied to the emergency trip valves. If either valve is caused to trip (i.e., move to the left), the protection fluid will be connected to drain via pipe A or pipe B. This results in the closure of all turbine steam valves. The pressure of the control fluid is maintained to avoid excess fluid consumption from the fire-resistant fluid (FRF) supply unit.

Spring-loaded trip plungers operate the emergency trip valves. During normal operation, a spigot maintains the spring in compression. The spigot is held in place by the Y-shaped trip arm and latch. When the overspeed trip is initiated, the manual trip or the solenoid trip releases the spring-loaded latch. Thus, the protection fluid at high pressure in the chamber located at the left-hand end of the emergency trip valve is released to drain. It causes the valves to move to the tripped position. It should be noted that when one overspeed trip occurs, the fluid on the corresponding side of the interlock unit will go to drain. The piston in the interlock unit will move, forcing the second emergency trip valve to trip. Additional hydraulic units (not shown) are used to reset the trip plungers and latches before

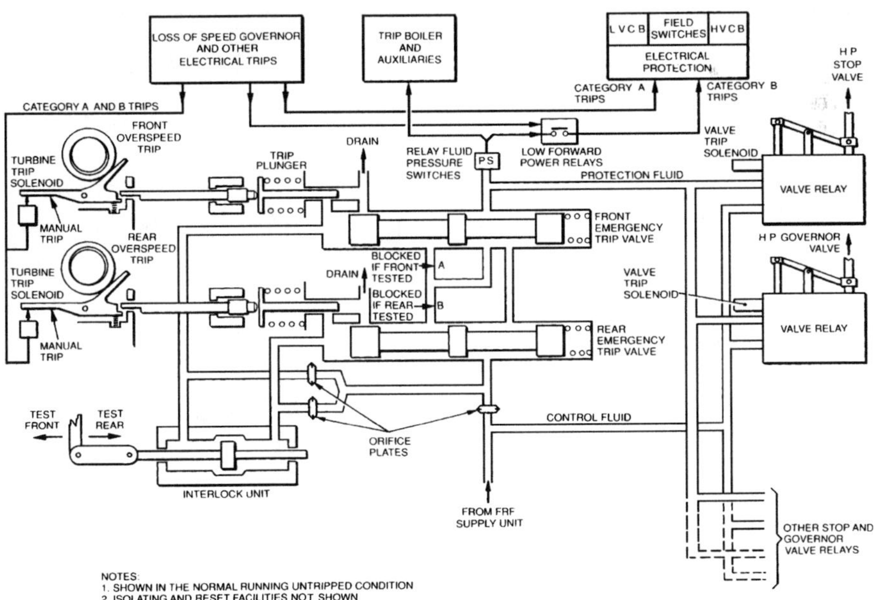

FIGURE 6.1 Hydraulic trip unit—simplified block diagram. *Notes:* (1) Shown in the normal-running, untripped condition. (2) Isolating and reset facilities not shown.

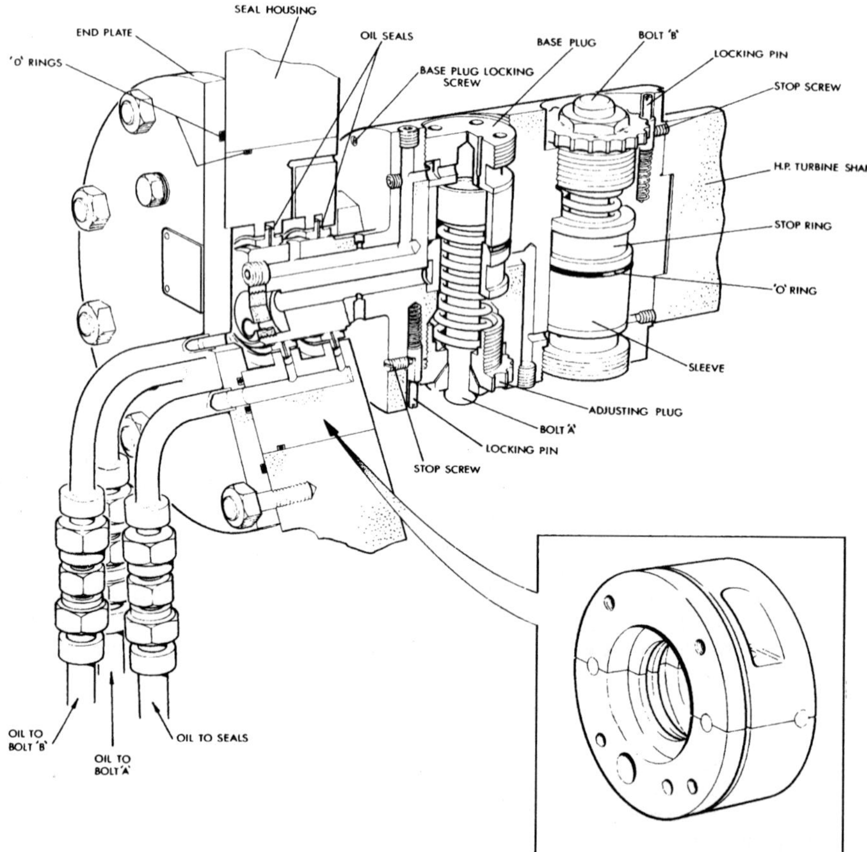

FIGURE 6.2 Overspeed governor.

subsequent trip run-up. Regular on-load testing is done to identify and rectify any faults in the tripping system.

OVERSPEED TRIP

The overspeed trip is initiated when the governing system fails to limit the speed rise of the turbine shaft. It is the final line of defense to prevent a catastrophic failure of the turbine. Turbine overspeed can occur following a load rejection (when the unit becomes disconnected from the grid). It can also occur when the unit is operating in the islanding (unsynchronized) mode. If the governing system fails, higher steam flow can enter the turbine, leading to overspeed.

If the overspeed becomes excessive (approaching 100 percent), the centrifugal forces acting on the rotating parts become extremely high. The blades will start to rupture and penetrate through the casing. The manufacturer normally performs an overspeed test at

120 percent of the speed. This speed is significantly lower than the design limit at which blade rupture could occur (180 to 200 percent overspeed). The overspeed trip is normally set in the range from 110 to 112.5 percent speed.

A pair of spring-loaded trip bolts are used to detect the overspeed. They are mounted in an extension of the shaft at the HP turbine end (Fig. 6.2). Each trip channel is associated with one trip bolt assembly. Each assembly can be tested on-load. The center of gravity of the bolt is located at a short distance from the axis of rotation. At normal speeds, the bolt is held in place by a spring. When the overspeed trip set point is reached, the centrifugal force acting on the bolt overcomes the spring force. The bolt extends beyond the shaft. It trips the static trip lever and releases a latch that trips the turbine. The tripping speed is adjusted when the turbine is stationary.

The overspeed trip test can be performed without actually overspeeding the turbine or taking the set off-load. The "front" or "rear" system is selected for testing. This action automatically isolates the associated emergency trip valve. A supply of lubricating oil under pressure is injected into the rotating turbine shaft. It flows through porting to the overspeed bolt being tested. The bolt moves out and trips its emergency trip valves via the lever and trip plunger. The test pressure is then released. The aforementioned items are reset, and the second bolt is tested.

REFERENCE

1. British Electricity International, *Modern Power Station Practice,* 3d ed., Pergamon Press, Oxford, United Kingdom, 1991.

CHAPTER 7
TURBINE INSTRUMENTATION

INSTRUMENTATION CATEGORIES

The six categories of turbine instrumentation are[1]

1. Supervisory instrumentation
2. Efficiency instrumentation
3. Auxiliary system instrumentation
4. Condition-monitoring instrumentation
5. Instrumentation associated with protection and control equipment
6. Instrumentation to provide postincident records

The most important of these six categories are supervisory and efficiency instrumentation. This is due to the significant role they play in monitoring plant safety and power production.

Supervisory Instrumentation

The supervisory instruments are required continuously to determine the condition of the main rotating and stationary components. The main functions of supervisory instruments include the following:

1. To ensure safe operation within acceptable limits.
2. To provide advanced warning of deterioration in the performance of the turbine generator. Maintenance or temporary restriction in the operating mode may be required. The measured parameters include the following:
   - *a. Rotor axial position.* These measurements provide the relative axial movement of the rotor. They are used to ensure that clearance margins are maintained under all operating conditions. These measurements are normally taken on each cylinder of the machine.
   - *b. Cylinder expansions.* These measurements provide the relative radial movement between the rotors and the stators. They are used to ensure that radial clearance margins are maintained under all operating conditions. These measurements are normally taken on each cylinder of the machine.
   - *c. Bearing pedestal vibrations.* These measurements are taken at each bearing. They continuously monitor the dynamic behavior of the machine.
   - *d. Shaft eccentricity.* The radial excursion of the rotor (peak-to-peak) relative to the stationary parts is measured on each rotor. This is done to indicate abnormal or unsafe conditions.

e. Shaft speed. The shaft speed is measured independently of the turbine governor. This measurement is used for operator reference. It is mainly used during run-up.

f. Steam valve positions. The position of each steam valve is measured. These measurements are used as a general reference for the operator. They are used to determine if the load can be increased or for diagnostic purposes.

g. Metal temperature measurements. The temperature of the turbines is measured during normal operation and transient states. The instruments are located in the high-pressure (HP) and interceptor steam valve chests, and in the cylinders of the HP and intermediate-pressure (IP) turbines.

h. Thrust bearing wear. These measurements are taken to ensure that the wear of the thrust pads is within acceptable limits. If the wear is higher than the acceptable limit, the turbine generator rotor will move with respect to the stator. This could have disastrous consequences on the machine.

All of the measured parameters are displayed continuously for the operator.

Efficiency Instrumentation

These instruments are used to determine or infer the thermal efficiency of the plant. The information is stored to determine the long-term trends. The temperatures and pressures of steam and water are measured at different locations throughout the plant. These measurements are taken to ensure that plant equipment is operating efficiently. For example, the conditions of steam and water at the inlet and outlet to the feedwater heaters are measured. Unsatisfactory operation will not likely result in shutdown of the plant; however, it will result in decreased efficiency.

REFERENCE

1. British Electricity International, *Modern Power Station Practice*, 3d ed., Pergamon Press, Oxford, United Kingdom, 1991.

CHAPTER 8
LUBRICATION SYSTEMS

LUBRICATION REQUIREMENTS AND TYPICAL ARRANGEMENTS

The turbine bearings must be lubricated to prevent damage that is caused by wear or increased temperatures.[1] It is necessary to lift the turbine generator shaft before starting to turn the shaft. The jacking oil system is used to provide this function.

The purposes of bearing lubrication are as follows:

1. To provide a hydrodynamic oil wedge between the bearing and the shaft.
2. To provide an oil flow to maintain the white metal of the bearing below 110°C. The sources of heat inside the bearing include:
   a. Thermal conduction
   b. Friction between the oil film, the journal (portion of the shaft inside the bearing), and the white metal of the bearing
   c. Turbulence within the oil itself

The oil temperature leaving the bearing is normally limited to 71°C. Older units used the same oil for lubrication and turbine control and protection (Fig. 8.1). Modern units use fire-resistant fluid (FRF) with a pressure of 7 to 17.5 Megapascals (MPa) for the turbine control system. Figure 8.2 illustrates the lubrication oil system of a modern unit. A directly driven centrifugal pump delivers oil at 1.1 MPa. The oil from this pump goes through an oil turbine. The oil pressure is reduced across the turbine to 0.3 MPa. The oil turbine drives a booster pump that supplies oil from the main tank to the suction of the centrifugal oil pump. The system is protected against overpressurization by a relief valve mounted on the oil tank. The relief valve is connected to the bearing oil supply line. During normal operation, the directly driven main oil pump provides a highly reliable source of lubrication oil. The alternating-current (AC) auxiliary oil pump provides lubrication during start-up and shutdown. The direct-current (DC) auxiliary pump provides lubrication during emergency shutdown (upon loss of AC supplies) or when the AC pump fails to start. Lubrication oil is also supplied to the generator hydrogen seals from this system. However, most modern units have a separate seal oil system to prevent contaminating the main oil with hydrogen. On these units, the supply from the main lubricating oil is used as a backup to the seal oil system. On modern units, the lubricating oil system supplies the following:

- Each journal bearing of the turbine, generator, and exciter.
- The main thrust surge bearing.
- The generator hydrogen seal (this is either a sole supply or a backup system).
- The bearings on the turbine-driven boiler feed pump (in plants having this feature).
- The lubricating oil system also has filters, strainer, coolers, and tank vents.

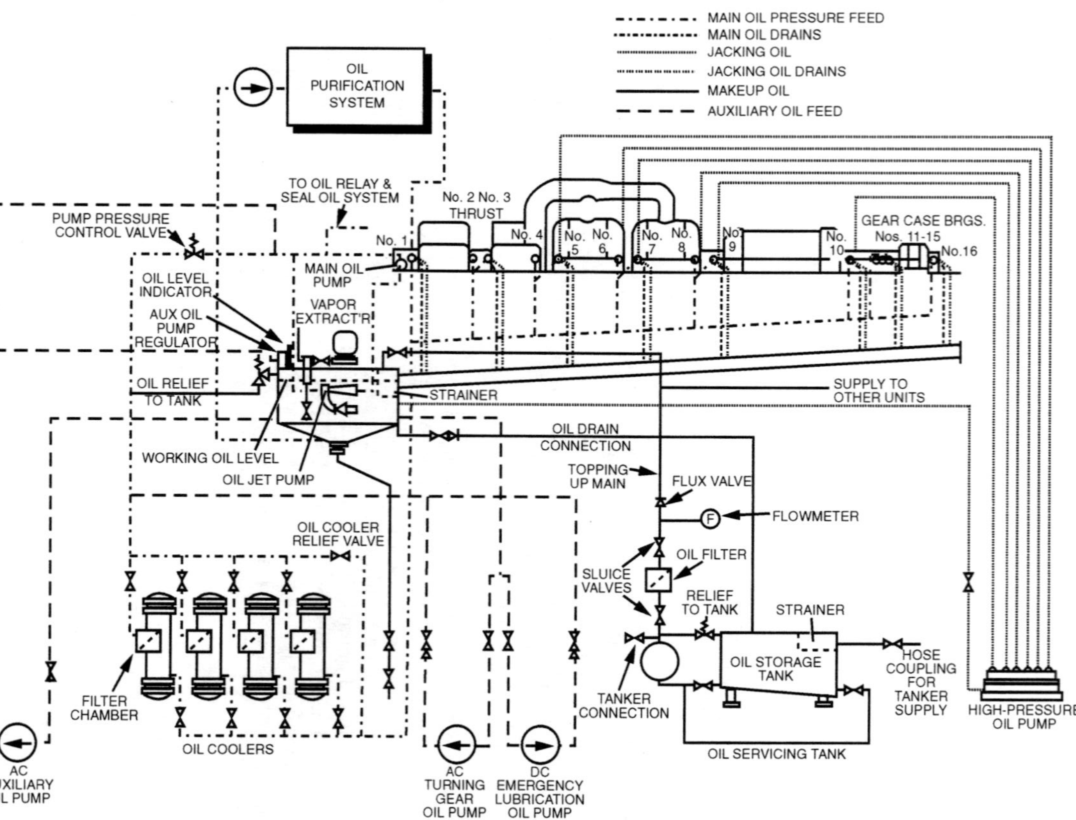

FIGURE 8.1 Lubricating and relay oil system for an older turbine generator plant.

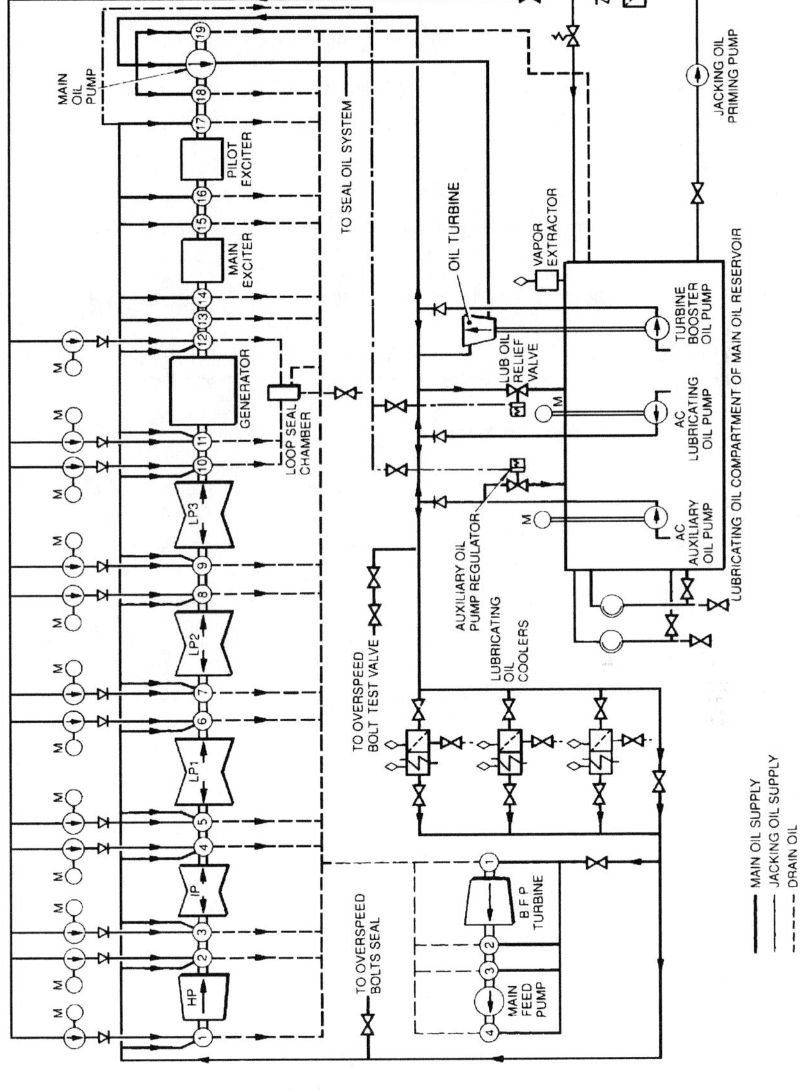

FIGURE 8.2 Lubricating oil system for a modern turbine generator plant.

The lubricating oil tank of the unit is connected to the following:

- Clean-oil tank
- Dirty-oil tank
- Oil purification system

The pumps and pipework permit the transfer of oil as follows:

- From the clean-oil tank to the unit oil tank through the oil purification unit
- From the used-oil tank to the unit oil tank through the oil purification unit
- To drain all of the oil in the system into the unit oil tank
- To move all of the oil from the unit oil tank to the station used-oil tank
- To move all of the oil from the road oil tanker into the station clean-oil tank
- To move the oil from the station used-oil tank to a road oil tanker
- To process the oil in the unit tank or the oil in the station clean-oil tank through the purifier
- To process the oil in the unit tank or the station clean-oil tank through a portable oil purifier unit

Figure 8.3 illustrates a schematic arrangement of the equipment used.

OIL PUMPS

Main Lubricating Oil Pump

The main lubricating oil pump is normally directly driven from the main shaft. This ensures a highly reliable oil supply. Figure 8.4 illustrates a typical centrifugal pump used as a main lubricating oil pump in modern units. The oil flow is around 100 L/s (for a 660-MW unit). The suction pressure is around 0.3 to 0.4 MPa.

Turbine-Driven Oil Booster Pump

The oil leaving the main oil pump goes through an oil turbine to increase the reliability of the lubricating oil supply. The oil turbine is mounted on top of the oil tank. It drives a submerged centrifugal pump, which delivers the oil to the suction of the main oil pump.

AC and DC Motor-Driven Auxiliary Oil Pumps

The AC auxiliary oil pump supplies oil to the bearings during start-up and normal shutdown. The DC pump supplies oil to the bearings during an emergency shutdown (when AC power is lost). These are centrifugal pumps with a submerged suction. They are also suspended from the top of the tank. Their arrangement is similar to the one in Fig. 8.5, but the oil turbine is replaced with an AC or DC motor. The AC auxiliary pump delivers the oil at around 0.3 MPa. It also primes the main oil pump. The AC and DC pumps have a capacity of around 7 to 12 L/s.

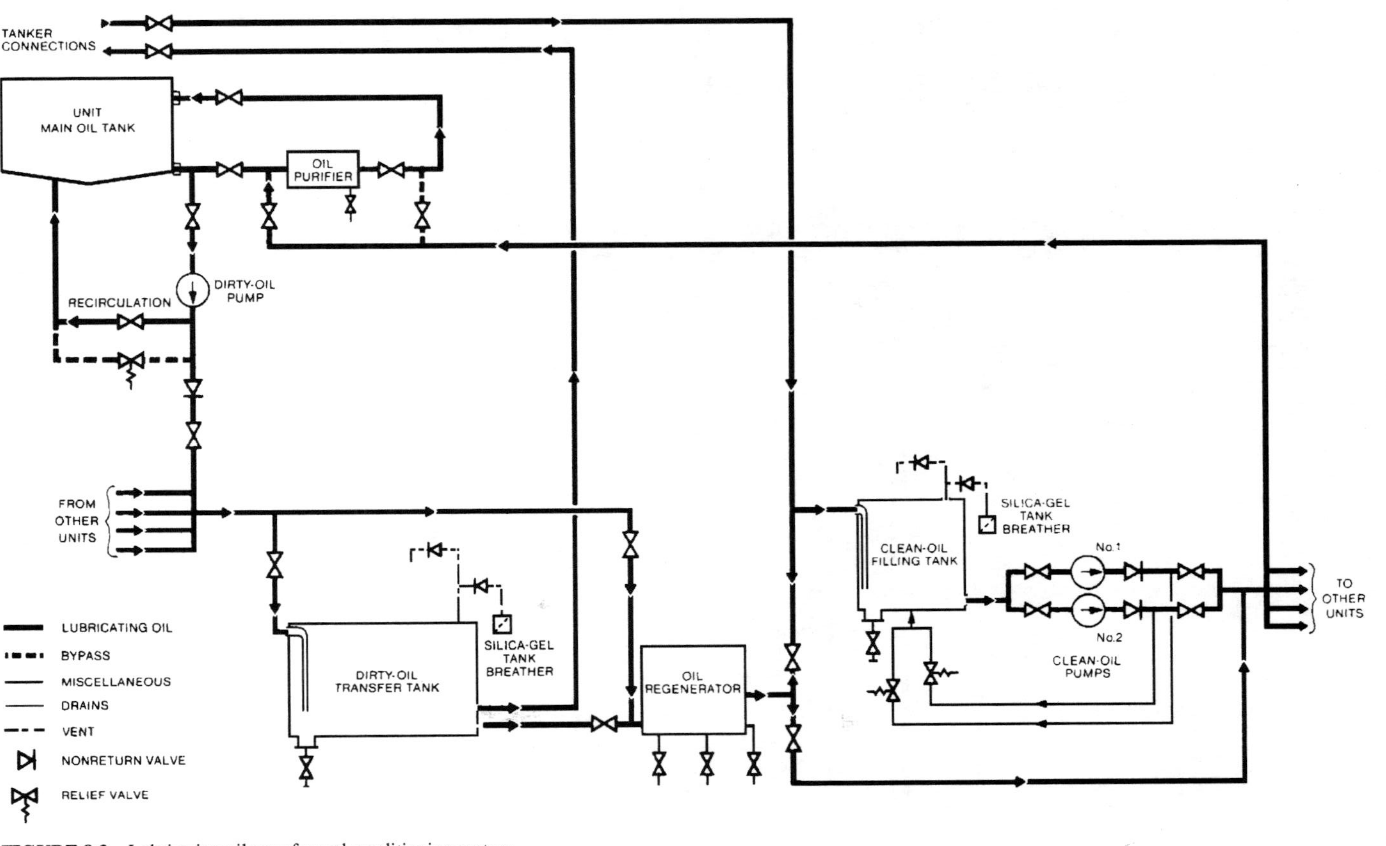

FIGURE 8.3 Lubricating oil transfer and conditioning system.

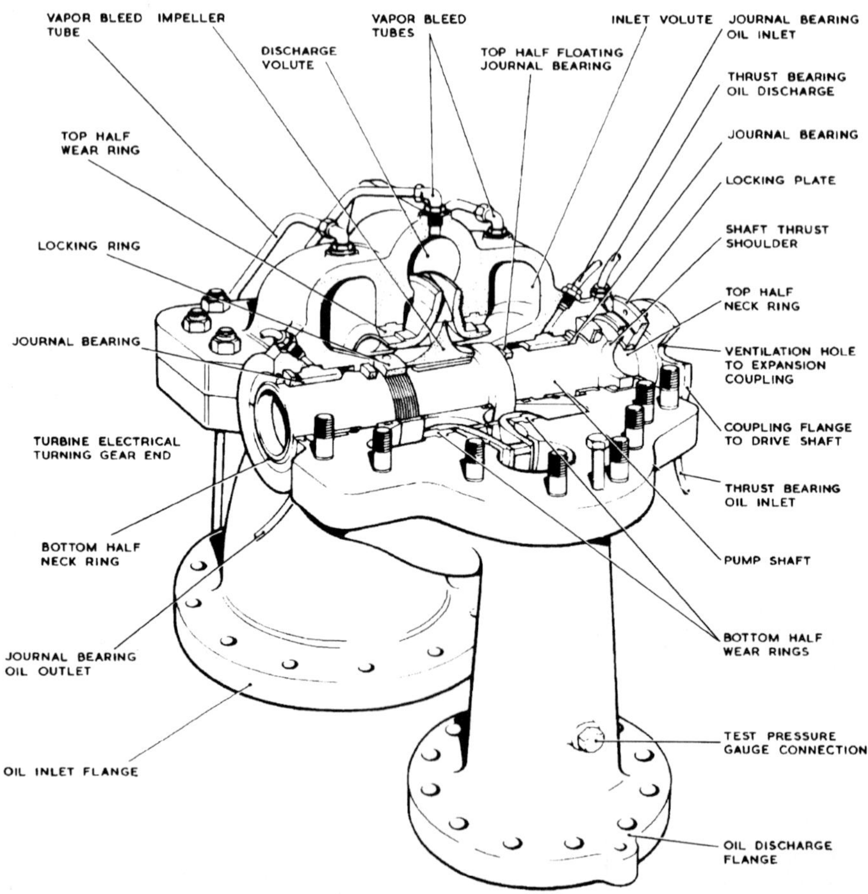

FIGURE 8.4 Main lubricating oil pump.

Jacking Oil Pumps and Priming Pumps

The jacking oil pumps deliver oil at around 30 MPa to the bearings. These are motor-driven positive-displacement pumps. They are either multiplunger pumps (Fig. 8.6) or two-shaft gear pumps (Fig. 8.7).

OIL TANKS

The main oil tank (Fig. 8.8) has a capacity of 75 m^3 in modern units. The normal working volume is around 50 m^3. Baffle plates separate the returning oil to the tank and the pump suction in order to assist in deaeration and settlement. It also prevents the formation of stagnant oil pockets. The tank is designed to provide around 7 min for oil transit time between return and suction. The trend in modern units is to provide a self-contained section of the tank for the hydrogen seal system. This is done to eliminate the possibility of hydrogen gas entering the main lubricating oil system. If the lubricating oil system is used to provide the

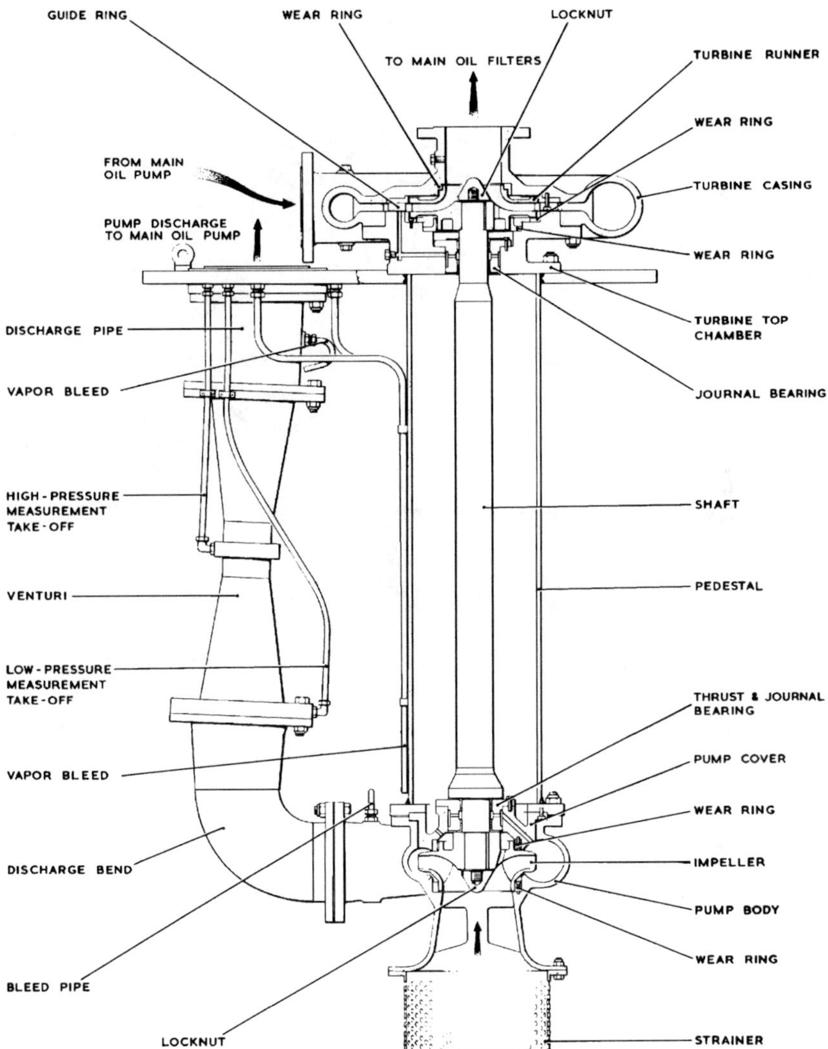

FIGURE 8.5 Turbine-driven oil booster pump.

seal oil for the generator, a detraining chamber is installed to remove all the hydrogen before mixing seal oil with the lubricating oil. All the oil returning to the tank goes through coarse-mesh strainers. This is done to assist in deaeration and to catch any large impurities. Many units experienced corrosion at the air/oil interface in the tank. This was caused by water and water vapor in the oil. The main oil tank is now being made from stainless steel or mild steel with a special phenolic paint protection against corrosion. The bearing oil pressure relief valves and two vapor extraction pumps are mounted on top of the tank beside the suspended oil pumps. One vapor extraction pump is used to remove water and oil vapor from the tank. The second is used to extract hydrogen and oil vapor from the detraining tank.

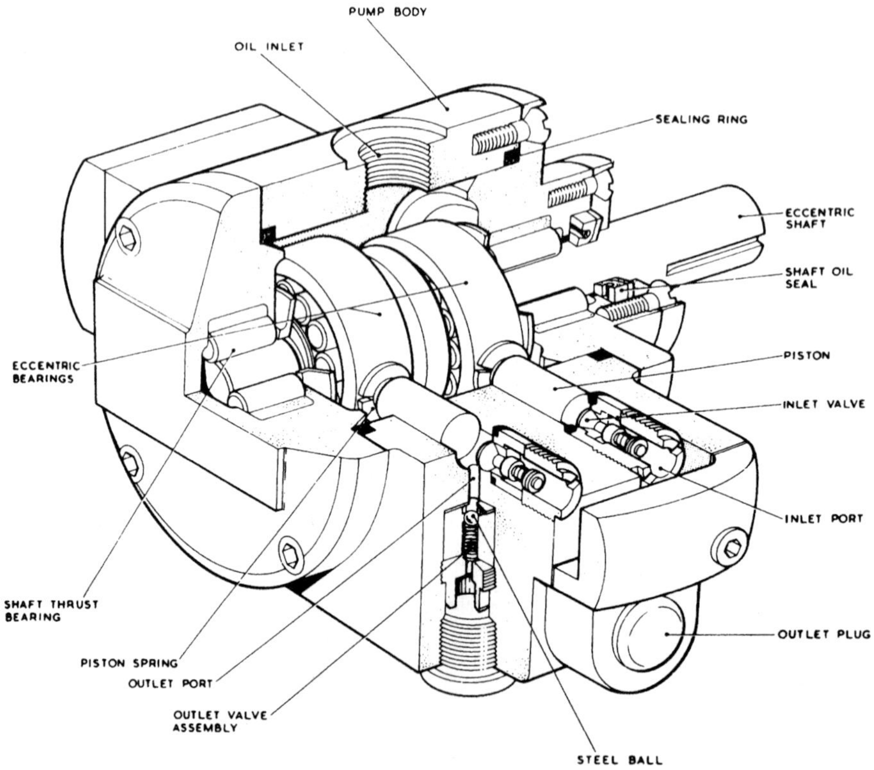

PUMP BODY
OIL INLET
SEALING RING
ECCENTRIC SHAFT
SHAFT OIL SEAL
PISTON
INLET VALVE
INLET PORT
OUTLET PLUG
ECCENTRIC BEARINGS
SHAFT THRUST BEARING
PISTON SPRING
OUTLET PORT
OUTLET VALVE ASSEMBLY
STEEL BALL

FIGURE 8.6 Multiplunger jacking oil pump.

END COVER
BODY
STRAIGHT CONNECTOR
O-RING
DRIVEN GEAR
WOODRUFF KEY
COMPOUND BUSH
BACKING WASHER
MOUNTING FLANGE
ELBOW CONNECTOR
DRIVE SHAFT AND GEAR
LOBE SEAL
BODY SEAL O-RING
OIL SEAL

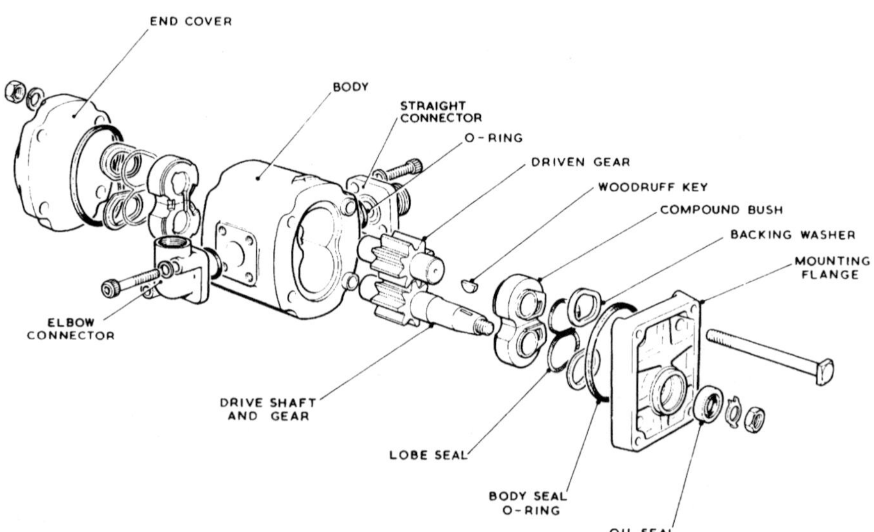

FIGURE 8.7 Gear-type jacking oil/priming pump.

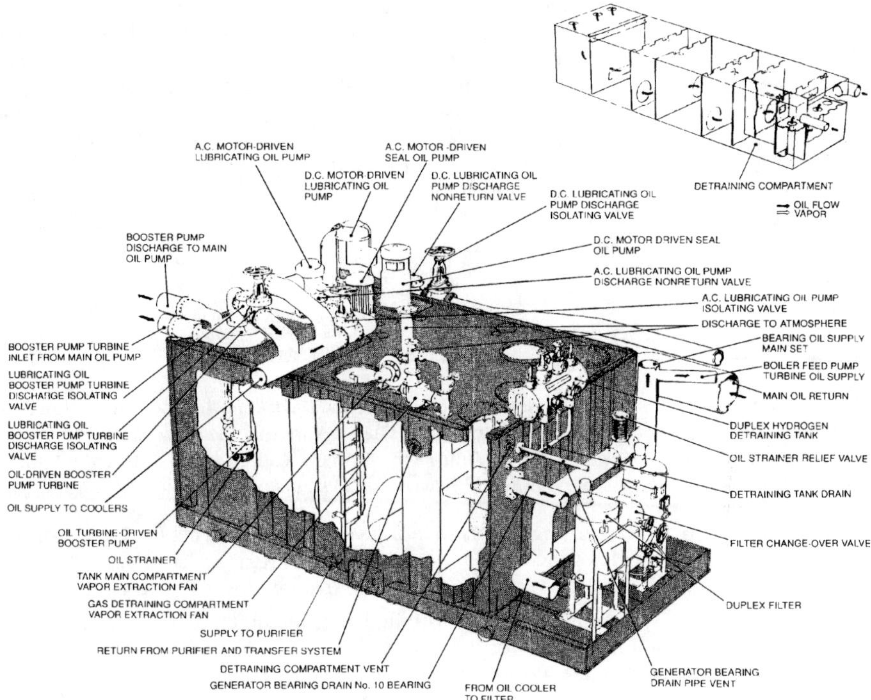

FIGURE 8.8 Main oil tank—general arrangement.

PIPING

Special design precautions against oil leakage and fire hazards are taken for piping used in jacking oil and lubricating oil systems. The oil piping is sized to have a velocity between 1 and 5 m/s. An enclosure or a duct is installed around the oil piping at the pump discharge. The number of pipe joints is minimized by maximizing the length of pipe runs. All pipe joints are welded class 1 type. At the exit from the ducted area, a protective pipe is installed around the pressure oil pipe. This is done to contain and detect any oil leakage. The piping between the pump and the filters is made of mild steel. Some units use stainless-steel piping after the filters to minimize corrosion. If the air is not vented through the bearings, an automatic air venting of the piping from its highest points to the oil tank is installed. Air vents to the oil tank are installed on the oil filters. They vent any air that accumulates during operation or maintenance to the oil tank.

OIL COOLERS

The function of the coolers (heat exchangers) is to lower the temperature of the oil leaving the bearings below the acceptable limit. Redundant coolers are provided to allow maintenance to be performed while the unit is operating. The normal arrangements are three 50 percent or two 100 percent coolers. The oil coolers are installed vertically. The water flows through the tube in a two-pass arrangement. The oil flows on the shell side of the coolers through a series of baffles. In modern units, the shells of the coolers are made of mild steel and the tubes of titanium. The tube bundle has a floating tube plate to accommodate thermal expansion. The coolers also have end plates. They permit cleaning of the coolers without dismantling the water pipes. The heat dissipated by each cooler is around 2 MW. The oil filters are integral with the cooler shell on some units (Fig. 8.9). An automatic bypass of the oil coolers is normally installed. It allows the oil to bypass the cooler upon an excessive pressure drop across the cooler. The automatic control system is based on the oil outlet temperature.

OIL STRAINER AND FILTERS

The oil strainers are basket-type assemblies made of coarse wire mesh. They are designed to catch large impurities entering the main oil tank. They ensure that the flow reaching the suction of the pump will not damage the pump. The strainers can be lifted out of the tank to remove and inspect the collected debris. The two main systems of lubricating oil filtration are

1. *Cartridge filters.* The cartridge filters fit into the casing of the oil cooler. Each cartridge is designed to filter 13 L/s of hot oil. The nominal particle size is 10 μm. Each cooler uses up to 4 disposable cartridges. Only two coolers are required for 100 percent duty.
2. *Duplex filters.* The duplex filters are installed after the oil coolers. Multiple disposable filters are used sometimes in this application. They have facilities for on-load replacement. Duplex plate filters are also used in this application. They can be

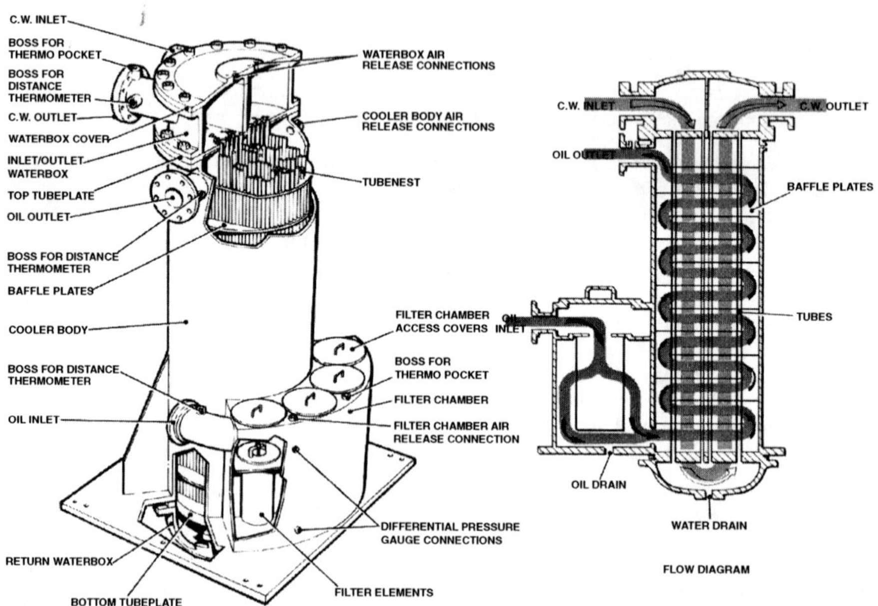

FIGURE 8.9 Oil cooler with integral filter.

cleaned on-load. There are two compartments in the plate-type filter. Each compartment has five filter assemblies. Each assembly is made of a series of plates and spacers. The degree of filtration is 75 μm. Each compartment receives half the oil flow. The filter has facilities to allow all the flow to go through one compartment. This configuration is used during on-load replacement, inspection, or maintenance of one compartment. During normal operation, the filter capacity is around 106 L/s under a pressure drop of 0.3 bar.

The filter is normally cleaned automatically when the pressure differential reaches 0.45 bar across the filter. Each plate filter assembly is rotated against a scraper bar. The debris from each filter falls into a sump at the bottom of the filter housing. The sump is cleaned out regularly. Figure 8.10 illustrates a typical plate-type filter. If a plate-type filter is used, additional filtration is required for the oil supply to:

- The thrust bearings
- The turning gear, jacking oil pump, gearing, and clutch
- The main oil pump, thrust bearing, and cooling sprays

The oil being supplied for these duties is taken from the discharge of the filter and passed through an additional duplex plate-type filter similar to the one shown in Fig. 8.10. There are four plate filter assemblies in each compartment of this additional filter. It can only be cleaned manually. The normal flow through the filter is 16 L/s under a pressure drop of 0.2 bar with both compartments in service.

OIL PURIFIERS AND COALESCERS

The steam leaking from the turbine glands represents the main source of contamination for the lubricating oil. The steam condenses when it comes in contact with the bearing housing. The condensate becomes dispersed through the oil. The used oil normally contains wear particles, oxides, soluble acids, and sludge. These impurities must be removed from the oil to extend its life and maintain adequate lubrication. During normal operation, there are two main systems used on bypass duty continuously. There is also an oil regeneration system. The on-line systems used include *centrifugal separation systems* and *static oil purifiers/coalescers.*

Centrifugal Separation Systems

The centrifugal separation systems have been used for many years. They require considerable maintenance and careful adjustment for best effectiveness. Figure 8.11 illustrates a typical arrangement of this system. It operates based on the principle that if a mixture is centrifuged, the fluids settle out radially with the fluid having the highest specific gravity outermost. Dirty oil from the main oil tank is delivered to the purifier. It passes through a regenerative heater/cooler. It is heated to 75°C. This is the best temperature for centrifugal separation. The oil enters the separator bowl. Centrifugal force separates the mixture into its different densities. The clean oil is collected by inverted cones (Fig. 8.12). It is delivered to the clean-oil outlet. The water and acids are discharged from the separator. The solids accumulate at the bottom of the bowl and are discharged regularly. The clean hot oil enters the regenerative heater or cooler. It is then returned to the main oil tank. The oil flow rate through the purifier is around 10 percent of the total oil inventory per hour.

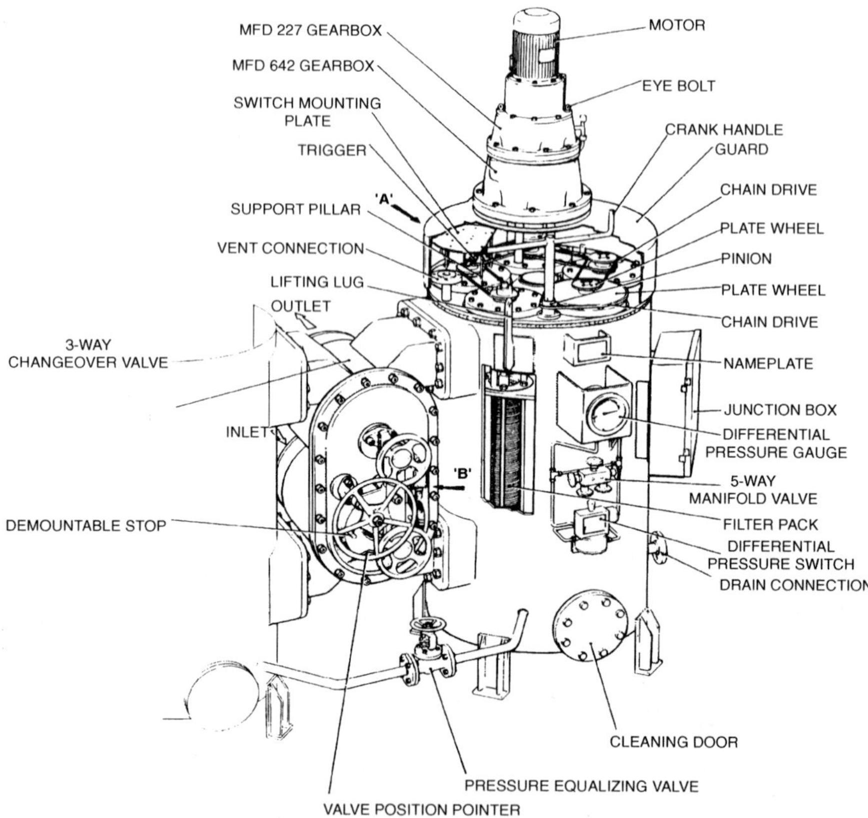

FIGURE 8.10 Plate-type oil filter.

Static Oil Purifiers/Coalescers

Figure 8.13 illustrates an oil purifier. This is a new system. The oil flow through the purifier is about 17 percent of the total oil inventory per hour. The oil flow enters initially through a series of fine-mesh sloping screens. The water coalesces on the screens. It falls down to the bottom of each screen, then goes to drain. The oil enters through a series of polyolefinic bags. The particulate matter is filtered out. Finally, the oil goes through a 5-μm pressure filter. It is then delivered back to the main oil tank. Since the oil is not heated when it enters the purifier, there is a higher risk of bacterial and fungal growth. The used oil is regenerated within the oil transfer system in the station. The oil is taken for regeneration from the unit oil tank or the station dirty-oil tank. It flows at about 1.1 m^3/h through a regeneration plant that is similar to the one shown in Fig. 8.14.

The oil is heated in the regeneration plant to 54.4°C. It is then sprayed into a vacuum chamber maintained at an absolute pressure of 87 mbar (913 mbar below atmospheric pressure). At this pressure, the water evaporates, and is then removed by a vacuum pump and condensed. The dry oil leaving the vacuum chamber goes through a 10-μm filter. The filter is made of perforated steel plates with a pack of nylon-backed filter papers clamped between them. The oil leaving the filter enters the clean-oil tank.

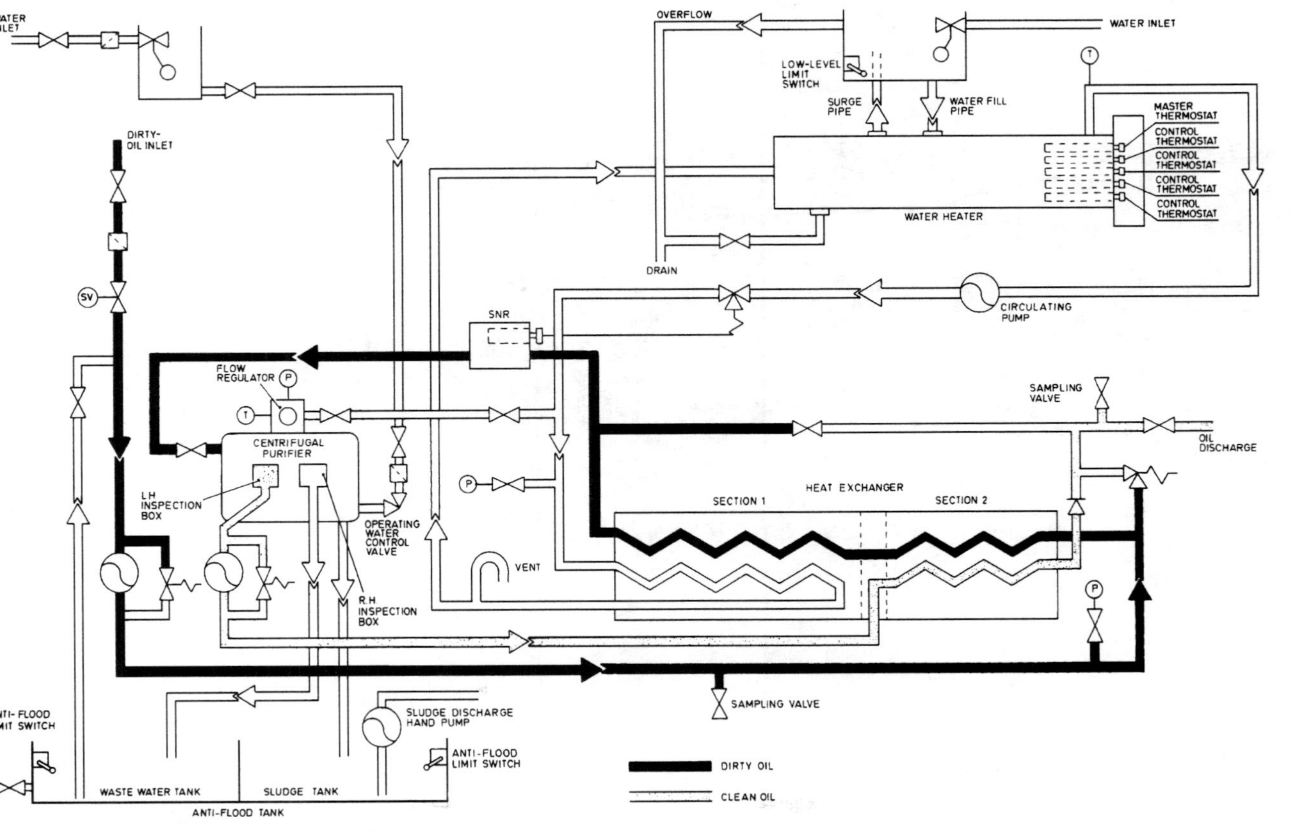

FIGURE 8.11 Oil purifying system.

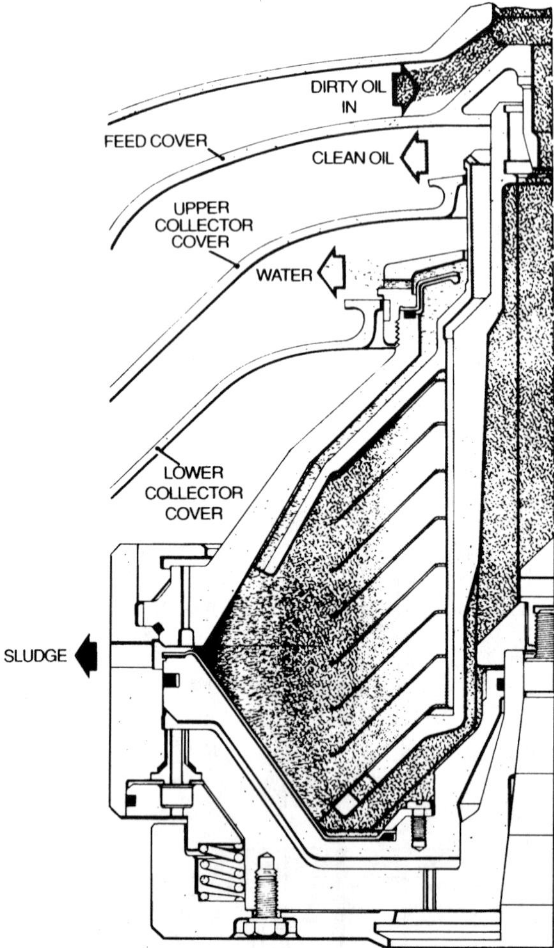

FIGURE 8.12 Oil purifier bowl operation.

OILS AND GREASES

Oils

The oils used for steam turbines must provide the following functions:

- Heat removal
- Removal of impurities from the bearings
- Minimization of corrosion and oxidation

The turbine lubricating oil requirements are outlined in Table 8.1. The oil contains additives for the prevention of oxidation, corrosion, and foaming. A summary of their functions is as follows:

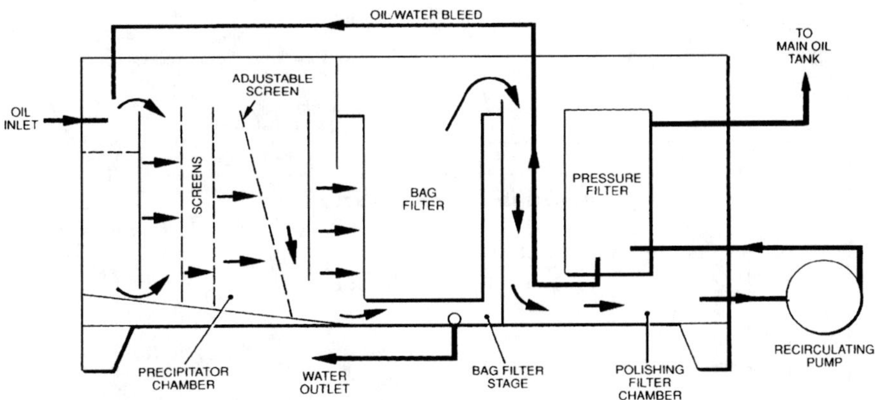

FIGURE 8.13 Static oil purifier.

1. *Oxidation inhibitor.* Stabilizes the rate of oxidation. It also passivates the metals that act catalytically to increase the rate of oxidation. These inhibitors maintain low acidity (neutralization number) in the oil for many years.
2. *Rust inhibitor.* Protects the carbon-steel surfaces from rusting when they come in contact with water entrained with the oil.
3. *Detergent additives.* Reduce the rate of high-temperature oxidation, formation of sludge at low temperature, and deposition of contaminants.
4. *Viscosity index improvers.* Reduce the decrease in viscosity with increase in temperature.
5. *Pour-point depressants.* Reduce the solidification temperature of the oil.
6. *Antifoaming agents.* Suppress foaming of aerated oil. They also assist in the release of air from the oil.

New oils normally have an acidity (total) of 0.02 to 0.1 mg of KOH/g. The acidity of new oils will be slightly higher if the oil contains additives. During operation, the total acidity of the oil increases. This is caused by the fact that oil oxidizes to organic acids. Thus, the level of acidity in the oil is a good indicator about the condition of the oil. Its need for purification and conditioning will be based on the level of acidity. Water ingress into the turbine oil is a common problem. Water presence could lead to bacterial and fungal contamination in the oil systems. This contamination appears as a yellow or black material similar to grease. This growth occurs in sediment in the oil system. It is very difficult to remove it from the system.

The required precautions that need to be taken include:

- Minimizing the water content in the oil by using an oil purification system. The concentration of water in the oil should be maintained at less than 0.05 percent.
- Removing the sludge from the sumps of the oil system regularly.

If bacterial or fungal growth occurs, a correct amount of biocide should be added to kill it.

Greases

The three types of greases used in turbine systems are

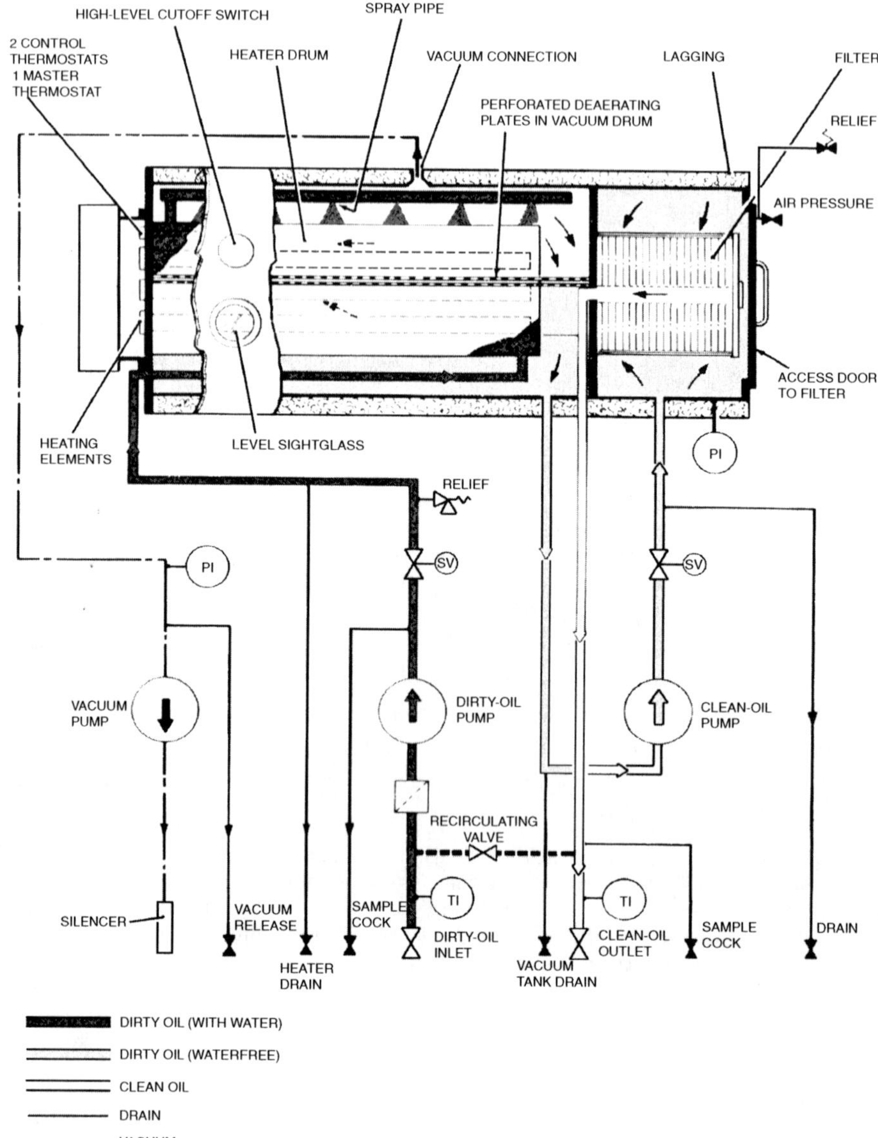

FIGURE 8.14 Oil regeneration plant—flow diagram.

1. *Silicon-based grease.* It contains molybdenum disulphide. Its operating temperature is between −50°C to 300°C.
2. *Mineral oil with Bentone filler.* The upper temperature limit of this grease is 260°C.
3. *Lithium-based grease.* They have a wide range of application, including ball and roller bearings.

TABLE 8.1 Turbine Lubricating Oil Requirements

Type prefix ISO VG grade designation (BS4231)		TO 32	TO 46	TO 68	TO 100
Viscosity, kinematic at 40°C, mm^2/s (cSt)	Min	28.8	41.4	61.2	90
	Max	35.2	50.6	74.8	110
Viscosity index	Min	70	70	70	70
Flashpoint, closed, °C, Pensky-Martens	Min	168	168	168	168
Pour point, °C	Max	−6	−6	−6	−6
Total acidity, mg KOH/g	Max	0.20	0.20	0.20	0.20
Copper corrosion, classification (3 h at 100°C)	Max	2	2	2	2
Rust-preventing characteristics		Rusting absent	Rusting absent	Rusting absent	Rusting absent
Demulsification number, s	Max	300	300	360	360
Foaming tendency					
Foam, mL					
at 24°C	Max	450	450	600	600
at 93.5°C	Max	50	50	100	100
at 24°C after test at 93.5°C	Max	450	450	600	600
Foam stability after 300 s					
Foam, mL					
at 24°C	Max	Nil	Nil	100	100
at 93.5°C	Max	Nil	Nil	25	25
at 24°C after test at 93.5°C	Max	Nil	Nil	100	100
Air release properties, minutes to 0.2% air content at 50°C		5	6	7	10
Oxidation characteristics					
Total oxidation products (TOP) with sludge limited to 40% of the determined TOP					
No catalyst, % (duration of tests 164 hours)	Max	0.1	0.1	0.1	0.1
Solid copper catalyst, % (duration of tests 164 hours)	Max	1.0	1.0	1.0	1.0
Soluble metal catalysts, % (duration of tests 164 hours)	Max	1.0	1.0	1.0	1.0

The first two types of grease are used for lubricating high-temperature sliding surfaces. The main applications are turbine palms and pivots of steam valves.

JACKING OIL SYSTEMS

The oil cannot separate the turbine generator shaft from the babbitt of the bearings when the shaft rotates at low speed. If separation is not achieved, the bearings and the shaft could become damaged. However, the oil is able to maintain separation between the shaft and the babbitt of the bearings when the speed exceeds 100 r/min. A hydrodynamic oil wedge is maintained between the shaft and the babbitt above this speed. The jacking oil system injects high-pressure oil into the bottom of the bearings. It continues the injection of oil until the turbine generator floats on an oil film. The jacking oil system is needed until an oil wedge is established. This normally occurs above 200 r/min. The jacking oil system generates a pressure of 30 MPa to lift the turbine generator rotor. The mineral oil used in the system represents a fire hazard due to the proximity of high-temperature components. Special precautions are needed to reduce the fire hazard. A single pump was used in older stations. Long pipelines were used to connect the pump to each bearing. This arrangement was prone to oil leakage. Modern stations install the high-pressure pump on the bearing pedestals (Fig. 8.15). The discharge line of each pump has a pressure relief valve. It prevents overpressurization of the liner. The bearings of the turning gear are also provided with jacking oil during start-up and shutdown. The pipework of the jacking oil system uses class 1–type welded pipe joints. The high-pressure pipework is mounted near the pedestal. Figure 8.16 illustrates a typical arrangement of a jacking oil pump for a turning gear.

GREASING SYSTEMS

The following components require greasing to ensure smooth movements between various parts:

- Turbine pedestals/base plates
- Gear pivots of steam valves

Some power plants attempted to provide automatic greasing systems. They used multipiston pumps with long pipelines to deliver the grease to the equipment. Unfortunately, these systems malfunction regularly due to hardening of the grease in the pipelines. Modern plants provide manual greasing for their equipment. Figure 8.17 illustrates the greasing points on the main gear pivots of the steam valves.

REFERENCE

1. British Electricity International, *Modern Power Station Practice*, 3d ed., Pergamon Press, Oxford, United Kingdom, 1991.

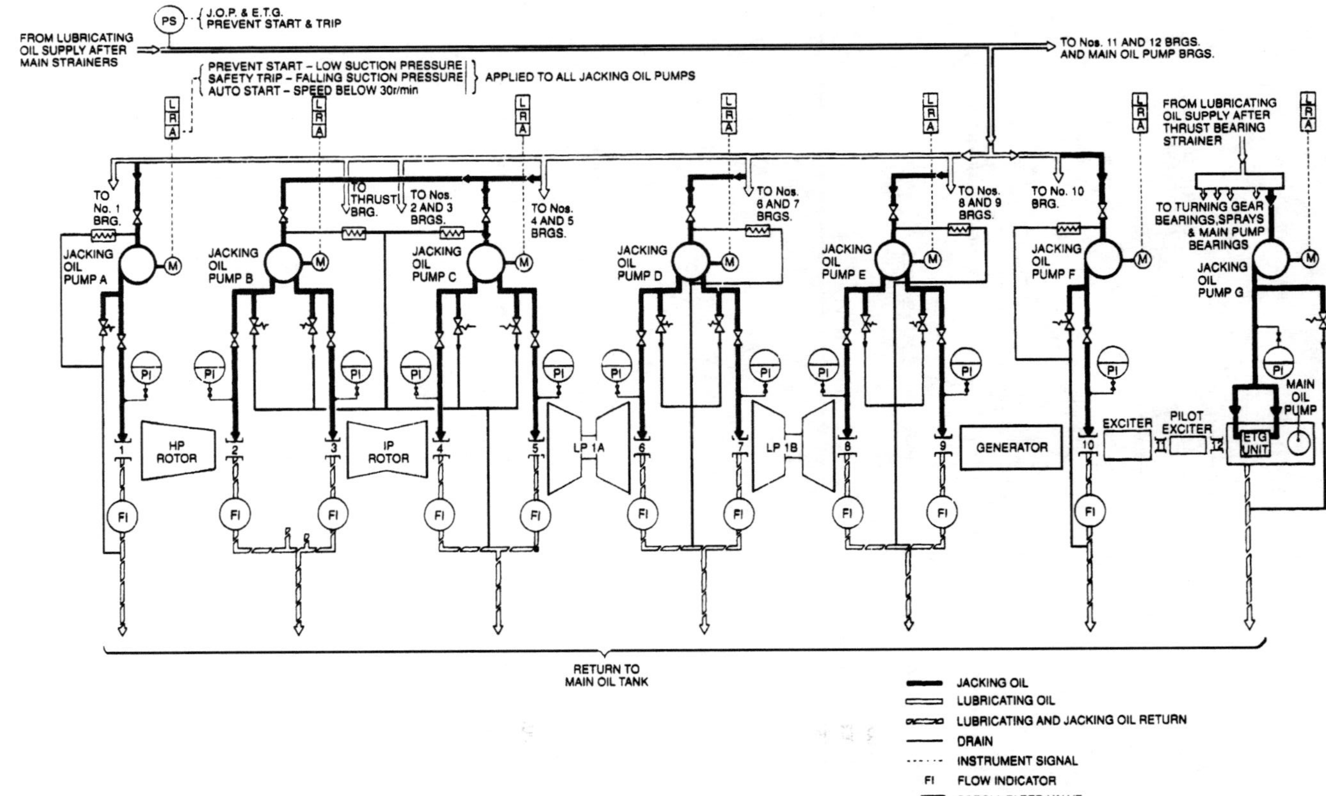

FIGURE 8.15 Jacking oil system.

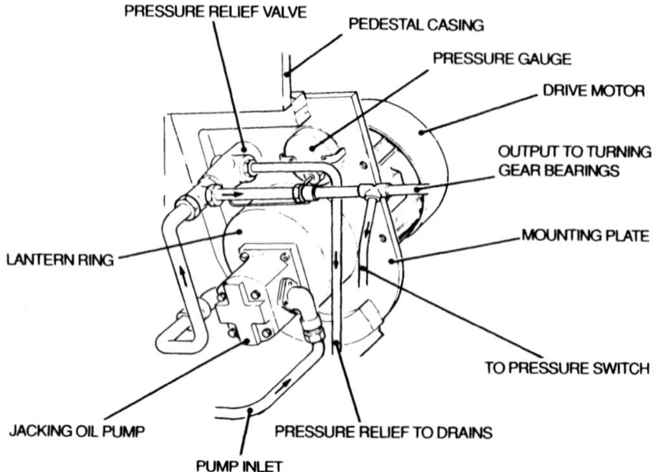

FIGURE 8.16 Shaft-turning gear, jacking oil pump.

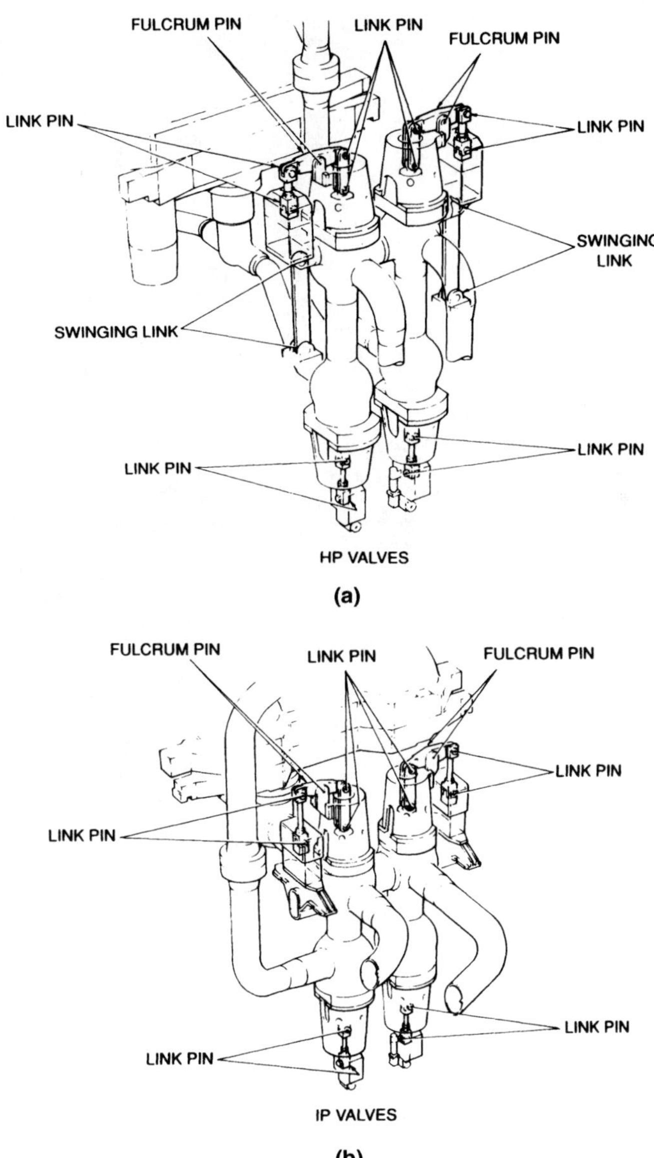

FIGURE 8.17 Main and reheat steam valves location of grease points. (*a*) HP valves, (*b*) IP valves.

CHAPTER 9
GLAND SEALING SYSTEM

FUNCTION AND SYSTEM LAYOUT

The two functions of the turbine glands and seals are:[1]

1. To prevent or reduce steam leakage between the rotating and stationary components of the turbines if the steam pressure is higher than atmospheric.
2. To prevent or reduce air ingress between the rotating and stationary components of the turbines if the steam pressure is less than atmospheric. The last few stages in the low-pressure (LP) turbines are normally under vacuum.

The leakage of steam or air could occur where the shaft is extended through the turbine endwalls to atmosphere. A power loss is associated with steam leakage or air ingress. Thus, the design of glands and seals is optimized to reduce any leakage.

Modern steam turbines use labyrinth glands to restrict steam and air leakage. However, the carbon ring gland is still used on some older turbines.

LABYRINTH SEALS

The labyrinth gland can withstand higher steam conditions than the carbon ring gland. Figure 9.1 (*a*) illustrates a simple form of a labyrinth seal. It consists of a ring having a series of machined fins. The fins form a number of fine annular restrictions. An expansion chamber follows each restriction. When the steam enters a restriction, the velocity increases and the pressure decreases (conversion of pressure energy into kinetic energy—the first law of thermodynamics). When the steam enters the expansion chamber, the kinetic energy is converted by turbulence into heat. The pressure is not recovered. The pressure is progressively reduced when the steam goes through successive restrictions. The finned ring and the shaft are usually stepped to enhance the conversion of energy [Fig. 9.1 (*b*)]. This type of gland is used where there is small axial differential expansions between the rotor and the casing.

Figure 9.1 (*c*) illustrates an alternative arrangement of stepped labyrinth glands. Figure 9.1 (*d*) illustrates a vernier gland. It is independent of differential expansion. The shaft and the seal ring are both finned. This design has the advantage of providing a greater restriction because the fins will always be directly opposite.

Figure 9.2 (*a*) illustrates a form of a labyrinth gland having fins in the axial and radial direction. This design increases the number of restrictions in a given gland length.

The thickness of the gland tips is kept to a minimum in order to minimize the heat generated if an accidental "rub" occurs between the shaft and the gland. Heavy rubbing would generate a significant amount of heat and could result in bending the shaft and making it unbalanced.

The radial clearance of the labyrinth gland is kept to a minimum in order to minimize the leakage across the gland (the leakage is proportional to the leakage area). The

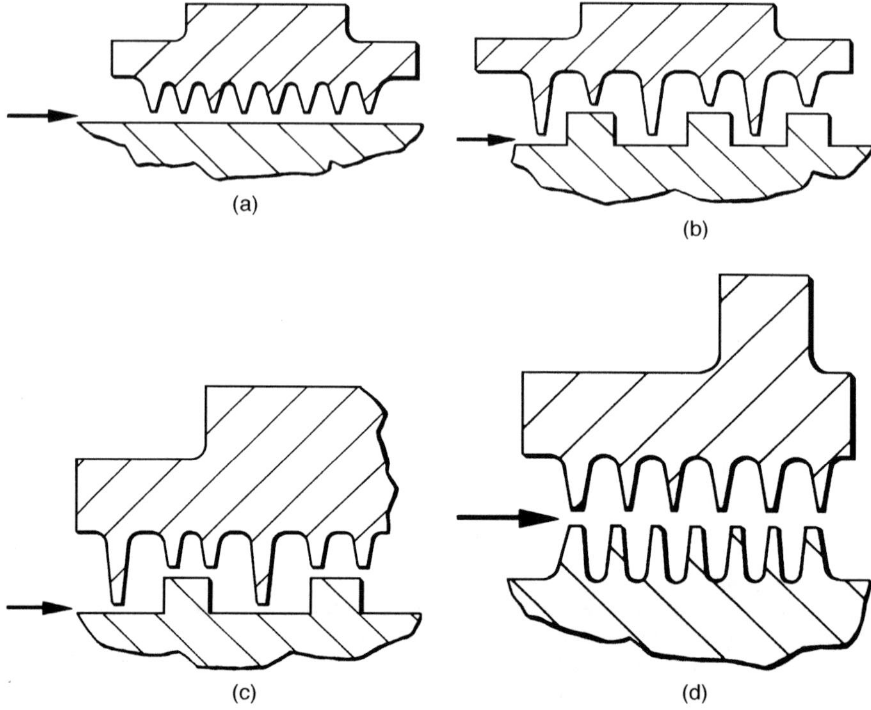

FIGURE 9.1 Labyrinth seals. (*a*) Plain; (*b*) stepped; (*c*) double-stepped; (*d*) vernier.

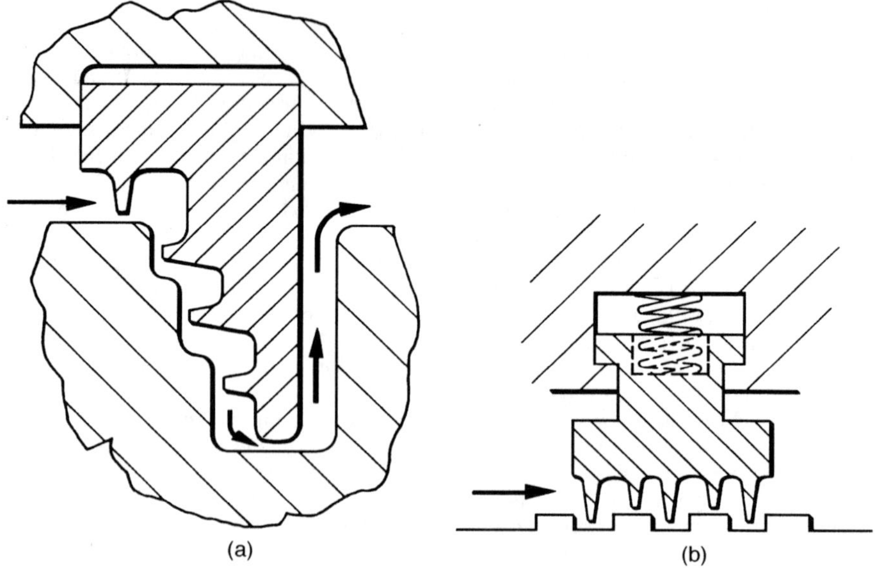

FIGURE 9.2 Labyrinth glands. (*a*) Axial radial labyrinth; (*b*) spring-back labyrinth.

minimum radial clearance used in modern turbines is 0.5 mm. The effects of a "rub" are minimized in close-clearance glands by making the glands spring-loaded [Fig. 9.2 (*b*)]. The gland rings are normally made of four or more segments. The gland sealing system supplies steam to seal the turbine shaft glands under all operating conditions. It also extracts leak-off steam from the glands.

SYSTEM LAYOUT

Figure 9.3 illustrates a typical gland sealing system. The system is normally divided into two parts. One part supplies steam to the glands of the high-pressure (HP) and intermediate-pressure (IP) turbines. The second supplies steam to the glands of the LP turbine. This is done to accommodate the range of temperatures experienced throughout the turbine.

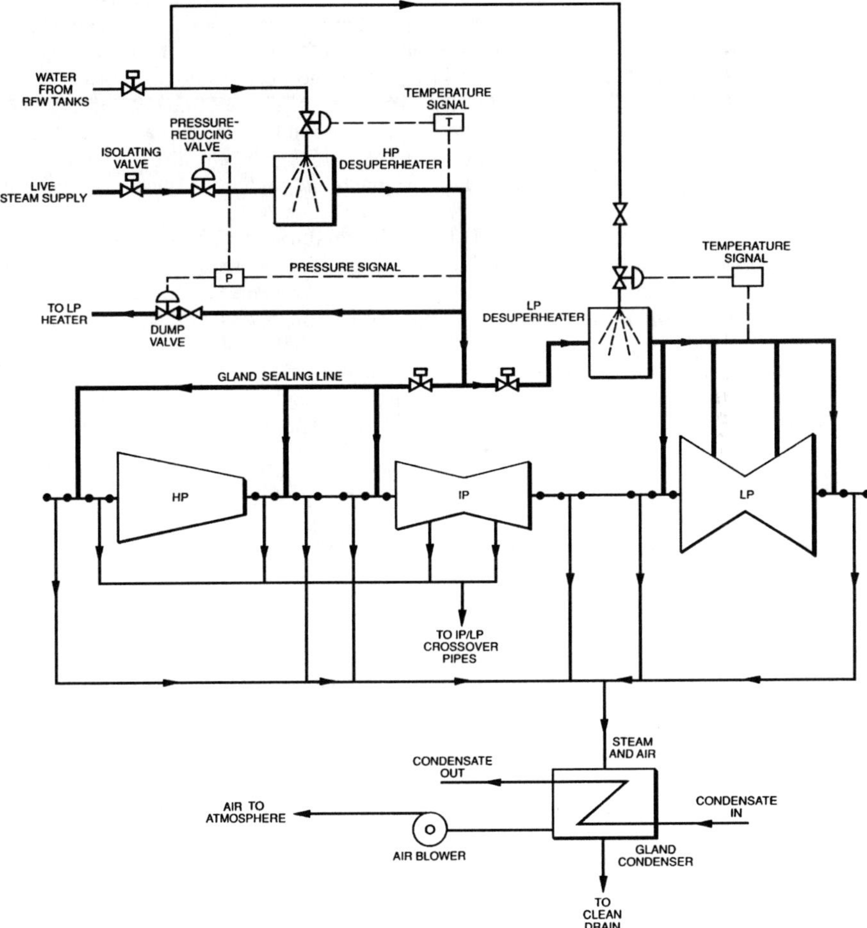

FIGURE 9.3 Typical gland sealing system.

The gland sealing system has two modes of operation. The first supplies steam at the outlet conditions of the superheater. This is known as *live steam.* It is used during start-up, shutdown, and when the unit is operating at low loads. The second mode of operation involves taking steam from the HP and IP turbine and using it to seal the glands of the LP turbine during normal power operation. The use of steam from the HP and IP turbines rather than live steam results in increased efficiency. The changeover from one source of steam to the other is entirely automatic.

A desuperheater is used to lower the temperature of the steam supplied to the glands. An HP desuperheater controls the temperature of the steam supplied to the glands of HP and IP turbines. An LP desuperheater controls the temperature of the steam supplied to the glands of the LP turbines.

The glands are normally divided into sections. After each section, the steam is fed back to an appropriate stage in the turbine or to a feedheater. Thus, energy is returned to the cycle to improve the efficiency. Figure 9.4 (*a*) illustrates the final section of a gland in an HP turbine.

The HP leak-off steam is normally connected to the IP turbine. Its pressure is maintained at the IP exhaust pressure. The steam pressure at the packing leak-off point is normally maintained slightly above atmosphere. The steam taken from the leak-off is normally used to seal the gland of the LP turbine [Fig. 9.4 (*b*)]. Since the steam is moving outward in the gland, it prevents air ingress into the turbine and condenser. The last line in all of the glands is connected to the gland steam condenser. The pressure in this line is maintained slightly below atmospheric to prevent steam leaks from the turbine. There is also a continuous air flow inward through the outboard section of the gland due to the subatmospheric pressure in the line.

At low loads, live steam enters the HP desuperheater through a pressure-reducing valve. The steam is cooled in the HP desuperheater to an acceptable temperature by the HP/IP glands. The steam then enters the HP/IP glands on its way to the LP desuperheater where the steam is then cooled to an acceptable temperature by the LP glands.

At higher loads, the glands of the HP/IP turbines are self-sealing. Excess steam from these glands enters the LP desuperheater to seal the glands of the LP turbines. Two strainers are used to prevent impurities from entering the glands. The first is used for the HP/IP system. The second is used for the LP system. These strainers are installed after the desuperheaters.

TEMPERATURE AND PRESSURE CONTROL

Temperature Control

Two desuperheaters are used to control the steam supplies to the glands. The first is for the HP/IP system and the second is for the LP system. The desuperheaters are normally of the waterspray type (Fig. 9.5).

Pressure Control

During start-up and shutdown, a pressure-regulating valve is used to control the pressure of the live steam reaching the glands. The steam flow to the glands of the HP/IP turbines becomes reduced as the load increases. The steam flow to the glands eventually reverses direction when leak-off steam becomes available. As the pressure in the glands increases, the pressure-regulating valve of the live steam closes progressively (the function of

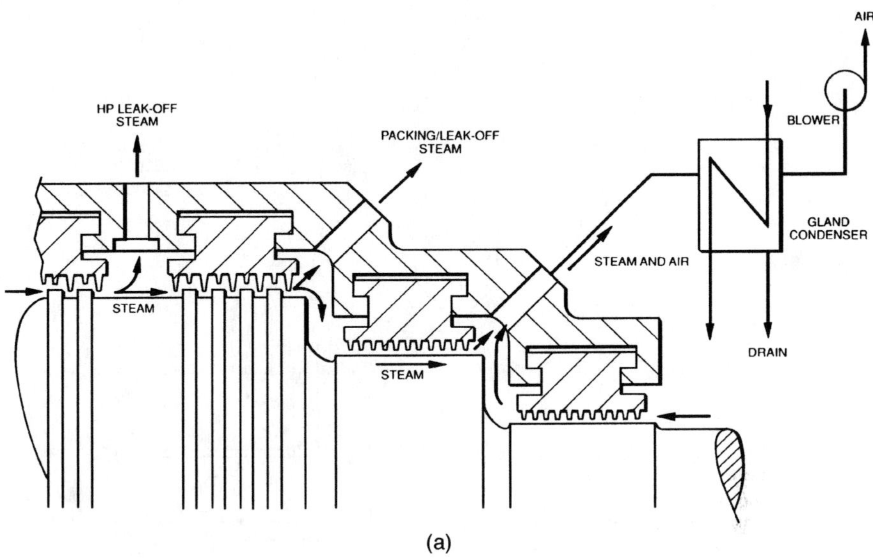

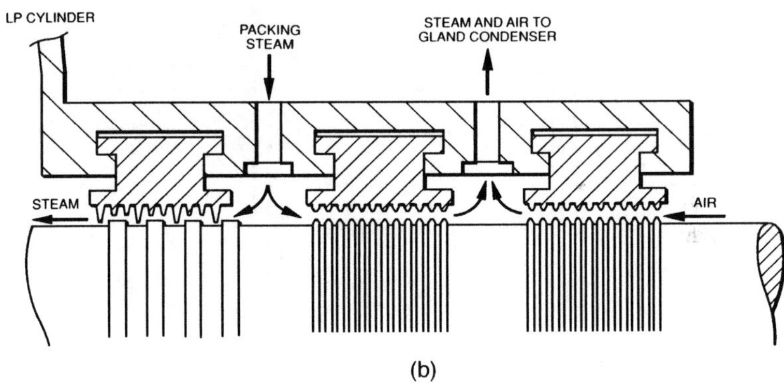

FIGURE 9.4 Glands. (*a*) HP final glands; (*b*) LP glands.

the pressure-regulating valve is to maintain constant pressure at the glands). The pressure-regulating valve eventually closes completely when the pressure at the glands reaches a predetermined value. At this stage, the steam leaking from the glands of the HP and IP turbines is used to seal the glands of the LP turbines. A leak-off valve controls the pressure at the glands by dumping steam to an LP heater. This configuration ensures the following:

- That the pressure at the glands is controlled by one regulating valve at any one time
- That there is an automatic changeover from live steam to leak-off steam

The pressure of the steam in the sealing line is displayed locally and in the control room. Alarms annunciate low-pressure conditions.

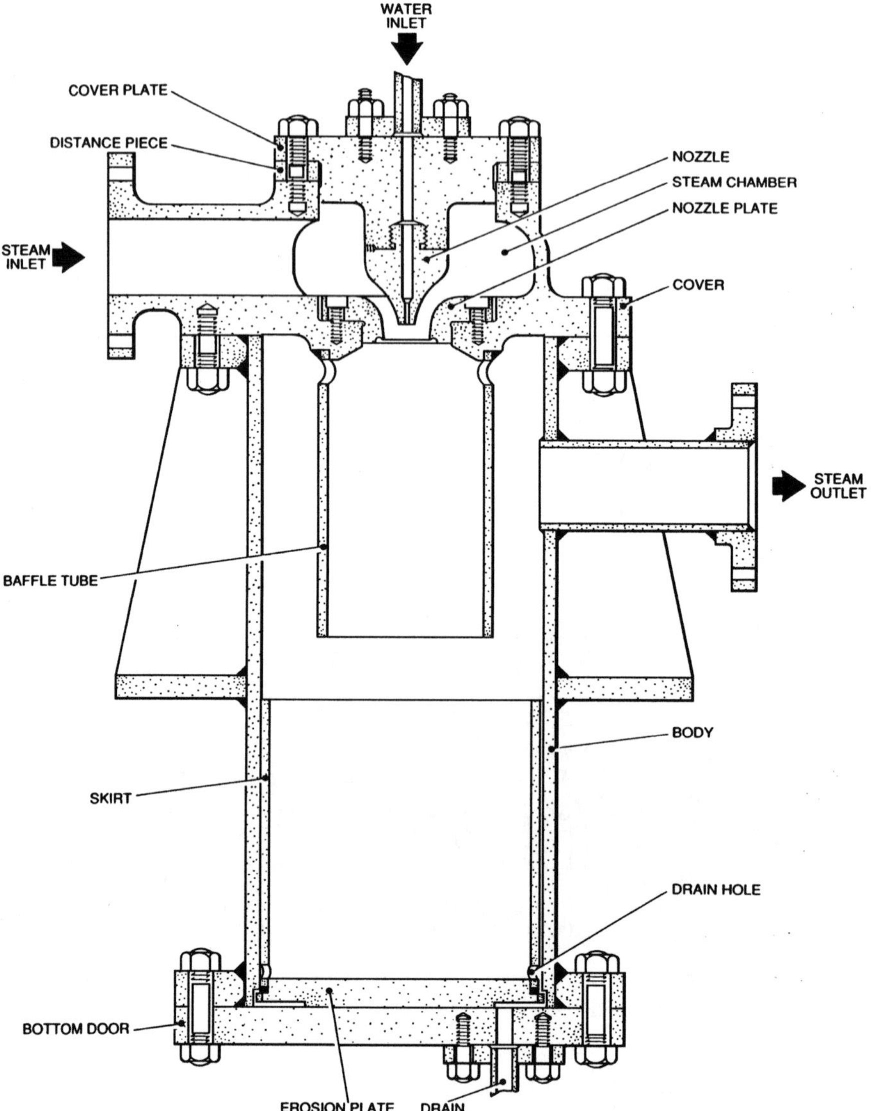

FIGURE 9.5 Gland steam desuperheater.

GLAND STEAM CONDENSER

The gland steam condenser maintains a subatmospheric pressure at the leak-off line of the glands. Thus, it prevents steam leakage from the turbines. A blower is used to vent the condenser to the atmosphere. Air is drawn into the glands due to the small vacuum created by the blower. The air mixes with the steam leaking from the turbine. The air is separated from

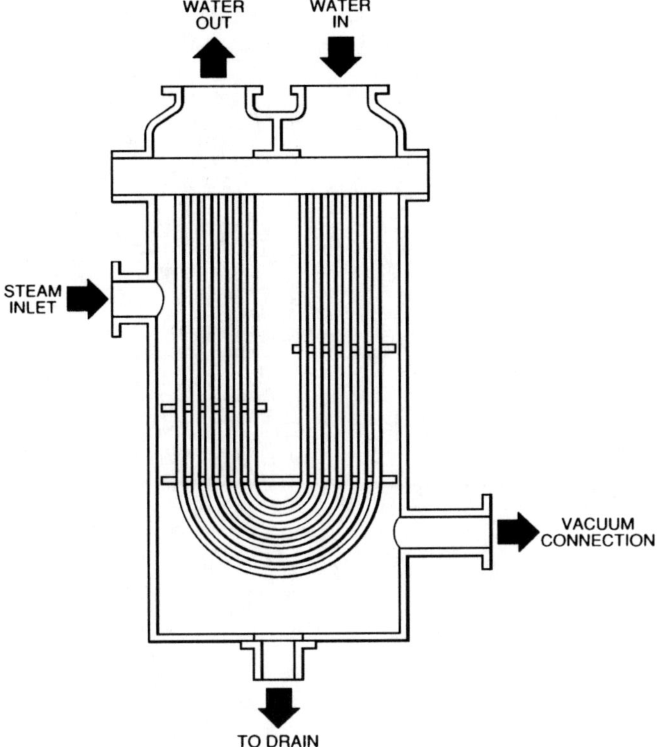

FIGURE 9.6 Gland steam condenser.

the steam in the gland condenser. It is passed back to the atmosphere by the vent fans. The condensed steam is sent to the main condenser (Fig 9.6).

REFERENCE

1. British Electricity International, *Modern Power Station Practice,* 3d ed., Pergamon Press, Oxford, United Kingdom, 1991.

CHAPTER 10
AN OVERVIEW OF GAS TURBINES

INTRODUCTION

Gas turbines are used in a wide range of services.[1,2] They power aircraft of all types and drive mechanical equipment such as pumps, compressors, and generators in electric utilities. They also generate power for peak loads and base-load duties. Recently, the interest in gas turbines has grown significantly in combined-cycle plants. These plants use combinations of gas and steam turbines in various configurations of turbines, heat recovery steam generators, and regenerators.

Gas turbines have these advantages over steam plants:

- They are small in size, mass, and initial cost per unit output.
- Their delivery time is relatively short and they can be installed quickly.
- They are quick starting (as low as 10 s), often by remote control.
- They are smooth running and have a capacity factor (percent of time the unit is operating at full power) of 96 to 98 percent.
- They can use a wide variety of liquid and gaseous fuels including gasified coal and synthetic fuels.
- They are subject to fewer environmental restrictions than other prime movers.

Figure 10.1 illustrates a simple cycle gas turbine. The compressor raises the pressure of inlet air 15 to 25 times. The work required by the compressor appears in the flow in the form of increased temperature. The discharge temperature of the compressor is about 750 to 870°F (400 to 465°C). The combustors burn the fuel to increase the temperature of the compressed air to between 2500 and 2600°F (1370 to 1427°C). The turbine nozzles (stationary blades) convert the high-enthalpy air to high velocity. The turbine buckets (moving blades) convert this energy into rotary motion. The turbine discharge temperature is around 900 to 1180°F (482 to 638°C).

The categories of gas turbines are:

1. Industrial heavy-duty gas turbines
2. Aircraft-derivative gas turbines
3. Medium-range gas turbines
4. Small gas turbines

The efficiency of modern gas turbines has reached 43 to 44 percent with a firing temperature (inside the combustors) of 2500°F (1371°C). The limiting factor for the efficiency of the gas turbine is the metallurgy of the first stage of moving blades in the turbine. New

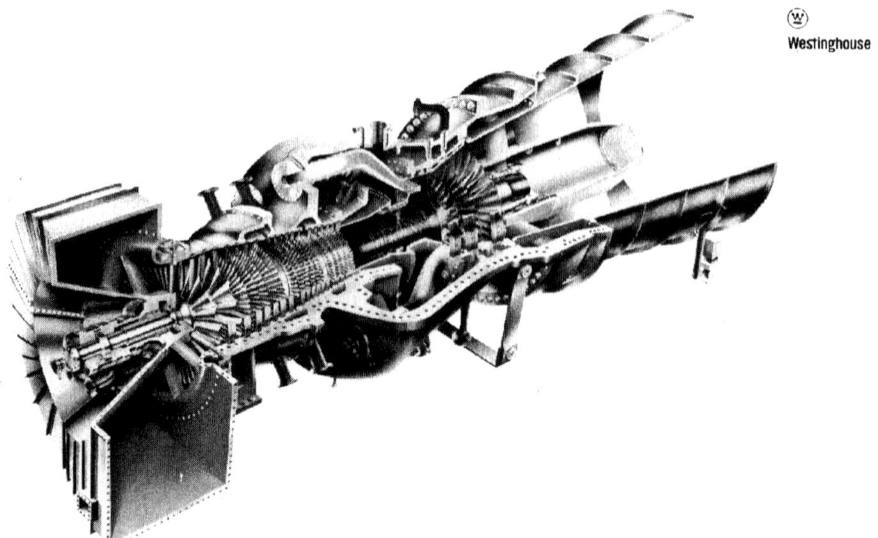

FIGURE 10.1 Combustion turbine, Model CW251B11/12.

The combustion turbine is a single shaft, two-bearing, solid coupling, simple cycle unit containing:

Multistage (19) axial-flow air compressor featuring:

- Variable inlet guide vanes.
- Horizontally split casing giving access to internal parts.
- Individually removable stainless steel blading.
- Accessible pressure-lubricated, pivoted-pad journal bearing.
- Double acting Kingsbury-type thrust bearing.
- Cold-end drive with solid coupling to main reduction gear.

Combustion system including the following:

- Eight can-type combustors in a circular array.
- Combustors removable with cylinder cover in place.
- Optional multiple fuels capability.
- Ignition system with retractable igniters.

Three-stage reaction-type turbine featuring:

- Horizontally split casing giving access to internal parts.
- Alloy turbine blades individually removable.
- Cooled by air-to-air cooler, with cooling air filtered.
- Individual first-stage vanes removable with cylinder cover in place.
- Accessible pressure-lubricated, pivoted-pad journal bearing.
- Low loss axial-exhaust system ideal for waste heat applications.

air-cooling methods and breakthroughs in the metallurgy of turbine blades allowed gas turbines available in research laboratories today to operate at 2800 to 3000°F (1538 to 1649°C). These gas turbines have higher efficiency than the modern gas turbines used in industry. Regeneration* has lowered the heat rate.† However, the best heat rate has been achieved by combining the gas turbine cycle with a steam turbine cycle. The arrangement is called *combined cycles*. Its heat rate is around 5000 to 7000 Btu/kWh. The efficiency of a gas turbine is affected by the firing temperature and pressure ratio across the compressor. For every 100°F (56°C) increase in firing temperature, the work output and efficiency increase by 10 percent and 1.5 percent, respectively.

Figures 10.2 and 10.3 illustrate a performance map of a simple-cycle and a regenerative cycle gas turbine as a function of pressure ratio and turbine inlet temperature. The pressure ratio has the opposite effect in a regenerative cycle compared to that experienced in a simple cycle. Regenerators can increase the efficiency of a modern gas turbine by about 15 to 20 percent. The optimum pressure ratio for a modern regenerative system is about 7:1 compared to 18:1 for a simple cycle gas turbine.

THE BRAYTON CYCLE

The Brayton cycle governs the behavior of gas turbines. Figure 10.4 illustrates an ideal Brayton cycle. It has two adiabatic-reversible (isentropic) processes and two constant-pressure processes.

*Regeneration consists of using a heat exchanger that recovers the heat from the air being discharged from the turbine. The temperature of the air discharged from the turbine is around 900 to 1180°F (482 to 638°C).

†The heat rate is the inverse of the efficiency (1/efficiency). It represents the amount of heat consumed (in Btu) to generate 1 kWh.

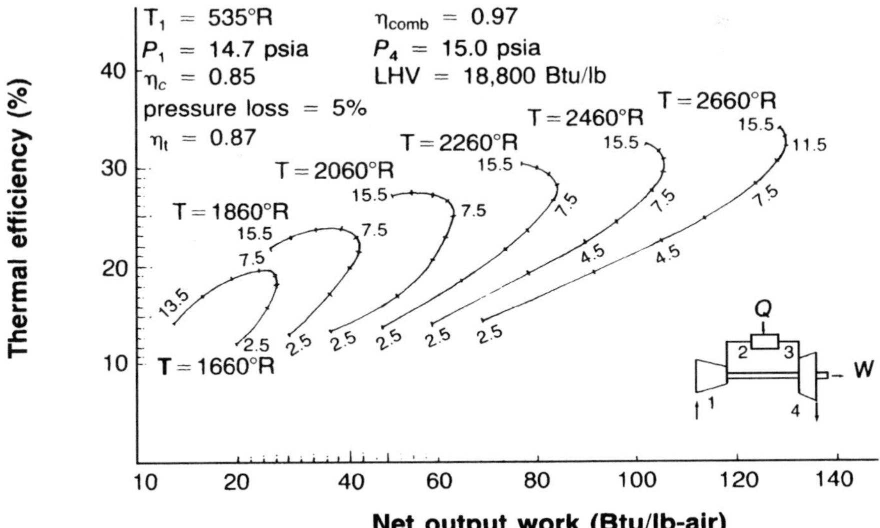

FIGURE 10.2 Performance map of a simple cycle.

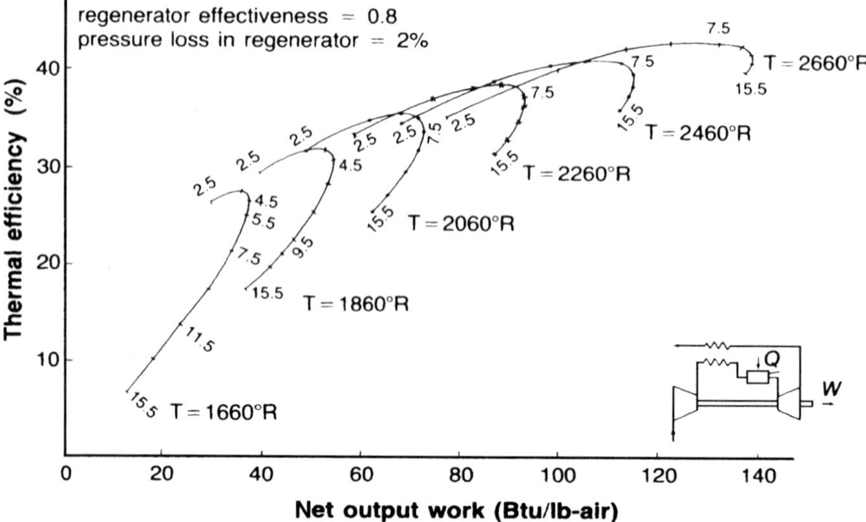

FIGURE 10.3 Performance map of a regenerative cycle.

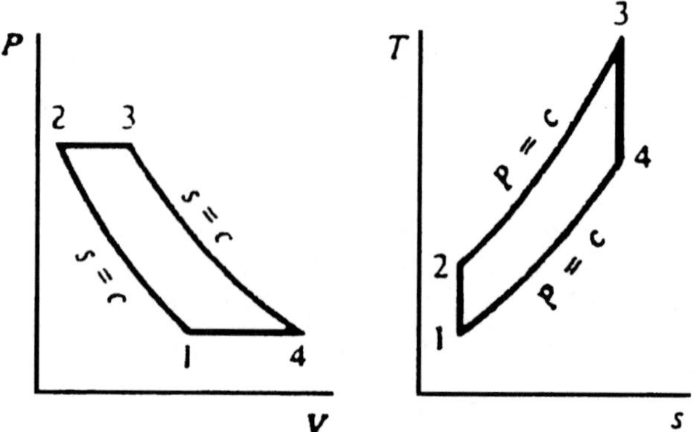

FIGURE 10.4 P-V and T-s diagrams of an ideal Brayton cycle.

The work done in the turbine W_T is equal to the rate of change of its enthalpy. Thus,

$$\dot{W}_T = \dot{H}_3 - \dot{H}_4 = \dot{m}(h_3 - h_4) \tag{10.1}$$

where $\dot{H}$ = total enthalpy of flowing gas, Btu/h or W
h = specific enthalpy, Btu/lb_m or J/kg
$\dot{m}$ = mass rate of flow of gas, lb_m/h or kg/s

Figure 10.5 illustrates a simple-cycle, two-shaft gas turbine. The power turbine, also known as the *low-pressure turbine,* operates on a different shaft than the high-pressure turbine and compressor. This feature allows the power turbine to drive a load at a wide range of speeds. Thus, the two-shaft machines are suitable for applications requiring variable speed.

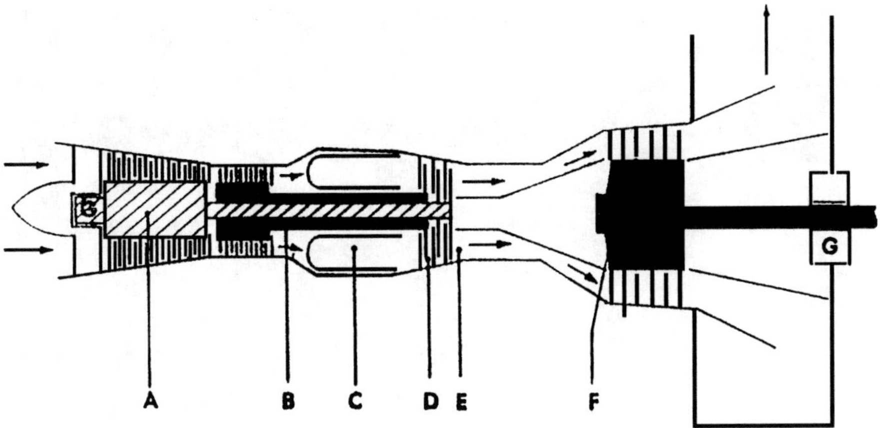

FIGURE 10.5 Dual-shaft gas turbine. *A:* LP compressor; *B:* HP compressor; *C:* combustors; *D:* HP compressor turbine; *E:* LP compressor turbine; *F:* power turbine; *G:* bearings.

The portion of the gas turbine consisting of compressors, combustors, and high-pressure (HP) turbine is called the *gas generator.* All the power developed by the HP turbine is used to drive the compressors. The requirements for starting this gas turbine are less than the ones for a single-shaft gas turbine. The reason is the reduced inertia of the spool carrying the compressor and HP turbine.

The ideal (isentropic) efficiency and specific work of a gas turbine are given by:

$$\eta_{th} = 1 - \frac{1}{r_p^{(k-1)/k}}; \quad \frac{\dot{W}_n}{\dot{m}} = c_p\left[T_1\,(1 - r_p^{(k-1)/k} + T_3\left(1 - \frac{1}{r_p^{(k-1)/k}}\right)\right] \tag{10.2}$$

$$r_{pT} = \frac{P_3}{P_4}; \quad k = \frac{c_p}{c_v}; \quad \frac{T_3}{T_4} = r_{pT}^{(k-1)/k}$$

INDUSTRIAL HEAVY-DUTY GAS TURBINES

Industrial heavy-duty gas turbines entered the market in the early 1950s. These ground-based units did not have restrictions on weight and space. Their design characteristics included heavy-wall casings, sleeve bearings, large-diameter combustors, thick airfoil sections for moving and stationary blades, and large frontal areas. The pressure ratio for these gas turbines increased from 5:1 for earlier units to 15 to 25:1 for modern units. The turbine inlet temperature for a modern unit is around 2000 to 2500°F (1093 to 1371°C). Projected temperatures approach 3000°F (1649°C) and when achieved, would result in a significant increase in the efficiency of these machines. The industrial heavy-duty gas turbines normally use axial-flow compressors and turbines. In most North American designs, the combustors are can-annular as shown in Figs. 10.6(*a*) and 10.6(*b*). European designs use single-stage side combustors as shown in Fig. 10.7. The combustors of these units normally have heavy walls and are very durable. The liners are designed to produce low smoke and low NO_X* emissions. Most

*NO_X is a term used to describe the mixture of NO and NO_2.

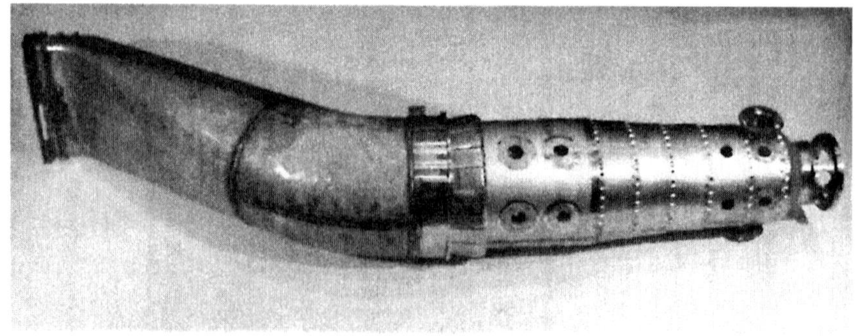

(a)

(b)

FIGURE 10.6 (*a*) Can-annular combustor with transition piece. (©*Rolls-Royce Limited*) (*b*) A typical diffusion flame, can-annular, reverse-flow combustor. (*Courtesy General Electric Company*)

of these units have dual fuel flexibility. The velocity of the inlet air drops in the large frontal areas resulting in a reduction of air noise. The auxiliary equipment includes heavy-duty pumps and motors that have been tested for long hours. Heavy-duty governors are also used in the control system. Electronic governors are being used in some newer models. The following are the advantages of heavy-duty gas turbines:

- High availability
- Long life
- Slightly higher efficiencies when compared with other types of gas turbines
- Significantly lower noise levels than aircraft-type gas turbines

These machines are used normally in electric utilities to deliver base load power.

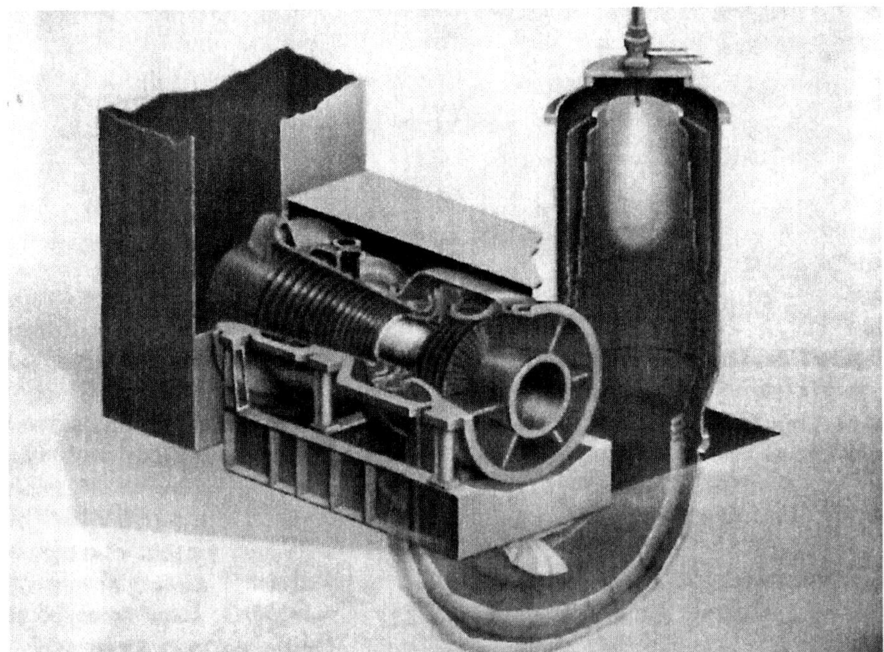

FIGURE 10.7 Side combustor can. (*Courtesy of Brown Boveri Turbomachinery, Inc.*)

AIRCRAFT-DERIVATIVE GAS TURBINES

Jet gas turbines consist of an aircraft-derivative gas generator and a free-power turbine. The gas generator produces the gas energy or gas horsepower. It consists of a compressor, combustors and a turbine. The turbine generates sufficient power to drive the compressor only. The combustion gas products leaving the gas generator are around 30 psi (206 kPa) and 1100°F (593°C). The free-power turbine converts the thermal energy in the gas to mechanical energy (torque x rotational speed) or brake horsepower. This mechanical energy is used to drive the load (see Fig. 10.8).

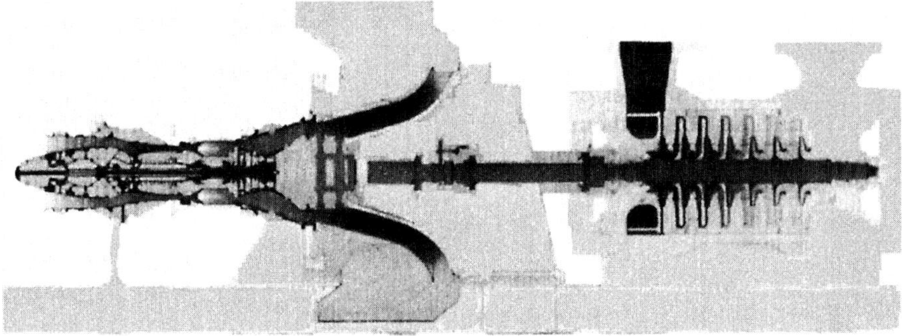

FIGURE 10.8 Aircraft-derivative gas turbine driving a centrifugal gas compressor. (©*Rolls-Royce Limited*)

Aircraft-type turbines are mainly used in the gas transmission industry and as peaking units in power plants. These are their main benefits:

- Relatively low installation cost
- They can easily be operated unattended by remote control due to the following reasons:
  - Their auxiliary systems are not complex.
  - They do not require water cooling (oil-to-air heat exchangers are used for cooling).
  - Their starting device, which is normally a gas expansion motor, requires little power.
  - Their performance can be monitored remotely. Maintenance is initiated upon degradation in performance.

MEDIUM-RANGE GAS TURBINES

Medium-range gas turbines are rated between 5000 to 15,000 hp (3.7 to 11.2 MW). These units have relatively high efficiency at part-load operation. The gasifier (section that generates the hot gas) operates at maximum efficiency, while the power turbine operates at variable speed. The compressor has normally 10 to 16 stages. Its pressure ratio (discharge pressure/inlet pressure) is around 5 to 11. Most American manufacturers use can-annular (5 to 10 combustor cans mounted on a circular ring) or annular-type combustors. European manufacturers normally use side combustors. The turbine inlet temperature of most European designs is normally lower than in American counterparts. Most gasifiers use a 2 to 3 stage axial turbine. Its first-stage nozzles (stationary blades) and buckets (moving blades) normally are air-cooled. Most power turbines have one or two stages.

These units are normally used on offshore platforms and in petrochemical plants. Regenerators are used with these turbines to improve their efficiency.

SMALL GAS TURBINES

Small gas turbines are rated below 5000 hp (3.7 MW). Their design is similar to the larger turbines discussed earlier. However, they normally use centrifugal compressors or combinations of centrifugal and axial compressors and radial-inflow turbines. These units have an efficiency of around 20 percent due to the following reasons:

- Centrifugal compressors have lower efficiency than their axial counterparts.
- The turbine inlet temperature is limited to around 1700 °F (927°C) due to lack of blade cooling.

The efficiency of these units can be improved by recovering the exhaust heat from the turbine.

MAJOR GAS TURBINE COMPONENTS

Compressors

Gas turbines use axial and centrifugal compressors. Small gas turbines use centrifugal compressors while all the larger ones use axial compressors.

Axial-Flow Compressors. Axial-flow compressors increase the pressure of the fluid by accelerating it in the rotating blades and then diffusing* it in the stationary blades. A compressor stage consists of one row of stationary blades and one row of moving blades. An additional row of fixed blades (inlet guide vanes) is normally installed at the inlet to the compressor to direct the air at the desired angle to the first-stage of rotating blades. An additional diffuser is installed at the compressor discharge. It diffuses the fluid further before entering the combustors. Figure 10.1 shows a 19-stage axial flow compressor. The overall pressure increase across a compressor of a modern gas turbine varies between 20:1 and 40:1. These compressors are generally more efficient than centrifugal compressors. They are also usually much smaller and run at higher speeds.

Centrifugal Compressors. Figure 10.9 illustrates the impellers of a centrifugal compressor. Air is taken at the center or "eye" of the rotor. It is accelerated by the blades due to high rotational speeds of the rotor and forced radially out of the rotor at high velocities. The air is then received by the diffuser, which converts the high velocity to high pressure.

A single compressor stage consists of an impeller mounted on the rotor and a diffuser mounted in the stator. The air enters the compressor at the inducer (see Fig. 10.10). It goes through a 90° turn and is discharged into a diffuser which normally has a vaneless space followed by a vaned section. The air leaves the diffuser and enters a scroll or collector. The pressure increase per stage of a centrifugal compressor varies between 1.5:1 and 12:1. Centrifugal compressors have lower efficiency than axial-flow compressors. However,

*A diffuser is a component of increasing cross-sectional area. The fluid pressure increases across it due to decrease in velocity.

FIGURE 10.9 Closed impeller. (*Courtesy Elliott Company, Jeannette, PA*)

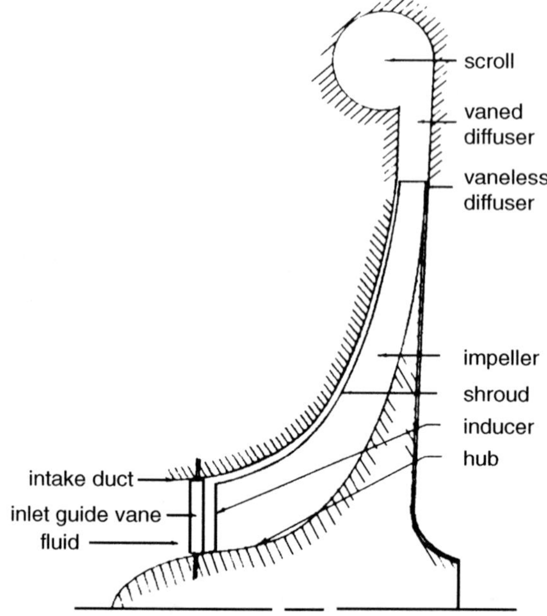

FIGURE 10.10 Schematic of a centrifugal compressor.

they are not as prone to a reduction in efficiency due to the build-up of deposits as in axial-flow compressors. Their main advantages are simplicity, strength, and short length.

Compressor Materials

The compressor casings are usually made of cast iron or aluminum alloy. The rotors are usually made of good-quality ferrite steel, and the compressor blades will be stainless steel or titanium alloys.

Two-Stage Compression

The compression process requires less work if heat is removed from the gas during the process. This improves the efficiency of the gas turbine. A two-stage compression is often used with an intercooler between the stages (see Fig. 10.11).

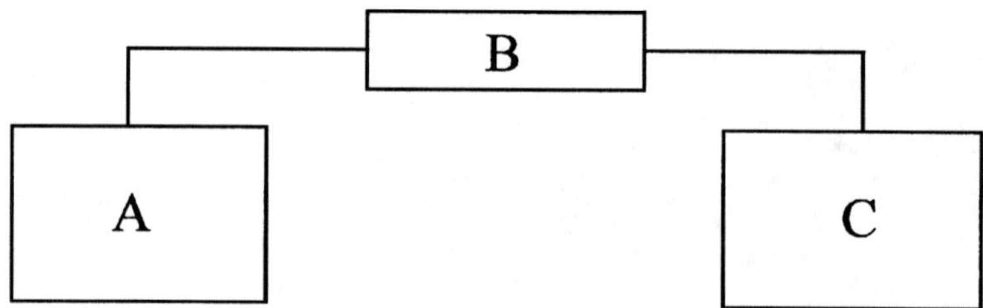

FIGURE 10.11 Two-stage compression. *A:* compressor; *B:* intercooler; *C:* compressor.

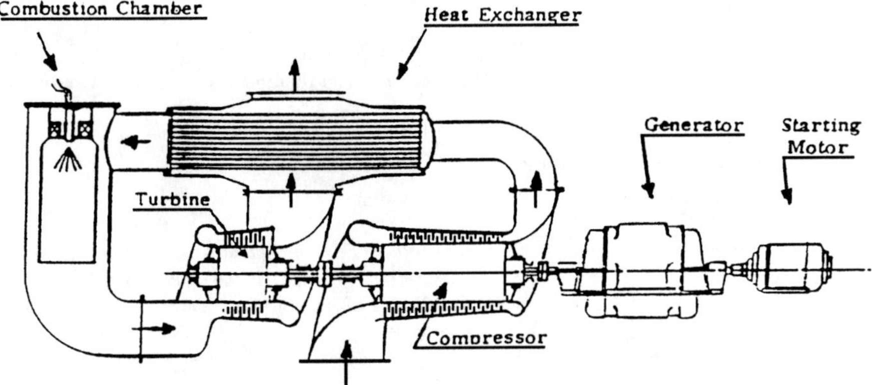

FIGURE 10.12 Gas turbine with regenerator.

Regenerators

In simple gas turbines, the gases exhausted from the turbine are still at a high temperature, 900 to 1180°F (482 to 638°C). The thermal efficiency of the gas turbine will improve if some of the heat in the exhaust gases is transferred to the compressed air before the air enters the combustor. This is accomplished by adding a heat exchanger called a *regenerator* to the basic cycle (see Fig. 10.12).

The regenerator (see Fig. 10.13) is a shell-and-tube heat exchanger having the turbine exhaust gases flowing in the tubes or on the shell side. The temperature of the exhaust gases from the turbine is reduced to 500°F (260°C) by transferring heat to the air in the regenerator. The air enters the regenerator at 392°F (200°C) and leaves at about 698°F (370°C). The regenerator can recover up to 75 percent of the exhaust heat, resulting in increase in efficiency.

Heavy-duty regenerators are used in large gas turbines in the 5000 to 100,000 hp (3.7 to 74.6 MW) range. They increase the efficiency of the unit by reducing the fuel consumption by up to 30 percent. Despite this increase in efficiency, regenerators are only used by a small number of manufacturers for these reasons:

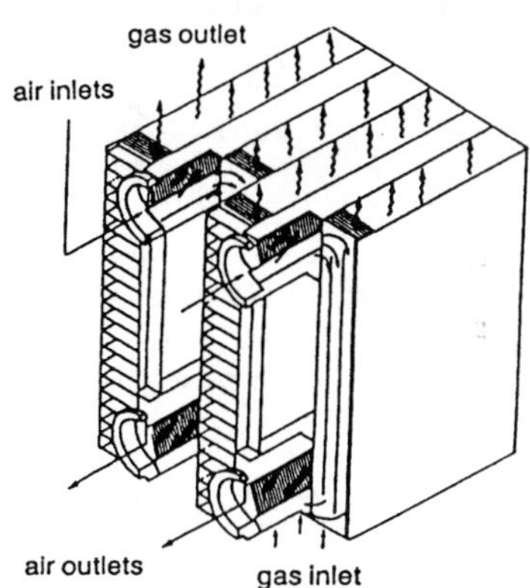

FIGURE 10.13 A typical plate-fin industrial regenerator for gas turbines.

- The increase in efficiency caused by using regenerators decreases steadily as the unit is operated due to build-up of deposits inside the regenerator.
- Regenerators are only used by turbines having low pressure increase across their compressors. The reason for this is that gas turbines having a large pressure increase across their compressors will also have a large temperature increase across them (the work required to increase the pressure across a compressor is proportional to the temperature increase across it). Since the temperature of the gas leaving the turbine is around 482°C (900°F), units having large pressure increase across their compressors will have limited benefit from a regenerator because the exit temperature of the compressor will approach the exit temperature of the turbine.
- Regenerators have relatively high cost, space, and maintenance requirements.

Combustors

The purpose of the combustor is to increase the temperature of the high-pressure gas. There is a slight pressure drop across the combustors. The four categories of combustors are:

- Tubular (side combustors)
- Can-annular
- Annular

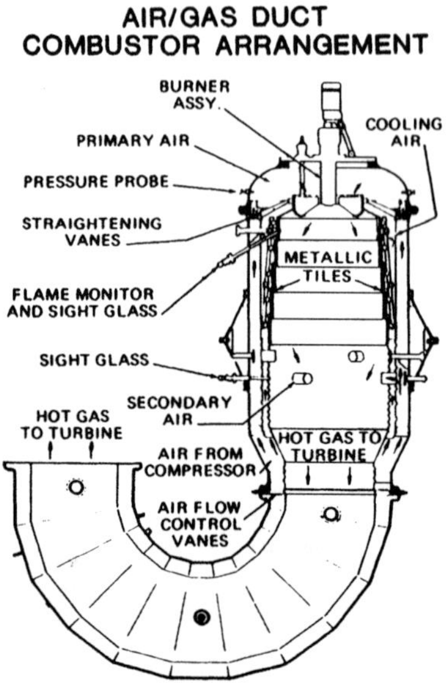

FIGURE 10.14 A typical single-can side combustor for an industrial turbine. (*Courtesy Brown Boveri Turbomachinery, Inc.*)

Tubular (side combustors). These combustors (see Figs. 10.7 and 10.14) are normally installed on large European industrial turbines. Their advantages are:

- Simple design
- Ease of maintenance
- High longevity

They could be of a "straight-through" or "reverse-flow" design. In the reverse-flow type, air enters the annulus between the combustor can and the housing. This design has minimal length.

Can-Annular and Annular. Most industrial heavy-duty gas turbines designed in the United States use can-annular combustors [see Figs. 10.6(*a*) and (*b*)]. Can-annular (known also as *tubo-annular,* Figs. 10.15 and 10.16) and annular (Fig. 10.17) combustors are used in aircraft engines due to their favorable radial and circumferential

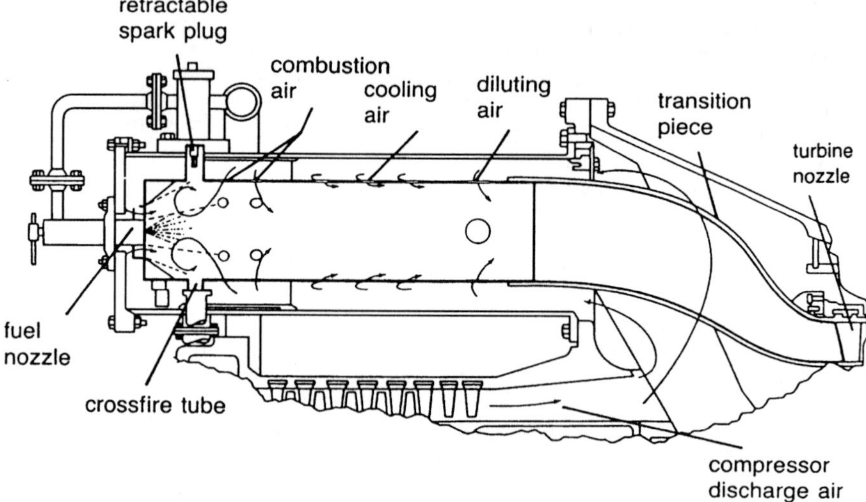

FIGURE 10.15 Tubo-annular or can-annular combustor for a heavy-duty gas turbine. (*Courtesy of General Electric Company*)

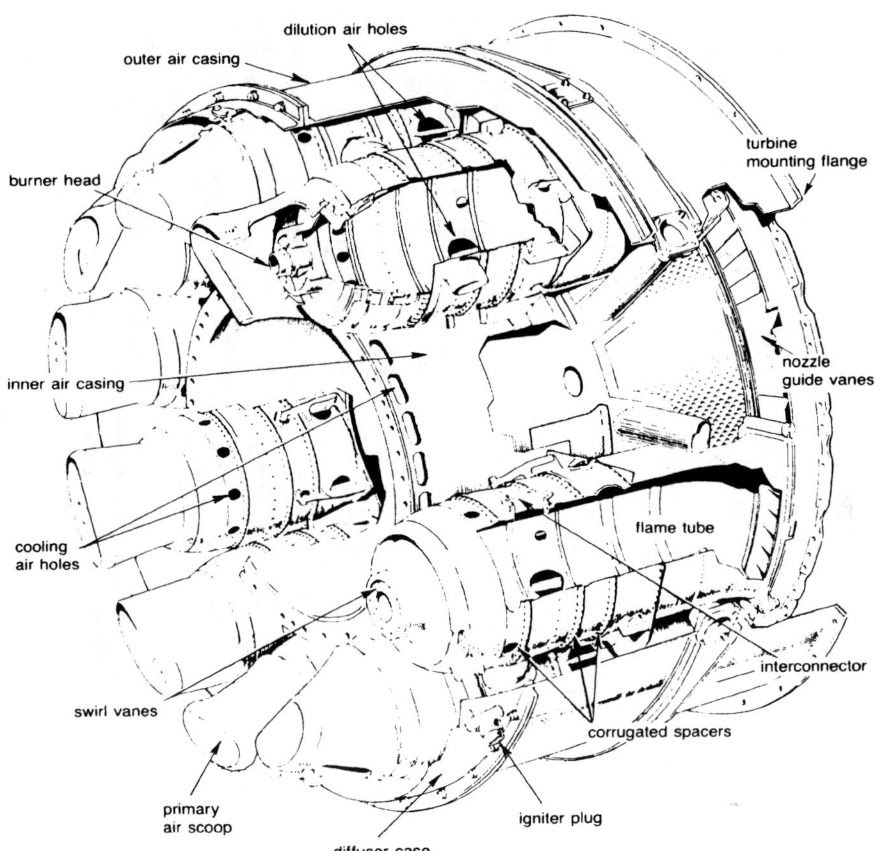

FIGURE 10.16 Tubo-annular combustion chamber for aircraft-type gas turbines. (©*Rolls-Royce Limited*)

profiles. These designs are suited for the large number of fuel nozzles employed in these applications. Annular combustors are used more commonly in applications having higher temperatures and low-heat-content (low-Btu) gases.

There are straight-through and reverse-flow can-annular combustors. The can-annular cans used in the aircraft industry are of the straight-through design. The reverse-flow design is normally used in industrial engines. Annular combustors are normally straight-through design.

Combustor Operation. In multiple-type combustors, there is a fuel supply to each flame tube, but there are only a couple of igniters for all the tubes. When ignition occurs in the flame tubes having the igniters, the crossfire tubes takes the hot gases from the hot flame tube to ignite the remainder. This occurs in a matter of one second. Once the flame detectors confirm stable ignition, the igniter will shut down. The manufacturers of gas turbines confirm that any fuel can be used if the necessary changes are made to the fuel system.

Turbines

Axial-flow and radial-inflow turbines are used in gas turbine applications. However, more than 80 percent of gas turbines use axial-flow turbines.

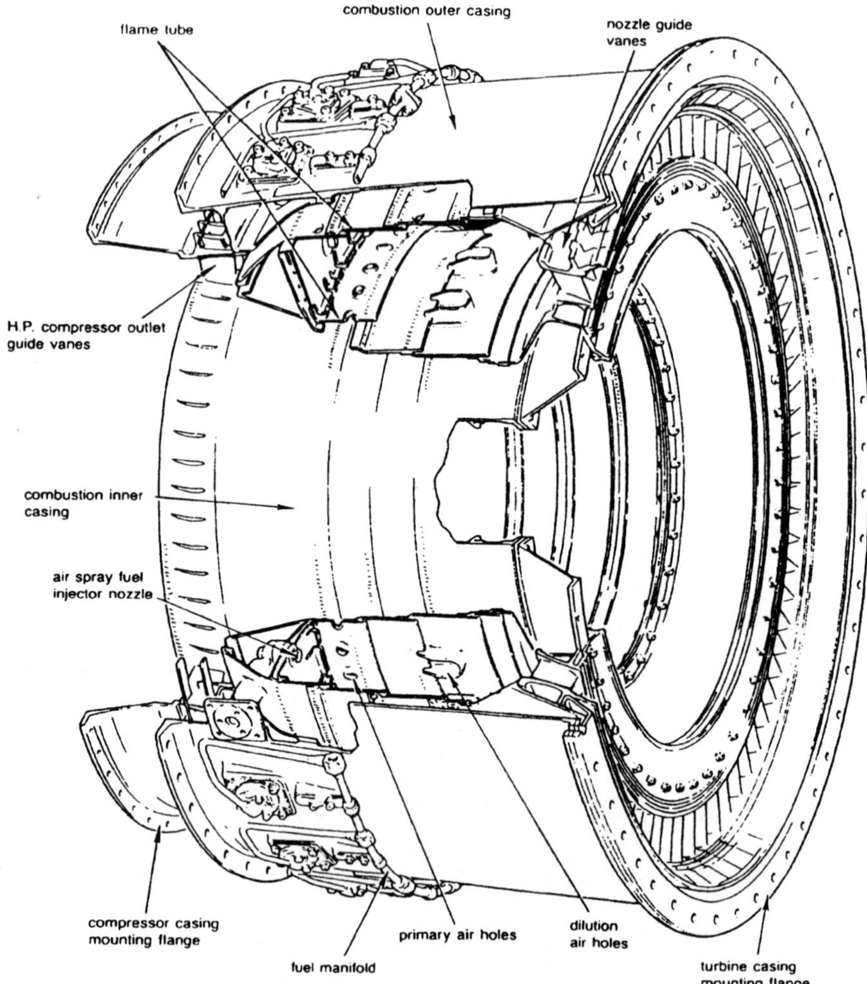

FIGURE 10.17 Annular Combustion Chamber. (©*Rolls-Royce Limited.*)

Axial-Flow Turbines. The flow in an axial-flow turbine (Fig. 10.18) and its counterpart, the axial-flow compressor, enters and leaves in the axial direction. These turbines can be of the impulse type or the reaction type. In an impulse turbine, the enthalpy drops entirely (the energy available in the high temperature and pressure is converted into velocity) in the nozzles (stationary blades). Thus, the velocity of the gas entering the rotor is very high. In a reaction turbine, the enthalpy drops in the nozzles and the buckets (moving blades).

Radial-Inflow Turbine. The radial-inflow turbine, or inward-flow radial turbine, consists of a centrifugal compressor having reverse flow and opposite rotation. These turbines are used for smaller loads and over a narrower operating range than the axial turbine. Axial turbines are normally suited for aircraft and power generation applications. However, they are much longer than radial turbines. This makes them unsuitable for certain applications. Radial turbines are normally used for turbochargers and in some types of expanders.

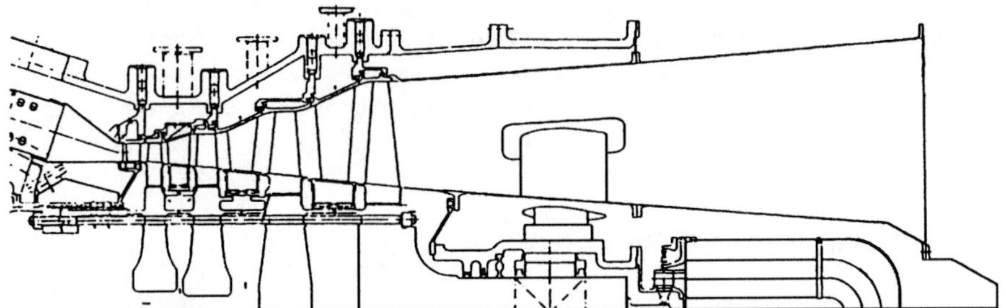

FIGURE 10.18 Schematic of an axial-flow turbine. (*Courtesy of Westinghouse Electric Corporation.*)

Heat Recovery Steam Generators

Most of the heat available in the exhaust gases [normally around 482 to 638°C (900 to 1180°F)] of a gas turbine can be recaptured in a heat recovery steam generator (HRSG). The steam can be used in the following applications:

- To drive a steam turbine in a combined cycle* plant
- For heating purposes in a cogeneration plant
- For a process in an industry such as a petrochemical plant

The HRSG (Fig. 10.19) is a counterflow heat exchanger used to generate steam by convection.

The following are its main components:

- The superheater: This is the first component exposed to the exhaust gases from the gas turbine. It superheats the saturated steam leaving the boiler.

*A combined cycle consists of a gas turbine working in conjunction with a steam power plant through an HRSG.

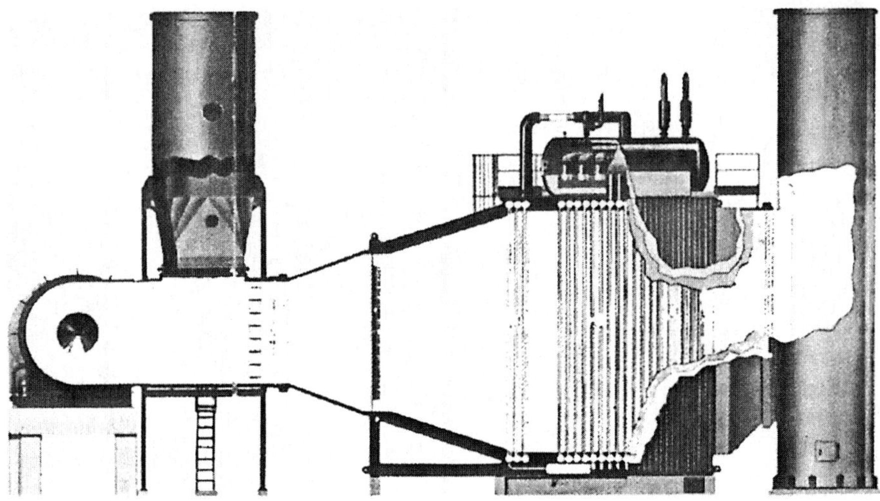

FIGURE 10.19 Supplementary fired exhaust gas steam generator. (*Courtesy of Henry Vogt Machine Company.*)

- The boiler: This component is exposed to the hot gases leaving the superheater. It provides the latent heat required to evaporate the saturated water leaving the economizer.
- The economizer: This component is exposed to the hot gases leaving the boiler. It provides the heat required to raise the temperature of the subcooled water entering the HRSG to saturation.

TOTAL ENERGY ARRANGEMENT

Gas turbines have been used in cogeneration and combined cycles plants to produce electricity and steam. In some cases, the steam is used in absorption chillers to produce cold water, which is used for cooling buildings with the aid of a cooling tower. This is known as a *total energy arrangement* due to the generation of steam, electricity, and cold water.

GAS TURBINE APPLICATIONS

Gas turbines have been used to produce power as well as an engine to drive pumps, compressors, emergency equipment, etc. It is common to use gas turbines in power plants and hospitals to produce instant emergency power for essential services when the main power supply is interrupted. Gas turbines are ideal for use as an unmanned and remotely controlled unit that can be started by a telephone or radio link.

COMPARISON OF GAS TURBINES WITH OTHER PRIME MOVERS

Modern gas turbines compare very favorably with other machines on the grounds of fuel consumption, efficiency, and power/mass/size ratios. Gasoline engines operating on the Otto cycle have efficiencies of 20 to 25 percent. The diesel and Rankine cycles (steam plant) have an efficiency of 30 to 35 percent. The modern gas turbine, which operates on the Brayton cycle, has an efficiency of 44 percent.

REFERENCES

1. Boyce, Meheran P., Gas Turbine Engineering Handbook, Golf Publishing Company, Houston, Tex., 1995.
2. El-Wakil, M. M., Power Plant Technology, McGraw-Hill, New York, 1984.

CHAPTER 11
GAS TURBINE COMPRESSORS

CENTRIFUGAL COMPRESSORS

When compared with axial compressors, centrifugal compressors have the following five advantages:

1. They occupy a smaller length than the equivalent axial compressors.
2. They are not liable to loss of performance by buildup of deposits on the surfaces of the air channel when working in a contaminated atmosphere.
3. They are able to operate efficiently over a wider range of mass flow at any particular rotational speed (i.e., they alleviate problems of matching operational conditions with those of the associated turbine).
4. They are used mainly in small power units because the higher isentropic efficiency of axial compressors cannot be maintained for small machines.
5. Titanium is the preferable material because of its high resistance to corrosion.

Principle of Operation

The centrifugal compressor consists of a stationary casing containing a rotating impeller, which increases the velocity of the air, and a number of diffusers that decelerate the air converting a part of its kinetic energy to pressure. Figure 11.1 illustrates a centrifugal compressor.

Compressor Characteristics

Figure 11.2 illustrates the variation in the pressure ratio when a valve placed in the delivery line of the compressor running at constant speed is slowly opened. When the valve is shut and the flow is zero, the pressure ratio will have a value *A*. This is the pressure head that is produced by the action of the impeller on the air trapped between the vanes. As the valve is opened and the flow increases, the maximum efficiency is reached at point *B*. Any further increase in flow will result in a decrease of the pressure ratio. If the flow is increased significantly beyond the design flow, the efficiency decreases rapidly. A hypothetical case is reached at point *C* where the pressure ratio drops to unity (i.e., all the power absorbed by the compressor is dissipated in friction losses). In reality, point *A* could be obtained if desired. However, most of the curve between points *A* and *B* could not be obtained due to the phenomenon of surging. Surging is associated with a sudden drop in delivery pressure, and with violent aerodynamic pulsations that are transmitted throughout the machine. Assume that the compressor is operating at some point *D*. A decrease in mass flow should be accompanied by a fall of delivery pressure. If the pressure of the air downstream of the

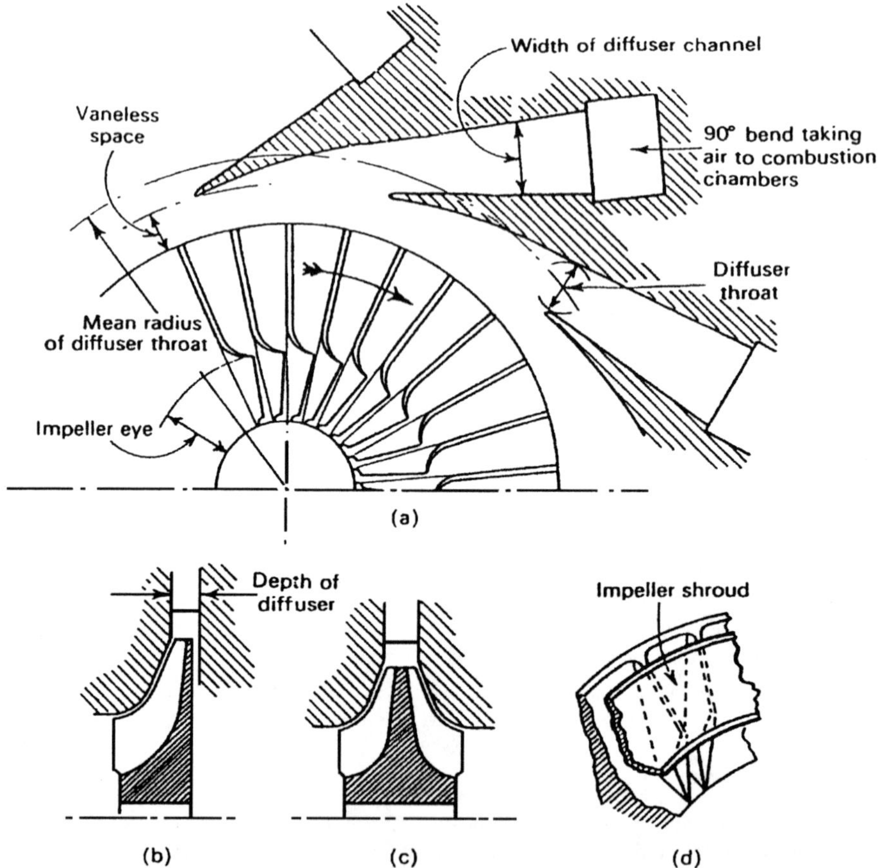

FIGURE 11.1 Diagrammatic sketches of centrifugal compressors. (*a*) Impeller and diffuser of a centrifugal compressor; (*b*) impeller of a centrifugal compressor; (*c*) different compeller of a centrifugal compressor; (*d*) impeller shroud.

compressor does not fall quickly enough, the air will flow backward due to the pressure gradient. This results in a rapid drop in pressure ratio. The pressure downstream of the compressor drops as well until the compressor reestablishes the flow. The surging of the air may not happen immediately as the operating point moves to the left of point *B* in Fig. 11.2. This is because the pressure downstream of the compressor may fall at a greater rate than the delivery pressure. As the mass flow is reduced, the flow reversal will occur. The conditions between points *A* and *B* are inherently unstable. If the operating point is on the part on the curve having negative slope, a decrease in mass flow results in increase in delivery pressure. The flow characteristic in this region is stable.

In a gas turbine, the swallowing capacity of the components downstream of the compressor (e.g., the turbine) and the way the swallowing capacity varies over the range of operating conditions determines the actual point at which surging occurs. An additional limitation exists in the operating range between points *B* and *C*. As the mass flow increases and the pressure decreases, the density is reduced and the radial component of velocity must increase ($m = \rho AV$). Point *E* is reached where no further increase in mass flow can be

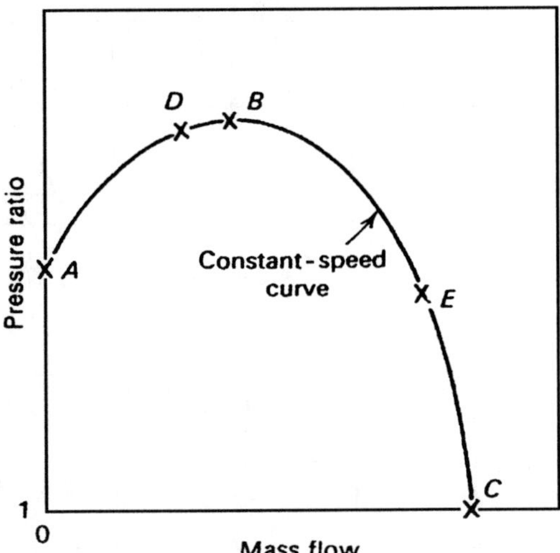

FIGURE 11.2 Theoretical characteristic.

obtained and choking occurs. This point represents the maximum flow obtainable at the particular rotational speed. Other curves can be obtained for different speeds.

Figure 11.3 (*a*) illustrates the actual variation of pressure ratio over the complete range of mass flow and rotational speed. The left-hand extremities of the constant-speed curves are joined up to form what is known as the *surge line.* The right-hand extremities represent the points where choking occurs.

Since the isentropic *p-T* relation is given by:

$$T_2/T_1 = r^{(\gamma-1)/\gamma} = T_3/T_4$$

where r is the pressure ratio $P_2/P_1 = r = P_3/P_4$.

Therefore, the form of the curves of the temperature ratio plotted on the same basis will be similar to the pressure ratio plotted in Fig. 11.3 (*a*). The isentropic efficiency curves are plotted in Fig. 11.3 (*b*). The efficiency varies with the mass flow at a given speed in a similar manner to the pressure ratio. However, the maximum value for all speeds is approximately the same. A curve representing the locus of operating points at maximum efficiency is shown in Fig. 11.3 (*a*). Gas turbines are usually designed to operate on this curve.

AXIAL-FLOW COMPRESSORS

The performance of axial-flow compressors exceeds that of the centrifugal compressors. Axial-flow compressors are used in the greater proportion of gas turbines of all applications. This type of compressor is described as "the reversed multistage axial flow turbine." In axial compressors, the flow is decelerating or diffusing by causing the fluid to pass through a series of expanding passages where the pressure rise is obtained by reduction in velocity. For good performance, the blades of the compressor rotor form series of diverging passages. In the case of a turbine, the passages are converging. Figure 11.4 illustrates the fundamental differences between the two types. Stalling troubles are prevalent in axial-flow compressors. Stalling occurs when the relevant angle of incidence between the flow direction and the

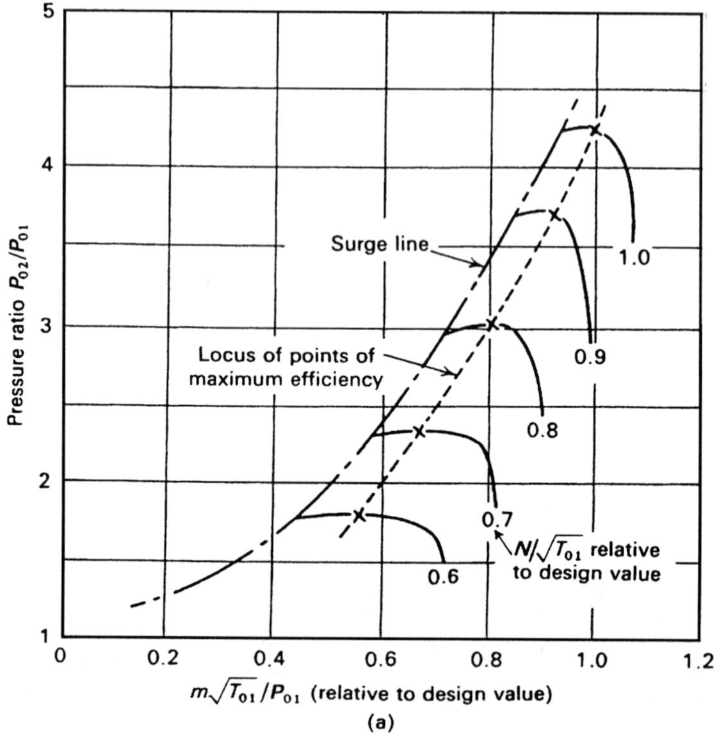

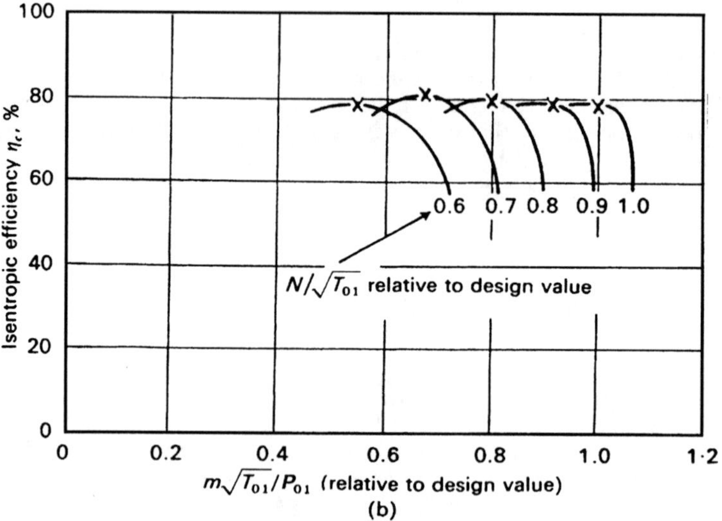

FIGURE 11.3 Centrifugal compressor characteristics. (*a*) Variation of pressure ratio in a centrifugal compressor; (*b*) variation of isentropic efficiency in a centrifugal compressor.

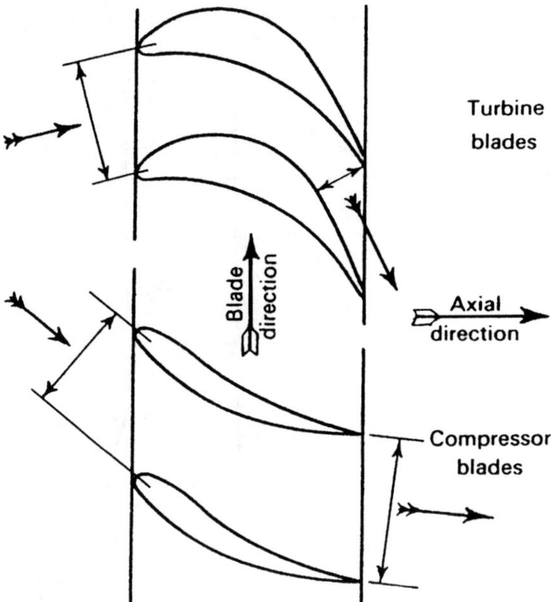

FIGURE 11.4 Comparison of typical forms of turbine and compressor rotor blades.

blades becomes excessive. Since the pressure gradient is acting against the direction of the flow, there is always danger to the stability of the flow pattern. Breakdown can easily occur at conditions of mass flow and rotational speed that are different from the ones for which the blades were designed.

The axial-flow compressor has two main components: (1) the rotor and (2) the stator. The rotor carries the moving blades and the stator the stationary rows. The stationary rows convert the kinetic energy imparted to the working fluid by the rotor blades to pressure increase. Also, the stationary rows redirect the flow into an angle that is suitable for entry to the next row of moving blades. Each stage consists of a stationary row followed by a rotating row. A row of inlet guide vanes is usually provided to the stator upstream of the first stage. They direct the flow correctly into the first row of rotating blades. The characteristic curves of an axial-flow compressor are similar to those of a centrifugal compressor. Figure 11.5 illustrates the axial compressor flow characteristics.

Blowoff valves are used sometimes to prevent surging when it is expected to occur near the rear of the compressor. Air is discharged from the compressor at some intermediate stage through a valve to reduce the mass flow through the later stages. Figure 11.6 illustrates the effects of the blowoff valve on the compressor characteristics. Figure 11.7 illustrates the effect of the blowoff valve and increased nozzle area on the compressor characteristics. A twin-spool compressor is another technique used to prevent surging by splitting the compressor into two (or more) sections, each being driven by a separate turbine at a different speed.

Figure 11.8 illustrates the effects of acceleration and deceleration on the compressor characteristics. Smooth starting and part load control therefore require devices such as variable

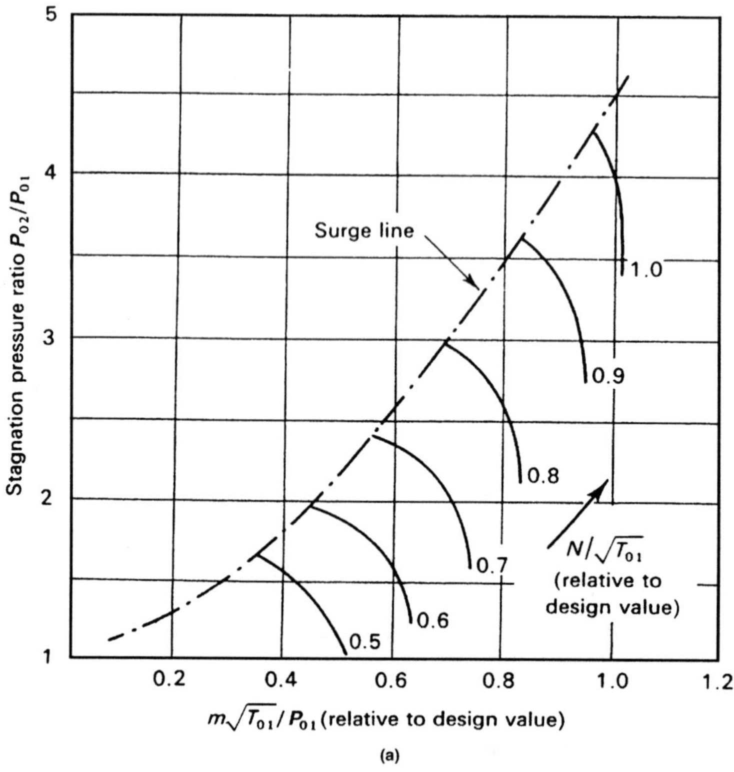

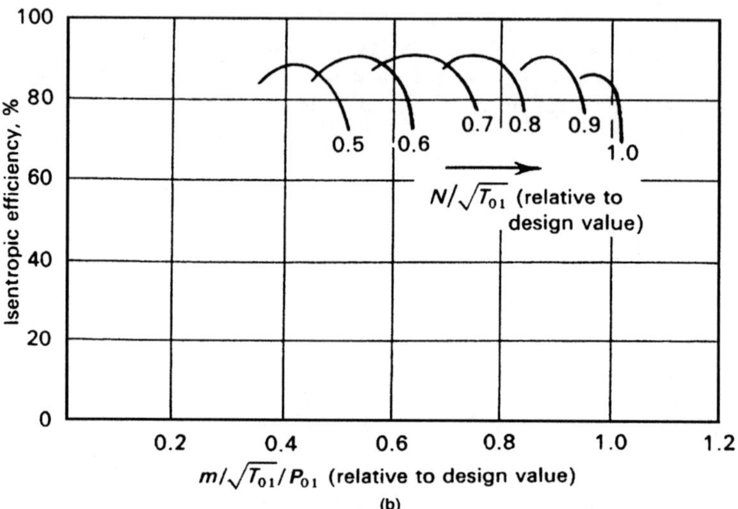

FIGURE 11.5 Axial-flow compressor characteristics. (*a*) Variation of pressure ratio in an axial flow compressor; (*b*) variation of isentropic efficiency in an axial flow compressor.

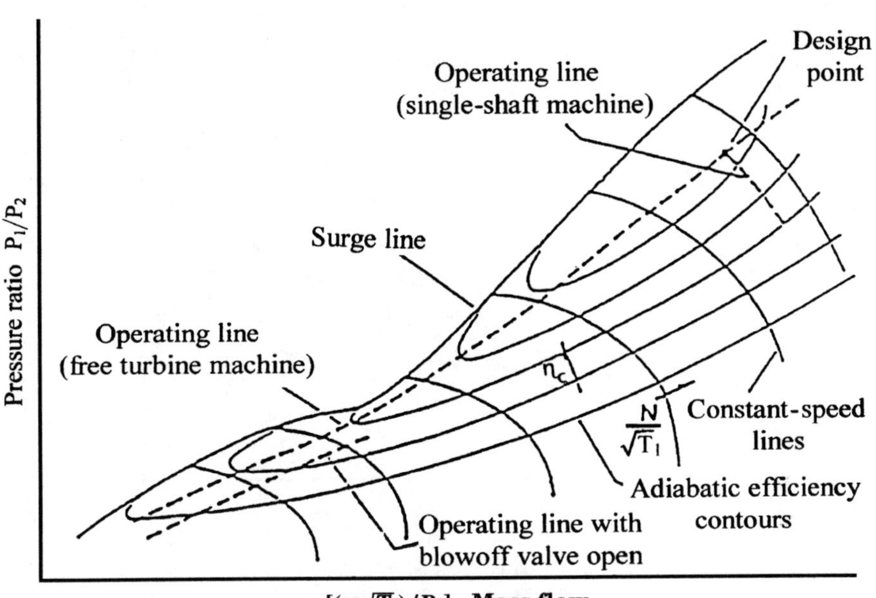

FIGURE 11.6 Typical gas turbine compressor characteristic. The basis of gas turbine design and engine governing requirements.

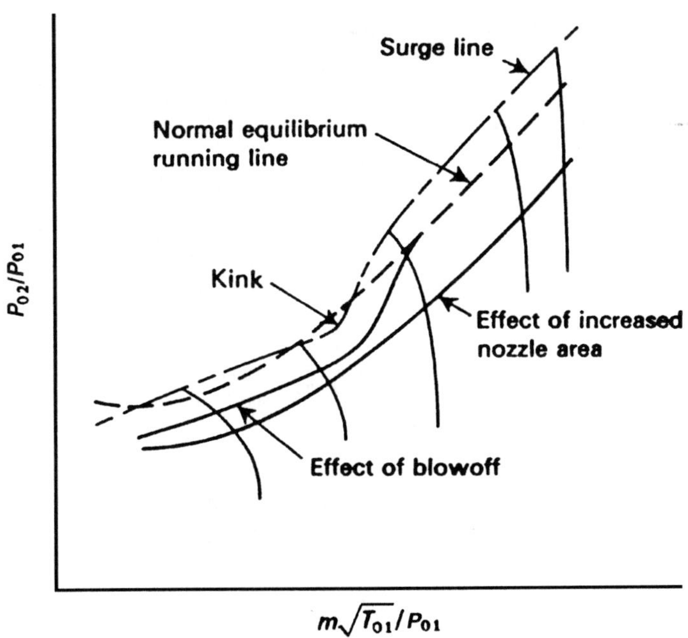

FIGURE 11.7 Effect of blow-off and increased nozzle area.

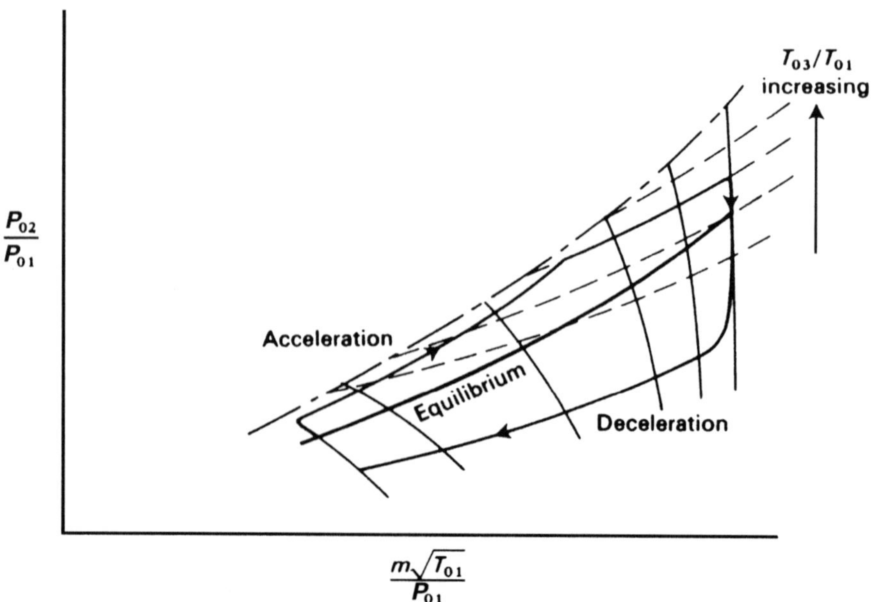

FIGURE 11.8 Transient trajectories on compressor characteristics (two-shaft machine). Acceleration moves the operating line toward surge. Deceleration moves the operating line away from surge.

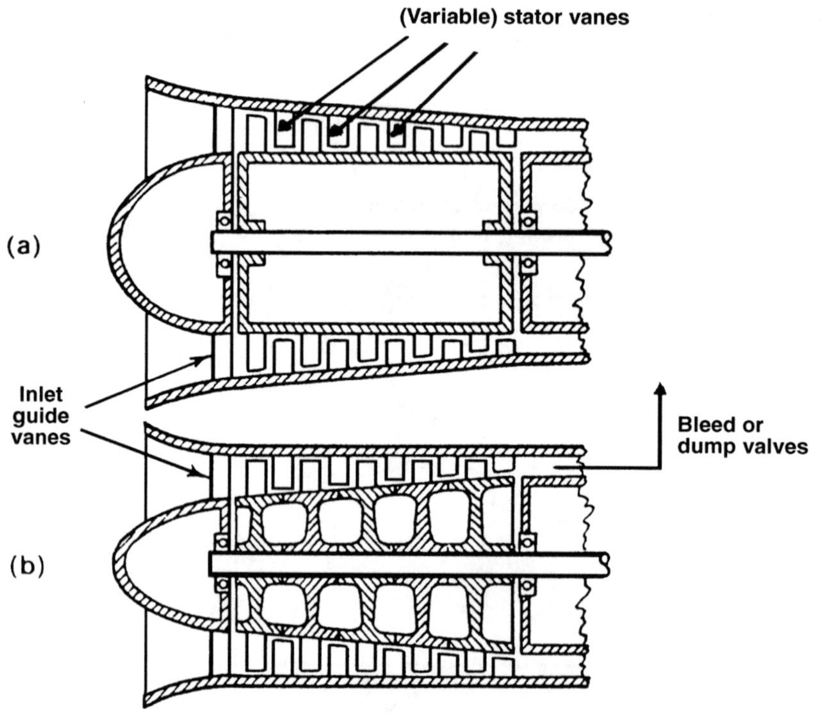

FIGURE 11.9 Axial-flow compressor construction. (*a*) Variable stator vanes; (*b*) bleed or dump valves.

inlet guide vanes (VIGVs), variable stator vanes (VSVs), or variable controlled bleed or dump valves (VBVs). All these devices avoid surge. They are illustrated in Fig. 11.9.

NOMENCLATURE

These are the most widely used symbols in this chapter.

m = mass flow
r = pressure ratio
η_c = isentropic efficiency
ρ = density
γ = ratio of specific heats
A = cross-sectional area
P = absolute pressure
N = speed of rotation
T = absolute temperature
V = flow velocity

Suffixes

0 = stagnation value
1, 2, 3, etc. = reference planes

CHAPTER 12
GAS TURBINE COMBUSTORS

The heat is added to the air flowing through the gas turbine in the combustors.[1] The air leaving the compressor enters the combustors. Its temperature increases while the pressure drops slightly across the combustors. Thus, combustors are direct-fired air heaters. The fuel is burned almost stoichiometrically with 25 to 35 percent of the air entering the combustors. The combustion products mix with the remaining air to arrive at a suitable temperature for the turbine. The three major types of combustors are tubular, tuboannular, and annular. All combustors, despite their design differences, have the following three zones:

1. Recirculation zone
2. Burning zone
3. Dilution zone

The fuel is evaporated and partially burned in the *recirculation zone.* The remainder of the fuel is burned completely in the *burning zone.* The dilution air is mixed with the hot gas in the *dilution zone.* If the combustion is not complete at the end of the burning zone, the addition of dilution air can chill the hot gas. This prevents complete combustion of the fuel. However, there is evidence that some combustion occurs in the dilution zone if the burning zone is run overrich.

The fuel-to-air ratio varies during transient conditions. It is high during the acceleration phase and low during the deceleration phase. Thus, the combustor should be able to operate over a wide range of mixtures. The combustor performance is measured by efficiency, pressure drop across the combustor, and evenness of the outlet temperature profile.

The combustor efficiency is a measure of combustion completeness. It affects the fuel consumption directly because the unburned fuel is wasted. The combustor efficiency is the ratio of the increase in gas enthalpy and the theoretical heat input of the fuel. It is given by

$$\eta_c = \frac{\Delta h_{\text{actual}}}{\Delta h_{\text{theoretical}}} = \frac{(\dot{m}_a + \dot{m}_f)\, h_3 - \dot{m}_a h_2}{\dot{m}_f (\text{LHV})}$$

where η_c = combustor efficiency
$\dot{m}_a$ = mass flow of gas
$\dot{m}_f$ = mass flow of fuel
h_3 = enthalpy of gas leaving the combustor
h_2 = enthalpy of gas entering the combustor
LHV = fuel heating value

The pressure drop across the combustor affects the fuel consumption and power output. It is normally around 2 to 8 percent of the static pressure. This pressure drop is equivalent to a decrease in compressor efficiency. It results in an increase in the fuel consumption and a lower power output from the machine.

The combustor outlet temperature profile must be uniform. Any nonuniformity in this temperature profile causes thermal stress on the turbine blades, which could lead to fracture.

It also results in a decrease of the efficiency and power output of the machine. Satisfactory operation of the combustor is achieved by having a self-sustaining flame and stable combustion over a wide range of fuel-to-air ratio to prevent loss of ignition during transient operation.

The temperature gradients, carbon deposits, and smoke should be minimized due to the following reasons:

- Temperature gradients cause warps and cracks in the liner.
- Carbon deposits increase the pressure loss and distort the flow patterns.
- Smoke is environmentally objectionable.

During the last half-century, the operating conditions of gas turbine combustors have changed significantly. Following is a summary of these changes:

- Combustion pressures have increased from 5 to 50 atmosphere (atm) (73.5 to 735 psi).
- Inlet air temperatures have increased from 572 to 1472°F (300 to 800°C).
- Combustor outlet temperatures have increased from 1620 to 3092°F (900 to 1700°C).

Despite these major changes in operating conditions, today's combustors operate at almost 100 percent combustion efficiency over their normal operating range and during idling conditions. They also provide a substantial reduction in pollutant emissions. In addition, the life expectancy of aeroderivative (aero) engine liners has increased from a few hundred hours to many tens of thousands of hours. Although many problems have been overcome, improvements are still required in the following areas:

- To further reduce pollutant emissions, ideas and technology are still needed.
- To accommodate the growing requirements of many industrial engines having multifuel capability.
- To deal with the problem of acoustic resonance. This problem occurs when combustion instabilities become coupled with combustor acoustics.

COMBUSTION TERMS

The following is a list of definitions of some of the terms used with combustors:

Reference velocity. The theoretical flow velocity of air through an area equal to the maximum cross section of the combustor casing. It is around 80 to 135 ft/s (24.5 to 41 m/s) in a straight-through-flow turbojet combustor.

Profile factor. This is the ratio of the maximum exit temperature and the average exit temperature.

Traverse number (temperature factor). (1) The maximum gas temperature minus the average gas temperature divided by the average temperature increase in a nozzle design. (2) The difference between the maximum and the average radial temperature. The traverse number should be between 0.05 and 0.15.

Stoichiometric proportions. The proportions of the reactants (fuel and oxygen) are such that there is exactly enough oxygen to complete the reaction (combustion of the fuel).

Equivalence ratio. The ratio of oxygen content at stoichiometric conditions and actual conditions:

$$\phi = \frac{\text{(Oxygen/fuel at stoichiometric conditions)}}{\text{(Oxygen/fuel at actual conditions)}}$$

Pressure drop. The pressure drop across the combustor is around 2 to 10 percent of the compressor outlet pressure. It reduces the efficiency of the unit by the same percentage.

COMBUSTION

Combustion is a chemical reaction between the fuel (carbon or hydrogen) and oxygen. Heat is released during this reaction. The combustion products are carbon dioxide and water. The combustion of natural gas is given by

$$\underset{\text{(methane + oxygen)}}{CH_4 + 4O} \rightarrow \underset{\text{(carbon dioxide + water + heat)}}{CO_2 + 2H_2O + \text{heat}}$$

Since the chemical composition of air is 21 percent oxygen and 79 percent nitrogen, there are four molecules of nitrogen for every molecule of oxygen in air. Thus, the complete combustion reaction of methane can be written as follows:

$$\underset{\text{(methane + air)}}{1CH_4 + 2(O_2 + 4N_2)} \rightarrow \underset{\text{(carbon dioxide + nitrogen + water + heat)}}{1CO_2 + 8N_2 + 2H_2O + \text{heat}}$$

Therefore, the combustion of 1 m^3 of methane requires 2 m^3 of oxygen and 8 m^3 of nitrogen. During the combustion of methane, another chemical reaction occurs, leading to the formation of nitric acid. It is written as follows:

$$2N + 5O + H_2O \rightarrow \underset{\substack{\text{nitric}\\ \text{oxide}}}{2NO} + 3O + H_2O \rightarrow \underset{\substack{\text{nitric}\\ \text{acid}}}{2HNO}$$

This reaction indicates that the formation of nitric acid can be reduced by controlling the formation of nitric oxide. Reducing the combustion temperature can achieve this goal. The combustion temperature is normally around 3400 to 3500°F (1870 to 1927°C). The volumetric concentration of nitric oxide in the combustion gas at this temperature is around 0.01 percent. This concentration will be substantially reduced if the combustion temperature is lowered. A reduction in the combustion temperature to 2800°F (1538°C) at the burner will reduce the volumetric concentration of nitric oxide to below 20 parts per million (ppm) (0.002 percent). This level is reached in some combustors by injecting a noncombustible gas (flue gas) around the burner to cool the combustion zone.

If the fuel contains sulfur (e.g., liquid fuels), sulfuric acid will be a by-product of the combustion. Its reaction can be written as follows:

$$H_2S + 4O \rightarrow \underset{\substack{\text{sulfuric}\\ \text{oxide}}}{SO_3} + H_2O \rightarrow \underset{\substack{\text{sulfuric}\\ \text{acid}}}{H_2SO_4}$$

The amount of sulfuric acid cannot be reduced during combustion. The formation of sulfuric acid can be eliminated by removing the sulfur from the fuel. There are two different sweetening processes to remove the sulfur from the fuel that will be burned.

As mentioned earlier, the ideal volumetric ratio of air to methane is 10:1. If the actual volumetric ratio is lower than 10:1, the combustion products will contain carbon monoxide. This reaction can be written as follows:

$$1CH_4 + 11/2\,(O_2 + 4N_2) \rightarrow 2H_2O + 1CO + 6N_2 + \text{heat}$$

The volumetric ratio of air to methane in gas turbines is maintained normally above 10:1. Thus, carbon monoxide is not a problem.

COMBUSTION CHAMBER DESIGN

The simplest combustor consists of a straight-walled duct connecting the compressor and turbine. This combustor is impractical due to the excessive pressure drop across it. The pressure drop from combustion is proportional to the square of the air velocity. Since the compressor air discharge velocity is around 558 ft/s (170 m/s), the pressure drop will be around one-third of the pressure increase developed by the compressor. This pressure loss can be reduced to an acceptable value by installing a diffuser. Even with a diffuser, the air velocity is still high to permit stable combustion. A low-velocity region is required to anchor the flame. This is accomplished by installing a baffle (Fig. 12.1). An eddy region forms behind the baffle. It draws the gases in to be burned completely. This steady circulation of the flow stabilizes the flame and provides continuous ignition.

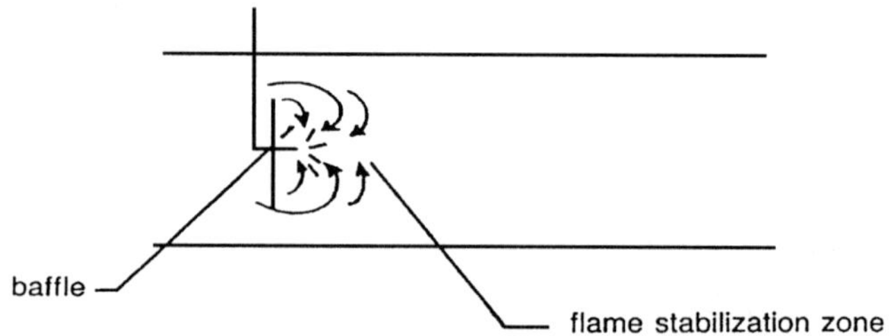

FIGURE 12.1 Baffle added to straight-walled duct to create a flame stabilization zone.

Other methods are used to stabilize the flame in the primary zone. Figures 12.2 and 12.3 illustrate two such designs. A strong vortex is created by swirl vanes around the fuel nozzle in the first design. The second design relies on formation of another flow pattern by admitting combustor air through rings of radial jets. The jet impingement at the combustor axis results in the formation of a torroidal recirculation zone that stabilizes the flame.

The air velocity has a significant effect on the stabilization of the flame. Figure 12.4 is a general stability diagram. It illustrates the decrease in the range of burnable mixtures as velocity increases. The size of the baffle also affects the limits of burnable mixtures and the pressure drop across the combustor. The flow velocity in the combustor is maintained well

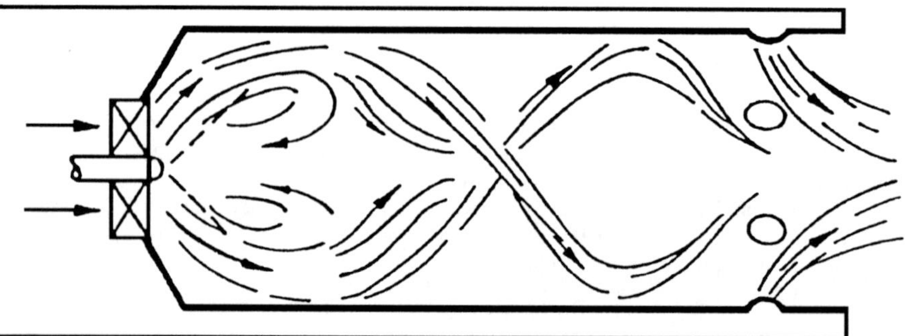

FIGURE 12.2 Flame stabilization region created by swirl vanes.

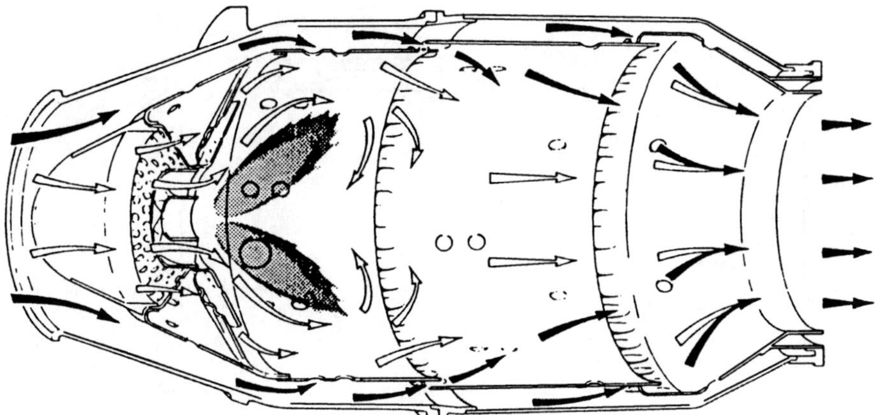

FIGURE 12.3 Flame stabilization created by impinging jets and general airflow pattern. (© *Rolls-Royce Limited.*)

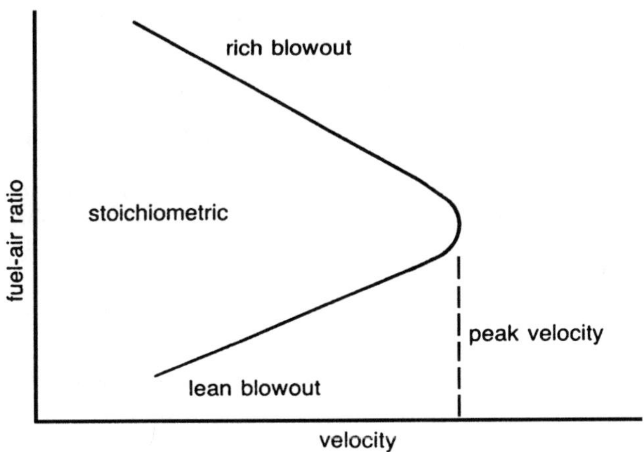

FIGURE 12.4 Range of burnable fuel-to-air ratios versus combustor gas velocity.

below the blowout limit to accommodate a wide operating range of fuel-to-air ratios. The air velocity does not normally vary with the load, because the compressor operates at a constant speed. In some applications, the mass flow varies with the load. In these applications, the static pressure varies in a similar fashion to the load. Thus, the volumetric flow rate remains almost constant.

The fuel-to-air ratio is around 1:60 in the primary zone of the combustor. The remaining air (known as *secondary,* or *dilution, air*) is added when the primary reaction is completed. The dilution air should be added gradually to prevent quenching of the reaction. This is accomplished by adding a flame tube (Fig. 12.5). The flame tubes are designed to produce a desirable outlet temperature profile. Their adequate life in the combustor environment is assured by film cooling of the liner.

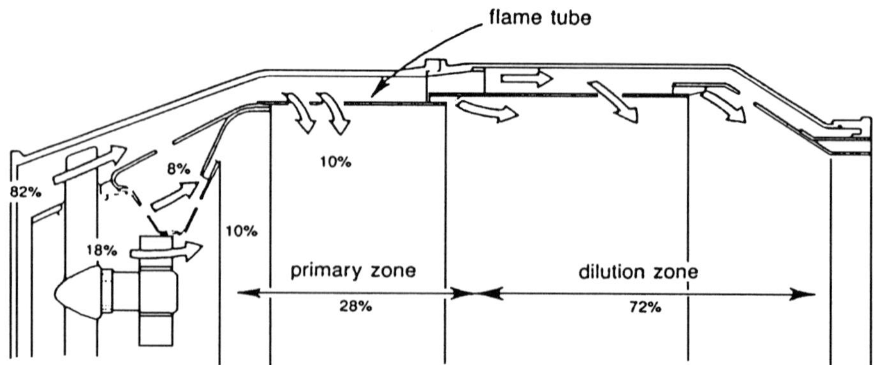

FIGURE 12.5 Addition of a flame tube distributes flow between the primary and dilution zones.

The air flowing in the annulus between the liner and the casing enters the space inside the liner through holes and slots. This air provides film cooling of the liner. The holes and slots are designed to divide the liner into distinct zones for flame stabilization, combustion, and dilution.

Flame Stabilization

Swirl vanes around the fuel nozzle generate a strong vortex flow in the combustion air within the combustor (Fig. 12.6). The flame is recirculated toward the fuel nozzle due to the creation of a low-pressure region at the combustor axis. Air flows to the center of the vortex through radial holes around the liner. This allows the flame to grow to some extent. The jet impingement along the combustor axis generates upstream flow, which forms a torroidal recirculation zone that stabilizes the flame.

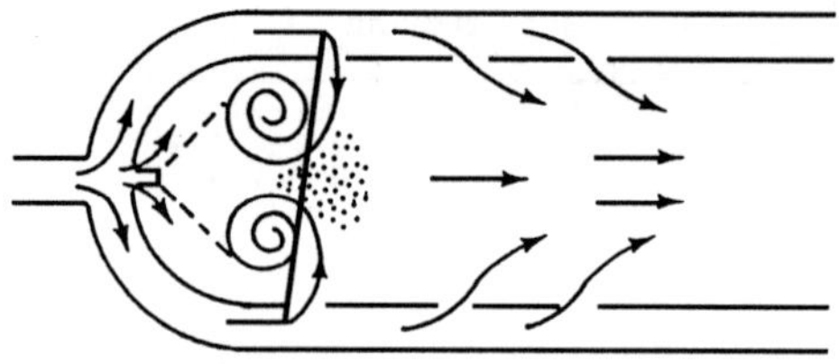

FIGURE 12.6 Flow pattern by swirl vanes and radial jets.

Combustion and Dilution

Combustors will not generate smoke when the equivalence ratio in the primary zone is below 1.5. Visible smoke is considered an air pollution problem. Following combustion, the rich burning mixture leaves the combustion zone and mixes with the air jets entering the liner, resulting in intensive turbulence throughout the combustor. Dilution air enters through holes in the liner and mixes with the combustion products to lower the temperature of the products. The mixture enters the turbine at a suitable temperature for the blade materials.

Film Cooling of the Liner

The liner is exposed to the highest temperature in the gas turbine due to combustion and heat radiated by the flame. The life of the liner is extended by using material having a high resistance to thermal stress and fatigue and by cooling the liner using an air film. This cooling is accomplished by admitting air through rows of small holes in the liner.

Fuel Atomization and Ignition

The liquid fuel used in gas turbines should be atomized in the form of a fine spray when it is injected into the combustors. Figure 12.7 illustrates a typical low-pressure fuel atomization nozzle.

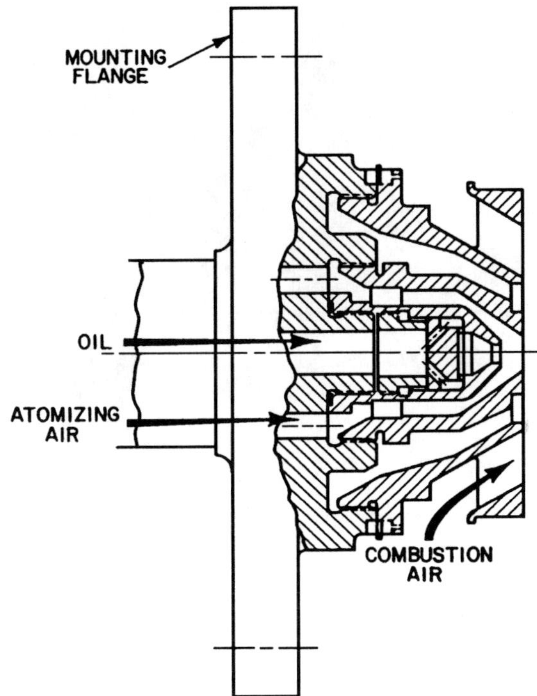

FIGURE 12.7 Air atomized liquid fuel nozzle. (*Courtesy of General Electric Company.*)

The flow rate in a pressure-atomizing fuel nozzle varies with the square root of the pressure. Some gas turbines require atomizers having a wide capacity range. This is accomplished using a *dual-orifice atomizer,* which has two swirl chambers. The first, known as the *pilot,* has a small orifice. The second is the *main swirl chamber.* It has a much larger orifice. When the flow is low, the fuel is supplied through the pilot orifice. This ensures good-quality atomization. When the flow increases, the fuel pressure increases as well. A valve opens at a predetermined pressure. The flow is now diverted through the main atomizer. This arrangement provides satisfactory atomization over a wide range of flows.

Interconnecting tubes connect all of the combustors together. When ignition is established in one combustor, the flame spreads to the remaining combustors immediately. Igniters are only installed in a few combustors. Figure 12.8 illustrates an igniter plug. It is a surface discharge plug. Thus, the energy does not jump over an air gap. A semiconductive material covers the end of the plug. It permits an electrical leakage to the body from the central high-tension electrode. This discharge provides a high-intensity flash from the electrode to the body.

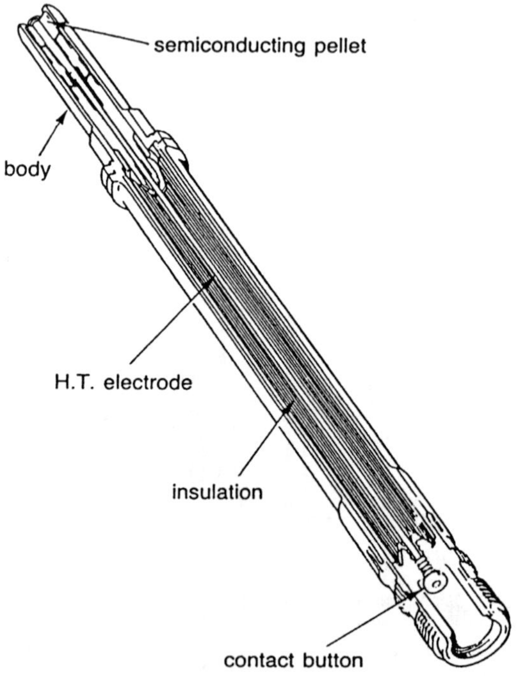

FIGURE 12.8 An igniter plug. (© *Rolls-Royce Limited.*)

Gas Injection

Few problems occur during combustion of gaseous fuels having a high heat content [British thermal unit (Btu)], such as natural gas. However, gaseous fuels having a low heat content may cause problems. The fuel flow rate could reach 20 percent of the total combustor mass flow. This will generate a significant mismatch between the flow in the compressor and the flow in the turbine. This problem will be more significant if the gas turbine was intended for a multifuel application. Low-heat-content gases also have a low burning rate. This may require larger combustors. An additional increase in the size of the combustors is needed to accommodate the large volumetric flow of fuel. Difficulties can also occur in achieving the correct mixing rate in the combustors. The gaseous fuel is normally injected through orifices, swirlers, or venturi nozzles.

Wall Cooling

The liner contains the combustion products. It also facilitates distribution of the correct amount of air to the various zones inside the combustor. The liner must have the mechanical strength to withstand the buckling force created by a difference in pressure across its wall. It must also be able to withstand the cyclical thermal stresses. These requirements are accomplished by the following:

- Making the liner of a high-temperature, oxidant-resistant material.
- Using the cooling air effectively. Most modern combustors use up to 40 percent of the total airflow for cooling the liner wall.

The temperature of the liner wall is determined by the following heat balance:

- Heat received by radiation and convection from the combustion of hot gases
- Heat removed from the liner by convection to the surrounding air and by radiation to the casing

It has become increasingly difficult to provide effective cooling for the liner wall. This stems from the increase in temperature of the inlet air entering the combustors. During the last 60 years, the pressure ratio in gas turbines has increased from 7 to 45, and the firing temperature has increased from 1500°F (815°C) to 2600°F (1427°C). This increase in temperature is mainly caused by an increase in compressor discharge pressure. There is a corresponding increase in temperature at the discharge of the compressor as a result of the increased pressure. The temperature in modern combustors is reaching higher values to increase the thermal efficiency in the gas turbine.

Wall Cooling Techniques

A louver cooling technique was used on many early gas turbines. The combustors were made in the form of cylindrical shells. They had a series of annular passages at the intersection points of the shells. A film of cooling air was injected through these passages along the hot side of the liner wall. It provided a thermal barrier from the hot gases. Simple wigglestrip louvers were used to control the heights of the annular gaps. This technique had major problems with controlling airflow.

Splash cooling devices were also used. They did not provide any problems with flow control. In this system, a row of small-diameter holes was drilled through the liner. The air entered the liner through the holes. A skirt acted as an impingement baffle for the flow. It deflected the cooling airflow along the liner wall. Both techniques (i.e., wigglestrip louvers and splash cooling) were used until annular combustors were introduced.

Angled-effusion cooling (AEC) is used on some modern combustors. Different patterns of small holes are drilled through the liner wall at a shallow angle to the surface. The cooling air enters the liner through the holes. It removes the heat from the liner and also provides a thermal barrier to the wall. This technique is among the best used in modern gas turbines. Combustors of the GE-90 use this technique. It reduced the air cooling requirement by 30 percent. Its main disadvantage is an increase in the weight of the liner by around 20 percent. This is mainly caused by the need for an increased thickness in the wall to meet the buckling stress.

Some large industrial gas turbines use refractory brick to shield the liner wall from heat. This technique is used on these engines because their size and weight are of minimal importance. However, most industrial and aero engines cannot use this technique due to the significant increase in weight. Some engines use metallic tiles for this application. For example, the Pratt & Whitney PW-4000 and the V-2500 use metallic tiles in their combustors. The tiles are capable of handling the thermal stresses. The liner handles the mechanical stresses. The tiles are usually cast from alloy materials used for the turbine blades. This material has a much higher temperature rating, at least 100°C higher than typical alloys used for combustor liners. Also, the liner can be made of relatively inexpensive alloys because it remains at a uniform low temperature. The main disadvantage of using tiles is the significant increase in weight.

Spraying a protective coating on the inner wall of the liner enhances the liner cooling. This coating acts as a thermal barrier. It can reduce the temperature of the liner wall by up to 100°C. These coatings are used on most modern combustors. The materials used for existing combustor liners are nickel- or cobalt-based alloys, such as Niminic 263 or Mastelloy X. Research is underway to develop new liner materials that can withstand the increasing requirements of modern combustors. Possibilities for future combustor material include carbon composites, ceramics, and alloys of high-temperature materials such as columbium. None of these materials are at the stage of development that would permit industrial application.

COMBUSTOR DESIGN CONSIDERATIONS

Cross-sectional area. The combustor cross section is obtained by dividing the volumetric flow by a reference velocity that has been selected for a particular turbine based on a proven performance in a similar unit.

Length. The combustor should have adequate length to provide flame stabilization, combustion, and mixing with dilution air. The length-to-diameter ratio for a typical liner is between 3 and 6. The length-to-diameter ratio for a casing is between 2 and 4.

Combustor material. The material selected for combustors normally has a high fatigue resistance (e.g., Nimonic 75, Nimonic 80, and Nimonic 90). Nimonic 75 is an alloy with 80 percent nickel and 20 percent chromium. Its stiffness is increased by adding a small amount of titanium carbide. It has excellent oxidation and corrosion resistance at high temperatures, adequate creep strength, and good fatigue resistance. It is also easy to press, draw, and mold.

AIR POLLUTION PROBLEMS

Smoke

Smoke is generated normally in fuel-rich combustors. It is normally eliminated by having a leaner primary zone. It is also eliminated by supplying a quantity of air to overrich zones inside the combustors.

Hydrocarbon and Carbon Monoxide

Incomplete combustion generates hydrocarbon (HC) and carbon monoxide (CO). This occurs normally during idle conditions. The idling efficiency of modern units has been improved by providing better atomization and higher local temperatures to eliminate HC and CO.

Oxides of Nitrogen

Combustion produces the main oxide of nitrogen NO (90 percent) and NO_2 (10 percent). These products are pollutants due to their poisonous characteristics, especially at full load. The concentration of nitrogen oxides increases with the firing temperature.

The concentration of nitrogen oxides can be reduced by one of the following three methods:

1. Minimizing the peak flame temperature by operating with a very lean primary zone
2. Injecting water or steam into the combustors to lower the firing temperature
3. Injecting an inert gas into the combustors to lower the firing temperature

The injection of steam or water into the combustors has proven to be an effective method in reducing NO_X emissions by 85 percent (from 300 to 25 ppm).

TYPICAL COMBUSTOR ARRANGEMENTS

The three major categories of combustors are

1. Tubular (single can)
2. Tuboannular
3. Annular

Most of the gas turbines manufactured in Europe use tubular or single-can combustors. These combustors have a simple design and a long life. They can be up to 10 ft (3 m) in diameter and 40 ft (12 m) high. These combustors use special tiles as liners. Damaged tiles can easily be replaced. Tubular combustors can be *straight-through* or *reverse-flow* designs. The air enters these combustors through the annulus between the combustor can and the hot gas pipe, as shown in Fig. 12.9. The air then flows between the liner and the hot

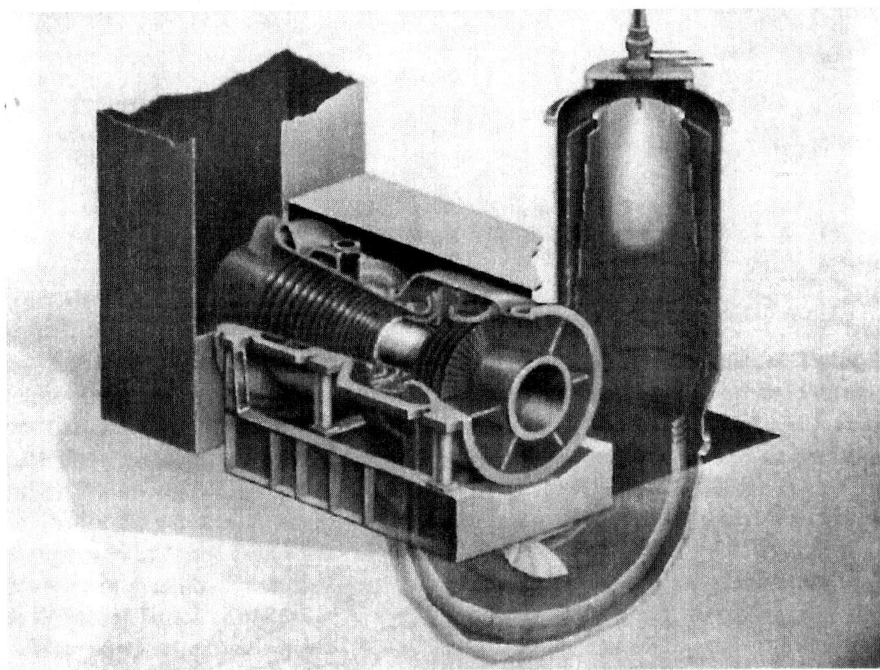

FIGURE 12.9 Single-can combustor. (*Courtesy of Brown Boveri Turbomachinery, Inc.*)

gas pipe and enters the combustion region through the various holes shown. Only 10 percent of the air enters the combustion zone. Around 30 to 40 percent of the air is used for cooling. The rest of the air is used for dilution purposes. Combustors having reverse-flow designs are much shorter than the ones having straight-through designs. These large combustors normally have a ring of nozzles placed in the primary zone area.

Tuboannular combustors are the most popular type of combustors used in gas turbines. Figure 12.10 illustrates the tuboannular or can-annular type of combustors. These combustors are easy to maintain. Their temperature distribution is better than side single-can combustors. They can be a straight-through or reverse-flow design. Most industrial gas turbines use the reverse-flow type.

Figure 12.11 illustrates the straight-through tuboannular combustors. These combustors are used in most aircraft engines. They require a much smaller frontal area than the reverse-flow-type tuboannular combustor. However, they require more cooling air than a single or annular combustor due to their large surface area. The amount of cooling air required can easily be provided in gas turbines using high-heat-content (high-Btu) gas. However, gas turbines using low-Btu gas require up to 35 percent of the total air in the primary zone. Thus, the amount of cooling air will be reduced.

Single-can and annular combustors are more attractive at higher firing temperatures due to their relatively smaller surface area. However, the tuboannular combustors have a more even flow distribution.

Figure 12.12 illustrates an annular combustor. This type of combustor is normally used in aircraft gas turbines. These combustors are usually of the straight-through design. The compressor casing radius is the same as the combustor casing. These combustors require less cooling air than the tuboannular combustors. Thus, they are growing in popularity in high-temperature applications. However, the maintenance of annular combustors is relatively more difficult, and their temperature and flow profiles are less favorable than tuboannular combustors. Annular combustors will become more popular in applications having higher firing temperatures and low-Btu gases.

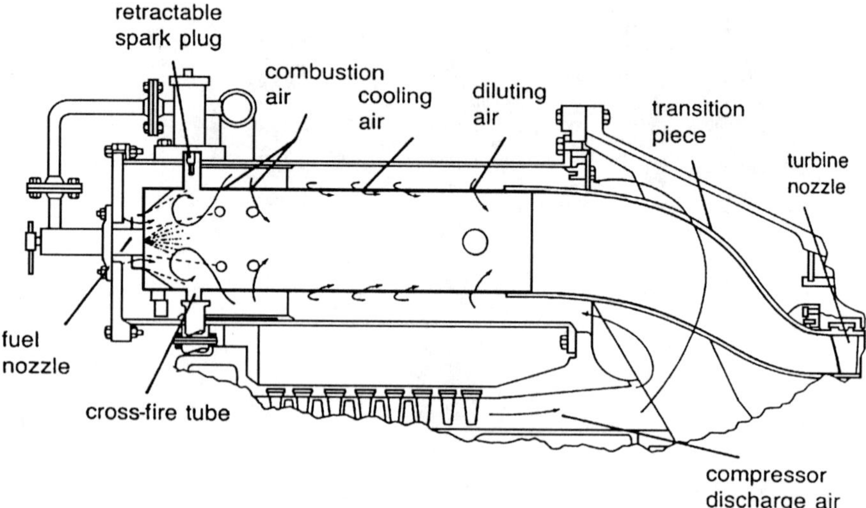

FIGURE 12.10 Can-annular, reverse-flow combustor for a heavy-duty gas turbine. (*Courtesy of General Electric Company.*)

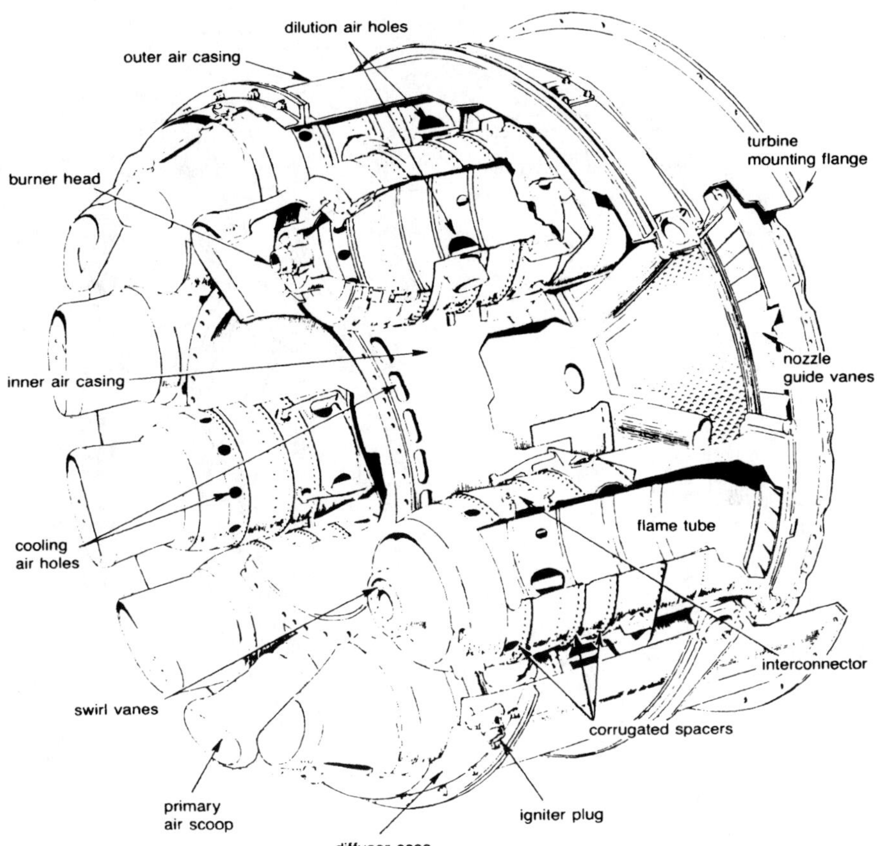

FIGURE 12.11 Straight-through flow-type can-annular combustors. (© *Rolls-Royce Limited.*)

COMBUSTORS FOR LOW EMISSIONS

There is a conflict among some of the combustor requirements. For example, the modification required to reduce the smoke and nitric oxides (NO and NO_2, termed NO_X) will increase the emissions from carbon monoxide (CO) and unburned hydrocarbon (UHC), and vice-versa. Throttling the airflow to the combustor can solve this problem. A device having a variable cross-sectional area is used to control the flow. Large quantities of air are admitted at high pressures, resulting in minimized formation of soot and nitric oxide. At low pressures, the cross-sectional area is reduced, leading to an increase in the fuel-to-air ratio and a reduction in the velocity of the flow. This change improves the ignition characteristics and increases the combustion efficiency, resulting in a reduction in the CO and UHC emissions. This technique of variable cross-sectional areas has been used on a few large industrial gas turbines. Its main disadvantage is the requirement of complex control systems that result in increasing the weight and cost and reducing reliability. This method has been ruled out for small gas turbines and aeronautical applications.

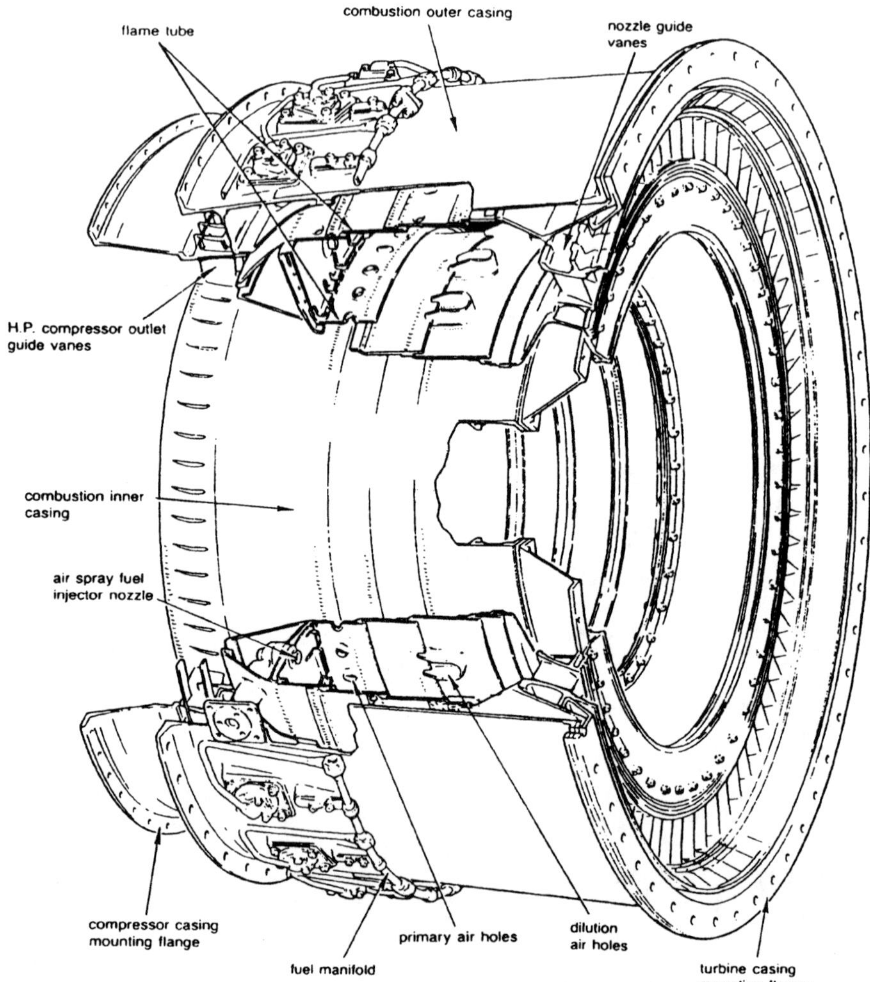

FIGURE 12.12 Aircraft-type annular combustion chamber. (© *Rolls-Royce Limited.*)

Staged combustion is an alternative solution for achieving all of the requirements of modern combustors. The staging could be *axial* or *radial.* In both cases, two separate zones are used. Each zone is designed specifically to improve certain features of the combustion process. Figure 12.13 illustrates the principle of axial staging. The primary zone (zone 1) is lightly loaded. It operates at a high equivalence ratio ϕ of around 0.8 ($\phi = 0.8$ indicates that the amount of air available is slightly more than needed for combustion). This is done to improve the combustion efficiency and minimize the production of CO and UHC. Zone 1 provides all of the power requirements up to operating speed. It acts as a pilot source of heat for zone 2 at higher power levels. Zone 2 is the main combustion zone. The air and fuel are premixed before entering zone 2. The equivalence ratio in both zones is maintained around 0.6 at full power. This is done to minimize the NO_X and smoke emissions.

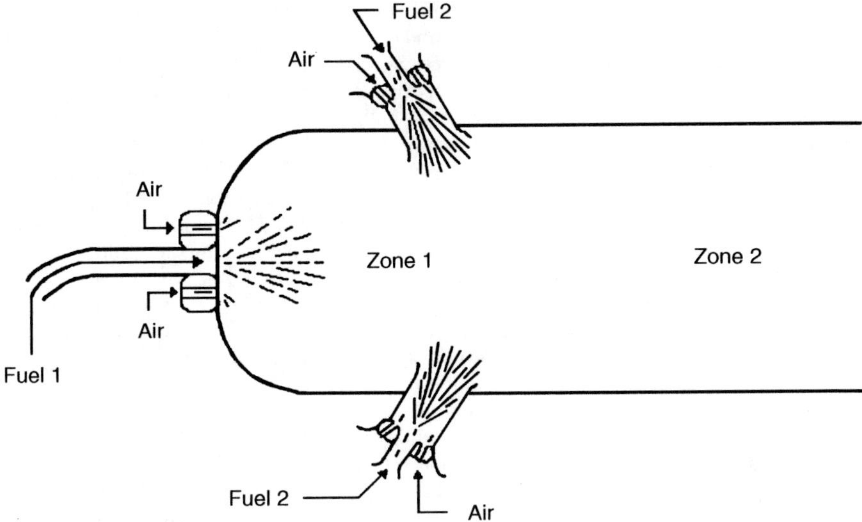

FIGURE 12.13 Principle of axial staging. Low power: $\phi_1 = 0.8$; $\phi_2 = 0.0$. High power: $\phi_1 = 0.6$; $\phi_2 = 0.6$.

Most modern gas turbines use staged combustion when burning gaseous fuels. This method is used to reduce the emission of pollutants without requiring steam or water injection. Some gas turbines use a *lean premix prevaporize* (LPP) *combustor* for liquid fuels. This technique seems to be the most promising for generating an ultralow level of NO_X. Figure 12.14 illustrates this concept. The objectives include:

- To evaporate all the fuel
- To mix the fuel and air thoroughly before combustion

The emissions of nitric oxide are drastically reduced for the following reasons:

- This technique avoids the burning of liquid droplets, resulting in a reduction in the flame temperature and elimination of the hot spots from the combustion zone (i.e., the concentration of nitric oxide drops with temperature).
- The combustion has a lean fuel-to-air ratio.

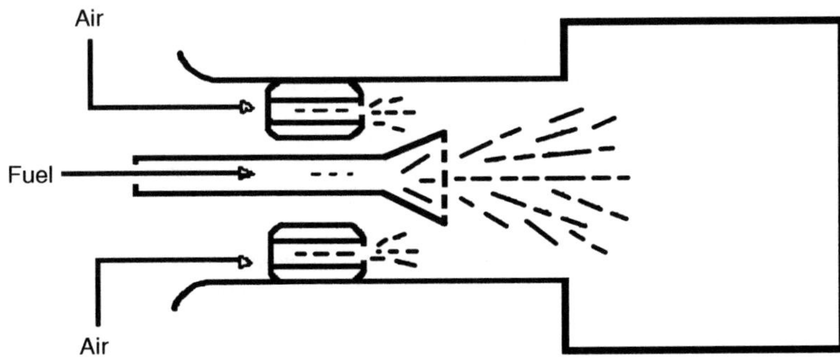

FIGURE 12.14 LPP.

The main disadvantage of the LPP system is the possibility of autoignition or flashback in the fuel preparation duct. This phenomenon could occur at the high pressures and inlet temperatures reached during full-power operation. It is caused by the long time needed to fully vaporize and mix the fuel at low power conditions. These problems can be solved by using staged combustors and/or variable cross-sectional areas to throttle the inlet air. Other concerns with the LPP systems are in the areas of durability, maintainability, and safety.

The *rich-burn/quick-quench/lean-burn* (RQL) *combustor* is another alternative for achieving ultralow NO_X emissions. This design has a fuel-rich primary zone. The NO_X formation rate in this zone is low due to the low temperature combustion and oxygen depletion. Additional air is injected downstream of the primary zone. It is mixed rapidly with the efflux from the primary zone. If the mixing process were slow, pockets of hot gas would last for a sufficient period to generate significant amounts of NO_X. Thus, the effectiveness of the quick-quench mixing section is essential for the success of the RQL combustors.

The catalytic combustor appears to be the most promising device for low NO_X emissions. It involves prevaporizing the fuel and premixing it with air at a very low equivalence ratio (i.e., the amount of air is much more than needed to participate in combustion). The homogeneous mixture of air and fuel is then passed through a catalytic reactor bed. The catalyst allows the combustion to occur at a very low concentration of fuel. The concentration of fuel is lower than the lean flammability limit. Thus, the reaction temperature is extremely low. Therefore, the resulting NO_X concentration is minimal. Most modern gas turbines have a thermal reaction zone downstream of the catalytic bed. The functions of the thermal reaction zone are as follows:

- To increase the gas temperature (the thermal efficiency increases with temperature)
- To reduce the concentration of CO and UHC

The capability of catalytic reactors for producing a very low emission level of pollutants has been known for more than 30 years. However, the harsh environment in combustors limited the development of this option in gas turbines. The durability and lifetime of the catalyst were always a problem. Considerable research is underway on catalysts. However, it is unlikely that it will be applied to aero engines in the near future. Considerable experience on stationary gas turbines is required before implementing this feature in aero engines. It is expected that it will be in the form of a radially staged, dual-annular combustor (Fig. 12.15) when it will be implemented. The outer combustor is used for easy ignition and low emissions when the engine is idling. At higher power levels, the mixture of air and fuel is supplied to the inner combustor. The catalytic reactor is embedded inside the inner combustor. This is the reactor that provides most of the temperature increase during full-load operation.

COMBUSTORS FOR SMALL ENGINES (LESS THAN 3 MW)

High shaft speeds of small gas turbines require close coupling of the compressor and turbine. This is necessary to reduce the problems with shaft whirling. This requirement has led to the development of annular reverse-flow or annular radial-axial combustors. This design is used almost universally in small engines. The Allison T63 engine is an exception. It has a single tubular combustor installed at the end of the engine to facilitate inspection and maintenance. Figure 12.16 illustrates an annular reverse-flow combustor. The main advantages are as follows:

- The combustion volume is used efficiently.
- The fuel injectors are accessible.

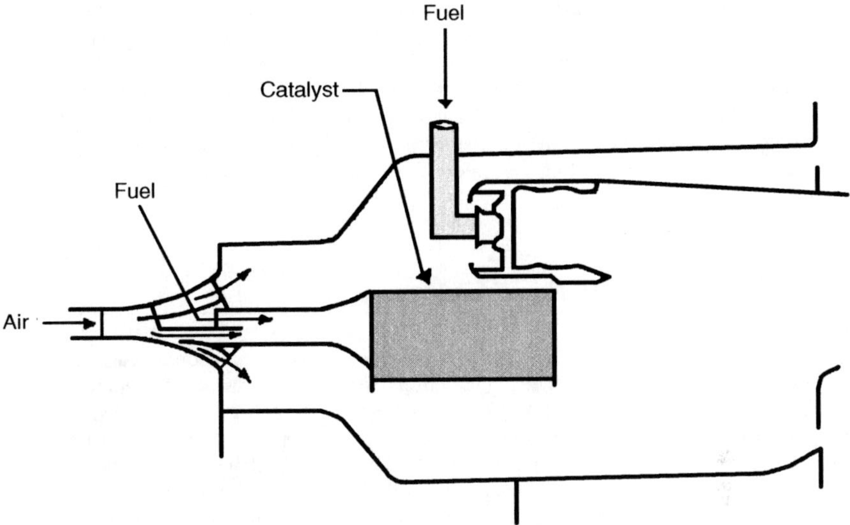

FIGURE 12.15 Combination of catalytic and conventional staged combustors.

These advantages are in addition to the significant reduction in shaft length. Small combustors have problems in ignition, wall cooling, and fuel injection. The size and weight of the ignition equipment is relatively large. However, they cannot be reduced, because this will lead to a reduction in reliability. Difficulties have been experienced in providing adequate cooling for the liner wall of small annular combustors. These stem from the relatively large surface area that must be cooled. The problem is compounded by the low velocities in the annulus. These are associated with centrifugal compressors (small gas turbines use centrifugal rather than axial-flow compressors because small axial-flow compressors drop in efficiency, but centrifugal compressors maintain their efficiency for small sizes). This results in poor convective cooling of the external surface of the liner. Angled effusion cooling appears to be the most suited for this application.

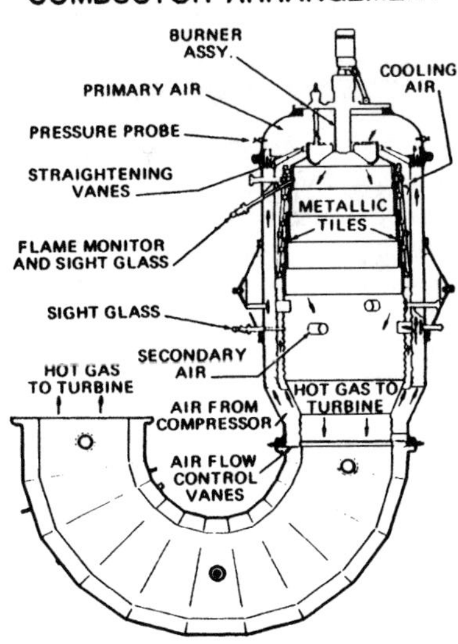

FIGURE 12.16 A typical single-can side reverse-flow combustor for an industrial turbine. *(Courtesy Brown Boveri Turbomachinery, Inc.)*

The fuel injection methods for small, straight-through annular chambers have not been completely satisfactory yet. The problem is caused by the need to use a large number of fuel injectors. This is necessary to meet the requirements of high combustion efficiency, low emissions, and good pattern factor. However, the size of the fuel injector decreases as the number of injectors increases. Industrial experience proved that small passages and orifices (<0.5 mm) are prone to erosion and blockage. Thus, the minimum size of the atomizer is limited.

Solar developed an airblast atomizer for their small annular combustors. The atomizer is installed on the outer liner wall. It injects fuel tangentially across the combustion zone. A small number of injectors is needed for each combustor. This design is known for providing good atomization even at start-up. The trend in the development of gas turbines is for higher pressure in the combustors and turbine inlet temperature. Research is underway in the areas of wall cooling, fuel preparation and distribution, miniaturized ignition devices, and high-temperature materials including ceramics. This will address the special requirements of small annular combustors.

INDUSTRIAL CHAMBERS

The most important criteria for industrial engines are reliable and economical operation for long periods of time without requiring attention. Compactness is not a consideration in this case. Thus, these engines must provide fuel economy, low pollutant emissions, and capital cost. Ease of maintenance and maximization of capacity factor (percent of time the unit is operating at full power) will play a major role in determining the market share of a specific engine.

To meet these objectives, industrial engine combustors are normally larger than the ones in aeronautical engines. Thus, the residence time inside the combustors is longer. This is an advantage when the fuel quality is poor. Also, the pressure drop across the combustors is smaller due to a lower velocity of the flow. The two categories of industrial engines are the following:

1. *Heavyframe machines.* They are designed to burn gaseous fuels, heavy distillates, and residual oils. They do not follow aeronautical practice.
2. *Industrialized aero engines.* They normally burn gaseous and/or light to medium distillate fuels. They follow aircraft practice closely.

The GE MS-7001, 80-MW gas turbines are one of the most successful industrial engines. There are 10 sets of combustion hardware in each machine. Each set includes a casing, an end cover, a set of fuel nozzles, a flow sleeve, a combustion liner, and a transition piece, as shown in Fig. 12.17. The flow sleeve has a cylindrical shape. It surrounds the liner and aids in distributing the air uniformly to all liners. Each combustor has one fuel nozzle in the conventional MS-7001. Multiple fuel nozzles are used for each combustor in the more advanced DLE versions. Some industrial engines have a single large combustor. It is installed outside the engine, as illustrated in Fig. 12.18. This design allows the combustor to meet the requirements of good combustion performance. The outer casing of the unit can be designed to withstand the high pressure. This arrangement has another advantage. It is the ease of inspection, maintenance, and repair. They can all be performed without removing the large components in the casing. The two types of liners are as follows:

1. *An all-metal liner having fins.* It is cooled by a combination of convection and film cooling.
2. *A tube of nonalloy carbon steel.* It has a refractory brick lining. This design requires less cooling air than the all-metal type.

It is preferable to use multiple fuel injectors (burners) for these combustors for the following two reasons:

1. They provide a shorter flame
2. The gases flowing into the dilution zone will have a more uniform temperature distribution.

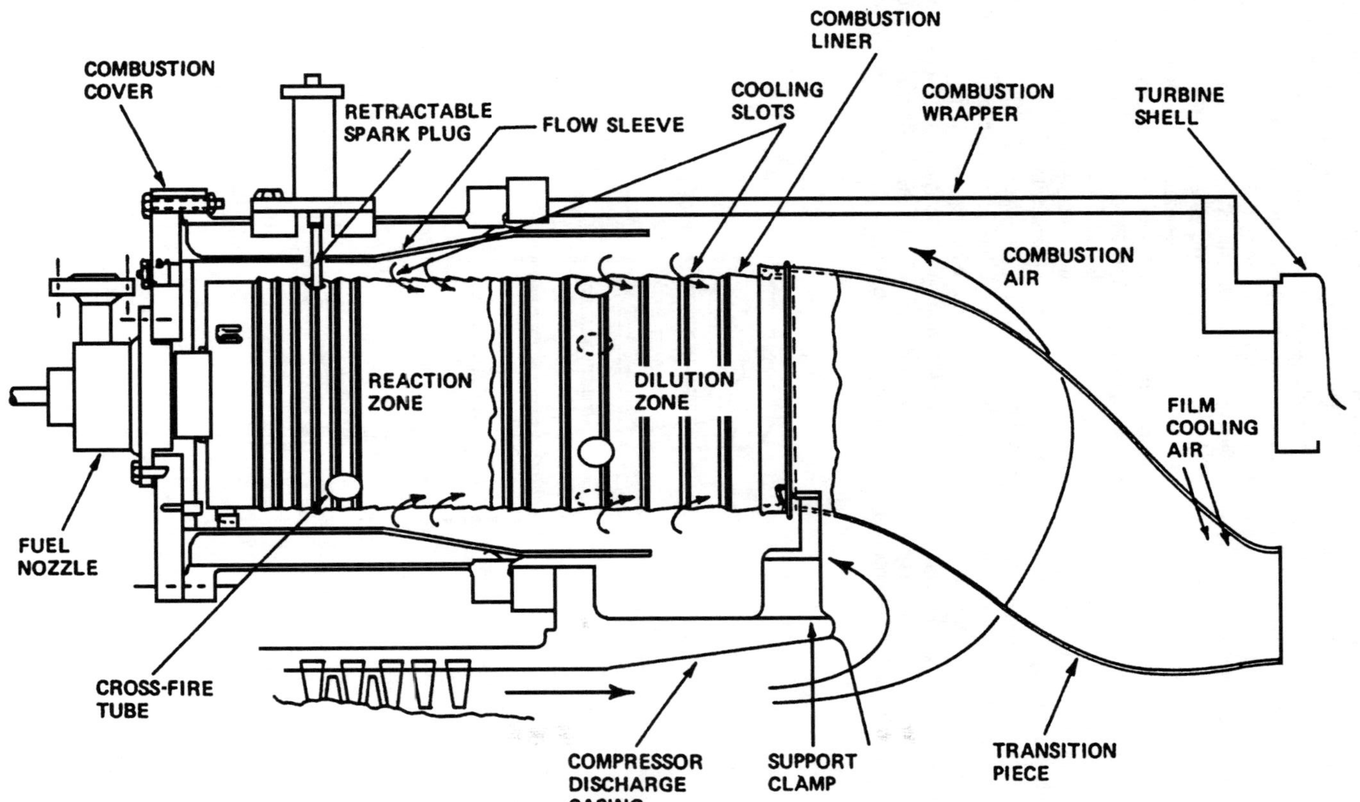

FIGURE 12.17 MS7001 combustion system. (*Courtesy of General Electric Company.*)

A number of "hybrid" burners are installed on the Siemens Silo combustors. They burn natural gas in either diffusion or premix modes. They emit a low level of pollutants over a wide range of loads. At low loads, the system operates as a diffusion burner. At high loads, it operates as a premix burner. Siemens used the same fuel burner in their silo-type combustors for engines having different power ratings. They only changed the number of burners to accommodate the changes in the size of the engine. However, the number of burners in their new annular combustors was fixed at 24. This was done to provide good pattern factor. The main disadvantage of this design is that the size of the burners must vary with the rating of the machine. However, the basic design remained the same. The Siemens hybrid burner has been proven to provide low emissions for engines in the 150-MW rating. This design has also been used by MAN GHH to its THM-1304 engine, which is a 9-MW gas turbine. It has two tubular combustion chambers. They are mounted on top of the casing.

ABB has developed a conical premix burner called the *EV burner.* It burns gas and liquid fuels satisfactorily and has been proven to provide low NO_X emissions in different applications. The ABB GT11N gas turbine has a silo combustor. It has 37 of these burners. They all operate in a premix mode. Fuel is supplied to some of these burners only during part-load operation. The annular combustors use the same technology. The ABB GT10 (23 MW) combustor has 18 EV burners in a single row. The ABB GT13E2 is a heavy-duty gas turbine (>150 MW). It has 72 EV burners. They are arranged in two staggered circumferential rows.

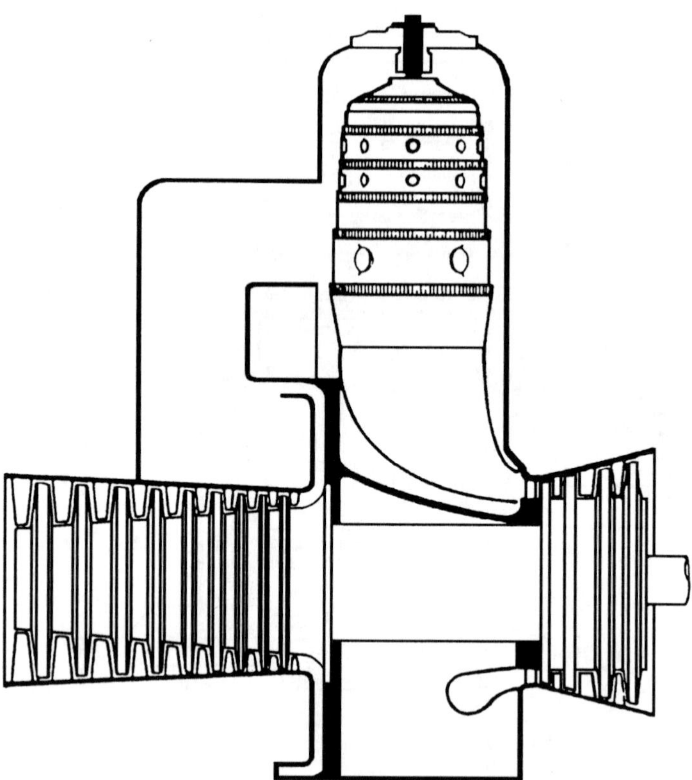

FIGURE 12.18 Industrial engine featuring single tubular combustor.

AERODERIVATIVE ENGINES

The modifications of aero engines to suit industrial and marine applications have been used for more than 30 years. For example, the Allison 501 engine is basically their T56 aero engine. It has been modified to burn DF2 fuel instead of kerosene (aviation fuel). The initial design of this engine had six tubular (can) combustors. However, the modern 501-K series of engines has a can-annular configuration. It has six tubular cans. They are located within an annular casing. The combustor version for dry low emission (DLE) burns natural gas using a dual-mode technique. It meets its emission goals without using water or steam injection. Many other companies used the same method to convert aero engines to industrial and transport applications. For example, Rolls-Royce developed industrial versions of their Avon, Tyne, and Spey aero engines. The fuel injectors were changed sometimes to handle multi-fuels. They were also modified to allow the injection of water or steam to reduce NO_X. The primary-zone pattern of airflow was modified to add more air. This was done for two reasons:

1. To take advantage of the absence of the requirement to relight at high altitude
2. To reduce the formation of soot and smoke

These simple modifications to an aero combustor will not be adequate in the future, mainly because emission regulations are becoming stricter. More sophisticated techniques will be required. Modern industrial DLE combustors achieve their emissions targets by using fuel staging and fuel-air premixing. The aero GE LM-6000 and RR-211 DLE industrial engines both use staged-combustion gaseous mixtures of fuel and air. These two engines were derived from successful high-performance aero engines. Their existing aero combustors were replaced by DLE combustors having the same length. Figure 12.19 illustrates the RB-211. The Trent is one of the most recent aero industrial engines manufactured by Rolls-Royce (Fig. 12.20). It uses three separate stages of premixed fuel-air injection.

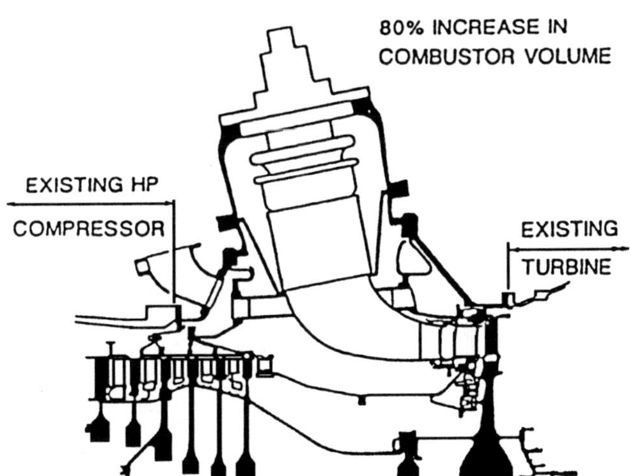

FIGURE 12.19 Industrial RB-211 DLE combustor. (*Courtesy of Rolls-Royce Limited.*)

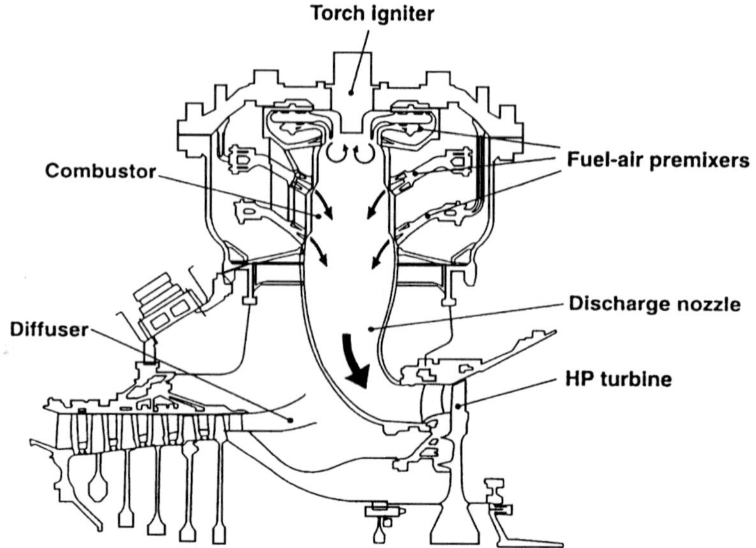

FIGURE 12.20 Industrial Trent DLE combustor. (*Courtesy of Rolls-Royce Limited.*)

REFERENCE

Boyce, M. P., *Gas Turbine Engineering Handbook,* Gulf Publishing Company, Houston, Tex., ©1982, reprinted July 1995.

CHAPTER 13
AXIAL-FLOW TURBINES

Axial-flow turbines are used in most applications involving compressible fluids.[1] They power most gas turbines except the smaller ones. Their efficiency is higher than radial-inflow turbines in most operating ranges. Axial-flow turbines are also used in steam turbine applications. However, there are significant differences between the design of axial-flow turbines used in gas turbines and those used in steam turbine applications.

There are *impulse* and *reaction-type* steam turbines. Most reaction-type steam turbines have a 50 percent reaction level. This design has proven to be very efficient. The reaction level varies considerably in the blades of gas turbines. Axial-flow turbines used today have a high work factor (ratio of stage work to square of blade speed). This is done to achieve lower fuel consumption and to reduce noise from the turbine.

TURBINE GEOMETRY

The important state points used to analyze the flow within a turbine are indicated at the following locations in Fig. 13.1:

0—The nozzle entrance

1—The rotor entrance

2—The rotor exit

The fluid velocity is an important parameter for analyzing the flow and energy transfer within a turbine. The fluid velocity relative to a stationary point is called the *absolute velocity,* **V.** This is an important term for analyzing the flow across a stationary blade such as a nozzle.* In turbine applications, the stationary blades of the turbine are called *nozzles.*

The relative velocity, **W,** is used when analyzing the flow across a rotating element such as a rotor blade. It is defined as:

$$\mathbf{W} = \mathbf{V} - \mathbf{U} \tag{13.1}$$

where **U** is the tangential velocity of the blade. Figure 13.2 illustrates this relationship. Subscripts z and o denote the axial and tangential component of velocity, respectively.

*A nozzle is defined as a channel of decreasing cross-sectional area.

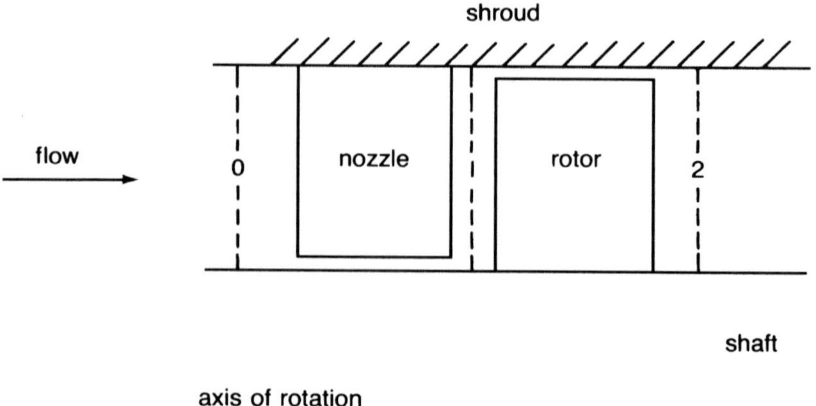

FIGURE 13.1 Axial turbine flow.

Degree of Reaction

The *degree of reaction* in an axial flow turbine having a constant axial velocity and a rotor with a constant radius is given by:

$$R = \frac{(W_4^2 - W_3^2)}{(V_3^2 - V_4^2) + (W_4^2 - W_3^2)} \tag{13.2}$$

For an impulse turbine (zero reaction), the relative exit velocity W_4, must be equal to the relative inlet velocity W_3. The degree of reaction of most turbines is between 0 and 1. Negative reaction turbines are not normally used due to their lower efficiencies.

Utilization Factor

The turbine cannot convert all of the energy supplied into useful work. There is some energy discharged due to the exit velocity. The *utilization factor* is defined as the ratio of ideal work to the energy supplied. For a turbine having a single rotor with constant radius, the utilization factor is given by:

$$E = \frac{(V_3^2 - V_4^2) + (W_4^2 - W_3^2)}{V_3^2 + (W_4^2 - W_3^2)} \tag{13.3}$$

Work Factor

The *work factor* is used to determine the blade loading. It is given by the following expression for a turbine having a constant radius:

$$\Gamma = \frac{V_{\phi 3} - V_{\phi 4}}{U} \tag{13.4}$$

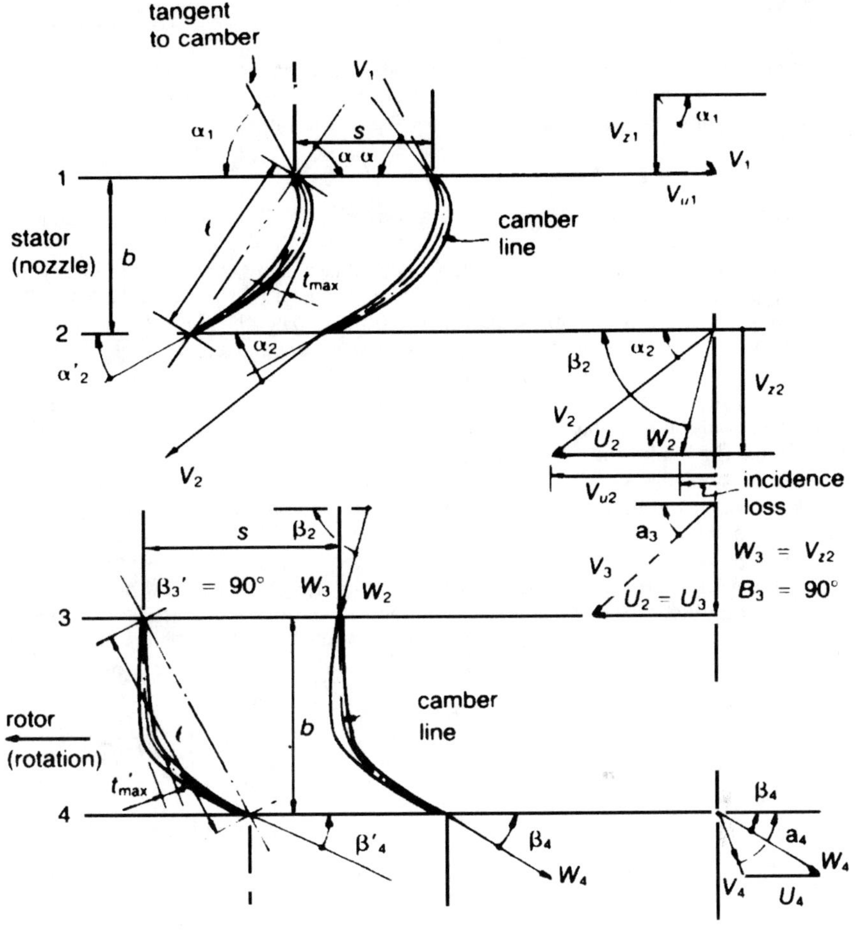

Stator: incidence $t_s = \alpha_1 - \alpha_1'$ $t_s > 0$ when $\alpha_1 > \alpha_1'$
deviation $\sigma_s = \alpha_2' - \alpha_2$
deflection $t_s = \alpha_1 + \alpha_2$ camber $\theta_s = \alpha_1' + \alpha_2'$
Rotor: incidence $t_r = \beta_2 - \beta_3'$ $t_r > 0$ when $\beta_2 > \beta_3'$
deviation $\sigma_r = \beta_4' - \beta_4$
deflection $t_r = \beta_2 - \beta_4$ camber $\theta_r = \beta_3' + \beta_4'$

FIGURE 13.2 Stage nomenclature and velocity triangles.

For an impulse turbine (zero reaction) with a maximum utilization factor, the value of the work factor is 2. The value of the work factor for a 50 percent reaction turbine with a maximum utilization factor is 1.

Modern turbines have a high work factor. This indicates that the blade loading of the turbine is high. The efficiency of the turbine tends to decrease as the work factor increases.

IMPULSE TURBINE

The impulse turbine has the simplest design. The gas is expanded in the nozzles (stationary blades). The high thermal energy (high temperature and pressure) is converted into kinetic energy. This conversion is given by the following relationship:

$$V_3 = \sqrt{2\Delta h_0} \tag{13.5}$$

where V_3 is the absolute velocity of the gas entering the rotor and Δh_0 is the change of enthalpy across the nozzles.

The high-velocity gas impinges on the rotating blades. Most of the kinetic energy in the gas stream will be converted to turbine shaft work. Figure 13.3 illustrates the velocity and pressure distribution in a single-stage impulse turbine. The absolute velocity of the gas increases in the nozzle due to the decrease in static pressure and temperature. The absolute velocity is then decreased across the rotating blades. However, the static pressure and the relative velocity remain constant. The maximum energy is transferred to the blades when they rotate at around one-half the velocity of the gas jet. Most turbines have two or more rows of moving blades for each nozzle. This is done to obtain low stresses and low speed at the tip of the blades. Guide vanes are installed in between the rows of the moving blades to redirect the gas from one row of moving blades to another (see Fig. 13.4). This type of turbine is known as the *Curtis* turbine.

The *pressure compound* or *Ratteau turbine* is another type of impulse turbine. In this design, the work is broken down into stages. Each stage consists of a row of nozzles and a row of moving blades. The kinetic energy in the jet leaving the nozzles is converted into useful work in the turbine rotor. The gas leaving the moving blades enters the nozzles of the next stage where the enthalpy decreases further and the velocity increases. The kinetic

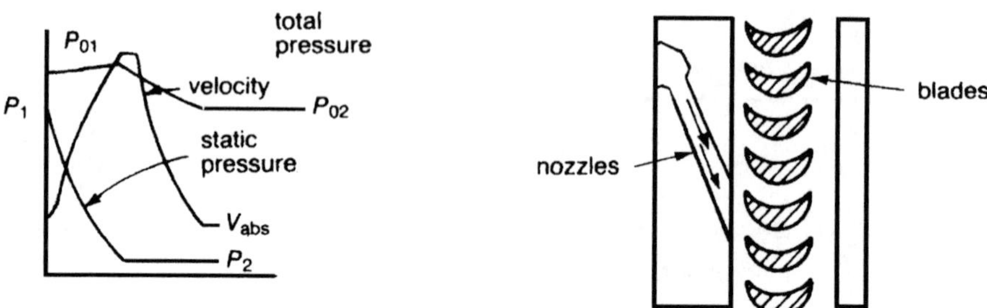

FIGURE 13.3 View of a single-stage impulse turbine with velocity and pressure distribution.

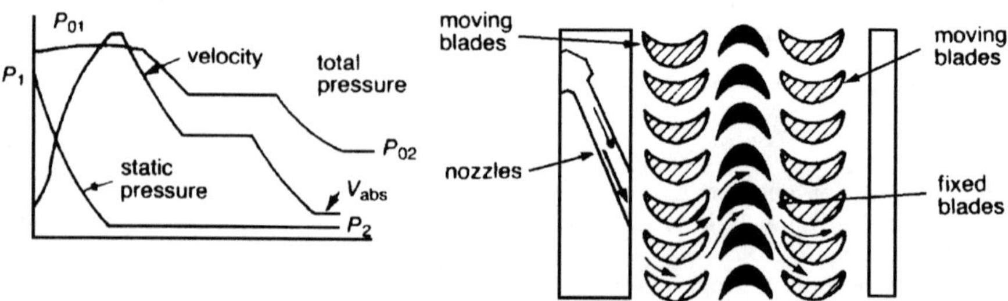

FIGURE 13.4 Pressure and velocity distributions in a Curtis-type impulse turbine.

energy of the gas leaving the nozzles of this stage is converted by the associated row of moving blades. Figure 13.5 illustrates a Ratteau turbine.

The degree of reaction in an impulse turbine is equal to zero. This indicates that the entire enthalpy drop of a stage is taken across the nozzles, and the velocity leaving the nozzles is very high. Since there is no change of enthalpy across the moving blades, the relative velocity entering them equals the relative velocity at the exit.

THE REACTION TURBINE

The axial-flow reaction turbine is the most common one throughout industry. The nozzles and moving blades of this turbine act as expanding nozzles. Therefore, the enthalpy (pressure and temperature) decreases in both the fixed and moving blades. The nozzles direct the flow to the moving blades at a slightly higher velocity than the moving blades. The velocities in a reaction turbine are normally much lower than the impulse turbine, and the relative velocities entering the blades are almost axial. Figure 13.6 illustrates a view of a reaction turbine.

Reaction turbines usually have a higher efficiency than impulse turbines. However, the amount of work generated by impulse turbines is higher than reaction turbines. Therefore, most modern multistage turbines have the impulse design in the first few stages to maximize the pressure drop while the remaining stages are 50 percent reaction. This combination has proven to be an excellent compromise.

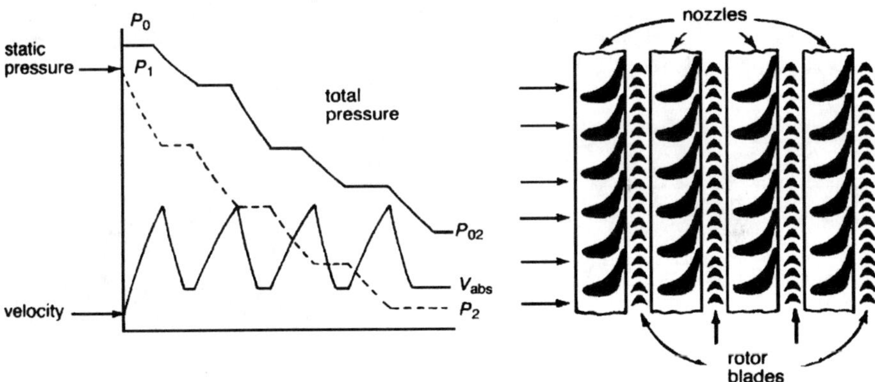

FIGURE 13.5 Pressure and velocity distributions in a Ratteau-type impulse turbine.

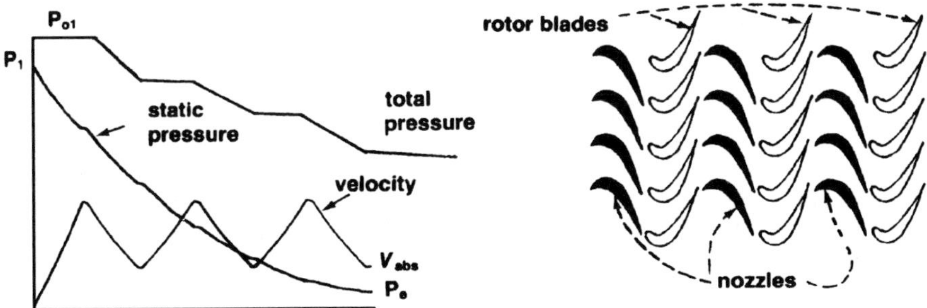

FIGURE 13.6 Velocity and pressure distribution in a three-stage reaction turbine.

TURBINE BLADE COOLING METHODS

During the last few decades, the turbine inlet temperatures of gas turbines have increased from 1500°F (815°C) to around 2500°F (1371°C). This trend will continue due to the increase in specific power and efficiency associated with the increase in turbine inlet temperature. This increase in temperature has been made possible by advancements in metallurgy and the use of advanced cooling techniques for the turbine blades. The cooling air is taken from the compressor discharge and directed to the rotor, stator, and other parts of the machine to provide adequate cooling. Figure 13.7 illustrates the five basic methods used for cooling in gas turbines:

1. Convection cooling
2. Impingement cooling
3. Film cooling
4. Transpiration cooling
5. Water cooling

Convection Cooling

Convection cooling is achieved by having the flow of cooling air inside the turbine blade to remove heat across the wall. The airflow is normally radial. It makes multiple passes through a serpentine channel from the hub to the tip of the blade. Convection cooling is the most common technique used in gas turbines.

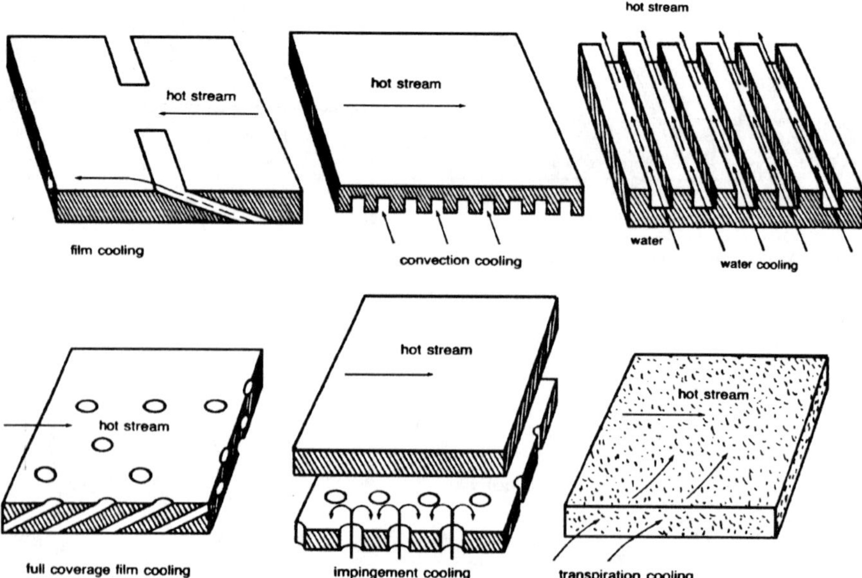

FIGURE 13.7 Various suggested cooling schemes.

Impingement Cooling

Impingement cooling is a form of convection cooling where the cooling air is blasted on the inner surface of the airfoil by high-velocity air jets. This increases the heat transfer from the metal surface to the cooling air. This technique can be limited to desired sections of the airfoil to maintain even temperatures over the entire surface. For example, the leading edge of the blade requires more cooling than the midchord section or trailing edge. Thus, the cooling air is impinged at the leading edge to enhance the cooling in this section.

Film Cooling

Film cooling is achieved by allowing the cooling air to establish an insulating layer between the hot gas stream and the blade. This technique is also used to protect the combustor liners from the hot gases.

Transpiration Cooling

Transpiration cooling is achieved by passing the cooling air through the porous wall of the blade. The air cools the hot gases directly. This method is effective at very high temperatures because the entire blade is covered with coolant flow.

Water Cooling

Water cooling involves passing water through tubes embedded in the blade. The water is then discharged from the tip of the blade as steam. The water must be preheated before entering the blade to prevent thermal shock. This method lowers the blade temperature below 1000°F (538°C).

TURBINE BLADE COOLING DESIGNS

The following are five different blade-cooling designs:

1. *Convection and Impingement Cooling/Strut Insert Design.* Figure 13.8 illustrates a strut insert design. Convection cooling is applied to the midchord section through horizontal fins, and impingement cooling is applied to the leading edge. The coolant exits through a split trailing edge. The air flows upward in the central cavity formed by the strut insert and through holes at the leading edge of the insert to cool the leading edge of the blade by impingement. The air then enters through horizontal fins between the shell and strut and discharges through slots at the trailing edge of the blade. Figure 13.9 illustrates the temperature distribution for this design.
2. *Film and Convection Cooling Design.* Figure 13.10 illustrates this blade cooling design. The midchord region is cooled by convection and the leading edges by convection and film cooling. The cooling air is injected through three ports from the base of the blade. It circulates up and down through a series of vertical channels and then passes through a series of small holes at the leading edge. It impinges on the inside surface of the leading edge and passes through holes to provide film cooling. The air discharging through slots cool the trailing edge by convection. Fig. 13.11 illustrates the temperature distribution for this design.

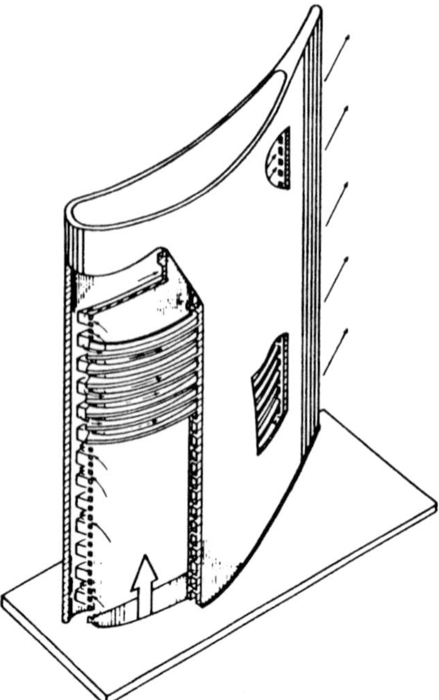

FIGURE 13.8 Strut insert blade.

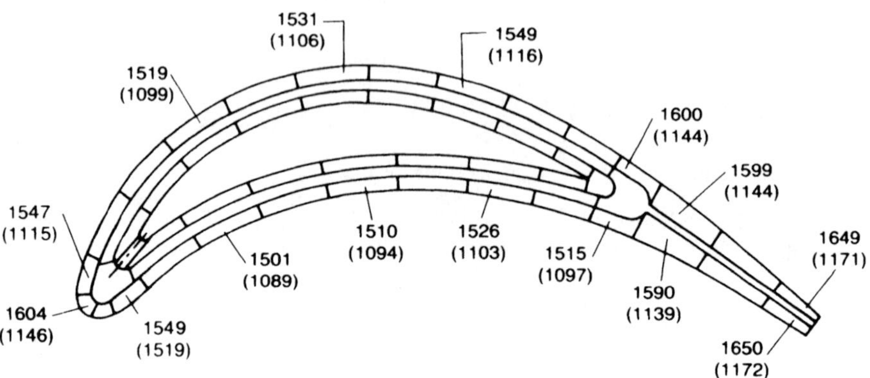

FIGURE 13.9 Temperature distribution for strut insert design, °F (cooled).

3. *Transpiration Cooling Design.* The blades cooled by this method have a strut-supported porous shell (see Fig. 13.12). The cooling air enters the blade through the central plenum of the strut, which has different-size metered holes on its surface. The air passes through the porous shell that is cooled by a combination of convection and film cooling. This technique is effective due to the infinite number of pores in the shell. Figure 13.13 illustrates the temperature distribution. Oxidation closes some of the pores during normal operation, causing uneven cooling and high thermal stresses. Thus, there is a higher probability of blade failure when this design is used.

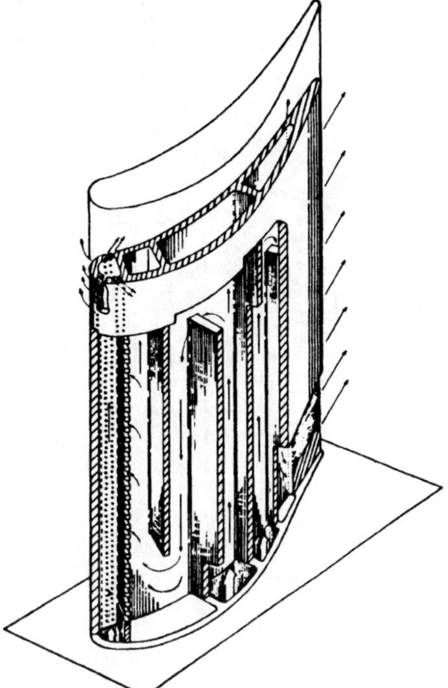

FIGURE 13.10 Film and convection-cooled blade.

4. *Multiple Small-Hole Design.* In this design, cooling air is injected through small holes over the airfoil surface (Fig. 13.14). The cooling is mainly achieved by film-cooling. Figure 13.15 illustrates the temperature distribution. These holes are much larger than the ones used for transpiration cooling. Thus, they are less susceptible to clogging by oxidation. Cross-ribs are used in this design to support the shell. This technique is considered to be among the best in modern gas turbines.

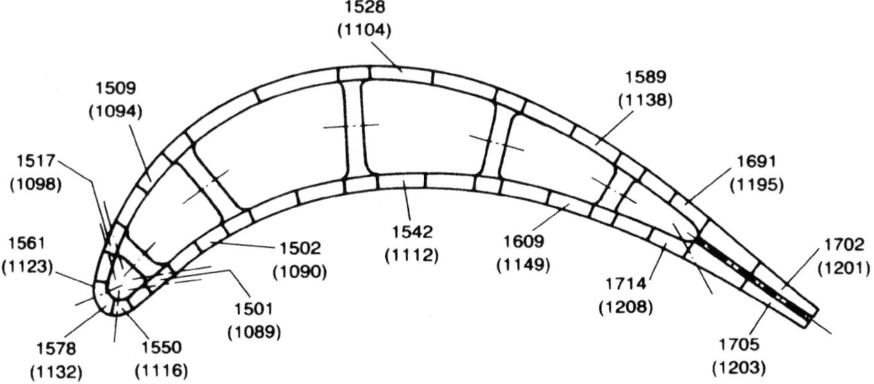

FIGURE 13.11 Temperature distribution for film convection-cooled design, °F (cooled).

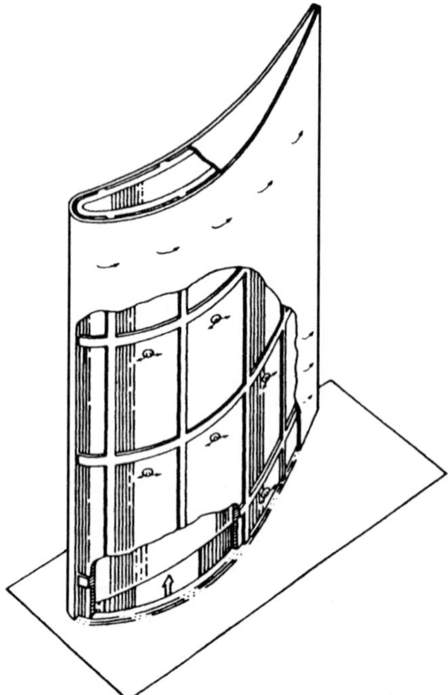

FIGURE 13.12 Transpiration-cooled blade.

5. *Water-Cooled Turbine Blades.* This technique has a number of water tubes embedded inside the blade (Fig. 13.16). The tubes are normally made of copper to provide good heat transfer. The water must be preheated before entering the blade to prevent thermal shock. It evaporates when it reaches the tip of the blade. The steam is then injected into the flow stream. This design is very promising for future gas turbines where the turbine inlet temperature is expected to be around 3000°F (1649°C). This technique will keep the blade temperature below 1000°F (538°C). Thus, there will be no problems with hot-corrosion.

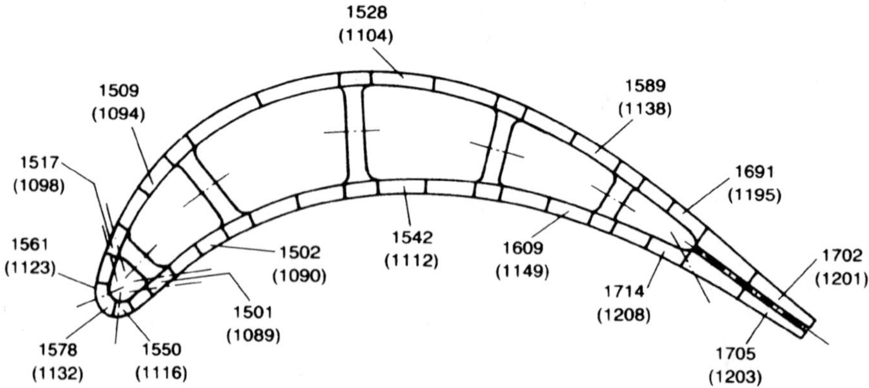

FIGURE 13.13 Temperature distribution for film transpiration-cooled design, °F (cooled).

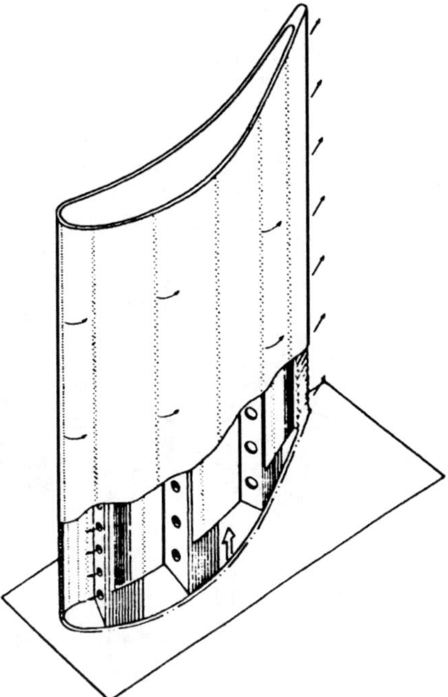

FIGURE 13.14 Multiple small-hole transpiration-cooled blade.

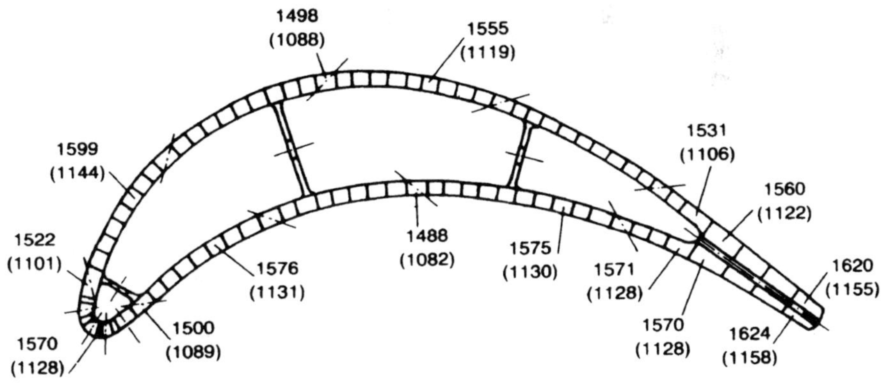

FIGURE 13.15 Temperature distribution for a multiple small-hole design, °F (cooled).

COOLED-TURBINE AERODYNAMICS

The efficiency of the turbine decreases when cooling air is injected into the rotor or stator (Fig. 13.17). However, the injection of cooling air into the turbine allows higher temperature in the combustors. This results in increase in the overall efficiency of the gas turbine.

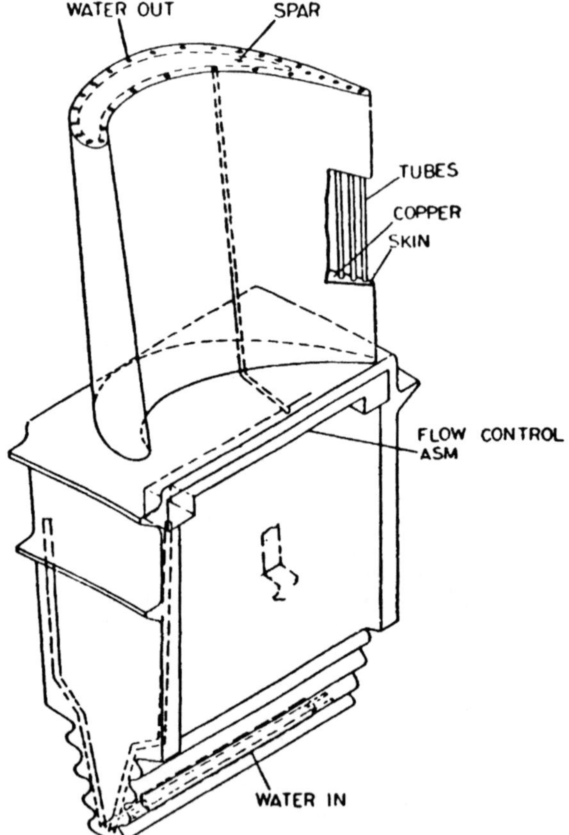

FIGURE 13.16 Water-cooled turbine blade. (*Courtesy General Electric Company*)

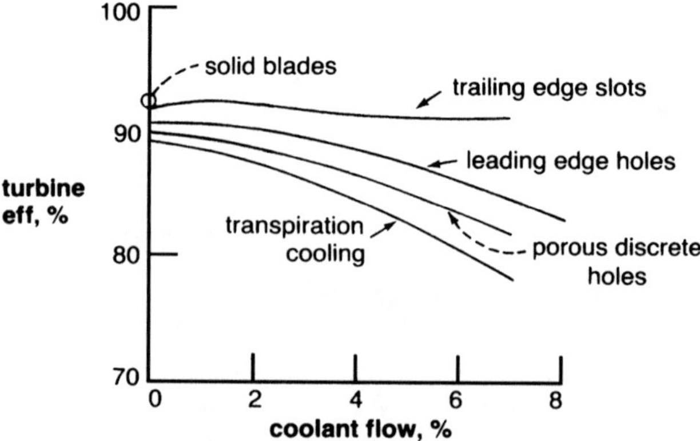

FIGURE 13.17 The effect of various types of cooling on turbine efficiency.

REFERENCE

Boyce, Meheran P., *Gas Turbine Engineering Handbook,* Gulf Publishing Company, Houston, Tex., © 1982, reprinted July 1995.

CHAPTER 14
GAS TURBINE MATERIALS

The efficiency of a gas turbine is limited by the highest temperature achieved in the combustors. Figures 14.1(*a*) and 14.1(*b*) illustrate how a higher turbine inlet temperature decreases the air consumption and increases the efficiency (by decreasing the specific fuel consumption). Materials and alloys that can withstand high temperatures are very expensive. Figure 14.1(*c*) illustrates the relative cost of raw material. Thus, the cooling methods for the turbine and combustor liners play an important role in reducing the cost of the unit.

Gas and steam turbines experience similar problems. However, the magnitude of these problems is different. Turbine components must operate under different stress, temperature, and corrosive conditions. The temperature in the compressor is relatively low, but the stress on the blades is high. The temperature inside the combustor is relatively high, but the stress is low. The turbine blades experience severe conditions of stress, temperature, and corrosion. In gas turbines, these conditions are more extreme than in steam turbine applications. Therefore, the selection of materials for individual components is based on different criteria in gas and steam turbines.

The success of a design is determined by the performance of the materials selected for the components. In modern, high-performance, long-life gas turbines, the critical components are the combustor liner and the turbine blades. The required material characteristics for a turbine blade to achieve high performance and long life include low creep, high rupture strength, high resistance to corrosion, good fatigue strength, low coefficient of thermal expansion, and high thermal conductivity to reduce thermal strains.

Creep and corrosion are the primary failure mechanisms in a turbine blade. They are followed by thermal fatigue. High performance, long life, and minimal maintenance are achieved when these design criteria for turbine blades are satisfied.

GENERAL METALLURGICAL BEHAVIORS IN GAS TURBINES

Creep and Rupture

The strength of different metals varies significantly with temperature. In the low temperature region, all materials deform elastically,* then plastically, and are independent of time. However, at higher temperatures deformation occurs under constant load conditions. This

*Elastic deformation is defined as temporary deformation that occurs when stress is applied to a piece of metal. This deformation will disappear when the stress is removed. Plastic deformation is defined as permanent deformation of a piece of metal that occurs when subjected to a stress.

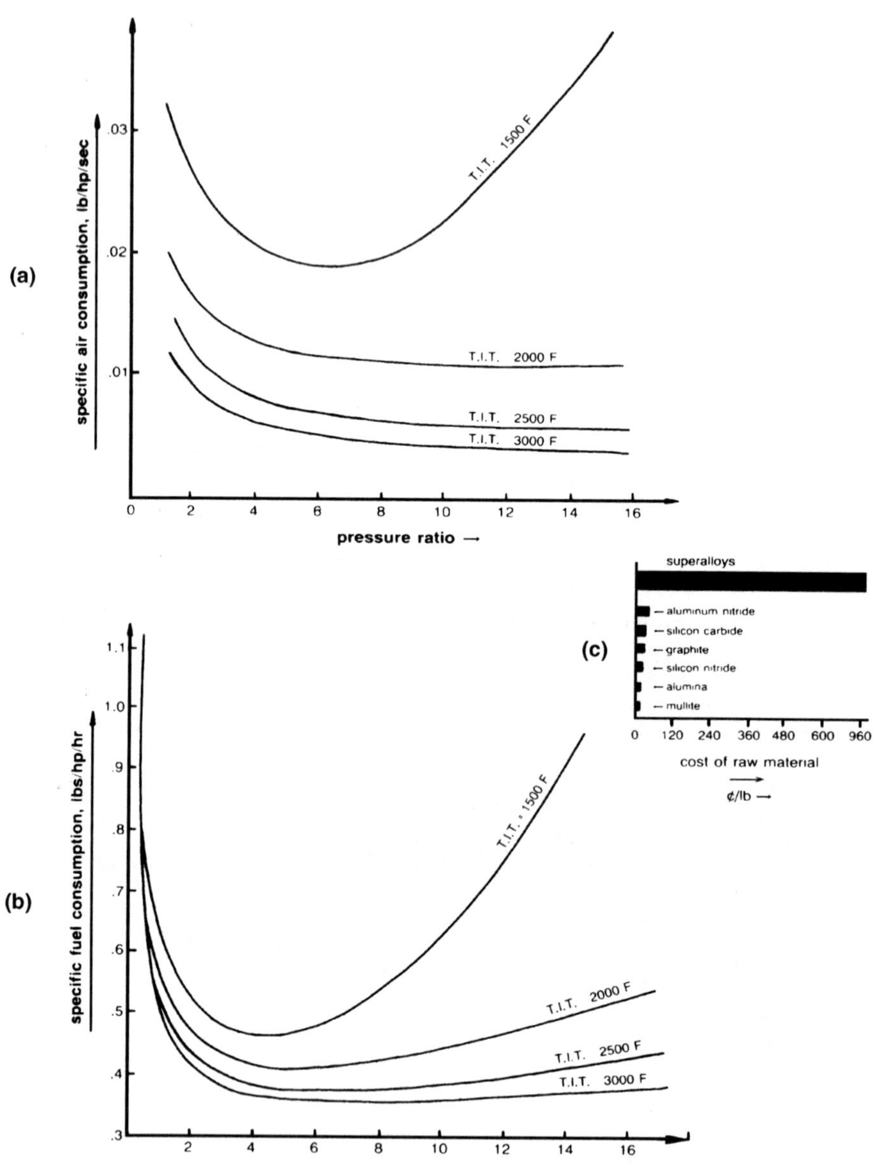

FIGURE 14.1 Specific air (*a*) and fuel (*b*) consumption versus pressure ratio and turbine inlet temperatures for a vehicular gas turbine, with raw material costs (*c*).

time-dependent characteristic of metals under high temperature is called *creep rupture.* Figure 14.2 illustrates the various stages of creep. The first region is the elastic strain, followed by the plastic strain region. Then, a constant-rate plastic strain region is followed by a region of increasing strain rate to fracture.

Creep varies with the material, stress, temperature, and environment. Low creep (less than 1 percent) is desirable for a gas turbine blade. Cast superalloys fail in brittle fracture with only a slight elongation. This type of failure occurs even at elevated temperature.

The Larson-Miller curve describes the stress-rupture characteristics of an alloy over a wide range of temperature, life, and stress. It is also used to compare the capabilities of many alloys at elevated temperature. The Larson-Miller parameter is given by:

$$P_{LM} = T(20 + \log t) \times 10^{-3}$$

where P_{LM} = Larson-Miller parameter
T = temperature, °R
t = time until rupture, hr

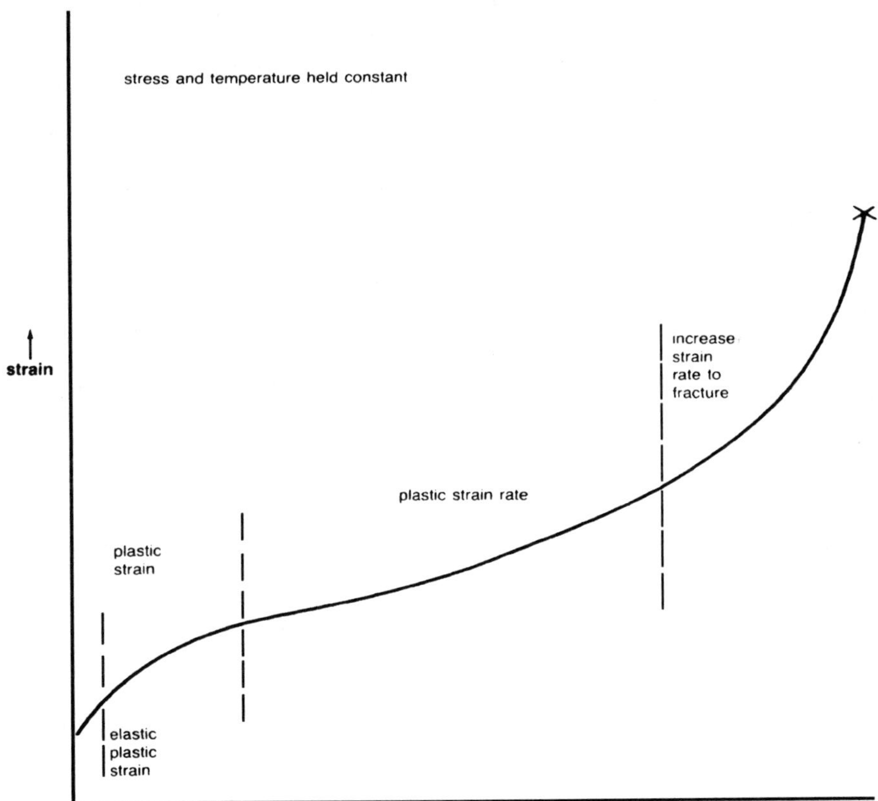

FIGURE 14.2 Time-dependent strain curve under constant load.

Figure 14.3 illustrates the Larson-Miller parameters for turbine blade alloys. A comparison of the operational life (hrs) of different alloys can be performed for similar stress and temperature conditions.

Ductility and Fracture

Ductility is the amount of elongation that a metal experiences when subjected to stress. Cast superalloys have very little creep at high temperature or stresses. They fail with just a small extension.

There are two important elongations in the time-creep curve. The first is to the plastic strain rate region and the second is until fracture occurs. Ductility is not always repeatable. It has erratic behavior even under laboratory conditions. Ductility of a metal is affected by the grain size, the shape of the specimen, and the manufacturing technique. A fracture resulting from elongation can be brittle or ductile. A brittle fracture is intergranular having little or no elongation. A ductile fracture is trangranular and normally typical of ductile tensile fracture. The alloys used for turbine blades normally have low ductility at operating temperatures. Thus, surface notches initiated by erosion or corrosion could easily lead to cracks that propagate rapidly.

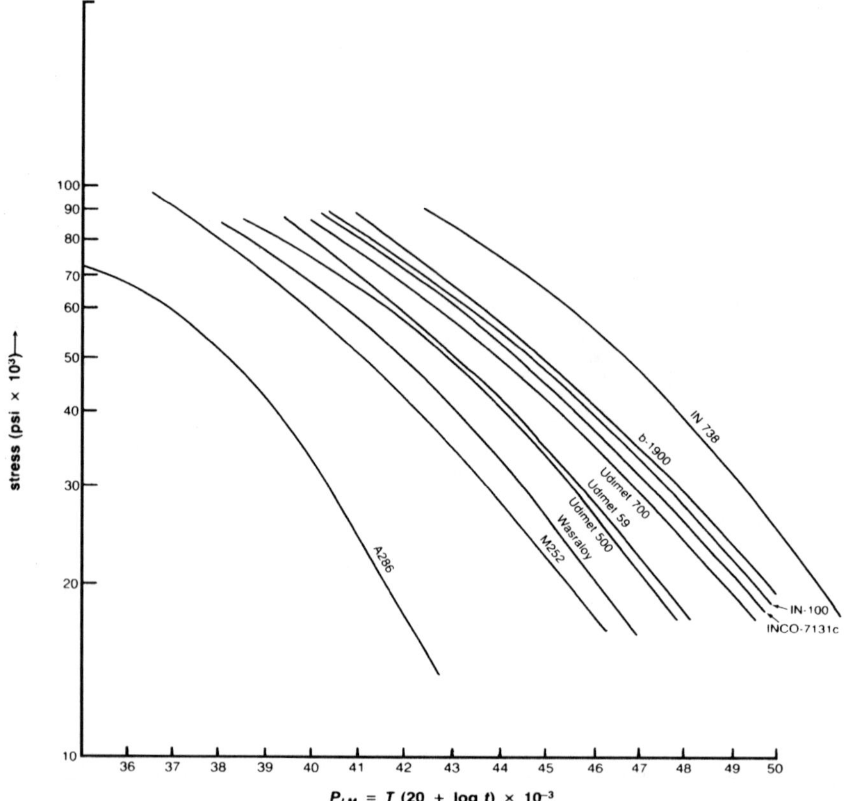

FIGURE 14.3 Larson-Miller parameters for turbine blade alloys.

Thermal Fatigue

Thermal fatigue is a secondary failure mechanism in turbine blades. Temperature differentials that occur during start-up and shutdown produce thermal stress. Thermal fatigue is the cycling of these stresses. It is low-cycle and similar to the failure caused by creep-rupture. The analysis of thermal fatigue is a heat transfer problem involving properties such a modulus of elasticity, coefficient of thermal expansion, and thermal conductivity. Highly ductile materials tend to have higher resistance to thermal fatigue and to crack initiation and propagation.

The life of the blades is directly affected by the number of starts per hour of operation. Table 14.1 shows that a higher number of starts decrease the life of the blades.

Corrosion

The two mechanisms that cause deterioration of the turbine blade material are erosion and corrosion. Erosion is caused by the impingement of hard particles on the turbine blade and removal of material from the blade surface. These particles may have passed through the gas turbine filter or they could be loosened scale deposits from the combustor. The two types of corrosion experienced in gas turbines are hot corrosion and sulfidication processes.

Hot corrosion is an accelerated oxidation of metal resulting from the deposition of Na_2SO_4.* Oxidation is caused by the ingestion of salts in the unit and sulfur from the fuel. *Sulfidication corrosion* is a form of hot corrosion in which the residue contains alkaline sulfates.

The two mechanisms of hot corrosion are:

1. *Accelerated oxidation.* During initial stages—blade surface clean

$$Na_2SO_4 + Ni\ (\text{metal}) \rightarrow NiO\ (\text{porous})$$

2. *Catastrophic oxidation.* Occurs with No, W, and V present—reduces NiO layer—increases oxidation rate

Reactions—Ni-Base Alloys

Protective oxide films

$$2\,Ni + O_2 \rightarrow NiO$$

$$4Cr + 3O_2 \rightarrow 2Cr_2O_3$$

Sulfate

$$2Na + S + 2O_2 \rightarrow Na_2SO_4$$

where Na is from NaCl (salt) and S is from fuel.

Other oxides

$$2\,Mo + 3O_2 \rightarrow 2\,MoO_3$$

$$2\,W + 3O_2 \rightarrow 2\,WO_3$$

$$4V + 5O_2 \rightarrow 2\,V_2O_5$$

*The following are the chemical elements used in this section: Nickel (Ni), Sodium (Na), Sulfur (S), Oxygen (O), Molybdenum (Mo), Tungsten (W), Vandium (V), Chromium (Cr), Aluminum (Al), Carbon (C), Nitrogen (N).

TABLE 14.1 Operation and Maintenance Life of an Industrial Turbine

	Type inspection (hrs. of operation)				Expected life (replacement) (hrs. of operation)		
Type of application fuel	Starts/h	Service	Minor	Major	Comb. liners	1st-stage nozzle	1st-stage buckets
Base	*	+	+	+	+	+	+
Nat. gas	1/1000	4500	9000	28,000	30,000	60,000	100,000
Nat. gas	1/10	2500	4000	13,000	7500	42,000	72,000
Distillate oil	1/1000	3500	7000	22,000	22,000	45,000	72,000
Distillate oil	1/10	1500	3000	10,000	6000	35,000	48,000
Residual	1/1000	2000	4000	5000	3500	20,000	28,000
Residual	1/10	650	1650	2300			
System Peaking X							
Nat. gas	1/10	3000	5000	13,000	7500	34,000	
Nat. gas	1/5	1000	3000	10,000	3800	28,000	
Distillate	1/10	800	2000	8000			
Distillate	1/5	400	1000	7000			
Turbine Peaking X							
Nat. gas	1/5	800	4000	12,000	2000	12,000	
Nat. gas	1/1	200	1000	3000	400	9000	
Distillate	1/5	300	2000	6000			
Distillate	1/1	100	800	2000			

*1/5 = One start per five operating hours
X No residual usage due to low load factor and high capital cost
Base = Normal maximum continuous load
System peaking = Normal maximum load of short duration and daily starts
Turbine peaking = Extra load resulting from operating temperature 50–100°F above base temperature for short durations
Service = Inspection of combustion parts, required downtime approximately 24 hours
Minor = Inspection of combustion plus turbine parts, required downtime approximately 80 hours
Major = Complete inspection and overhaul, required downtime approximately 160 hours
Note: Maintenance times are arbitrary and depend on manpower availability and training, spare parts and equipment availability, and planning. Boroscope techniques can help reduce downtime.

The Ni-base alloy surface normally has a protective layer made of an oxide film, Cr_2O_3. The metal ions diffuse to the surface of the oxide layer and combine with the molten Na_2SO_4. This results in the formation of Ni_2S and Cr_2S_3 (sulfidication):

$$NaCl\ (\text{sea salt}) \rightarrow Na + Cl$$

$$Na + S\ (\text{fuel}) + 20_2 \rightarrow Na_2SO_4$$

Cl grain boundaries *cause intergranular corrosion.* The rate of corrosion depends on the amount of nickel and chromium in the alloy. The oxidation rate increases (accelerated oxidation) when the oxide films become porous and nonprotective.

The presence of Na_2SO_4 with MO, W and/or V results in catastrophic oxidation. Crude oil has high concentration of V and more than 65 percent of ash is V_2O_5. A galvanic cell is generated as follows:

MoO_3

>———WO_3——— cathode - anode ———< Na_2SO_4

V_2O_5

Galvanic corrosion removes the protective oxide film from the blade and increases the rate of oxidation.

The corrosion problem includes the following four mechanisms:

- Erosion
- Sulfidation
- Intergranular corrosion
- Hot corrosion

Cr increases the oxidation resistance in an alloy. For example, alloys having 20 percent Cr have higher oxidation resistance than alloys having 16 percent Cr (Inconel 600). Cr reduces the grain boundary oxidation of an alloy. However, alloys having high Ni content tend to oxidize along the grain boundaries. Gas turbine blades having 10 to 20% Cr tend to corrode (sulfidation) at temperatures higher than 1400°F (760°C). Ni_2S forms in the grain boundaries of the alloy. The addition of cobalt to the alloy increases the temperature at which corrosion occurs. The rate of corrosion can be reduced by increasing the amount of Cr or applying a coating of Al or Al and Cr.

The strength at an elevated temperature of an alloy is increased by increasing the amount of nickel. It is also desirable to have a chromium content exceeding 20 percent for corrosion resistance. The corrosion rate is affected by the composition of the alloy, stress level, and environment. A corrosive atmosphere normally contains chloride salts, vanadium, sulfides, and particulate matter. Combustion products such as NO_x, CO, and CO_2 also contribute to the rate of corrosion. Each fuel type produces different combustion products that affect the rate of corrosion in a different way.

GAS TURBINE BLADE MATERIALS

The first-stage blades in a gas turbine must withstand the most severe conditions of temperature, stress, and environment. The advances made for these blades allowed the turbine inlet temperature to increase from 1500°F (815°C) to 2600°F (1427°C) during the last half century. This resulted in the corresponding improvements for each increment of 15°F (8°C):

1. An increase in power output of 1.5 to 2.0 percent.
2. An increase in efficiency of 0.3 to 0.6 percent.

Thus, the development of new alloys for the blades has a significant financial reward. This improvement achieved is a combined result of metallurgical advancements and design development such as better blade cooling techniques, hollow-blade designs, improved aerodynamics of the turbine and compressor blades, and improved combustion technology.

Nickel-base alloys have been preferred over cobalt-base alloys for turbine nozzles due to the higher attainable strength. These blades are made of vacuum-cast nickel-base alloys that have been strengthened through solution and precipitation-hardening heat treatments. The following are some of the alloys used in turbines.

IN-738. This alloy is currently used in the first-stage blades of most two-stage high-performance turbines and some second stages of three-stage high-performance turbines. The corrosion life of the IN-738 has been extended by 50 to 100 percent by applying a coating to the blades.

U-500. The U-500 and nimonic are being used for the last stage blades of some turbine. Both alloys are precipitation-hardened, nickel-base alloys that were used previously for first stages. Their application for first-stage buckets was stopped due to the higher firing temperature, which requires higher creep-rupture strength and oxidation resistance.

Turbine Wheel Alloys

Cr-Mo-V. Single-shaft heavy-duty turbine wheels and spacers are made of 1 percent Cr, 1 percent Mo, and 0.25 percent V steel. This alloy is also used in most high-pressure steam turbine rotors. It is normally quenched and tempered to enhance the toughness of the bore. Figure 14.4 illustrates the stress rupture properties of this alloy.

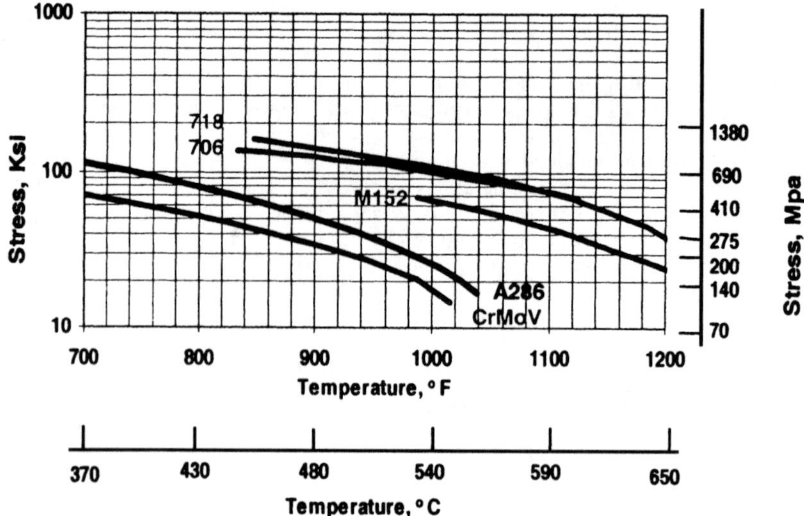

FIGURE 14.4 Turbine wheel material properties. (*Courtesy of General Electric Company.*)

12 Cr alloys. These alloys have good ductility at high strength, uniform properties throughout thick sections, and good hot-strength at temperatures up to 650°F (343°C). This makes them suitable material for turbine wheels.

M-152. A member of this family of alloys having 2 to 3 percent nickel. It has excellent fracture toughness in addition to the common properties of alloys in this family. It also has intermediate rupture strength (see Fig. 14.4), and higher tensile strength than Cr-Mo-V or A-286. It is normally used for turbine discs.

A-286. This is an austenitic iron-base alloy that has been used for several decades in aircraft engines and industrial gas turbine applications. It has been used successfully in industrial discs. Table 14.2 shows the compositions of commonly used high-temperature alloys.

Coatings for Gas Turbine Materials

Hot corrosion is greatly accelerated in the presence of sodium sulfate (Na_2SO_4), which is a product of combustion. Significant hot corrosion damage will occur in the presence of only a few parts per million (ppm) of sodium and sulfate. Sulfur is normally present in the fuel as a contaminant. Sodium can also be a contaminant in the fuel or in the air of sites located in the vicinity of salt water.

Hot corrosion occurring in aircraft engines is distinctly different from the one that occurs in heavy-duty gas turbines. Thus, the coating used for aircraft engines are different from the ones used for heavy-duty gas turbines. Composite plasma, RT-22, and clad have been commonly used as coating in heavy-duty gas turbines. Coated blades last many times longer than uncoated blades in service.

REFERENCE

1. Boyce, Meheran P. *Gas Turbine Engineering Handbook,* Gulf Publishing Company, Houston, Tex., 1982, reprinted July 1995.

TABLE 14.2 High-Temperature Alloys—Nominal Compositions (%)

	Cr	Ni	Co	Fe	W	Mo	Ti	Al	Cb	V	C	B	Ta
Blades													
S816	20.0	20	BAL	4.0	4.0	4.0			4.0		0.40		
NIM 80A	20.0	BAL		4.0			2.30	1.00			0.05		
M-252	19.0	BAL	10.0	2.0		10.0	2.50	0.75			0.10		
U-500	18.5	BAL	18.5			4.0	3.00	3.00			0.07	0.006	
RENE 77	15.0	BAL	17.0			5.3	3.35	4.25			0.07	0.020	
IN 738	16.0	BAL	8.3	0.2	2.6	1.75	3.40	3.40	0.9		0.11	0.010	1.75
GTD 111	14.0	BAL	9.5	4.0	1.5	3.00	5.00				0.11	0.010	3.00
Partitions—1st													
X-40	25	10	BAL	1	8.0						0.50	0.01	
X-45	25	10	BAL	1	8.0						02.5	0.01	
FSX	29	10	BAL	1	7.0						0.25	0.01	
N-155	21	20	20	BAL	2.5	3					0.20		
Turbine Wheels													
Cr-Mo-V	0.1	0.5		BAL		1.25				0.25	0.30		
A-286	0.15	25.0		BAL		1.20	2.0	0.3		0.50	0.08	0.006	
										0.25			
M-152	0.12	2.5		BAL		1.70				0.3	0.12		
IN 706	0.16	41.0		BAL			1.7	0.4	3.0		0.06	0.006	

CHAPTER 15
GAS TURBINE LUBRICATION AND FUEL SYSTEMS

GAS TURBINE LUBRICATION SYSTEMS

A single lubricating system is usually used for heavy-frame gas turbines and driven equipment using mineral oil. Some applications use synthetic lubricating oil due to its fire-resistant property. Common oils used in these machines have a viscosity of 32 centistokes (cSt). However, higher-viscosity oils can be used in high-ambient-temperature areas. Heavy-frame and power turbines use oil-film bearings.

Aeroderivative (aero) gas turbines have two lubricating systems. The first is for the aero gas generator where the rotors are carried on ball-and-roller antifriction bearings. This system uses the same synthetic oil that was used in the parent aero engine. Most aeronautical oils used today meet or are very similar to two military specifications, MIL-7808 and MIL-23699. Modern engines use the latter oil due to its high-temperature capability. The second lubricating system is used for power turbines and driven equipment using oil similar to that used in heavy-frame machines. The system for the aero gas generator uses an oil cooler to reject the heat removed from the engine to the atmosphere or to a glycol-and-water cooling loop, which rejects the heat to atmosphere. In some liquid-fueled installations, the lubricating oil is cooled in a shell-and-tube heat exchanger by the incoming fuel.

Heavy-frame machines, power turbines, and driven equipment of most aero installations have a separate lubricating system tank with heaters to maintain the required temperature. The main pump is driven by an alternating current (AC) motor or by the shaft while the auxiliary pump is usually driven by an AC motor. A smaller emergency pump is driven by a direct current (DC) motor. The smaller units used an oil-to-air, oil-to-glycol/water mixture (which is cooled by air), or oil-to-cooling-water heat exchanger. An oil-to-cooling-water heat exchanger is normally used for large units. The water is usually cooled in a cooling tower.

Since most installations experience very low temperatures in the winter, the DC pump is used to keep the system reasonably full and warm, ready for an emergency start. This pump is used during start-up (black-start capability). When the generator reaches the rated frequency and voltage, the AC pump is started and the DC pump is stopped.

The oil makeup should be monitored and routine sampling and analysis of the oil should be carried out to ensure proper operation. During long outages, the tank should be drained and cleaned (the sludge and sediments at the bottom should be removed), and the heater elements should be checked for cleanliness before the tank is refilled.

COLD-START PREPARATIONS

The prestart requirements for cold engines vary significantly depending on the engine, installation type, and location. Most aero engines using synthetic lubricating oil do not require prelubrication during start-up. The normal flow of the oil meets the requirements on starting (the engine parent was designed for this mode of operation during its aeronautical use). The normal enclosure heating should keep the oil at a higher temperature than the one encountered in aircraft installations.

There are no requirements for prelubrication with heating oil prior to start-up for heavy-frame engines and most power turbines used with aero gas generators because they use oil-film bearings. Electrical heaters are used to keep the oil in the tank heated. The oil is sometimes heated by steam or hot water in a heat exchanger. The starter is not allowed to rotate the machine unless the temperature and pressure (at the bearings) are above prescribed values (permissives).

A circulating pump is used sometimes in extremely low temperatures to keep the oil in the lube system warm while the unit is not operating. In some cases, the lube oil is directed through the cooling heat exchanger (cooler). This is done to prevent excessive pressure drop across the cooler during start-up. In cold areas, the oil-to-air coolers are located inside the building. The louvers in the building wall are closed while the unit is not operating to isolate the cooler from outside air.

Heaters are normally installed in the stator frame of generators for protection against condensation and changes in electrical resistance. Space heaters in the enclosure around the machine maintain a specified minimum temperature.

Heaters are installed in the day tank of liquid fuel systems to maintain the fuel at a specified minimum temperature. The fuel-forwarding system from the main tank to the engine has heaters as well. The fuel must be heated to keep it above the temperature at which wax will form to prevent blockage in the filter elements. The fuel must also receive additional heating to maintain it at the viscosity required for correct spray pattern and atomization from the fuel nozzles. Gas fuel systems are not as sensitive to temperature. However, they must be kept within the operating temperature of the equipment.

The machine should be loaded gradually to reduce the thermal stress on the blades. The reduction in thermal stresses increase the engine life. The gradual loading ensures that the thermal growth of the rotating components matches that of the stationary components to prevent rubbing between them. Some engines have a specified warm-up period while idling before they are loaded.

FUEL SYSTEMS

The petroleum-based liquid fuels are naphtha (used in India and China), number 6 fuel oil (commonly called Bunker "C"), and crude oil. Naphtha is a very light fuel having extremely low lubricity. Thus, pump problems (high wear due to low lubricity) are encountered, but the combustion is clean. Number 6 fuel oil is a thick and a highly viscous fuel, with a very wide viscosity range. It requires heating before it can be pumped and used. Since it is heavy, it collects all the heavy-metal components from the crude oil. It requires treatment before it can be used. The treatment consists of the addition of chemicals to counteract the corrosive effects of the combustion products containing these metallic elements, especially sodium and vanadium. Similar problems are encountered with crude oil.

Heavy-liquid fuels, such as numbers 4 through 6, and crude oil are used in heavy-frame machines only. They require heating in order to be pumped. Diesel fuels also require heating to prevent blockage of the filter by waxes at the specified viscosity. Aero gas turbines typically use number 1 or 2 diesel-grade fuel oil. Number 3 fuel oil is used in some engines under special circumstances.

LIQUID FUELS

The ratings used for liquid fuels are viscosity or distillation ranges. These are specifications for diesel fuel, heating fuel oils, and gas turbine fuels, which have similar viscosity and distillation ranges. Table 15.1 lists typical specifications for liquid fuels.

TABLE 15.1 Liquid Fuel Specifications

Water and sediment	1.0% (V%) max.
Viscosity	20 centistokes at fuel nozzle
Pour point	About 20° below min. ambient
Carbon residue	1.0% (wt) based on 100% of sample
Hydrogen	11% (wt) minimum
Sulfur	1% (wt) maximum

Typical ash analysis and specifications

Metal	Lead	Calcium	Sodium and potassium	Vanadium
Spec. max. (ppm)	1	10	1	0.5 untreated
Naphtha	0–1	0–1	0–1	500 treated
Kerosene	0–1	0–1	0–1	0–0.1
Light distill.	0–1	0–1	0–1	0–0.1
Heavy distill. (true)	0–1	0–1	0–1	0–0.1
Heavy distill. (blend)	0–1	0–5	0–20	0.1/80
Residual	0–1	0–20	0–100	5/400
Crude	0–1	0–20	0–122	0.1/80

Source: M. P. Boyce, *Gas Turbine Engineering Handbook,* Gulf Publishing Company, Houston, Tex., 1982.

The heating grade of fuel does not have provision for riders to control parameters that are significant to gas turbine combustion. For example, the specifications for standard diesel fuel and heating fuel do not carry reference to luminometer number. A radiant flame is highly undesirable in gas turbines, but it could be satisfactory for heating. Gas turbine fuel has restriction also on metallic ion content which is required to reduce hot corrosion while heating fuel does not.

The metallic ion content of a fuel is affected by its mode of transportation from the refinery to the location of use. Aeronautical fuels are transported in dedicated tankers or tankers that have been rigorously cleaned after being used for a different fuel. The transportation of commercial fuels does not have the same restrictions. This fuel can become contaminated during sea transport if the vessel carried residual grades of fuel, heavy crude oil, or salt water (used as ballast) on a previous trip. It is important to note that the specifications of the fuel at site may be different from the ones at the refinery.

Water and Sediment

The presence of water and sediment in the fuel leads to fouling of the fuel-handling system. Sediment tends to accumulate in storage tanks and on filter screens, leading to obstruction of the fuel flow. Water can also cause corrosion and emulsions.

Sodium, potassium, and calcium can be present in water. These salts are not soluble in the fuel. Water washing is effective in removing these salts. Vanadium salts are soluble in oil but not in water. Thus, they cannot be removed by water washing.

Carbon Residue

This parameter is an indicator of the carbonaceous material left in a fuel after vaporizing all the volatile components in the absence of air. It indicates the susceptibility of a gas turbine for carbon residue or varnish to form in the nozzles. Combustion systems that use lighter grades of fuel may require a limit on carbon residue.

Trace Metallic Constituents and Sulfur

The contaminants in fuel may be soluble or insoluble. The following are the most common constituents:

Vanadium. The presence of vanadium can form low-melting compounds such as vanadium pentoxide, which melts at 1275°F (691°C). It causes severe corrosive attack on the turbine blades, which are made of high-temperature alloys.

If the fuel contains vanadium, a weight ratio of magnesium to vanadium higher than 3 must be maintained to control corrosion. This ratio must be limited to 3.5 due to the formation of ash at higher ratios.

Lead. The presence of lead can cause corrosion and spoil the effect of magnesium. However, the presence of lead is rare in crude oil. It is normally caused by contamination.

Sodium and potassium. These substances combine with vanadium to form eutectics that melt around 1050°F (566°C). They can also combine with sulfur in the fuel to produce sulfates ($-SO_4$) that melt during normal operation. The levels of sodium and potassium must be limited. Fuel contamination during sea transport is a major problem.

Calcium. This substance does not have harmful corrosion effects. In reality, it reduces the effect of vanadium. However, it can produce hard, bonded deposits, which cannot be removed by water washing. These deposits degrade the performance but do not cause material damage. Water washing of the fuel will reduce the calcium content.

Sulfur. The sulfur normally becomes sulfur dioxide when burned. It can also oxidize partially to form sulfur trioxide, which can combine with sodium and potassium to form substances that can react with the oxide layer on hot end components. This will leach away the layer and allow the nickel in the high-temperature alloys to be attacked, resulting in sodium sulfate or "green rot" corrosion.

In general, it is impractical to prevent corrosion by limiting the level of sulfur in the fuel. The rate of corrosion is controlled by limiting the levels of sodium and potassium. The rotating blades and stationary vanes normally have a protective coating to reduce the impact of corrosion.

Sulfuric acid can form in the exhaust of the heat recovery systems when the exhaust gas contains sulfur dioxide or trioxide. Limestone injection is used to reduce the impact on the metals.

GASEOUS FUELS

Fully treated pipeline natural gas is the most common gaseous fuel. Some units operate on landfill or sewage digester gas. These fuels have heating values of 25 to 60 percent of the heating value of natural gas. Gas produced from coal gasification is also used. It normally has 10 percent of the heating value of natural gas. Table 15.2 is a summary of gaseous fuel specifications.

TABLE 15.2 Gaseous Fuel Specifications

Heating value	300–500 Btu/ft^3
Solid contaminants	<30 ppm
Flammability limits	2.2:1
Composition—S, Na, K, Li	<5 ppm
(Sulfur + sodium + potassium + lithium)	(When formed into alkali metasulfate)
H_2O (by weight)	<25%

Source: M. P. Boyce, *Gas Turbine Engineering Handbook,* Gulf Publishing Company, Houston, Tex., 1982.

GAS FUEL SYSTEMS

Liquid fuel droplets cannot be tolerated in the gas. These droplets have heating values 20 to 70 times higher than gas fuel. Some fuel nozzles are designed for gas only. They are not atomizing nozzles as the ones used for liquids. Liquid droplets passing through these nozzles tend to burn on the surface of combustors and turbine blades. They cause extremely high thermal stresses, metal melting, and component damage.

Compressors are used to increase the pressure of gas entering the combustors. These compressors are normally subjected to high wear. Pulsation dampeners are required for reciprocating compressors. Oil separators are required for oiled screw compressors. Gas coolers are required for most of them.

STARTING

There are two basic sources of energy used for starting a gas turbine:

1. *Stored energy.* This includes batteries, compressed air in bottles, compressed gas from gas pipelines, and hydraulic oil from an accumulator.
2. *Active energy.* This includes electricity from the grid to either the starting motor or directly to the generator that will act as a motor during start-up, an internal combustion engine to start the gas turbine directly.

The advantage of stored-energy systems is the ability to provide *black-start* capability. However, they have practical size limitations. Most black-start systems require the capability for three starts in case the initial attempts are unsuccessful. Small units (up to 6 MW) use electric batteries for start-up. Larger units use air or hydraulic starter motors. Compressed gas from pipelines is used with units up to 25 MW. However, this method is becoming less popular due to environmental and cost concerns associated with exhausting larger amounts of natural gas to the atmosphere. An electric motor powered from the grid can be used to drive a hydraulic pump or air compressor to provide high-pressure oil or air to the starting device. An internal combustion engine can also be used to start the unit. This provides black-start capability.

The engine-starting systems are used to rotate the engine for compressor washing. Some units use the starter to cool the engine by air following an emergency trip before a restart can be attempted.

A small DC motor is normally used to drive heavy-frame machines at very low speeds through a speed reduction gearbox as the engine cools down. This is done to prevent "sag" of the rotor between the bearings as the engine cools. A typical barring speed is 6 r/min, which is maintained for 4 h at least. It is essential to maintain lubrication of the bearings to remove the heat that is generated during the barring phase.

INTAKE SYSTEM

Impurities in inlet air build up on the internal components of the engine. They change the compressor characteristics and can lead to surge conditions. They also reduce the efficiency of the compressor. Coarse dirt in the inlet air erodes the coatings of the components. Poor filtration results in blocking the cooling passages to the rotor blades.

Inertial filtration is normally used to remove large particles. It is normally followed by self-cleaning filters, which detect the increase in pressure drop across the filter and release air pulses to remove the dirt. Most filtration systems have a "blow-in" door located downstream of the filter. It opens automatically when the differential pressure between the area downstream of the filter and the outside exceeds a preset value. This door prevents excessive and damaging differential pressure across the filter. However, when the door opens, unfiltered air enters the engine. This increases fouling and possible bug and bird entry into the engine.

The ambient air conditions should be evaluated carefully to determine the particle size and concentration in the area before specifying the type of filtration required. Most axial compressor fouling is caused by particles in the 0.3- to 3-μm range. The filtration system should be specified to remove the whole range of particles encountered.

The flexible sealing bands between sections of the intake should be checked routinely for cracks. Unfiltered air enters the engine through such cracks causing damage to the engine.

COMPRESSOR CLEANING

Dirt accumulation on the compressor blades changes the compressor characteristics and reduces the output power. The exhaust temperature increases when the output power decreases (conservation of energy). The compressor can be cleaned using these five methods:

1. Disassemble the compressor partially to clean the blades of the rotor. This method gives excellent results, but it is very time-consuming.
2. Some manufacturers recommend cleaning the compressor by using ground shell injected into the inlet by a high-velocity air stream. They remove buildup by an abrasive fashion. This method cannot be used with engines having coating on the blades, because they will be eroded. This method is normally done while the compressor is being rotated by the starter. Many users have difficulty with this method because the ground shell enters the hydraulic fluid of the governing system and the pressurizing air for seals and bearings, thus blocking passages. This method cannot be used with units having air-cooled turbine blades (rotating or stationary).

3. Liquid wash while the compressor rotor is on starter. Demineralized water mixed with a detergent is injected to wash the contaminants off the blades. This is followed by a demineralized water rinse and an air-dry cycle while the machine is on starter. Another technique (called soak-wash cycle) involves injecting demineralized water while the engine is stopped. The water is allowed to soak to loosen the dirt accumulation before injecting the mixture of demineralized water and detergent into the engine.
4. A "crank cleaning" method involves a soak, followed by an abrasive shell cleaning, a rinse, and a drying cycle.
5. A recent method was developed for on-wing cleaning of aircraft engines (on-line or fired washing). It involves washing the gas generator by spraying a special cleaning liquid into the compressor inlet while the engine is running. The speed of rotation during the cycle and the cleaning liquid are specified by the manufacturer.

The methods that include injection of liquids use a set of liquid spray nozzles at several positions around the inlet to ensure uniform spray pattern into the compressor. Transcanada Pipelines recommends a compressor cleaning of a 1500- to 2500-h interval using a soak wash cycle to recover the full performance of the engine. Some heavy-frame machines use a turbine wash cycle while the engine is shut down to remove deposits off the hot-end components.

CHAPTER 16
GAS TURBINE BEARINGS AND SEALS

BEARINGS

Journal bearings provide radial support for the rotating equipment and thrust bearings provide axial positioning for them. Ball and roller bearings are used in some aircraft jet engines. However, all industrial gas turbines use journal bearings.

Journal bearings can be split or full-round. Large-size bearings used for heavy machinery normally have heavy lining. Precision insert-type bearings used commonly in internal combustion engines have a thin lining. The majority of sleeve bearings are of the split type for convenience in maintenance and replacement. Figure 16.1 provides a comparison of different types of journal bearings. The following is a description of the most common types of journal bearings:

1. *Plain journal.* The bearing is bored with equal amounts of clearance between 1.5×10^{-3} in (3.8×10^{-3} cm) and 2×10^{-3} in (5×10^{-3} cm) per inch of journal diameter between the journal (portion of the shaft inside the bearing) and the bearing.
2. *Circumferential grooved.* This bearing has the oil groove at half the bearing length. This design provides better cooling. However, it reduces the load capacity by dividing the bearing into two parts.
3. *Cylindrical bore.* This bearing type is commonly used in turbines. It has a split design. The two axial oil-feed grooves are at the split.
4. *Pressure or pressure dam.* This is a plain journal bearing with a pressure pocket in the unloaded half. The pocket has the following dimensions:

   Depth: 0.031 in (0.079 cm)

   Length: 50 percent of bearing length

   Width: arc of 135°

   The arc terminates abruptly in a sharp-edge dam. The shaft rotation is such that the oil is pumped through the channel toward the sharp edge. These bearings have only one direction of rotation. They are known to have good stability.
5. *Lemon bore or elliptical.* This is bored at the split line. The bore shape is similar to an ellipse, having a major axis approximately twice the length of the minor axis. These bearings are used in both directions of rotation.
6. *Three-lobe.* These bearings have moderate load-carrying capability and can operate in both directions. They are not commonly used in turbo machines.
7. *Offset halves.* This bearing is similar to the pressure dam bearing. It has good load-carrying capability. However, it is limited to one direction of rotation.

8. *Tilting-pad.* This is the most popular type in modern machines. It has several bearing pads located around the circumference of the shaft. These pads can tilt to assume the most effective operating position. Its main advantage is the ability for self-alignment. This bearing provides the greatest increase in fatigue life due to these advantages:

   - Self-aligning to provide optimum shaft alignment.
   - The backing material has good thermal conductivity. It dissipates the heat developed in the oil film

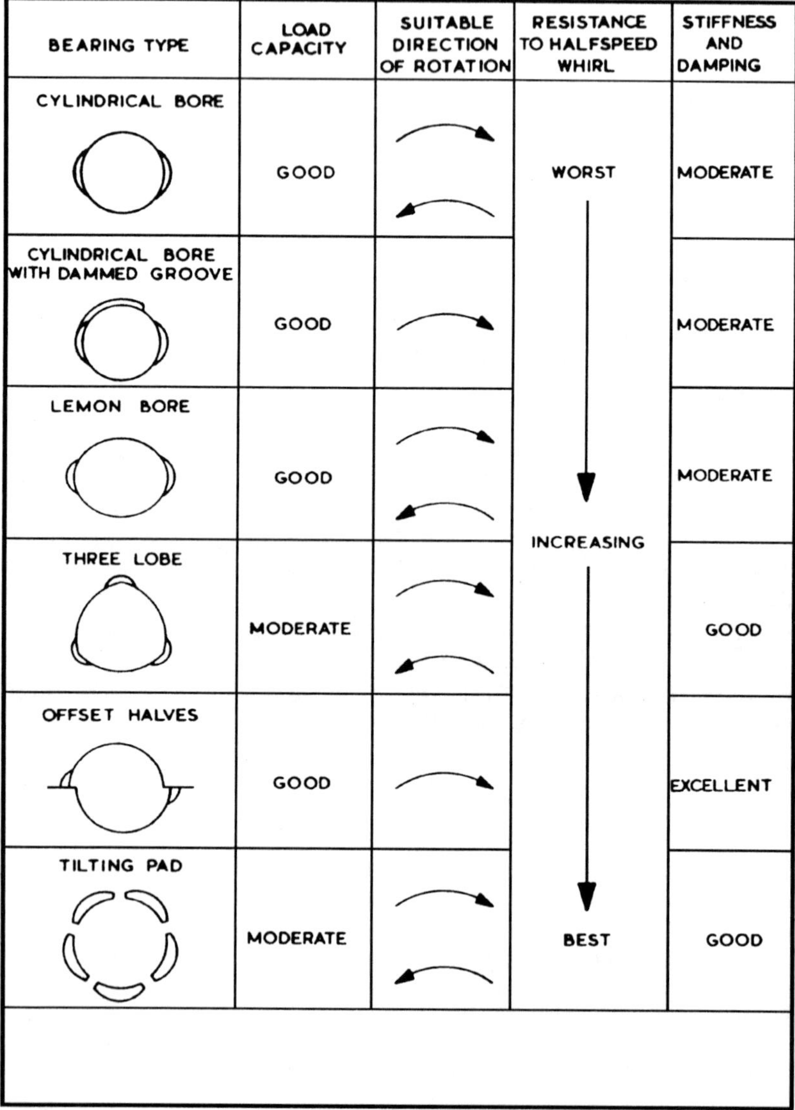

BEARING TYPE	LOAD CAPACITY	SUITABLE DIRECTION OF ROTATION	RESISTANCE TO HALFSPEED WHIRL	STIFFNESS AND DAMPING
CYLINDRICAL BORE	GOOD		WORST	MODERATE
CYLINDRICAL BORE WITH DAMMED GROOVE	GOOD			MODERATE
LEMON BORE	GOOD			MODERATE
THREE LOBE	MODERATE		INCREASING	GOOD
OFFSET HALVES	GOOD			EXCELLENT
TILTING PAD	MODERATE		BEST	GOOD

FIGURE 16.1 Comparison of general bearing types.

- The Babbitt layer is thin [around 0.005 in (0.013 cm)]. Thick babbitts reduce the bearing life significantly. Babbitt thickness around 0.01 in (0.025 cm) reduces the bearing life by more than half.
- The thickness of the oil film has a significant effect on the bearing stiffness. In tilted-pad bearings, the thickness of the oil film can be changed by the following methods:

  Changing the number of pads
  Changing the axial length of the pads
  Directing the load on or in-between the pads

These are the most common types of journal bearings. They are listed in the order of growing stability. As the stability increases, the cost and efficiency of the bearing decreases. All anti-whirl bearings impose a parasitic load on the journal. This generates higher power losses, requiring larger oil flow to cool the bearing.

BEARING DESIGN PRINCIPLES

In a journal bearing, a full film of fluid separates the stationary bushing from the rotating journal. This separation is achieved by pressurizing the fluid in the clearance space until the fluid forces balance the bearing load. The fluid must flow continuously into the bearing and maintain the pressure in the film space. Figure 16.2 illustrates the four methods of

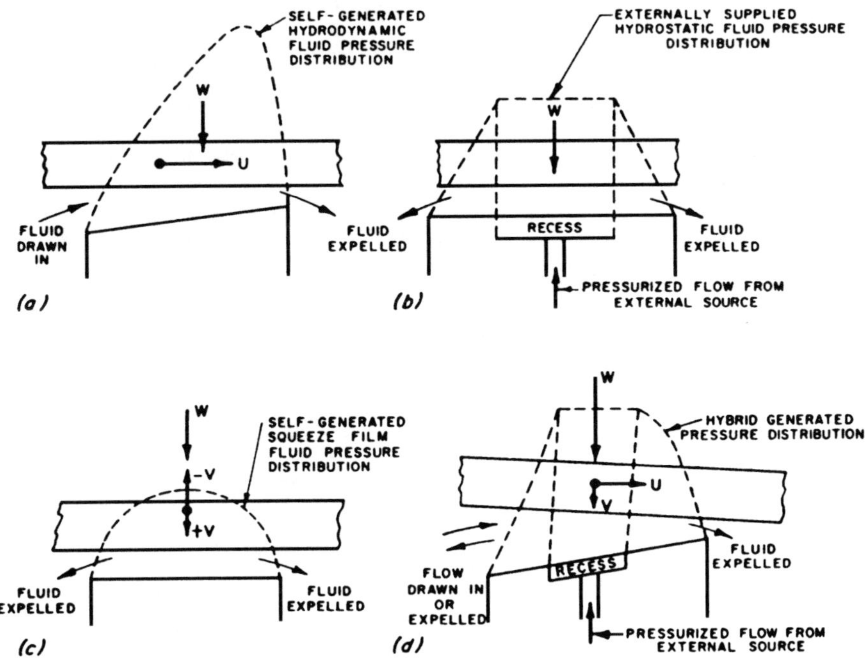

FIGURE 16.2 Modes of fluid-film lubrication: (*a*) hydrodynamic, (*b*) hydrostatic, (*c*) squeeze film, and (*d*) hybrid.

lubrication in a fluid-film bearing. The most common method is the *hydrodynamic*. It is known as a *self-acting* bearing.

Figure 16.3 illustrates the natural wedge formed by a journal bearing and the pressure distribution inside the bearing. The thickness of the fluid-film varies from 0.0001 to 0.001 in (0.00025 to 0.0025 cm) depending on the lubrication method and application. There are peaks and valley in every surface regardless of its finish. The average asperity height is around 5 to 10 times the RMS surface finish reading. When a surface is abraded, an oxide film will form on it almost immediately.

Figures 16.4(*a*), (*b*), and (*c*) illustrate three types of separation between the journal and the babbitt in a bearing:

a. Full-film

b. Mixed-film (intermediate zone)

c. Boundary lubrication

If a full-film exists, the bearing life would be almost infinite. The limitation in this case would be due to lubricant breakdown, surface erosion, and fretting of various components. Figures 16.4(*d*) and 16.4(*e*) illustrate the effect of oil additives, which are considered contaminants that form beneficial surface films.

Figure 16.5 describes the bearing health by plotting the coefficient of friction versus ZN/P, where Z is the lubricant viscosity in centipoises; N, the rpm of the journal; and P, the projected area unit loading. The lowest friction is reached when the full-film is

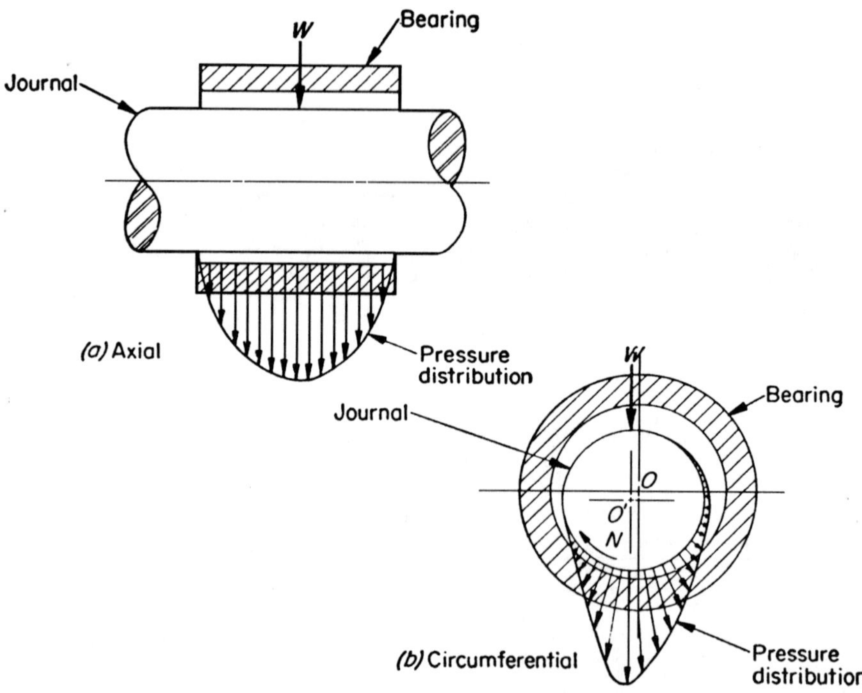

FIGURE 16.3 Pressure distribution in a full journal bearing.

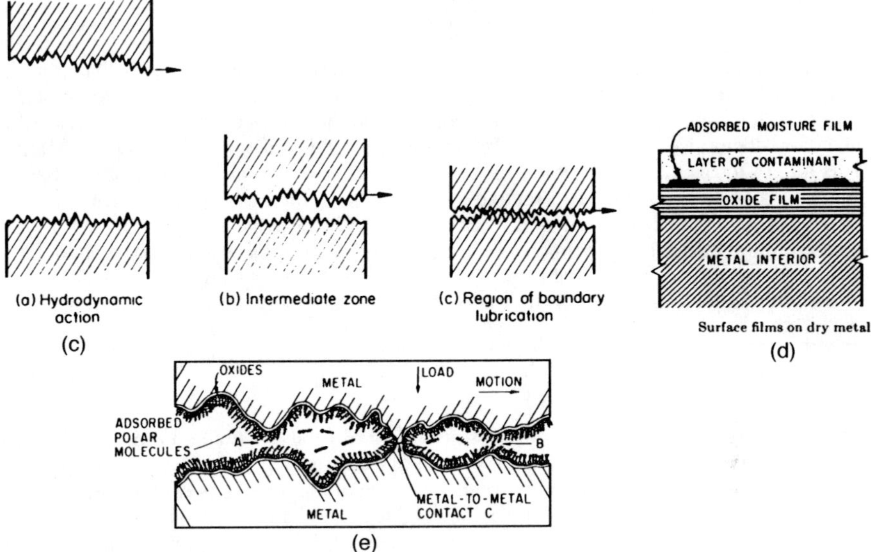

FIGURE 16.4 Enlarged views of bearing surfaces.

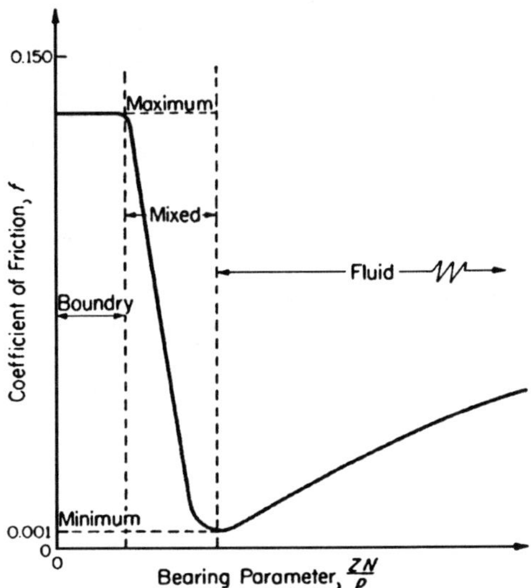

FIGURE 16.5 Classic *ZN/P* curve.

established. At higher speeds, the friction increases due to an increase in the shear force of the lubricant.

The transition from laminar to turbulent flow in the bearing is assumed to occur at around a Reynold number of 800. At higher speed, turbulence starts to increase in the bearing. It manifests itself in heat generation within the bearing and in a significant increase in frictional losses.

TILTING-PAD JOURNAL BEARINGS

Tilting-pad journal bearings are selected for applications having light shaft loads due to their great ability to resist oil whirl vibration. However, these bearings can normally carry very high loads. Their pads can tilt to accommodate the forces developed in the oil film. Therefore, they can operate with an optimum thickness of the oil-film for a given application. This ability to operate over a wide range of loads is very useful for applications having high-speed gear reductions. The second advantage of tilting-pad journal bearings is their ability to accommodate shaft misalignment easily. These bearings should be used for high-speed rotors (which normally operate above the first critical speed) due to the advantages just listed and their dynamic stability.

Bearing preload is defined as the ratio of bearing assembly clearance to the machined clearance:

$$\text{Preload ratio} = \frac{C'}{C} = \frac{\text{Concentric pivot film thickness}}{\text{Machined clearance}} \tag{16.1}$$

This is an important design criterion for tilting-pad bearings. A preload ratio of 0.5 to 1.0 provides stable operation due to the production of a converging wedge between the bearing journal and the bearing pads. The installed clearance of the bearing is C′. It depends on the radial position of the journal. For a given bearing, C is fixed. Figure 16.6 illustrates different preloading on two pads of a five-pad tilting-pad bearing. Pad 1 has a preload ratio less than 1, while Pad 2 has a preload ratio of 1.0. The solid line in Fig. 16.6 represents the position of the journal before applying the load. The dashed line represents the position of the journal after applying the load.

Pad 1 operates with a good converging wedge, while Pad 2 operates with a diverging film. This indicates that it is completely unloaded. Bearings operating with a preload ratio of 1 or higher will have some of their pads completely unloaded. This reduces the overall stiffness

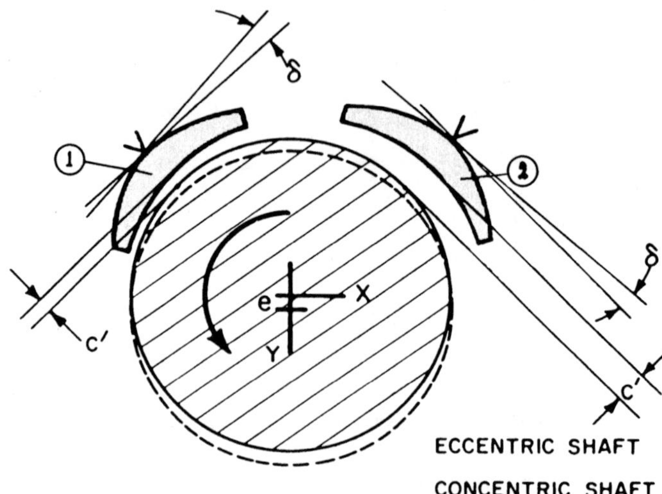

FIGURE 16.6 Tilting-pad bearing preload.

of the bearing and decreases its stability. Unloaded pads experience flutter, which leads to a phenomenon known as *leading-edge lockup*. In this situation, the pads would be forced against the shaft and maintained in this position by the friction of the shaft and the pad. Therefore, bearings should be designed with a preload, especially when the lubricant viscosity is low.

BEARING MATERIALS

Babbitt is the soft material in the stator of the bearing that faces the journal. It has excellent nonscoring characteristics and is outstanding for embedding dirt. However, it has low fatigue strength, especially at elevated temperatures and when its thickness is more than 0.038 cm (0.015 in). Babbitts will not be damaged by momentary rupture of the oil film. They will also minimize the damage to the journal in the event of a complete failure. Tin babbitts are preferred over lead-based material due to their higher corrosion resistance. They are also easier to bond to a steel shell.

The maximum design temperature of Babbitts is around 300°F (149°C). However, most applications are limited to 250°F (121°C). This metal tends to experience creep as the temperature increases. Creep normally forms ripples on the bearing surface. Tin babbitts experience creep from around 375°F (190°C) and for bearing loads below 200 psi (1.36 MPa) to 270°F (132°C) and for steady loads of 1000 psi (6.8 MPa). This range can be improved by using very thin layers of Babbitt as in automotive bearings.

BEARING AND SHAFT INSTABILITIES

Journal bearings encounter a serious form of instability known as *half-frequency whirl*. This phenomenon is caused by vibration characterized by rotation of the shaft center around the bearing center at a frequency of half the shaft rotational speed (Fig. 16.7).

Any increase in speed following this phenomenon will produce more violent vibration until eventual seizure occurs. Unlike a critical speed, the shaft cannot "pass through" this region. As the shaft speed increases, the frequency of instability remains at half the shaft speed. This problem occurs mainly at high speed in lightly loaded bearings. This problem can be predicted accurately and avoided by changing the design of the bearing. This problem does not occur in tilted-pad bearings. However, these bearings can become unstable due to the problem of pad flutter. The main cause of bearing failure is its inability to resist cyclic stresses. The severity charts in Fig. 16.8 show the level of vibration that can be tolerated by bearings.

THRUST BEARINGS

The main function of a thrust bearing is to resist any axial force applied to the rotor and maintain it in its position. Figure 16.9 illustrates three types of thrust bearings. The plain washer bearing is not normally used with continuous loads. Its applications are limited to thrust loads of very short duration, at standstill, or low speed. This type of bearings is used also for light loads [less than 50 psi (340 kPa)].

Thrust bearings designed to handle significant continuous loads require a fluid film between the bearing surface and the rotor. The tapered-land thrust bearing can match the load handled by the tilting-pad thrust bearing. However, tilting-pad thrust bearings are preferred for variable speed operation. The main reason for this is the ability of the pads

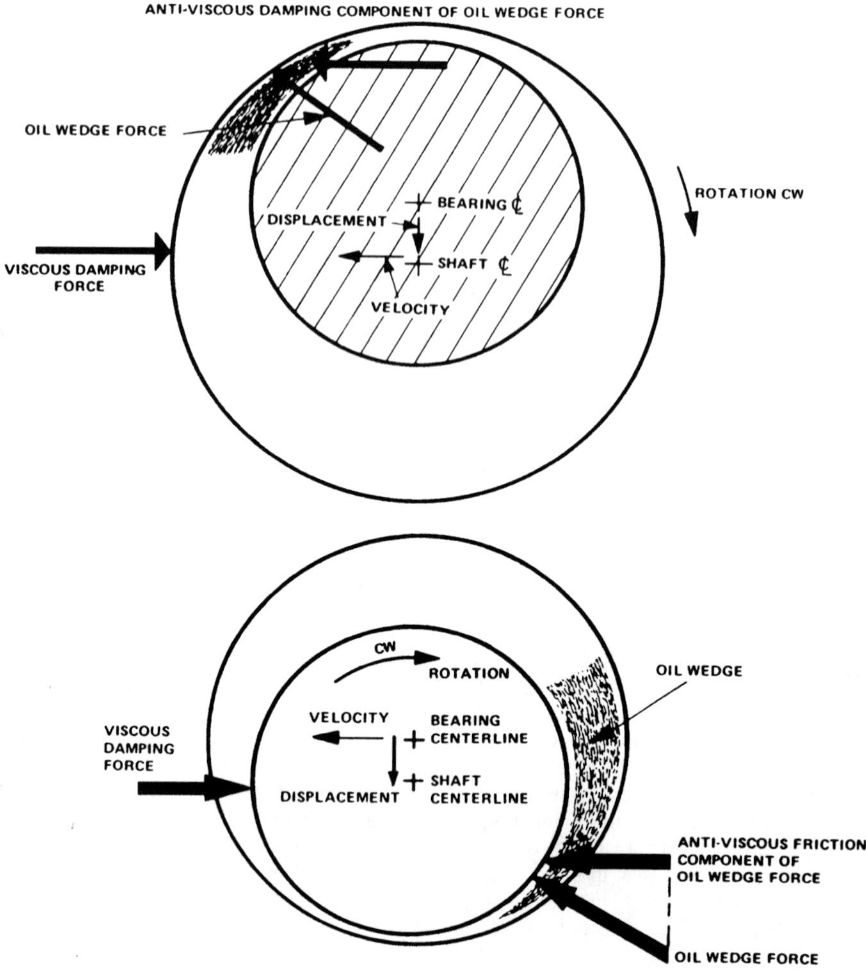

FIGURE 16.7 Oil whirl.

to pivot freely to form a suitable angle for lubrication over a wide speed range. The self-leveling feature equalizes the loads on the individual pads and allows the bearing to tolerate larger shaft misalignments. The main disadvantage of this bearing design is that it requires more axial space than nonequalizing thrust bearings.

Factors Affecting Thrust Bearing Design

Tests have proven that the load capacity of a thrust bearing is limited by the strength of the babbitt surface at the highest temperature in the bearing. The normal capacity of a steel-backed babbitted tilting-pad thrust bearing is around 250 to 500 psi (1700 to 3400 kPa). This capacity can be improved by maintaining the flatness of the pads and removing heat

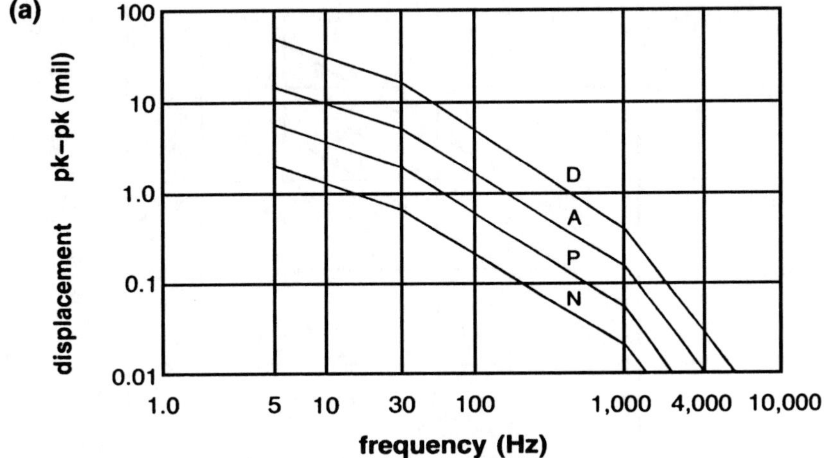

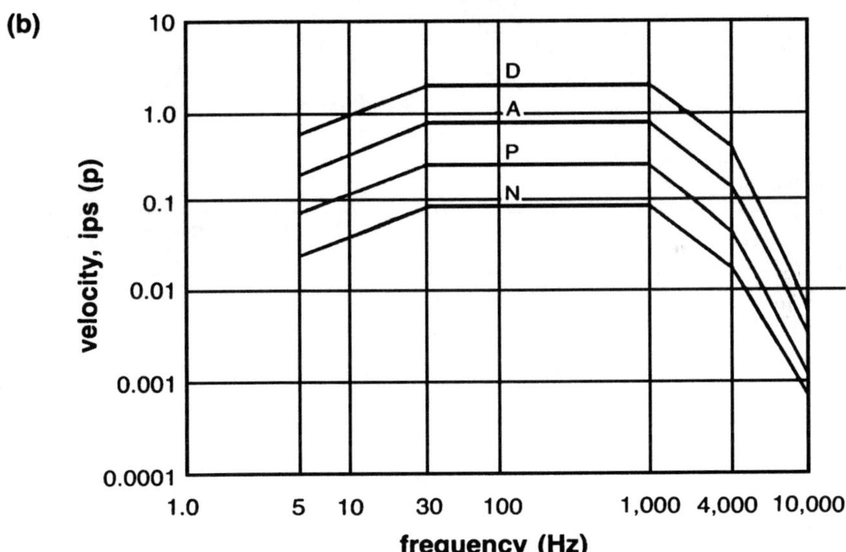

D = Dangerous, shutdown.

A = Abnormal, will deteriorate. Inspect as early as possible.

P = Problems, keep close watch.

N = Normal.

FIGURE 16.8 Severity charts: (*a*) displacement and (*b*) velocity.

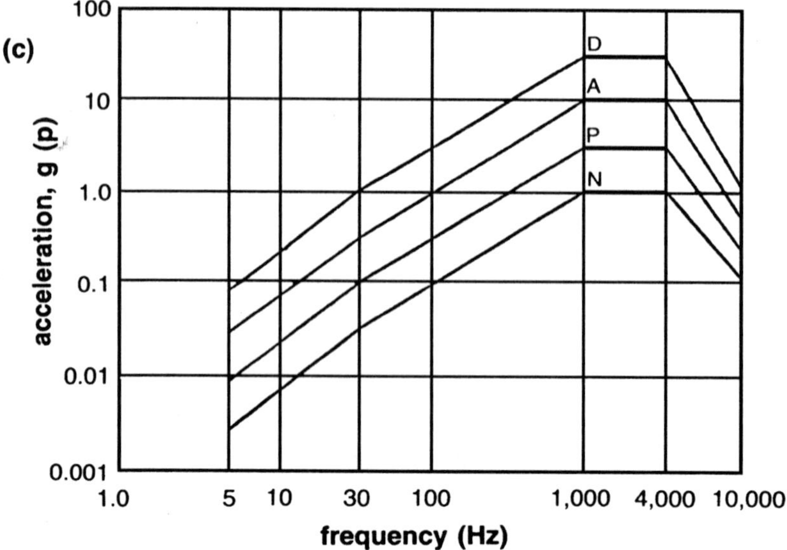

D = Dangerous, shutdown.

A = Abnormal, will deteriorate. Inspect as early as possible.

P = Problems, keep close watch.

N = Normal.

FIGURE 16.8 (*Continued*) Severity charts: (*c*) acceleration.

BEARING TYPE		LOAD CAPACITY	SUITABLE DIRECTION OF ROTATION	TOLERANCE OF CHANGING LOAD/SPEED	TOLERANCE OF MISALIGNMENT	SPACE REQUIRMENT
PLAIN WASHER		POOR		GOOD	MODERATE	COMPACT
TAPER LAND	BIDIRECTIONAL	MODERATE		POOR	POOR	COMPACT
	UNIDIRECTIONAL	GOOD		POOR	POOR	COMPACT
TILTING PAD	BIDIRECTIONAL	GOOD		GOOD	GOOD	GREATER
	UNIDIRECTIONAL	GOOD		GOOD	GOOD	GREATER

FIGURE 16.9 Comparison of thrust-bearing types.

from the loaded area. The use of backing materials with proper thickness and high thermal conductivity can increase the maximum continuous thrust to more than 1000 psi (6800 kPa).

The use of backing material having high thermal conductivity, such as copper or bronze, allows the thickness of the Babbitt to be reduced to 0.01 to 0.03 in (0.025 to 0.076 cm). Thermocouples and resistive thermal detectors (RTD's) embedded in the bearing will signal distress when they are properly positioned. Temperature monitoring systems have proven to have a higher accuracy than axial position indicators, which tend to have problems with linearity at high temperatures.

Thrust Bearing Power Loss

The power consumed in a thrust bearing must be accurately predicted to determine the turbine efficiency and the requirements of the oil supply. Figure 16.10 illustrates the typical power consumption in a thrust bearing with shaft speed. The total power loss is around 0.8 to 1.0 percent of the total rated power of the machine. Newly tested vectored lube bearings show preliminary indications of reducing the power loss by 30 percent.

SEALS

Seals are critical components in turbomachinery, especially when the unit operates at high pressure and speed. The two categories of sealing systems between the rotor and the stator are (1) *noncontacting seals* and (2) *face seals*.

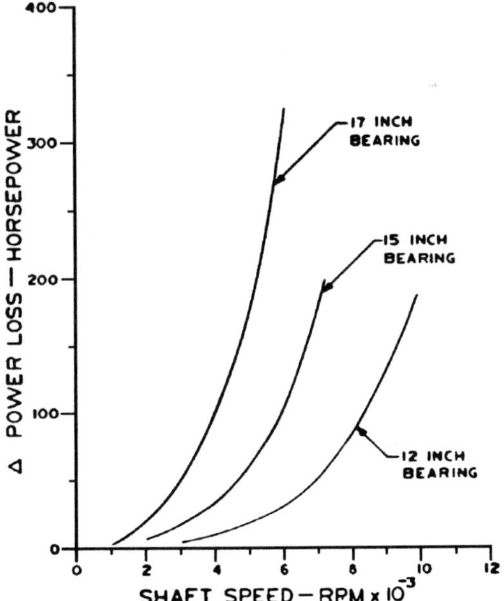

FIGURE 16.10 Difference in total power loss data—test minus catalog frictional losses versus shaft speed for 6 × 6 pad double-element thrust bearings.

Noncontacting Seals

Noncontacting seals are reliable and commonly used in high-speed turbomachinery. The two types of noncontacting seals (or clearance seals) are *labyrinth seals* and *ring seals.*

Labyrinth Seals. A labyrinth seal consists of a series of metallic circumferential strips that extend from the shaft or from the shaft housing to form a series of annular orifices. Labyrinth seals have higher leakage than clearance bushings, contact seals, or film riding seals. Thus, labyrinth seals are used in applications that can tolerate a small loss of efficiency. They are also used sometimes in conjunction with a primary seal. The advantages of labyrinth seals are:

- Simplicity
- Reliability
- Tolerance to impurities
- System adaptability
- Very low power consumption
- Flexibility of material selection
- Minimal effects on the rotor
- Reduction of reverse diffusion
- Ability to handle very high pressures
- Tolerance to large temperature variations

Their disadvantages are:

- Relatively high leakage
- Loss of efficiency
- Possible ingestion of impurities with resulting damage to other components such as bearings
- Possible clogging
- Inability to meet the seal standards of the Environmental Protection Agency (EPA)

Many modern machines are relying on other types of seals due to these disadvantages.

Labyrinth seals can easily be manufactured from conventional materials. Figure 16.11 illustrates some of the modern seals. The grooved seal shown in Fig 16.11(*b*) is tighter than the simple seal shown in Fig 16.11(*a*). Figures 16.11(*c*) and 16.11(*d*) show rotating labyrinth-type seals. Figure 16.11(*e*) shows a buffered, stepped labyrinth seal. This design is normally tighter than the one described earlier. Figure 16.11(*f*) shows a buffered-vented straight labyrinth seal. The pressure of the buffered gas is maintained at a higher value than the process gas, which can be under vacuum or above atmospheric conditions. The buffered gas produces a fluid barrier that seals the process gas. The eductor sucks the buffered gas and atmospheric air into a tank maintained under vacuum.

The matching stationary seal is normally made from soft material such as babbitt or bronze, while the rotating labyrinth lands are made of steel. This arrangement allows the seal to have minimal clearance. During operation, the lands can cut into the softer material without causing extensive damage to the seal. In a labyrinth seal, the high fluid pressure is converted into high velocity at the throats of the restrictions. The kinetic (velocity) energy is then dissipated into heat by turbulence in the chamber after each throat. The clearances of a large turbine is around 0.015 to 0.02 in (0.038 to 0.51 cm).

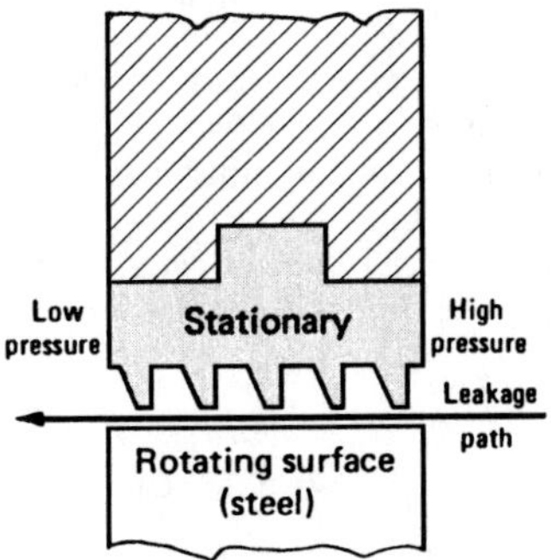

(a.) Simplest design. (Labyrinth materials: aluminum, bronze, babbitt or steel)

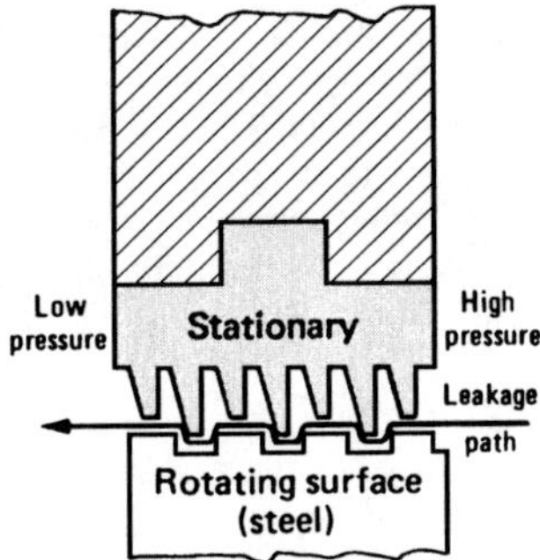

(b.) More difficult to manufacture but produces a tighter seal. (Same material as in a.)

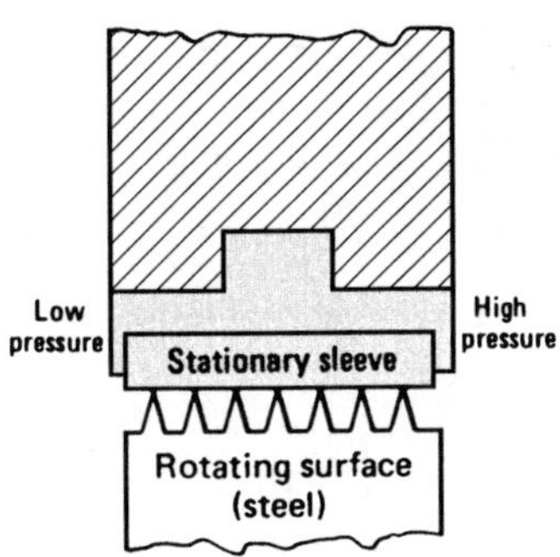

(c.) Rotating labyrinth type, before operation. (Sleeve material: babbitt, aluminum, nonmetallic or other soft material)

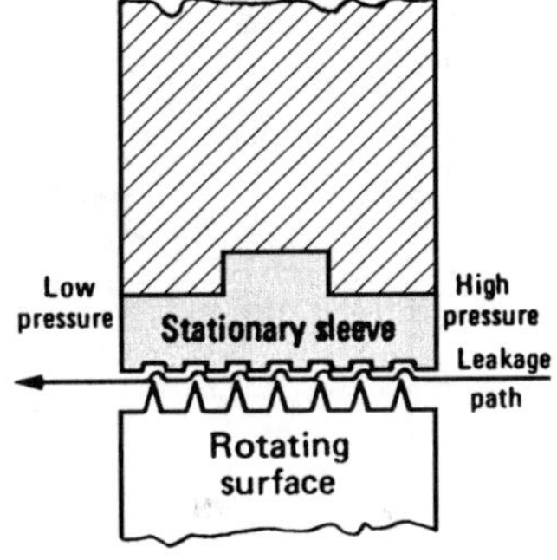

(d.) Rotating labyrinth, after operation. Radial and axial movement of rotor cuts grooves in sleeve material to simulate staggered type shown in b.

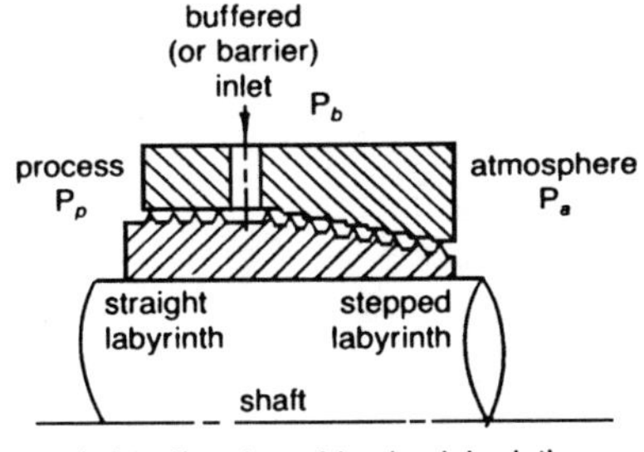

(e.) buffered combination labyrinth

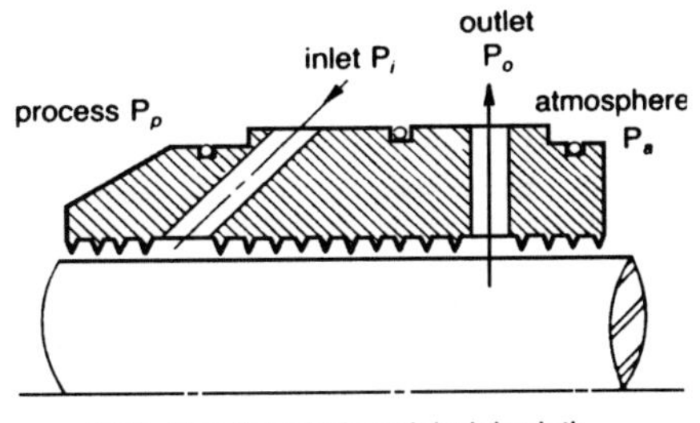

(f.) buffered-vented straight labyrinth

FIGURE 16.11 Various configurations of labyrinth seals.

Ring (Bushing) Seals. This seal consists of a series of sleeves having a small clearance around the shaft. The leakage across the seal is limited by the flow resistance. This design allows the shaft to expand axially when the temperature increases without affecting the integrity of the seal. The segmented and rigid types of this seal are shown in Figs. 16.12(*a*) and 16.12(*b*), respectively. This seal is ideal for high-speed rotating machinery due to the minimal contact between the stationary ring and the rotor.

The seal ring is normally made from babbitt-lined steel, bronze, or carbon. The main advantage of carbon is its self-lubricating properties. If the fluid is a gas, carbon seal rings

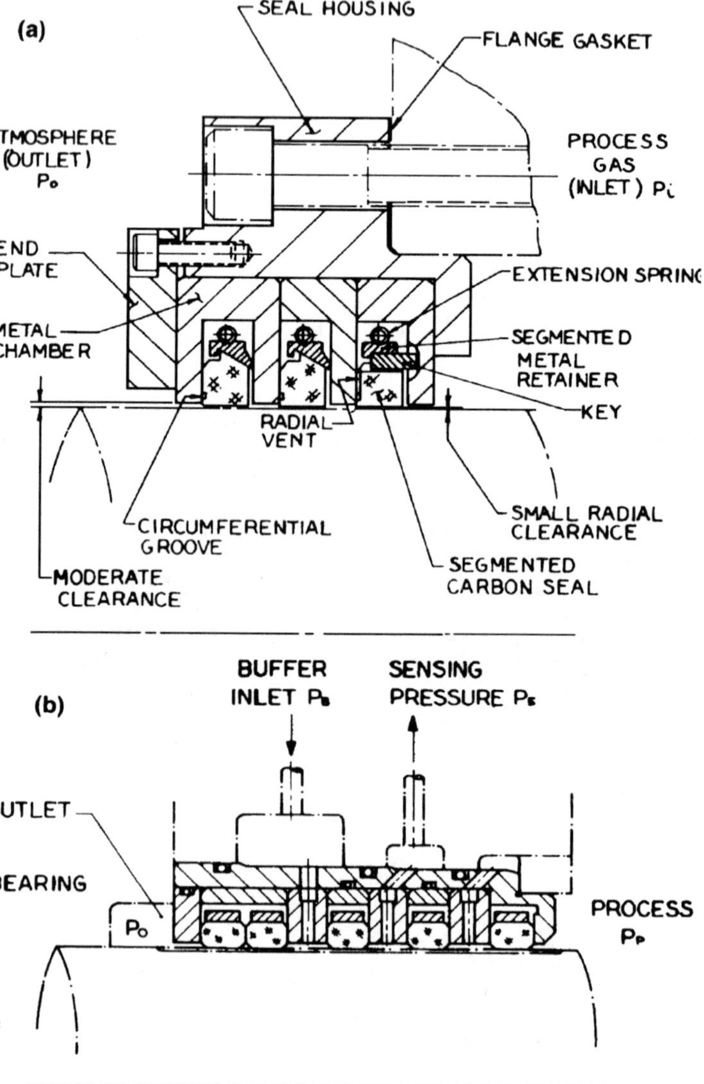

FIGURE 16.12 Floating-type restrictive ring seal.

should be used. Flow through the seal provides the cooling required. In some applications, seal rings are made from aluminum alloys or silver.

Mechanical (Face) Seals

The main purpose of a mechanical (face) seal is to prevent leakage. It consists of the following subcomponents:

- A stationary seal ring mounted around the shaft known as the *stator* of the seal
- A rotating seal ring mounted on the shaft known as the *rotor* of the seal
- Springs to push the rotating ring against the stationary ring
- Static seals (o-rings)

The sealing surfaces of the rotor against the stator are normally in a plane perpendicular to the shaft. The forces that hold these surfaces together are parallel to the shaft. Figure 16.13

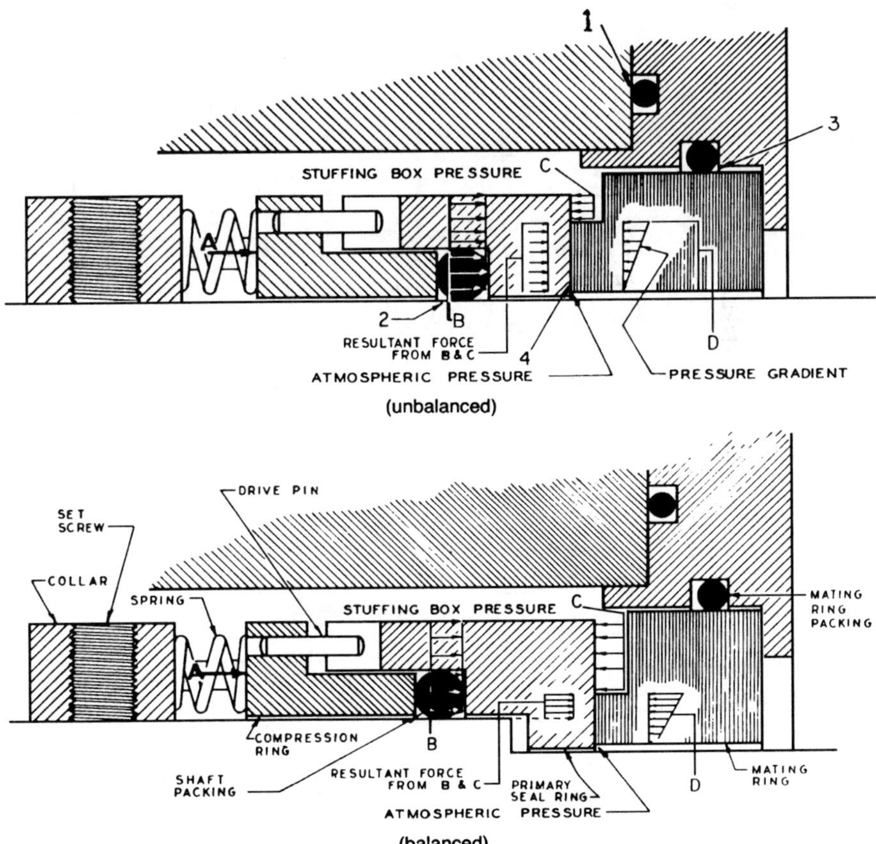

FIGURE 16.13 Unbalanced seal and balanced seal with step in shaft.

illustrates the four sealing points that must be sealed to ensure adequate operation of the seal:

1. The stuffing-box face
2. Leakage along the shaft
3. The mating ring in the gland plate
4. The dynamic faces (rotary to stationary)

The basic units of the seal (Fig. 16.14) are the *seal head* and the *seal seat.* The seal head unit includes the housing, the end-face member, and the spring assembly. The seal seat is the member that mates the seal head. The faces of the seal head and seal seat are lapped to ensure a flatness of $3 \times 10^{-6} - 15 \times 10^{-6}$ in ($8 \times 10^{-6} - 38 \times 10^{-6}$ cm). The head or the seat must rotate, while the other remains stationary. During normal operation, the sealing surfaces are kept closed by the hydraulic pressure. The spring is only needed to close the sealing surfaces when the hydraulic pressure is lost. The degree of *seal balance* (Fig. 16.15) determines the load on the sealing area. A completely balanced seal will only have the spring force acting on the sealing surfaces (i.e., there is no net hydraulic pressure on the sealing surfaces).

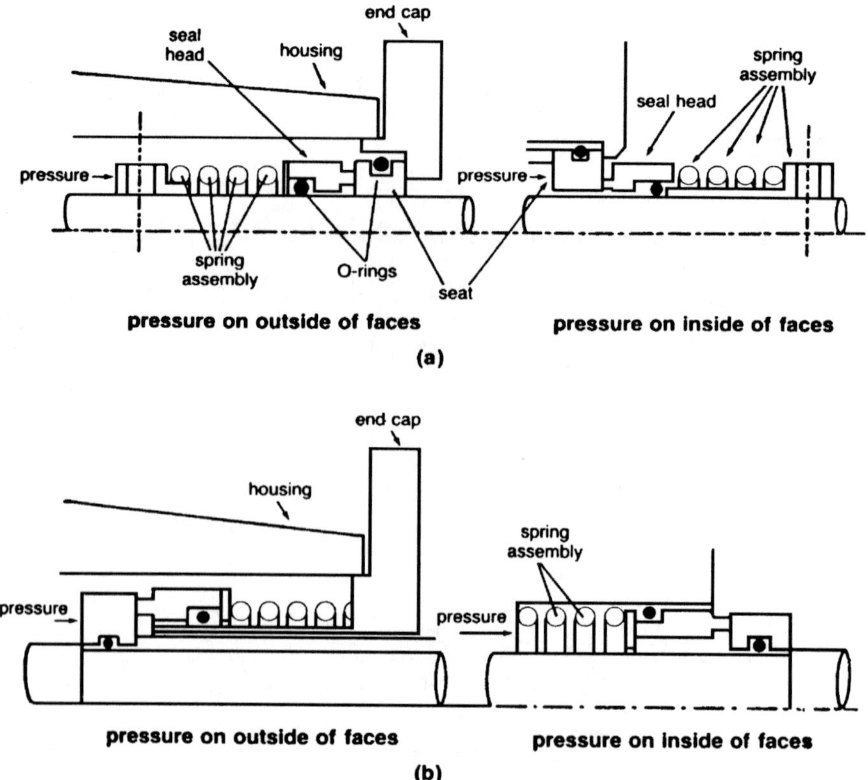

FIGURE 16.14 (*a*) Rotating and (*b*) stationary seal heads.

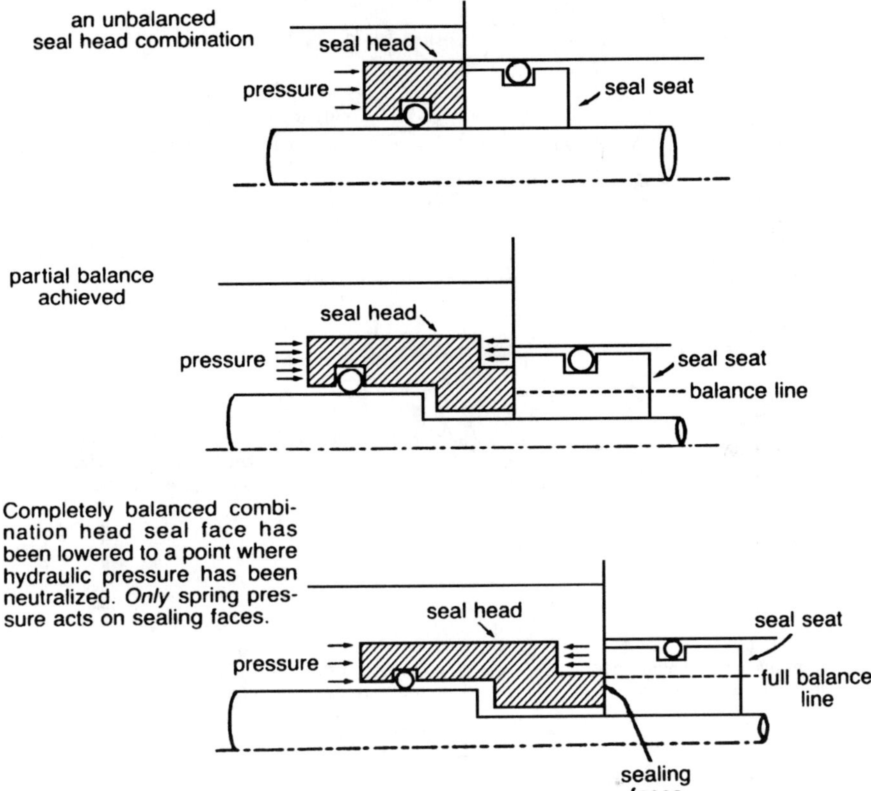

FIGURE 16.15 The seal balance concept.

During the last decade, magnetic seals (Fig. 16.16) have proven to be reliable under severe operating conditions for a variety of fluids. They use magnetic force to produce a face loading. Their advantages are that they are compact, relatively lighter, provide an even sealing force, and are easy to assemble. The two groups of shaft seals are:

- *Pusher-type seal.* It includes o-ring, v-ring, U-cup, and wedge configuration (Fig. 16.17).
- *Bellow-type seals.* They form a static seal between themselves and the shaft.

The two main elements of a mechanical contact shaft seal (Fig. 16.18) are: the oil-to-pressure-gas seal and the oil-to-uncontaminated-seal-oil-drain seal known as *breakdown bushing.* A buffer gas is injected at a port inboard of the seal. During shutdown, the carbon ring remains tightly sandwiched between the rotating seal ring and the stationary sleeve to prevent gas in the compressor from leaking out when the seal oil is not applied.

During operation, the seal oil is maintained at a pressure of 35 to 50 psi (238 to 340 kPa) higher than the process gas. The seal oil enters from the top of the seal and fills the seal cavity completely. A small oil flow is forced across the seal faces of the carbon ring to provide lubrication and cooling for the seal. The oil that crossed the seal faces contacts the process gas. It is called *contaminated oil.* The majority of the oil flows out from the uncontaminated seal oil

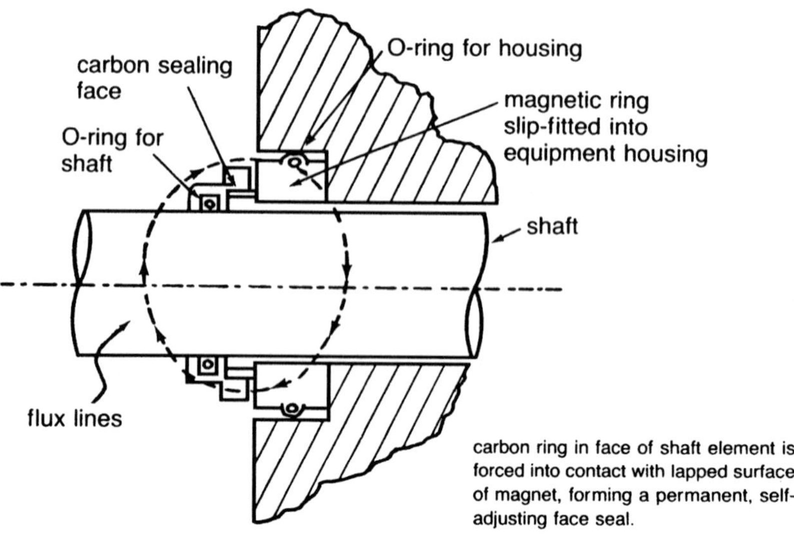

FIGURE 16.16 Simple magnetic-type seal.

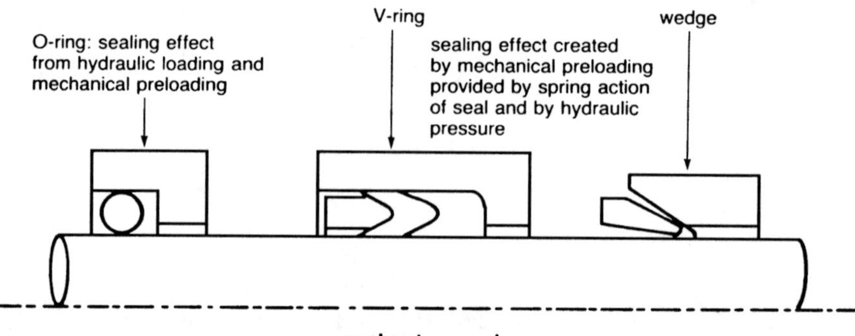

FIGURE 16.17 Various types of shaft sealing elements.

drain line (item 9). The contaminated oil leaves through the drain (item 6) to be purified in the degasifier. In some applications, the bearing oil is combined with the uncontaminated seal oil. However, a separate system for the bearing oil will increase the life of the bearings.

SEAL SYSTEMS

Modern sealing systems have become more sophisticated to meet recent government regulations. Figure 16.19 illustrates a simple seal having a buffered gas and an eductor. The buffer gas pressure must be subatmospheric. Problems have occurred with these systems due to the low capacity of the eductor and variations in the buffer gas pressure. Figure 16.20 illustrates a modern complex seal that incorporates three different types of seals to provide the most effective sealing arrangement. The labyrinth seal prevents the polymers in the

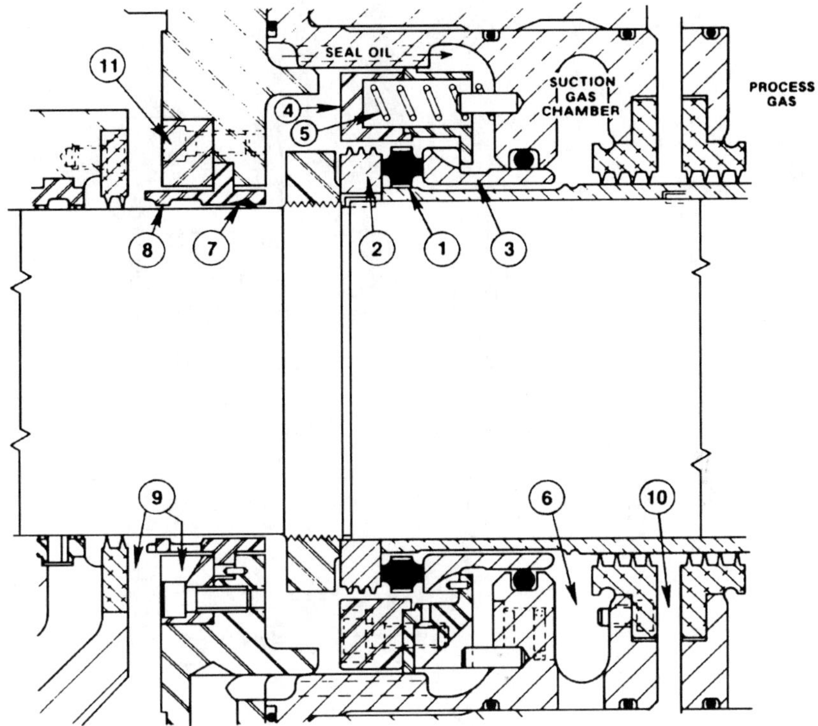

1. ROTATING CARBON RING
2. ROTATING SEAL RING
3. STATIONARY SLEEVE
4. SPRING RETAINER
5. SPRING
6. GAS AND CONTAMINATED OIL DRAIN
7. FLOATING BABBITT-FACED STEEL RING
8. SEAL WIPER RING
9. SEAL OIL DRAIN LINE
10. BUFFER GAS INJECTION PORT
11. BYPASS ORIFICE

FIGURE 16.18 Mechanical contact shaft seal.

process gas from clogging the seal rings. Following the labyrinth seal there are two segmented circumferential contact seals and four segmented restrictive-ring seals. This combination makes the primary seal. Four circumferential-segmented seal rings follow the primary seal. A buffer gas is injected at the first set of circumferential contact seals. An eductor is also installed at the rear circumferential seals. Thus, this assembly is very effective in providing a tight seal in most applications.

REFERENCE

1. Boyce, Meheran P., *Gas Turbine Engineering Handbook,* Gulf Publishing Company, Houston, Tex., 1982, reprinted July 1995.

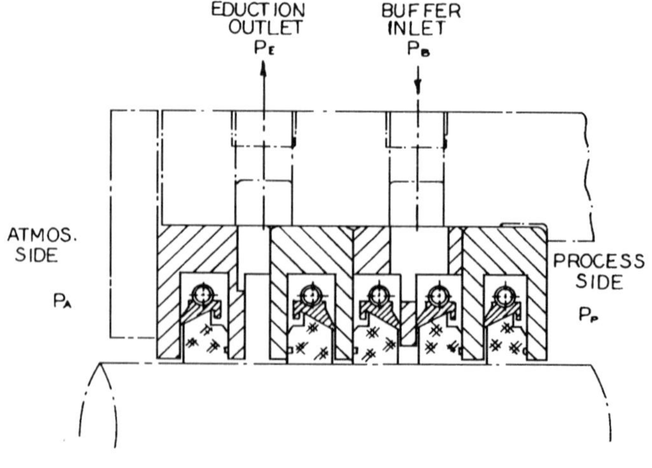

FIGURE 16.19 Restrictive ring seal system with both buffer and education cavities.

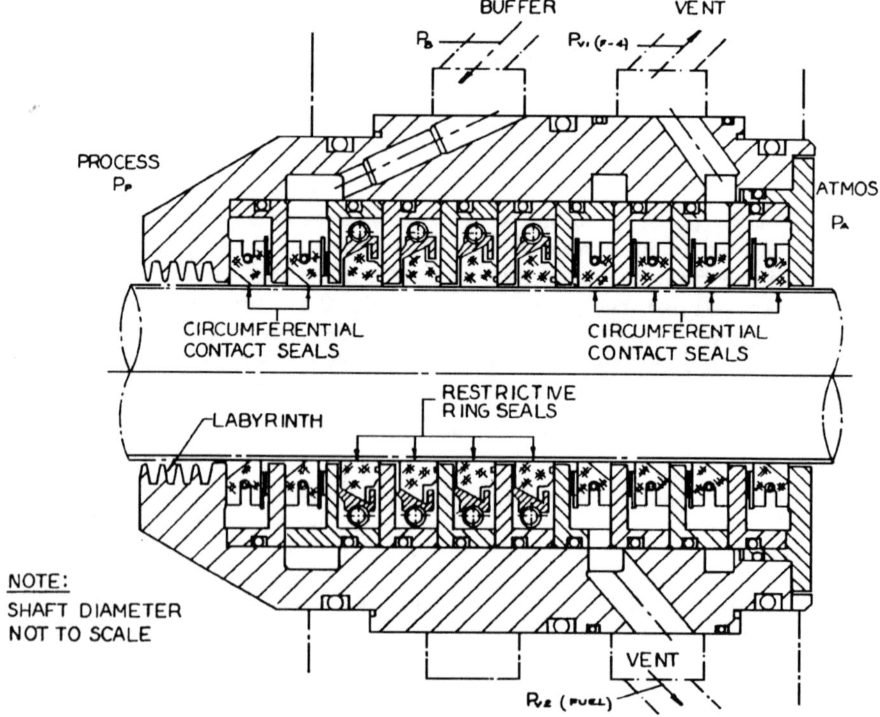

FIGURE 16.20 Multiple combination segmented gas seal system.

CHAPTER 17
GAS TURBINE INSTRUMENTATION AND CONTROL SYSTEMS

Modern gas turbine instrumentation and control systems provide advanced monitoring and diagnostics designed to prevent damage to the unit and to enable it to operate at its peak performance. The following sections describe the various measurements and instrumentation used in gas turbines.

VIBRATION MEASUREMENT

Machine vibration is monitored using:

- Displacement probes
- Velocity pickup detectors
- Accelerometers (measurement of acceleration)

Displacement probes are used to measure the movement of the shaft in the vicinity of the probe. They cannot measure the bending of the shaft away from the probe. Displacement probes indicate problems such as unbalance, misalignment, and oil whirl.

Velocity pickup detectors have a flat response of amplitude as a function of frequency. This means that their alarm setting remains unchanged regardless of the speed of the unit. Their diagnostic role is somewhat limited. The velocity pickup detectors are very directional. They provide different values for the same force when placed in different directions.

Accelerometers are normally mounted on the casing of the machine. They pick up the spectrum of vibration problems transmitted from the shaft to the casing. Accelerometers are used to identify problems having high frequency response such as blade flutter, dry frictional whirl, surge, and gear teeth wear.

Figure 17.1 illustrates a chart used to convert from one type of measurement to another. The vibration limits are also shown on this chart. It demonstrates that the velocity measurement is independent of the frequency, except at very low frequencies where the displacement amplitude is constant.

PRESSURE MEASUREMENT

Pressure transducers consist of a diaphragm and strain gauges. The deflection of the diaphragm is measured by strain gauges when pressure is applied. The output signal varies

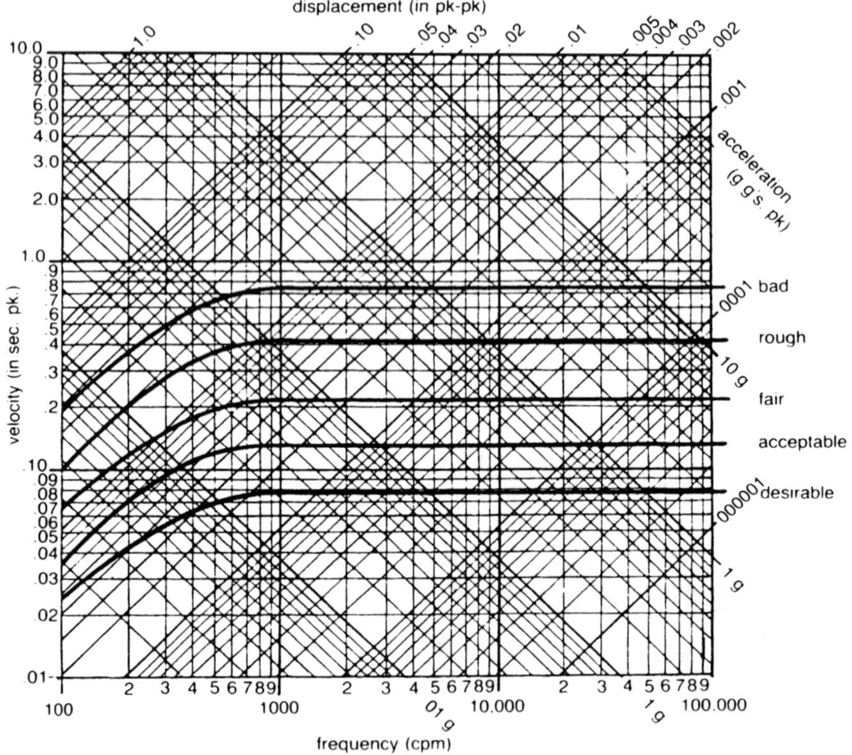

FIGURE 17.1 Vibration nomograph and severity chart.

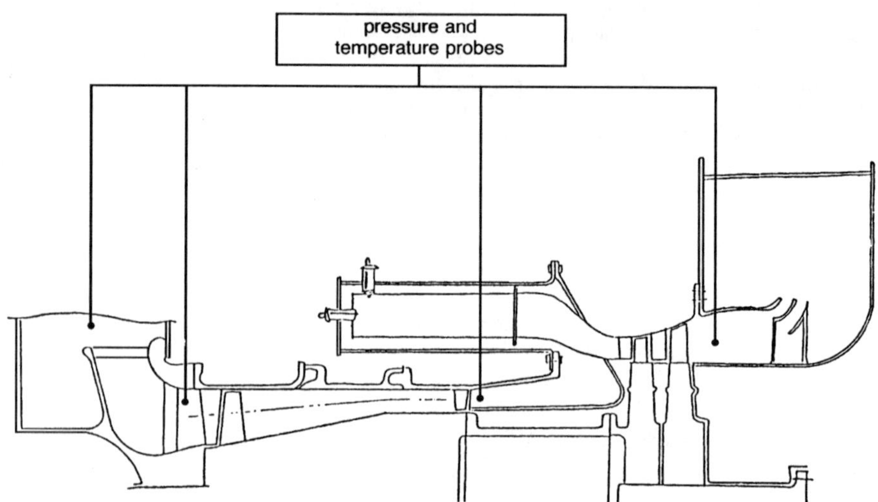

FIGURE 17.2 Locations of pressure and temperature probes on a typical gas turbine.

linearly with the change in pressure over the operating range. Transducers having an operating temperature below 350°F (177°C) are located outside the machine due to temperature constraints. In these cases, a probe is installed inside the machine to direct the air to the transducer. Most modern gas turbines provide probes to measure the compressor inlet and outlet pressure, and turbine exhaust pressure. These probes are normally installed along the shroud of the unit. Some gas turbines have probes installed in each bleed chamber in the compressor and on each side of the inlet air filter. Figure 17.2 illustrates the locations of pressure and temperature probes in a typical gas turbine.

TEMPERATURE MEASUREMENT

Temperature detectors such as thermocouples (used for high-temperature measurement) and resistive thermal detectors (RTDs) are installed in the following locations in a typical gas turbine:

1. Turbine exhaust temperature. Thermocouples are installed around the periphery at the exhaust of the turbine. Two thermocouples are installed at each location to improve the reliability of the measurements. Some gas turbines install thermocouples in two different planes at the turbine exhaust. The first set of thermocouples (e.g., 16) is installed about 0.5 in (1.3 cm) downstream of the last-stage blades of the turbine. These thermocouples measure the *blade path* temperature of the turbine. Differences between the readings obtained between thermocouples located at different locations around the periphery indicate differences in air temperature leaving the combustors. This differential temperature between the combustors creates significant thermal stresses on the blades of the turbine. Most control systems reduce the load or trip the gas turbine when the differential temperature readings exceed predetermined values.
2. The second set of thermocouples (e.g., 16) are installed at the exhaust of the gas turbine, a few meters downstream of the blade path thermocouples. They measure the air temperature leaving the machine. In heat recovery applications (e.g., cogeneration and combined cycle plants), this is the air temperature entering the heat recovery steam generators (HRSG). This temperature is monitored to prevent overheating of the turbine components. The temperature inside the combustors (firing temperature) is not normally monitored due to the following constraints:
   - Thermocouples that are able to detect a temperature around 2400 to 2600°F (1315 to 1427°C) are very expensive.
   - Turbine damage could occur if a thermocouple were to break and pass through the turbine blades.

   Thus, the firing temperature is normally obtained by measuring the exhaust temperature of the turbine and calculating the firing temperature based on the design characteristics (expected temperature drop) of the turbine.
3. Redundant RTDs are embedded in the babbitt (white metal) of the bearing to monitor the oil temperature in the bearings. The unit is tripped on high lube oil temperature. It is also prevented from starting on a low lube oil temperature.
4. The compressor inlet and discharge temperatures are measured to evaluate the compressor performance.

Thermocouples and RTDs are used as temperature detectors. Each one of them has advantages and disadvantages. The following paragraphs describe the features of each type of temperature detectors.

Thermocouples

Thermocouples provide transducers used for measuring temperatures from −330 to 5000°F (−201 to 2760°C). Figure 17.3 shows the useful range of each type of thermocouples. They operate by producing a voltage proportional to the temperature difference between two junctions of dissimilar metals. Thermocouples measure this voltage to determine the temperature difference. The temperature at one of the junctions is known. Thus, the temperature at the other junction can be determined. Since they produce a voltage, there is no need for an external power supply.

Resistive Thermal Detectors

Resistive thermal detectors (RTDs) determine the temperature by measuring the change in resistance of an element due to a change in temperature. Platinum is normally used in RTDs due to its mechanical and electrical stability. Platinum RTDs are used for measuring temperatures from −454 to 1832°F (−270 to 1000°C). The RTD requires an electrical current source to operate. Its accuracy is within ±0.02°F (±0.01°C).

CONTROL SYSTEMS

The control system of a gas turbine performs the following functions:

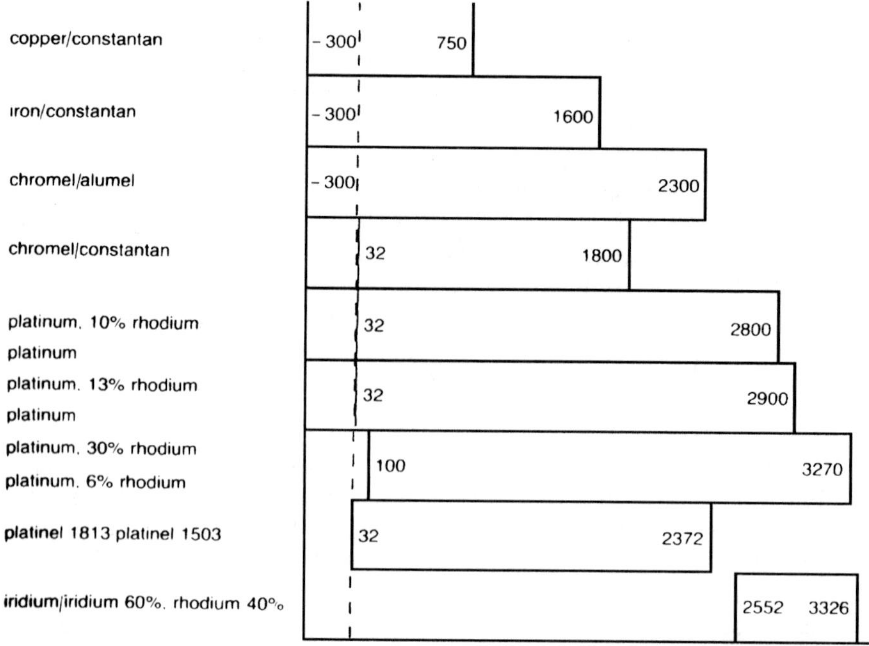

FIGURE 17.3 Ranges of various thermocouples.

- Provides speed and temperature control in the machine
- Control the unit during normal operation
- Provide protection to the gas turbine
- Perform start-up and shutdown sequence of events

Speed Control

Magnetic transducers measure the speed of the shaft at a toothed wheel mounted on the shaft. The transducers provide an output in the form of AC voltage having a frequency proportional to the rotational speed of the shaft. A frequency-to-voltage converter is used to provide a voltage proportional to the speed. This measured value of the speed is then compared to the desired value of the speed (speed setpoint). The difference between these two values is called the *error.* If there is an error, the control system will adjust the opening of the fuel valve to eliminate it. It relies on a proportional-integral-derivative (PID) algorithm (mathematical expression) to eliminate the error within minimal time and without instabilities (oscillations in the speed).

Temperature Control

A series of thermocouples mounted around the periphery at the exhaust of the turbine provides an input to the control system. They are normally made from iron-constantan or chromel-alumel fully enclosed in magnesium oxide sheaths to prevent erosion. Two thermocouples are frequently mounted for each combustion can. The redundancy improves the reliability of the control system. The output of the thermocouples is generally averaged. The control system compares this measured value of the turbine exhaust temperature with the desired value of *setpoint.* The difference between these values is called the *temperature error.* If the temperature error is different from zero, the control system will adjust the opening of the fuel valve to eliminate it. It relies also on PID algorithm to eliminate the error within minimal time and without instabilities.

Protective Systems

The protective systems provide protection during the following events:

- Overspeed
- Overtemperature
- Vibration
- Loss of flame
- Loss of lubrication

The overspeed protection relies on a transducer mounted on the accessory gear or shaft. It trips the unit at around 110 percent of the operating speed. The overtemperature protection system relies on thermocouples similar to the ones used for temperature control. The flame detection system consists of at least two ultraviolet flame detectors that provide the status of the flame in the combustion cans.

In gas turbines having multiple-combustor cans, the flame detectors are mounted in cans, which are not equipped with spark plugs (igniters) to ease the propagation of the flame between cans during the ignition phase. During normal operation, a detector indicating a loss of flame in one can will only annunciate an alarm in the control room. At least two detectors must indicate a loss of flame to trip the machine.

The vibration protection system normally relies on velocity transducers to provide a constant trip setpoint throughout the complete speed range. Two transducers are normally installed on the gas turbine with additional transducers on the driven equipment (e.g., generator). Vibration monitors provide an alarm at a specified level and a trip at a higher level. Most control systems provide a warning in the event of an open-circuit, ground, or short-circuit fault.

START-UP SEQUENCE

The gas turbine control system performs the start-up sequence. It consists of ensuring that all subsystems of the gas turbine perform satisfactorily, and the turbine rotor temperature does not increase too rapidly or overheat during start-up. The control system is designed to start the unit remotely, accelerate it to operating speed, synchronize it automatically with the grid, and increase the load to the desired setting. The start-up sequence for a typical large gas turbine includes the following.

Starting Preparations

The following steps are required to prepare the equipment for a typical start-up:

- Close all control and service breakers.
- Close the computer breaker if it has been de-energized, and enter the time of day. Under normal conditions, the computer operates continuously.
- Acknowledge any alarms.
- Confirm that all lockout relays are reset.
- Place the "Remote-Local" switch to the desired position.

Start-up Description

When all the preparations to start the unit are complete and the unit is ready to go through the start-up process, the "Ready to Start" lamp will energize. At this stage, the operation of the start-up push button will initiate the start-up sequence. Following are the initial steps in the start-up sequence:

1. Energizing the auxiliary lubrication oil pump (see note)
2. Energizing the instrument air solenoid valve

Note: The auxiliary lubricating oil pump is normally powered from an AC power supply. It is used during the start-up and shutdown phase to provide lubrication to the machine. The main lubricating oil pump is normally shaft driven. It provides lubrication to the unit during normal operation. However, some units use two fully redundant lubricating oil pumps powered from an AC power supply. An emergency DC oil pump is also used in most gas turbines. It relies on power from a battery bank to provide sufficient lubrication for safe shutdown and turning gear operation when the normal AC power fails.

When the pressure downstream of the auxiliary lubricating oil pump reaches a predetermined value, the turbine turning gear is started. If the pressure downstream of the auxiliary lubricating oil pump does not reach the predetermined value within 30 s, the unit is shut down. When the signal indicating adequate operation of the turning gear is received, the start-up sequence continues.

At this stage, the starting device (e.g., starting motor) is activated if the lubricating oil pressure is sufficient (above the predetermined value). The turning gear motor is de-energized at around 15 percent of the operating speed. When the turbine reaches the firing speed (when ignition should start), the turbine overspeed trip solenoid and vent solenoid are energized to reset. When the oil pressure is sufficient, the overspeed trip bolts will be reset. These bolts are used to trip the unit at around 12.5 percent overspeed. They initiate the trip when the governing system fails to limit the overspeed to a lower value. When the overspeed trip bolts are reset, the ignition circuit is energized. It will initiate or energize the following:

- Ignition transformers.
- Ignition timer. (The unit is allowed 30 s to establish the flame on both detectors; otherwise, the unit will shut down after several tries.)
- Appropriate fuel system (depending on the type of fuel selected—liquid or gas).
- Atomizing air.
- Timer to de-energize the igniters at the proper time.

At around 50 percent of the operating speed, the starting device is stopped. This is called the *self-sustaining speed* of the gas turbine. At this stage, the turbine is generating enough power to drive the compressor and continue the increase in speed. The bleed valves, which bleed air from the compressor during start-up to prevent surge, close around 92 percent of the operating speed.

Following fuel injection and confirmation of ignition, the speed reference (known as the *no-load speed setpoint*) is increased. The fuel valve will open further to increase the speed of the unit. The shaft is accelerated at a desired rate that is limited by the maximum permissible blade path and exhaust temperatures. The unit is tripped if the desired acceleration is not maintained due to the following reasons:

- If the acceleration is high, compressor surge could occur, leading to extensive damage in the machine.
- If the acceleration is high, the rotor could overheat at a much higher rate than the stator. The rotor blades would expand at a higher rate than the stator blades. This could lead to rubbing between the blades, resulting in a significant damage to the turbine.

When the unit reaches the operating speed, it can be synchronized manually or automatically. Following synchronization, the speed reference becomes a load reference. In other words, since the speed of the unit cannot increase while the unit is synchronized, an increase in speed reference will result in an increase in the load. The speed/load reference is increased at a predetermined rate. This leads to further opening in the fuel valve until the desired load is reached. The computer will store the number of starts and operating hours at various loads. This information is used for maintenance scheduling.

Shutdown

Following a local or remote shutdown request, the fuel is reduced at a predetermined rate until zero load is reached. At this stage, the main circuit breaker connecting the unit to the grid and the circuit breaker connecting it to its own auxiliary loads (*field circuit breaker*) are opened and the fuel valves are tripped. During an emergency shutdown (e.g., a load rejection following a fault on the grid), the circuit breakers and fuel valves are tripped immediately without waiting for the load to be reduced. The turbine speed and the oil pressure from the motor-driven pump will drop. The DC auxiliary lubricating oil pump will start. At around 15 percent of the operating speed, the turning-gear motor will be restarted. When the unit reaches the turning-gear speed (around 5 r/min), the turning-gear overrunning clutch will engage the shaft to rotate the rotor slowly.

The unit must be purged completely of any fuel before it can be restarted. This is done by moving air through it. The air flow must be greater than five times the volume of the turbine. The unit must be left on turning gear for up to 60 h. At this stage, sagging and hogging are no longer a concern due to low rotor temperature. The turning gear and auxiliary lube oil pump are stopped and the shutdown sequence is complete. The computer stores all the contact status and analog values. They can be displayed if required.

FUEL SYSTEM

Hot-corrosion problems have been encountered in modern gas turbines. Techniques have been developed to detect and control the parameters that cause these problems. They include the monitoring of the water content and corrosive contaminants in the fuel line. Any changes in the quality of the fuel can be identified and corrective measures taken. This technique relies on monitoring the water content in the fuel. Since sodium (Na) contaminants in the fuel are caused by external sources such as seawater, monitoring the water content will indicate the sodium content in the fuel. This on-line technique is used for lighter distillate fuels. For heavier fuels, a complete analysis of the fuel should be performed at least monthly using the batch-type system. The results of the analysis should be stored in the computer. The turbine efficiency should be determined with the aid of a fuel Btu (heat content) meter. A water capacitance probe is used to detect water in the fuel line. The corrosive condition of the fuel is monitored by a corrosion probe, which operates based on detecting metal in the fuel.

BASELINE FOR MACHINERY

Mechanical Baseline

The *vibration baseline* for a gas turbine is defined as the normal vibration encountered when there are no problems with the machine. It is normally represented on a vibration spectrum plot showing the frequency on the x-axis and amplitude (peak-to-peak displacement, peak velocity, or peak acceleration) on the y-axis. This vibration spectrum varies significantly with the location on the machine. Thus, when portable vibration equipment is used, the detector should be placed at the same location every time the vibration readings are taken. Baseline vibration measurements should also be taken at different machine speeds and conditions (e.g., different loads). When the operating vibration levels exceed the baseline values by a predetermined amount, an alarm should annunciate and the condition should be investigated.

Aerothermal Baseline

A gas turbine has an *aerothermal performance baseline* in addition to its vibration baseline spectrum. It represents its normal operating aerothermal characteristic. Any deviation from the aerothermal performance baseline beyond a predetermined value should trigger an alarm. When a compressor operates close to the surge line, an alarm should annunciate. Figure 17.4 illustrates a typical compressor characteristic. Other monitoring and operating outputs of a compressor include loss in compressor flow, loss in pressure ratio, and increase in operating fuel cost due to operation at off-design conditions or with a dirty compressor.

The aerothermal characteristic of compressors and turbines is very sensitive to variations in inlet temperature and pressure. Thus, the aerothermal performance parameters (e.g., flow, speed, horsepower) should be normalized to standard-day condition. If these corrections to standard conditions are not used, the performance of the unit may appear to have degraded when, in reality, the performance changed because of a change in ambient pressure or temperature. Table 17.1 shows some of the equations used for obtaining corrections to standard-day conditions.

DATA TRENDING

The data trending technique involves monitoring for a change in the slope of a curve derived from the received data. The slope of the curve is normally calculated for both a long-term trend (168 h) and a short-term trend based on the last 24 h. If the difference between the short-term slope and long-term slope is more than a predetermined value, this

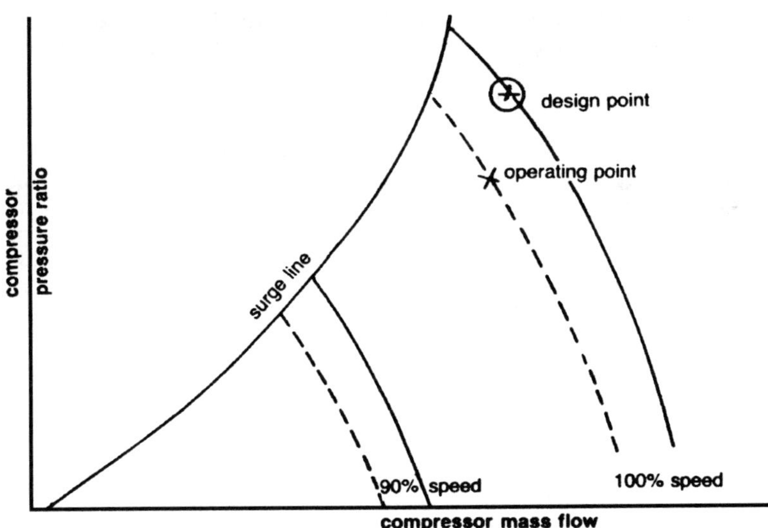

DATA INPUT
Ambient Pressure
Compressor Inlet Pressure
Compressor Discharge Pressure
Compressor Inlet Temperature
Compressor Discharge Temperature
Compressor Speed
Compressor Inlet or Discharge Flow if Available

DIAGNOSTICS OUTPUTS
Compressor Efficiency Lower than Design
Compressor Approaching Surge Conditions
Compressor Approaching Choke Conditions
Dirty Compressor

CONDITION MONITORING OUTPUTS
Loss in Compressor Flow Through Put
Loss in Compressor Pressure Ratio
Fuel Cost Penalty
Projected Increase in Fuel Cost After One Month Operation
Surge Point Deterioration Trend and Anticipated Outage Date

FIGURE 17.4 Aerothermal condition monitoring for compressors.

TABLE 17.1 Gas Turbine Aerothermal Performance Equations for Correction to Standard-Day Conditions

Factors for correction to standard-day temperature and pressure conditions	
Assumed standard-day pressure	14.7 psia
Assumed standard-day temperature	60°F (520°R)
Conditions of test	
Inlet temperature T_i°R	
Inlet pressure P_i psia	
Corrected compressor discharge temperature = (observed temperature) $520/T_i$)	
Corrected compressor discharge pressure = (observed pressure) ($14.7/P_i$)	
Corrected speed = (observed speed) $\sqrt{520/T_i}$	
Correct airflow = (observed flow) ($14.7/P_i$) $\sqrt{T_i\ 520}$	
Corrected horsepower = (observed power) ($14.7/P_i$) $\sqrt{T_i/520}$	

is an indication that the rate of deterioration has changed. The maintenance schedule will be affected because of this change. Figure 17.5 illustrates a difference between the slope of a short-term and a long-term trend.

The trended data is used to predict the scheduled maintenance. For example, Fig. 17.6 is used to predict when the compressor cleaning is required. The data presented in this figure were obtained by recording the compressor exit temperature and pressure each day. These points are then joined and a line is projected to predict when cleaning will be required.

It should be noted that as the pressure at the exit of the compressor decreases, the temperature at the exit increases. The reason for this is that as the pressure at the exit of the compressor drops due to fouling buildup on the compressor blades, the efficiency of the compressor drops. This results in increased turbulence. Thus, a higher portion of the input mechanical energy from the turbine will be converted to temperature increase (rather than pressure increase) at the exit of the compressor.

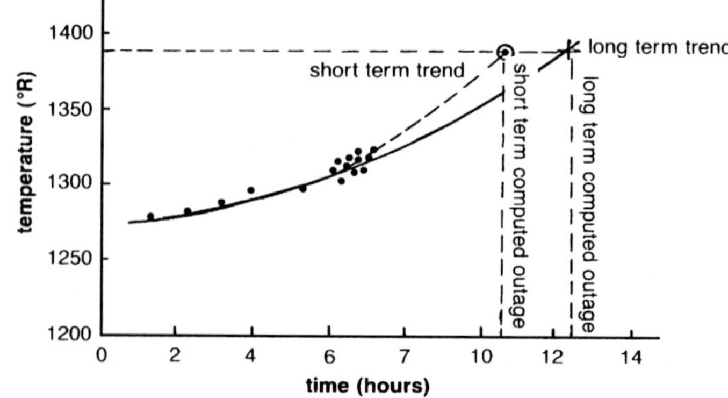

FIGURE 17.5 Temperature versus expected outage time.

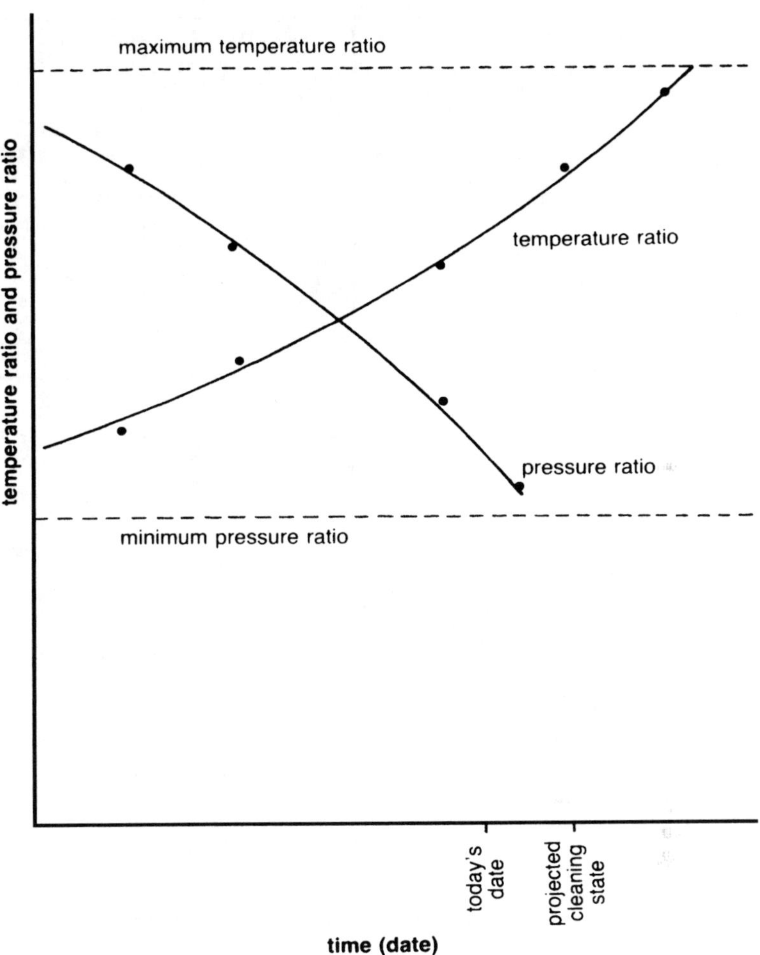

FIGURE 17.6 Data trending to predict maintenance schedules.

COMPRESSOR AEROTHERMAL CHARACTERISTICS AND COMPRESSOR SURGE

Figure 17.7 illustrates a typical performance characteristic for a centrifugal compressor (axial compressors have a similar characteristic). It shows constant aerodynamic speed lines and constant efficiency lines. It can be seen that the pressure ratio changes with the flow and speed. Compressors operate normally on a line, known as *operating line* of the compressor, separated by a safety margin from the surge line. Compressor surge is a situation of unstable operation that results in flow reversal, high vibrations, overheating, and possible damage to the compressor. Therefore, it should be avoided during operation of the unit.

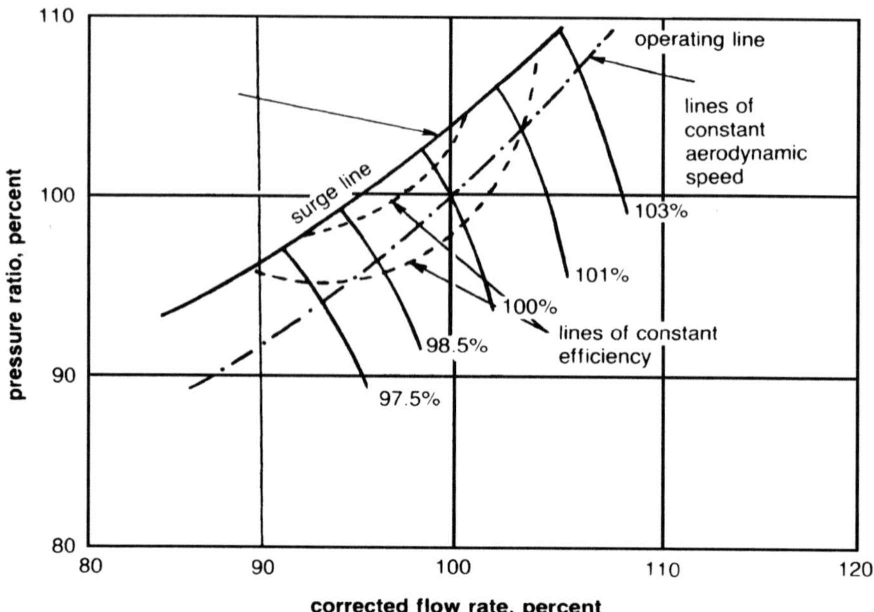

FIGURE 17.7 Typical compressor map.

FAILURE DIAGNOSTICS

Gas turbine failures can be diagnosed. The following sections show how some of the problems are diagnosed.

Compressor Analysis

The following parameters are monitored to perform a compressor analysis:

- Inlet and exit pressures and temperatures
- Ambient pressure
- Vibration at each bearing
- Pressure and temperature of the lubricating system

Table 17.2 shows how some problems affect the various parameters of the compressor. Monitoring these parameters allows the identification of the following problems:

- *Clogged air filter.* A clogged air filter is normally identified by an increase in the pressure drop across the filter.
- *Compressor surging.* Compressor surge is normally identified by a rapid increase in shaft vibration and instability in the discharge pressure. The pressure in the bleed air chamber will also fluctuate.
- *Compressor fouling.* This is normally indicated by a decrease in pressure and an increase in temperature at the discharge of the compressor. If the buildup of deposits on the blades is excessive, the vibration level will increase.

TABLE 17.2 Compressor Diagnostics

	ηc	P_2/P_1	T_2/T_1	Mass flow	Vibration	ΔT bearing	Bearing pressure	Bleed chamber pressure
Clogged filter	↓		↓					
Surge	↑	Variable		↓	High fluctuating	↑	↑	Highly fluctuating
Fouling	↓	↓	↑	↓	↑			
Damaged blade	↓	↓	↑	↓	↑			Highly fluctuating
Bearing failure					↑	↑	↓	

- *Bearing failure.* This is normally indicated by a loss of lubrication pressure in the bearing, an increase in temperature difference across the bearing, and an increase in vibration level.

Combustor Analysis

The measured parameters in the combustors are pressure of the fuel and evenness of combustion noise. The inlet temperature to the turbine is not normally measured due to the very high temperatures in the combustors. Table 17.3 shows how various problems affect the combustor parameters. The measurement of these parameters permit the identification of the following problems:

- *Plugged nozzle.* This is identified by an increase in the fuel pressure and unevenness of combustion noise. This problem is common when the unit burns residual fuels.
- *Cracked or detached liner.* This is identified by an increase in the reading of the acoustic meter and a large difference in the exhaust temperature of the combustors.
- *Combustor inspection or overhaul.* This is based on the equivalent engine hours, which depends on the number of starts, fuel type, and temperature inside the combustors. Figure 17.8 illustrates the effect of these parameters on the life of the unit. The strong effect of the fuel type and number of starts has on the life of the engine should be noted.

Turbine Analysis

Turbine analysis is done by monitoring the pressures and temperatures across the turbine, shaft vibration, and the lubricating system temperature and pressure. Table 17.4 shows the effects various problems have on the turbine parameters. Monitoring these parameters will allow the identification of the following problems:

- *Turbine fouling.* This is indicated by an increase in the exhaust temperature of the turbine. The vibration amplitude will also increase if the fouling is excessive and causes a rotor unbalance.
- *Damaged turbine blades.* This is indicated by a large increase in vibration amplitude and an increase in the exhaust temperature of the turbine.
- *Bowed nozzle.* This results in an increase in the exhaust temperature and possibly an increase in turbine vibration.

TABLE 17.3 Combustor Diagnostics

	Fuel pressure	Unevenness of combustion (sound)	Exhaust temperature spread	Exhaust temperature
Clogging	↑	↑	↑	↑
Combustor fouling	↑ or ↓	↑	↑	↓
Crossover tube failure	↑ or ↓	—	↑+	—
Detached or cracked liner	↑ or ↓	↑	↑	—

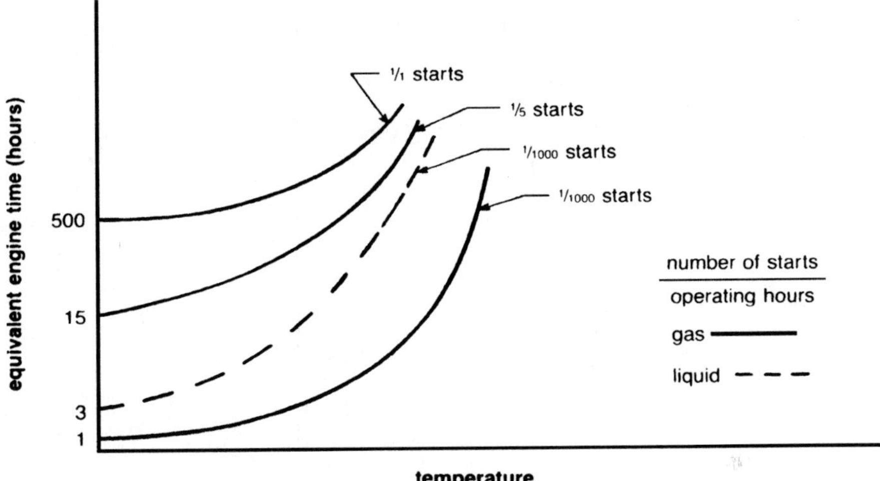

FIGURE 17.8 Equivalent engine time in the combustor section.

- *Bearing failure.* Turbine bearing problems have the same symptoms as compressor bearing problems.
- *Cooling air failure.* Problems with the blade cooling system are normally detected by an increase of the pressure drop in the cooling line.
- *Turbine maintenance.* The *equivalent engine time* is used to determine the turbine maintenance schedule. It is a function of temperature, type of fuel, and number of starts. Figure 17.9 illustrates the effect of these parameters on the life of the unit. The strong effect of the fuel type and number of starts on the life of the unit should be noted.

Turbine Efficiency

Significant fuel savings can be achieved by monitoring the efficiency of the gas turbine equipment and correcting for operational problems. Some of these problems are very simple to correct, such as cleaning of the compressor blades. Others may require a more complex solution to maximize the overall efficiency of the plant equipment.

Figure 17.10 illustrates the significant profits gained by operating at a slightly higher efficiency.

MECHANICAL PROBLEM DIAGNOSTICS

Table 17.5 shows a chart used for vibration diagnosis. It consists of general guidelines used for diagnosing mechanical problems. The vibration data collected is normally stored in the computer system. Previous vibration data is recalled and compared with recent data to identify problems in the machine.

TABLE 17.4 Turbine Diagnostics

	ηc	P_3/P_4	T_3/T_4	Vibration	ΔT bearing	Cooling air pressure	Wheelspace temperature	Bearing pressure
Fouling	↓		↓	↑			↑	
Damaged blade	↓		↓	↑				
Bowed nozzle	↓	↓	↓	↑			↑	
Bearing failure				↑	↑			↓
Cooling air failure					↑	↓	↑	

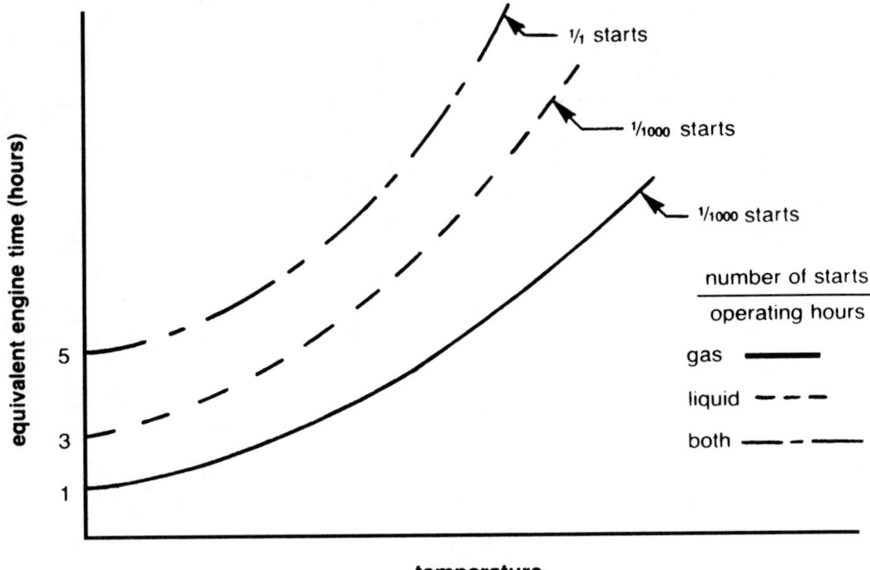

FIGURE 17.9 Equivalent engine time in the turbine section.

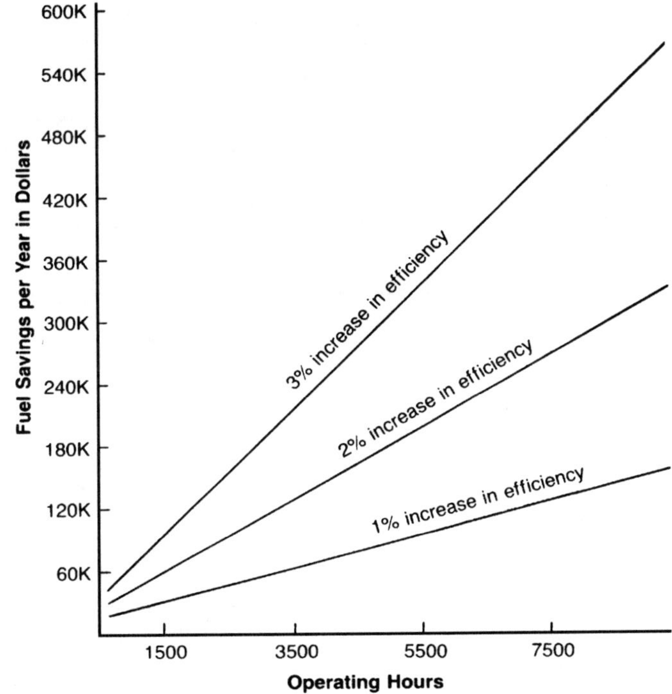

FIGURE 17.10 Savings versus efficiency. Fuel cost of \$2.7/million Btu approximately \$1/gal (based on a unit consuming 280×10^6 Btu/h). For a 15-MW gas turbine unit.

TABLE 17.5 Vibration Diagnostics

Usual Predominant Frequency*	Cause of vibration
Running frequency at 0–40%	Loose assembly of bearing liner, bearing casing, or casing and support Loose rotor shrink fits Friction-induced whirl Thrust bearing damage
Running frequency at 40–50%	Bearing support excitation Loose assembly of bearing liner, bearing case, or casing and support Oil whirl Resonant whirl Clearance induced vibration
Running frequency	Initial unbalance Rotor bow Lost rotor parts Casing distortion Foundation distortion Misalignment Piping forces Journal and bearing eccentricity Bearing damage Rotor bearing system critical Coupling critical Structural resonances Thrust bearing damage
Odd frequency	Loose casing and support Pressure pulsations Vibration transmission Gear inaccuracy Valve vibration
Very high frequency	Dry whirl Blade passage

*Occurs in most cases predominately at this frequency; harmonics may or may not exist.

INSTRUMENTATION AND CONTROL SYSTEMS OF A TYPICAL MODERN GAS TURBINE

Modern Gas Turbine Control Systems

Microprocessor-based distributed digital control systems are used for control and monitoring of modern gas turbines and combined cycle power plants. The instrumentations are normally triplicated with 2 out of 3 voting logic. The start-up and shutdown of the gas turbine is fully automatic. The supervisory system of the gas turbine includes monitoring of the speed, vibration, temperature, and flame as well as an operating data counter. The human system interface (HIS) is provided locally (near the gas turbine) and remotely in the control room. It consists of operator station(s) with monitor, keyboard, mouse, printer, and sequence-of-event recorders. Operator intervention is not required, except for selecting the fuel type and the setting of the load. The controls are done in a sequential mode. All steps are monitored for execution. An incomplete step can prevent the program from advancing further. The cause of the incomplete step is indicated on the monitor. The active step of the program is also indicated.

Closed-Loop Controllers

The function of a closed-loop controller is to continuously monitor and adjust process variables (e.g., temperatures, pressures, flow) in the gas turbine to match their setpoints. They are used to control many parameters in the gas turbine, including the following:

- Start-up and shutdown speed, fuel flow, and so forth
- Frequency and load
- Exhaust temperature
- Position of the guide vanes

PROTECTIVE SYSTEMS

The gas turbine instrumentation and control system vary significantly between different machines. However, most gas turbines are protected against the following:

- *Low lube oil pressure.* The pressures downstream of the lube oil pump and the bearing oil pressures are monitored. The turbine trips when the oil pressure in the bearing header drops.
- *High vibration.* Dual radial sensors monitor the vibration and trip the unit on high vibrations.
- *Turbine overspeed.* A triple-redundant system protects the unit against shaft overspeed. Magnetic pickup sensors are mounted near the toothwheel on the rotor inside the inlet bearing cavity (near the thrust and journal bearings) to monitor the speed. They trip the unit on overspeed. Overspeed bolts are also used to trip the unit when the overspeed becomes around 12.5 percent.
- *High lube oil temperature.* Redundant RTDs are embedded in the babbitt (white metal) of the bearings to monitor the temperature. They trip the unit on high lube oil temperature. The reason for this is that the oil viscosity drops with increased temperature, resulting in higher friction in the bearings. The temperature inside the bearings will increase, leading to bearing damage.
- *Exhaust temperature.* The exhaust temperature of the air leaving the gas turbine is monitored by 16 thermocouples. They trip the unit on high exhaust temperature.
- *Blade path temperature.* The blade path temperatures are monitored by 16 thermocouples installed around 1.3 cm (0.5 in) downstream of the last-stage blades of the turbine. The thermocouples are installed around the circumference of the turbine. They monitor the temperature difference between the combustor baskets. These thermocouples cannot be installed at the discharge of the combustors due to the high temperature [around 2500°F (1371°C)]. However, they can still monitor the difference in temperature between the combustor baskets due to a relationship between the location of the baskets and the location of the thermocouples. For example, the air stream leaving a combustor flows through the turbine and is discharged from it at a 40° angle away from the combustor. Therefore, the temperature difference between two neighboring thermocouples

would be representative of the temperature difference between two combustors. The concern about having a high difference in blade path temperatures is thermal cycling and fatigue. An alarm is received when the blade path temperature difference is 90°F (50°C); the unit is unloaded when the difference is 120°F (67°C); and the unit is tripped when the temperature difference is 130°F (72°C).

- *High acceleration.* Acceleration detectors trip the turbine on high shaft acceleration. They are used during start-up to prevent compressor surge. They are also used during normal operation to prevent overspeed following a load rejection (i.e., when the circuit breaker connecting the generator to the grid opens suddenly following a fault on the grid).
- *High thrust pad temperature.* The shaft is prevented from moving axially in either direction at the thrust bearing. Tilted pads are installed at both sides of the shaft collar to prevent axial movement of the shaft. An oil film is established between the shaft collar and the pads at both sides of the collar. When the pads wear out, the shaft starts to move axially. This causes higher friction inside the bearing leading to increase in oil temperature. The RTDs trip the turbine on high thrust pad temperature. An alternative method relies on proximity probes to trip the turbine following axial movement.
- *Low or high gas turbine inlet vacuum.* The pressure at the inlet to the gas turbine is below atmospheric (under vacuum). A pressure switch monitors it. The control system trips the unit when the vacuum drops (normally caused by a damaged filter) and when the vacuum increases (normally caused by a clogged filter).
- *High turbine exhaust pressure.* The unit is tripped on high turbine exhaust pressure. This trip is needed in case there is a restriction in the airflow downstream of the turbine (e.g., in a boiler).

PERMISSIVES (INTERLOCKS)

Permissives, also known as *interlocks,* are conditions that must be satisfied so that the control system can permit the continuation of the start-up sequence or continued operation. The following are some of the permissives normally used in gas turbines:

- *Combustor outfire.* The combustion is monitored by ultraviolet detectors (flame scanners) located in the upper combustors. They interrupt the fuel to the turbine if combustion is not confirmed a few seconds after the fuel is injected into the combustors.
- *Low compressor discharge pressure.* The discharge pressure of the compressor is monitored by a pressure switch. When there is sufficient air flow to support combustion, the compressor discharge pressure will be higher than a predetermined value [e.g., 0.6 psi (4 kPa)]. At this stage, the control system opens the fuel valve. This condition (compressor discharge pressure higher than a predetermined value) is called a *permissive* or *interlock.* If it is not satisfied, the control system will stop the startup sequence.
- *Low lube oil temperature.* The start-up sequence is stopped on low lube oil temperature. The reason for this is the difficulty encountered in pumping the oil to the bearings due to increased viscosity at low temperature.
- *Low lube oil pressure.* The turning gear is prevented from operating when the bearing oil pressure is low. This is done to prevent damage to the unit due to high friction inside the bearings.
- *High and low gas supply pressure.* The unit is prevented from starting when the gas supply pressure is high or low. This is done to prevent high or low gas flow into the combustors.

LIQUID FUEL SUPPLY

Many gas turbines have a liquid fuel supply in addition to the gas fuel supply. The following are its main protective features:

- *Low fuel pump suction pressure.* The fuel pump is tripped on low suction pressure to prevent cavitation damage in the pump.
- *High and low differential pressure across fuel manifold.* The differential pressure across the fuel manifold is monitored. This is the pressure difference between the inlet to the liquid fuel manifold and the compressor discharge. It is used to confirm that sufficient flow is entering the combustors. The unit is tripped when this differential pressure becomes very high (overfueling) or very low (underfueling).
- *Fuel transfer failure.* The transfer from gas to liquid fuel is monitored by a pressure switch in the liquid fuel line. The unit is tripped upon a fuel transfer failure.

START-UP SEQUENCE OF THE GAS TURBINE

Prior to starting the gas turbine, all of the auxiliaries must be in the automatic position. The turning gear and oil pumps must be operating. The fuel system must also be ready. Following are the steps required to start a simple-cycle gas turbine:

Cranking Phase

- The starting motor is energized.
- The rotor is accelerated to the ignition speed. It is around 1000 r/min (the compressor normally operates at 5400 to 8000 r/min).
- The fuel valves are opened.
- The igniters are energized (normally, there are two igniters located in the bottom combustor baskets).
- The flame is established. It is confirmed by the flame scanners, which are normally located in the upper combustor baskets.

Acceleration Phase

- The start ramp controller accelerated the rotor to 89 percent of the operating speed. This is an open-loop controller that increases the speed over a 20-min period.
- The starting motor is stopped at around 66 percent of the operating speed.
- The speed controller accelerates the rotor from 89 to 100 percent of the operating speed. This is a closed feedback controller.

Synchronization Phase

Synchronization should not be attempted until the following conditions are met:

- The generator frequency is slightly higher (e.g., by 0.05 Hz) than the frequency in the grid.
- The generator voltage is matched to the voltage in the grid.
- The generator-phase voltage is matched to the grid-phase voltage. It should be noted that during commissioning of the unit (before the generator is synchronized to the grid for the

first time), an additional condition must be met. It is ensuring that the phase sequence of the generator is the same as the phase sequence in the grid. In other words, the A, B, and C phases in the generator are being connected to the same phases in the grid. Problems have occurred when one of the generator phases was connected to a different phase in the grid.

- The synchronous acceptor relay must also provide an independent confirmation that all the conditions required for synchronization are met before the circuit breaker can be closed.
- The generator circuit breaker is closed manually or automatically. An automatic synchronizer is used normally to change the speed and voltage to match the grid. It initiates a signal to close the generator circuit breaker after ensuring that all the conditions required for synchronization are met. However, the breaker does not close until the synchronous acceptor confirms that the unit is in synchronism with the grid.

Loading Phase. The load is increased by opening the fuel valve further until the desired load is reached.

Operation Phase. Some units are operated based on an exhaust temperature control system. This control system operates as follows:

- It measures the compressor discharge pressure and transmits this measurement to a controller.
- The controller uses a predetermined relationship between the compressor discharge pressure and the setpoint of the exhaust temperature to determine the new setpoint of the exhaust temperature. Based on this predetermined relationship, the setpoint of the exhaust temperature decreases when the compressor discharge pressure increases. For example, when the ambient temperature decreases, the air becomes denser, resulting in an increase in the compressor discharge pressure. The controller will decrease the setpoint of the exhaust temperature. Since the actual exhaust temperature is higher than the new setpoint of the exhaust temperature (the controller would have matched the actual exhaust temperature and the previous setpoint of the exhaust temperature), the controller will send a signal to reduce the flow through the fuel valve. Thus, the power output from the gas turbine remains at 100 percent while the fuel flow has been reduced. In other words, the gas turbine is operating more efficiently due to a reduction in ambient temperature. It should be noted that this control system is not controlling the output power based on the ambient temperature. The reason for this is that the compressor discharge pressure is affected by other parameters, including the following:
  - Fouling of the compressor blades
  - Condition of the compressor blades (cracks and dents in the compressor blades reduce the efficiency and hence the discharge pressure of the compressor)
  - Ambient pressure
  - Ambient humidity

  Thus, this control system relies on the compressor discharge pressure to determine the setpoint of the exhaust temperature because it includes the effects of all the variables upstream of the compressor discharge. This design has great advantages. It maintains constant output power despite variations in all the parameters mentioned earlier. This ensures that the gas turbine is operating at its best efficiency point (100 percent load). The capital cost of a gas turbine using this control system is normally lower than others having the same output power. The reason for this is that other gas turbines may use a control system that allows the output power to exceed 120 percent when the ambient temperature drops.

These gas turbines must have a rating for all of their components exceeding 120 percent. This results in an increase in the capital cost of these gas turbines.

Inlet Guide Vanes. The variable inlet guide vanes (IGVs) are installed upstream of the first-stage compressor blades. They are normally partially closed (40° angle) when the output power is less than 10 MW. The control system opens them gradually when the power is between 10 and 22 MW. When the power is more than 22 MW, they are fully open.

The control system throttles the IGVs closed in some combined cycle applications. This increases the exhaust temperature of the gas turbine and improves the efficiency of the steam power plant. This feature is normally used when the gas turbine is at part-load.

Compressor Bleed Valves. The compressor bleed valves are not normally controlled by the control system. They are mechanical valves that vent air from the compressor during start-up to prevent compressor surge. They normally close when the unit reaches 92 percent of the speed. (At this stage, the pressure inside the compressor is higher than the spring force of the valve.)

Transmitters. Temperature and pressure transmitters provide a 4- to 20-mA signal over the temperature or pressure range specified. They do not have a control function (e.g., they do not cause a trip). They are used to inform the operator of the actual values of temperature and pressure across the machine.

REFERENCE

1. Boyce, M. P., *Gas Turbine Engineering Handbook,* Gulf Publishing Company, Houston, Tex., 1982, reprinted 1995.

CHAPTER 18
GAS TURBINE PERFORMANCE CHARACTERISTICS

THERMODYNAMIC PRINCIPLES

The ambient conditions around a gas turbine vary with time and location.[1,2] Standard conditions are required for comparative purposes. The gas turbine industry uses these standard conditions: 59°F (14°C), 14.7 psia (1.013 bar), and 60 percent relative humidity. These conditions are established by the International Organization for Standardization (ISO) and are generally referred to as *ISO Standards.*

Figure 18.1 illustrates a simple-cycle gas turbine. Ambient air enters the compressor of the gas turbine. The pressure increase across the compressor is from 12- to 45-fold. The temperature also increases across the compressor as a result of the compression process. The discharge temperature from the compressor is between 650 and 900°F (345 and 480°C). The air leaving the compressor enters the combustors. The combustion process occurs at almost a constant pressure. In reality, there is a slight decrease in pressure across the combustors. There is significant increase in temperature in the combustors to between 2200 and 3000°F (1200 and 1650°C). The turbine converts the energy in the hot gases to mechanical work. This conversion occurs in two steps. First, the velocity of the hot gases increases in the stationary blades (nozzles) of the turbine. A portion of the thermal energy is converted into kinetic energy (first law of thermodynamics). Second, the rotating blades of the turbine (buckets) convert the kinetic energy to work. The work developed by the turbine drives the compressor and the load. The compressor normally requires from 55 to 67 percent of the total work developed by the turbine.

The single-shaft gas turbine illustrated in Fig. 18.1 has one continuous shaft. Thus, all the components operate at one speed. This design is normally used to drive a generator. It is used for this application because there is no need to vary the speed.

THERMODYNAMIC ANALYSIS

The laws of thermodynamics can be used to analyze the Brayton cycle. Figure 18.2 illustrates the results of this analysis. The cycle efficiency is plotted versus the specific output (output power per pound of airflow) at different firing temperatures (in the combustors) and pressure ratios. The specific output per pound of airflow is an important parameter. The increase in this parameter indicates that the required gas turbine can be smaller for the same output power. Simple-cycle gas turbines [Fig. 18.2 (*a*)] increase in efficiency at a given firing temperature when the pressure ratio increases. Also, the increase in firing temperature results in increase in specific output for a given pressure ratio. The pressure ratio has less

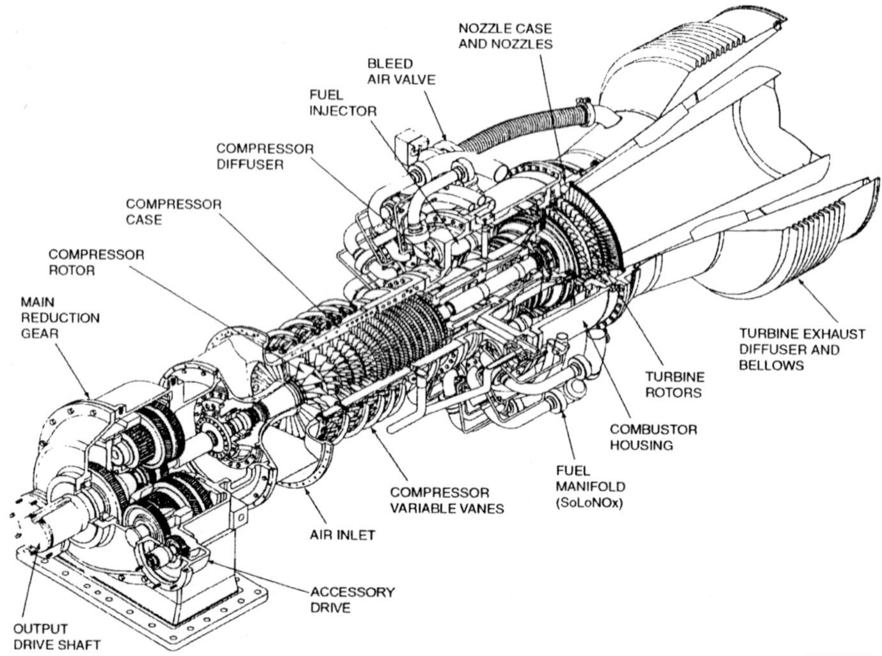

FIGURE 18.1 Cutaway view of the Taurus 70 gas turbine. (*Courtesy of Solar Turbines.*)

effect on efficiency in combined cycles [Fig. 18.2 (*b*)]. The specific output decreases when the pressure ratio increases. The thermal efficiency increases with increasing firing temperature. Note the significant differences between the two curves. The parameters giving optimum performance are different between simple and combined cycles. Increasing the pressure ratio increases the efficiency in simple cycles. Having a relatively modest pressure ratio and higher firing temperature increases the efficiency in combined cycles. For example, the GE MS-7001-FA design parameters are a pressure ratio of 14:1 and a firing temperature of 2350°F (1288°C). The combined-cycle efficiency of this machine is optimized. However, its simple-cycle efficiency is not. On the other hand, the pressure ratio of the LM-6000 is 24:1. Its simple-cycle efficiency is 40 percent.

FACTORS AFFECTING GAS TURBINE PERFORMANCE

The performance of the gas turbine is heavily affected by ambient conditions. Any parameter affecting the mass flow of the air entering the gas turbine will have an impact on the performance of the gas turbine. Figure 18.3 illustrates how the ambient temperature affects the

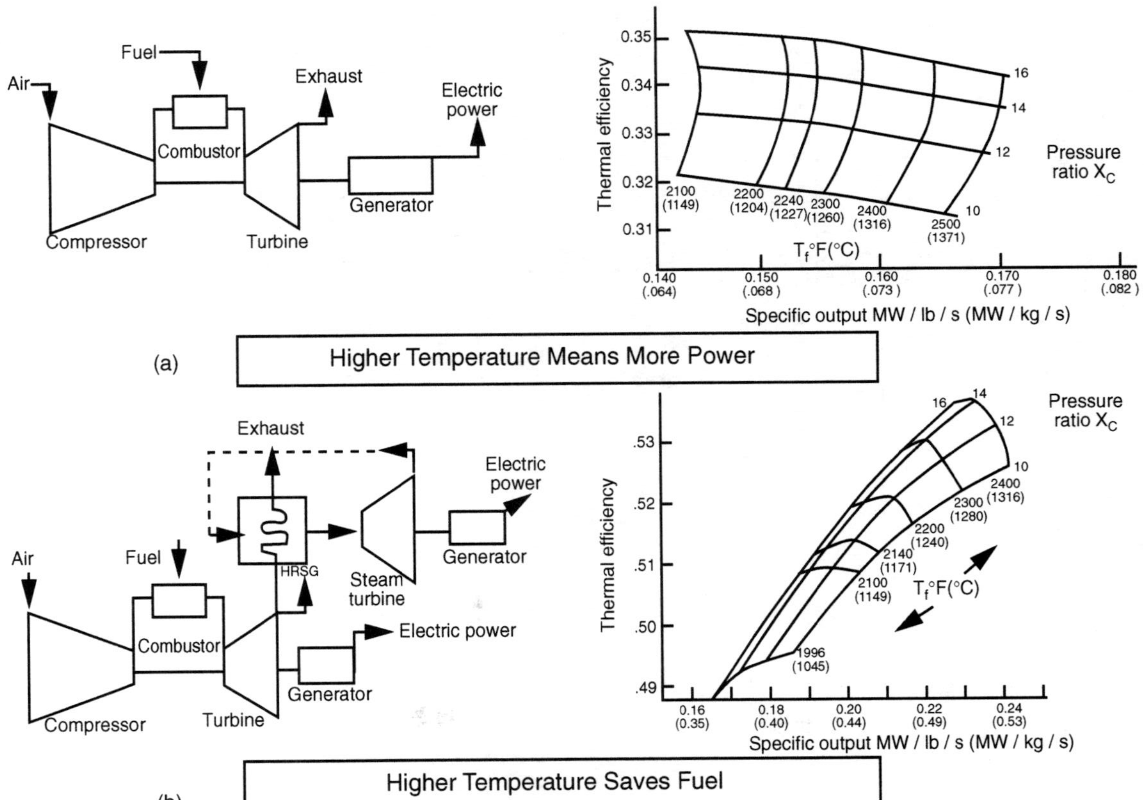

FIGURE 18.2 Gas turbine thermodynamics. (*a*) Simple cycle; (*b*) combined cycle. (*Courtesy of General Electric.*)

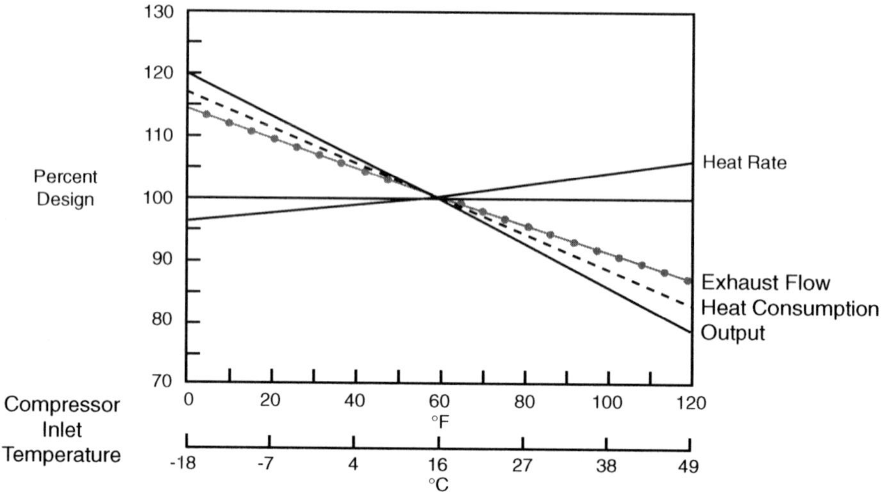

FIGURE 18.3 Effect of ambient temperature. (*Courtesy of General Electric.*)

output power, heat rate (one/(thermal efficiency)), heat consumption, and the exhaust flow for a typical single-shaft heavy-duty gas turbine. The airflow and power output of a gas turbine decrease with increasing altitude due to a decrease in barometric pressure. The reduction in these parameters is proportional to the decrease in the air density. A typical decrease in airflow and output power of a gas turbine is 1 percent per 100-m increase in altitude. The heat rate and the remaining cycle parameters are not affected.

The density of humid air is lower than dry air. An increase in ambient humidity will reduce the power output and efficiency of a gas turbine. An increase in specific humidity of 0.01 kg water vapor/kg dry air will typically reduce the power output and efficiency by 0.0015 and 0.0035 percent, respectively. In the past, this effect was considered negligible. In modern gas turbines, it has a greater significance because the flow of water or steam injected for nitric oxide (NO_X)control is being changed, depending on the level of humidity. This humidity effect is mainly caused by the control system approximation of the firing temperature. Some gas turbine control systems reduce the power when ambient humidity increases. However, on some aeroderivatives, the control system uses the discharge temperature from the gas generator to control the fuel flow. This control system will actually increase the power. The fuel flow is increased to raise the temperature of the moist air (containing humidity) to the setpoint (required temperature). The increase in fuel flow will increase the gas generator speed. (This is a two-spool engine.) The gas generator can operate at different speeds from the power turbine. The increase in fuel flow compensates for the decrease in air density.

Pressure losses in the system are caused by inserting air filtration, silencing, evaporative coolers, chillers in the inlet, or exhaust heat recovery devices. The effects of pressure drop vary with the unit. A pressure drop of 4 in (10 mbar) of water at the inlet to a gas turbine will decrease the output power and efficiency by around 1.5 and 0.5 percent, respectively. The same pressure drop at the exhaust of a gas turbine will reduce the output power and efficiency by around 0.4 percent. The fuel type has an effect on performance. Natural gas produces more output then distillate oil. The difference is almost 2 percent. The reason is that the combustion products of natural gas have higher specific heat. This is caused by a higher concentration of water vapor resulting from a higher hydrogen-carbon ratio in methane.

The gas turbine performance is affected significantly by gaseous fuels having lower heating values than natural gas. The fuel flow must increase when the heating value drops to provide the required heat. The compressor does not compress the additional mass flow. It increases the turbine and the output power of the machine. The compressor power is not affected by this change. The five side effects include the following:

1. The increase in mass flow through the turbine increases the power developed by the turbine. The compressor takes some of this increase in power. This results in an increase in the pressure ratio across the compressor, driving it closer to the surge limit.
2. The increase in turbine power could take the turbine and all the equipment in the power train above their 100 percent rating. Equipment rated at higher limits may be required in some cases.
3. The size and cost of the fuel piping and valves will increase due to an increase in the volume of the fuel. Coal gases [low or medium heating value (Btu)] are normally supplied at high temperatures. This increases their volumetric flow further.
4. Gases having low heating values (Btu) are normally saturated with water before delivery to the turbine. This results in an increase in the heat transfer coefficients of the combustion products, leading to an increase in the metal temperature in the turbine.
5. The amount of air required to burn the fuel increases as the heating value decreases. Gas turbines having high firing temperatures may not be able to operate using low-heating-value fuel.

As a result of these effects, each model of a gas turbine has a set of application guidelines. They specify the flows, temperatures, and output power to preserve the life of the machine. In most applications involving lower-heating-value fuel, it is assumed that the efficiency and power output will be equal to or higher than the ones obtained using natural gas. In applications involving higher-heating-value fuels, such as refinery gases, the efficiency and output power will be equal to or less than those obtained using natural gas.

Water and steam injection have been used during the last few decades to reduce NO_X emissions. This technique involves injecting water or steam in the cap area, or "head end," of the combustor liner. The output power and efficiency will increase due to the additional mass flow. However, each machine has limits on the amount of water or steam injected. These are imposed to protect the combustor and turbine section. Steam injection can increase the output power and efficiency by 20 and 10 percent, respectively. Water injection can increase the output power by 10 percent. However, it has very little effect on efficiency because more fuel is needed to raise the water to combustor temperature.

AIR EXTRACTION

Some gas turbine applications require air from the compressor. In general, up to 5 percent of the flow can be extracted from the discharge casing of the compressor. This can be done without modification to the casings or on-base piping. Higher flow (from 16 to 20 percent) can be extracted from the compressor. However, this requires modifications to the casings, piping, and controls. Air extraction has a significant effect on the performance of the machine. The rule of thumb is that every 1 percent of air extraction causes 2 percent of reduction in power output.

PERFORMANCE ENHANCEMENTS

Two possibilities can be considered to enhance the performance when additional power is required:

1. Inlet cooling
2. Steam and water injection for power augmentation

Inlet Cooling

Figure 18.3 shows that there is an improvement in power output and heat rate when the inlet temperature to the compressor decreases. The installation of an evaporative cooler or inlet chiller in the inlet ducting (downstream of the inlet filters) will lower the inlet temperature to the compressor. Inadequate operation of this equipment can result in condensation or carryover of water into the compressor. This increases compressor fouling and degrades the performance. Moisture separators, or coalescing pads, are generally installed to reduce the possibility of moisture carryover. Figure 18.4 illustrates the effect of evaporative cooling on power output and heat rate. It indicates that hot, low-humidity climates gain the most from evaporative cooling. It should be noted that evaporative cooling is limited to an ambient temperature higher than 59°F (15°C). The reason is concern about potential formation of ice on the compressor blades. The information presented in Fig. 18.4 is based on the evaporative cooler having an effectiveness of 85 percent. The effectiveness is measured by how close the cooler exit temperature is to the ambient wet-bulb temperature. For most applications, a cooler effectiveness of between 85 and 90 percent provides the most economic benefit.

Chillers do not have the same characteristics as evaporative coolers. The wet-bulb temperature does not limit them. The temperature achieved is limited by the capacity of the chiller.

Steam and Water Injection for Power Augmentation

The injection of steam or water into the combustor to reduce NO_X emissions results in increasing the mass flow. Therefore, the power output will increase. The amount of steam

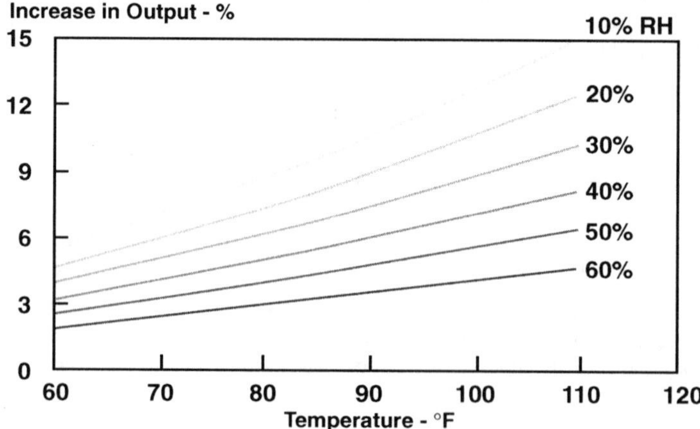

FIGURE 18.4 Effect of evaporative cooling on output and heat rate.

or water injected is limited to the amount required to meet the NO_X requirement. It is around 1.1 kg of steam/1 kg of fuel or 1 kg of water/1 kg of fuel.

Steam injection was used for power augmentation for more than 30 years. The steam is normally injected into the compressor discharge casing and combustor. It can increase the power output by up to 20 percent and the efficiency by 10 percent. Most machines are designed to allow up to 5 percent of the compressor airflow for steam injection. The steam must have around 50°F (28°C) superheat. It is normally premixed with the fuel before being injected in the combustor.

PEAK RATING

The performance values for a machine are normally given for base load ratings. The American National Standards Institute (ANSI) B133.6 Ratings and Performance[3] define the following:

- *Base load.* Operation of 8000 h/year with 800 h per start
- *Peak load.* Operation of 1250 h/year with 5 h per start

Since the peak-load operating hours are shorter, increasing the firing temperature can increase the power output. This mode of operation requires shorter inspection intervals. Despite this penalty, running a gas turbine at peak could be a cost-effective way of operation. Additional power is generated in periods of higher power cost. Generators also have peak ratings. These are obtained by operating at a higher power factor or temperature increase. The ratings of the peak cycle are customized to the turbine mission. They consider the starts and hours of operation. The firing temperature can be selected between the base and the peak. They are chosen to maximize the power output while remaining within the limits of the repair interval of the turbine hot section. For example, a typical heavy-duty gas turbine can operate for 24,000 h using gas fuel at base load. The hot-section repair interval is limited to 800 starts. The hot-section repair interval is also limited to 4000 h for peaking cycle of 5 h per start. This corresponds to a peak firing temperature operation. Turbine missions between 5 and 800 h per start will allow the firing temperature to increase above the base temperature. However, the firing temperature will remain below the peak temperature. This can be done without sacrificing time to the repair of the hot section. The water injection for power augmentation can also be factored into the rating of the peak cycle to further increase the power output.

PERFORMANCE DEGRADATION

The performance of all turbomachinery degrades with time. There are two types of degradation in gas turbines: recoverable and nonrecoverable loss. The compressor fouling is a recoverable loss. It can be recovered partially by water washing. This loss can be recovered fully by mechanical cleaning of the compressor blades and vanes after opening the unit. The increase in turbine and compressor clearances is a nonrecoverable loss. The changes in surface finish and airfoil contours are also nonrecoverable. This loss can only be recovered by replacement of the affected parts. After 24,000 h of operation (the normal recommended interval for inspection of the hot gas path), the total performance degradation is between 1 and 1.5 percent. Recent industrial experience shows that frequent off-line water washing will reduce the recoverable and nonrecoverable losses. In general, the machines that operate in hot, dry climates degrade less than those in humid climates.

VERIFYING GAS TURBINE PERFORMANCE

A performance test is normally conducted after the gas turbine is installed. The power, fuel, heat consumption, and so forth are recorded. This is done to allow these parameters to be corrected to the condition of the guarantee. The ASME Performance Test Code PTC-22-1985, "Gas Turbine Plants,"[4] describes the testing procedures and calculation methods. All the instruments used for data collection must be inspected and calibrated before the test.

REFERENCES

1. Brooks, F. J., *GE Gas Turbine Performance Characteristics,* GER-3567H, *GE Power Systems,* Schenectady, N.Y., 2000.
2. Boyce, M., *Gas Turbine Engineering Handbook,* Gulf Publishing Company, Houston, Tex., 1995.
3. American National Standards Institute (ANSI), "B133.6 Ratings and Performance," ANSI, Washington, D.C.
4. ASME, "Gas Turbine Plants," Performance Test Code PTC-22-1985, ASME International, New York, 1985.

CHAPTER 19
GAS TURBINE OPERATING AND MAINTENANCE CONSIDERATIONS

A good maintenance program is needed to maximize the availability of the equipment. Advance planning for maintenance is essential to reduce downtime. The parts that require the most careful attention are the combustors and the section exposed to the hot gases that are discharged from the combustors. These are known as the *hot-gas-path parts.* They include combustion liners, cross-fire tubes, transition pieces, turbine nozzles, turbine stationary shrouds, and turbine buckets.

The recommended maintenance of most manufacturers for heavy-duty gas turbines is oriented toward:

- Minimum downtime for inspection and overhauls
- On-site inspection and maintenance
- Use of site workers to disassemble, inspect, and reassemble

Periodic maintenance is also required for control devices, fuel-metering equipment, and gas turbine auxiliaries.

The main contributors of downtime are normally controls and accessories, combustor, turbine, generator, and the balance of the plant. The outages caused by controls and accessories normally have a short duration; however, they are frequent. The remaining systems normally cause longer-duration outages.

The maintenance and instruction manual outlines the inspection and repair requirements. Some manufacturers also provide a system of technical information letters (TILs). These TILs update the information that is included in the maintenance and instruction manual. This ensures optimum installation, operation, and maintenance of the unit. Some TILs provide technical recommendations to resolve problems and improve operation, safety, and reliability of the machine. It is advisable to follow the recommendations provided in the TILs.

GAS TURBINE DESIGN MAINTENANCE FEATURES

Most heavy-duty gas turbines can be maintained on-site. Only a few components should be repaired off-site, including certain parts in the hot-gas-path and rotor assemblies, which require special service. The following features are designed into most heavy-duty gas turbines to facilitate the on-site maintenance:

- All of the casings, shells, and frames on the machine are horizontally split along the centerline. The upper halves can be lifted individually to provide access to the internal parts.

- All of the stator vanes can be removed circumferentially out of the casing following removal of the upper-half of the compressor casing. They can be inspected or replaced without removing the rotor. Following removal of the upper half of the inlet casing, the variable inlet guide vanes (VIGVs) can be removed for inspection.
- The nozzle (stationary blades) assemblies can be removed for inspection, repair, or replacement without removal of the rotor following removal of the upper half of the turbine shell.
- The weight and weight profile of the turbine buckets (moving blades) are recorded. They are computer-charted in sets and can be replaced without needing to rebalance the rotor.
- The bearing housings and liners are horizontally split along the centerline and can be inspected and replaced if necessary. The bottom half of the bearing liner can be removed without removing the rotor.
- All of the packings for seals and shafts are separate from the main bearing housings and casing structures and can be readily removed and replaced.
- The fuel nozzles, combustion liners, and flow sleeves can be removed, inspected, and maintained without removing the combustors or lifting the casings.

Special inspection techniques can be conducted on most heavy-duty gas turbines. These techniques permit the visual inspection and clearance measurement of critical components inside the gas turbines without removing the outer casings and shells. They include borescopic inspection of the gas path and axial clearance measurement of the turbine nozzles.

BORESCOPE INSPECTION

Visual inspections of the internal components of most heavy-duty gas turbines can be performed using the optical borescope. Radially aligned holes in the compressor casings, turbine shell, and internal stationary turbine shrouds are available. The optical borescope penetrates the compressor and turbine through these holes.

If deficiencies are found during the inspection, the casings and shells from the turbine or compressor must be removed to perform the required repairs. A baseline inspection is needed on all machines. The borescope inspection is normally done during the combustion inspection to reduce the maintenance cost and increase the availability and reliability of the machine.

MAJOR FACTORS INFLUENCING MAINTENANCE AND EQUIPMENT LIFE

The main factors that determine the maintenance interval are the starting cycle, power level, fuel, and amount of steam or water injected. Most manufacturers use gas fuel, base-load operation with no water or steam injected as a baseline for maintenance planning. This condition determines the recommended, maximum maintenance interval. Maintenance factors are used when the operation is different from the baseline. They determine the reduction in maintenance interval. For example, a maintenance factor of 2 would indicate that the maintenance interval should be half of the baseline interval.

Starts and Hours Criteria

The life of peaking gas turbines is normally limited by thermal mechanical fatigue while creep, oxidation, and corrosion limit the life of continuous-duty machines. The interactions of these mechanisms are considered by most manufacturers; however, they are treated normally as second-order effects.

The maintenance requirements for gas turbines vary between manufacturers. Some manufacturers base their maintenance requirements on separate counts of machine starts and hours of operation. The maintenance interval is determined by the criteria limit reached first. Other manufacturers use an alternative approach, which consists of converting each start cycle to an equivalent number of operating hours (EOH). The inspection interval is determined by the number of equivalent hours. The maintenance intervals determined by both approaches are not normally very different.

Service Factors

The maximum (baseline) inspection intervals of a typical heavy-duty gas turbine are as follows:

- Hot-gas-path inspection: 24,000 h or 1200 starts
- Major inspection: 48,000 h or 2400 starts

These are based on the ideal case (continuous base load, gas fuel, and no steam or water injection). Maintenance factors are used to reduce the maintenance interval of gas turbines when they are subjected to harsh operating conditions. Maintenance factors are normally associated with each of the following parameters:

- Fuel type and quality
- Firing temperature
- Steam or water injection
- Number of trips
- Rate of start-up

The following sections will examine the effects of the main operating factors on maintenance intervals and parts refurbishment/replacement intervals.

Fuel

Gas turbines burn a wide variety of fuels. They vary from clean natural gas to residual oils. Natural gas has no effect on the maximum maintenance intervals. However, if residual fuels are used, the maintenance intervals should be reduced to a quarter of the maximum maintenance intervals. If crude-oil fuels are used, the maintenance intervals should be reduced to half of the maximum maintenance intervals. The radiant thermal energy of these fuels is higher than other fuels, which reduces the lifetime of the combustion system. These fuels also contain corrosive components (e.g., sodium, potassium, vanadium, and lead), which result in acceleration of the rate of hot corrosion in the turbine nozzles and buckets. In addition, some elements of these fuels generate deposits during the combustion process. These deposits reduce the efficiency of the machine. Frequent maintenance is required to remove these deposits.

Distillates do not normally have high levels of corrosive elements. However, they could contain harmful contaminants. Type 2 distillate fuel oil is normally contaminated by salt water used as ballast during sea transport. Distillate fuels can also be contaminated during transportation to site in tankers, tank trucks, or pipelines if this equipment was previously used to transport chemicals or contaminated fuel.

The maintenance intervals of gas turbines using distillate fuels should be around 70 percent of the maximum maintenance intervals. It should also be noted that contaminants in the liquid fuel can have effects on the life of the gas turbine and its auxiliaries (e.g., fuel pumps, etc.).

It is important to note that if a single shipment of contaminated fuel was undetected, it can cause significant damage to the hot gas path of the gas turbine. The potential for downtime and expensive repairs can be minimized by:

- *Providing a fuel specification to the fuel supplier.* Each shipment of liquid fuels should include a report identifying specific gravity, flash point, viscosity, sulfur content, pour point, and ash content of the fuel.
- *Establishing a regular program for sampling and analyzing the fuel quality.* This program should include on-line monitoring of water in the fuel. A portable fuel analyzer should also be used regularly to monitor the concentration of vanadium, lead, sodium, potassium, calcium, and magnesium.

Contaminants can also be entrained with the incoming air and with the steam or water injected to control nitric oxide (NO_X) emission or power augmentation. In some cases, the hot-gas-path degradation caused by these contaminants is as serious as the degradation caused by contaminants found in the fuel. Most manufacturers specify maximum concentrations of contaminants in the fuel, air, and water or steam. The limits specified normally are 1 ppm sodium plus potassium, 1 ppm lead, 0.5 ppm vanadium, and 2 ppm calcium in the fuel.

Firing Temperature

Peak load operation requires higher operating temperatures. This results in more frequent maintenance and replacement of the hot-gas-path components. It is normally assumed that each hour of operation at peak load [higher firing temperature by 100°F (56°C)] has the same effect on the moving blades of the turbine (buckets) as 6 h of operation at base load. This mode of operation has a maintenance factor of 6. A 200°F (111°C) increase in the firing temperature has a 40:1 equivalency.

Lower firing temperature increases the life of the parts. Some of the negative effects caused by operating at peak load (higher firing temperature) can be balanced by operating at part load. However, the operation at lower temperature does not have the same countereffect as higher-temperature operation of the same magnitude. For example, the machine should be operated for 6 h at 100°F (56°C) below the base-load conditions to compensate for 1 h of operation at 100°F (56°C) above the base conditions. It should also be noted that the firing temperature does not always decrease when the load is reduced. In heat recovery applications, where the plant efficiency is governed by steam generation, the load is first reduced by closing the VIGVs partially. This reduces the airflow while maintaining the maximum exhaust temperature. For these applications, the load must be reduced below 80 percent before the firing temperature changes. Conversely, a simple-cycle gas turbine experiences over a 200°F (111°C) reduction in its firing temperature when the load is reduced to 80 percent while maintaining the VIGVs fully open.

Steam or Water Injection

The injection of steam or water for emission control or power augmentation has an effect on the life of the parts and maintenance intervals. This effect is caused by the changes in the gas properties resulting from the added water. The increase on thermal conductivity of the gas and the resulting increase in heat transfer to the buckets (stationary blades) and nozzles (moving blades) of the turbine can lead to higher metal temperature. A decrease in the life of the parts by 33 percent is normally expected with a steam injection rate of 3 percent of the airflow.

The impact on the life of the parts resulting from steam or water injection is related to how the turbine is controlled. Most control systems of machines operating at base load reduce the firing temperature when water is injected. This compensates for the effect of higher heat transfer from the gas and results in no impact on the life of the blades.

Some control systems are designed to maintain a constant firing temperature when water is injected. This results in increasing the power output. However, the life of the parts in the hot gas path will decrease. Most of these units are used in peaking applications. The operating hours are low. However, the reduction in the life of the parts is justified by significant power advantage.

The steam or water injection has another effect on the machine. It increases the loading on the turbine components. This additional loading increases the deflection rate of the nozzles in the first three turbine stages, resulting in a reduced repair interval for these components. Some manufacturers developed a high-creep-strength alloy for the first three-stage nozzles. This alloy minimizes or eliminates the deflective effect on the nozzles.

Cyclic Effects

Operating conditions different from the normal start-up and shutdown sequence can potentially reduce the cyclic life of the hot-gas-path components and the maintenance interval. The edges of the turbine buckets and nozzles respond faster to changes in the gas temperature than the thicker bulk section. These temperature gradients produce thermal stresses in the blades. Cracking at the root of the blades will occur when the stresses are cycled.

Research about thermal mechanical fatigue indicates that the total strain range and the maximum metal temperature experienced by a part have a significant effect on the number of cycles that it can withstand before cracking occurs. Any operating condition that results in a significant increase in the strain range and/or the maximum metal temperature over the normal cycle conditions will reduce the fatigue life of the machine. For example, a trip cycle from full load causes significantly higher strain range than normal shutdown. This results in a life effect of eight normal shutdown cycles. Trips from part load will have a reduced effect due to lower metal temperatures.

Emergency starts and fast loading affect the maintenance interval in a similar way as do trips from load. This is caused by the increased strain range that results from these events. Emergency starts from standstill to full load within 5 min will have an effect equivalent to 20 normal starts on the life of the parts of the hot gas path. A normal start with fast loading has double the effect of a normal start with normal loading.

Air Quality

The quality of air entering the turbine has significant effects on the maintenance and operating costs. Dust, salt, and oil cause erosion, corrosion, and fouling of the compressor blades. The fouling of the compressor blades accounts typically for between 70 and 85 percent of the recoverable losses in performance. A reduction of 5 percent in airflow as a result of compressor fouling will reduce the power output by 13 percent and increase the heat rate by 5.5 percent. Fortunately, proper implementation of maintenance procedures minimizes fouling of the compressor blades. On-line compressor wash systems clean the blades during normal operation. Off-line systems are used for compressors that have heavy fouling.

The nonrecoverable losses in the compressor are normally caused by erosion of the blades. The increase in clearance of the bucket tips is the main cause of unrecoverable losses in the turbine. The regular monitoring and recording of the unit performance parameters provide a valuable diagnostic tool for possible performance degradation in the compressor.

COMBUSTION INSPECTION

The combustion inspection is a shutdown inspection of fuel nozzles, liners, transition pieces, cross-fire tubes and retainers, spark plug assemblies, flame detectors, and combustor flow sleeves. The typical combustion inspection requirements for a gas turbine include:

- Inspect and identify each cross-fire tube, retainer, and combustion liner for cracking, oxidation, corrosion, and erosion.
- Inspect the combustion chamber interior for debris and foreign objects.
- Inspect flow sleeve welds for cracking.
- Inspect the transition piece for wear and cracks.
- Inspect fuel nozzles for plugging, erosion of tip holes, and safety lock of tips.
- Inspect all fluid, air, and gas passages in the nozzle assembly for plugging, erosion, corrosion, and so forth.
- Inspect spark plug assembly for freedom from binding; check condition of electrodes and insulators.
- Replace all consumables and normal wear-and-tear items (e.g., seals, lockplates, nuts, bolts, gaskets, etc.).
- Perform visual inspection of first-stage turbine nozzle partitions and borescope-inspect turbine buckets to mark the progress of wear and deterioration of these parts. This inspection will help to determine the schedule for the hot-gas-path inspection.
- Enter the combustion wrapper and observe the condition of the blading in the aft end of the axial-flow compressor with a borescope.
- Inspect visually the compressor inlet and turbine exhaust areas, checking the condition of the VIGVs, VIGV bushings, last-stage buckets, and exhaust system components.
- Verify proper operation of purge-and-check valves. Confirm proper setting and calibration of the combustion controls.

Following the completion of the combustion inspection, the removed combustion liners and transition pieces can be bench-tested and repaired. The removed fuel nozzles can be cleaned and tested on-site, if test facilities are available.

HOT-GAS-PATH INSPECTION

The hot-gas-path inspection includes inspection of all components that were in contact with the hot gas for cracking, oxidation, corrosion, erosion, and abnormal wear. The top half of the turbine casing must be removed to perform this inspection. All combustion transition pieces and the first-stage turbine nozzle assembly must also be removed for this inspection. The inspection of the turbine buckets can normally be done in-place. A fluorescent penetrant inspection (FPI) is normally required for the bucket vane sections to detect any cracks. A complete set of internal turbine radial and axial clearances is also required during any hot-gas-path inspection.

The typical hot-gas-path inspection requirements for a gas turbine are:

- Inspect and record the condition of first three-stage buckets. The turbine buckets may have to be removed by following bucket removal and condition recording instructions. The condition of the coating of the first-stage buckets should be evaluated.
- Inspect and record the condition of first three-stage nozzles.
- Inspect and record the condition of later-stage nozzle diaphragm packings. Check the seals for rubs and deterioration of clearance.
- Record the bucket tip clearances. Inspect the bucket seals for clearance, rubs, and deterioration.
- Check the turbine stationary shrouds for clearance, cracking, erosion, oxidation, rubbing, and buildup of deposits.
- Check and replace any faulty wheelspace instrumentation.
- Enter the compressor inlet plenum and observe the condition of the forward section of the compressor. Pay specific attention to VIGVs, looking for corrosion, bushing wear evidenced by excessive clearance and vane cracking.
- Enter the combustion wrapper and, with a borescope, observe the condition of the blading in the aft end of the axial-flow compressor.
- Inspect visually the turbine exhaust area for any signs of cracking or deterioration.

The first-stage nozzles are subjected to the highest gas temperature in the turbine. They experience cracking and oxidation. The second- and third-stage nozzles experience deflection and closure of axial clearances due to high gas-bending loads. In general, these nozzles will require repair and refurbishment during the inspection.

Coatings of the turbine buckets play a major role in determining their useful life. The creep rate will accelerate if the base metal becomes exposed to the hot gases. Premature failure will occur due to a reduction in the strength of the material. Recoating is normally done for larger designs. However, it must be done before the base metal becomes exposed. The buckets for smaller gas turbines are normally replaced.

The condition of the turbine can be monitored by taking nozzle deflection measurements and performing a visual and borescopic examination of the hot gas parts during the combustion inspections. This provides more accurate part life predictions and allows adequate time to plan for replacement or refurbishment during the hot-gas-path inspection. All necessary spare parts should be available before starting the inspection. This is required to avoid an extension in the hot-gas-path inspection.

MAJOR INSPECTION

The major inspection includes examination of all of the internal rotating and stationary components, from the inlet to the exhaust of the machine. This inspection should be scheduled based on the recommendation provided in the maintenance manual and the results of previous borescopic and hot-gas-path inspections. All of the components subjected to wear during normal operation are inspected. This inspection includes the work covered by the combustion and hot-gas-path inspections. Depending on the coating condition, the first-stage buckets may require replacement during a major inspection. The requirements of a typical major inspection are:

- Check all radial and axial clearances against their original values.
- Inspect casings, shells, frames, and diffusers for cracks and erosion.
- Inspect the compressor inlet and compressor flow path for fouling, erosion, corrosion, and leakage. Inspect the VIGVs for corrosion, bushing wear, and vane cracking.
- Check the rotor and stator compressor blades for rubs, impact damage, corrosion pitting, bowing, and cracking.
- Check the turbine stationary shrouds for clearance, erosion, rubbing, cracking, and buildup of deposits.
- Inspect the seals and hook fits of the turbine nozzles and diaphragms for rubs, erosion, fretting, or thermal deterioration.
- Remove the turbine buckets and perform a nondestructive check of the buckets and wheel dovetails. Check the protective coating for the first-stage buckets. Replace those first-stage buckets that were not recoated at the hot-gas-path inspection.
- Inspect the bearing liners and seals for clearance and wear.
- Inspect the inlet systems for corrosion, cracked silencers, and loose parts.
- Inspect the exhaust systems for cracks, broken silencer panels, and insulation panels.
- Check alignment of the gas turbine to the generator, as well as of the gas turbine to the accessory gear.

CHAPTER 20
GAS TURBINE EMISSION GUIDELINES AND CONTROL METHODS

EMISSIONS FROM GAS TURBINES

Natural gas used to fuel gas turbines is one of the cleanest types of fuels used for power production. It produces little sulfur dioxide (SO_2) or carbon monoxide (CO). The high overall efficiency of modern gas turbines and combined cycles contributes to lower carbon dioxide (CO_2) emissions. However, since power and thermal efficiency increase with increasing firing temperature, modern gas turbines are emitting higher nitrogen oxides (NO, NO_2, termed NO_X). Figure 20.1 illustrates the increase in NO_X with combustion temperature.

Volatile organic compounds and sunlight combine with this pollutant to form ground-level ozone, or smog. Respiratory systems and vegetation are seriously affected by elevated ozone concentrations.

NO_X is also a contributor to acid rain, and it is implicated as a greenhouse gas. Its emissions are transported over long distances, causing harmful effects in other geographic areas. It is produced by high-temperature (2000°F) oxidation of nitrogen.

NO_X production is promoted by higher pressures and by long residence time of the very hot mixture, which ensures complete combustion of fuel to minimize CO and smoke. In general, the CO emissions increase as the NO_X emissions decline. Liquid fuels that have higher local-flame temperature and some nitrogen compounds also form NO_X. SO_2 emissions are also produced by liquid-fueled units, depending on the fuel sulfur content.

NO_X emissions are normally measured as a fraction of NO_2-equivalent measured in parts per million by volume (ppmv) in the exhaust stack, corrected to dry International Organization for Standardization (ISO) (15°C) conditions.

Machines built in the 1960s had lower firing temperatures and pressure ratios. In general, their full-load emissions are in the 50- to 100-ppmv range. However, today's units have higher firing temperatures [from 2400 to 2800°F (1315 to 1538°C)] in order to improve the efficiency. They have double the emission levels of the older units.

The NO_X levels drop off at a fast rate when the unit load is reduced due to less fuel flow and with lower compressor air mass flow and pressure ratio. The NO_X production at 80 percent load is typically only between 60 and 70 percent of full-load production.

The data in Table 20.1 show the uncontrolled emission levels of some common new types of base-loaded units (assuming 8000 operating h/year, half at full load, simple cycle, and gas fuel). The average emission is about 2 to 3 kg/MWh of operation.

Large gas turbines could become a major NO_X source. However, large units in combined-cycle operation use steam or water injection to reduce the NO_X levels by 70 percent (25- to 75-ppmv range).

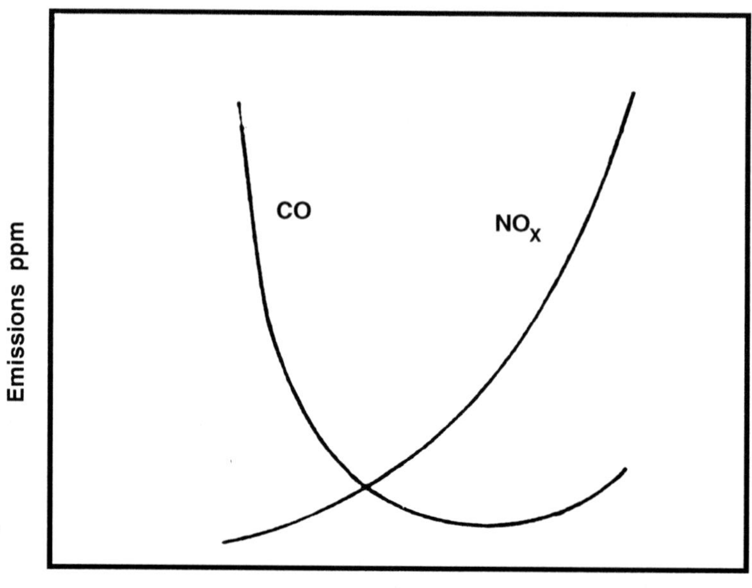

FIGURE 20.1 Influence of temperature on CO and NO_X emissions.

TABLE 20.1 Uncontrolled Emission Levels of Some Common New Types of Base-Loaded Units

Unit size (in MW)	ppmv	$g/GJ_{(out)}$	kg/h	t*/year
1	70	550	2	14
4	120	900	13	80
14	150	800	40	250
25	180	1000	90	550
50	200	1100	200	1250

*1 t = 1 tonne = 1000 kg.

In 1994, about 80 percent of the gas turbine NO_X emissions came from the gas transmission industry. The total national emissions from all sources are approximately 1900 kilotonnes (kt). This is split equally between fossil-fuel combustion for transportation and from stationary sources.

GENERAL APPROACH FOR A NATIONAL EMISSION GUIDELINE

In 1991, a multistakeholder working group was formed to develop the *Combustion Turbine National Emission Guideline* (Initiative N307 of the 1990 CCME NO_X/VOC Management Plan).[2] A guideline was developed and approved in August 1992. However, more stringent standards could be selected by regional or provincial regulators to deal with high local ground-level ozone or smog problems.

NO_X EMISSION TARGET LEVELS

The NO_X emission levels from gas turbines without NO_X controls are relatively high (from 100 to 400 ppmv). The regulated national Environmental Protection Agency (EPA) limits in the United States are 75 ppmv for electric power units having an output higher than 30 MW, and 150 ppmv for other units. These limits are based on a 25 percent efficiency correction (higher limits for more efficient plants). However, many regions in the United States are requiring ultralow levels, such as southern California (9 ppmv) and the Northeast (from 9 to 25 ppmv). Selective catalytic reduction (SCR) techniques as a back-end exhaust cleanup are used to attain these levels.

The N307 guideline has promoted high-efficiency applications of gas turbines, with a reasonably achievable low level of emissions of NO_X and CO. The guideline does not require ultralow NO_X levels, which are achievable with an SCR back-end cleanup system. The levels required by the guideline (from 30- to 50-ppmv range for most units) are expected to be achievable by the development and use of dry low-NO_X (DLN) combustors by most manufacturers. These levels are also achievable by moderate steam or water injection in cogeneration plants. More stringent regulations can be adopted by the regional regulatory agencies in response to local air quality problems.

The working group developed this standard reflecting reasonably attainable emission levels to facilitate the installation of improved combustion systems on existing units where applicable. The standard also avoids situations where the installation of high-efficiency combined cycles may be discouraged by the cost and efforts involved in meeting very low emissions.

The high cost of NO_X removal by large catalytic systems is only justifiable in serious nonattainment areas. For example, the annual cost of control to 30 ppmv by using steam injection or a DLN combustor is about $2000/t, whereas the cost of an SCR installation for additional control down to 10 ppmv is about 10 to 15 times higher.

POWER OUTPUT ALLOWANCE

The guideline NO_X emission targets for gaseous and liquid fuels are given in Table 20.2. These levels were then converted to an energy output basis using 1.7 grams per gigajoule (input) [$g/GJ_{(input)}$] per ppmv of NO_X for gas fuel, and a 1.77 factor for liquid fuel. For example, for a large unit having 30 percent efficiency:

$$25 \text{ ppmv} \times \left(\frac{1}{0.30}\right) \times 1.7 = 142 \text{ g/GJ}_{(output)} \qquad \text{(rounded to 140 g/GJ)}$$

TABLE 20.2 Guideline NO_X Emission Targets for Gaseous and Liquid Fuels

Size (in MW)	Base eff. (%)	Base emission targets (ppmv) Gas fuel	Liquid fuel
0–3	25	75	175
3–20	25	35	65
Over 20	30	25	65

The mass of NO_X emitted is related to the number of gigajoules (GJ) or megawatts (MW) of power output by this power output allowance. It applies to the normal operating conditions determined by the regulatory authority. Units meeting a base rating emission ppmv level are able to achieve the grams per gigajoule criteria under all conditions because both air mass flow and ppmv of NO_X tend to drop at reduced power.

A higher emission level is permitted through the heat recovery allowance (HRA) if the exhaust thermal energy is used for an additional application. For example, 70 percent higher emission targets (240 g/GJ) are set for units in the size range of 3 to 20 MW. This level is thought to be technically achievable for the smaller DLN combustors (Fig. 20.2).

Emission targets for liquid fuels are significantly higher for the following reasons:

- The local-flame temperature for liquid fuels, such as No. 2 oil, is higher.
- Most liquid fuels contain nitrogen compounds, which contribute to NO_X production.
- More research is required for DLN control, and most manufacturers are focusing on gas-fueled units, which represent the majority of applications.

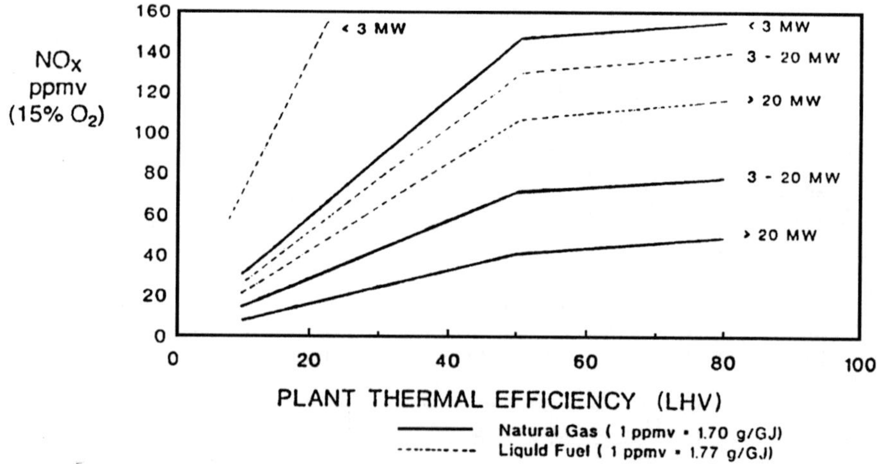

Power Output Allowance "A" (g/GJ)

	Natural gas	Liquid fuel
Nonpeaking turbines		
<3 MW	500	1250
3–20 MW	240	460
>20 MW	140	380
Peaking turbines		
<3 MW	Exempt	Exempt
>3 MW	280	530

Heat Recovery Allowance "B" (g/GJ)

For all units	
Natural gas	40
Liquid	60
Solid-derived	120

FIGURE 20.2 Gas turbine emission guidelines—sample conversion from g/GJ to ppmv (for nonpeaking units).

HEAT RECOVERY ALLOWANCE

A heat recovery allowance (HRA) was established in addition to the basic emission levels for electrical power output (determined by the power output allowance) to recognize the environmental benefits of increased energy efficiency. If useful energy is recovered from the unit's exhaust thermal energy, or "waster heat," the turbine is credited with NO_X emission saved from other combustion sources.

The HRA was established to be an emission rate of 40 g/GJ for natural gas and 60 g/GJ for liquid fuel. It would add from 5 to 10 ppmv to the emission target of a typical cogeneration plant. The rate is lower than that of the power output allowance because electrical power is more valuable than heat energy. Therefore, a slightly higher NO_X emission target is assigned to plants producing a larger proportion of power, versus heat extraction.

Most cogeneration plants have steam available, and may not need the higher allowance to operate. However, the NO_X control to 45 ppmv, instead of 40 ppmv, would reduce the amount of steam injection. This increases the overall efficiency and reduces associated emissions of CO. Additional fuel that is used in auxiliary duct burners in the heat recovery system is taken into account in assessing the overall plant thermal efficiency.

EMISSION LEVELS FOR OTHER CONTAMINANTS

The potential negative effects of other pollutants that may be emitted from gas turbines is also recognized by the guideline. The sources of these contaminants are certain NO_X control methods and the fuel that is being burned.

Carbon Monoxide

Large quantities of thermal NO_X are formed as a result of very high combustion temperatures, which are burning the carbon compounds and increasing the efficiency. The amount of CO and unburned hydrocarbons increases significantly when NO_X control methods are implemented.

Research has shown that the amounts of both NO_X and CO can be minimized in a narrow temperature range near 1500°F, which is substantially lower than normal combustion temperatures. The air and fuel mixed in stages within DLN combustors to take advantage of this narrow temperature range. This is done while ensuring flame stability during transient conditions. Good combustion efficiency in most gas turbines results in less than 5 ppmv of CO in the exhaust. A target of 50 ppmv was established when NO_X control methods (e.g., steam injection of DLN combustors) are employed.

Sulfur Dioxide

The sulfur dioxide (SO_2) emission targets were included to address SO_2 emissions from liquid fuels and any sulfur-containing fuels such as syngas (coal-derived or biomass). The emission targets were established to reflect levels for large utility boilers contained in the updated N305 guideline for thermal power plants. These targets were converted to energy output basis assuming 35 percent efficiency.

Other Contaminants

Other pollutants, such as ammonia, which is injected upstream of a catalyst bed in an SCR method for NO_X control, were considered (some unreacted ammonia is emitted in off-design conditions and catalyst degradation). However, it was decided that since SCR is not a technology required by the guideline, the ammonia emission limits were not included.

SIZE RANGES FOR EMISSION TARGETS

The emission targets developed by the working group were based on what is achievable with DLN combustors on various types of gas turbines. The limits on units having an output less than 3 MW were more lenient due to the following:

- The inherent difficulties in modifying their very small combustors.
- They compete with reciprocating engines that produce much more NO_X.
- The total contribution of these small units would represent only about 2 percent of the total NO_X production.

The emission limits for large gas turbines were determined based on what is achievable by steam injection or DLN combustors without using back-end cleanup (about two-thirds of the power produced in Canada comes from these units). These units substantially reduced uncontrolled emissions from between 150 and 250 ppmv down to between 25 and 35 ppmv.

Intermediate emission limits were established for medium-size gas turbines (between 3 and 20 MW). These units would reduce NO_X levels from between 100 and 200 ppmv down to between 40 and 50 ppmv. It was also agreed that multiple small units cannot be used to evade the intended emission targets.

PEAKING UNITS

Units that normally operate less than 1500 h/year are called *peaking units*. Emission targets for a 5-year, 7500-h period were developed with a caveat that these units cannot run excessively during the summer months (potentially high-ozone period).

There are no emission targets for very small units. All other peaking units have targets of between 40 and 60 ppmv (for natural gas), and between 75 and 100 ppmv on distillate fuel (which peaking units commonly use).

Well-developed DLN combustors are required to achieve the high start/acceleration reliability of peaking units. Standby and emergency units are exempt from the Guideline.

EMISSION MONITORING

New plants are required to monitor their emissions of NO_X and other contaminants to compare their performance to emission targets. The guideline stipulates that any electricity-producing unit larger than 25 MW should have continuous emission-monitoring (CEM) systems.

Other methods of comparable effectiveness approved by the regulatory authority (e.g., steam/water injection flow rate measurement) can also be used. The remaining units are required to have an annual emission test to confirm performance.

NO_X EMISSION CONTROL METHODS

Water and Steam Injection

The injection of water or steam into the combustion zone to lower the flame temperature is a common method for NO_X control. A high-quality distillation system is required to remove impurities from the water, which can damage the downstream engine components. A water-fuel mass ratio around 1.2 is normally used. A ratio of 1.0 achieves about 70 to 80 percent NO_X reduction. The combustion efficiency drops substantially when the ratio is higher than 1.1, and the CO concentration increases rapidly.

Water injection must be carefully monitored in frequent inspection because it contributes to pulsations and erosion in the combustion system. Common emission limits of 42 ppmv on gas-fired and 75 ppmv on distillate oil units were achieved using this control technology.

Water injection can reduce NO_X emission more effectively than steam due to the heat that is absorbed by vaporization of the droplets. However, vaporization requires additional fuel to be burned. In general, the heat rate degrades by approximately 3 percent when the ratio is 1:1. However, the output power increases by about 10 percent due to an increase in the mass flow.

When steam is not available, water injection is used. In general, this is common in simple-cycle applications, such as peaking duty or pipeline compression. The estimated cost of NO_X removal is between $2000 and $6000 per tonne for a water injection system installed on a new large unit. The upper end of this range is mainly for isolated areas where the cost of water acquisition and treatment are significant.

Small units incur a cost that is 50 percent higher on average. These amounts may double for retrofits due to modifications of the unit and the control system. Most of these costs are associated with the following:

- Transportation, treatment, and disposal of water
- Modifications to the combustor, turbine, and control system components
- Increased maintenance
- Fuel penalty

A preferable option on natural gas-fired combined cycles is steam injection because the steam is readily available from the exhaust heat recovery system. The steam-fuel mass ratio is about 50 percent higher than water injection for a given NO_X reduction. Steam has less serious effects on component deterioration. It is also more efficient because the heat required for vaporization is taken from the turbine exhaust instead of the combustor.

The mass flow increases when steam is injected into the combustor. It generates a 20 percent increase in output power, and a subsequent improvement in heat rate of up to 10 percent. Some units add large amounts of steam downstream of the combustor to increase the mass flow through the power turbine. This results in up to 50 percent power increase for peaking applications.

The cost-effectiveness of steam injection for NO_X control varies depending on the application, but it is usually in the same range.

Selective Catalytic Reduction (SCR)

Since the mid-1980s, SCR (also known as a *back-end cleanup system*) has been used on large units, particularly in California. Ammonia is sprayed into the exhaust gas, which is sent through a catalyst bed in the heat recovery steam generator. In the presence of a catalyst, the ammonia reacts with the NO_X in a temperature range of between 300 and 400°C to form nitrogen and water vapor.

A heat recovery steam generator (HRSG) is required for the SCR system to reduce the exhaust from between 500 and 600°C down to the required reaction temperature range. Therefore, it is only practical for combined-cycle applications where the load is fairly constant.

The NO_X removal efficiency of an SCR system is about 80 percent. It is typically used after water-steam injection to reduce emissions from 50 to 10 ppmv.

A reliable CEM system and adequate controls are required to keep the ammonia injection rate at the required level, and to ensure the appropriate reaction temperature. Otherwise, emissions of unreacted ammonia, which is a pollutant, will increase over the normal 10-ppmv range.

Different designs of catalyst beds are available, depending on the required NO_X emission targets and the temperature range. Titanium oxide, vanadium pentoxide, or platinum are mounted on a substrate in a catalyst bed designed for optimum flow velocity.

For applications requiring a wider, higher temperature range (250 to 500°C), zeolite materials have been used. This material could potentially be used on simple-cycle applications. However, it is more expensive than conventional materials.

Units using liquid fuel cannot use an SCR system due to the presence of sulfur, which leads to plugging of the downstream HRSG section and catalyst bed with sulfates of ammonia. The lifespan of the SCR catalyst has been increased from 3 to 5 years when clean fuel is used. The disposal of spent catalyst structures could be expensive if they are classified as hazardous waste. The capital cost for SCR systems is around $50 per kW installed for large units. The cost of NO_X control from 150 ppmv down to 40 ppmv on large units is about $2000 per tonne. If steam injection is used to control down to 50 ppmv, and SCR down to 10 ppmv, the marginal cost of the SCR portion would be much higher.

Dry Low-NO_X Combustors

The high local peak-flame temperatures can be minimized by rearranging the airflow of the fuel mixture inside the combustor. Operational difficulties with water injection and SCR have led to the development of this technology. Development of DLN for large industrial gas turbines started in the early 1980s, where staging of the fuel-air mixture to meet the U.S. EPA requirement of 75 ppmv is possible due to the availability of enough space in the combustor.

The NO_X reductions in recent developments have reached a range of between 25 and 30 ppmv for small- to medium-sized units, and 7 ppmv for very large machines. Many existing units are proposed to be retrofitted with the new systems.

The combustors of most Canadian gas turbines are annular or canannular. DLN consists of new, lean premix combustors. The compressor discharge air is mixed with the fuel to achieve a uniform mixture, prior to entering the combustion zone. The fuel-air ratio is quite lean to minimize NO_X formation. However, this must be closely controlled during off-design conditions to prevent flameout.

For large industrial units, General Electric has a two-stage premix combustor can arrangement for the Frame 6 and Frame 7 lines. Westinghouse has developed low-NO_X combustor cans for its W-251 and W-501 units. European companies such as Asea Brown Boveri have achieved NO_X reductions down to the 10- to 25-ppmv level by selectively using a large number of premix conical burners.

REFERENCES

1. Klein, M., *Development of National Emission Guidelines for Stationary Combustion Turbines,* Industrial Programs Branch, Environment Canada, Ottawa, 1995.

2. *Combustion Turbine National Emission Guideline,* Initiative 307, CCME NO_X/VOC Management Plan, 1990.

CHAPTER 21
COMBINED CYCLES

THE NONIDEAL BRAYTON CYCLE

The Brayton cycle with fluid friction is shown in Figure 21.1 by area 1-2-3-4.

$$\eta_c = \text{compressor polytropic efficiency} = \frac{\text{ideal work}}{\text{actual work}}$$

$$= \frac{h_{2s} - h_1}{h_2 - h_1}$$

If we assume constant specific heats

$$\eta_c = \frac{T_{2s} - T_1}{T_2 - T_1}$$

and

$$\eta_T = \text{turbine polytropic efficiency} = \frac{\text{actual work}}{\text{ideal work}}$$

$$= \frac{h_3 - h_4}{h_3 - h_{4s}}$$

and for constant specific heats

$$\eta_T = \frac{T_3 - T_4}{T_3 - T_{4s}}$$

The net power of the cycle is

$$\dot{W}_n = \text{power of turbine} - |\text{power of compressor}|$$

For constant specific heats

$$\dot{W}_n = \dot{m}c_p\,[(T_3 - T_4) - (T_2 - T_1)] \tag{21.1}$$

or

$$\dot{W}_n = \dot{m}c_p\left[(T_3 - T_{4s})\,\eta_T - \frac{T_{2s} - T_1}{\eta_c}\right] \tag{21.2}$$

This equation can be written in terms of the initial temperature T_1, a chosen metallurgical limit T_3, and the compressor and turbine efficiencies [Eqs. (21.1) and (21.2)] to give

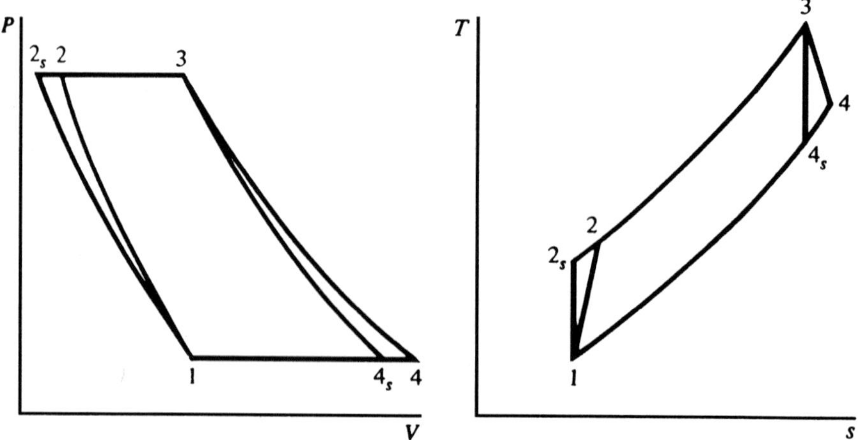

FIGURE 21.1 *P-V* and *T-s* diagrams of ideal and nonideal Brayton cycle.

$$\dot{W}_n = \dot{m}c_pT_1\left[\left(\eta_T \frac{T_3}{T_1} - \frac{r_p^{(k-1)/k}}{\eta_c}\right)\left(1 - \frac{1}{r_p^{(k-1)/k}}\right)\right] \tag{21.3}$$

The second quantity in parentheses is the efficiency of the corresponding ideal cycle.

As in the case of the ideal cycle, the specific power of the nonideal cycle, $\dot{W}_n/\dot{m}$, reaches a maximum value at some optimum pressure ratio. The heat added in the cycle is given by:

$$\dot{Q}_A = \dot{m}c_p(T_3 - T_2) = \dot{m}c_p\left[(T_3 - T_1) - \left(T_1\frac{r_p^{(k-1)/k} - 1}{\eta_c}\right)\right] \tag{21.4}$$

The efficiency of the nonideal cycle can be obtained by dividing Eq. (21.3) by Eq. (21.4). Although the efficiency of the ideal cycle is independent of cycle temperatures, the efficiency of the nonideal cycle is very much a function of the cycle temperatures. The efficiency of the nonideal cycle reaches a maximum value at an optimum pressure ratio. The two optimum pressure ratios, for specific power and for efficiency, have different values. Therefore, a compromise in design is necessary.

Other irreversibilities (e.g., fluid friction in heat exchangers, piping, etc.) have not been included in Fig. 21.1. There is a pressure drop between points 2 and 3. Also, the pressure at point 4 is greater than at point 1. Further irreversibilities occur due to bearings friction and auxiliaries, heat losses from combustion chambers, and air bypass to cool the turbine blades.

Figure 21.2 illustrates the calculation results for efficiency and specific work of a simple cycle (solid lines) and one with a regenerator (dashed lines).

The following data were used for the simple cycle:

$T_1 = 15°C = 59°F =$ constant

$P_1 = 1.013$ bar $= 1$ atm $=$ constant

$\eta_c = 90\%$; $\eta_T = 87\%$

Mechanical losses = 1%

Combustion chamber losses = 2%

Air bypass = 3%

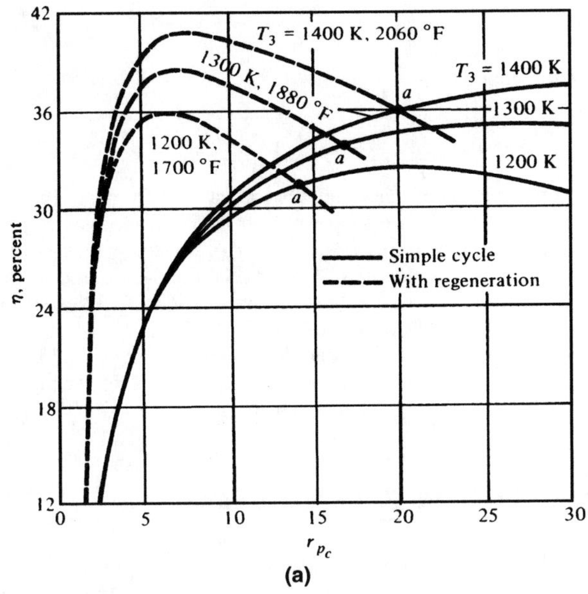

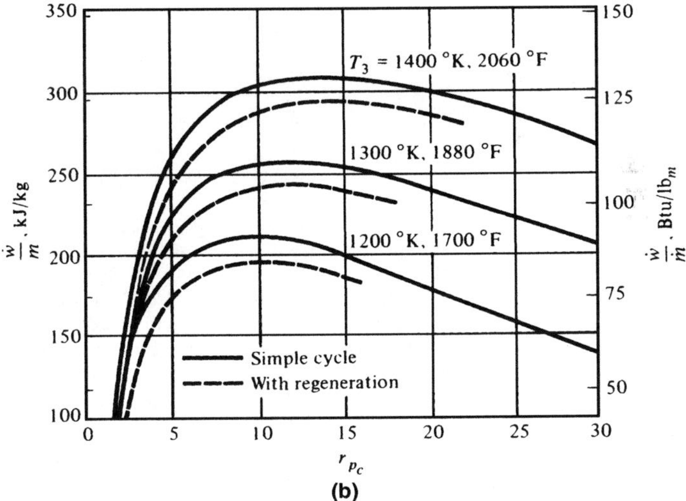

FIGURE 21.2 (*a*) Efficiency versus compressor pressure ratio of a nonideal Brayton cycle, showing effects of maximum temperature and regeneration. (*b*) Specific power versus compressor pressure ratio of a nonideal Brayton cycle, showing effects of maximum temperature and regeneration. [*Source: El-Wakil, M. M. (Ref. 1).*]

Pressure losses:

At inlet = 1%

In combustion chamber = 3%

At outlet = 2%

In regeneration = 4%

Actual, variable properties of air and combustion gases were used. Figure 21.2 indicates that the efficiency and specific work depends strongly on the maximum temperature *T*, which occurs at the inlet to the turbine.

Figure 21.3 illustrates a single-shaft, direct-cycle, open-air combustion gas turbine. A 16-stage axial compressor, 1 of 10 combustion chambers, and a 3-stage turbine are shown. A diesel engine for starting is shown on the left.

The power plant, General Electric model MS-6001, produces 35.75 MW, is 30.50 percent efficient, runs at 5100 r/min, and has overall dimensions, including electric generator (not shown), of 38 m (122 ft) long, 11 m (36 ft) high, and 8 m (26 ft) wide.

MODIFICATIONS OF THE BRAYTON CYCLE

The simple gas turbine cycle is economically adequate for peaking units and jet transport. However, base-loaded units require modifications to improve their efficiency. Some modifications required, besides increasing the combustor outlet temperature, include the following:

- Regeneration
- Compressor intercooling
- Turbine reheat
- Water injection

Regeneration

Regeneration is the internal exchange of heat within the cycle. The turbine outlet temperature is usually higher than the compressor outlet temperature. Figure 21.4 illustrates the flow and *T-s* diagrams of a closed, nonideal Brayton cycle with regeneration. The compressed gas at point 2 is preheated by the exhaust gases at point 4 in a heat exchanger called a *regenerator,* sometimes *recuperator.*

If the regenerator were 100 percent effective, the gas temperature entering the combustor would be raised from T_2 to $T_{2''}$ (T_4). The heat added would be reduced from $H_3 - H_2$ to $H_3 - H_{2''}$. In reality, the compressed gas is heated to $T_{2'}$ because the regenerator effectiveness is always less than 100 percent.

The regenerator effectiveness, ε_R, is:

$$\varepsilon_R = \frac{T_{2'} - T_4}{T_4 - T_2} \tag{21.5}$$

Figure 21.2 (*a, b*) shows the effect of adding a regenerator with $\varepsilon_R = 0.75$.

There is a significant increase in efficiency. However, the optimum pressure ratio for efficiency shifts to lower values. This is because as the pressure ratio decreases, the

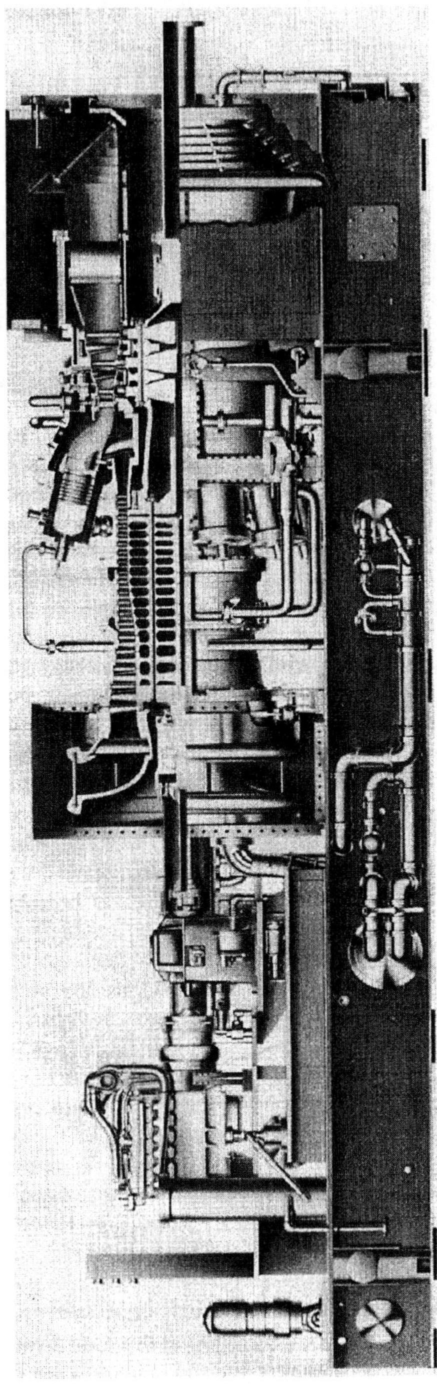

FIGURE 21.3 35.75-MW direct-cycle gas-turbine powerplant. *(Courtesy Gas Turbine Division, General Electric Company, Schenectady, New York.)*

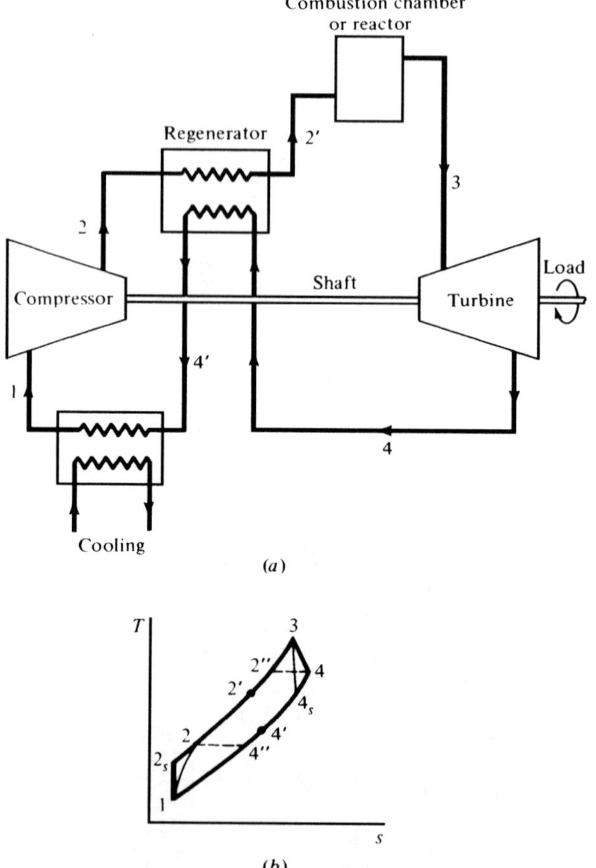

FIGURE 21.4 (*a*) Flow and (*b*) *T-s* diagrams of a closed, nonideal Brayton cycle with regeneration.

difference between T_4 and T_2 increases. This results in a greater reduction in cycle heat input.

At a very low pressure ratio (r_p), the effect of reduced cycle work predominates and the efficiency drops significantly. The efficiency curves for a cycle with regenerator cross the simple-cycle curves at points such as point *a*. This is the point beyond which the effect of a regenerator on efficiency is negative. These points represent pressure ratios at which the turbine exhaust gases temperature (T_4) is lower than those after compression (T_2).

Compressor Intercooling

The work in a compressor or a turbine is given by:

$$W = -\int_1^2 V\,dP \tag{21.6}$$

For a perfect gas where $PV = mRT$, this equation can be written as

$$W = -\int_1^2 mRT \frac{dP}{P} \tag{21.7}$$

For a given dP/P, the work is directly proportional to temperature. A compressor working between points 1 and 2 would expend more work as the gas approaches point 2. Therefore, it is advantageous to keep T as low as possible while reaching P_2.

Figure 21.5 shows two stages of intercooling. There is a net increase in work and efficiency. The increase in work is given by area 2-1′-2′-1″-2″-x-2. The heat added has also increased by $h_x - h_{2''}$. However, there is a net improvement in efficiency.

Turbine Reheat

The turbine work can be increased by keeping the gas temperature in the turbine as close as possible to the turbine inlet temperature, T_3. Figure 21.5 shows one stage of reheat. The

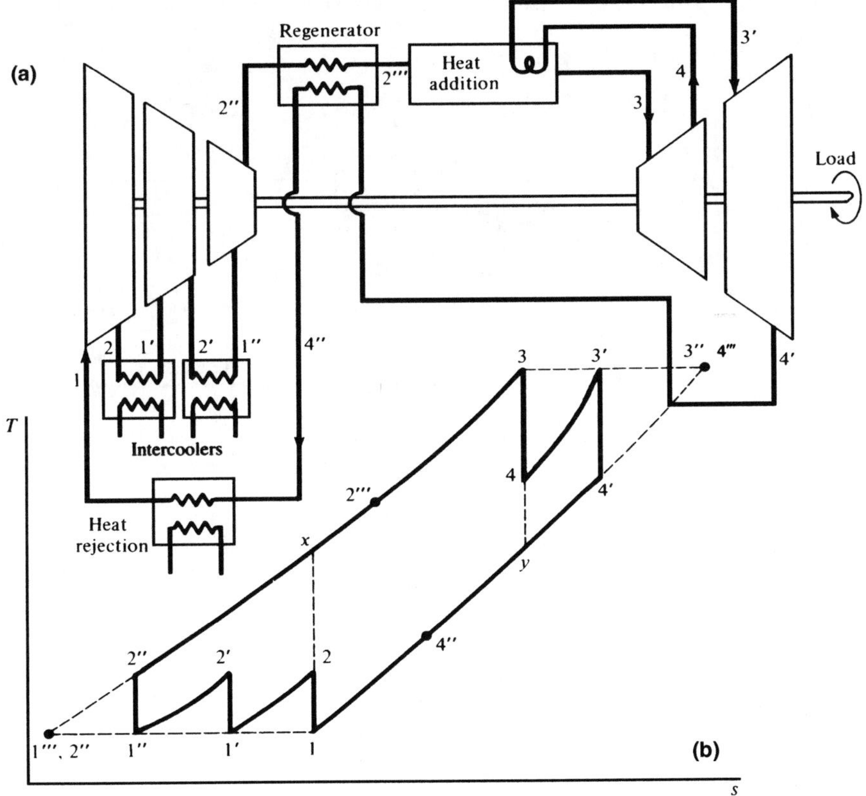

FIGURE 21.5 (*a*) Flow and (*b*) *T-s* diagrams of a closed, ideal Brayton cycle with two stages of intercooling, one stage of reheat, and regeneration.

increase in cycle work is given by area 4-3′-4′-*y*. The heat added has increased by $H_{3'} - H_4$. However, there is a net increase in work and efficiency. The efficiency increases when the number of reheat and intercooling stages increases. However, the capital investment and plant size would increase.

Water Injection

Water injection is a method used to increase the power output of a gas turbine significantly and to have marginal increase in efficiency. In some aircraft propulsion units, water is injected into the compressor. It evaporates when the air temperature rises through the compression process. The heat of vaporization reduces the compressed air temperature, resulting in a decrease in compressor work.

Figure 21.6 (*a, b*) shows flow and *T-s* diagrams of a gas turbine cycle with water injection and regeneration. Area 1-2-4-5-7-9′-1 represents the cycle without water injection. Point 9′ represents the exhaust gas at the outlet of the regenerator.

When water in injected, the compressed air at point 2 is cooled at nearly constant pressure by the evaporating water at point 3. The regenerator preheats the compressed air at point 3 to point 4. The added heat required to increase the temperature of the moist air from point 3 to point 2 is obtained from the exhaust gases between points 9′ and 9.

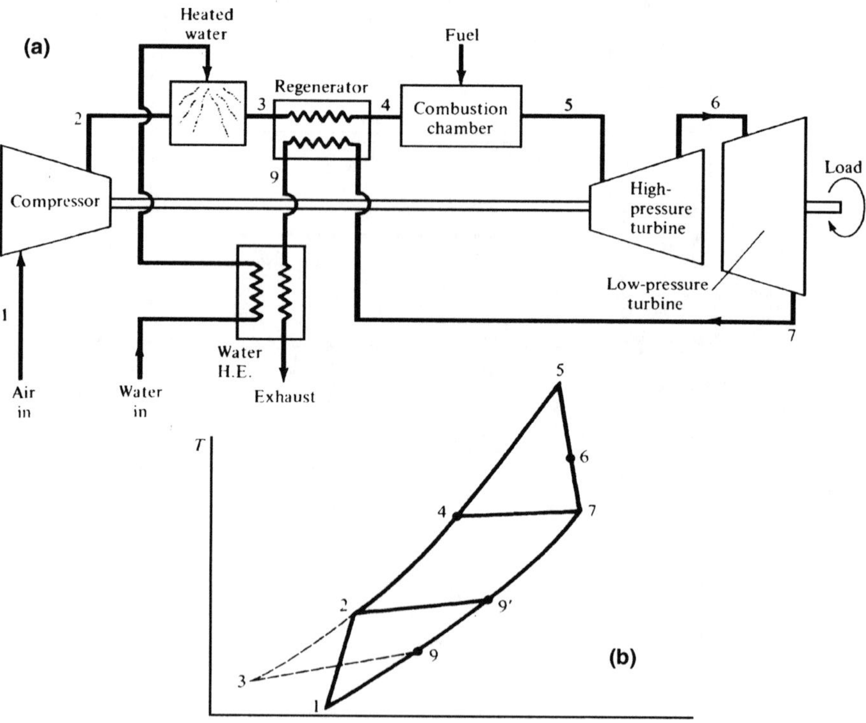

FIGURE 21.6 (*a*) Flow and (*b*) *T-s* diagrams of a two-shaft gas turbine cycle with water injection and regeneration.

The quantity of water vapor injected is enough to saturate the air at T_3. Any further increase in the quantity of water vapor would reduce the efficiency and increase the net work. The increase in water will lead to fouling in the regenerator, local severe temperature differences, and associated thermal stresses. The increase in work due to water injection is due to an increase in turbine work caused by the increased mass flow rate.

DESIGN FOR HIGH TEMPERATURE

Higher efficiencies can be achieved by increasing the turbine inlet temperature. The optimum pressures increase with increasing turbine inlet temperatures for both efficiency and power. The potential for corrosion increases with higher temperatures.

A turbine inlet temperature of between 2800 and 3000°F (1540 and 1650°C) has been reached.

These temperatures are significantly higher than the temperature at the inlet of the modern steam turbine, which are between 1000 and 1200°F (540 and 650°C).

Materials

The turbine first-stage blades (fixed and moving) suffer most from a combination of high temperatures, high stresses, and chemical attack. They must resist corrosion, oxidation, and thermal fatigue. The two recent advances are heat-resistant material and precision casting. They are largely attributable to aircraft engine developments.

The turbine first-stage fixed blades are made of cobalt-based alloys. These alloys are being supplemented by vacuum-cast nickel-based alloys, which are strengthened through solution- and precipitation-hardened heat treatment. The moving blades are made of cobalt-based alloys and high chromium content. Ceramic materials have been used for the turbine inlet fixed blades. However, problems were encountered due to inherent brittleness.

Cooling

Early gas turbines operated without any cooling. Operation at high temperatures in modern gas turbines requires cooling. The thermal stresses in the turbine moving blades are caused by the following:

- High rotational speeds
- Uneven temperature distributions in the different blade cross sections
- Static and pulsating gas forces that may result in dangerous vibrational stresses
- Load changes, start-up and shutdown

Therefore, the thermal stresses are caused by steady-state, as well as transient, operation. The transient operation will lead to low-cycle fatigue. This reduces the blade life significantly. Additional problems are encountered due to creep rupture, high-temperature corrosion, and oxidation.

In general, the blade surfaces should be kept below 1650°F (900°C) to reduce corrosion to an acceptable level. Cooling of the blades is done by making them hollow to allow the coolant to circulate through them. A hollow blade is lighter than a solid blade. It also has a more uniform temperature distribution than a solid blade. Air has been used as a coolant in

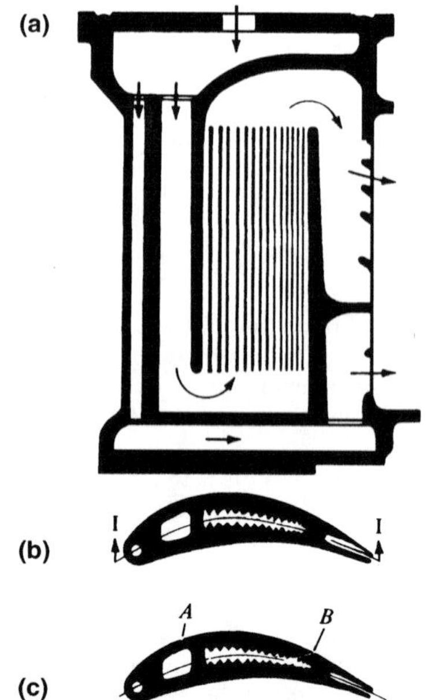

FIGURE 21.7 Air-cooled gas turbine fixed blade.

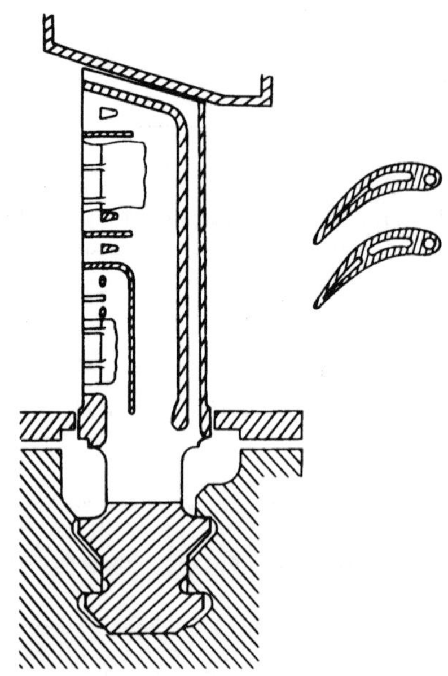

FIGURE 21.8 Air-cooled gas turbine moving blade.

gas turbines up to 2100°F (1150°C). Water has been used for gas temperature above 2400°F (1315°C).

Air Cooling. The cooling air is obtained directly from the compressor to the turbine. It bypasses the combustor.

In *convection cooling,* the air flows inside the hollow blade. It enters at the leading edge and leaves at the trailing edge to enter the main gas stream.

Film cooling is used in conjunction with convection cooling. Air flows through holes from inside the blade to the outside boundary layer to form a protective insulating film between the blade and the hot gases. This method helps prevent corrosion of the blades in addition to cooling.

Figure 21.7 illustrates air cooling of inlet fixed blades. The upper vertical cross section [Fig. 21.7 (*a*)] shows air entering from the stator at the top. It flows downward by the leading edge in two parallel paths. It changes direction a few times and leaves at the trailing edge.

Figure 21.7 (*b*) illustrates the middle horizontal cross section through the blade. It shows the internal path in pure convection cooling. Figure 21.7 (*c*) illustrates two rows of holes, *A* and *B,* on the side of the blade for film cooling.

Figure 21.8 illustrates the air cooling in the moving blades. The air enters the blade root from the rotor. It flows through the hollow blades in ducts and leaves through slots from the blade trailing edge.

Water Cooling. When the air temperature reaches 2100°F (1150°C), air cooling becomes ineffective due to the significant increase in cooling air that bypasses the combustion chamber. Water cooling is very effective when the gas temperature exceeds 2400°F (1315°C). Lower metal temperatures are reached due to the high heat transfer capability of water. It reduces hot corrosion and deposition from contaminated fuels. Water cooling also eliminates the need of passages through the blades (film cooling), which could be plugged by contamination.

Experiments using heavy ash-bearing fuels have showed lower metal temperatures and reduction in ash accumulation on the blades with water cooling. The fixed blades or nozzles are hollow. They contain series of parallel flow paths. The water circulates in, through, and out of these paths in a closed loop. The heat removed from these blades is recovered in a heat exchanger for use in the steam portion of a combined cycle. The inlet water temperature is relatively high to prevent thermal shock. Its pressure is high to prevent boiling.

The moving blades are cooled by an open-loop system. The water enters the blades at lower pressures and is allowed to boil. The steam is ejected from the blade tips to mix with the gas stream.

FUELS

Liquid fuels have been used in gas turbines. However, they are viscous and form sludge when overheated. Their high carbon content leads to excessive carbon deposits in the combustion chamber. Their contents of alkali metals, such as sodium, combine with sulfur to form sulfates that are corrosive. Their metals, such as vanadium, form corrosive combustion products. They have a high ash content that deposits mainly on the inlet fixed blades, resulting in reduction in gas flow and power output.

Fuel additives, such as magnesium, have been found to neutralize vanadium. Other additives and protective coatings are also used to reduce corrosion.

The pressurized-fluidized-bed combustion (PFBC) makes coal, which is cheap, abundant, and readily available as a gas turbine fuel. In the PFBC, the addition of limestone will remove enough sulfur to meet environmental regulations. Further research is required to reduce particulate matter from the gaseous products of PFBC, which can destroy the turbine blades. Another alternative for coal usage is the use of synthetic fuels from coal gasification and liquidation.

COMBINED CYCLES

Steam and gas turbines are used to supply power in combined-cycle power plants. The idea has originated from the need to improve the Brayton cycle efficiency by utilizing the waste heat in the turbine exhaust gases.

The large quantity of energy leaving with the turbine exhaust is used to generate steam for a steam power plant. This is a suitable arrangement because the gas turbine is a relatively high-temperature machine (2000 to 3000°F, 1100 to 1650°C) while the steam turbine is a relatively low-temperature machine (1000 to 1200°F, 540 to 650°C).

Combined cycles have high efficiency, as well as high power, outputs. They are characterized by flexibility and quick part-load starting. They are also suitable for both base-load and cyclic operation, and have a high efficiency over a wide range of loads.

The most common types of combined cycles include those with heat recovery boilers (HRBs), the steam-and-water (STAG) combined-cycle power plant, and combined cycles with multipressure steam.

Combined Cycles with Heat Recovery Boiler

Figure 21.9 illustrates a schematic flow diagram of a combined cycle with an HRB. The gas turbine exhaust is going to an HRB to generate superheated steam. The HRB consists of an

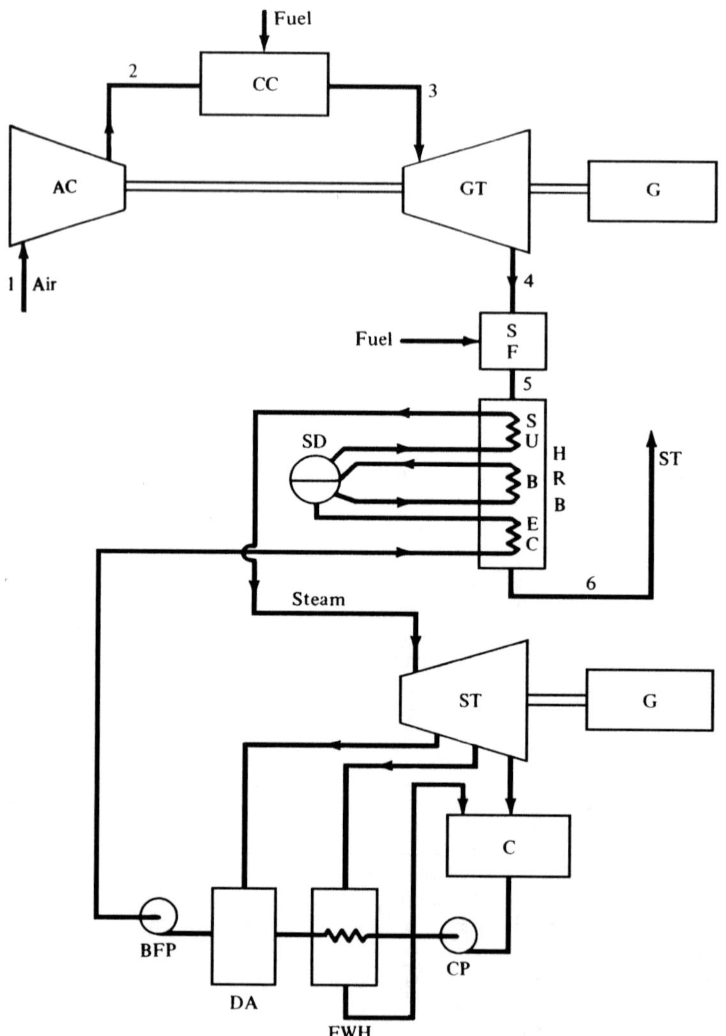

FIGURE 21.9 Schematic flow diagram of a combined cycle with a heat recovery boiler (HRB).

economizer (*EC*), boiler (*B*), steam drum (*SD*), and superheater (*SU*). The gas leaves the HRB to the stack. The gas turbine is operated with a high air-fuel ratio to make sufficient air available in the gas turbine exhaust for further combustion.

To increase the output for short periods during load peaks, supplementary fuel (SF) burners are fitted to the HRB to increase the steam mass-flow rate. This can also be done on a continuous basis.

A forced fan may be installed ahead of SF to operate the steam cycle on its own when the gas turbine is cut off. The fuel that is used in the supplementary firing can be the same as the high-grade fuel that is used in the gas turbine or it can be lower-grade fuels, such as heavy oil or coal. However, the high-grade fuel is preferred because it causes fewer problems in the SF and HRB.

The STAG Combined-Cycle Powerplant

The steam and gas (STAG) is a 330-MW combined-cycle power plant built for the Jersey Central Power and Light Company. It is a cyclic plant designed by General Electric Company. It consists of four GE Model-7000 gas turbines exhausting to supplementary firing in the form of auxiliary burner sections within four HRBs. The HRBs provide the superheated steam to one steam turbine. Figure 21.10 illustrates the plant layout.

The STAG is an operationally flexible combined-cycle power plant. Each of the four gas turbines and the steam turbine can be started, controlled, and loaded independently from a control room. Either one or more gas turbines can be operated with its HRB supplement fired or unfired. Steam pressures of 600, 800, 1000, and 1250 pounds per square inch gauge (psig) (4.08, 5.4, 6.8, and 8.5 MPa) are obtained with one, two, three, and four gas turbines. The plant data are as follows:

Gas turbines:	Four GE Model-7000, each rated at 49.5 MW (base) and 54.9 MW (peak) at 80°F (27°C) inlet.
Turbine exhaust:	970°F (521°C). Dampers used to bypass gas to atmosphere when operating alone, or to direct gas to the HRB when operating in combined-cycle mode. Silencers are located ahead of bypass stack and HRB.
HRB:	Four single-pressure, burner-and-steam generator sections are factory-assembled modules for site erection. Forced recirculation in boiler section.
Feedwater:	267°F (130°C) at economizer inlet.
Steam:	1250 psig (87 bar), 950°F (510°C), 995,220 lb_m/h (125 kg/s).

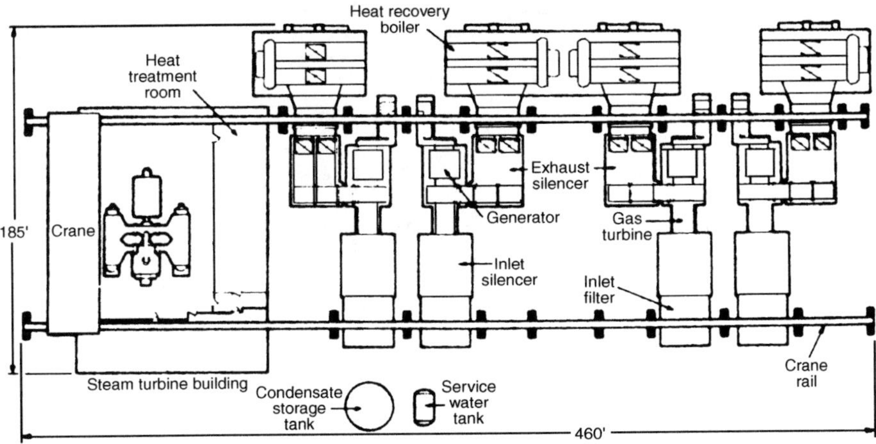

FIGURE 21.10 Layout of the STAG combined-cycle power plant.

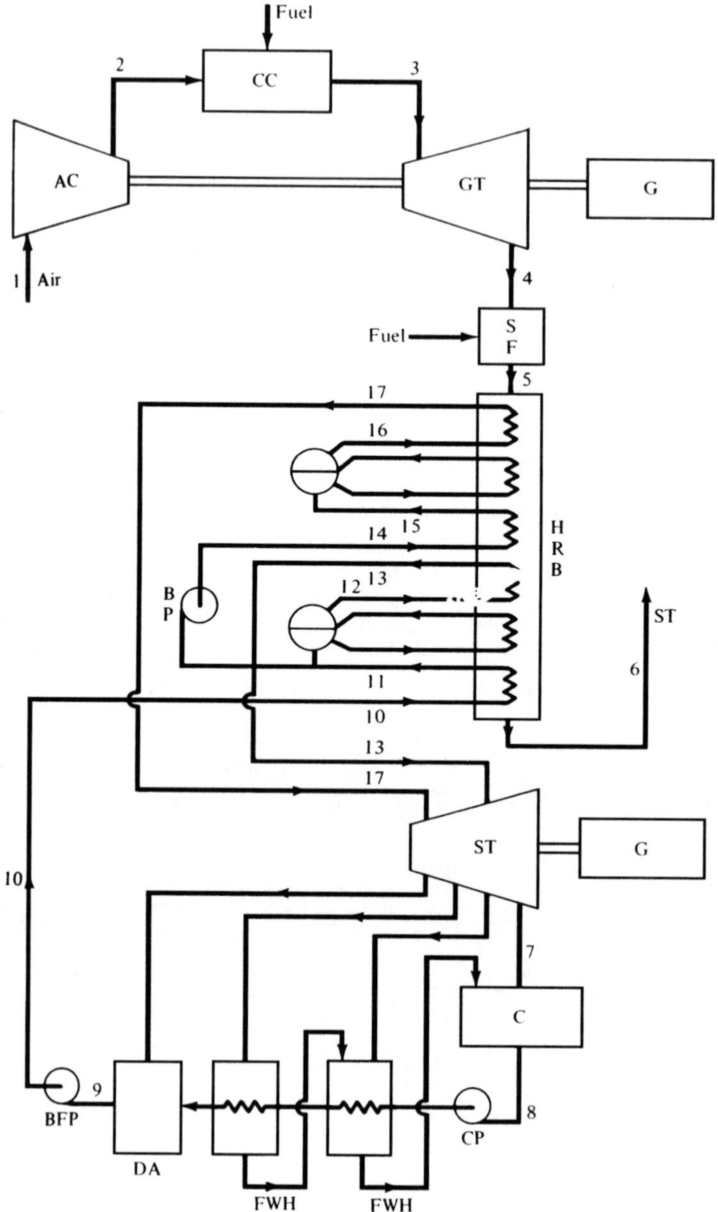

FIGURE 21.11 A schematic diagram for a dual-pressure combined cycle.

Steam turbine: One high-pressure and one double-flow, low-pressure, tandem-compound section, non-reheat, rated at 129.6 MW with 3.5 inHg (0.12 bar) back pressure.

Fuel: No. 2 distillate oil initially. Corrosion-resistant first-stage gas turbine materials allow future use of heavier fuel.

When the gas turbines are exhausting to atmosphere, the efficiency is 26.3 to 25.3 percent. When the HRB is firing and the steam turbine is at very wide-open throttle, the efficiency is 39.3 percent.

Combined Cycles with Multipressure Steam

The temperature of the gas leaving the HRB is reduced in a combined cycle having multipressure steam. This results in an increase in the efficiency of the plant. With steam cycles operating around 1300 psia (90 bar), the gas temperature leaving the HRB to the stack is around 300 to 400°F (150 to 200°C). Some of the energy leaving with the gas can be utilized in a multipressure steam cycle.

A *dual-pressure cycle* is shown in Fig. 21.11. The HRB has two steam circuits in it:

1. *High-pressure circuit.* It feeds steam to the steam turbine at its inlet.
2. *Low-pressure circuit.* It feeds steam to the turbine at a lower stage.

The corresponding temperature-enthalpy diagram of both gas and steam circuits in the HRB is shown in Fig. 21.12. Line 10-11 is a feedwater heating in a low-pressure economizer. It is followed by evaporation to point 12 and superheat to point 13. Water is pumped by a booster pump (BP) from the low-pressure steam drum at point 11 to point 14.

Figure 21.12 shows also that a single high-pressure steam circuit is represented by lines 10′-15-16-17 with the gas leaving to the stack at 6′.

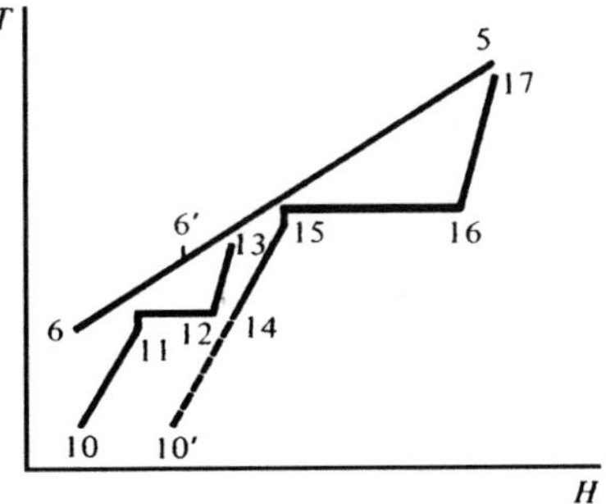

FIGURE 21.12 Temperature-enthalpy (*T-H*) diagram of the heat recovery boiler of the dual-pressure combined cycle shown in Fig. 21.11.

The addition of the low-pressure circuit allowed the gas to leave at a lower temperature (point 6). This indicates that more energy has been extracted from the gas, resulting in an increase in overall cycle efficiency. The efficiency is 46.1 percent when the air temperature is 15°C.

REFERENCES

1. El-Wakil, M. M., *Power Plant Technology*, McGraw-Hill, New York, 1984.

CHAPTER 22
SELECTION CONSIDERATIONS OF COMBINED CYCLES AND COGENERATION PLANTS

Gas (combustion) turbine research performed in the 1970s hinted that high pressure ratios and very high temperatures are required to achieve high efficiency. However, modern engine technology proved that the Carnot cycle's fundamentals are valid. Only high temperatures are required to achieve high efficiencies. Modern gas turbines reached efficiencies higher than 44 percent for a simple cycle by operating at elevated temperatures (over 2500°F).

Modern design is concentrating on increasing the *turbine inlet temperature* (TIT) to improve performance, and the bulk of the development is focused on improving the metallurgy and cooling. The economics of operating a gas turbine alone and selling power to the local utility are not favorable because utilities use elaborate and expensive large thermal plants based on steam turbine technology and very low-cost fuel.

Combined-cycle plants use the high volume and temperature in the exhaust of gas turbines in a boiler to make steam suitable for steam turbines and other industrial and commercial applications. Modern combined cycles have achieved efficiencies around 60 percent for electrical power production only and over 85 percent for electrical power and steam production.

THE HEAT RECOVERY STEAM GENERATOR

The concept of recovering waste heat is not new. In 1948, Westinghouse built a gas turbine for a railroad locomotive intended for fast passenger service, nicknamed "Blue Goose." The gas turbine had a small boiler installed in its exhaust duct to make steam for heating the passenger cars. Initially, the boilers were called *heat recovery boilers,* and their purpose was to produce saturated steam for secondary uses.

Since that time, a great deal of effort was spent on trying to maximize the performance of the gas turbine, and little attention was paid to the back end of the cycle. In the late 1960s, the emphasis changed to maximizing the *cycle* efficiency, and engineers started designing gas turbines with a waste heat boiler in mind. When a large superheater was added, the name changed to *heat recovery steam generator* (HRSG). Figure 22.1 illustrates an HRSG manufactured by Foster Wheeler having a superheater, a boiler, and an economizer.

This change was made to highlight the substantial superheat in the steam, which greatly improved the efficiency of the steam (bottoming) part of the cycle. Stack temperatures can be reduced as low as 120°F (49°C). However, these temperatures cause problems if the fuel in the turbine contains sulfur. Sulfur dioxide (SO_2) will form during combustion and dissolve in water vapor to form H_2SO_4 (sulfuric acid) in the stack, which has a direct effect on the metallurgy of the boiler. Supplementary treatment of the exhaust gases with limestone slurry injection or other techniques may be required depending on the local environment and the amount of acid.

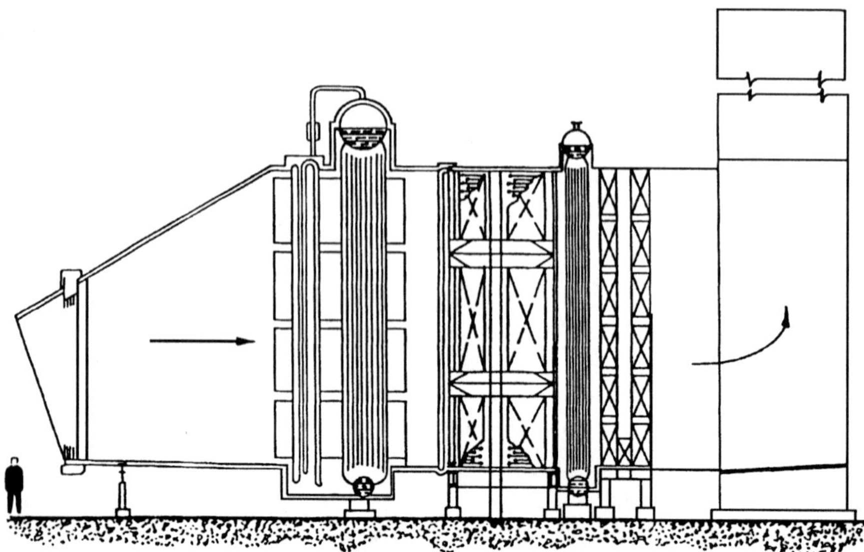

FIGURE 22.1 Modern HRSGs like this one are in three sections: a superheater (in the hottest part of the airstream), a boiler/evaporator (middle), and an economizer (in the coolest part), which is actually a heater for the feedwater. (*Courtesy of Foster Wheeler.*)

The casing of the HRSG is designed to handle the significant thermal stresses that are caused by fast temperature transients during start-up and shutdown. A large diffuser is installed at the inlet to reduce the high velocity in the gas turbine exhaust to levels that the tube banks can withstand. Supplementary firing can be added in the diffuser to provide additional steam production in off-design operations and/or for steam superheat control.

The HRSG operates normally with two pressures [one substantially superheated and one (lower pressure) section with little or no superheat]. A steam turbine generator set can be installed to balance steam flows in the attached plant. The HRSGs can be designed to handle multiple pressures, but it is rarely economical to use more than three.

The once-through design where a single tube is used for heat recovery is relatively new. It does not have boiler drums, and the controls are greatly simplified. Feedwater at full pressure enters the finned boiler tube in the coolest part of the boiler and is heated. The water starts to boil at some point, and the steam is superheated in the hottest part of the boiler (at the gas inlet). The feedwater flow is easily controlled on either a pressure or superheater outlet temperature basis. The latter approach provides the most efficient operation of the steam turbine generator set. This has the potential to increase the plant viability and reduce complexity. Also, a side benefit is easy operation.

COGENERATION STEAM CONSIDERATIONS

Many manufacturing processes commonly use steam as an exceptionally stable source of heat. In cogeneration plants, steam is commonly made at a much higher pressure than required by the process to allow the turbine generator to exhaust the incremental energy in it.

Such "topping" cycles are inherently very efficient because any inefficiency in the turbomachinery (i.e., failure to convert some of the high-enthalpy energy in the steam to mechanical power) results in the uncaptured energy remaining in the steam flow, where it can be captured by the downstream process as heat.

When designing a cogeneration plant, it is tempting to consider maximizing the efficiency by implementing Carnot cycle rules. This can be done by maximizing the turbine inlet enthalpy (maximum inlet temperature and pressure). Unfortunately, in the real world, the thermodynamics of power plants can be misleading when considered exclusively. This is due to several considerations, the discussion of which follows.

Requirement of Chrome-Moly Steel

When boiler outlet temperatures exceed 750°F (400°C), carbon steel would not be adequate. The cost of the boiler, main steam piping, and the turbine start to rise rapidly due to the need for steels with chrome and molybdenum alloying. For example, the cost of steam turbine inlet cylinder castings *doubles* when specified for 900 psi (6.1 MPa) and 900°F (482°C), compared with 600 psi (4.08 MPa), and 750°F.

Misleading Thermodynamics

Although the thermodynamics suggests that the efficiency of the plant can be maximized by maximizing the turbine inlet enthalpy, selecting lower conditions results in increasing the generation capability of the steam flow ($Q = \dot{m}C_P\Delta T$). This offsets most of the loss caused by decreasing the turbine inlet enthalpy. The actual decrease in cycle efficiency is fairly small.

Equipment Availability

For most industrial sizes of steam turbines (up to 30 MW) back-pressure designs, and 60 MW condensing, turbine designs are readily available for inlet conditions in the 600 psi (4.08 MPa), 750°F (400°C) range. The turbomachinery of these applications does not require higher temperatures and pressures.

Maintenance Cost

The maintenance of the whole cycle is reduced when modest temperatures and pressures are selected. This is because bolted (flanged) joints are completely satisfactory for the steam cycle. However, as the temperatures and pressures increase, more and more of the joints should be welded to ensure that the risk of leaks is minimized.

Operational Cost

Higher inlet enthalpies require more sophisticated feedwater chemistry (addition of hydrazine and morphiline). This increases the operating cost. (This is in addition to the higher construction cost of the equipment.) The cost is particularly important in applications where steam is not recovered after being used in a process. The makeup treatment cost can be substantial.

Turbine Cost

A high enthalpy drop in the turbine requires additional stages in order to handle the energy drop. This increases the capital cost significantly and results in a longer time to pay a return on the investment.

If the steam flow and the resultant power are low in, for example, a 2-MW back-pressure turbine generator set, one turbine stage is needed for steam at 600 psi (4.08 MPa) and 750°F (400°C). However, in condensing applications, a multistage turbine (at least three stages) is required to handle the same power. This increases the capital cost substantially.

If the inlet is at 850 psi (5.8 MPa) and 750°F (400°C), a six-stage (or more) turbine is required. The capital cost of the turbine generator is determined almost entirely by the size and complexity of the hardware, and the output power is largely irrelevant.

Operating Staff

The existing legislation for most jurisdictions in Canada requires operating staff for conventional drum-type boilers. This creates a significant continuous cost, which is unrelated to the output power.

If the addition of the steam cycle to the cogeneration plant requires highly educated staff, this will reduce the return on the investment. Recent studies indicate that at least 20 MW of power generation is required to pay incremental staff cost. However, if the generation site already uses large amounts of steam, the incremental cost is very small.

Heat of Condensation

Since a substantial amount of the heat in a cogeneration plant must be used for an industrial application (process), it is essential to have the process capture the heat of condensation. Generating steam to go through a condensing turbine (little or no process heat being extracted) is actually a miniature version of the thermal plants that the local utility uses. However, the economics of scale work strongly against the cogeneration plant.

The capital cost structure and taxation are also equally bad for these cogeneration plants. It is impossible to generate a profit using this approach.

Pipework to Steam Host

If long runs of steam pipework are required due to the plant layout design, elevated pressures will allow smaller piping diameter. This reduces the heat loss and eventually the cost. However, higher pressures are associated with higher temperatures. This should be evaluated carefully because substantial pipe insulation may be required. The designer must choose between thick insulation on small (alloy-steel) pipe or less insulation on larger-diameter (carbon-steel) pipe.

Requirement of Steam Host

The type of fuel has a large impact on the economics of cogeneration plants. If the fuel is free (i.e., municipal garbage), it is possible to build a relatively small cogeneration plant that will generate a profit. If there is any cost for the fuel, the availability of a customer paying for process steam becomes crucial. The economics of cogeneration plants are optimized when the process demand is 100 percent (i.e., a back-pressure turbine is selected).

COMBINED CYCLE

Since the Carnot cycle efficiency is quite high when the peak cycle temperature is over 2000°F (1093°C) [impossible on a steam-only cycle due to dissociation of water molecules around 1200°F (649°C)], gas turbines with firing temperatures up to 2800°F (1538°C) are excellent when operated in a combined cycle with a steam turbine. These cycles reach efficiencies up to 60 percent for power generation only (40 percent from the gas cycle and 20 percent from the steam cycle).

Note: A combined cycle having an efficiency of 60 percent for power production only is considered to have more valuable product than a cogeneration plant having an efficiency of 83 percent, where 20 percent is electrical product and 63 percent is thermal. However, the capital cost of such a combined cycle would be significantly higher than a cogeneration plant having the same heat input. In general, the economics of a cogeneration plant producing 100 percent of the process steam from a back-pressure turbine are more favorable than a combined cycle.

SELECTION AND ECONOMICS OF COMBINED CYCLES

It is tempting to select a gas turbine for combined-cycle applications that will completely eliminate purchased power. It is also possible to buy a gas turbine, add a waste heat boiler and a steam turbine with a controlled extraction for the process, and specify a condensing exhaust that will handle the surplus steam. The two advantages of this approach are

1. High efficiency of the combined cycle
2. Production of process steam at low cost

However, this approach has the following two disadvantages:

1. Low efficiency of the condensing exhaust steam cycle
2. Substantial increase in capital cost due to the condensing turbine and condenser (or cooling towers)

A better approach for selecting a combined cycle would consist of the following four considerations:

1. Determine the process heat demand (work backward) and the steam flow that are required to meet that demand.
2. Select a back-pressure turbine to handle the flow (plus a small margin).
3. Size a boiler to make the required steam.
4. Select a gas turbine that produces the right amount of exhaust heat. It is also possible to select a gas turbine that is a little smaller than the maximum load and add a supplementary firing for occasional peaks.

In summary, the preceding four considerations lead to these four reasonable guidelines:

1. Match the steam plant size to real process steam (heat) demand. Do not oversize.
2. Resist the temptation to consider condensing turbines in spite of the high power they can generate.

3. Select modest steam conditions for the turbine inlet to reduce the cost of the turbine, piping, and operation (boiler feedwater chemistry).
4. Search for minimum fuel cost. Waste heat from gas turbines is increasingly attractive. However, operation of a gas turbine alone is rarely attractive due to high fuel cost and relatively low efficiency.

GUIDELINES

When it becomes necessary to add a steam turbine to a plant, follow these three guidelines:

1. If the steam leaving the turbine is going to a process for use as a source of heat, then the economics are favorable. If the steam is going into a condenser under vacuum and the steam cycle is used only for power production, then the whole project should be reconsidered. This is not cogeneration. The economics are generally not favorable, and the cycle is more complicated.

2. Burning a high-quality fuel (e.g., natural gas) in a boiler to make steam is convenient and practical. However, the economics of this process are not favorable. Combined cycles should be considered in this case. The gas is burned in the gas turbine, and the exhaust heat is used to make steam in a slightly different boiler. The capital cost would increase significantly, but the efficiency of the combined cycles would also increase.

Low-grade, cheap fuels (e.g., waste coal, groundwood, and municipal garbage) can be attractive in a suitable boiler. However, these cheap-fuel plants tend to generally have a very high investment in fuel handling.

3. Waste heat boilers are commonly used with new gas turbines. They can also be retrofitted to many existing exothermic processes with suitable choices in materials and construction. In general, they can produce steam at an exceptionally low cost.

CHAPTER 23
APPLICATIONS OF COGENERATION AND COMBINED-CYCLE PLANTS

GUIDELINES FOR ADDITION OF A STEAM TURBINE

The following is a list of questions and answers that provide some guidelines to determine if the addition of a steam turbine is justified.

1. *Where is the steam that is leaving the turbine going to?* If the steam is going to a process for use as a heat source, then proceed. If the steam is entering a condenser and the steam cycle is used to produce power only, then the project should be reconsidered. This is not cogeneration and the economics are generally bad.

2. *What is the source of the steam?* Burning high-quality fuel like natural gas to generate steam is convenient and practical but not very economical. Combined cycles are recommended in this case. Burn the gas in a gas turbine and use the exhaust (waste) heat to make steam. The capital cost has increased significantly, but the efficiency of the combined cycles is much higher (around 60 percent for power generation only). Low-grade, cheap fuels (e.g., waste coal, groundwood, and municipal garbage) are very attractive. However, plants using these cheap fuels tend to have a very high investment in fuel handling.

3. *Is it a waste heat steam generator?* In general, these are installed with new gas turbines. However, they can be retrofitted to many exothermic processes with suitable choices in materials and construction. The cost of steam produced is exceptionally low.

4. *What is the turbine arrangement required?* Until recently, the complexity, poor accuracy, and high maintenance of control systems and turbine generator sets created many problems. The use of *programmable logic controllers* (PLCs) and *distributed control systems* (DCSs) allowed a variety of arrangements to be used. Some examples follow.

SCENARIO A—FOOD PROCESSING PLANT

Three gas-fired boilers generate steam at 550 psi (3.7 MPa). The steam is distributed throughout a food processing plant having desuperheaters and local pressure-reducing stations. Two of the boilers are small and in need of expensive repairs, while the third is large, new, and in excellent condition. The steam is used at 180 psi (1.2 MPa) and other slightly lower pressures. There is no power generation on site. However, there is an unreliable and expensive local utility. An older (retired) steam generator set is available (free). The turbine is in poor condition while the generator is in fair condition.

Solution

Install a new coal-fired boiler that generates steam at 900 psi (6.1 MPa) and 800°F (427°C). The steam was fed into a new turbine that is coupled to the rewound generator. The two old boilers were scrapped. The custom-built turbine also *admits* steam at 550 psi (3.7 MPa) from the existing boiler. The steam is exhausted from the turbine at 200 psi (1.4 MPa) to feed the existing processes.

Half the plant electrical load is generated internally. The remainder is purchased. All of the critical loads of the plant are supplied from the internally generated power by a new dedicated power bus (in general, the internally generated power is considered more reliable than purchased power).

The utility bus supplies noncritical loads and the two buses are tied together by a tie-breaker, which is closed during normal operation. The tie-breaker opens when utility upsets occur to protect the critical loads of the plant. The steam turbine is unusual but not unique (it has incoming steam in the extraction lines). A custom-built governor (Woodward 43027) was used for this application.

SCENARIO B—REPOWERING A POWER GENERATING PLANT

A power generating corporation having several relatively small steam turbine generator sets is owned by a municipality. Natural gas has been used as a fuel for many years. The boilers and the stack are in rough shape, while the turbine generator sets are still in a good condition.

Solution

Scrap the old stack and boilers. Install a few relatively large gas turbines and waste heat steam generators to make the steam needed for the existing turbine generator sets. The fuel consumption increases by 16 percent, while the net power from the plant doubles due to the much higher combined-cycle efficiency. This is known as *repowering*. It is becoming a very attractive option for municipal power producers.

SCENARIO C—CHEMICAL PLANT

A chemical plant burns sulfur as a part of its process. Steam jackets are built into the walls of the combustors to generate steam at 45 psig for use in a process that concentrates sulfuric acid. A high-pressure steam generator was installed several years ago to supply steam to a small turbine generator set (10 MW), which is normally synchronized to the local utility. The generator can disengage from the grid when it becomes unstable. When the generator set is not synchronized, it supplies some of the critical loads required for safe shutdown of the plant. The power cost of the local utility is high. It would be desirable to generate additional power. Violent lightning storms occur throughout the summer. Therefore, the reliability of in-plant power should be improved.

Solution

An elaborate heat recovery system was added to the combustors to generate steam at 600 psi (4.1 MPa) and 620°F (327°C). This temperature is considered low for a new controlled extraction-condensing turbine generator set due to formation of high moisture in the last few stages, which leads to significant erosion. Thus, supplementary gas firing was added to increase the temperature to 720°F (382°C). The exhaust moisture is around 11 (>10 percent), but tolerable. The controlled extraction supplies the process steam header at 45 psi (0.3 MPa).

Since the high-pressure steam production varies slightly (five combustion furnaces are used), the governor is designed for inlet pressure control and simultaneous extraction pressure control. Thus, the turbogenerator set will follow the availability of high-pressure steam. Purchased power is almost eliminated by installing this heat recovery system. A sophisticated power plant distributed control system (DCS) is installed. It monitors the amount of power purchased and maintains a "hot list" of lower-priority loads that could be dropped without warning and with little or no impact on plant performance. When lightning strikes near the plant, the tie breaker opens and the "hot-list" loads are dropped instantly. The turbine generator set goes into isochronous mode at 60 Hz, regardless of load. Plant operation continues without power from the utility (there is enough power to continue operation). A frequency feedback control system is available to indicate that additional loads should be dropped if the turbine generator set is unable to carry the remaining load. However, operating experience indicates that this backup system is not required.

SCENARIO D—PULP AND PAPER PLANT

A pulp and paper producer having several paralleled boilers is planning on installing a conventional extraction back-pressure turbine generator set. This approach is highly efficient but is tightly integrated into the process. It is not possible to generate full power unless the normal (design) steam flow is being used. This means the downstream processes must take the steam at "normal" levels.

The local utility has a severe penalty clause if purchased power exceeds the limit specified in the contract (a higher rate is applied on purchased power for the entire month). Thus, large demand peaks will turn into large penalties. An extraction-condensing turbine generator set was proposed initially as an alternative solution to handle peak demands. Unfortunately, it would have had high penalties on cycle performance for most of the time.

Solution

A controlled-extraction, noncondensing turbine generator set is installed. The control system monitors and controls the extraction and exhaust pressure simultaneously. Control valves are used to adjust the steam flow to maintain pressures at their setpoints. A computer was added to the plant control system to monitor the amount of power purchased and to calculate trends.

If a demand peak is about to occur (high electrical load and low steam demand occurring simultaneously), the control system opens a valve to a dump condenser (which operates well above atmospheric pressure). This increases the steam flow and power production temporarily until the peak is trimmed off. Some coordination between the plant and turbine generator control is required.

CHAPTER 24
COGENERATION APPLICATION CONSIDERATIONS

COGENERATION

Cogeneration is defined as the simultaneous generation of heat and power. Cogeneration plants became popular due to their high thermal efficiency (e.g., 84 percent). They can be arranged as topping or bottoming cycles. In a topping cycle, power is generated before delivering heat to the process. The following are typical examples of topping cycles:

- Noncondensing steam turbines (commonly used in the pulp and paper industry).
- Gas turbine heat recovery and combined cycles. In these applications, the exhaust heat from gas turbines is recovered and used as an efficient source of heat.

Power is generated in a bottoming cycle by recovering heat from kilns, process heaters, and furnaces. This design normally has low thermal efficiency. This is mainly due to the low temperature of the steam used for power generation.

The thermal efficiency of a modern coal-fired power plant is around 35 percent. Most of the remaining energy (65 percent) is discharged to the environment (e.g., lake, ambient air). Thus, for every megawatt (MW) electric generated in a coal-fired power plant, almost 2 MW of heat is discharged to the ambient. Cogeneration plants use most of the heat input in a useful manner. Only a small amount of energy is lost (e.g., 16 percent). This is due to their high thermal efficiency (e.g., 84 percent).

The thermal efficiency of a cogeneration plant decreases significantly as the process steam is diverted to power generation. For example, the thermal efficiency of a cogeneration plant will decrease from 84 to 35 percent if the amount of electrical power generated increases from 10 to 35 percent (i.e., the cogeneration plant is generating electricity only). It should be noted that this decrease in thermal efficiency does not necessarily result in reduction of the revenue to the plant. In reality, the plant revenue will most likely increase due to the increase in power generated (1 MW of electricity can be 5 to 50 times more expensive than 1 MW of heat).

NET HEAT TO PROCESS AND FUEL CHARGEABLE TO POWER

Two concepts are used to evaluate and compare alternative cogeneration plants. They are the net heat to process (NHP) and fuel chargeable to power (FCP). These parameters account for the heat transfer inside the cogeneration plant. They are used to compare the performance of different plants. They are also provided as input for every economic model used to study cogeneration plants.

The NHP is the net energy provided by the cogeneration plant to the process load. It is given by

$$\mathrm{NHP} = W_p H_p - W_c H_c - W_{mu} h_{mu} \tag{24.1}$$

where W_p = mass flow to the process
H_p = enthalpy of steam going to process
W_c = mass flow of condensate returning from the process
H_c = enthalpy of condensate returning from the process
W_{mu} = makeup mass flow
h_{mu} = enthalpy of makeup flow

The FCP is a parameter used to define the thermal performance of a topping cogeneration plant. It is defined as the incremental fuel for the cogeneration plant relative to the fuel that is needed for a plant supplying steam only, divided by the net incremental power generated by the cogeneration plant. In summary, the FCP is the incremental fuel divided by the incremental power (i.e., the incremental heat rate). If the plant were generating electric power only, the FCP would be identical to the net plant heat rate. The units of the FCP are British thermal units per kilowatthour (Btu/kWh) or kilojoules per kilowatthour (kJ/kWh).

STEAM TURBINES FOR COGENERATION

The various types of steam turbines used to generate power and provide steam to a process include:

- *Back-pressure turbine (noncondensing).* Steam is discharged from the turbine directly to the process.
- *Condensing turbine.* The turbine is followed by a condenser where steam is condensed.
- *Uncontrolled extraction turbine.* Steam is extracted from some specified stages in the steam turbine. Control valves are not used to control the steam flow. The steam flows are determined by the size of the extraction lines.
- *Automatic extraction turbine (also known as controlled extraction turbine).* A control valve inside the turbine controls the extraction flow. There are two types: condensing and noncondensing.

Expanding the steam in a noncondensing turbine can maximize the efficiency of cogeneration plants using steam turbines. The steam is delivered to the process from an extraction line and/or the exhaust of the turbine. The FCP of these plants is around 4000 to 4500 Btu/kWh (4220 to 4750 kJ/kWh) based on HHV.

The amount of power generated in the most efficient cogeneration plants using a steam turbine without a condensing section will not usually exceed 85 kW per million Btu (0.6 kW/10^9 J) of net heat supplied. This amount will not meet the electrical energy requirements of most industrial plants. Thus, it is necessary for cogeneration plants that use steam turbines to purchase power or install condensing steam turbines to meet the electrical demands of the industrial plants.

The efficiency of plants using condensing steam turbines is low (around 33 percent). This is caused by the significant amount of heat that the condenser discharges to the lake. The amount of heat discharged by the condenser, $\mathrm{MW}_{thermal}$, is almost twice as large as the electrical energy generated, $\mathrm{MW}_{electrical}$. However, the use of condensing steam turbines is economically justifiable in many industrial applications. The economics of steam turbines are favorable in the following applications:

- The power generated from condensing steam turbines is used to limit the amount of purchased power.
- The availability of low-cost fuels or process by-product fuels.
- The availability of low-level process energy for a bottoming cogeneration plant.
- The power generated from condensing steam turbines cannot be interrupted (e.g., applications where loss of electric power can disrupt the operation and/or safety of the plant).
- The plants where power has an economical advantage over heat, particularly if the fuel cost is low.

GAS TURBINE POWER ENHANCEMENT

Evaporative coolers are used to increase the output of gas turbines operating at high ambient temperature and low humidity. This system evaporates water into the inlet airflow upstream of the compressor, resulting in a decrease in the compressor inlet temperature. This method is economically justifiable for both base- and peak-load applications. The output of heavy-duty machines can increase by up to 9 percent when the ambient temperature is 90°F/32°C at relative humidity of 20 percent. Aeroderivative machines using an evaporative cooler operating at 85 percent effectiveness will increase the output by about 22 percent at 90°F/32°C ambient temperature and 20 percent relative humidity.

Inlet chillers are also used mainly on aeroderative engines to enhance the power output. The incoming air is cooled in this method to increase the output. It is usually desirable to chill the incoming air to the maximum power output. This occurs at an inlet temperature around 45 to 50°F (7.2 to 10°C). An absorption refrigeration system is normally used for this application. The steam is delivered to the absorption system from the low-pressure section of the heat recovery steam generator (HRSG).

GAS TURBINE EXHAUST HEAT RECOVERY

The economics of cogeneration plants depend heavily on recovering the heat from the exhaust of the gas turbine. The recovered heat normally represents between 60 and 70 percent of the inlet fuel energy. The cogeneration plant efficiency increases as the exhaust stack temperature decreases due to effective heat recovery. This energy is normally used to generate steam in HRSGs, with fired as well as unfired designs.

HEAT RECOVERY STEAM GENERATORS

The overall FCP of a cogeneration plant using a gas turbine HRSG depends on the amount of energy recovered from the exhaust of the gas turbine. As the amount of energy recovered increases, the stack temperature of the HRSG and the FCP will decrease (a decrease in the FCP is an improvement due to a reduction in the amount of fuel consumed). Thus, plants using a gas turbine HRSG should use the lowest possible feedwater temperature in the economizer (the last section of the HRSG) to recover the highest amount of energy. However, limits are imposed on the minimum feedwater temperature due to condensation of corrosive substances on the stack. If corrosion is not a concern (i.e., the fuel does not contain sulfur), the stack temperature can be reduced to 120°F/49°C. However, if the fuel contains sulfur, the feedwater temperature should be kept above 270°F/132°C to ensure that condensation of sulfuric products will not occur on the stack.

Unfired HRSG

The steam conditions in an unfired HRSG vary from 150 pounds per square inch gauge (psig)/10.3 bars saturated to 1450 psig/100 bars, and 950°F/510°C superheated. The steam temperature is usually around 50°F/28°C below the turbine exhaust temperature. Modern gas turbine technology allows superheated steam temperatures of between 1000 and 1050°F/538 and 566°C. Reheaters are also used in some plants. The unfired units are economically designed to recover around 95 percent of the heat in the turbine exhaust. When higher steam conditions are used in unfired units for combined-cycle applications, the HRSG will have multiple-pressure units to increase the amount of recovered heat. In applications using natural gas, three pressure cycles are used in some HRSGs to enhance the system performance.

Supplementary—Fired HRSG

Supplementary fuel firing upstream of the HRSG is used to increase the steam production rate. The combustion can be sustained upstream of the HRSG due to abundance of oxygen in the discharge of the gas turbine. A supplementary-fired HRSG is defined as a unit fired to an average temperature not exceeding 1800°F/982°C.

Fully Fired HRSG

The definition of a fully fired HRSG is a unit having the same amount of oxygen in its stack gases as an ambient-air-fired power boiler. The steam production rate of a fully fired HRSG (10 percent excess air) is up to six to seven times higher than an unfired HRSG. Since a fully fired unit uses preheated combustion air, its fuel requirement is around 7.5 to 8 percent lower than an ambient-air-fired boiler providing the same incremental steam generation rate.

Fully fired units are rarely used in industry despite their high steam production rate. Economic evaluations proved that unfired and supplementary-fired HRSGs are preferable due to their higher power-to-heat ratio.

CYCLE CONFIGURATIONS

The simplest form of a gas turbine cogeneration plant consists of a gas turbine coupled to a generator and its exhaust flow fed to an HRSG. The exhaust heat from the gas turbine is used to generate steam at the conditions required by the process. However, steam can be generated at higher conditions than the ones required by the process. This arrangement requires the use of an induction steam turbine. This turbine admits the higher-pressure steam at its inlet and the lower-pressure steam at a specified location downstream. This configuration provides a higher power-to-heat ratio than the previous one.

The latter configuration is known as a multipressure combined cycle. It is used commonly with unfired and moderately fired (1200°F/654°C) HRSGs. The multipressure HRSG recovers more heat from the exhaust of the gas turbine. This improves the FCP of these cycles. For example, a single-pressure, unfired HRSG used in a combined cycle supplying steam to a process at 150 psig (10.3 bars) will give an FCP of 6030 Btu/kWh HHV (6360 kJ/kWh HHV), whereas an unfired multipressure HRSG would have an FCP of 5150 Btu/kWh HHV (5430 kJ/kWh HHV).

Cogeneration plants can deliver different amounts of power ($MW_{electrical}$) and steam ($MW_{thermal}$). For example, a cogeneration plant having a thermal efficiency of 84 percent will deliver 24 percent of its output in power and 60 percent in steam. As the amount of steam diverted to power generation increases, the thermal efficiency drops. For example, a combined cycle can have a thermal efficiency of 70 percent. The amount of power and steam delivered in this case are around 50 and 20 percent, respectively. A combined cycle that generates power only will have a thermal efficiency of around 60 percent.

The FCP of cogeneration plants having a high-thermal-efficiency (e.g., 84 percent) "thermal match" is usually lower than plants having lower efficiencies. The per-unit cost of power generated from plants having high efficiencies is normally about 20 to 30 percent lower than plants having lower efficiencies. Despite this difference, site-specific fuels and power costs or power sales opportunities may dictate combined-cycle plants having considerable condensing power as the best economic choice. For example, the selection of combined cycles delivering higher amounts of power will become more attractive when the power cost increases.

COGENERATION OPPORTUNITIES

Cogeneration should be considered under the following circumstances:

- Availability of a steam host
- Development or expansion of industrial, residential, or commercial facilities such as universities, hospitals, and shopping malls needing power, heating, and cooling
- Replacement of old steam generators
- Changes in the cost of energy (fuel and power)
- Opportunities to sell power

Any industrial plant or major expansion to an existing facility requiring power and heat provides an ideal opportunity to evaluate cogeneration. In these cases, cogeneration is compared with a base case where heat is produced on-site and power is purchased from the utility. An incremental investment over the base case is required for a cogeneration plant. However, the payback period in most cases is less than 3 to 4 years.

Replacement of aged steam generators also provides an attractive opportunity for cogeneration plants. The steam generators can be replaced by a gas turbine/HRSG system. This results in an increase in the system power-to-heat ratio at an attractive FCP. The economics of such a project are normally favorable. Cogeneration should also be examined if the cost of energy is expected to change. This is especially true in cases where the cost of purchased power is increasing at a higher rate than fuel costs.

Favorable power sales opportunities have led to the development of many cogeneration projects. Some projects involved a simple displacement of purchased power; others were based on large-process heat demands. They resulted in a significant amount of electric power generation in excess of plant requirements.

CHAPTER 25

ECONOMIC AND TECHNICAL CONSIDERATIONS FOR COMBINED-CYCLE PERFORMANCE—ENHANCEMENT OPTIONS

The output and efficiency of combined-cycle plants can be increased during the design phase by selecting the following features:[1]

- Higher steam pressure and temperature
- Multiple steam pressure levels
- Reheat cycles

Additional factors are considered if there is a need for peak power production. They include gas turbine power augmentation by water or steam injection or a supplementary-fired heat recovery steam generator (HRSG). If peak power demands occur on hot summer days, gas turbine inlet evaporative cooling or chilling should be considered. Fuel heating is another technique that has been used to increase the efficiency of combined-cycle plants.

The ability of combined-cycle plants to generate additional power beyond their base capacity during peak periods has become an important design consideration. During the last decade, premiums were paid for power generated during the summer peak periods. The cost of electricity during the peak periods can be 70 times more expensive than off-peak periods. Since the cost during the peak periods is much higher, most of the plant's profitability could be driven by the amount of power generated during these peak periods. Thus, plants that can generate large quantities of power during the peak periods can achieve the highest profits.

ECONOMIC EVALUATION TECHNIQUE

The addition of most power enhancement techniques to a combined-cycle plant will have a negative impact on the base-load performance. Thus, the net revenue of the plant will be affected adversely during nonpeak periods. In general, the economics of the plant are determined by the efficiency during nonpeak periods and by the capacity during peak periods.

An economic study using a cost-of-electricity (COE) model is normally done to determine the enhancement option that provides the best overall life cycle benefit for the plant. The model includes both the peak and nonpeak performance levels, operating hours, premium paid for power generated during the peak period, cost of fuel, plant capital cost, incremental capital cost of the enhancement, and the cost of operating and maintaining the plant. This COE model is then used to determine the best enhancement option for the plant.

Most power enhancement alternatives exist in the topping cycle (gas turbine), as opposed to the bottoming cycle (HRSG/steam turbine). The supplementary direct firing within the HRSG is the only power enhancement option for the bottoming cycle. However, most performance enhancement options for the gas turbine result in improvement in the bottoming cycle due to an associated increase in the exhaust energy from the gas turbine.

OUTPUT ENHANCEMENT

The two major categories of plant output enhancements are (1) gas turbine inlet air cooling and (2) power augmentation.

Gas Turbine Inlet Air Cooling

Industrial gas turbines operating at constant speed have a constant volumetric flow rate. Since the specific volume of air is directly proportional to temperature, cooler air has a higher mass flow rate. It generates more power in the turbine. Cooler air also requires less energy to be compressed to the same pressure as warmer air. Thus, gas turbines generate higher power output when the incoming air is cooler.

A gas turbine inlet air cooling system is a good option for applications where electricity prices increase during the warm months. It increases the power output by decreasing the temperature of the incoming air. In combined-cycle applications, it also results in improvement in thermal efficiency. A decrease in the inlet dry-bulb temperature by 10°F (5.6°C) will normally result in around 2.7 percent power increase of a combined cycle using heavy-duty gas turbines. The output of simple-cycle gas turbines is also increased by the same amount.

The two methods used for reducing the gas turbine inlet temperature are (1) evaporative cooling and (2) chilling. Evaporative coolers rely on water evaporation to cool the inlet air to the turbine. Chilling of the inlet air is normally done by having cold water flowing through a heat exchanger located in the inlet duct. The wet-bulb temperature limits the effectiveness of evaporative cooling. However, chilling can reduce the inlet air temperature below the wet-bulb temperature. This provides additional output power, albeit at significantly higher costs.

Evaporative Cooling. Evaporative cooling is a cost-effective method to increase the power output of a gas turbine when the ambient temperature is high and the relative humidity is reasonably low.

Evaporative Cooling Methods. There are two methods for providing evaporative cooling. The first utilizes a wetted-honeycomb type of medium known as an *evaporative cooler.* The second is the *inlet fogger.*

Evaporative Cooling Theory. Evaporative cooling uses water evaporation to cool the airstream. Energy is required to convert water from liquid to vapor. This energy is taken from the airstream. This results in cooler air having higher humidity. Figure 25.1 illustrates a psychrometric chart. It is used to explore the limitations of evaporative cooling.

In theory, the lowest temperature achieved by adding water to air is the ambient wet-bulb temperature. In reality, it is difficult to achieve this level of cooling. The actual temperature

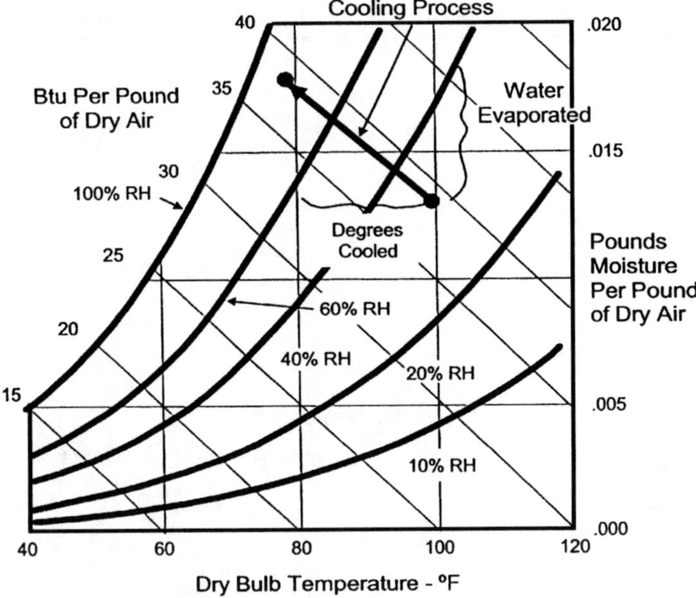

FIGURE 25.1 Psychrometric chart, simplified.

achieved depends on both the equipment design and atmospheric conditions. The evaporative cooler effectiveness depends on the surface area of the water exposed to the airstream and the residence time. The cooler effectiveness is defined as:

$$\text{Cooler effectiveness} = \frac{T1_{DB} - T2}{T1_{DB} - T2_{WB}} \tag{25.1}$$

where 1 = inlet conditions
2 = exit conditions
DB = dry-bulb temperature
WB = wet-bulb temperature

The typical effectiveness of a cooler is between 85 and 95 percent. If the effectiveness is 85 percent, the temperature drop will be

$$\text{Temperature drop} = 0.85\,(T1_{DB} - T2_{WB}) \tag{25.2}$$

For example, assume that the ambient temperature is 100°F (37.8°C) and the relative humidity is 32 percent. The cooling process is illustrated on the psychrometric chart (Fig. 25.1). It follows a constant-enthalpy line as sensible heat is exchanged for latent heat of evaporation. The corresponding wet-bulb temperature is 75°F (23.9°C). The drop in temperature through the cooler is then 0.85 (100 – 75), or 21°F (11.7°C). Thus, the compressor inlet temperature is 79°F (26°C). The effectiveness of an evaporative cooler is normally around 85 percent and of the foggers is between 90 and 95 percent.

The actual increase in power from the gas turbine as a result of air cooling depends on the design of the machine, site altitude, as well as ambient temperature and humidity. However, the information provided in Fig. 25.2 can be used to make an estimate of the effect of evaporative coolers. The highest improvement is achieved in hot, dry weather.

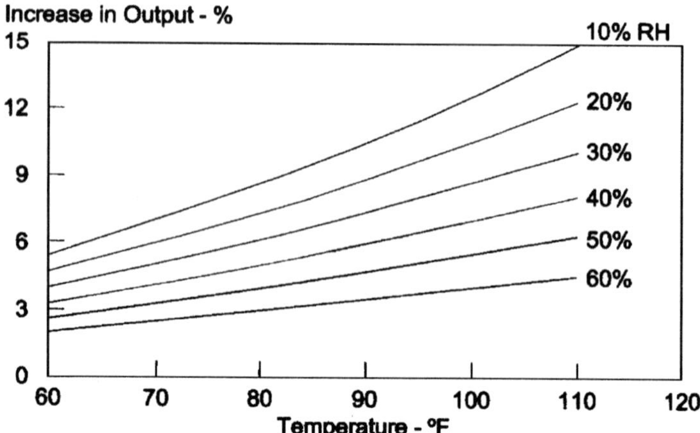

FIGURE 25.2 Effect of evaporative cooler on available output—85 percent effective.

Wetted-Honeycomb Evaporative Coolers. Conventional evaporative coolers use a wetted-honeycomb-like medium to maximize the evaporative surface area and the cooling effectiveness. The medium used for gas turbines is typically ≥12 in thick. It covers the entire cross section of the filter house or the inlet air duct. The pressure drop across it is around 1 in of water. The plant output and efficiency decrease due to this pressure drop. The reduction in gas turbine and combined-cycle output is 0.35 and 0.3 percent, respectively. The increase in heat rate is 0.12 and 0.04 percent for gas turbine and combined cycles, respectively.

A controller is provided to prevent operation of the evaporative cooler system below 60°F (15.6°C). Icing could form if the system is allowed to operate below this temperature. The whole system must be deactivated and drained to avoid damage to the water tank and piping if the ambient temperature is expected to fall below freezing.

Water Requirements for Evaporative Coolers. Evaporative coolers have the highest effectiveness in arid regions where water has a higher concentration of dissolved solids. As water evaporates and makeup water enters the tank, the amount of minerals present in the tank will increase. These minerals would precipitate out on the media, reducing the rate of evaporation. The hazard of having minerals getting entrained with the air entering the gas turbine will also increase. This hazard is minimized by continuously bleeding down the tank to reduce the concentration of minerals. This is known as *blowdown.* Water is added as makeup for evaporation and blowdown. The rate of evaporation depends on the ambient temperature and humidity, altitude, cooler effectiveness, and airflow through the gas turbine.

Foggers. Gas turbines started to use foggers in the mid-1980s. These systems atomize the supply of water into billions of tiny droplets. The size of the droplets plays an important role in determining the surface area of water exposed to the airstream and, therefore, to the speed of evaporation. For example, water atomized into 10-μm droplets produces 10 times more surface area than the same amount atomized to 100-μm droplets. The water droplets should be atomized to less than 40 μm in foggers. Retrofit installation of foggers requires minor modification. The installation can be completed within a 1- or 2-day outage. Condensation of the fog can occur in the inlet duct. A drainline should be installed downstream of the fog nozzles to prevent collection of water.

Demineralized water is used to reduce compressor fouling or nozzle plugging. However, it necessitates the use of a high-grade stainless steel for all wetted parts.

Two methods are used for water atomization. The first relies on compressor air in the nozzles to atomize the water. The second uses a high-pressure pump to force the water through a small orifice. Air-atomized nozzles require less water pressure. However, they result in lower power output due to the air extraction from the gas turbine. The typical air-to-water mass ratio is 0.6 (volume ratio is 500).

Some high-pressure pumps use swirlers to break the water into small droplets. Others force the water on an impingement pin to generate the same effect. A typical high-pressure pumped-fog system has an operating pressure of between 1000 and 3000 psi (6.8 and 20.4 MPa).

Evaporative Intercooling. *Evaporative intercooling,* also known as *overspray* or *overcooling,* consists of additional injection of fog into the inlet airstream beyond what can be evaporated by a given ambient climate condition. Nonevaporated fog droplets are carried into the airstream entering the compressor. The higher temperatures in the compressor evaporate the droplets. This cools the air and makes it denser, resulting in a decrease in the relative work of the compressor and an increase in the total mass flow of the air. The output power of the machine will increase. The power increase obtained from fog intercooling is higher than the amount obtained from a conventional evaporative cooling system. The only possible drawback of intercooling is that if the water droplets are too large, erosion of the compressor blade will occur due to liquid impaction.

Intercooling is also done by fog-spraying atomized water between compressor sections. The atomization is done using high-pressure air taken from the eighth-stage bleed. The water injection reduces the outlet temperature of the compressor significantly, resulting in higher output and better efficiency. During a 90°F (32°C) day, the output and efficiency increase by more than 20 and 3.9 percent, respectively. This method allows recovery of most of the power lost on hot days without incurring the capital and operating costs of chillers. A review of the design limits of the gas turbine components, control algorithms, generator, steam turbine, and auxiliaries must be done before evaporative intercooling is applied.

Inlet Chilling. The two types of inlet chilling systems are (1) *direct chillers* and (2) *thermal storage.* Liquefied natural gas (LNG) systems use the cooling generated by the vaporization of liquefied gas in the fuel supply. Thermal storage systems use off-peak power to store thermal energy in the form of ice. During peak power periods, the ice is used to perform inlet chilling. Direct chilling systems use mechanical or absorption chillers. All these options can be installed in new plants or retrofitted in older plants.

The chilling achieved by using cooling coils depends on the design of the equipment and ambient conditions. Unlike evaporative coolers, cooling coils are capable of lowering the temperature below the wet-bulb temperature. The capacity of the inlet chilling device, the compressor's acceptable temperature and humidity limits, and the effectiveness of the coils limit the actual reduction in temperature. Figure 25.3 illustrates a typical cooling process from an ambient dry-bulb temperature of 100°F (37.8°C) and 20 percent relative humidity. The initial cooling process follows a line of constant humidity ratio. As the air approaches saturation, condensation starts to occur. Additional cooling results in further condensation. Drift eliminators should be installed downstream of the coils to prevent condensed water from entering the gas turbine. The desired gas turbine output and the capacity of the chilling system will determine the end of the cooling process. The air can be cooled below the ambient wet-bulb temperature. However, the compressor inlet temperature should be limited to 45°F (7.2°C) with a relative humidity of 95 percent. Icing will form at lower temperatures, resulting in possible equipment damage.

Inlet Chilling Methods. Direct cooling provides an almost instantaneous power increase by cooling the air at the inlet to the gas turbine. Large mechanical chillers driven by electricity are used with heat exchangers (chiller coils) in the inlet to the gas turbine. The pressure drop across these heat exchangers is around 1 in of water. Absorption chillers are also used if waste heat is available. The air temperature at the inlet to the gas turbine can be

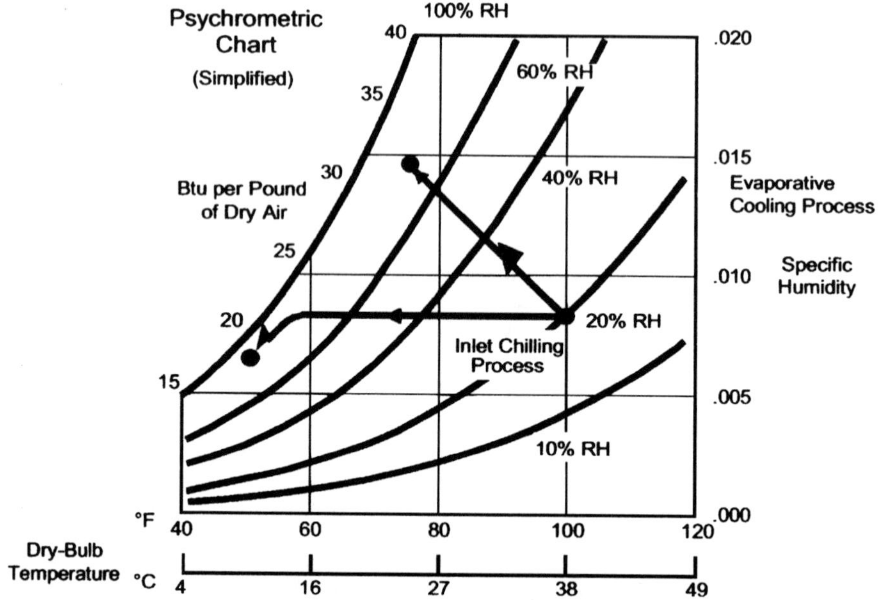

FIGURE 25.3 Inlet cooling process.

reduced to 45°F (7.2°C). The net gain of mechanical chillers is lower than absorption systems due to their high electrical consumption.

Direct cooling is accomplished by two methods: (1) direct-expansion and (2) chilled-water systems. Direct-expansion systems use a refrigerant in the cooling coil installed in the inlet air duct. Chilled-water systems use water or a mixture of water and glycol as a secondary heating fluid between the refrigerant and the air entering the gas turbine. It should be noted that these systems provide the maximum benefit on the hottest days. Their benefit decreases as ambient temperature is reduced. Also, these systems reduce the power output when the temperature drops below 45°F (7.2°C) due to an increase in pressure drop at the inlet to the gas turbine.

Off-Peak Thermal Energy Storage. Off-peak thermal energy storage is used where the cost of electricity during daytime peak periods is very high. Ice or cold water is produced during off-peak hours and weekends by mechanical chillers and stored in large tanks. The power increase lasts for a few hours each day. The inlet air to the gas turbine is chilled during periods of peak power demand by the melted ice or cold water. The gas turbine inlet air temperature is reduced to between 50 and 60°F by this system. However, large storage space is required for ice or cold water.

Gas Vaporizers of Liquefied Petroleum Gases. Liquefied petroleum gases (LPGs) should be vaporized before use in gas turbines. They are normally delivered at 50°F (10°C) to the gas turbine. The inlet air can provide the heat needed to vaporize the liquid fuel. Glycol is used as an intermediate fluid. The inlet air to the gas turbine heats the glycol. Its temperature drops during this process. The glycol heats the fuel. The typical drop in inlet air temperature is 10°F (5.6°C). Thus, the energy in the incoming air to the gas turbine is used in a useful manner.

Power Augmentation

The three methods used for power augmentation are: (1) water or steam injection, (2) HRSG supplementary firing, and (3) peak firing.

Gas Turbine Steam or Water Injection. The steam or water injection into the combustors for nitric oxide (NO_X) control increases the mass flow of the air, resulting in increased power output. The amount of steam or water injected is normally limited by the amount required to control NO_X. This is done to minimize the operating and maintenance costs and impact on inspection intervals. The steam injected is normally mixed with the fuel entering the combustors. It can also be injected into the compressor discharge casing of the gas turbine. In combined-cycle applications, the heat rate increases with steam or water injection. The reasons for this change are

- *For water injection.* Significant amount of heat is required to vaporize the water.
- *For steam injection.* Steam is taken from the bottoming cycle (HRSG/steam turbine) to be injected in the gas turbine. This reduces the efficiency of the steam cycle.

Most machines allow up to 5 percent of the compressor airflow for steam injection. The steam must have at least 50°F (28°C) superheat and be at a similar pressure to the fuel gas. Most control systems allow only the steam flow required until the unit is fully loaded. At this stage, additional steam or water is admitted for further increase in power.

Supplementary-Fired HRSG. Since only a small percentage of the air entering the gas turbine participates in the combustion process, the oxygen concentration in the discharge of the gas turbine allows supplementary firing in the HRSG. The definition of a supplementary-fired unit is an HRSG fired to an average temperature of, not exceeding, about 1800°F (982°C). Supplementary-fired HRSGs are installed in new units. However, it is not practical to retrofit them on existing installations due to the space requirements of duct burners and significant material changes.

Peak Firing. Some gas turbines can be operated at a higher firing temperature than their base rating. This is called *peak firing*. The output of the simple cycle and combined cycle will increase. This mode of operation results in a shorter inspection interval and increased maintenance. Despite this penalty, operating at higher firing temperatures for short periods is cost-effective due to the increase in power output.

Output Enhancement Summary. Several output enhancement methods have been discussed. Table 25.1 shows the effect on performance for each method on a day that is 90°F (32.2°C), with 30 percent RH. The capability of each piece of equipment in the plant, including gas turbine, steam turbine, and generator, must be reviewed to ensure that the design limits will not be exceeded. For example, the capability of the generator may be limited on hot days due to inadequate cooling capability.

EFFICIENCY ENHANCEMENT

Fuel Heating

Low-grade heat can be used to increase the temperature of gaseous fuels. This results in increasing the plant efficiency by reducing the amount of fuel consumed to increase the fuel temperature to the combustion temperature. This method has minimal impact on the output of

TABLE 25.1 Effect on Performance of Power Enhancement Option on Combined Cycles Compared with the Base Case

Power enhancement option	Change in power output	Change in efficiency
Evaporative cooling of inlet air	+5%	—
Chilling of inlet air	+11%	−1.5%
Peak load of gas turbine	+5%	—
Steam injection (5% of air flow through the gas turbine)	+3.5%	−4.3%
Water injection in gas turbine	+6%	−5%
Supplementary-fired HRSG	+30%	−10%

gas turbines. However, it results in a limited reduction in the output of combined cycles due to using energy to heat the fuel rather than for steam production. The temperature of the fuel can be increased up to 700°F (370°C) if the fuel constituents are acceptable, before carbon deposits start to form on heat transfer surfaces and the remainder of the fuel delivery system. Fuel temperatures of between 300 and 450°F (150 and 230°C) are considered economically optimal for combined-cycle application. A typical gain in efficiency for a large combined-cycle plant is around 0.3.

It is important to prevent the fuel from entering the steam system because the temperature of the steam is normally higher than the autoignition temperature of gas fuels. This can be accomplished by implementing the following modifications:

- Maintaining the water pressure above the fuel pressure in direct fuel-to-steam heat exchangers to ensure that any leakage will occur into the fuel system.
- Design and operational requirements to prevent the fuel from entering the steam system when the steam pressure is low.
- Using an intermediate heat transport fluid so that any leak in the fuel heat exchanger will not affect the steam system.

CONCLUSION

Economic analyses of combined-cycle performance enhancement options normally reveal that HRSG duct firing is the best option for the plant. It is followed by inlet fogging, evaporative cooling, and inlet air chilling. However, these analyses were focused on capacity-driven economics resulting from premiums paid for short periods of peak power generation. These economic drivers exist in today's market environment. However, as the market condition changes due to an increase in the installed capacity, escalation of fuel prices, and deregulation in the power generation industry, the emphasis will shift to plant efficiency. Thus, plants designed with moderate increase in capacity and high efficiency could provide the highest life cycle profitability.

REFERENCE

1. Jones, C., and J. Jacobs, III, "Economic and Technical Considerations for Combined-Cycle Performance-Enhancement Options," *GE Power Systems*, GER-4200, October 2000.

CHAPTER 26
FUNDAMENTALS OF ELECTRICAL SYSTEMS

CAPACITORS

Figure 26.1 illustrates a capacitor.[1] It consists of two insulated conductors, a and b. They carry equal and opposite charges, $+q$ and $-q$, respectively. All lines of force that originate on a terminate on b. The capacitor is characterized by the following parameters:

- q, the magnitude of the charge on each conductor
- V, the potential difference between the conductors

Both q and V are proportional to each other in a capacitor, or $q = CV$. C is the constant of proportionality. It is called the *capacitance* of the capacitor. C depends on the following parameters:

- Shape of the conductors
- Relative position of the conductors
- Medium that separates the conductors

The unit of capacitance is the coulomb/volt or farad (F). Thus

$$1\text{ F} = 1\text{ coulomb/volt}$$

It is important to note that:

$$\frac{dq}{dt} = C\,\frac{dV}{dt}$$

but since

$$\frac{dq}{dt} = i$$

Thus,

$$i = C\,\frac{dV}{dt}$$

This means that the current in a capacitor is proportional to the rate of change of the voltage with time.

In industry, the following submultiples of farad are used:

- Microfarad (μF): $1\ \mu\text{F} = 10^{-6}\text{ F}$
- Picofarad (pF): $1\text{ pF} = 10^{-12}\text{ F}$

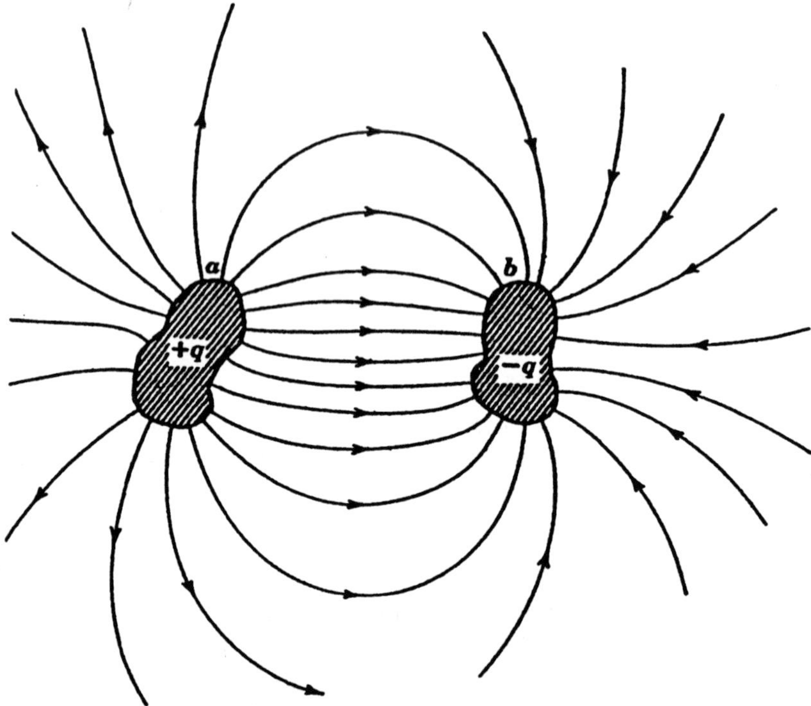

FIGURE 26.1 Two insulated conductors (a and b), totally isolated from their surroundings and carrying equal and opposite charges, form a capacitor.

Capacitors are very useful electric devices. They are used in the following applications:

- *To store energy in an electric field.* The energy is stored between the conductors of the capacitors, which are normally called *plates.* The electrical energy that is stored in the capacitor is given by

$$U_E = \frac{1}{2}\frac{q^2}{C}$$

- To reduce voltage fluctuations in electronic power supplies
- To transmit pulsed signals
- To generate or detect electromagnetic oscillations at radio frequencies
- To provide electronic time delays

Figure 26.2 illustrates a parallel-plate capacitor in which the conductors are two parallel plates of area A separated by a distance d. If each plate is connected momentarily to the terminals of the battery, a charge $+q$ will appear on one plate and a charge $-q$ on the other. If d is relatively small, the electric field E between the plates will be uniform.

The capacitance of a capacitor increases when a dielectric (insulation) is placed between the plates. The *dielectric constant* κ of a material is the ratio of the capacitance with dielectric

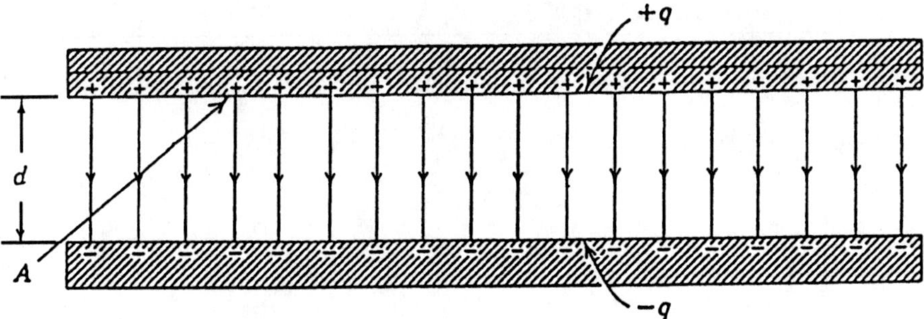

FIGURE 26.2 A parallel-plate capacitor with conductors (plates) of area A.

TABLE 26.1 Properties of Some Dielectrics*

Material	Dielectric constant	Dielectric strength† (kV/mm)
Vacuum	1.00000	∞
Air	1.00054	0.8
Water	78	—
Paper	3.5	14
Ruby mica	5.4	160
Porcelain	6.5	4
Fused quartz	3.8	8
Pyrex glass	4.5	13
Bakelite	4.8	12
Polyethylene	2.3	50
Amber	2.7	90
Polystyrene	2.6	25
Teflon	2.1	60
Neoprene	6.9	12
Transformer oil	4.5	12
Titanium dioxide	100	6

*These properties are at approximately room temperature and for conditions such that the electric field E in the dielectric does not vary with time.

†This is the maximum potential gradient that may exist in the dielectric without the occurrence of electrical breakdown. Dielectrics are often placed between conducting plates to permit a higher potential difference to be applied between them than would be possible with air as the dielectric.

to that without dielectric. Table 26.1 illustrates the dielectric constant and dielectric strength of various materials.

The high dielectric strength of vacuum [infinity (∞)] should be noted. It indicates that if two plates are separated by vacuum, the voltage difference between them can reach infinity without having flashover (arcing) between the plates. This important characteristic of vacuum has led to the development of vacuum circuit breakers, which have proven to have excellent performance in modern industry.

CURRENT AND RESISTANCE

The *electric current* i is established in a conductor when a net charge q passes through it in time t.
Thus, the current is

$$i = \frac{q}{t}$$

The units for the parameters are

i = amperes (A)
q = coulombs (C)
t = seconds (s)

The *electric field* exerts a force on the electrons to move them through the conductor. A positive charge moving in one direction has the same effect as a negative charge moving in the opposite direction. Thus, for simplicity we assume that all charge carriers are positive. We draw the current arrows in the direction that positive charges follow (Fig. 26.3). A conductor is characterized by its resistance (the symbol -ww- in Fig. 26.3). It is defined as the voltage difference between two points divided by the current flowing through the conductor. Thus,

$$R = \frac{V}{i}$$

where V is in volts, i in amperes, and the resistance R is in ohms (Ω).

The current, which is the flow of charge through a conductor, is often compared with the flow of water through a pipe. The water flow occurs due to pressure difference between the inlet and outlet of a pipe. Similarly, the charge flows through the conductor due to voltage difference.

The resistivity ρ is a characteristic of the conductor material. It is a measure of the resistance that the material has to the current. For example, the resistivity of copper is $1.7 \times 10^{-8}\ \Omega\cdot\text{m}$; that of fused quartz is about $10^{16}\ \Omega\cdot\text{m}$. Table 26.2 lists some electrical properties of common metals. The temperature coefficient of resistivity (α) is given by

$$\alpha = \frac{1}{\rho}\frac{d\rho}{dT}$$

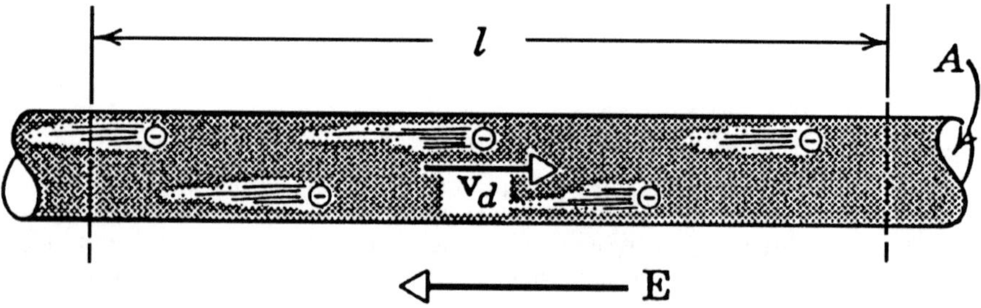

FIGURE 26.3 Electrons drift in a direction opposite to the electric field in a conductor.

TABLE 26.2 Properties of Metals as Conductors

Metal	Resistivity (at 20°C) $10^{-8}\ \Omega\cdot\text{m}$	Temperature coefficient of resistivity, α, per °C $(\times 10^{-5})^*$
Silver	1.6	380
Copper	1.7	390
Aluminum	2.8	390
Tungsten	5.6	450
Nickel	6.8	600
Iron	10	500
Steel	18	300
Manganin	44	1.0
Carbon†	3500	−50

*This quantity, defined from

$$\alpha = \frac{1}{\rho}\frac{d\rho}{dT}$$

is the fractional change in resistivity ($d\rho/\rho$) per unit change in temperature. It varies with temperature, the values here referring to 20°C. For copper ($\alpha = 3.9 \times 10^{-3}/°\text{C}$) the resistivity increases by 0.39 percent for a temperature increase of 1°C near 20°C. Note that α for carbon is negative, which means that the resistivity *decreases* with increasing temperature.

It represents the rate of variation of resistivity with temperature. Its units are 1/°C (or 1/°F). Conductivity, (σ), is used more commonly than resistivity. It is the inverse of conductivity, given by

$$\sigma = \frac{1}{\rho}$$

The units for conductivity are $(\Omega\cdot\text{m})^{-1}$.

Across a resistor, the voltage and current have the following relationship:

$$V = iR$$

The power dissipated across the resistor (conversion of electrical energy to heat) is given by

$$P = i^2R \quad \text{or} \quad P = \frac{V^2}{R}$$

where P is in watts, i in amps, V in volts, and R in ohms.

THE MAGNETIC FIELD

A *magnetic field* is defined as the space around a magnet or a current-carrying conductor. The magnetic field B, is represented by lines of induction. Figure 26.4 illustrates the lines of induction of a magnetic field B near a long current-carrying conductor.

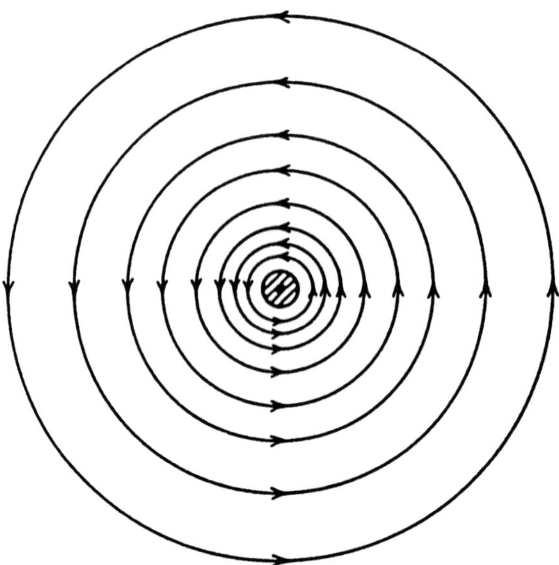

FIGURE 26.4 Lines of **B** near a long, circularly cylindrical wire. A current I, suggested by the central dot, emerges from the page.

The *vector* of the magnetic field is related to its lines of induction in two ways:

1. The direction of **B** at any point is given by the tangent to the line of induction.
2. The number of lines of induction per unit cross-sectional area (perpendicular to the lines) is proportional to the magnitude of **B.** B is large if the lines are close together, and it is small if they are far apart.

The flux Φ_B of magnetic field B is given by:

$$\Phi_B = \int \mathbf{B} \cdot d\mathbf{S}$$

The integral is taken over the surface for which Φ_B is defined.

The magnetic field exerts a force on any charge moving through it. If q_0 is a positive charge moving at a velocity **V** in a magnetic field **B,** the force **F** acting on the charge (Fig. 26.5) is given by

$$\mathbf{F} = q_0 \mathbf{V} \times \mathbf{B}$$

The magnitude of the force **F** is given by

$$\mathrm{F} = q_0 V B \sin \theta$$

where θ is the angle between V and B.

The force **F** will always be at a right angle to the plane formed by **V** and **B.** Thus, it will always be a sideways force. The force will disappear in two cases:

1. If the charge stops moving
2. If **V** is parallel or antiparallel to the direction of **B**

The force F has a maximum value if **V** is at a right angle to **B** ($\theta = 90°$).

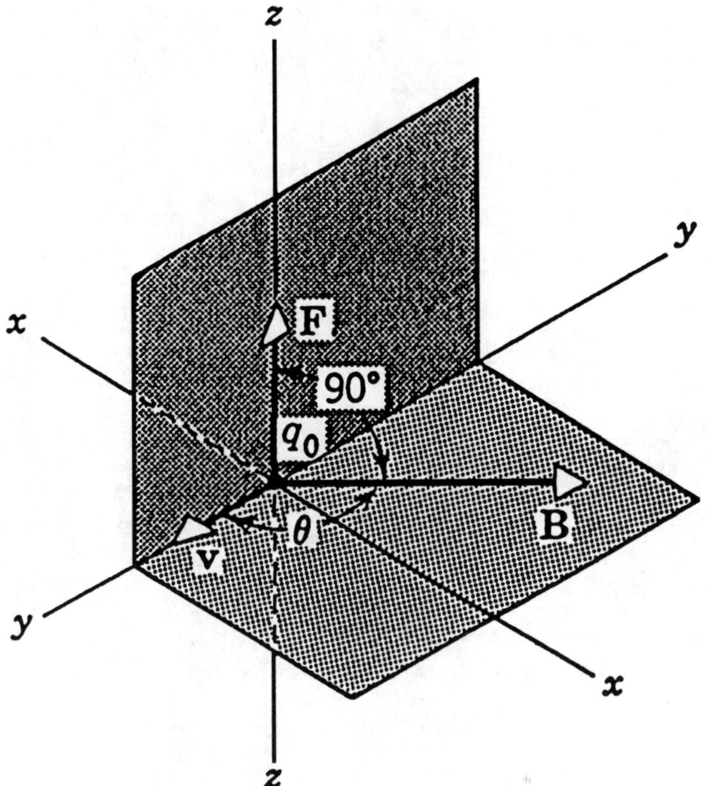

FIGURE 26.5 Illustrating $\mathbf{F} = q_0 \mathbf{V} \times \mathbf{B}$. Test charge q_0 is fired through the origin with velocity **v**.

Figure 26.6 illustrates the force that is created on a positive and a negative electron moving in a magnetic field **B** pointing out of the plane of the figure (the symbol ⊙). The unit of **B** is tesla (T) or weber per square meter (Wb/m^2). Thus,

$$1 \text{ T} = 1 \text{ Wb/m}^2 = 1 \text{ N/(A} \cdot \text{m)}$$

The force acting on a current-carrying conductor placed at a right angle to a magnetic field **B** (Fig. 26.7) is given by

$$F = ilB$$

where l is the length of the conductor placed in the magnetic field.

AMPÈRE'S LAW

Figure 26.8 illustrates a current-carrying conductor surrounded by small magnets. If there is no current in the conductor, all of the magnets will be aligned with the horizontal component of the earth's magnetic field. When a current flows through the conductor, the orientation of the magnets suggests that the lines of induction of the magnetic field form closed

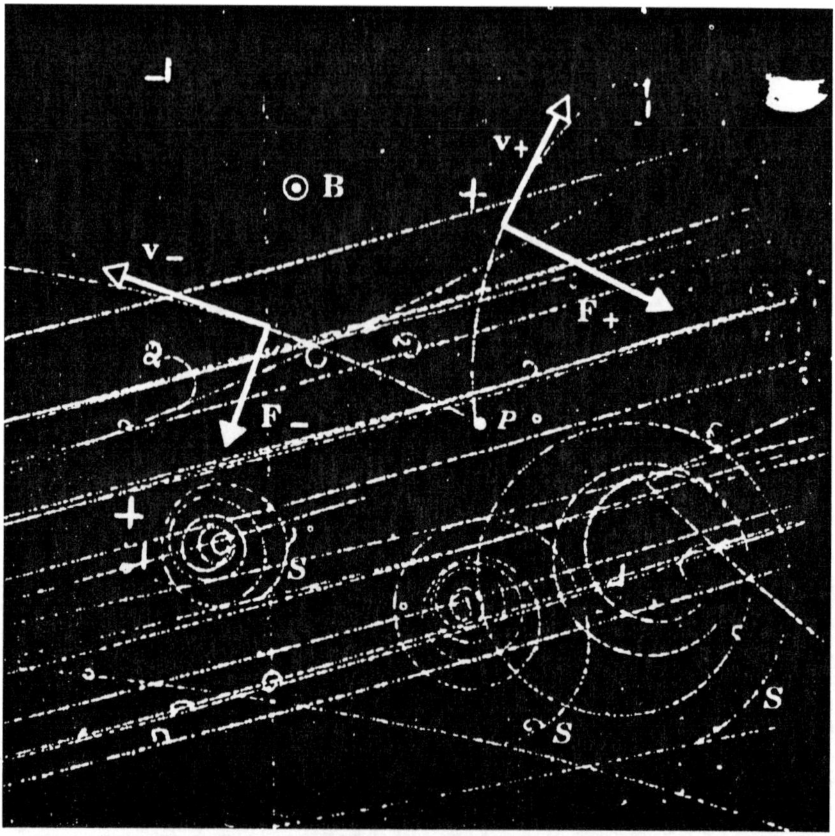

FIGURE 26.6 A *bubble chamber* is a device for rendering visible, by means of small bubbles, the tracks of charged particles that pass through the chamber. The figure is a photograph taken with such a chamber immersed in a magnetic field **B** and exposed to radiations from a large cyclotron-like accelerator. The curved V at point P is formed by a positive and a negative electron, which deflect in opposite directions in the magnetic field. The spirals S are tracks of three low-energy electrons.

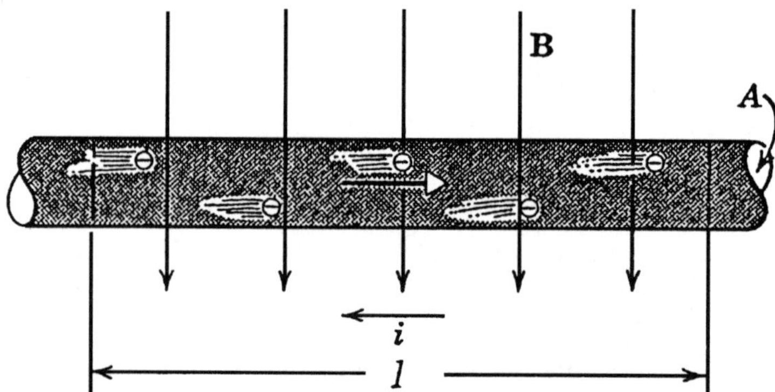

FIGURE 26.7 A wire carrying a current i is placed at right angles to a magnetic field **B.** Only the drift velocity of the electrons, not their random motion, is suggested.

circles around the conductor. This observation is reinforced by the experiment shown in Fig. 26.9. It shows a current-carrying conductor passing through the center of a horizontal glass plate with iron filings on it. Ampère's law states that:

$$\oint \mathbf{B} \cdot d\mathbf{l} = \mu_0 i$$

where **B** is the magnetic field, **l** is the length of the circumference around the wire, i is the current, μ_0 is the permeability constant ($\mu_0 = 4\pi \times 10^{-7}\,\text{T} \cdot \text{m/A}$). The integration is carried around the circumference.

If the current in the conductor shown in Fig. 26.8 reverses its direction, all the compass needles change their direction as well. Thus, the direction of **B** near a current-carrying conductor is given by the "right-hand rule": *If the current is grasped by the right hand and the thumb points in the direction of the current, the fingers will curl around the wire in the direction* **B.**

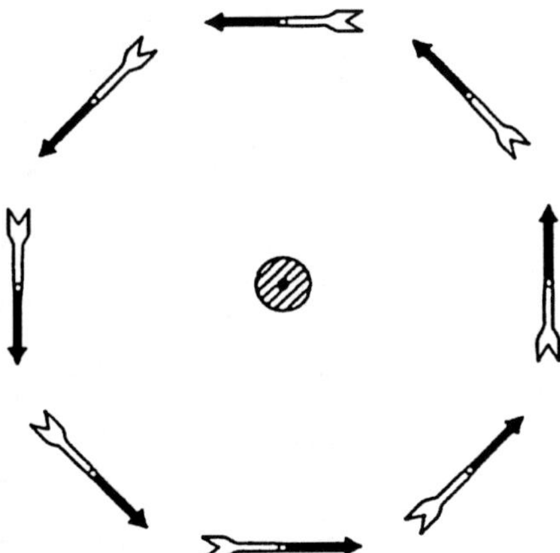

FIGURE 26.8 An array of compass needles near a central wire carrying a strong current. The black ends of the compass needles are their north poles. The central dot shows the current emerging from the page. As usual, the direction of the current is taken as the direction of flow of positive charge.

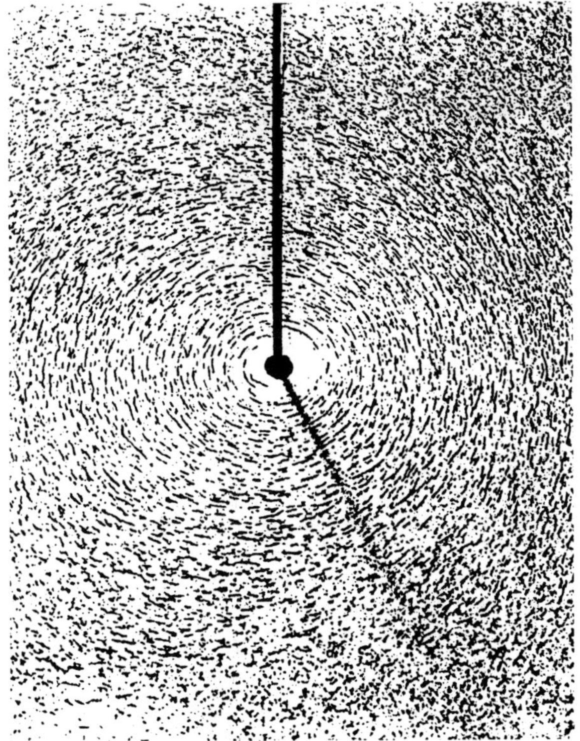

FIGURE 26.9 Iron filings around a wire carrying a strong current.

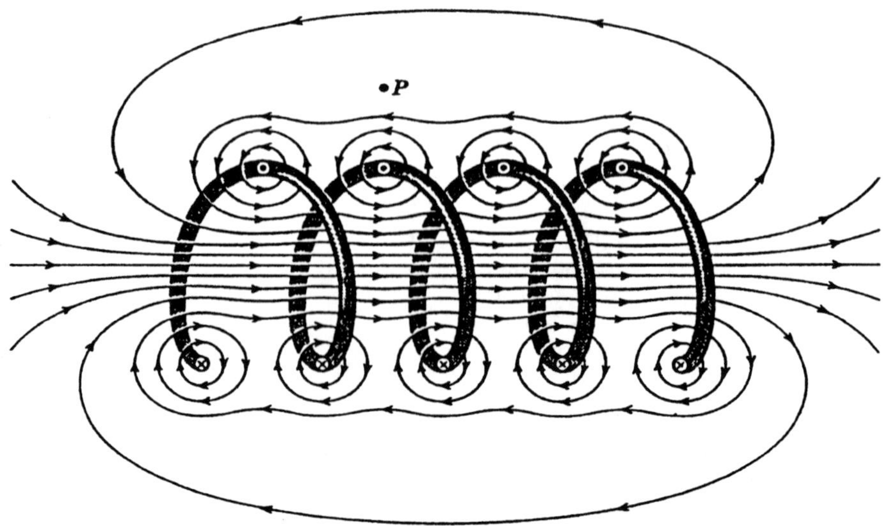

FIGURE 26.10 A loosely wound solenoid.

MAGNETIC FIELD IN A SOLENOID

A *solenoid* (an inductor) is a long current-carrying conductor wound in a close-packed helix. Figure 26.10 shows a solenoid having widely spaced turns. The fields cancel between the wires. Inside the solenoid, **B** is parallel to the solenoid axis. Figure 26.11 shows the lines of **B** for a real solenoid. By applying Ampère's law to this solenoid, we will have

$$B = \mu_0 \, i \, n$$

where n is the number of turns per unit length. The flux Φ_b for the magnetic field **B** will become

$$\Phi_B = \mathbf{B} \cdot \mathbf{A}$$

FARADAY'S LAW OF INDUCTION

Faraday's law of induction is one of the basic equations of electromagnetism. Figure 26.12 shows a coil connected to a galvanometer. If a bar magnet is pushed toward the coil, the galvanometer deflects. This indicates that a current has been induced in the coil. If the magnet is held stationary with respect to the coil, the galvanometer does not deflect. If the magnet is moved away from the coil, the galvanometer deflects in the opposite direction. This indicates that the current induced in the coil is in the opposite direction.

Figure 26.13 shows another experiment when the switch S is closed, thus establishing a steady current in the right-hand coil, the galvanometer deflects momentarily. When the switch is opened, the galvanometer deflects again momentarily, but in the opposite direction.

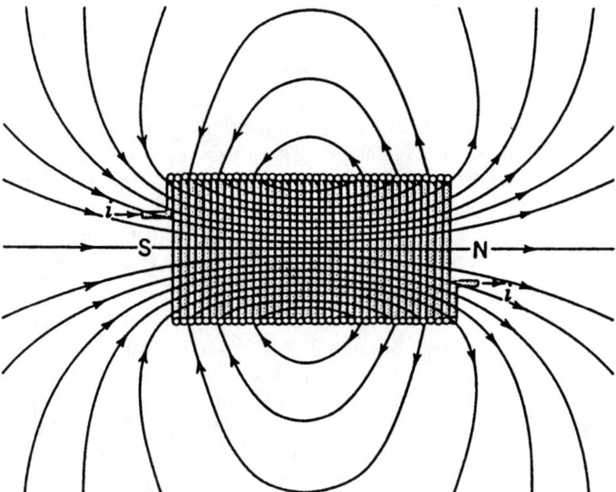

FIGURE 26.11 A solenoid of finite length. The right end, from which lines of **B** emerge, behaves like the north pole of a compass needle. The left end behaves like the south pole.

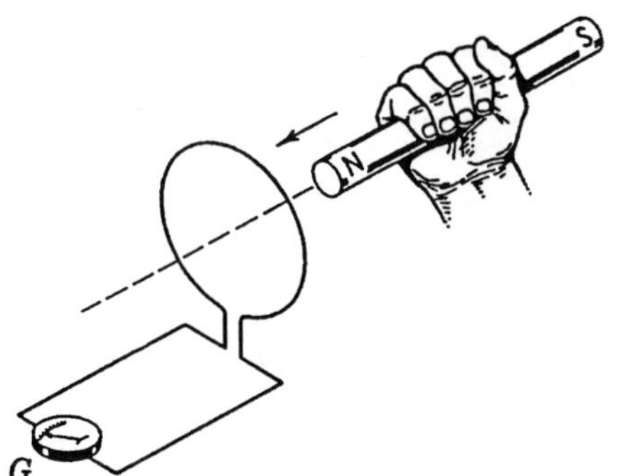

FIGURE 26.12 Galvanometer *G* deflects while the magnet is moving with respect to the coil. Only their relative motion counts.

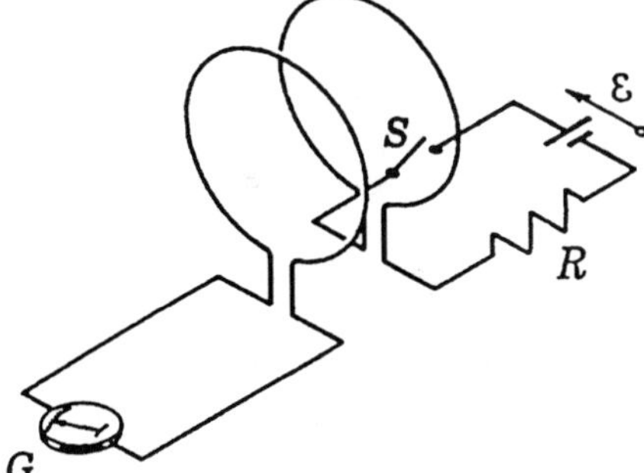

FIGURE 26.13 Galvanometer *G* deflects momentarily when switch *S* is closed or opened. No motion is involved.

This experiment proves that a voltage known as an *electromagnetic force* (emf) is induced in the left coil when the current in the right coil changes.

Faraday's law of induction is given by

$$\mathcal{E} = -N \frac{d\Phi_B}{dt}$$

where $\mathcal{E}$ is the emf (voltage), N is the number of turns in the coil, and $d\Phi_B/dt$ is the rate of change of the flux with time. The minus sign will be explained by Lenz's law.

LENZ'S LAW

Lenz's law states that *the induced current will be in a direction that opposes the change that produced it.* If a magnet is pushed toward a loop, as shown in Fig. 26.14, an induced current will be established in the loop. Lenz's law predicts that the current in the loop must be in a direction such that the flux established by it must oppose the change. Thus, the face of the loop toward the magnet must have the north pole. The north pole from the current loop and the north pole from the magnet will repel each other. The right-hand rule indicates that the magnetic field established by the loop should emerge from the right side of the loop. Thus, the induced current must be as shown. Lenz's law can be explained as follows: When the magnet is pushed toward the loop, this change induces a current. The direction of this current should oppose the push. If the magnet is pulled away from the coil, the induced current will create the south pole on the right-hand face of the loop because this will oppose the pull. Thus, the current must be in the opposite direction to the one shown in Fig. 26.14 to make the right-hand face a south pole. Whether the magnet is pulled or pushed, its motion will always be opposed. The force that moves the magnet will always experience a resisting force. Thus, the force moving the magnet will always be required to do work.

Figure 26.15 shows a rectangular loop of width l. One end of it has a uniform field **B** pointing at a right angle to the plane of the loop into the page (⊗ indicates into the page and ⊙ out of the page). The flux enclosed by the loop is given by

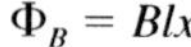

$$\Phi_B = Blx$$

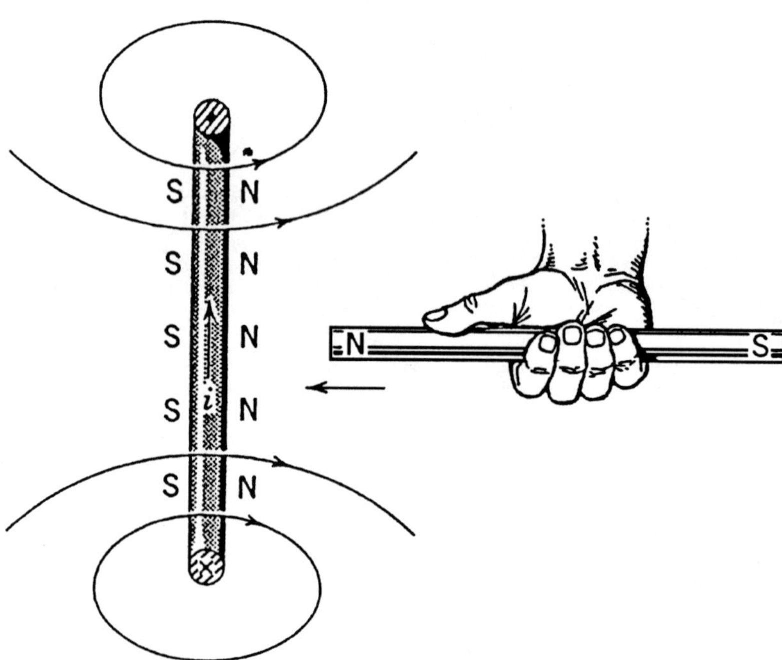

FIGURE 26.14 If we move the magnet toward the loop, the induced current points as shown, setting up a magnetic field that opposes the motion of the magnet.

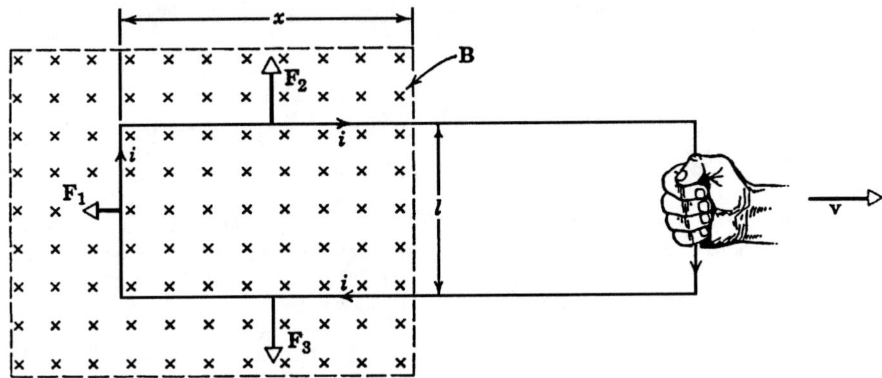

FIGURE 26.15 A rectangular loop is pulled out of a magnetic field with velocity **v**.

Faraday's law states that the induced voltage, or emf $\mathcal{E}$ is given by

$$\mathcal{E} = -\frac{d\Phi_B}{dt} = -\frac{d}{dt}(Blx) = -Bl\frac{dx}{dt} = Blv$$

where $-\dfrac{dx}{dt}$ is the velocity v of the loop being pulled out of the magnetic field. The current induced in the loop is given by

$$i = \frac{\mathcal{E}}{R} = \frac{Blv}{R}$$

where R is the loop resistance. From Lenz's law, this current must be clockwise because it is opposing the change (the decrease in Φ_B). It establishes a magnetic field in the same direction as the external magnetic field within the loop. Forces $\mathbf{F}_2$ and $\mathbf{F}_3$ cancel each other because they are equal and in opposite directions. $\mathbf{F}_1$ is obtained from the equation ($F = i\,\mathbf{l} \times \mathbf{B}$).

$$F_1 = ilB \sin 90° = \frac{B^2l^2v}{R}$$

The force pulling the loop must do steady work given by

$$P = F_1v = \frac{B^2l^2v^2}{R}$$

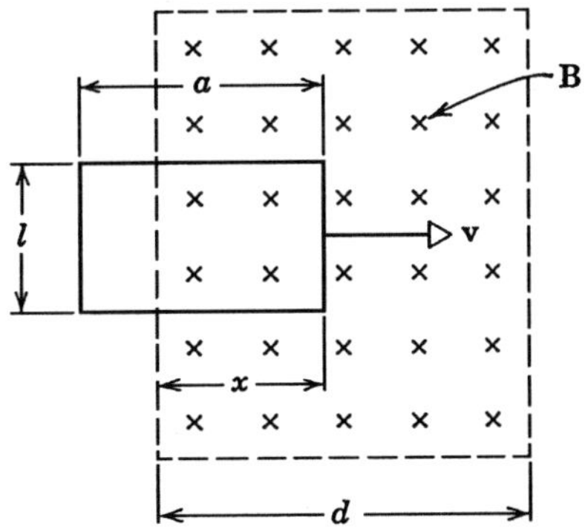

FIGURE 26.16 A rectangular loop is caused to move with a velocity **v** through a magnetic field. The position of the loop is measured by x, the distance between the effective left edge of the field **B** and the right end of the loop.

Figure 26.16 illustrates a rectangular loop of resistance R, width l, and length a being pulled at constant speed v through a magnetic field **B** of thickness d. There is no flux Φ_B when the loop is not in the field. The flux Φ_B is Bla when the loop is entirely in the field. It is Blx when the loop is entering the field. The induced voltage, or emf $\mathcal{E}$, in the loop is given by

$$\mathcal{E} = -\frac{d\Phi_B}{dt} = -\frac{d\Phi_B}{dx}\frac{dx}{dt} = -\frac{d\Phi_B}{dx}v$$

where $\left(\frac{d\Phi_B}{dx}\right)$ is the slope of the curve shown in Figure 26.17 (*a*).

The voltage $\mathcal{E}(x)$ is shown in Fig. 26.17 (*b*). Lenz's law indicates that $\mathcal{E}(x)$ is counterclockwise. There is no voltage induced in the coil when it is entirely in the magnetic field, because the flux Φ_B through the coil does not change with time. Figure 26.17 (*c*) shows the rate P of thermal energy generation in the loop. P is given by

$$P = \frac{\mathcal{E}^2}{R}$$

If a real magnetic field is considered, its strength will decrease from the center to the peripheries. Thus, the sharp bends and corners shown in Figure 26.17 will be replaced by smooth curves. The voltage $\mathcal{E}$, induced in this case, will be given by $\mathcal{E}_{max} \sin \omega t$ (a sine wave). This is exactly how AC voltage is induced in a real generator. It should also be noted that the prime mover has to do significant work to rotate the generator rotor inside the stator.

INDUCTANCE

When the current in a coil changes, an induced voltage appears in that same coil. This is called *self-induction.* The voltage, or emf, that is induced is called *self-induced emf.* It obeys Faraday's law of induction like any other induced emf's. For a closed-packed coil (an inductor) we have

$$N\Phi_B = Li$$

Where N is the number of turns of the coil, Φ_B is the flux, i is the current, and L is the inductance of the device. From Faraday's law, we can write the induced voltage (emf) as

$$\mathcal{E} = -\frac{d\,(N\Phi_B)}{dt} = -L\,\frac{di}{dt}$$

This relationship can be used for inductors of all shapes and sizes. In an inductor (the symbol ⌇⌇⌇⌇⌇, L depends only on the geometry of the device. The unit of inductance is the henry (H). It is given by

$$1\text{ H} = 1\text{ V}\cdot\text{s/A}$$

In an inductor, energy is stored in a magnetic field. The amount of magnetic energy stored, U_B, in the inductor is given by

$$U_B = \tfrac{1}{2} Li^2$$

In summary, an inductor stores energy in a magnetic field, and the capacitor stores energy in an electric field.

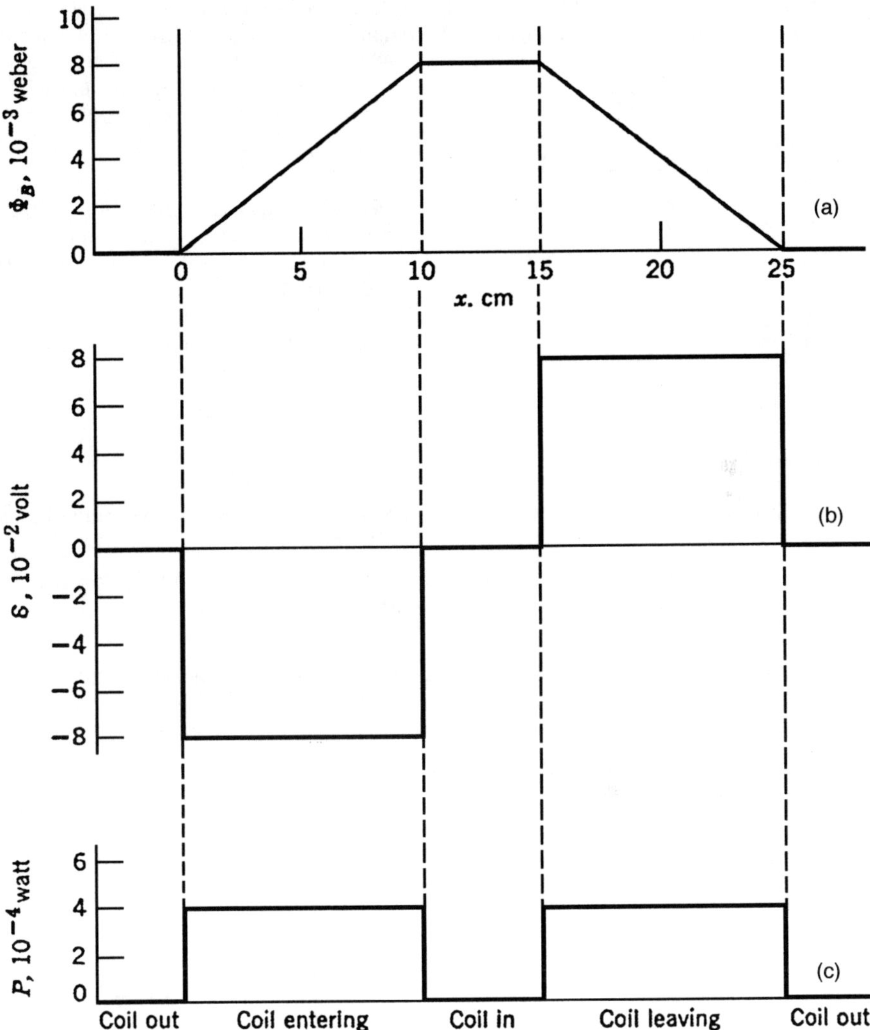

FIGURE 26.17 In practice, the sharp corners would be rounded. (*a*) Variation of flux with distance; (*b*) variation of voltage with distance; (*c*) variation of power with distance.

ALTERNATING CURRENTS

An alternating current in a circuit establishes a voltage (emf) that varies with time as

$$\mathcal{E} = \mathcal{E}_m \sin \omega t$$

where $\mathcal{E}_m$ is the maximum emf and $\omega = 2\pi\nu$, where ν is the frequency measured in hertz (Hz). This type of emf is established by an AC generator in a power plant. In North America, $\nu = 60$ Hz. In Western Europe and Australia, it is 50 Hz. The symbol for a source of alternating emf is -⊝-. This device is called an *alternating current generator* or an *AC generator.*

Alternating currents are essential for modern society. Power distribution systems, radio, television, satellite communication systems, computer systems, and so on would not exist without alternating voltages and currents.

The alternating current in the circuit shown in Fig. 26.18 is given by

$$i = i_m \sin(\omega t - \theta)$$

where i_m is the maximum amplitude of the current; ω is the angular frequency of the applied alternating voltage (or emf), and θ is the phase angle between the alternating current and the alternating voltage. Let us consider each component of the circuit separately.

$(\mathcal{E} = \mathcal{E}_m \sin \omega t)$

FIGURE 26.18 A single-loop *RCL* circuit contains an AC generator. V_R, V_C, and V_L are the time-varying potential differences across the resistor, the capacitor, and the inductor, respectively.

Resistive Circuit

Figure 26.19 (*a*) shows an alternating voltage applied across a resistor. We can write the following equations:

$$V_R = \mathcal{E}_m \sin \omega t \quad \text{and} \quad V_R = i_R R \quad \text{or} \quad i_R = \frac{\mathcal{E}_m}{R} \sin \omega t$$

A comparison between the preceding equations shows that the time-varying (instantaneous) quantities V_R and i_R are *in-phase*. This means that they reach their maximum and minimum

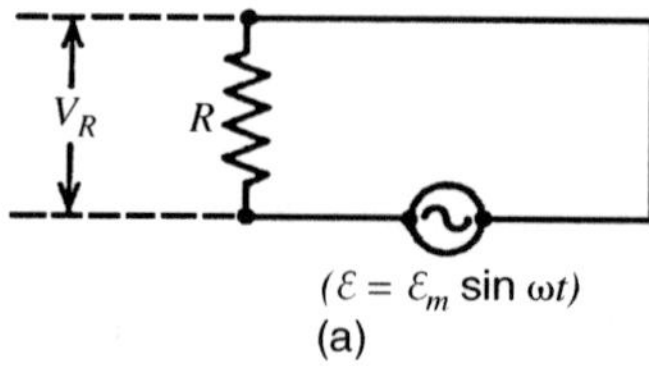

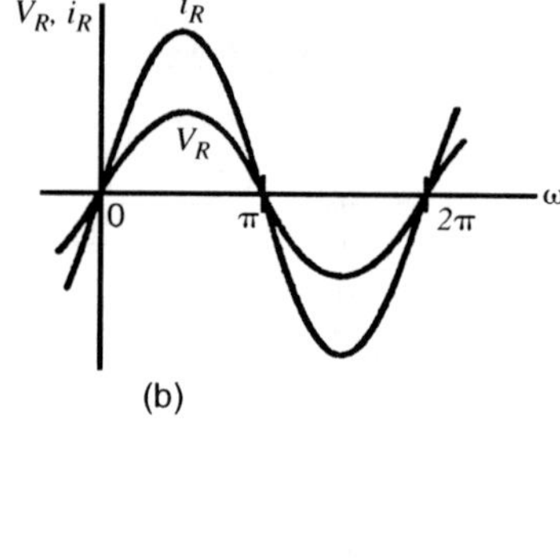

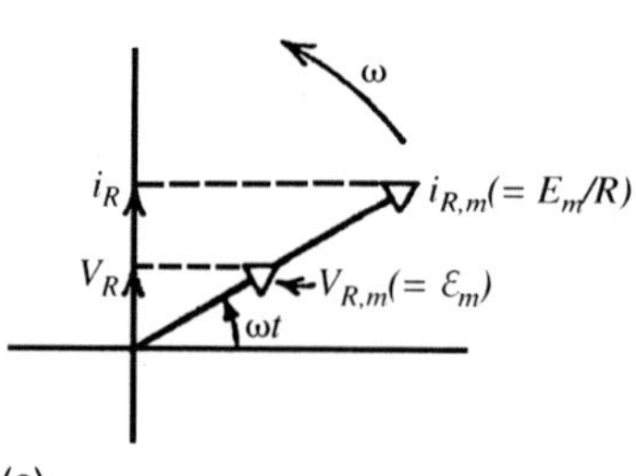

FIGURE 26.19 (*a*) A single-loop resistive circuit containing an AC generator. (*b*) The current and the potential difference across the resistor are in-phase ($\theta = 0$). (*c*) A phasor diagram shows the same thing. The arrows on the vertical axis are *instantaneous* values.

values at the same time. They also have the same angular frequency ω. These facts are shown in Fig. 26.19 (*b, c*).

Figure 26.19 (*c*) illustrates a *phasor diagram.* It is another method used to describe the situation. The phasors in this diagram are represented by open arrows. They rotate counterclockwise with an angular frequency ω about the origin. The phasors have the following two properties:

1. The length of the phasor is proportional to the *maximum* value of the alternating quantity described (i.e., $\mathcal{E}_m$ for V_R and $\mathcal{E}_m/R$ for i_R).
2. The projection of the phasors on the vertical axis gives the *instantaneous* values of the alternating parameter (current or voltage) described. Thus, the arrows on the vertical axis represent the instantaneous values of V_R and i_R. Since V_R and i_R are in-phase, their phasors lie along the same line [Fig. 26.19 (*c*)].

Capacitive Circuit

Figure 26.20 (*a*) illustrates an alternating voltage acting on a capacitor. We can write the following equations:

$$V_c = \mathcal{E}_m \sin \omega t \quad \text{and} \quad V_c = \frac{q}{C} \text{ (definition of } C)$$

From these relationships, we have

$$q = \mathcal{E}_m C \sin \omega t$$

or

$$i_c = \frac{dq}{dt} = \omega C \mathcal{E}_m \cos \omega t$$

A comparison between these equations shows that the instantaneous values of V_c and i_c are one-quarter cycle out of phase. This is illustrated in Fig. 26.20 (*b*).

V_c lags i_c (i.e., as time passes, V_c reaches its maximum after i_c does) by one-quarter cycle (90°). This is also shown clearly in the phasor diagram [Fig. 26.20 (*c*)]. Since the phasors rotate in the counterclockwise direction, it is clear that the $V_{c,m}$ phasor lags behind the $i_{c,m}$ phasor by one-quarter cycle. The reason for this lag is that the capacitor stores energy in its electric field. The current goes through it before the voltage is established across it. Since the current is given by

$$i = i_m \sin (\omega t - \theta)$$

θ is the angle between V_c and i_c. In this case, it is equal to −90°. If we put this value of θ in the equation of current, we obtain

$$i = i_m \cos \omega t$$

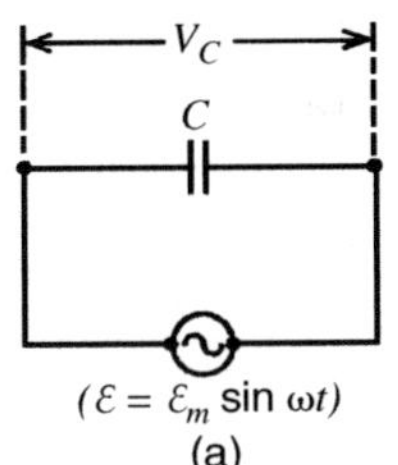

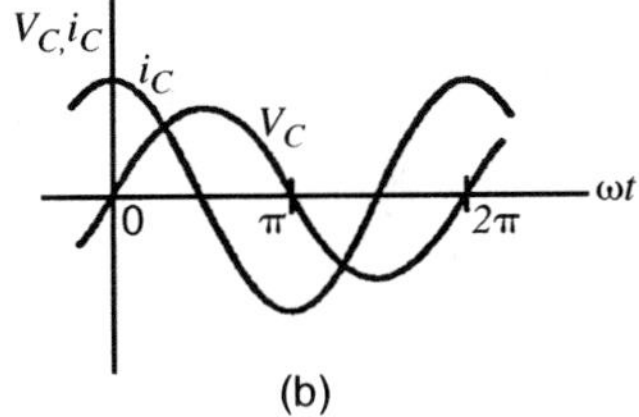

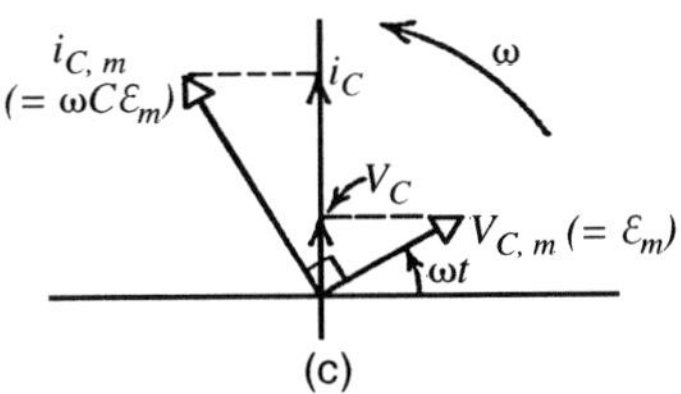

FIGURE 26.20 (*a*) A single-loop capacitive circuit containing an AC generator. (*b*) The potential difference across the capacitor lags the current by one-quarter cycle. (*c*) A phasor diagram shows the same thing. The arrows on the vertical axis are instantaneous values.

This equation is in agreement with the previous equation for current that we obtained

$$i_c = \frac{dq}{dt} = \omega C \mathcal{E}_m \cos \omega t$$

where $i_m = \omega C\, \mathcal{E}_m$.

i_c is also expressed as follows:

$$i_c = \frac{\mathcal{E}_m}{x_c} \cos \omega t$$

x_c is called the *capacitive reactance.* Its unit is the ohm (Ω). Since the maximum value of $V_c = V_{c,\,m}$ and the maximum value of $i_c = i_{c,\,m}$, we can write

$$V_{c,\,m} = i_{c,\,m}\, x_c$$

$V_{c,\,m}$ represents the maximum voltage established across the capacitor when the current is i.

Inductive Circuit

Figure 26.21 (*a*) shows a circuit containing an alternating voltage acting on an inductor. We can write the following equations:

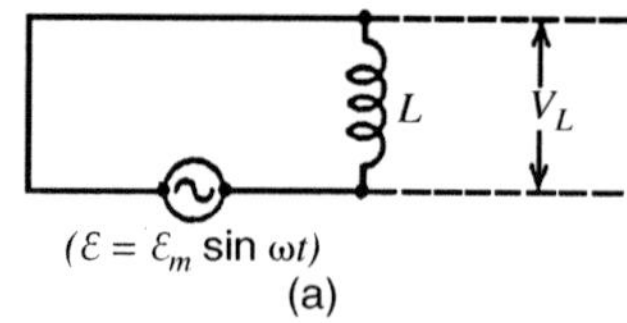

$$V_L = \mathcal{E}_m \sin \omega t$$

and

$$V_L = L\,\frac{di}{dt} \text{ (from the definition } L\text{)}$$

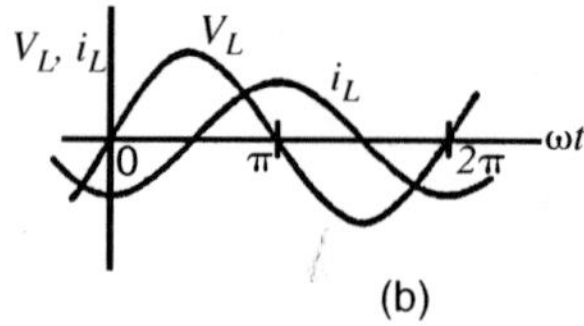

From these equations, we have

$$di = \left(\frac{\mathcal{E}_m}{L}\right) \sin \omega t\, dt$$

or

$$i_L = \int di = -\left(\frac{\mathcal{E}_m}{\omega L}\right) \cos \omega t$$

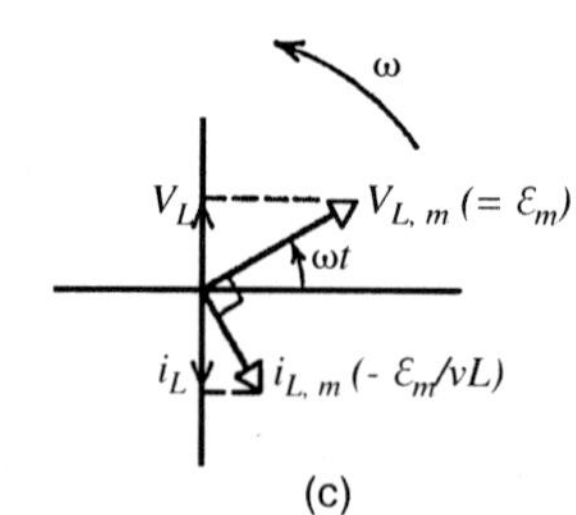

FIGURE 26.21 (*a*) A single-loop inductive circuit containing an AC generator. (*b*) The potential difference across the inductor *leads* the current by one-quarter cycle. (*c*) A phasor diagram shows the same thing. The arrows on the vertical axis are instantaneous values.

A comparison between the instantaneous values of V_L and i_L shows that these parameters are out of phase by a quarter-cycle (90°). This is illustrated in Fig. 26.21(*b*). It is clear that V_L *leads* i_L. This means that as time passes, V_L reaches its maximum before i_L does, by one-quarter cycle.

This fact is also shown in the phasor diagram of Fig. 26.21 (*c*). As the phasors rotate in the counterclockwise direction, it is clear that the $V_{L,m}$ phasor leads (precedes) $i_{L,m}$ by one-quarter cycle.

The phase angle θ, which is between V_L and i_L, in this case is +90°. If this value is put in the current equation:

$$i = i_m \sin (\omega t - \theta)$$

we obtain

$$i = -i_m \cos \omega t$$

This equation is in agreement with the previous equation of the current:

$$i_L = \int di = -\left(\frac{\mathcal{E}_m}{\omega L}\right) \cos \omega t$$

Again, for reasons of compactness of notation, we rewrite the equation as:

$$i_L = -\left(\frac{\mathcal{E}_m}{X_L}\right) \cos \omega t$$

where

$$X_L = \omega L$$

X_L is called the *inductive reactance.* As for the capacitive reactance, the unit for X_L is the ohm (Ω). Since $\mathcal{E}_m$ is the maximum value of V_L ($=V_{L,m}$), we can write

$$V_{L,m} = i_{L,m} X_L$$

This indicates that when any alternating current of amplitude i_m and angular frequency ω exists in an inductor, the maximum voltage difference across the inductor is given by

$$V_{L,m} = i_m X_L$$

We can now examine a circuit containing a resistor and an inductor, which is shown in Fig. 26.22.

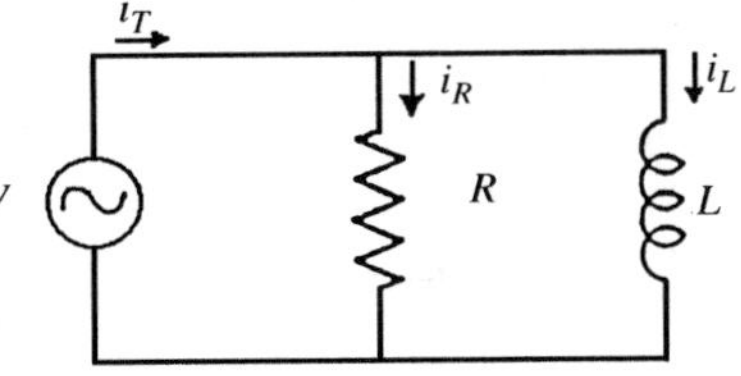

FIGURE 26.22 Circuit containing a resistor and an inductor.

Figure 26.23 illustrates the phasor diagram of the circuit. The total current, $\mathbf{i}_T = \mathbf{i}_R + \mathbf{i}_L$, θ, represents the angle between $\mathbf{i}_T$ and the voltage, **V.** It is called the *phase angle of the system.* An increase in the value of the inductance L will result in increasing the angle θ. The *power factor* (PF) is defined as

$$\text{PF} = \cos \theta$$

It is a measure of the ratio of the magnitudes of ($|\mathbf{i}_R|/|\mathbf{i}_T|$).

The circuit shown in Fig. 26.22 shows that the load supplied by a power plant has two natures, $\mathbf{i}_R$ and $\mathbf{i}_L$. Equipment such as motors, welders, and fluorescent lights require both types of currents. However, equipment such as heaters and incandescent bulbs require the resistive current, i_R only.

The power in the resistive part of the circuit is given by

$$P = Vi_R \quad \text{or} \quad P = Vi_T \cos \theta$$

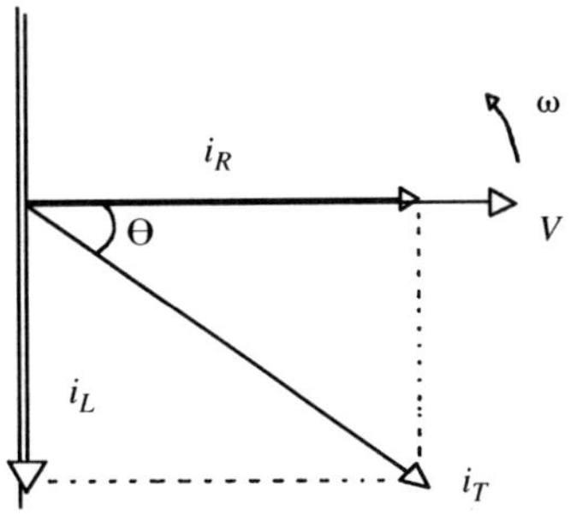

FIGURE 26.23 A phasor diagram of the circuit in Fig. 26.22.

This is the *real power* in the circuit. It is the energy that is dissipated by the resistor. This is the energy converted from electrical power to heat. This power is also used to provide the mechanical power (torque $\times$ speed) in a motor. The unit of this power is watts (W) or megawatts (MW).

The power in the inductor is given by

$$Q = Vi_L \quad \text{or} \quad Q = Vi_T \sin \theta$$

This is the *reactive or inductive power* in the circuit. It is the power that is stored in the inductor in the form of a magnetic field. This power is not consumed like the real power. It returns to the system (power plant and transmission lines) every half-cycle. It is used to create the magnetic field in the windings of the motor. The three main effects of reactive power on the system are as follows:

1. The transmission line losses between the power plant and the load are proportional to $i_T^2 R_T$, where $\mathbf{i}_T = \mathbf{i}_R + \mathbf{i}_L$ and R_T is the resistance in the transmission lines. Therefore, i_L is a contributor to transmission losses.
2. The transmission lines have a specific current rating. If the inductive current i_L is high, the magnitude of i_R will be limited to a lower value. This creates a problem for the utility because their revenue is mainly based on i_R.
3. If an industry has large motors, it will require a high inductive current to magnetize these motors. This creates a localized reduction in voltage (a voltage dip) at the industry. The utility will not be able to correct for this voltage dip from the power plant. Capacitor banks are normally installed at the industry to correct the power factor. Figures 26.24 and 26.25 illustrate the correction in power factor. θ' is smaller than θ. Therefore, the new PF (*cos* θ') is larger than the previous one PF (*cos* θ). Most utilities charge a penalty when the PF drops below between 0.9 and 0.92. This penalty is charged to the industry even if the PF drops once during the month below the limit that is specified by the utility. Most industries use the following methods to ensure that their PF remains above the limit that is specified by the utility:

   a. The capacitor banks are sized to give the industry a margin above the limit that is specified by the utility.

   b. The induction motors at the industry are started in sequence. This is done to stagger the inrush current required by each motor.

   Note: The *inrush current* is the starting current of the induction motor. It is normally from six to eight times larger than the normal running current. The inrush current is mainly an inductive current. This is due to the fact that the mechanical energy (torque × speed) developed by the motor and heat losses during the starting period of the motor are minimal (the real power provides the mechanical energy and heat losses in the motor).

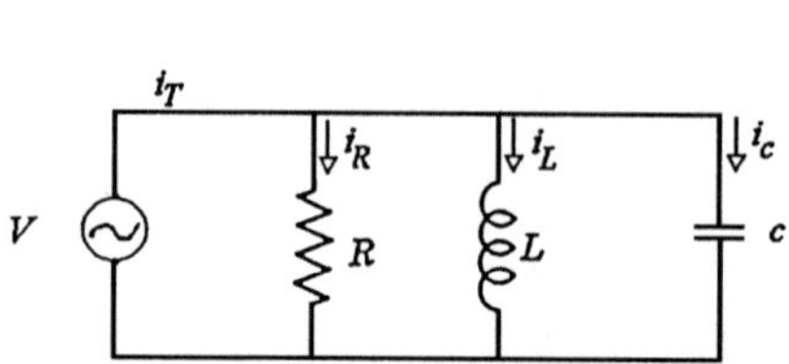

FIGURE 26.24 Addition of capacitor banks at an industry.

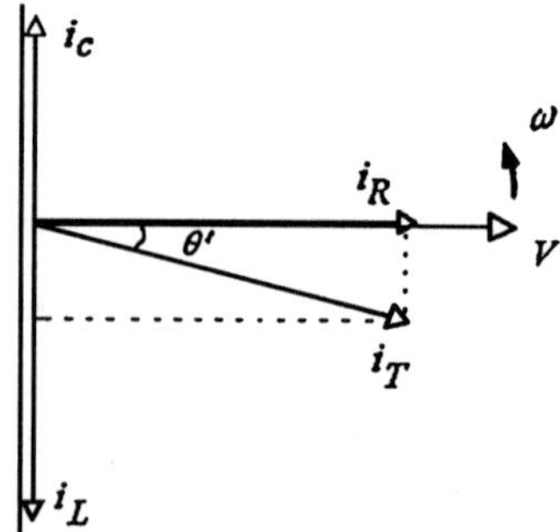

FIGURE 26.25 Correction of PF at an industry.

c. The synchronous motors are used in conjunction with induction motors. A synchronous motor is supplied by AC power to its stator. It is also supplied by DC power to its rotor. The DC current allows the synchronous motor to deliver reactive (inductive) power. Therefore, a synchronous motor can operate at a leading PF, as shown in Fig. 26.26. This allows the synchronous motors to correct the PF at the industry by compensating for the lagging PF generated by induction motors.

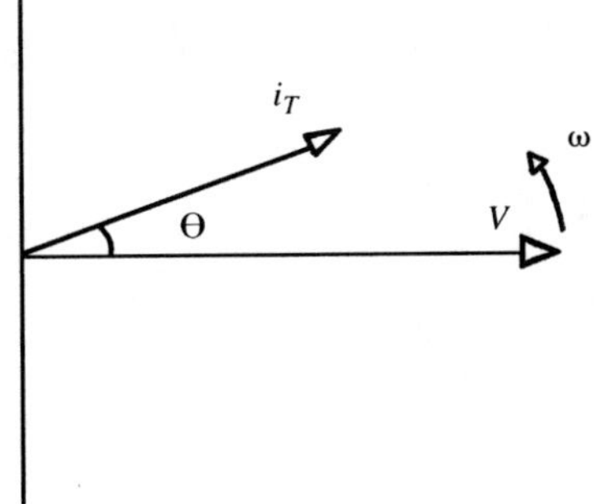

FIGURE 26.26 Phasor diagram of a synchronous motor.

The third form of power used is the *apparent power.* It is given by

$$S = i_T V$$

where $\mathbf{i}_T = \mathbf{i}_R + \mathbf{i}_L$. The unit of this power is voltamperes (VA) or megavoltamperes (MVA). This power includes the combined effect of the real power and reactive power. All electrical equipment (e.g., transformers, motors, generators, etc.) are rated by their apparent power. This is due to the fact that the apparent power specifies the total power (real and reactive) requirement of equipment.

REFERENCE

1. Halliday, D., and R. Resnick, *Physics, Part Two,* 3rd ed., John Wiley & Sons, 1978.

CHAPTER 27
INTRODUCTION TO MACHINERY PRINCIPLES

ELECTRIC MACHINES AND TRANSFORMERS

An *electric machine* is a device that can convert either mechanical energy to electric energy or electric energy to mechanical energy.[1] Such a device is called a *generator* when it converts mechanical energy to electric energy; it is called a *motor* when it converts electric energy to mechanical energy. Since an electric machine can convert power in either direction, any such machine can either be used as a generator or a motor. Thus, all motors and generators can be used to convert energy from one form to another using the action of a magnetic field.

A *transformer* is a device that converts alternating current (AC) electric energy at one voltage level to ac electric energy at another voltage level. Transformers operate on the same principles as generators and motors.

COMMON TERMS AND PRINCIPLES

θ = angular position of an object. It is the angle at which it is oriented. It is measured from one arbitrary reference point (units: radians or degrees).

ω = angular velocity = $d\theta/dt$. It is the rate of variation of angular position with time (units: radian or degrees).

f_m = angular velocity expressed in revolutions per second = $\omega_m/2\pi$.

α = angular acceleration = $d\omega/dt$. It is the rate of variation of angular velocity with time (units in rad/s^2).

τ = torque = (force applied) × (perpendicular distance) – (units in N·m).

τ = $J\alpha$ = Newton's law of rotation, where J is the moment of inertia of the rotor (units in kg·m^2).

W = work = $\tau\theta$ (if τ is constant) – (units in joules).

P = power = dW/dt. It is the rate of variation of work with time (watts): $P = \tau\omega$.

THE MAGNETIC FIELD

Energy is converted from one form to another in motors, generators, and transformers by the action of magnetic fields. There are four basic principles that describe how magnetic fields are used in these devices:

1. A current-carrying wire produces a magnetic field in the area around it.
2. A time-changing magnetic field induces a voltage in a coil of wire if it passes through that coil. (This is the basis of *transformer action.*)
3. A current-carrying wire in the presence of a magnetic field has a force induced on it. (This is the basis of *motor action.*)
4. A moving wire in the presence of a magnetic field has a voltage induced in it. (This is the basis of *generator action.*)

PRODUCTION OF A MAGNETIC FIELD

Ampere's law is the basic law that governs the production of a magnetic field:

$$\oint \mathbf{H} \cdot d\mathbf{l} = I_{net}$$

Where **H** is the magnetic field intensity produced by the current I_{net}. I is measured in amperes and **H** in ampere-turns per meter. Figure 27.1 shows a rectangular core having a winding of N turns of wire wrapped on one leg of the core. If the core is made of ferromagnetic materials (such as iron), most of the magnetic field produced by the current will remain inside the core.

Ampere's law becomes

$$\mathbf{H} l_c = Ni$$

Where l_c is the mean path length of the core. The magnetic field intensity **H** is a measure of the "effort" that the current is putting to establish a magnetic field. The material of the core affects the strength of the magnetic field flux produced in the core. The magnetic field intensity **H** is linked with the resulting magnetic flux density **B** within the material by

$$\mathbf{B} = \mu \mathbf{H}$$

where **H** = magnetic field intensity
μ = magnetic *permeability* of material
B = resulting magnetic flux density produced

Thus, the actual magnetic flux density produced in a piece of material is given by the product of two terms:

H = the effort exerted by the current to establish a magnetic field

μ = the relative ease of establishing a magnetic field in a given material

In SI, the units are: **H** (ampere-turn per meter); μ [henrys per meter (H/m)]; **B** [Webers per square meter, known as teslas (T)]. μ_0 is the permeability of free space. Its value is

$$\mu_0 = 4\pi \times 10^{-7} \text{ H/m}$$

The *relative permeability* compares the magnetizability of materials. For example, in modern machines, the steels used in the cores have relative permeabilities of 2000 to 7000. Thus, for a given current, the flux established in a steel core is 2000 to 7000 times stronger than

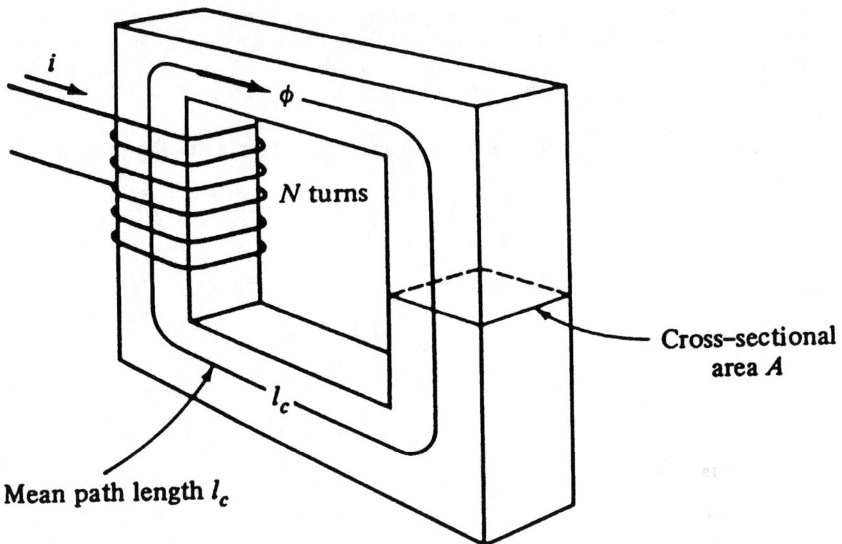

FIGURE 27.1 A simple magnetic core.

in a corresponding area of air (air has the same permeability as free space). Thus, the metals of the core in transformers, motors, and generators play an essential part in increasing and concentrating the magnetic flux in the device. The magnitude of the flux density is given by

$$B = \mu H = \frac{\mu N i}{l_c}$$

Thus, the total flux in the core in Fig 27.1 is

$$\boxed{\phi = BA = \frac{\mu N i A}{l_c}}$$

Where A is the cross-sectional area of the core.

MAGNETIC BEHAVIOR OF FERROMAGNETIC MATERIALS

The magnetic permeability is defined by the equation:

$$\mathbf{B} = \mu \mathbf{H}$$

The permeability of ferromagnetic materials is up to 6000 times higher than the permeability of free space. However, the permeability of ferromagnetic materials is not constant. If we apply a DC current to the core shown in Fig. 27.1 (starting with 0 A and increasing the current), Fig. 27.2 (*a*) illustrates the variation of the flux produced in the core versus the magnetomotive force. This graph is known as the *saturation curve,* or *magnetization curve.* At first, a slight increase in the current (magnetomotive force) results in a significant increase in the flux. However, at a certain point, a further increase in current results in no change in the flux. The region where the curve is flat is called the *saturation region.* The core has become *saturated.* The region where the flux changes rapidly is called the *unsaturated region.* The transition region between the unsaturated region and the saturated region is called the *"knee" of the curve.*

Figure 27.2 (*b*) illustrates the variation of magnetic flux density **B** with magnetizing intensity **H.** These are the equations:

$$H = \frac{Ni}{l_c} \qquad B = \frac{\phi}{A}$$

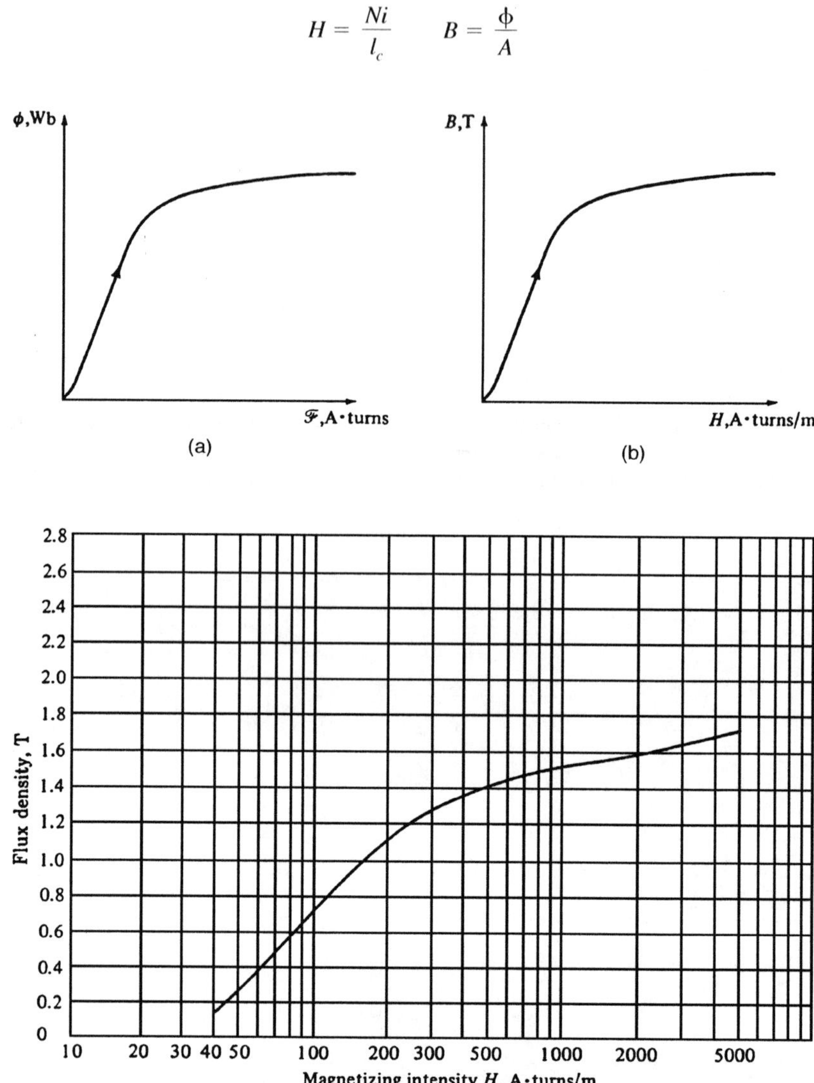

FIGURE 27.2 (*a*) Sketch of a DC magnetization curve for a ferromagnetic core; (*b*) the magnetization curve expressed in terms of flux density and magnetizing intensity; (*c*) a detailed magnetization curve for a typical piece of steel.

It can easily be seen that the magnetizing intensity is directly proportional to the magnetomotive force, and the magnetic flux density is directly proportional to the flux. Therefore, the relationship between **B** and **H** has the same shape as the relationship between flux and magnetomotive force. The slope of flux-density versus magnetizing intensity curve [Fig. 27.2 (*b*)] is by definition the permeability of the core at that magnetizing intensity. The curve shows that in the unsaturated region the permeability is high and almost constant. In the saturated region, the permeability drops to a very low value. Electric machines and transformers use ferromagnetic material for their cores because these materials produce much more flux than other material.

ENERGY LOSSES IN A FERROMAGNETIC CORE

If an AC [Fig. 27.3 (*a*)] is applied to the core, the flux in the core will follow path *ab* [Fig. 27.3 (*b*)]. This graph is the saturation curve shown in Fig. 27.2. However, when the current drops, the flux follows a different path from the one it took when the current increased. When the current decreases, the flux follows path *bcd.* When the current increases again, the flux follows path *deb.*

The amount of flux present in the core depends on the previous history of the flux in the core and the magnitude of the current applied to the windings of the core. The dependence on the history of the preceding flux and the resulting failure to retrace the flux path is called *hysteresis.* Path *bcdeb,* shown in Fig. 27.3 is called a *hysteresis loop.*

Notice that if a magnetomotive force is applied to the core and then removed, the flux will follow path *abc.* The flux does not return to zero when the magnetomotive force is removed. Instead, a magnetic field remains in the core. The magnetic field is known as the *residual flux* in the core. This is the technique used for producing permanent magnets. A magnetomotive force must be applied to the core in the opposite direction to return the flux to zero. This force is called the *coercive magnetomotive force,* $\mathcal{F}_c$.

To understand the cause of hysteresis, it is necessary to know the structure of the metal. There are many small regions within the metal, called *domains.* The magnetic fields of all the atoms in each domain are pointing in the same direction. Thus, each domain within the metal acts like a small permanent magnet. These tiny domains are oriented randomly within the material. This is the reason that a piece of iron does not have a resultant flux (Fig. 27.4).

When an external magnetic field is applied to the block of iron, all the domains will line up in the direction of the field. This switching to align all the fields increases the magnetic flux in the iron. This is the reason why iron has a much higher permeability than air.

When all the atoms and domains of the iron line up with the external field, a further increase in the magnetomotive force will not be able to increase the flux. At this point, the iron has become saturated with flux. The core has reached the saturation region of the magnetization curve (Fig. 27.2).

The cause of hysteresis is that when the external magnetic field is removed, the domains do not become completely random again. This is because energy is required to turn the atoms in the domains. Originally, the external magnetic field provided energy to align the domains. When the field is removed, there is no source of energy to rotate the domains. The piece of iron has now become a permanent magnet.

Some of the domains will remain aligned until an external source of energy is supplied to change them. A large mechanical shock, and heating are examples of external energy that can change the alignment of the domains. This is the reason why permanent magnets lose their magnetism when hit with a hammer, or when heated.

Energy is lost in all iron cores due to the fact that energy is required to turn the domains. The energy required to reorient the domains during each cycle of the alternating current is called the *hysteresis loss in the iron core.* The area enclosed in the hysteresis loop is directly proportional to the energy lost in a given ac cycle (Fig. 27.3).

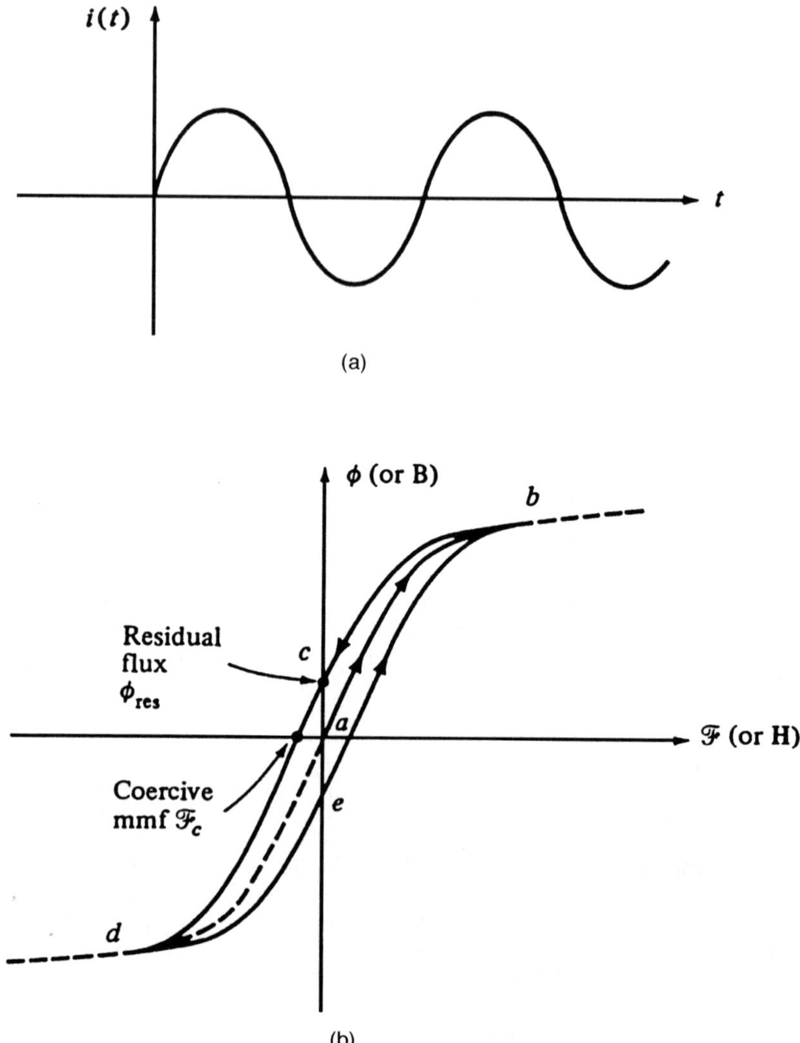

FIGURE 27.3 The hysteresis loop traced out by the flux in a core when the current $i(t)$ is applied to it.

FARADAY'S LAW—INDUCED VOLTAGE FROM A MAGNETIC FIELD CHANGING WITH TIME

Faraday's law states that if a flux passes through a turn of a coil of wire, a voltage will be induced in the turn of wire that is directly proportional to the *rate of change* of the flux with time. The equation is

$$e_{\text{ind}} = -\frac{d\phi}{dt}$$

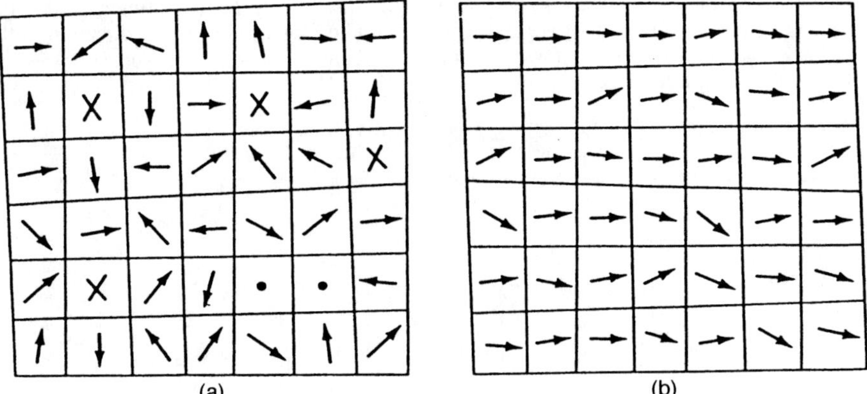

FIGURE 27.4 (*a*) Magnetic domains oriented randomly; (*b*) magnetic domains lined up in the presence of an external magnetic field.

e_{ind} is the voltage induced in the turn of the coil and ϕ is the flux passing through it. If the coil has N turns and if a flux ϕ passes through them all, then the voltage induced across the whole coil is

$$e_{ind} = -N \frac{d\phi}{dt}$$

where e_{ind} = voltage induced in the coil
N = number of turns of wire in the coil
ϕ = flux passing through the coil

Based on Faraday's law, a flux changing with time induces a voltage within a ferromagnetic core in a similar manner as it would in a wire wrapped around the core. These voltages can generate swirls of current inside the core. They are similar to the eddies seen at the edges of a river. They are called *eddy currents.* Energy is dissipated by these flowing eddy currents. The lost energy heats the iron core. Eddy current losses are proportional to the length of the paths they follow within the core. For this reason, all ferromagnetic cores subjected to alternating fluxes are made of many small strips, or *laminations.* The strips are insulated on both sides to reduce the paths of the eddy currents. Since hysteresis losses and eddy current losses occur in the core, their sum is called *core losses.*

PRODUCTION OF INDUCED FORCE ON A WIRE

A magnetic field induces a force on a current-carrying conductor within the field (Fig. 27.5). The force induced on the conductor is given by:

$$\mathbf{F} = i\,(\mathbf{l} \times \mathbf{B})$$

where i = magnitude of current in wire
$\mathbf{l}$ = length of wire, with direction of $\mathbf{l}$ defined to be in direction of current flow
$\mathbf{B}$ = magnetic flux density vector

The direction of the force is given by the right-hand rule. If the index finger of the right hand points in the direction of vector **l**, and the middle finger points in the direction of the flux density vector **B**, the thumb will point in the direction of the resultant force on the wire. The magnitude of the force is:

$$F = ilB \sin \theta$$

where θ is the angle between vectors **l** and **B**.

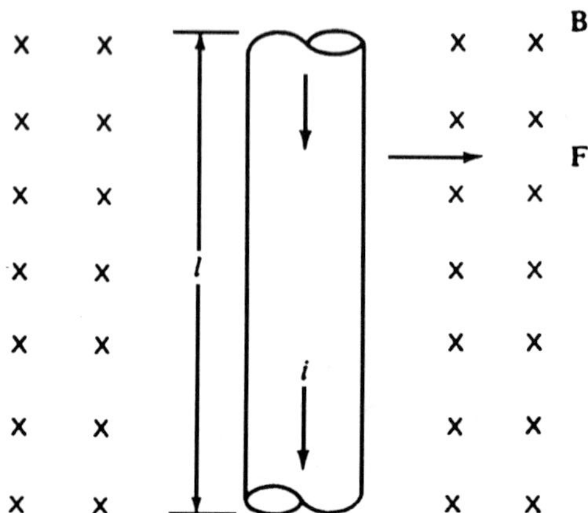

FIGURE 27.5 A current-carrying conductor in the presence of a magnetic field.

INDUCED VOLTAGE ON A CONDUCTOR MOVING IN A MAGNETIC FIELD

A magnetic field induces a voltage on a conductor moving in the field (Fig. 27.6). The induced voltage in the conductor is given by

$$e_{\text{ind}} = (\mathbf{v} \times \mathbf{B}) \cdot \mathbf{l}$$

where **v** = velocity of conductor
B = magnetic flux density vector
l = length of conductor in magnetic field, with direction defined to be in direction of current flow

REFERENCE

1. Chapman, S. J., *Electric Machinery Fundamentals*, 2d ed., McGraw-Hill, New York, 1991.

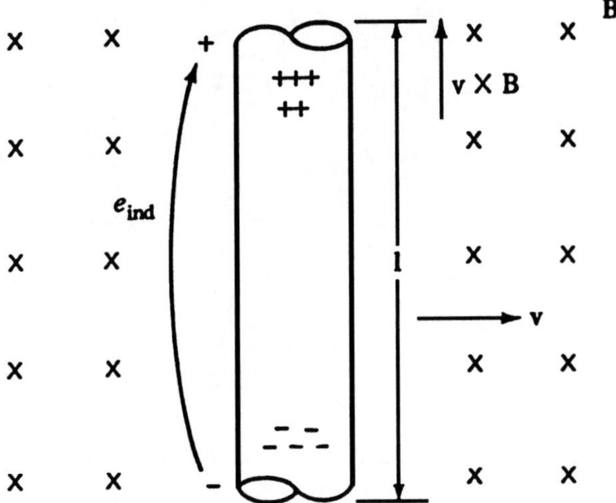

FIGURE 27.6 A conductor moving in the presence of a magnetic field.

CHAPTER 28
TRANSFORMERS

A *transformer* is a device that uses the action of a magnetic field to change alternating current (AC) electric energy at one voltage level to AC electric energy at another voltage level.[1] It consists of a ferromagnetic core with two or more coils wrapped around it. The common magnetic flux within the core is the only connection between the coils. The source of AC electric power is connected to one of the transformer windings. The second winding supplies power to loads. The winding connected to the power source is called *primary winding*, or *input winding*. The winding connected to the loads is called the *secondary winding*, or *output winding*.

IMPORTANCE OF TRANSFORMERS

When a transformer steps up the voltage level of a circuit, it decreases the current to keep the power equal. Therefore, AC power can be generated at one central station. The voltage is stepped up for transmission over long distances at very low losses. The voltage is stepped down again for final use. Since the transmission losses are proportional to the square of the current, raising the voltage by a factor of 10 will reduce the transmission losses by a factor of 100.

Also, when the voltage is increased by a factor of 10, the current is decreased by a factor of 10. This allows the use of much thinner conductors to transmit power.

In modern power stations, power is generated at 12 to 25 kilovolts (kV). Transformers step up the voltage to between 110 and 1000 kV for transmission over long distances at very low losses. Transformers then step it down to between 12 and 34.5 kV for local distribution and then permit power to be used in homes and industry at 120 V.

TYPES AND CONSTRUCTION OF TRANSFORMERS

The function of a transformer is to convert AC power from a voltage level to another voltage level at the same frequency. The core of a transformer is constructed from thin laminations that are electrically isolated from each other to reduce eddy current losses (Fig. 28.1). The primary and secondary windings are wrapped one on top of the other around the core with the low-voltage winding innermost. This arrangement serves two purposes:

1. The problem of insulating the high-voltage winding from the core is simplified.
2. It reduces the leakage flux compared if the two windings were separated by a distance on the core.

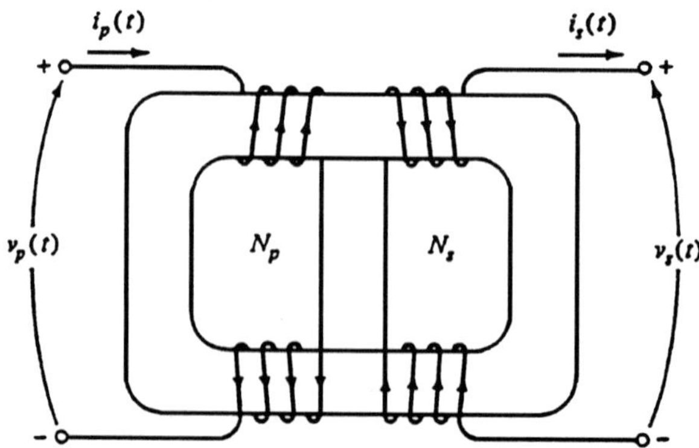

FIGURE 28.1 Core-form transformer construction.

The transformer that steps up the output of a generator to transmission levels (110+ kV) is called the *unit transformer.* The transformer that steps the voltage down from transmission levels to distribution levels (2.3 to 34.5 kV) is called a *substation transformer.* The transformer that steps down the distribution voltage to the final voltage at which the power is used (110, 208, 220 V, etc.) is called a *distribution transformer.*

There are also two special-purpose transformers used with electric machinery and power systems. The first is used to sample a high voltage and produce a low secondary voltage proportional to it (*potential transformers*). The potential transformer is designed to handle only a very small current. A *current transformer* is designed to give a secondary current that is much smaller than its primary current.

THE IDEAL TRANSFORMER

An ideal transformer does not have any losses (Fig. 28.2). The voltages and currents are related by these equations:

$$\boxed{\frac{v_P(t)}{v_S(t)} = \frac{N_P}{N_S} = a}$$

$$\boxed{N_P i_P(t) = N_S i_S(t)}$$

$$\boxed{\frac{i_P(t)}{i_S(t)} = \frac{1}{a}}$$

The equations of the phasor quantities are

$$\boxed{\frac{\mathbf{V}_P}{\mathbf{V}_S} = a} \qquad \boxed{\frac{\mathbf{I}_P}{\mathbf{I}_S} = \frac{1}{a}}$$

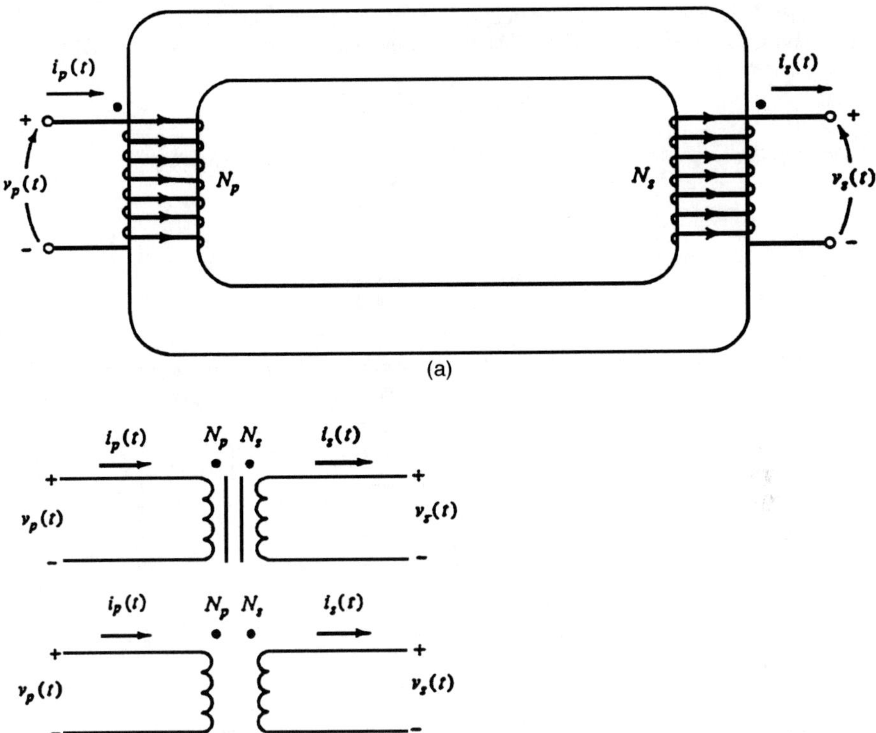

FIGURE 28.2 (*a*) Sketch of an ideal transformer; (*b*) schematic symbols of a transformer.

The phase angle of $\mathbf{V_P}$ is the same as the angle of $\mathbf{V_S}$ and the phase angle of $\mathbf{I_P}$ is the same as the phase angle of $\mathbf{I_S}$.

POWER IN AN IDEAL TRANSFORMER

The power given to the transformer by the primary circuit is

$$P_{\text{in}} = V_P I_P \cos \theta_P$$

where θ_P is the angle between the primary voltage and current. The power supplied by the secondary side of the transformer to its loads is

$$P_{out} = V_S I_S \cos \theta_S$$

where θ_S is the angle between the secondary voltage and current.

An ideal transformer does not affect the voltage and power angle, $\theta_P = \theta_S = \theta$. The primary and secondary windings of an ideal transformer have the *same power factor.* The power out of a transformer is

$$P_{out} = V_S I_S \cos\theta$$

Applying the turns-ratio equations gives $V_S = V_P/a$ and $I_S = aI_P$, so

$$P_{out} = \frac{V_P}{a} aI_P \cos\theta$$

$$\boxed{P_{out} = V_P I_P \cos\theta = P_{in}}$$

Therefore, *the output power of an ideal transformer is equal to its input power.*

The same relationship is applicable to the reactive power Q and apparent power S:

$$\boxed{Q_{in} = V_P I_P \sin\theta = V_S I_S \sin\theta = Q_{out}}$$

$$\boxed{S_{in} = V_P I_P = V_S I_S = S_{out}}$$

IMPEDANCE TRANSFORMATION THROUGH A TRANSFORMER

The *impedance* of a device is defined as the ratio of the phasor voltage across it to the phasor current flowing through it.

$$Z_L = \frac{\mathbf{V}_L}{\mathbf{I}_L}$$

Since a transformer changes the current and voltage levels, it also changes the impedance of an element. The impedance of the load shown in Fig. 28.3 (*b*) is

$$Z_L = \frac{\mathbf{V}_S}{\mathbf{I}_S}$$

the primary circuit apparent impedance is

$$Z'_L = \frac{\mathbf{V}_P}{\mathbf{I}_P}$$

Since the primary voltage and current can be expressed as

$$\mathbf{V}_P = a\mathbf{V}_S \qquad \mathbf{I}_P = \frac{\mathbf{I}_S}{a}$$

The apparent impedance of the primary is

$$Z'_L = \frac{\mathbf{V}_P}{\mathbf{I}_P} = \frac{a\mathbf{V}_S}{\mathbf{I}_S/a} = a^2\frac{\mathbf{V}_S}{\mathbf{I}_S}$$

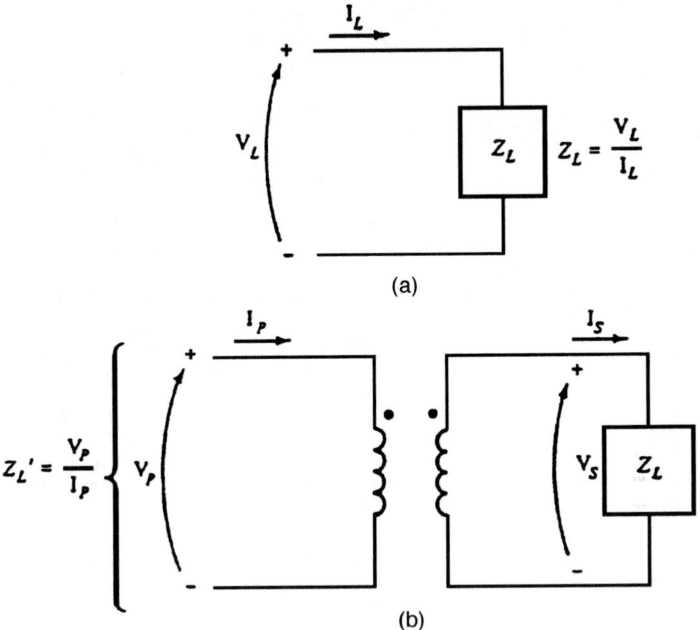

FIGURE 28.3 (*a*) Definition of impedance; (*b*) impedance scaling through a transformer.

$$\boxed{Z_L' = a^2 Z_L}$$

It is possible to match the magnitude of a load impedance to a source impedance by simply selecting the proper turns ratio of a transformer.

ANALYSIS OF CIRCUITS CONTAINING IDEAL TRANSFORMERS

The easiest way to analyze a circuit containing an ideal transformer is by replacing a portion of the circuit on one side of the transformer by an equivalent circuit with the same terminal characteristics. After substituting the equivalent circuit, the new circuit (without a transformer present) can be solved for its voltages and currents. The process of replacing one side of a transformer by its equivalent at the second side's voltage level is known as *reflecting,* or *referring,* the first side of the transformer to the second side. The solution for circuits containing ideal transformers is shown in Example 28.1.

EXAMPLE 28.1 A single-phase power system consists of a 480-V, 60-Hz generator supplying a load $Z_{load} = 4 + j3\Omega$ through a transmission line of impedance $Z_{line} = 0.18 + j0.24\Omega$. Answer the following questions about this system.

1. If the power system is exactly as previously described [Fig. 28.4 (*a*)], what will be the voltage at the load? What will the transmission line losses be?

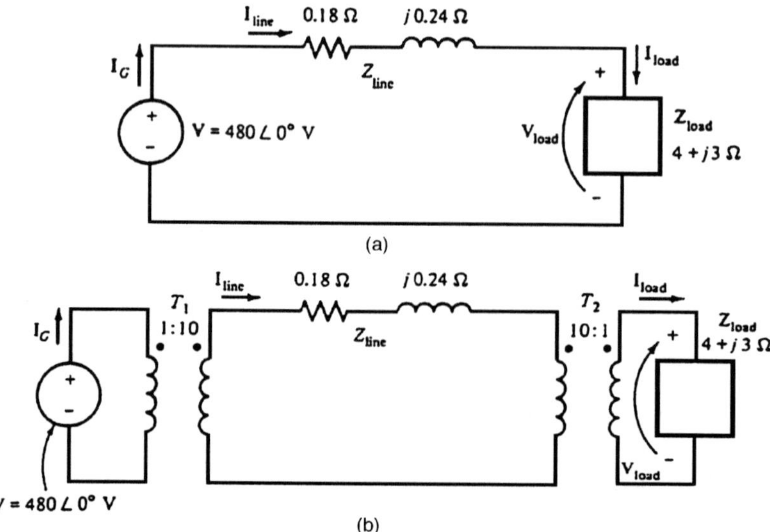

FIGURE 28.4 The power system of example 28.1, (*a*) without and (*b*) with transformers at the ends of the transmission line.

2. Suppose a 1:10 step-up transformer is placed at the generator end of the transmission line and a 10:1 step-down transformer is placed at the load end of the line [Fig. 28.4 (*b*)]. What will the load voltage be now? What will the transmission line losses be now?

Solution

1. Figure 28.4 (*a*) shows the power system without transformers. Here $\mathbf{I}_G = \mathbf{I}_{\text{line}} = \mathbf{I}_{\text{load}}$. The line current in this system is given by

$$
\begin{aligned}
\mathbf{I}_{\text{line}} &= \frac{\mathbf{V}}{Z_{\text{line}} + Z_{\text{load}}} \\
&= \frac{480 \angle 0^\circ \text{ V}}{(0.18\ \Omega + j0.24\ \Omega)\ (4\Omega + j3\Omega)} \\
&= \frac{480 \angle 0^\circ}{4.18 + j3.24} \\
&= \frac{480 \angle 0^\circ}{5.29 \angle 37.8^\circ} \\
&= 90.8 \angle -37.8^\circ \text{ A}
\end{aligned}
$$

Therefore the load voltage is

$$
\begin{aligned}
\mathbf{V}_{\text{load}} &= \mathbf{I}_{\text{line}}\, Z_{\text{load}} \\
&= (90.8 \angle -37.8^\circ \text{ A})\ (4\Omega + j3\Omega) \\
&= (90.8 \angle -37.8^\circ \text{ A})\ (5 \angle 36.9^\circ\ \Omega) \\
&= 454 \angle -0.9^\circ \text{ V}
\end{aligned}
$$

and the line losses are

$$P_{\text{loss}} = (I_{\text{line}})^2 R_{\text{line}}$$
$$= (90.8 \text{ A})^2 (0.18 \ \Omega)$$
$$= 1.484 \text{ W}$$

2. Figure 28.4 (*b*) shows the power system with the transformers. To analyze this system, it is necessary to convert it to a common voltage level. This is done in two steps:

a. Eliminate transformer T_2 by referring the load over to the transmission line's voltage level.

b. Eliminate transformer T_1 by referring the transmission line's elements and the equivalent load at the transmission line's voltage over to the source side.

The value of the load's impedance when reflected to the transmission system's voltage is

$$Z'_{\text{load}} = a^2 Z_{\text{load}}$$
$$= (^{10}/_1)^2 (4\Omega + j3\ \Omega)$$
$$= 400 + j300\ \Omega$$

The total impedance at the transmission line level is now

$$Z_{\text{eq}} = Z_{\text{line}} + Z'_{\text{load}}$$
$$= 400.18 + j300.24\ \Omega = 500.3\ \angle 36.88°\ \Omega$$

This equivalent circuit is shown in Fig. 28.5 (*a*). The total impedance at the transmission line level ($Z_{\text{line}} + Z'_{\text{load}}$) is now reflected across T_1 to the source's voltage level:

$$Z'_{\text{eq}} = a^2 Z_{\text{eq}}$$
$$= a^2 (Z_{\text{line}} + Z'_{\text{load}})$$
$$= (^1/_{10})^2 [(0.18 + j0.24) + (400 + j300)]\ \Omega$$
$$= (0.0018 + j0.0024) + (4 + j3)\ \Omega$$
$$= 5.003\ \angle 36.88°\ \Omega$$

Notice that $Z''_{\text{load}} = 4 + j3\Omega$ and $Z_{\text{line}} = 0.0018 + j0.0024\Omega$. The resulting equivalent circuit is shown in Fig. 28.5 (*b*). The generator's current is

$$\mathbf{I}_G = \frac{480\ \angle 0°\ \text{V}}{5.003\ \angle 36.88°\ \Omega} = 95.94\ \angle -36.88°\ \text{A}$$

Knowing the current $\mathbf{I}_G$, we can now work back and find $\mathbf{I}_{\text{line}}$ and $\mathbf{I}_{\text{load}}$. Working back through T_1, we get

$$N_{P1}\mathbf{I}_G = N_{S1}\,\mathbf{I}_{\text{line}}$$

$$\mathbf{I}_{\text{line}} = \frac{N_{P1}}{N_{S1}}\,\mathbf{I}_G$$
$$= {}^1/_{10}\ (95.94\ \angle -36.88°\ \text{A})$$
$$= 9.594\ \angle -36.88°\ \text{A}$$

Working back through T_2 gives

$$N_{P2}\,\mathbf{I}_{line} = N_{S2}\,\mathbf{I}_{load}$$

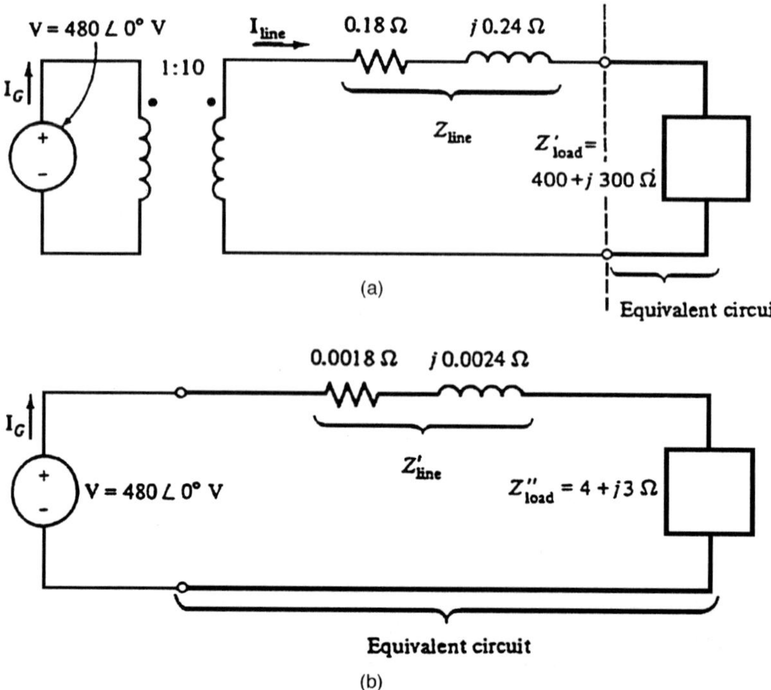

FIGURE 28.5 (*a*) System with the load referred to the transmission system voltage level; (*b*) system with the load and transmission line referred to the generator's voltage level.

$$\mathbf{I}_{load} = \frac{N_{P2}}{N_{S2}} \mathbf{I}_{line}$$

$$= {}^{10}\!/\!_{1}\ (9.594 \angle -36.88^\circ \text{ A})$$

$$= 95.94 \angle -36.88^\circ \text{ A}$$

It is now possible to answer the questions originally asked. The load voltage is given by

$$\mathbf{V}_{load} = \mathbf{I}_{load}\, Z_{load}$$

$$= (95.94 \angle -36.88^\circ \text{ A})\ (5 \angle 36.87^\circ\ \Omega)$$

$$= 479.7 \angle -0.01^\circ \text{ V}$$

and the line losses are given by

$$P_{loss} = (I_{line})^2 R_{line}$$

$$= (9.594 \text{ A})^2 (0.18\ \Omega)$$

$$= 16.7 \text{ W}$$

Notice that by stepping up the transmission voltage of the power system, the transmission losses have been reduced by a factor of 90. Also, the voltage at the load dropped significantly in the system with transformers compared to the system without transformers.

THEORY OF OPERATION OF REAL SINGLE-PHASE TRANSFORMERS

Figure 28.6 illustrates a transformer consisting of two conductors wrapped around a transformer core. Faraday's law describes the basis of transformer operation:

$$e_{\text{ind}} = \frac{d\lambda}{dt}$$

where λ is the flux linkage in the coil across which the voltage is being induced. λ is the sum of the flux passing through each turn in the coil added over all the coil turns:

$$\lambda = \sum_{i=1}^{N} \phi_{\text{i}}$$

The total flux linkage through a coil is not $N\phi$ (N is the number of turns). This is because the flux passing through each turn of a coil is slightly different from the flux in the neighboring turns. An average flux per turn in a coil is defined. If λ is the total flux linkage in all the turns of the coils, the *average flux per turn* is

$$\bar{\phi} = \frac{\lambda}{N}$$

where N is the number of turns.

Faraday's law can be written as

$$\boxed{e_{\text{ind}} = N\,\frac{d\bar{\phi}}{dt}}$$

THE VOLTAGE RATIO ACROSS A TRANSFORMER

The average flux present in the primary winding of a transformer is

$$\boxed{\bar{\phi} = \frac{1}{N_P}\int v_P(t)\,dt}$$

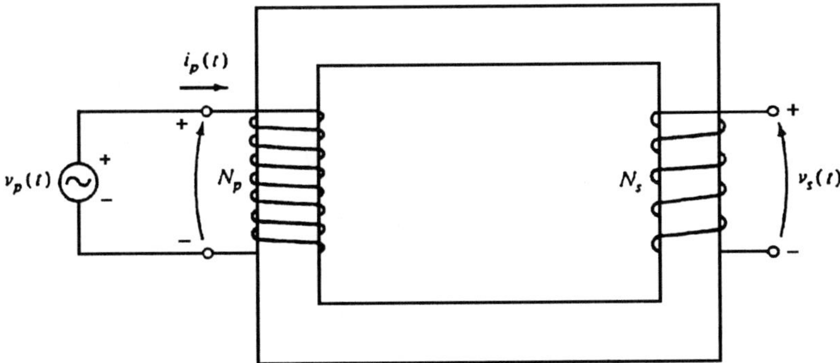

FIGURE 28.6 Sketch of a real transformer with no load attached to its secondary.

The effect of this flux on the secondary coil of the transformer depends on how much of the flux reaches the secondary coil. Only a portion of the flux produced in the primary coil reaches the secondary coil.

Some of the flux lines pass through the surrounding air instead of passing through the iron core (Fig. 28.7). The *leakage flux* is the portion of the flux that passes through one of the coils but not the other.

The flux in the primary coil can be divided into two components: (1) a *mutual flux,* which remains in the core and links both coils (windings), and (2) a small *leakage flux,* which passes through the primary winding and returns through air, bypassing the secondary winding:

$$\boxed{\bar{\phi}_P = \phi_M + \phi_{LP}}$$

where $\bar{\phi}_P$ = total average primary flux
ϕ_M = flux component linking both primary and secondary coils
ϕ_{LP} = primary leakage flux

Similarly, the flux in the secondary winding is divided between the mutual and leakage fluxes, which pass through the secondary winding and return through air, bypassing the primary winding:

$$\boxed{\bar{\phi}_S = \phi_M + \phi_{LS}}$$

where $\bar{\phi}_S$ = total average secondary flux
ϕ_M = flux component linking both primary and secondary coils
ϕ_{LS} = secondary leakage flux

The primary circuit can be expressed as

$$\begin{aligned} v_P(t) &= N_P \frac{d\bar{\phi}_P}{dt} \\ &= N_P \frac{d\phi_M}{dt} + N_P \frac{d\phi_{LP}}{dt} \end{aligned}$$

The first term is $e_P(t)$, and the second is $e_{LP}(t)$

$$v_P\,(t) = e_P\,(t) + e_{LP}\,(t)$$

The voltage in the secondary coil is expressed as

$$\begin{aligned} v_S\,(t) &= N_S \frac{d\bar{\phi}_S}{dt} \\ &= N_S \frac{d\phi_M}{dt} + N_S \frac{d\phi_{LS}}{dt} \\ &= e_S(t) + e_{LS}(t) \end{aligned}$$

the mutual flux is

$$\frac{e_P(t)}{N_P} = \frac{d\phi_M}{dt} = \frac{e_S(t)}{N_S}$$

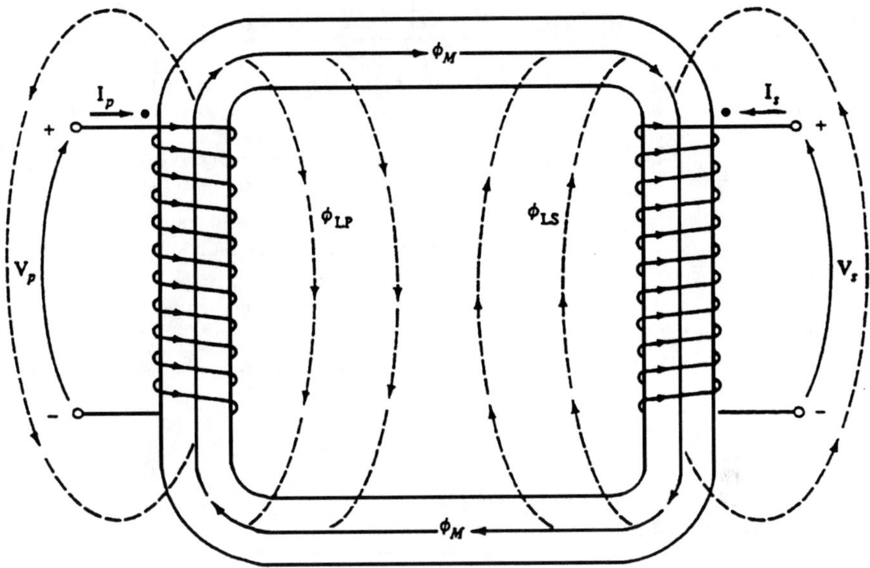

FIGURE 28.7 Mutual and leakage fluxes in a transformer core.

Therefore,

$$\boxed{\frac{e_P(t)}{e_S(t)} = \frac{N_P}{N_S} = a}$$

This equation indicates that the ratio of the *primary voltage caused by the mutual flux to the secondary voltage caused by the mutual flux is equal to the turns ratio of the transformer.*

In well-designed transformers, $\phi_M >> \phi_{LP}$ and $\phi_M >> \phi_{LS}$, the ratio of the total voltage on the primary and the total voltage on the secondary is approximately

$$\frac{v_P(t)}{v_S(t)} \approx \frac{N_P}{N_S} = a$$

THE MAGNETIZING CURRENT IN A REAL TRANSFORMER

When the AC power source is connected to a transformer, a current flows in the primary winding, *even when the secondary winding is open-circuited.* This is the current required to produce the flux in the ferromagnetic core. It consists of these two components:

1. *Magnetization current i_m.* The current required to produce the flux in the core of the transformer
2. *Core-loss current i_{h+e}.* The current required to make up for the hysteresis and eddy current losses

THE EQUIVALENT CIRCUIT OF A TRANSFORMER

Any accurate model of transformer behavior should show the losses that occur in real transformers. The four major items that should be considered in such a model include:

1. *Copper losses.* These are the resistive losses in the primary and secondary windings of the transformer. They are proportional to the square of the current in the windings.
2. *Eddy current losses.* These are the resistive heating losses in the core of the transformer. They are proportional to the square of the voltage applied to the transformer.
3. *Hysteresis losses.* These are associated with the rearrangement of the magnetic domains in the core during each half-cycle. They are the nonlinear function of the voltage applied to the transformer.
4. *Leakage flux.* The fluxes, ϕ_{LP} and ϕ_{LS}, which pass through only one winding, escaping the core. A self-inductance in the primary and secondary windings is associated with these escape fluxes. The effects of these inductances must be included in any transformer model.

THE EXACT EQUIVALENT CIRCUIT OF A REAL TRANSFORMER

The copper losses can be modeled by placing a resistor, R_P and R_S, in the primary and secondary circuits, respectively. A voltage e_{LP} is produced by the leakage flux in the primary winding ϕ_{LP}. It is given by

$$e_{LP}(t) = N_P \frac{d\phi_{LP}}{dt}$$

Similarly, in the secondary winding, the voltage produced is

$$e_{LS}(t) = N_S \frac{d\phi_{LS}}{dt}$$

Since the leakage flux passes through air, and air has *constant* reluctance much higher than the reluctance of the core, the flux ϕ_{LP} is proportional to the current in the windings:

$$\phi_{LP} = (\mathcal{P}N_P)\, i_P \qquad \phi_{LS} = (\mathcal{P}N_S)\, i_S$$

where $\mathcal{P}$ = permeance of flux path
N_P = number of turns on primary coil
N_S = number of turns on secondary coil

By substituting these equations into the previous ones, the result is

$$e_{LP}(t) = N_P \frac{d}{dt}(\mathcal{P}N_P)\, i_P = N_P^2 \mathcal{P} \frac{di_P}{dt}$$

$$e_{LS}(t) = N_S \frac{d}{dt}(\mathcal{P}N_S)\, i_S = N_S^2 \mathcal{P} \frac{di_S}{dt}$$

By lumping the constants together, then

$$e_{\mathrm{LP}}(t) = L_P \frac{di_P}{dt}$$

$$e_{\mathrm{LS}}(t) = L_S \frac{di_S}{dt}$$

where L_P and L_S are the self-inductances of the primary and secondary windings, respectively. Therefore, the leakage flux will be modeled as an inductor.

The magnetization current i_m is proportional (in the unsaturated region) to the voltage applied to the core but lags the applied voltage by 90°. Hence, it can be modeled as a reactance X_M connected across the primary voltage source.

The core-loss current i_{h+e} is proportional to the voltage applied to the core and in phase with it. Hence, it can be modeled as a resistance R_c connected across the primary voltage source.

Figure 28.8 illustrates the equivalent circuit of a real transformer. Although Fig. 28.8 represents an accurate model of a transformer, it is not a very useful one. The entire circuit is normally converted to an equivalent circuit at a single voltage level. This equivalent circuit is referred to its primary or secondary side (Fig. 28.9).

APPROXIMATE EQUIVALENT CIRCUITS OF A TRANSFORMER

In practical engineering applications, the exact transformer model is more complex than necessary in order to get good results. Since the excitation branch has a very small current compared to the load current of the transformers, a simplified equivalent circuit is produced. The excitation branch is moved to the front of the transformer, and the primary and secondary impedances are added, creating equivalent circuits [Fig. 28.10 (*a, b*)]. In some applications, the excitation branch is neglected entirely without causing serious error [Fig. 28.10 (*c, d*)].

REFERENCE

1. Chapman, S. J., *Electric Machinery Fundamentals*, 2d ed., McGraw-Hill, New York, 1991.

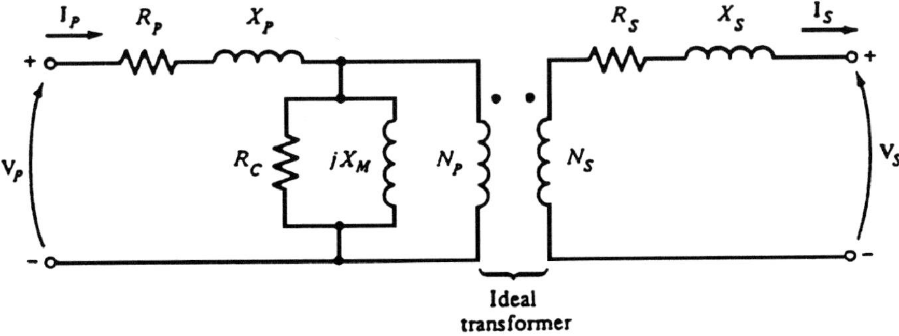

FIGURE 28.8 The model of a real transformer.

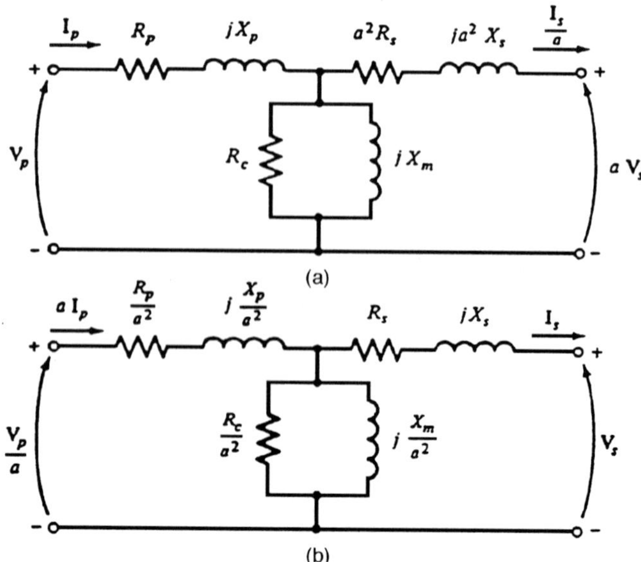

FIGURE 28.9 (*a*) The transformer model referred to its primary voltage level; (*b*) the transformer model referred to its secondary voltage level.

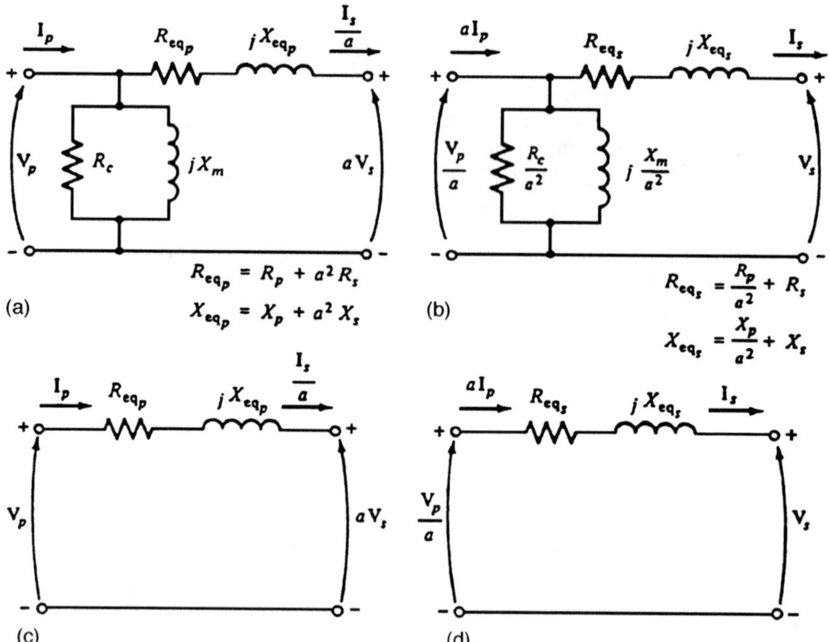

FIGURE 28.10 Approximate transformer models: (*a*) Referred to the primary side; (*b*) referred to the secondary side; (*c*) with no excitation branch, referred to the primary side; (*d*) with no excitation branch, referred to the secondary side.

CHAPTER 29
TRANSFORMER COMPONENTS AND MAINTENANCE

Electric power is generated most economically at 14 to 25 kV.[1] System loads such as motors, lights, and so on, require a voltage source of 440, 220, and 110 V. Transformers are needed to change the voltage level. They are also used for these reasons:

- To reduce transmission losses between power plants and the load by stepping up the voltage (when the voltage is stepped-up, the current will be stepped down. This results in reduction in transmission losses, which are proportional to the square of the current).
- To reduce the diameter of the transmission line (amount of copper or aluminum) due to a reduction in the current flowing in the line.

Typical transmission voltages are 13.2, 22, 66, 230, 345, and 500 kV. In general, the longer the distance, the higher the voltage used.

CLASSIFICATION OF TRANSFORMERS

The two types of transformers are: (1) air-cooled (dry-type), and (2) oil-filled. The transformer rating increases with improved cooling methods. These are the typical ratings for various types of transformers:

Dry Transformers

The two types of dry transformers are self-air-cooled and forced-air-cooled. The heat is removed by natural convection in self-air-cooled transformers. In forced-air-cooled, it is removed by blowers. The rating of dry-type transformers used to be limited to less than 1 MVA. However, modern technology pushed this rating to 20 MVA. This was mainly due to improvements in the quality of insulation and mechanisms of heat removal from the transformer.

Oil-Immersed Transformers

In this type of transformer, the windings and core are immersed in oil. The main types of oil-immersed transformers are

- Oil-immersed self-cooled (heat is removed by natural convection of the oil through radiators)

- Oil-immersed cooled by forced air (heat is removed by blowers blowing air on radiators)
- Oil-immersed cooled by water (the oil is cooled by an oil-water heat exchanger)

The lowest rating of oil-type transformers is around 750 kVA. Since modern dry-type transformers are being manufactured up to a rating of 20 MVA, they are replacing oil-type transformers. The main reason is that oil-immersed transformers constitute a fire hazard and they are very hard to maintain. Dry-type transformers are preferred in most industries.

The rating of oil-immersed, cooled-by-water transformers is normally higher than 100 MVA. However, they could be used for transformers having a rating as low as 10 MVA if the transformer is feeding a rectifier. *Harmonics* (deformation in the sine-wave of current and voltage) are normally generated in this application causing significant heat generation that necessitates cooling through a heat exchanger.

Most failures in transformers are caused by erosion of the insulating materials. Analysis of a transformer's oil can provide trends and early warning signs of premature failure.

Figure 29.1 illustrates a basic electric power system from the utility to the consumer.

MAIN COMPONENTS OF A POWER TRANSFORMER

Figure 29.2 illustrates the outline drawing of a transformer. Figure 29.3 illustrates a cut-away view of an oil-filled transformer.

The 17 main components of the transformer are as follows:

1. *Concrete base.* To provide support for the transformer. It must be leveled and fire-resistant.
2. *Core.* Provides a route for the magnetic flux and supports the low-voltage and high-voltage windings.
3. *Low-voltage winding.* It has fewer truns compared with the high voltage windings. Its conductor has a large diameter because it carries more current.
4. *High-voltage winding.* It has a larger number of turns, and its conductor has a smaller diameter than the low-voltage winding conductor. The high-voltage winding is usually wound around the low-voltage winding (only cooling ducts and insulation separate the windings). This is done to minimize the voltage stress on the core insulation.

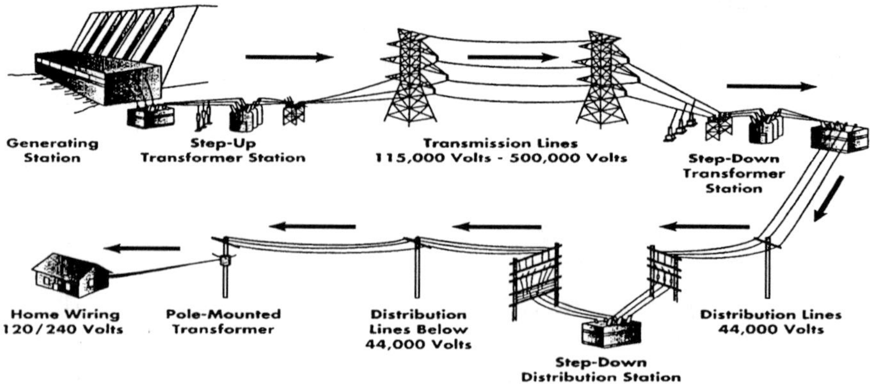

FIGURE 29.1 Basic electric power system.

5. *Tank.* Houses the windings, core, and oil. It must be strong enough to withstand the gas pressures and electromagnetic forces that could develop when a fault occurs.
6. *Oil.* It is a good-quality mineral oil. It provides insulation between the windings, core, and transformer tank. It also removes the heat generated. The oil is specially refined, and it must be free from impurities such as water, inorganic acid, alkali, sulphur, vegetable and mineral oil.

   Note: Some transformers use askarel, which is a nonflammable insulating and cooling medium instead of insulating oil. It gives good fire protection, which is a significant advantage when the transformer is located inside a building. However, askarel contains polychlorinated biphenals (PCBs). They have been linked to cancer-causing substances. Therefore, they have been banned. Most industries are now in the process of replacing transformers containing askarel with dry-type transformers or transformers containing mineral oil.
7. *Thermometer.* Measures the oil temperature and initiates an alarm when the temperature exceeds the alarm setpoint.
8. *Low/high-voltage bushing.* Ceramic bushing that carries the low/high-voltage conductor and insulates it from the tank. The high-voltage bushing is usually filled with oil to enhance the heat removal capability.
9. *Low/high-voltage connection.* Connects the low/high-voltage conductor to the circuit.
10. *Conservator tank.* It contains oil and has the capability of absorbing the swell of the oil when it becomes hot.
11. *Gas detector relay.* Electrical faults are characterized by the formation of gas. In the early stages of the fault, small quantities of gas are liberated. The amount of gas formed increases with time and a violent explosion could occur. Most of the damage and expense can be saved if the fault can be discovered and corrected in its early stages. The gas detector relay detects gas build-up in the tank. Any gas generation inside the transformer passes through it. It has two parts. One detects large rate of gas production which could be caused by a major fault (such as hydrogen, acetylene, and carbon monoxide). The second part detects the slow accumulation of air and gases which are released from the oil, when it gets warm or from minor arcs. When the gas level reaches a predetermined amount, an alarm is annunciated. The relay has also the capability to trip the transformer in case of a serious fault which would result in a sudden rush of oil or gas through it.
12. *Explosion vent.* It prevents the build-up of high pressure in the tank due to gas formation (caused by oil disintegration) when a fault occurs. A relief diaphragm at the end of the explosion vent, ruptures when the gas pressure reaches a certain predetermined value to relief the pressure to atmosphere.
13. *Oil level.* The oil level changes with the temperature of the oil. The core and winding must always be immersed in oil to ensure they are adequately cooled and insulated.
14. *Sight glass.* Indicate oil level.
15. *Breather.* Allows air movement to the conservator upon swell and shrinkage of the oil. It has a silica gel (air dryer) to remove moisture from the air entering the conservator tank. The transformer oil must be kept dry always. A water content of 8 p.p.m (parts per million) in the oil will reduce the dielectric strength to a dangerous level. Oxygen has also adverse consequences on the oil (it oxidizes it resulting in the formation sludge). Some transformers have a seal of inert gas (Nitrogen) between the oil and atmosphere to prevent oxygen and moisture from reaching the oil.
16. *Radiator.* It is a heat exchanger which cools the oil by natural circulation.
17. *Ground connection.* The tank is connected to ground (earth) to ensure safety of maintenance personnel.

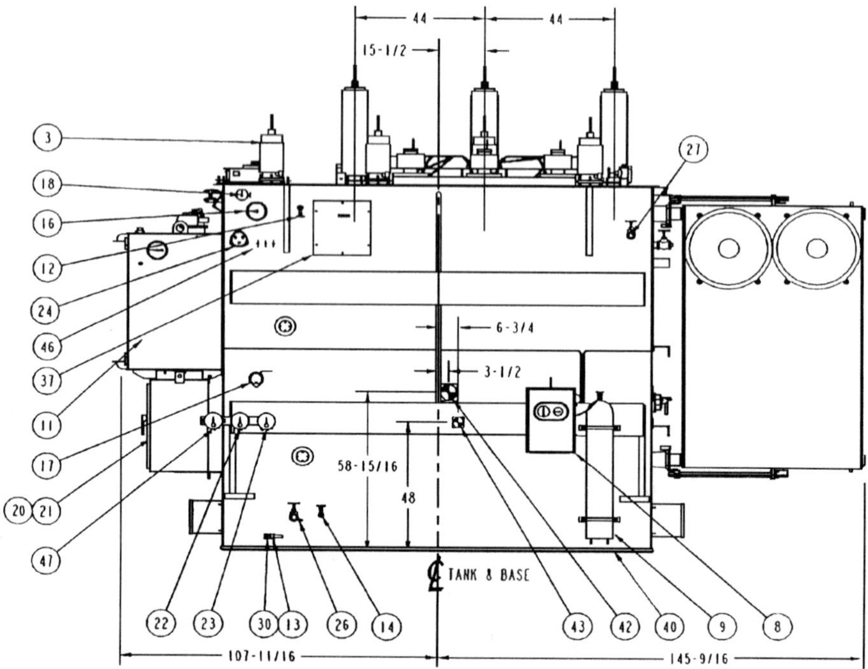

Legend for Outline Drawing

1. 3 H. V. bushings; 69 kV, 350 kV B.I.L. 400 amps, C/W 1.50″-12 silver-plated stud. 2″ usable thread length. LAPP Cat #B-88726-70. Internal bushing lead is drawlead connected. Shipping weight per bushing is 139 lb.
2. 3 L. V. bushings; 25 kV, 150 kV B.I.L. 2000 amps, C/W 1.50″-12 silver-plated stud. 2.5″ usable thread length. LAPP Cat # B-88723-70. Internal lead is bottom connected.
3. 1 L. V. neutral bushings; 25 kV, 150 kV B.I.L. 2000 amps, C/W 1.50″-12 silver-plated stud. 2.5″ usable thread length. LAPP Cat # B-88723-70. Internal lead is bottom connected.
4. 3 H. V. lightning arresters, 60 kV, 48 kV MCOV. Ohio brass polymer housed, station class PVN 314048-3001. Shipping weight of arrester is 53.6 lb.
5. H. V. lightning arrester supports C/W seismic bracing. Shipping weight of supports is 304 lb.
6. 3 L. V. lightning arresters, 9 kV, 7.65 kV MCOV. Ohio brass polymer housed, station class PVN 314008-3001. Shipping weight of arrester is 21.3 lb.
7. L. V. lightning arrester supports C/W seismic bracing. Shipping weight of supports is 138 lb.
8. Nitrogen preservation system, ABB Type RNB, In a hinged, lockable door compartment C/W regulators, cylinder pressure gauge, empty cylinder alarm switch, transformer tank pressure/vacuum gauge, high- & low-tank-pressure alarm switches & tank gas space sampling valve. Connected to a nitrogen cylinder.
9. Nitrogen cylinder.
10. Deenergized tap changer handle C/W position indicator & provision for padlocking.
11. Load tap changer, Reinhausen Type RMV-II, C/W Qualitrol Self-Sealing Pressure Relief Device # 208-60U, C/W deflector, alarm contacts & semaphore, liquid level indicator C/W contacts, 1-1/2″ NPT drain valve with sampler, dehydrating breather, vacuum interrupters and monitoring system. (See wiring diagram.)
12. 2 - 1″ globe valves located approximately 6′ below cover.
13. Ground connectors, Anderson # SW11-025-B.
14. 1″ globe valve and plug.
15. 2 - Multiaxis impact recorders (one at each end). To be returned to Ferranti-Packard.
16. Magnetic liquid level indicator C/W contacts. (See wiring diagram.)

FIGURE 29.2 Transformer outline drawing, Los Medanos Energy Center. *(Courtesy of VA Tech Ferranti-Packard Transformers.)*

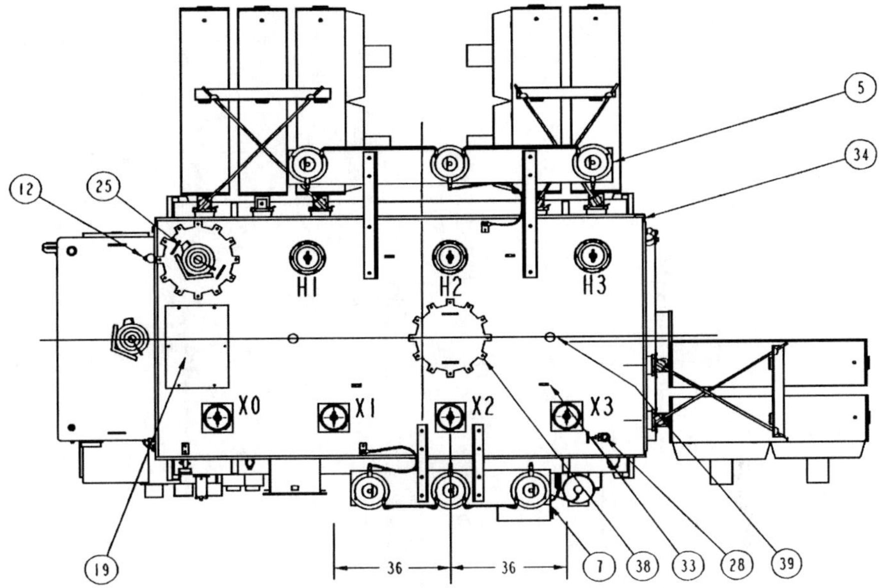

Legend for Outline Drawing (*cont.*)

17. Rapid pressure rise relay C/W contacts. Located under oil. (See wiring diagram.)
18. Pressure vacuum gauge C/W bleeder.
19. C. T. outlet box for current transformer leads continued to control cabinet.
20. Weatherproof control cabinet C/W LTC motor drive and C/W 7″ × 21-1/4″ opening(s) in bottom.
21. Nameplate.
22. Liquid temperature indicator C/W contacts. (See wiring diagram.)
23. Winding temperature indicator C/W Contacts. (See wiring diagram.)
24. Thermowell for liquid temperature indicator and winding temperature indicator.
25. Qualitrol Self-Sealing Pressure Relief Device # 208-60U C/W deflector, alarm contacts & semaphore. (See wiring diagram.)
26. 2″ NPT globe valve for draining C/W sampler.
27. 2″ NPT top filter press globe valve.
28. 2″ NPT globe valve located on tank cover for vacuum filling.
29. 2″ NPT globe valve (for F.P. Use).
30. Copper-faced ground pads.
31. 4 - Transformer lifting lugs, each C/W a 2-1/2″ dia. hole. Use slings with minimum leg length of 12 ft.
32. 4 - Transformer jacking steps.
33. Cover lifting lugs.
34. Tank cover (welded on).
35. 7 Detachable cooling radiators C/W shutoff valves, lifting lugs, 1″ NPT top vent C/W brass plug and 1″ NPT bottom drain plug. Shipping weight per radiator is 1336 lb.
36. 9 Cooling fans C/W guards, 2 stages. (See wiring diagram.) Shipping weight per fan is 35 lb.
37. Accessible core ground(s), inside box C/W 5-kV bushings.
38. 2 - 18″ dia. manholes.
39. Safety harness anchor rod (for F.P. use).
40. Slab base suitable for skidding and rolling in both directions.
41. 2 sets of seismic radiator bracing per radiator bank (1 at top & 1 at bottom). Shipping weight per set is 41 lb.)
42. Center of gravity—operation.

FIGURE 29.2 (*Continued*) Transformer outline drawing, Los Medanos Energy Center. *(Courtesy of VA Tech Ferranti-Packard Transformers.)*

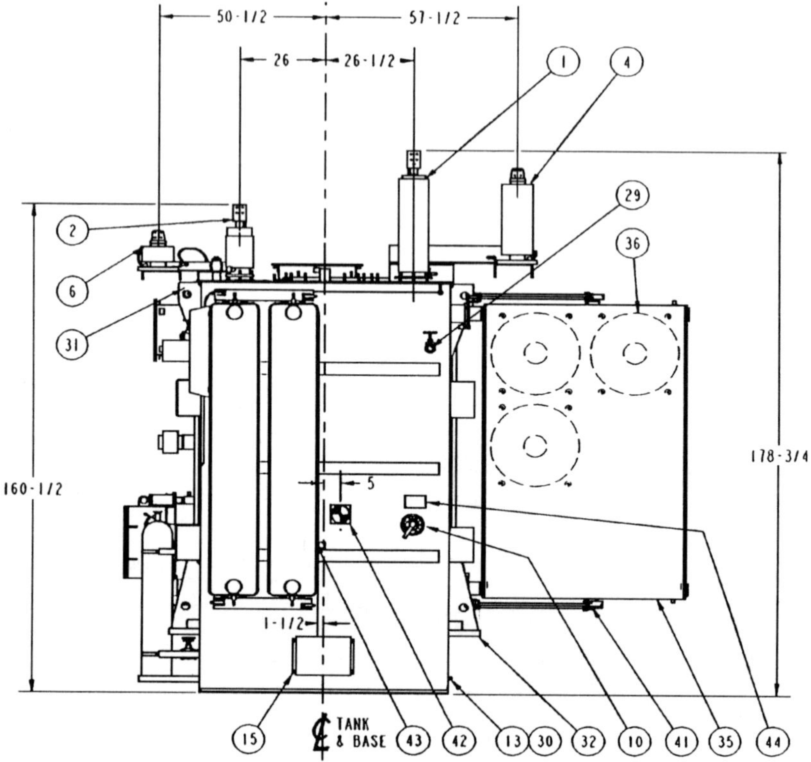

Legend for Outline Drawing (*cont.*)

43. Center of gravity—shipping.
44. Warning plate—deenergized tap changer.
45. Bushing terminal connectors on HV, LV & neutral bushings are SEFCOR # SNFT-44-4B-SND (tin plated).
46. Liquid cover mark (+ + +).
47. Thermal load gauge center. (See wiring diagram.)

Notes:

- [Bracketed] Items in legend are removed for shipping.
- Oil is removed for shipping.

Transformer rating data	Estimated mass of components		
Oil-filled transformer	Core & windings		44,855 lb
3-phase 60 Hz 55°/65°C rise	Tank & fittings		24,257 lb
Type: OA / FA / FA	Removable pads		9,353 lb
MVA: 18 / 24 / 30		U.S. Gal.	
H.V. - 67000 delta	Liquid (trans)	4969	36,111 lb
L.V. - 12470 wye	Liquid (rads)	492	3,574 lb
Tank characteristics	Liquid (LTC)	280	2,032 lb
Tank strength: ±14.7 P.S.I.	Total liquid	5741	41,717 lb
Tank size: 73 × 145 × 133-1/2″	**Total mass**		120,183 lb
Paint: ANSI 70 gray	**Shipping mass**		72,000 lb

FIGURE 29.2 (*Continued*) Transformer outline drawing, Los Medanos Energy Center. *(Courtesy of VA Tech Ferranti-Packard Transformers.)*

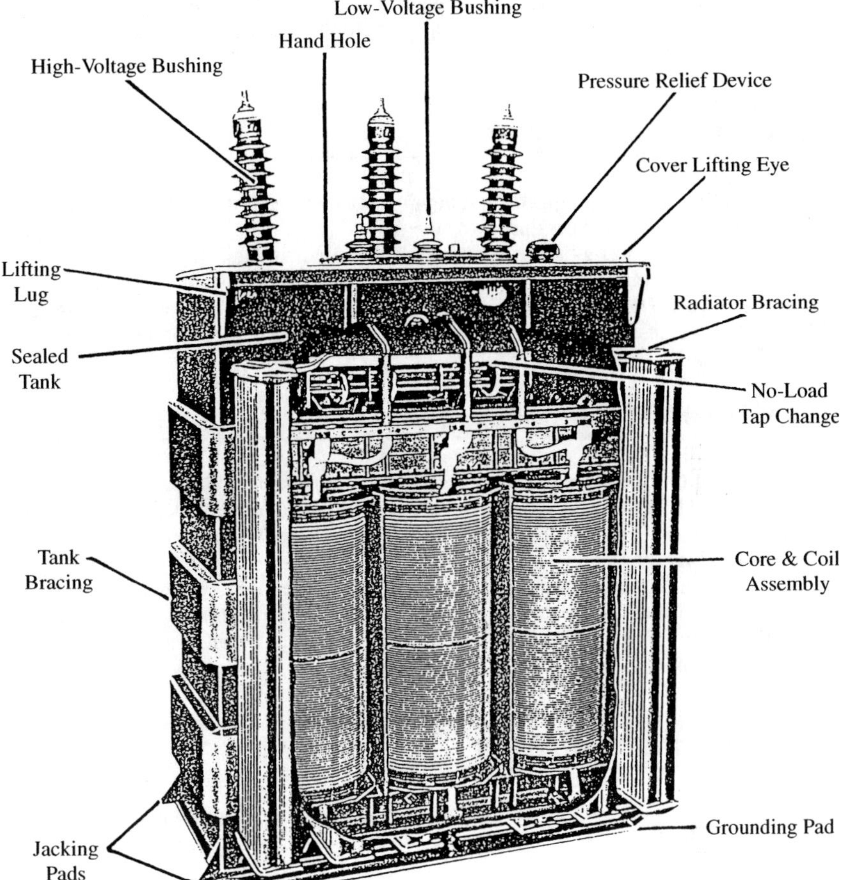

FIGURE 29.3 Cut-away view of a power transformer.

TRANSFORMER CORE

The core is made from thousands of laminations of grain-oriented steel. The thickness of a lamination is around 12 mils. Each lamination is coated with a thin layer of insulating material. The windings have a circular cross section. They are normally concentric. The lowest-voltage winding is placed next to the core to reduce the voltage stress. There is a layer of insulation between the low-voltage winding and the core. There are also oil ducts and insulating barriers between the coils. The core is grounded at one point. The ground connection is normally accessible externally for test purposes.

WINDINGS

The windings must be able to withstand the large mechanical forces created by a short circuit. The winding insulation must be able to withstand the highest operating temperature without excessive degradation. The cooling fluid must be able to flow freely through spaces between the windings to remove the heat. The windings are arranged concentrically. The highest voltage is located on the outside.

NITROGEN DEMAND SYSTEM

Many transformers are equipped with an automatic nitrogen demand system. It regulates the pressure in the transformer during the thermal cycles of the oil (swell and shrinkage of the oil). Nitrogen is used as a buffer gas between the oil and the air. Its purpose is to separate outside air (containing water vapor) from contacting the oil. The water vapor has devastating effects on the oil. The dew point of nitrogen is less than $-50°C$ to ensure that it is very dry. Most units have an alarm indicating low nitrogen pressure in the cylinder.

CONSERVATOR TANK WITH AIR CELL

The conservator air cell preservation system is an expansion tank located above the main transformer tank. It provides a head of oil so that the transformer tank is always filled. The quality of oil in the transformer is preserved by sealing it from contaminants such as moisture and oxygen (Fig. 29.4).

Air is drawn into the air cell (part 1) or expelled through the breather (part 2) as the oil level changes. The air cell prevents the transformer oil from coming in direct contact with atmospheric air. The air cell will inflate and deflate as the oil volume changes in the conservator tank.

CURRENT TRANSFORMERS

Current transformers (CT) are auxiliary transformers used normally for metering or operation of auxiliary equipment and relays. They could be located inside or outside the tank assembly.

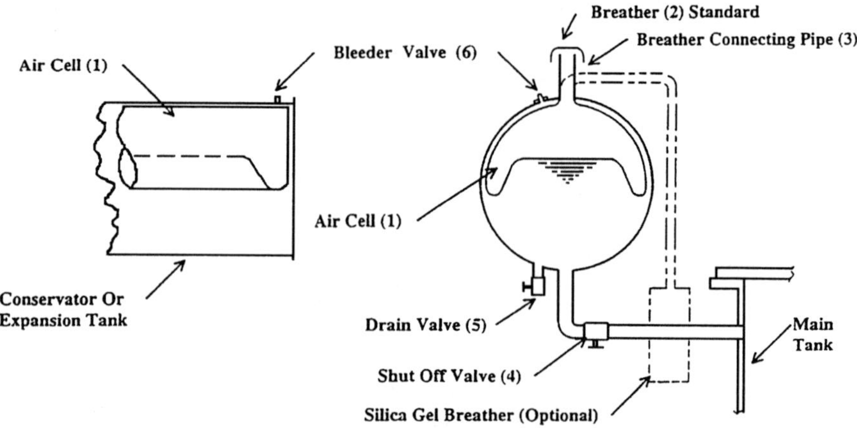

FIGURE 29.4 Conservator tank with air cell.

BUSHINGS

A *bushing* is an insulated conductor passing through a cover of a piece of enclosed electrical equipment. The bushing carries the current through it and seals the opening against weather or oil pressure. It also supports the leads and provides protection against flashover due to overvoltage or heavy contamination (Fig. 29.5).

A bushing having a voltage of less than 35 kV consists of a current-carrying conductor, an epoxy or porcelain insulator, and a mechanical assembly to hold it all together. It also has terminals on the top and bottom for connection. The bushing is filled with oil for cooling.

TAP CHANGERS

Many transformers have on-load or off-load tap changers. They change the effective number of the windings in the transformer to maintain the secondary voltage constant.

INSULATION

Figure 29.6 shows the main components of a power transformer and the major uses of Kraft paper. The winding insulation is normally made of paper. Cellulose board is also used as internal insulation in liquid-filled transformers. Cellulose insulation is impregnable with the insulating fluid of the transformer. This maintains a uniform dielectric stress throughout the transformer.

Types and Features of Insulation

1. Low-density calendared board, available in flat and formed parts in thicknesses of up to 0.188 in.
2. Laminated low-density calendared board using dextrin resin.
3. High-density precompressed board designed for high mechanical strength and dimensional stability. The dimensional stability is important for the long life of the transformer. It ensures that the windings do not loosen over time. This insulation is used for space ducts in the transformer.
4. Laminated high-density boards using polyester resin. This material is typically used for clamping plates at each end of the transformer windings. It is completely impregnable with oil despite its high density. This ensures freedom from partial discharge.

Aramid is another type of insulation used in power transformers. It is chemically similar to nylon. It is completely impregnable with oil. It is generally known as Nomex. It has high strength and it can withstand an operating temperature of 170°C without deterioration (cellulose insulation can only withstand 105°C). However, Nomex is very expensive (about 10 times more than cellulose insulation). In general, Nomex is not cost-effective for use as a major insulation in a power transformer.

Reasons for Deterioration

Insulation deteriorates due to the following:

- Heat

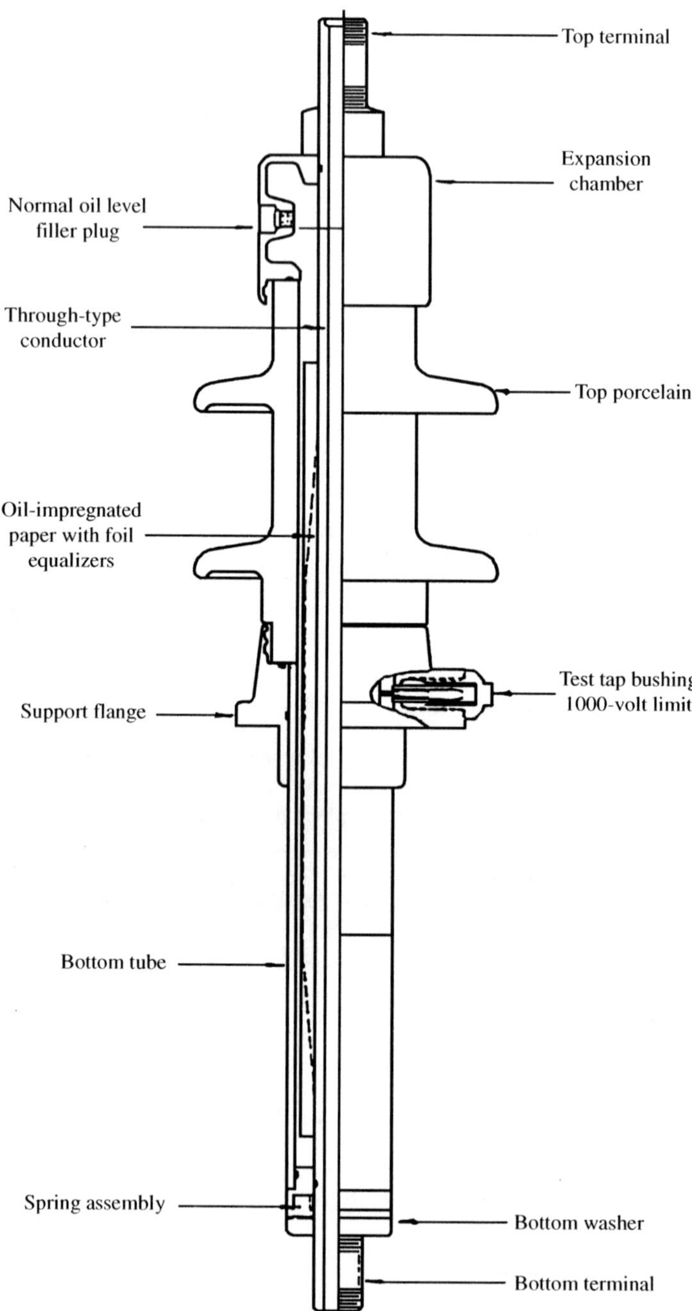

FIGURE 29.5 Typical bushing construction.

Kraft paper providing turn to turn insulation of winding coil.
Conductor tap leads wrapped in paper insulation.
End rings using dense pressboard to aid in mechanical strength. Spaced to also provide for cooling of the inner winding(s).
Dense pressboard used for support.

FIGURE 29.6 Three-phase power transformer (75/125 MVA).

- Contamination such as dirt, moisture, or oxygen
- Electrical stress
- Mechanical stress and strain

Insulation deterioration normally results in the loss of its mechanical properties. As the insulation weakens, it loses flexibility and becomes brittle. It would not be able to resist the mechanical stresses resulting from the magnetic forces, differential temperature expansion, and vibration. The insulation disintegrates, leading to electrical faults.

FORCES

During normal operation, the axial and radial forces between the windings are moderate. These forces become severe during a short circuit. The transformer must be able to withstand fault conditions. This includes forces 10 times higher than normal. Figure 29.7 illustrates damaged top and bottom coils in a transformer.

CAUSE OF TRANSFORMER FAILURES

Most transformers fail due to mechanical reasons. The windings are subjected to physical forces that operate in all directions. These forces can become astronomical under short-circuit conditions. For example, a 16-MVA transformer will develop a 500,000-lb vertical force and a hoop force (horizontal) of 3 million lb. Therefore, the windings must be braced to withstand these forces. If the windings are not properly braced, physical movement occurs. Short circuit is developed leading to transformer failure. Therefore, the root cause of electrical faults is mechanical in nature.

When the Kraft paper is impregnable with a good, clean, dry oil, it becomes one of the best dielectrics known in the industry. Water has devastating effects on Kraft paper. Most transformers fail due to the presence of water. The water that weakens the Kraft paper is the *microscopic* droplets formed by paper degradation and oil oxidation (Fig. 29.8). The water droplets are produced by the inner layers of paper and oil that are trapped between the coil (copper or aluminum) and the paper. The water acts as a solvent to dissolve and weaken the paper by

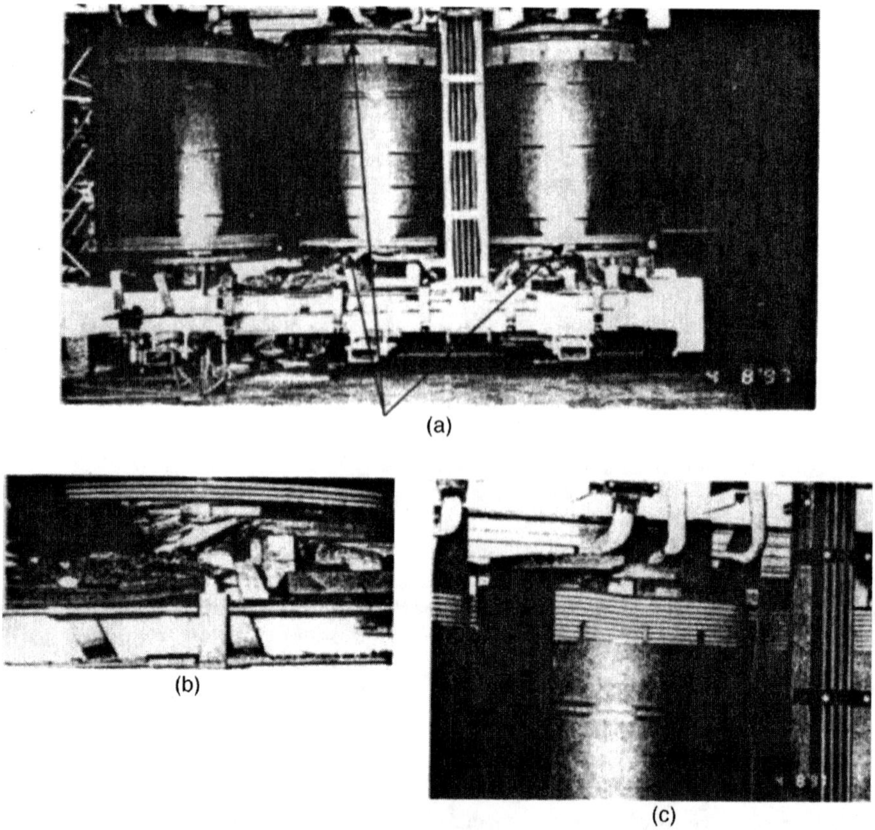

(a)

(b)

(c)

FIGURE 29.7 (*a*) Examples of damage to top and bottom coils in a transformer; (*b*) bottom view of coil; (*c*) top view of coil.

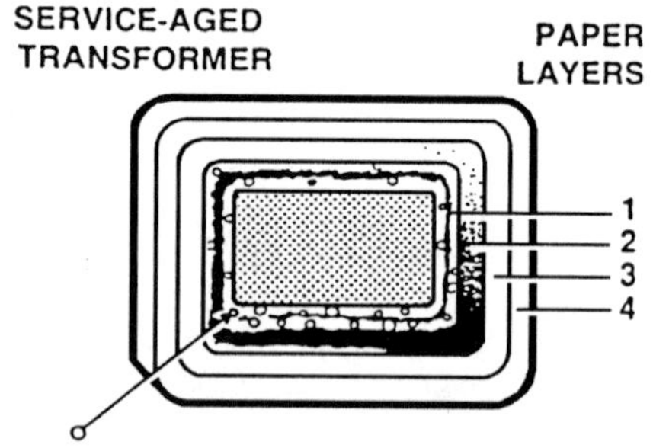

FIGURE 29.8 Water in microscopic droplets that cause the Kraft paper to dissolve from oil decay products.

destroying the fiber of the Kraft paper. This results in loosening the windings. The paper insulation will get abraded by the constant moving of the windings. A total failure is created by having a failure in an extremely small amount of the paper in the transformer. Adequate measures must be taken early, and promptly, to protect the transformer.

The water generated in the "innards of the transformer" that causes the destruction of the unit is significantly below the level of detection through oil test procedures and/or electrical testing. Therefore, advanced deterioration would have already occurred by the time the evidence appears in the test data. A suitable solution involves continuous dehydration of the transformer during normal operation. A less expensive solution involves servicing the transformer every 3 to 5 years.

The amount of moisture in the paper of a transformer is expressed as the *percentage of moisture by dry weight* (% M/dw). The aging factor is controlled by controlling the % M/dw. The upper limit of 0.5% M/dw should be specified when a transformer is selected. If this limit is not specified, the moisture content could be as high as 1.5 to 2.0% M/dw.

Figure 29.9 illustrates the aging factor versus % M/dw. As shown, moisture weakens the Kraft paper. This weakening is measured and expressed by the *aging factor* (AF). Notice the significant increase of the AF with % M/dw. Figure 29.10 illustrates the significant decrease in transformer life expectancy with % M/dw.

Most transformers fail at the bottom due to a high % M/dw. This is caused by the fact that paper has up to 3000 times higher affinity for water than oil does at lower temperatures.

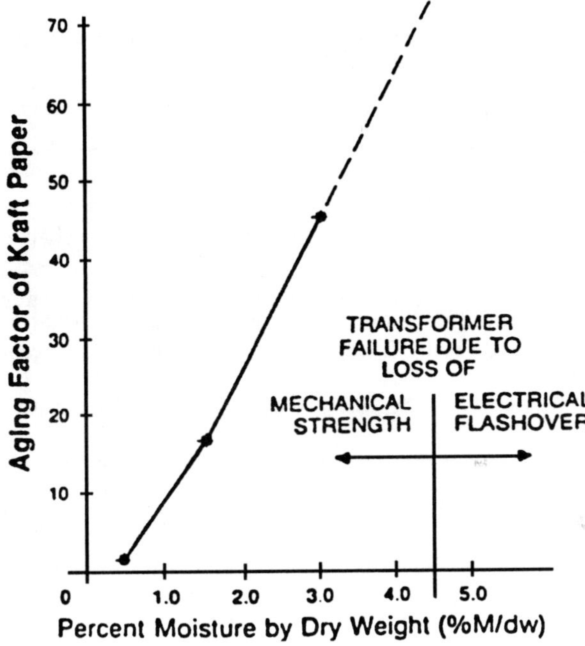

FIGURE 29.9 Variation of AF with % M/dw.

TRANSFORMER OIL

The oil acts as an insulation and cooling medium for the transformer. The mineral oil used in transformers normally has these six features:

1. A high flash point to minimize fire hazard.
2. It is nonvolatile at operating temperatures to avoid evaporation losses.
3. It has a low pour point.
4. It remains as a liquid at the lowest ambient temperatures expected.
5. It is stable and inert.
6. It resists oxidation, which increases acidity and formation of sludge.

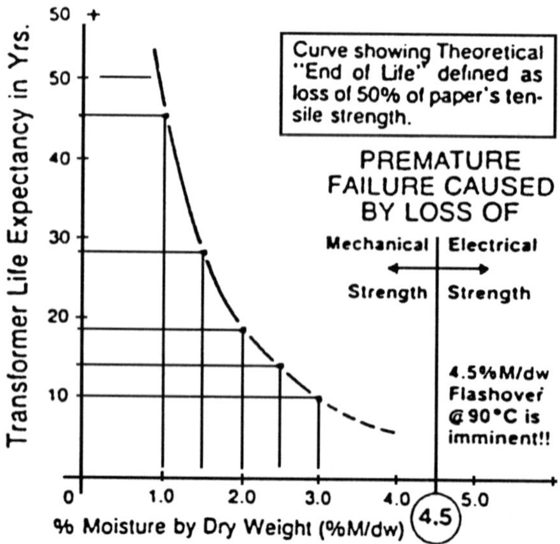

FIGURE 29.10 Variation of transformer life expectancy with % M/dw.

Table 29.1 lists all the oil tests and when they are normally performed. The private industry usually performs the following tests only: dielectric breakdown, neutralization number (NN), interfacial tension (IFT), specific gravity, color, and visual exams. The remaining tests may be done when necessary.

The visual examination consists of checking the color of the oil . The color varies from the following:

[Clear (like water). Acidity: 0.01 to 0.03 mgKOH/g. Interfacial tension: 30 to 45 dynes/cm.]

to

[Black. Acidity: 1.01 mgKOH/g and higher. Interfacial tension: 6 to 9 dynes/cm.]

The acceptable conditions range from clear to amber (acidity: 0.15 mgKOH/g; interfacial tension: 22 dynes/cm).

TESTING TRANSFORMER INSULATING OIL

The functions of the oil in the transformer are

- Provide insulation
- Provide efficient cooling
- Protect the windings and core from chemical attack
- Prevent the buildup of sludge in the transformer

The condition of the oil in the transformer determines the transformer life. Annual testing is the *minimum* requirement to ensure acceptable dielectric strength for the oil. These are the benefits of annual testing:

- *Indicate the internal condition of the transformer.* It detects the presence of sludge. The sludge must be purged before it can precipitate on the windings and other surfaces inside the transformer.

TABLE 29.1 Insulating Oil Tests Available

ASTM test method	Test name	Units	Used oil	New oil	Aging analysis	Fault analysis
D-877/D-1816	Dielectric breakdown	kV		♦		
D-974	Neutralization number	Mg KOH/g	♦	♦		
D-924	Power factor@100°C	%		♦		
D-924	Power factor @25°C	%	♦			
D-971	Interfacial tension	Dynes/cm	♦	♦		
D-1500	Color	Scale 0.5–8.0	♦	♦		
D-1298	Specific gravity	@15°C	♦	♦		
	PCB	ppm	♦	♦		
	Water content	ppm	♦	♦		
D-97	Pour point	°C	♦	♦		
D-1935	Steam emulsion	Seconds		♦		
D-92	Flash point	°C		♦		
D-445	Viscosity	°C		♦		
D-2440	Stability test			♦		
	Carbon content	Ppm (g/kg)				♦
	Metal particles					♦
	Oxidation inhibitors				♦	
	Furans	ppb			♦	
	Degree of polymerization	Units P_v			♦	

- *Indicate any deteriorating trends.* The naphthenic insulating oils used in transformers today have been used for more than 50 years. The deteriorating trend of these oils is well known. Many data are available to permit the comparison between normal and abnormal oil.
- *Prevent a forced outage.* Incipient problems are detected early. Corrective action is scheduled with minimal disruption. The tests that are required for transformer oil are listed in Table 29.2. The results of one test only cannot indicated the condition of the oil. The true condition of the oil is obtained by considering the combined results of the eight tests together (especially the first four tests).

The ASTM D-877 (flat-disc electrode) is the classical test for determining the dielectric strength of the oil. It will detect contaminants such as free water, dirt, or other conducting particles. However, it will not detect the presence of dissolved water, acid, or sludge.

CAUSES OF DETERIORATION

Oxygen, heat, and moisture have adverse effects on oil. Oxygen is derived from the air that entered the transformer and from the transformer oil. Oxygen is liberated in some cases by the effect of heat on cellulose insulation. The natural oxygen inhibitors in new insulating oil depletes gradually with time. Thus, the oxidation rate of the oil increases steadily while the oil is in service.

Pure hydrocarbons do not oxidize easily under normal conditions. The American Society for Testing and Materials (ASTM) has established that oil oxidation results generally from a process that starts when oxygen combines with unstable hydrocarbon impurities. The metals in the transformer act as a catalyst for this combination. Acids, peroxides, alcohols, and ketones are the products of oxidation. The oxidation process results in continuous detrimental action on the insulating materials of the transformer. Sludge will eventually form. Greater damage will be caused by sludge formation. This is due to the inability of the sludge to circulate and remove the heat buildup.

The most important of the eight ASTM tests listed in Table 29.2 are neutralization number (NN) and the D-971 for interfacial tension (IFT). This is because these tests deal directly with the acid content and the presence of sludge. The two tests provide a quantitative description of the condition of the oil.

The Neutralization Number Test

The NN test (ASTM D-974) determines the acid content of the oil. An oil sample of known quantity is titrated with the base potassium hydroxide (KOH) until the acid in the oil has been neutralized. NN is expressed as the amount of KOH in milligrams required to neutralize 1 gram of oil. A high NN indicates high acid content.

The acid formation in the transformer begins as soon as the oil is placed in service. Figure 29.11 illustrates the increase of NN with time and temperature. Electromechanical vibration, mechanical shock, and especially heat will accelerate the normal deterioration of

TABLE 29.2 The Eight Most Important ASTM Tests for In-Service Transformer Oil*

ASTM test method	Criteria for evaluating test results	Information provided by test
D-877—Dielectric breakdown strength	New oil should not break down at 30 kV or below.	Free water present in oil.
D-974—Neutralization (or acid) number (NN)	Milligrams of potassium hydroxide required to neutralize 1 g oil ($\leq$0.03 g new oil).	Acid present in oil.
D-971—Interfacial tension (IFT)	Dynes per centimeter ($\geq$40 for new oil).	Sludge present in oil.
D-1524—Color	Compared against color index scale of 0.5 (new oil) to 8.0 (worst case).	Marked change from one year to next indicates a problem.
D-1298—Specific gravity	Specific gravity of new oil is approximately 0.875.	Provides a quick check.
D-1524—Visual evaluation of transparency/opacity	Good oil is clear and sparkling, not cloudy.	Cloudiness indicates presence of moisture or other contaminants.
D-1698—Sediment	None/slight/moderate/heavy.	Indicates deterioration and/or contamination of oil.
D-924—Power factor	Power factor of new oil is $\leq$0.05.	Reveals presence of moisture, resin varnishes, or other products of oxidation in oil, or of foreign contaminants such as motor oil or fuel oil.

**Note:* For comparative purposes, specifications of new insulating oil can be obtained from ASTM publication D-3487-77, *Standard Specifications for Mineral Insulating Oil in Electrical Apparatus*, available from the American Society for Testing and Materials, 1916 Race St., Philadelphia, PA 19103.

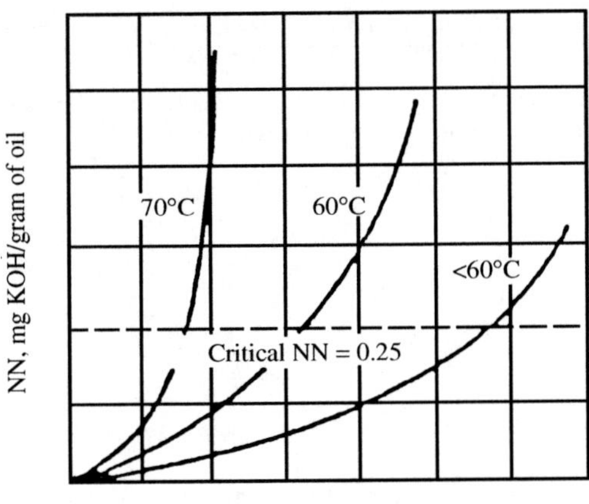

FIGURE 29.11 Typical pattern of increase in NN as a function of time is exhibited by the curve for transformer oil operated at 60°C. The exponential rise in NN at the critical point results from the catalytic action of acids and the depletion of the oxidation inhibitors. Heat is the greatest accelerator of oil deterioration; deterioration is most marked above 60°C. Beyond 60°C, the rate of deterioration approximately doubles for each 10°C increase.

the oil. Even minute amounts of water will enhance the oxidation process and the formation of acids. The copper or copper alloys in the windings will act as a catalyst for this reaction.

The Interfacial Tension Test

The ASTM D-971 test for interfacial tension (IFT) determines the concentration of sludge. In this test, a platinum ring is drawn through the interface between distilled water and the oil sample. A delicate balance (Cenco DuNuoy tensiometer) is used to draw the ring. The test results are expressed in dynes per centimeter (dynes/cm). This test gives a good indication about the presence of oil decay products. The IFT of new oil is more than 40 dynes/cm; the IFT of badly deteriorating oil is less than 18 dynes/cm.

THE MYERS INDEX NUMBER

A high IFT indicates that the oil is relatively sludge-free. Therefore, it will be purer than an oil with a low IFT.

Conversely, when the oil has a high acid content and bad deterioration, it will have a high NN. An excellent indicator of the oil condition is obtained by dividing the IFT by the NN. This ratio is known as the *Myers Index Number* (MIN) or *oil quality index number.* For example, the MIN for a new oil is around 1500.

$$\text{MIN} = \frac{\text{IFT}}{\text{NN}}$$

$$= \frac{45.0 \text{ (typical new oil)}}{0.03 \text{ (typical new oil)}} = 1500$$

THE TRANSFORMER OIL CLASSIFICATION SYSTEM

The seven classifications of the transformer oil are presented in Table 29.3. These seven classifications, or categories, include the following:

1. "Good oils"
2. "Proposition A oils"
3. "Marginal oils"
4. "Bad oils"
5. "Very bad oils"
6. "Extremely bad oils"
7. "Oils in a disastrous condition"

They are based on the oil's ability to perform its four intended functions (cooling, insulation, protection against chemical attack, and prevention of sludge buildup).

The oils in the first classification, or category ("good oils"), can perform efficiently all four functions. They do not require attention other than periodic testing.

TABLE 29.3 Transformer Oil Classifications

Oil condition	NN*	IFT*	Color	MIN*
1. "Good oils"	0.00–0.10	30.0–45.0	Pale yellow	300–1500
2. "Proposition A oils"	0.05–0.10	27.1–29.9	Yellow	271–600
3. "Marginal oils"	0.11–0.15	24.0–27.0	Bright yellow	160–318
4. "Bad oils"	0.16–0.40	18.0–23.9	Amber	45–159
5. "Very bad oils"	0.41–0.65	14.0–17.9	Brown	22–44
6. "Extremely bad oils"	0.66–1.50	9.0–13.9	Dark brown	6–21
7. "Oils in a disastrous condition"	1.51 or more		Black	

*IFT, interfacial tension; MIN, Myers Index Number; NN, neutralization number.

Preventive maintenance is required for the oils in the second ("Proposition A oils") and third ("marginal oils") categories. The decrease of the IFT to 27.0 indicates the start of sludge in solution. At this stage, the oil is less than ideal, but does not require immediate attention.

Oil in the third category (marginal) is not providing adequate cooling and winding protection. At this stage, fatty acids have begun to coat the winding insulation. The sludge has also begun to build up in the insulation voids. Numerous studies of transformer failures for oils in the second and third categories revealed sludge in the voids of the insulation system. This is the reason for not deferring transformer maintenance when they contain marginal oil.

Transformers containing oils in categories 4 ("bad oils"), 5 ("very bad oils"), and 6 ("extremely bad oils") should be serviced promptly. Sludge has already been deposited on most of the winding and core in category 4. Considerable insulation shrinkage and blockage of cooling vents would have occurred in categories 5 and 6 (extremely bad) due to oil deterioration. The transformer should be replaced if the oil is found in category 7 ("oil in a disastrous condition").

There is some overlap of MIN ranges in the first three categories. This overlap is due to the fact that the oil should meet the criteria for both minimum IFT and maximum NN for the category, in addition to falling within the range given for the MIN.

Table 29.4 summarizes the results of a study on 500 transformers to determine the relationship between IFT, NN, and the sludge content in transformers. The transformers have been selected from different industrial environments. All 500 transformers experienced visible sludge buildup when the NN exceeded 0.6 mgKOH/g, or when the IFT dropped below 14.0 dynes/cm.

TABLE 29.4 Correlation of Neutralization Number and Interfacial Tension to Transformer Sludging*

Neutralization number (NN), mg KOH/g of oil	Number of units found sludged
0.00–0.10	0
0.11–0.20	190
0.21–0.60	360
0.60 or higher	500
Interfacial tension (IFT), dynes/cm	
24 or higher	0
22–24	150
20–22	165
18–20	175
16–18	345
14–16	425
14 or less	500

*Study conducted by ASTM from 1946 to 1957 on 500 transformers that had been in service for some time. Study is described in ASTM Special Publication No. 218, *Evaluation of Laboratory Tests as indicators of the Service Life of Uninhibited Electrical Insulating Oils* (1957).

Figure 29.12 illustrates the relationship between NN, IFT, and the condition of transformer oil. If a sickeningly sweet odor is detected while the oil sample is taken, additional tests are needed. Degradation products released by arcing can cause this odor. However, the odor of arc-over products can be masked by the odor of acid if the oil has a high acid content. The oil should be tested by gas chromotography if there is a reason to suspect that dissolved combustible gases are present.

METHODS OF DEALING WITH BAD OIL

There are two options when tests indicate the oil is in the "Proposition A" (second classification) range or worse. They are replacement or reclamation of the oil. The reclamation process involves three steps:

1. Dissolving the sludge on the internals of the transformer
2. Purging the sludge from the transformer
3. Filtering the sludge from the oil to restore it to like-new condition

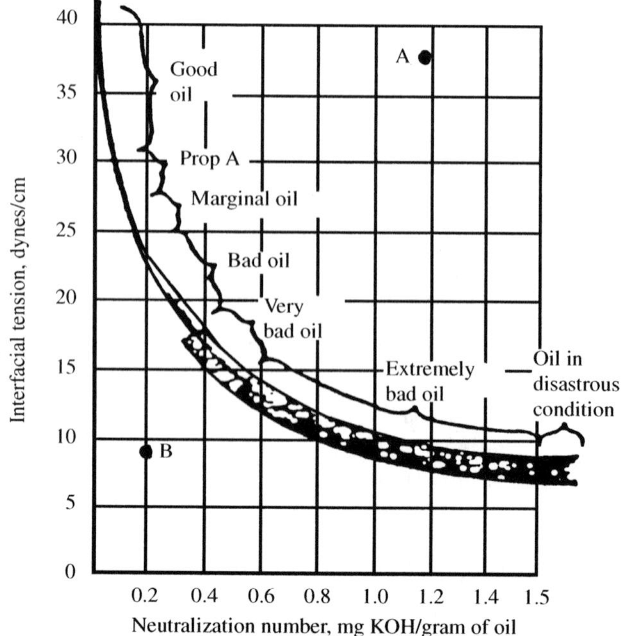

FIGURE 29.12 Plot shown was developed from the results of more than 10,000 IFT/NN tests. If a plot of IFT versus NN for a given oil sample does not fall within the range shown on either side of the median line (as in the case of points *A* and *B*), further investigation is in order. Additional tests (see Table 29.2) should be conducted. The results should be evaluated in combination to get a true picture of the condition of both the oil and the transformer.

The sludge deposited on the internal components of the transformer will not be removed when the oil is replaced. Simple replacement will only put new oil into a contaminated container. There are also handling and disposal problems with the replacement option.

The same process and equipment are used to reclaim the oil regardless of the degree of deterioration. Reclamation is relatively simple if the oil is in the "Proposition A" range. If the oil has deteriorated further, a more extensive treatment will be required.

The reclamation process is performed in a *closed loop*. Special equipment is used to continuously heat the oil, filter it through absorbent beds, and recirculate it in the transformer. The heated oil is maintained at its aniline point (82°C) during the process. The hot oil acts as a strong solvent for decay products. The sludge is removed usually by 6 to 10 recirculation cycles. Twenty recirculations may be required to desludge the transformer if it is badly sludged (oil with NN > 0.3 and IFT < 18).

Many separate reclamation/desludging treatments are needed if the transformer is in extremely sludged condition (NN > 1.5). It is recommended to consider replacing the transformer at this stage. Reclamation/desludging should be performed before NN exceeds 1.5 and IFT drops below 24.0 to ensure adequate operation and minimum deterioration of the insulation. The oil can be reclaimed/desludged while the transformer is on-line (energized and in-service) by properly equipped maintenance contractors. Therefore, there is no reason to allow the oil to deteriorate until an expensive treatment is required.

It is essential to have adequate cleanliness and quality control while obtaining the test results. Dirty containers or laboratory equipment should not be used for the oil sample. It is very important to protect the sample from light, air, and moisture. The sample should be taken quickly, sealed in a container, and tested within hours. It must not be exposed to sunlight. Aging will accelerate the sample if it is exposed to sunlight. The results of the sample could be misleading in this case.

GAS-IN-OIL

The analysis of dissolved combustible gases in transformers is highly indicative of possible trouble. All transformers will develop a certain amount of gases over their lifetime. The two principle causes of gas formation within an operating transformer are thermal and electrical disturbances. Heat losses from the conductors produce gases from decomposition of the oil and solid insulation. Gases are also generated from the decomposition of oil and insulation exposed to arc temperatures. The following paragraph was extracted from the *IEEE Guide for the Interpretation of Gases Generated in Oil-Immersed Transformers:*[2]

> The detection of certain gases generated in an oil filled transformer is frequently the first available indication of a malfunction that may eventually lead to failure if not corrected. Arcing, corona discharge, low-energy sparking, severe overloading, pump motor failure, and overheating in the insulation system are some of the possible mechanisms. These conditions occurring singly, or as several simultaneous events, can result in decomposition of the insulating materials and the formation of some gases. In fact, it is possible for some transformers to operate throughout their useful life with substantial quantities of combustible gas present. Operating a transformer with large quantities of combustible gas present is not a normal occurrence but it does happen, usually after some degree of investigation and an evaluation of possible risk.

The generated gases in the transformer can be found dissolved in the oil, in the gas blanket above the oil, or in gas-collecting devices. If an abnormal condition is detected, an evaluation is required to determine the amount of generated gases and their continuing rate of generation. When the composition of the generated gases is determined, some indication of the source of the gases and the kind of insulation involved will be gained.

There are many techniques for detecting and measuring gases. However, the interpretation of the significance of these gases is not a science at the present time. It is an art subjected to variability. It is difficult to establish a consensus due to the variability of acceptable gas limits. The main reason for not developing an exact science for fault interpretation is the lack of correlation between the fault-identifying gases with faults found in actual transformers. Table 29.5 provides a general description of the various fault types with associated developing gases.

GAS RELAY AND COLLECTION SYSTEMS

Most utilities and large industries have a gas relay mounted on their power transformers. As mentioned earlier, gases are generated by the chemical and electrical phenomena associated with the development of faults in oil-filled transformers. A significant amount of gas is normally formed in the early stage of the fault.

The gases generated and the air expelled from the oil by the fault rise to the top of the equipment and is collected in a gas relay. Figure 29.13 illustrates a gas collection system. It ensures that gases trapped in various pockets are allowed to escape and travel to the gas relay.

TABLE 29.5 A General Description of the Various Fault Types with Associated Developing Gases

Fault type	Description
Arcing	Arcing is the most severe of all fault processes. Large amounts of hydrogen and acetylene are produced, with minor quantities of methane and ethylene. Arcing occurs through high-current and high-temperature conditions. Carbon dioxide and carbon monoxide may also be formed if the fault involved cellulose. In some instances, the oil may become carbonized.
Corona	Corona is a low-energy electrical fault. Low-energy electrical discharges produce hydrogen and methane, with small quantities of ethane and ethylene. Comparable amounts of carbon monoxide and dioxide may result from discharges in cellulose.
Sparking	Sparking occurs as an intermittent high-voltage flashover without high current. Increased levels of methane and ethane are detected without concurrent increases in acetylene, ethylene, or hydrogen.
Overheating	Decomposition products include ethylene and methane, together with smaller quantities of hydrogen and ethane. Traces of acetylene may be formed if the fault is severe or involves electrical contacts.
Overheated cellulose	Large quantities of carbon dioxide and carbon monoxide are evolved from overheated cellulose. Hydrocarbon gases, such as methane and ethylene, will be formed if the fault involved an oil-impregnated structure. A furanic compound and/or degree of polymerization analysis may be performed to further assess the condition of the insulating paper.

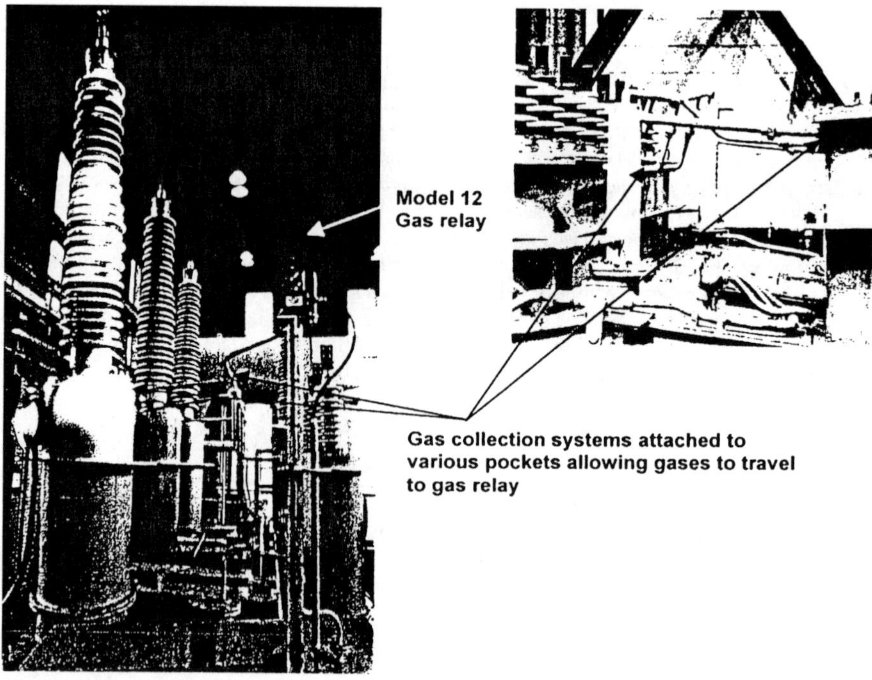

FIGURE 29.13 Gas relay and gas collection systems.

Gas Relay

The gas detector relay (Fig. 29.14) gives an early indication of faults in oil-filled transformers. There are two types of faults:

1. *Minor faults that result in a slow evolution of gases.* These faults may result from the following:
   - Local heating
   - Defective insulation structures
   - Improperly brazed joints
   - Loose contacts
   - Ground faults
   - Short-circuit turns

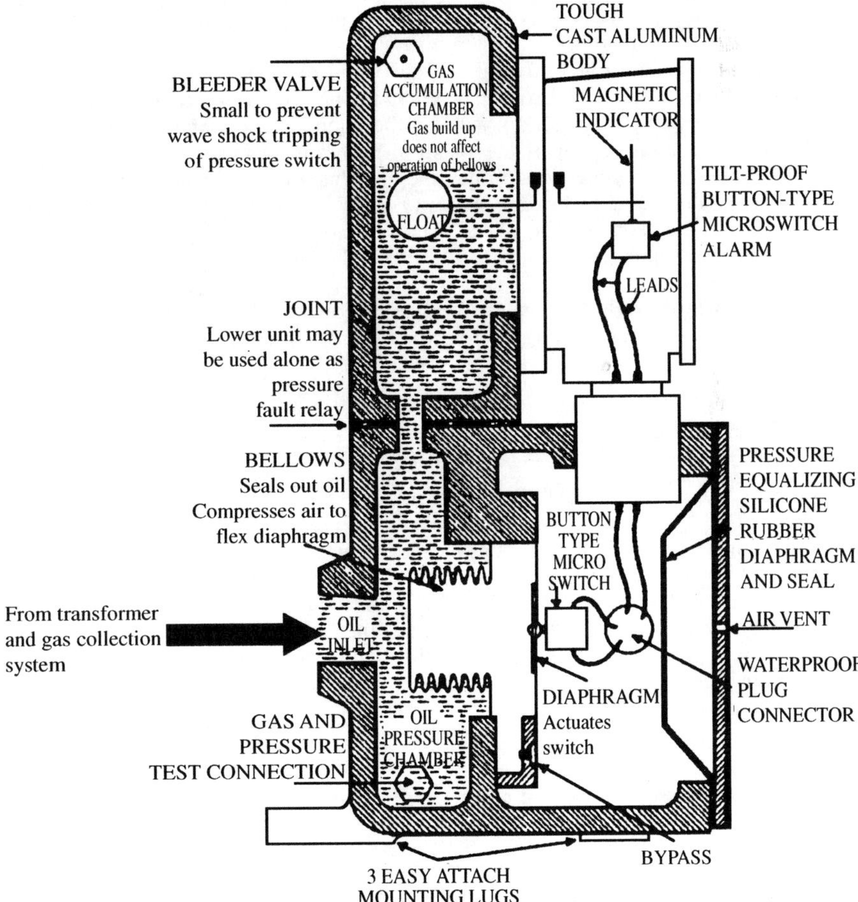

FIGURE 29.14 Cross-sectional view of CGE Model 12 gas relay.

- Opening or interruption of a phase current
- Burnout of core iron
- Release of air from oil
- Leakage of air into the transformer

2. *Major faults that result in a sudden increase in pressure.* These faults are normally caused by flashover between parts. The relay will detect both types of faults.

The relay has two sections:

1. *A gas accumulation chamber located at the top of the relay.* It consists of an oil chamber with a gas bleeder needle valve. A float in the oil chamber operates a magnetic oil gauge with an alarm switch.
2. *A pressure chamber at the bottom of the relay.* It has two parts: an oil chamber at the rear of the relay. The chamber is connected to the transformer by a pipe entering the back of the relay. A test valve is located at the base. It is used for making operation checks. Sensitive brass bellows separate the first section from the second.

There is an air chamber in the front. It contains stops for the bellows to prevent overtravel, a flexible diaphragm, and a microswitch. When the bellows move, they compress the air behind the diaphragm. This action actuates the microswitch, which is fastened to the diaphragm. When arcing occurs in the transformer, it causes a rapid evolution of gas in the oil. A pressure wave is generated through the oil. This wave will reach the relay through the pipe. It will compress the flexible bellows. The air in the chamber is compressed by the displacement of the bellows. Since the air cannot pass quickly through the bypass valve, it forces the flexible diaphragm to close the contact of the trip switch. This action disconnects the transformer.

It is essential to find the fault when the pressure contact trips the transformer. The fault should be corrected before putting the transformer back in service.

RELIEF DEVICES

Very high pressure is generated following an electrical fault under oil. These pressures could easily burst the steel tank if they are not relieved. An explosion vent was used until the early 1970s. It consisted of a large-diameter pipe extending slightly above the conservator tank of the transformer and curved in the direction of the ground. A diaphragm (made of glass, usually) is installed at the curved end. It ruptures at a relatively low pressure releasing any force that builds up inside the transformer. Since the early 1970s, a self-resetting pressure relief vent was installed on transformers. When the pressure in the transformer reaches a predetermined level following a fault, it forces the seal open under spring pressure. This relieves the pressure to atmosphere.

INTERCONNECTION WITH THE GRID

Figures 29.15 and 29.16 illustrate interconnections of power plants with the grid. The transformer that connects the plant with the grid is normally called the main output transformer (MOT) or generator step-up transformer. The transformer that connects the output of the generator with the plant itself (feeding power back to the plant) is called the unit service

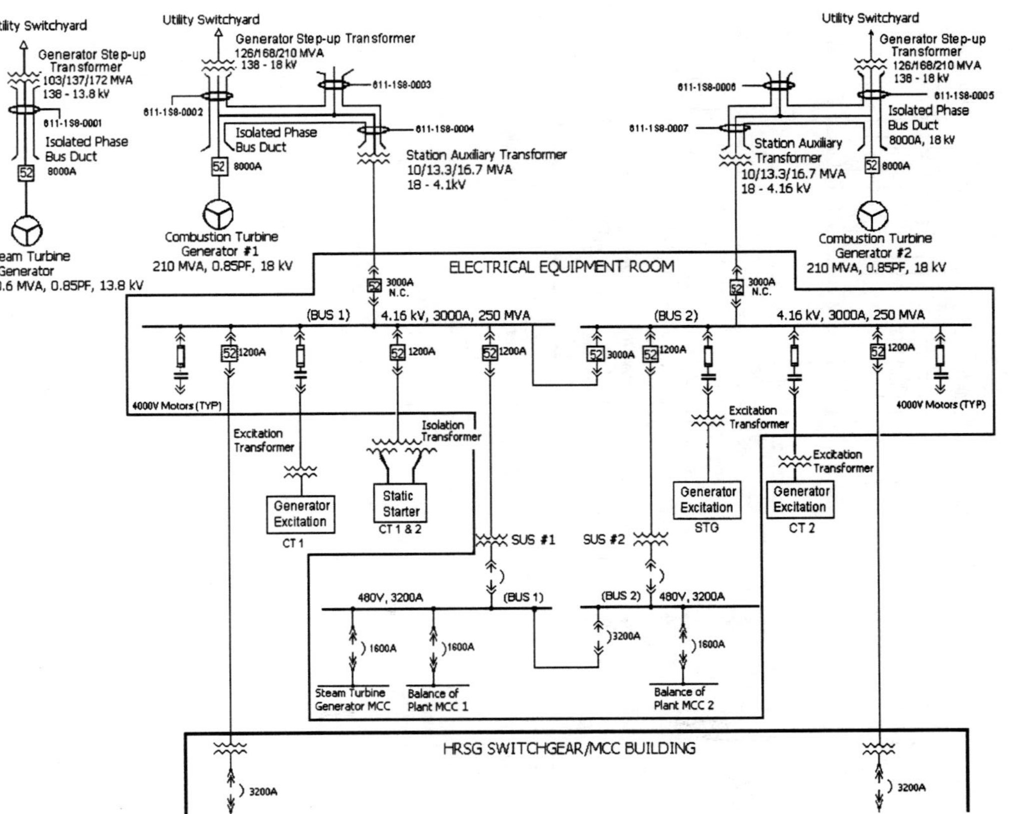

FIGURE 29.15 Interconnection of a combined cycle with the grid.

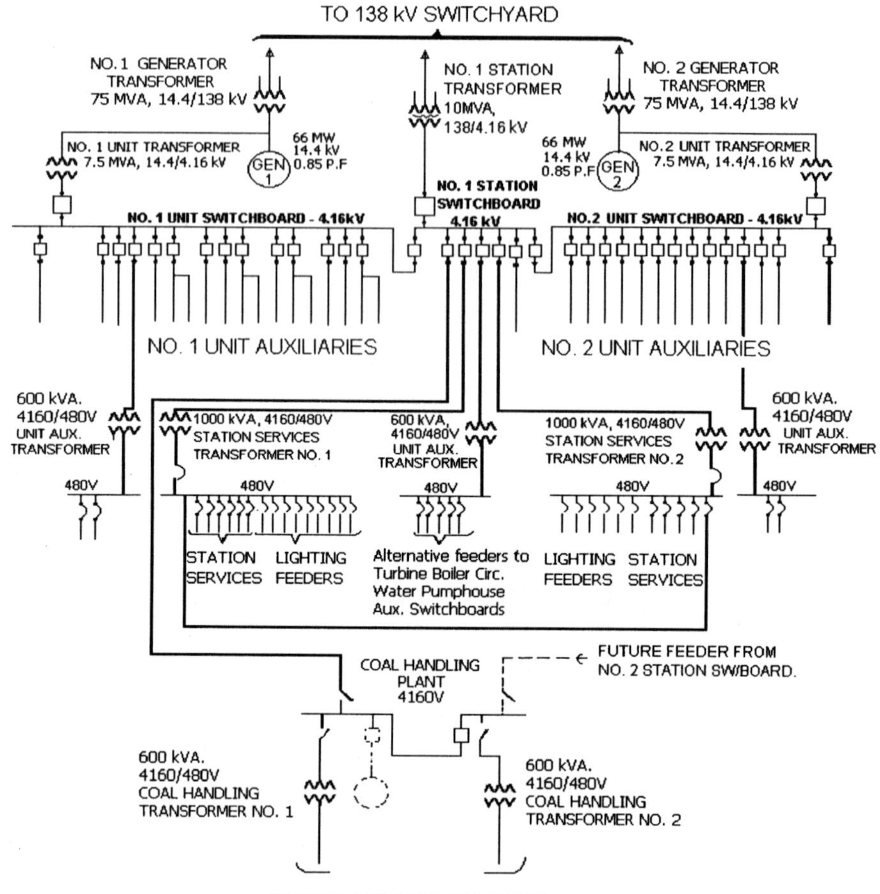

FIGURE 29.16 Power station AC single-line diagram.

transformer (UST) or station auxiliary transformer. The rating of the UST is normally about 6 to 7 percent of the MOT. The transformer that connects the grid to the station loads (allowing power to be fed back to the unit) is called the station service transformer (SST). The design philosophy for supplying power to the loads in the plant varies. Some power plants supply half their loads through the UST and the second half through the SST. However, modern power plants have opted to supply all their power through the UST. They use the incoming power through the SST as backup. In the plants where the plant loads are supplied equally from the UST and SST (Fig. 29.16), the tie breakers connecting the buses inside the plant close when the unit is disconnected from the grid. This is done to ensure that the loads inside the plant continue to be supplied with power when the unit is taken off-line.

Some plants install the generator breaker before the line feeding power from the output of the generator back into the plant. In this design, the plant loads are supplied from another source (e.g., the grid) when the breaker opens. Other plants install the generator breaker after the line feeding power from the output of the generator back into the plant. When the generator breaker opens (due to a load rejection), a significant load shedding occurs (about

94 percent of the load is taken off within a fraction of a second). This results in a significant reduction in counter-torque on the generator shaft (about 94 percent reduction). Since the driving torque from the turbine has not changed, the turbine-generator shaft will accelerate. The governing system will limit the overspeed normally to 8 percent. However, since the generator is still supplying the plant loads at higher frequency (up to 8 percent higher), the synchronous speed of the motors inside the plant will increase. The currents pulled by these motors from the power supply will increase. This results in tripping of these motors in some plants on overload.

Transformers are used inside the plant to provide power to the loads requiring lower voltage. Some steam power plants use separate gas turbines as backup power (standby generators), They feed the 4-kV and 600-V buses inside the plant when the normal power from the UST and SST is lost. This type of power is considered more reliable than the power supplied from the UST or SST. Most plants use large battery banks to supply emergency loads (e.g., turbine emergency dc lube oil pump, generator stator emergency dc water cooling pump, and generator emergency dc seal oil pump). Some plants use inverters to supply emergency AC power from the battery bank to plant loads. The reliability of power supplies in descending order is as follows:

1. Power from the battery banks (DC or AC through inverters)—most reliable
2. Standby generators
3. Power through UST or SST—least reliable

REFERENCES

1. Myers, S. D., and J. J. Kelly, Transformer Maintenance Institute, Division of S.D. Meyers, Inc., Cuyahoga Falls, OH.
2. Institute of Electrical and Electronics Engineers (IEEE), *Guide for the Interpretation of Gases Generated in Oil-Immersed Transformers,* Standard C57.104-1991, IEEE, New York, 1991.

CHAPTER 30
AC MACHINE FUNDAMENTALS

Alternating current (AC) machines are motors that convert AC electric energy to mechanical energy, and generators that convert mechanical energy to AC electric energy. The two major classes of AC machines are (1) synchronous and (2) induction machines.

The field current of *synchronous machines* (motors and generators) is supplied by a separate direct current (DC) power source while the field current of *induction machines* is supplied by magnetic induction (transformer action) into the field windings.

The AC machines differ from DC machines by having their *armature windings* almost always located on the stator while their *field windings* are located on the rotor. A set of three-phase AC voltages is induced into the stator armature windings of an AC machine by the rotating magnetic field from the rotor field windings (generator action). Conversely, a set of three-phase currents flowing in the stator armature windings produces a rotating magnetic field within the stator. This magnetic field interacts with the rotor magnetic field to produce the torque in the machine (motor action).

THE ROTATING MAGNETIC FIELD

The main principle of AC machine operation is a three-phase set of currents, flowing in an armature winding, each of equal magnitude and differing in phase by 120°, produces a rotating magnetic field of constant magnitude. The stator shown in Fig. 30.1 has three coils, each 120° apart.

The currents flowing in the stator are given by

$$i_{aa'}(t) = I_M \sin \omega t \quad \text{A}$$

$$i_{bb'}(t) = I_M \sin (\omega t - 120°) \quad \text{A}$$

$$i_{cc'}(t) = I_M \sin (\omega t - 240°) \quad \text{A}$$

The resulting magnetic flux densities are

$$B_{aa'}(t) = B_M \sin \omega t \angle 0° \quad \text{Wb/m}^2$$

$$B_{bb'}(t) = B_M \sin (\omega t - 120°) \angle 120° \quad \text{Wb/m}^2$$

$$B_{cc'}(t) = B_M \sin (\omega t - 240°) \angle 240° \quad \text{Wb/m}^2$$

The direction of these fluxes is given by the right-hand rule. When the fingers of the right hand curl in the direction of the current in a coil, the thumb points in the direction of the resulting magnetic flux density.

An examination of the currents and their corresponding magnetic flux densities at specific times is used to determine the resulting net magnetic flux density. For example, at time $\omega t = 0°$, the magnetic field from coil aa' will be

$$B_{aa'} = 0$$

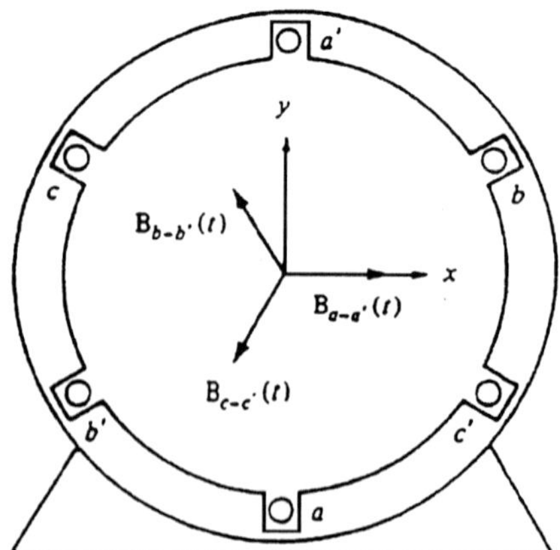

FIGURE 30.1 A simple three-phase stator. Currents in this stator are assumed positive if they flow into the unprimed and out of the primed ends of the coils.

The magnetic field from coil bb' will be

$$B_{bb'} = B_M \sin(-120°) \angle 120°$$

and the magnetic field from coil cc' will be

$$B_{cc'} = B_M \sin(-240°) \angle 240°$$

The total magnetic field from all three coils added together will be

$$\begin{aligned} B_{net} &= B_{aa'} + B_{bb'} + B_{cc'} \\ &= 0 + \left(-\frac{\sqrt{3}}{2} B_M\right) \angle 120° - \frac{\sqrt{3}}{2} B_M \angle 240° \\ &= 1.5 B_M \angle -90° \end{aligned}$$

As another example, look at the magnetic field at time $\omega t = 90°$. At that time, the currents are

$$i_{aa'} = I_M \sin 90° \quad \text{A}$$

$$i_{bb'} = I_M \sin(-30°) \quad \text{A}$$

$$i_{cc'} = I_M \sin(-150°) \quad \text{A}$$

and the magnetic fields are

$$B_{aa'} = B_M \angle 0°$$

$$B_{bb'} = -0.5 B_M \angle 120°$$

$$B_{cc'} = -0.5 B_M \angle 240°$$

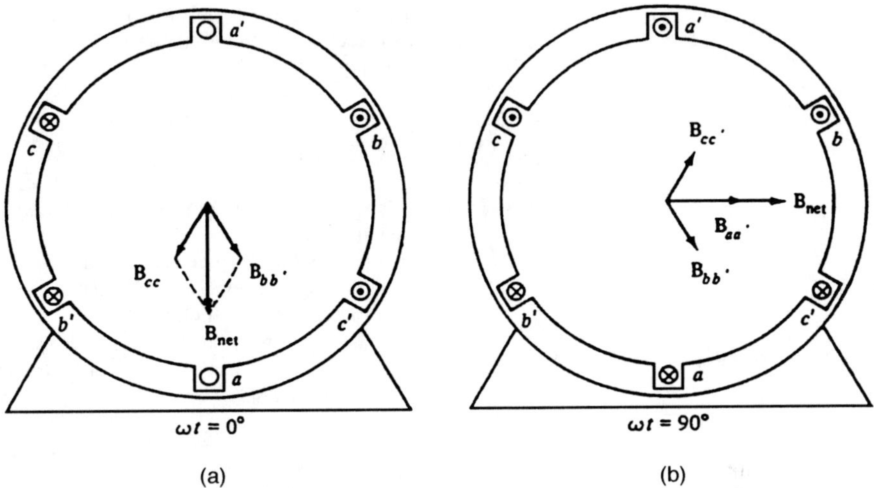

FIGURE 30.2 (*a*) The vector magnetic field in a stator at time $\omega t = 0°$. (*b*) The vector magnetic field in a stator at time $\omega t = 90°$.

the resulting net magnetic field is

$$B_{\text{net}} = B_M \angle 0° + (-0.5)\, B_M \angle 120° + (-0.5)\, B_M \angle 240°$$

$$= 1.5 B_M \angle 0°$$

The resulting magnetic flux is shown in Fig. 30.2. Notice that the direction of the magnetic flux has changed, but its magnitude remained constant. The magnetic flux is rotating counterclockwise, while its magnitude remained constant.

PROOF OF THE ROTATING MAGNETIC FLUX CONCEPT

At any time t, the magnetic flux has the same magnitude, $1.5B_M$. It continues to rotate at angular velocity ω. A proof of this concept is presented in Ref. 1.

THE RELATIONSHIP BETWEEN ELECTRICAL FREQUENCY AND THE SPEED OF MAGNETIC FIELD ROTATION

Figure 30.3 illustrates that the rotating magnetic field in the stator can be represented as a north and a south pole. The flux leaves the stator at the north pole and enters the stator at the south pole. The magnetic poles complete one entire revolution around the stator surface for each electrical cycle of the applied current. Therefore, the mechanical

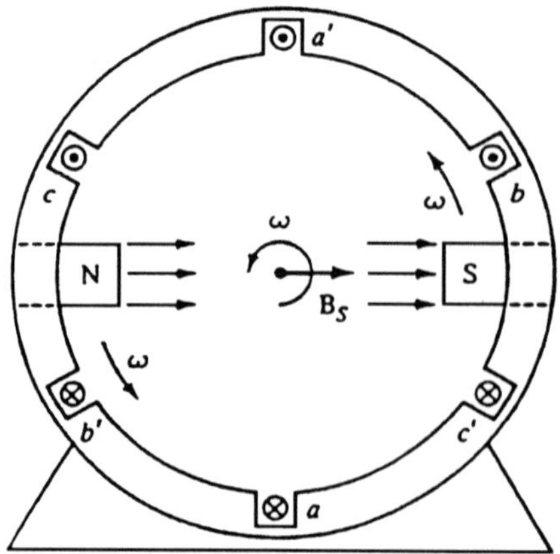

FIGURE 30.3 The rotating magnetic field in a stator represented as moving north and south stator poles.

angular speed of rotation in revolutions per second is equal to the electrical frequency in hertz:

$$f_e = f_m \qquad \text{two poles}$$

$$\omega_e = \omega_m \qquad \text{two poles}$$

where f_m and ω_m are the mechanical speed of rotation in revolutions per second and in radians per second, respectively. f_e and ω_e are the electrical frequency (speed) in hertz and in radians per second.

The windings on the two-pole stator shown in Fig. 30.1 occur in the order (taken counterclockwise)

$$a\text{-}c'\text{-}b\text{-}a'\text{-}c\text{-}b$$

If this pattern were repeated twice within the stator, the pattern of windings becomes

$$a\text{-}c'\text{-}b\text{-}a'\text{-}c\text{-}b'\text{-}a\text{-}c'\text{-}b\text{-}a'\text{-}c\text{-}b'$$

Figure 30.4 illustrates the *two* north poles and *two* south poles that are produced in the stator when a three-phase set of currents is applied to the stator. In this stator, the pole moves around half the stator surface in one electrical cycle. Since the mechanical motion is 180° for a complete electrical cycle (360°), the electrical angle θ_e is related to the mechanical angle θ_m by

$$\theta_e = 2\theta_m \qquad \text{four poles}$$

Therefore, for a four-pole stator, the electrical frequency is double the mechanical frequency of rotation:

$$f_e = 2f_m \qquad \text{four poles}$$

$$\omega_e = 2\omega_m \qquad \text{four poles}$$

In general, if *P* is the number of magnetic poles on the stator, then there are *P*/2 repetitions of the windings. The electrical and mechanical quantities of the machine are related by:

$$\boxed{\theta_e = \frac{P}{2}\,\theta_m}$$

$$\boxed{f_e = \frac{P}{2}\,f_m}$$

$$\boxed{\omega_e = \frac{P}{2}\,\omega_m}$$

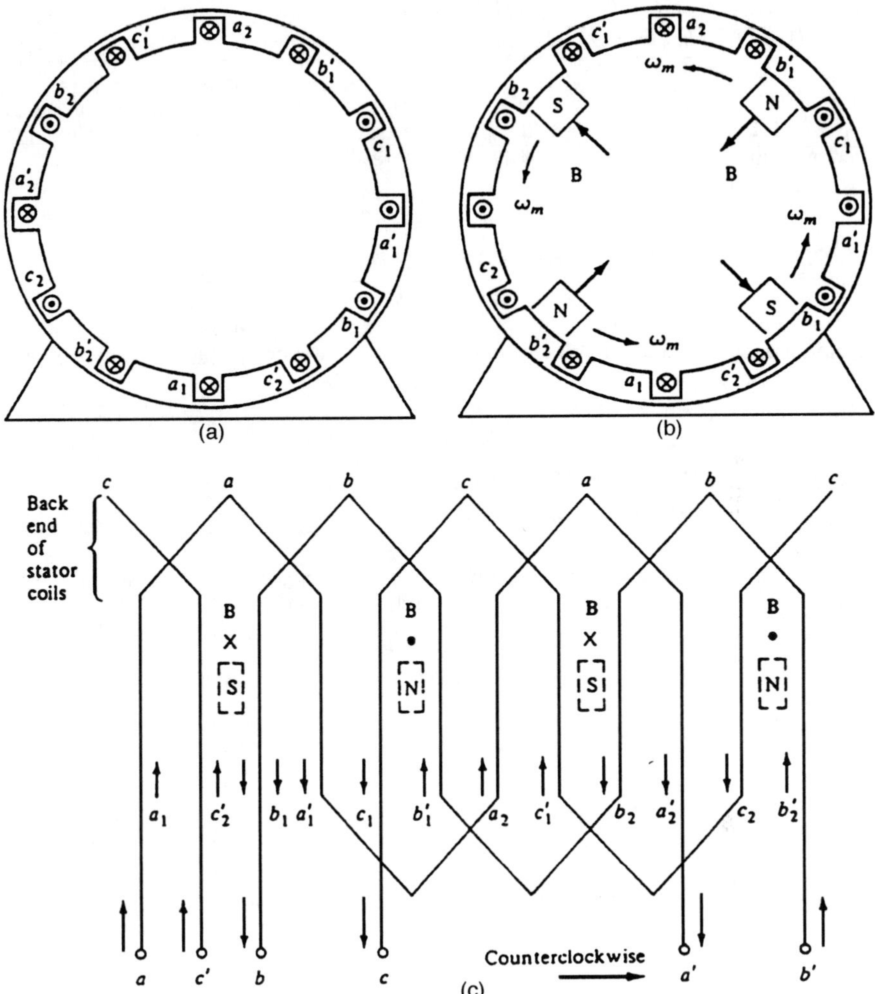

FIGURE 30.4 (*a*) A simple four-pole stator winding. (*b*) The resulting stator magnetic poles. Notice that there are moving poles of alternating polarity every 90° around the stator surface. (*c*) A winding diagram of the stator as seen from its inner surface, showing how the stator currents produce north and south magnetic poles.

Since the mechanical frequency $f_m = n_m/60$, the electrical frequency in hertz is related to the mechanical speed of the magnetic fields in revolutions per minute by

$$\boxed{f_e = \frac{n_m P}{120}}$$

REVERSING THE DIRECTION OF THE MAGNETIC FIELD ROTATION

The direction of the magnetic field's rotation is reversed when the current in any two of three coils is swapped. Therefore, it is possible to reverse the direction of rotation of an AC motor by just switching any two of the three phases.[1]

INDUCED VOLTAGE IN AC MACHINES

Just as a rotating magnetic field can be produced by a three-phase set of currents in a stator, a three-phase set of voltages in the coils of a stator can be produced by a rotating magnetic field.

THE INDUCED VOLTAGE IN A COIL ON A TWO-POLE STATOR

Figure 30.5 illustrates a *stationary* coil with a *rotating* magnetic field moving in its center. The induced voltage in a wire is given by the following equation:

$$e_{\text{ind}} = (v \times B) \cdot l$$

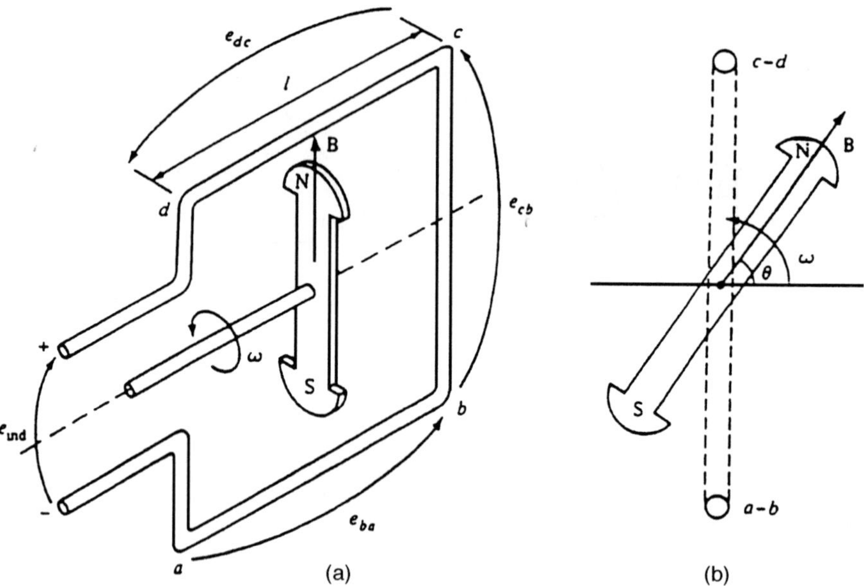

FIGURE 30.5 A rotating magnetic field inside a fixed coil. (*a*) Perspective view; (*b*) end view.

where v = velocity of wire *relative to the magnetic field*
B = magnetic flux density of field
l = length of wire

This equation was derived for a *wire moving within a stationary magnetic field.* In AC machines, the magnetic field is moving and the wire is stationary.

Figure 30.6 illustrates the velocities and vector magnetic field from the point of view of a moving wire and a stationary magnetic field. The voltages induced in the four sides of the coil in Fig. 30.6 are as follows:

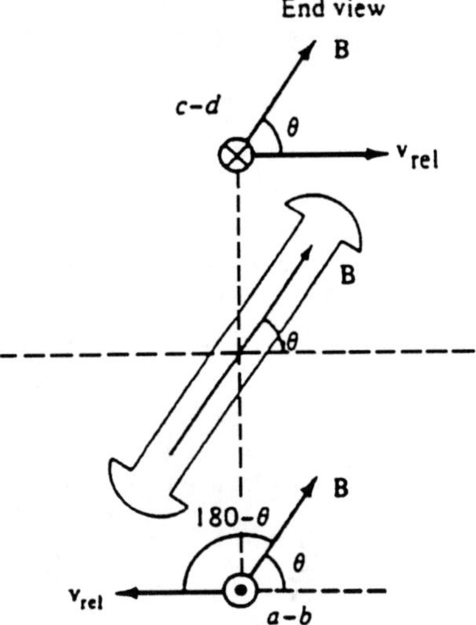

FIGURE 30.6 The magnetic fields and velocities of the coil sides as seen from a frame of reference in which the magnetic field is stationary.

1. *Segment ab.* The angle between v and B in segment bc is $180° - \theta$, while the quantity $v \times B$ is in the direction of l, so

$$e_{ba} = (v \times B) \cdot l$$

$$e_{ba} = vBl \sin (180° - \theta) \quad \text{directed } \textit{into} \text{ the page}$$

The direction of e_{ba} is given by the right-hand rule. By trigonometric identity, $\sin (180° - \theta) = \sin \theta$, so

$$e_{ba} = vBl \sin \theta$$

2. *Segment bc.* The voltage on segment bc is zero, since the vector quantity $v \times B$ is perpendicular to l:

$$e_{cb} = (v \times B) \cdot l$$
$$= 0$$

3. *Segment cd.* The angle between υ and B in segment cd is θ, while the quantity $v \times B$ is in the direction of l, so

$$e_{dc} = (v \times B) \cdot l$$
$$= vBl \sin \theta \qquad \text{directed } \textit{out of} \text{ the page}$$

4. *Segment da.* The voltage on segment da is zero, for the same reason as in segment bc:

$$e_{ad} = 0$$

the total voltage induced within a single-turn coil is given by

$$e_{ind} = 2vBl \sin \theta$$

Since angle $\theta = \omega_e t$, the induced voltage can be rewritten as

$$e_{ind} = 2vBl \sin \omega_e t$$

Since the cross-sectional area A of the turn is $2rl$, and the velocity of the end conductors is given by $v = r\omega_m$, the equation can be rewritten as

$$e_{\text{ind}} = 2\,(r\omega_m)\,Bl \sin \omega_e t$$

$$= (2rl)\,B\omega_m \sin \omega_e t$$

$$= AB\omega_m \sin \omega_e t$$

The maximum flux passing through the coil is $\phi = AB$. For a two-pole stator, $\omega_m = \omega_e = \omega$, the induced voltage is

$$\boxed{e_{\text{ind}} = \phi\omega \sin \omega t}$$

This equation describes the voltage induced in a single-turn coil. If the coil (phase) has N_c turns of wire in it, the total induced voltage will be

$$\boxed{e_{\text{ind}} = N_e\,\phi\omega \sin \omega t}$$

THE INDUCED VOLTAGE IN A THREE-PHASE SET OF COILS

Figure 30.7 illustrates three coils, each of N_c turns, placed around the rotor magnetic field. The voltage induced in each of them has the same magnitude but differs in phase by 120°. The resulting voltages in the three phases are

$$e_{aa'}(t) = N_c\,\phi\omega \sin \omega t \quad \text{V}$$

$$e_{bb'}(t) = N_c\,\phi\omega \sin (\omega t - 120^\circ) \quad \text{V}$$

$$e_{cc'}(t) = N_c\,\phi\omega \sin (\omega t - 240^\circ) \quad \text{V}$$

Therefore, a set of three-phase currents generates a rotating uniform magnetic field within the stator of the machine, and a uniform magnetic field induces a set of three-phase voltages in such a stator.

THE RMS VOLTAGE IN A THREE-PHASE STATOR

The peak voltage in any phase is

$$E_{\max} = N_c\,\phi\omega$$

Since $\omega = 2\pi f$, the rms voltage in any phase is:

$$E_A = \frac{2\pi}{\sqrt{2}}\,N_c\,\phi f$$

$$\boxed{E_A = 2\,\pi N_c\,\phi f}$$

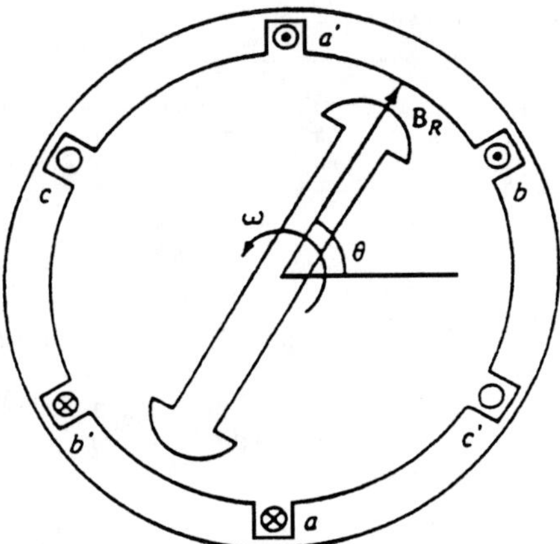

FIGURE 30.7 The production of three-phase voltages from three coils spaced 120° apart.

The rms voltage at the terminals of the machine depends on whether the stator is Y- or Δ-connected. If the machine is Y-connected, the terminal voltage is 3 times E_A. In Δ-connected machines, the terminal voltage is the same as E_A.

THE INDUCED TORQUE IN AN AC MACHINE

During normal operation of AC machines (motors and generators), there are two magnetic fields: (1) a magnetic field from the rotor and (2) another from the stator. A torque is induced in the machine due to the interaction of the two magnetic fields.

A synchronous machine is illustrated in Fig. 30.8. A magnetic flux density B_R is produced by the rotor, and a magnetic flux density B_S is produced by the stator. The induced torque in a machine (motors and generators) is given by

$$\tau_{\text{ind}} = kB_R \times B_S$$

$$\tau_{\text{ind}} = kB_R B_S \sin\gamma$$

where τ_{ind} = induced torque in machine
B_R = rotor flux density
B_S = stator flux density
γ = angle between B_R and B_S

The net magnetic field in the machine is the vector sum of the fields from the stator and rotor:

$$B_{\text{net}} = B_R + B_S$$

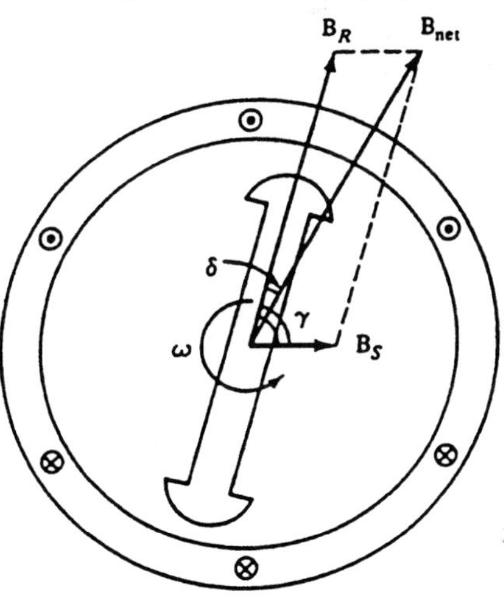

FIGURE 30.8 A simplified synchronous machine showing its rotor and stator magnetic fields.

The induced torque can be expressed as

$$\tau_{\text{ind}} = kB_R \times B_{\text{net}}$$

The magnitude of the torque is

$$\tau_{\text{ind}} = kB_R B_{net} \sin \delta$$

The magnetic fields of the synchronous machine shown in Fig. 30.8 are rotating in a counter-clockwise direction. What is the direction of the induced torque on the rotor of the machine?

By applying the right-hand rule to the equation of the induced torque, we see that the induced torque is clockwise. It is opposing the direction of rotation of the rotor. Therefore, this machine is working as a generator.

WINDING INSULATION IN AC MACHINES

In AC machine design, one of the most critical parts is the insulation of the windings. When the insulation breaks down, the machine shorts out. The repair of machines with shorted insulation is expensive, and sometimes impossible.

The temperature of the windings should be limited to prevent the insulation from breaking down due to overheating. This can be done by providing circulation of cool air over the windings. The continuous power supplied by the machine is usually limited by the maximum temperature of the windings.

The increase in temperature usually degrades the insulation, causing it to fail by another cause, such as shock, vibration, or electrical stress. A rule of thumb indicates that the life of an AC machine is halved for a temperature rise of 10 percent above the rated temperature of the windings.

The temperature limits of machine insulation have been standardized by the National Electrical Manufacturers Association (NEMA). A series of insulation system classes have been defined. Each insulation system class specifies the maximum temperature rise allowed for the insulation. The most common NEMA insulation classes for AC motors are B, F, and H. Each class has a higher permissible winding temperature than the one before it. For example, the temperature rise above ambient of the armature windings in continuously operating induction machines is limited to 80°C for class B, 105°C for class F, and 125°C for class H insulation. Similar standards have been defined by the International Electrotechnical Commission (IEC) and by other national standards organizations.

AC MACHINE POWER FLOWS AND LOSSES

A power-flow diagram is a convenient tool to analyze AC machines. Figure 30.9 illustrates the power-flow diagram of an AC generator and an AC motor.

The losses in AC machines are as follows:

- Rotor and stator copper (I^2R) losses
- Core losses
- Mechanical losses
- Stray losses

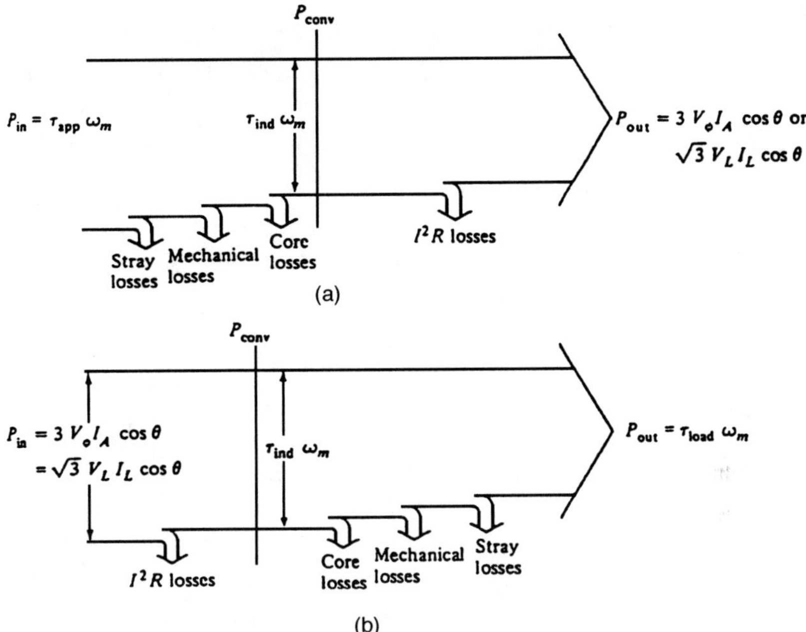

FIGURE 30.9 (*a*) Power-flow diagram of a three-phase AC generator; (*b*) power-flow diagram of a three-phase AC motor.

The *stator copper losses* in AC machines are the heat losses from the conductors of the stator. They are given by

$$P_{\text{SCL}} = 3I_A^2 R_A$$

where I_A is the current flowing in each armature phase, and R_A is the resistance of the conductor in each armature phase.

The *rotor copper losses* are given by

$$P_{\text{RCL}} = I_F^2 R_F$$

The *mechanical losses* are caused by bearing friction and windage effects, while the *core losses* are caused by hysteresis and eddy currents. These losses are called the *no-load rotational losses* of the machine. All the input power at no load is used to overcome these losses. Therefore, these losses can be obtained by measuring the power to the stator at no load.

Stray-load losses are all miscellaneous losses that do not fall into one of these categories. They are taken by convention as 1 percent of the output power of the machine.

The overall efficiency of an AC machine is the useful power output to the total input power:

$$\eta = \frac{P_{\text{out}}}{P_{\text{in}}} \times 100\%$$

REFERENCE

1. Chapman, S. J., *Electric Machinery Fundamentals,* 2d ed., McGraw-Hill, New York, 1991.

CHAPTER 31
SYNCHRONOUS GENERATORS

Synchronous generators or *alternators* are synchronous machines that convert mechanical energy to alternating current (AC) electric energy.[1]

SYNCHRONOUS GENERATOR CONSTRUCTION

A direct current (DC) is applied to the rotor winding of a synchronous generator to produce the rotor magnetic field. A prime mover rotates the generator rotor to rotate the magnetic field in the machine. A three-phase set of voltages is induced in the stator windings by the rotating magnetic field.

The rotor is a large electromagnet. Its magnetic poles can be *salient* (protruding or sticking out from the surface of the rotor), as shown in Fig. 31.1, or *nonsalient* (flush with the surface of the rotor), as shown in Fig. 31.2. Two- and four-pole rotors have normally nonsalient poles, while rotors with more than four poles have salient poles.

Small generator rotors are constructed of thin laminations to reduce eddy current losses, while large rotors are not constructed from laminations due to the high mechanical stresses encountered during operation. The field circuit of the rotor is supplied by a DC current. The common methods used to supply the DC power are

1. By means of *slip rings* and *brushes*
2. By a special DC power source mounted directly on the shaft of the rotor

Slip rings are metal rings that encircle the rotor shaft but are insulated from it. Each of the two slip rings on the shaft is connected to one end of the DC rotor winding and a number of brushes ride on each slip ring. The positive end of the DC voltage source is connected to one slip ring, and the negative end is connected to the second. This ensures that the same DC voltage is applied to the field windings regardless of the angular position or speed of the rotor. Slip rings and brushes require high maintenance because the brushes must be checked for wear regularly. Also, the voltage drop across the brushes can be the cause of large power losses when the field currents are high. Despite these problems, all small generators use slip rings and brushes because all other methods used for supplying DC field current are more expensive.

Large generators use *brushless exciters* for supplying DC field current to the rotor. They consist of a small AC generator having its field circuit mounted on the stator and its armature circuit mounted on the rotor shaft.

The exciter generator output (three-phase alternating current) is converted to direct current by a three-phase rectifier circuit also mounted on the rotor. The DC current is fed to the main field circuit. The field current for the main generator can be controlled by the small DC field current of the exciter generator, which is located on the stator (Figs. 31.3 and 31.4).

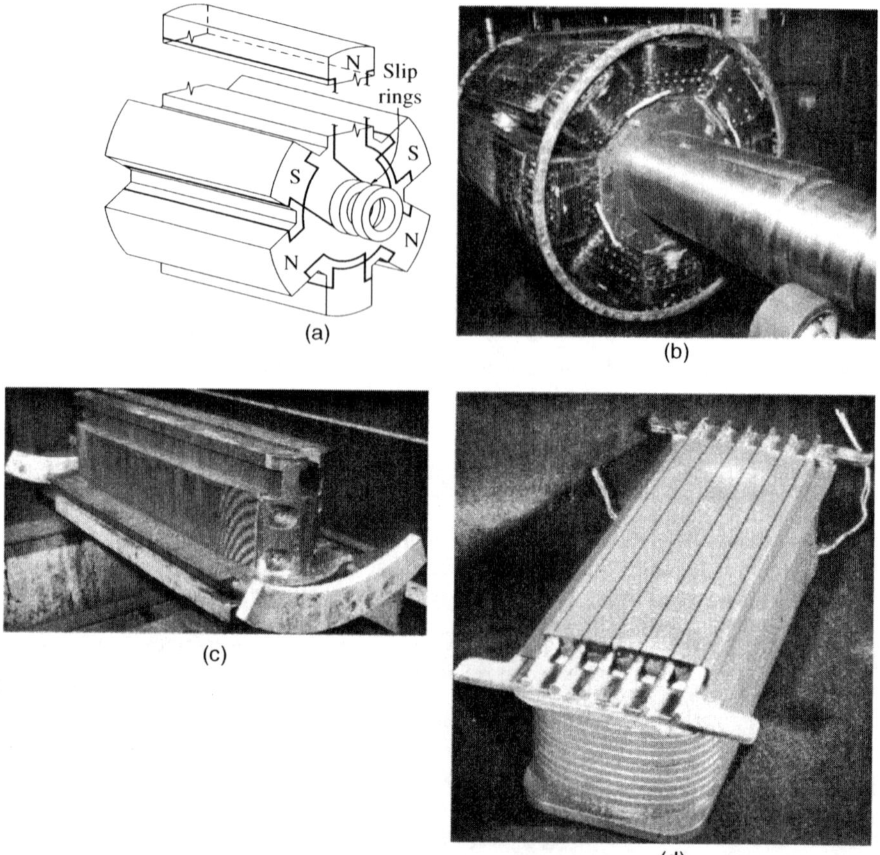

N
Slip
rings
S
S
N
N
(a)
(b)
(c)
(d)

FIGURE 31.1 (*a*) A salient six-pole rotor for a synchronous machine. (*b*) Photograph of a salient eight-pole synchronous machine rotor showing the windings on the individual rotor poles. (*Courtesy of General Electric Company.*) (*c*) Photograph of a single salient pole from a rotor with the field windings not yet in place. (*Courtesy of General Electric Company.*) (*d*) A single salient pole shown after the field windings are installed but before it is mounted on the rotor. (*Courtesy of Westinghouse Electric Company.*)

$\mathbf{B}_R$
N
S
N
(a)
End view
(b)
Side view

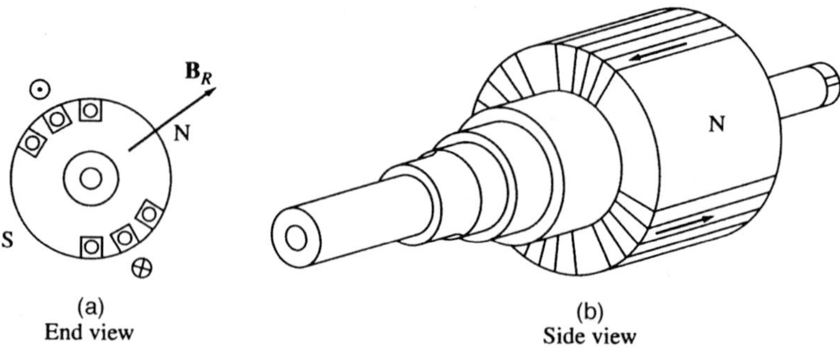

FIGURE 31.2 A nonsalient two-pole rotor for a synchronous machine. (*a*) End view; (*b*) side view.

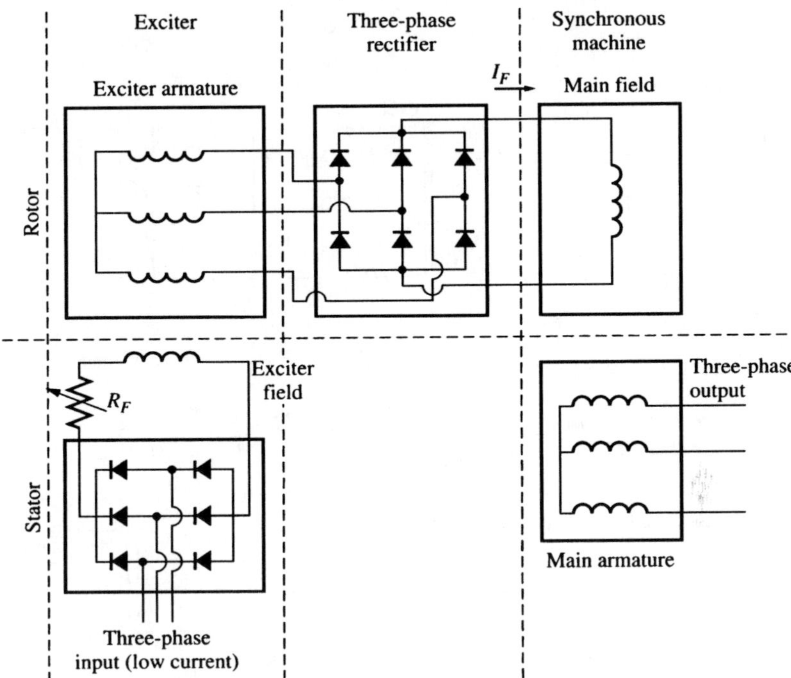

FIGURE 31.3 A brushless exciter circuit. A small three-phase current is rectified and used to supply the field circuit at the exciter, which is located on the stator. The output of the armature circuit of the exciter (on the rotor) is then rectified and used to supply the field current of the main machine.

FIGURE 31.4 Photograph of a synchronous machine rotor with a brushless exciter mounted on the same shaft. Notice the rectifying electronics, which are visible next to the armature of the exciter.

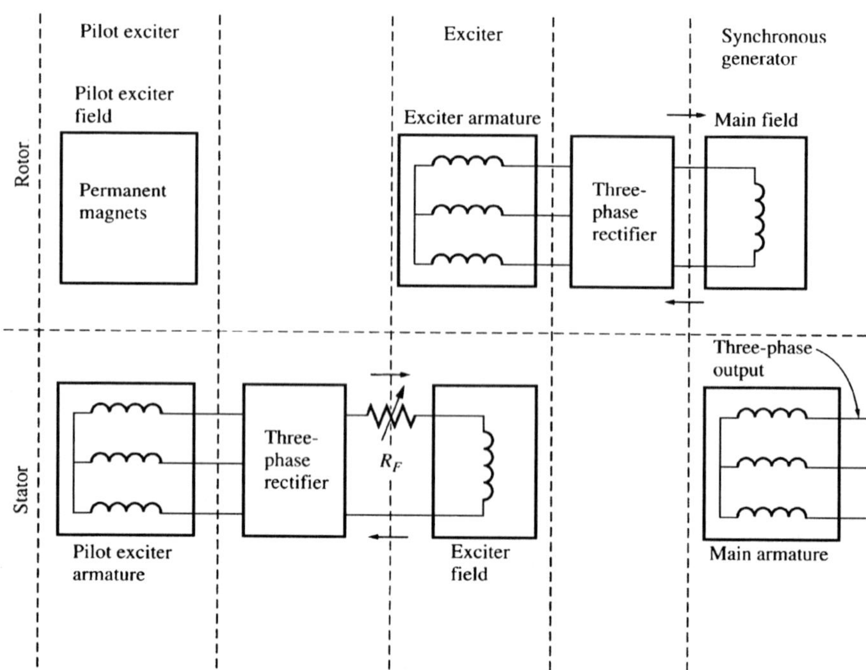

FIGURE 31.5 A brushless excitation scheme that includes a pilot exciter. The permanent magnets of the pilot exciter produce the field current of the exciter, which in turn produces the field current of the main machine.

A brushless excitation system requires much less maintenance than slip rings and brushes because there is no mechanical contact between the rotor and the stator. The generator excitation system can be made *completely* independent of any external power sources by using a small pilot exciter. It consists of a small AC generator with *permanent magnets* mounted on the rotor shaft and a three-phase winding on the stator. The pilot exciter produces the power required by the field circuit of the exciter that is used to control the field circuit of the main generator. When a pilot exciter is used, the generator can operate without any external electric power (Fig. 31.5).

Most synchronous generators that have brushless exciters also use slip rings and brushes as an auxiliary source of field DC current in emergencies. Figure 31.6 illustrates a cutaway of a complete large synchronous generator with a salient-pole rotor with eight poles and a brushless exciter.

THE SPEED OF ROTATION OF A SYNCHRONOUS GENERATOR

The electrical frequency of synchronous generators is synchronized (locked in) with the mechanical rate of rotation. The rate of rotation of the magnetic fields (mechanical speed) is related to the stator electrical frequency by:

$$\boxed{f_e = \frac{n_m P}{120}}$$

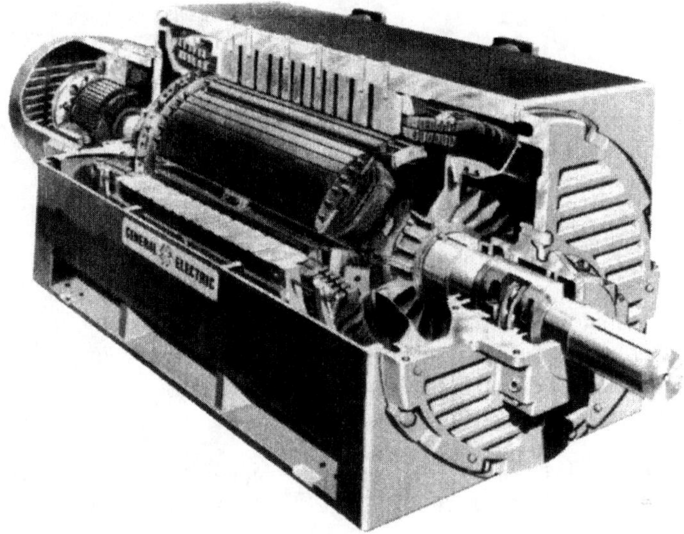

FIGURE 31.6 A cutaway diagram of a large synchronous machine. Notice the salient-pole construction and the on-shaft exciter. (*Courtesy of General Electric Company.*)

where f_e = electrical frequency, Hz
n_m = mechanical speed of magnetic field, r/min (= speed of the rotor for synchronous machines)
P = number of poles

For example, a two-pole generator rotor must rotate at 3600 r/min to generate electricity at 60 Hz.

THE INTERNAL GENERATED VOLTAGE OF A SYNCHRONOUS GENERATOR

The magnitude of the voltage induced in a given stator phase is given by:

$$E_A = K\phi\omega$$

where K is a constant that depends on the generator construction, ϕ is the flux in the machine, and ω is the frequency or speed of rotation.

Figure 31.7 (*a*) illustrates the relationship between the flux in the machine and the field current I_F. Since the internal generated voltage E_A is directly proportional to the flux, the relationship between the E_A and I_F is similar to the one between ϕ and I_F [Fig. 31.7 (*b*)]. The graph is known as the *magnetization curve* or *open-circuit characteristic* of the machine.

THE EQUIVALENT CIRCUIT OF A SYNCHRONOUS GENERATOR

The variable E_A is the internal generated voltage induced in one phase of a synchronous generator. However, this is not the usual voltage that appears at the terminals of the generator.

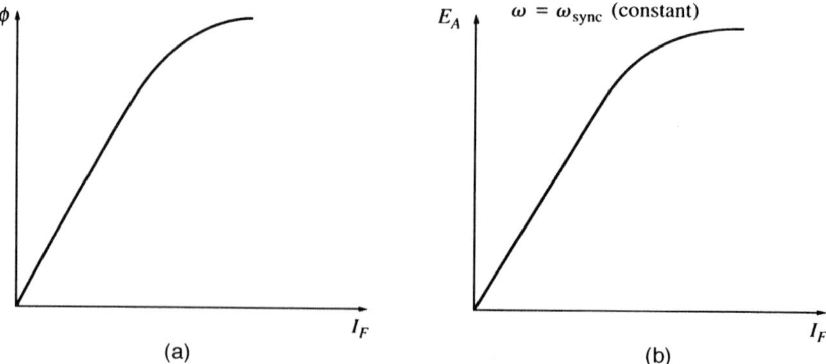

FIGURE 31.7 (*a*) Plot of flux versus field current for a synchronous generator. (*b*) The magnetization curve for the synchronous generator.

In reality, the internal voltage E_A is the same as the output voltage V_ϕ of a phase only when there is no armature current flowing in the stator. The three factors that cause the difference between E_A and V_ϕ are

1. The *armature reaction,* which is the distortion of the air-gap magnetic field by the current flowing in the stator
2. The self-inductance of the armature (stator) windings
3. The resistance of the armature windings

The armature reaction has the largest impact on the difference between E_A and V_ϕ. The voltage E_A is induced when the rotor is spinning. If the generator's terminals are attached to a load, a current flows.

The three-phase current flowing in the stator will produce its own magnetic field in the machine. This *stator* magnetic field distorts the magnetic field produced by the rotor resulting in a change of the phase voltage. This effect is known as the *armature reaction* because the current in the armature (stator) affects the magnetic field that produced it in the first place.

Figure 31.8 (*a*) illustrates a two-pole rotor spinning inside a three-phase stator when there is no load connected to the machine. An internal generated voltage E_A is produced by the rotor magnetic field $\mathbf{B}_R$ whose direction coincides with the peak value of E_A. The voltage will be positive out of the top conductors and negative into the bottom conductors of the stator.

When the generator is not connected to a load, there is no current flow in the armature. The phase voltage V_ϕ will be equal to E_A. When the generator is connected to a lagging load, the peak current will occur at an angle behind the peak voltage [Fig. 31.8 (*b*)]. The current flowing in the stator windings produces a magnetic field called $\mathbf{B}_s$, whose direction is given by the right-hand rule [Fig. 31.8 (*c*)].

A voltage is produced in the stator E_{stat} by the stator magnetic field $\mathbf{B}_s$. The total voltage in a phase is the sum of the internal voltage E_A and the armature reaction voltage E_{stat}:

$$V_\phi = E_A + E_{stat}$$

The net magnetic field $\mathbf{B}_{net}$ is the sum of the rotor and stator magnetic fields:

$$\mathbf{B}_{net} = \mathbf{B}_R + \mathbf{B}_S$$

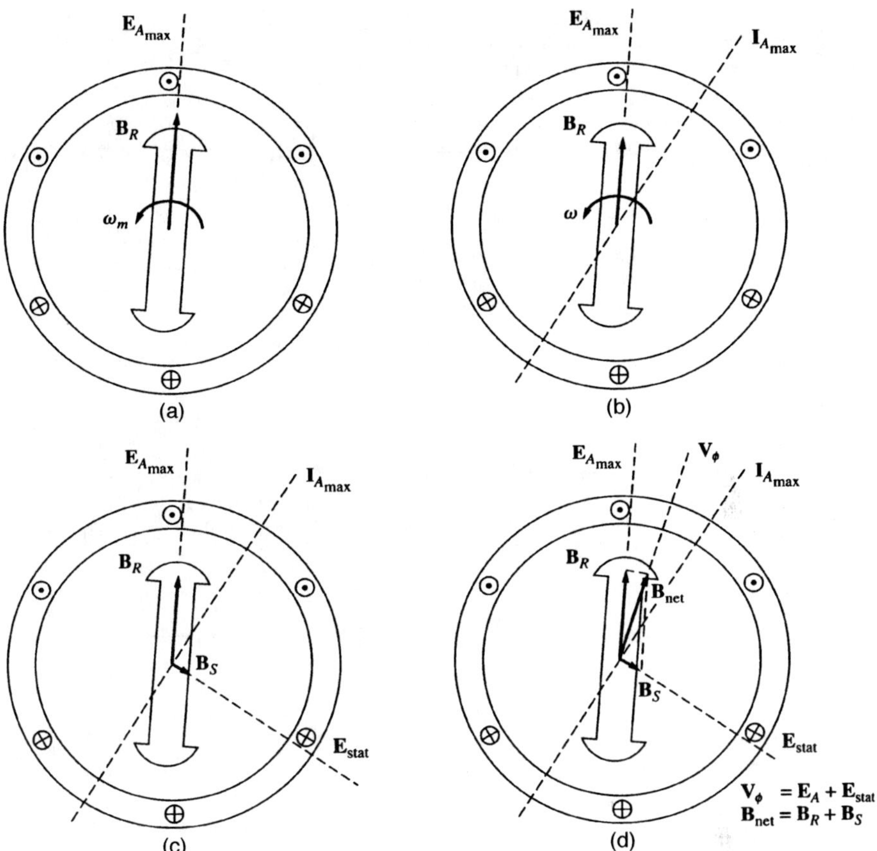

FIGURE 31.8 The development of a model for armature reaction. (*a*) A rotating magnetic field produces the internal generated voltage $\mathbf{E}_A$. (*b*) The resulting voltage produces a lagging current flow when connected to a lagging load. (*c*) The stator current produces its own magnetic field $\mathbf{B}_S$, which produces its own voltage $\mathbf{E}_{\text{stat}}$ in the stator windings of the machine. (*d*) The field $\mathbf{B}_S$ adds to $\mathbf{B}_R$, distorting it into $\mathbf{B}_{\text{net}}$. The voltage $\mathbf{E}_{\text{stat}}$ adds to $\mathbf{E}_A$, producing $\mathbf{V}_\phi$ at the output of the phase.

The angle of the resulting magnetic field $\mathbf{B}_{\text{net}}$ coincides with the one of the net voltage V_ϕ [Fig. 31.8 (*d*)].

The angle of voltage E_{stat} is 90° behind the one of the maximum current I_A. Also, the voltage E_{stat} is directly proportional to $\mathbf{I}_A$. If X is the proportionality constant, the *armature reaction* voltage can be expressed as

$$E_{\text{stat}} = -jXI_A$$

The voltage of a phase is

$$V_\phi = E_A - jXI_A$$

Figure 31.9 shows that the armature reaction voltage can be modeled as an inductor placed in series with the internal generated voltage.

When the effects of the stator windings self-inductance L_A (and its corresponding reactance X_A) and resistance R_A are added, the relationship becomes

$$V_\phi = E_A - jXI_A - jX_A I_A - R_A I_A$$

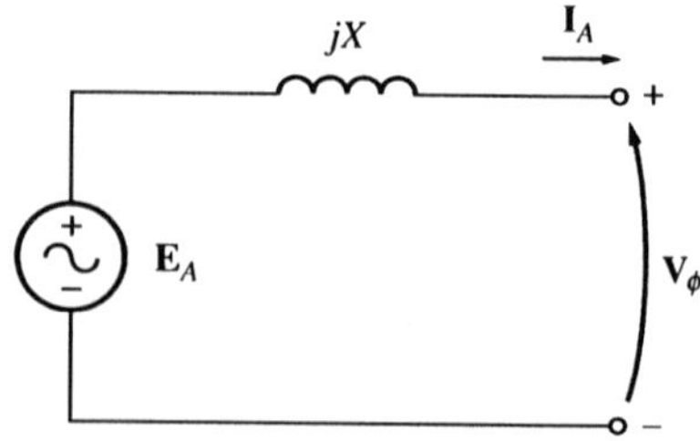

FIGURE 31.9 A simple circuit (see text).

When the effects of the armature reaction and self-inductance are combined (the reactances are added), the *synchronous reactance* of the generator is

$$X_S = X + X_A$$

The final equation becomes

$$V_\phi = E_A - jX_S I_A - R_A I_A$$

Figure 31.10 illustrates the equivalent circuit of a three-phase synchronous generator. The rotor field circuit is supplied by DC power, which is modeled by the coil's inductance and resistance in series. The adjustable resistance R_{adj} controls the field current. The internal

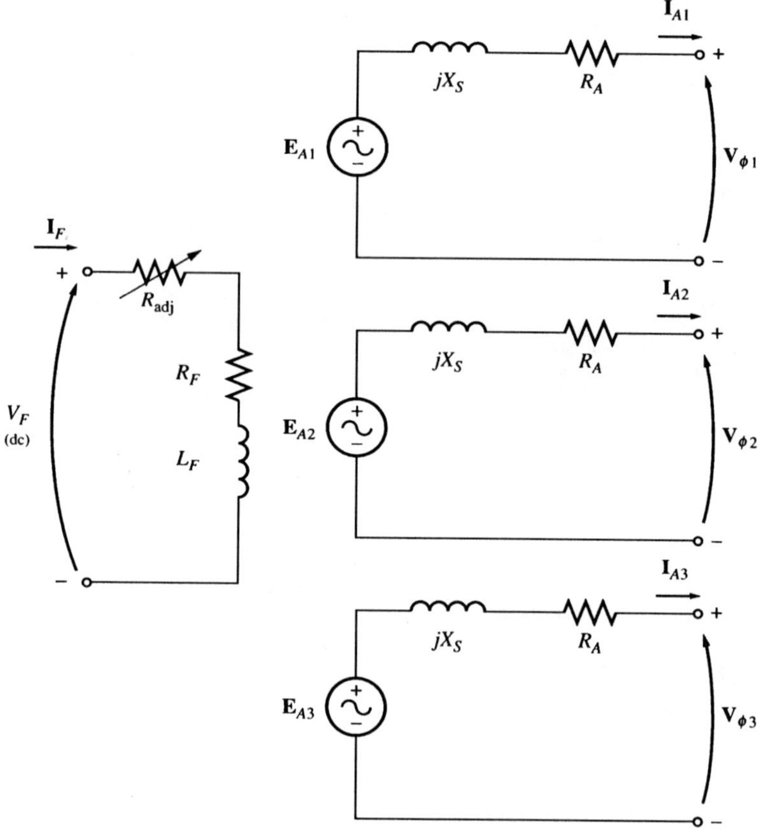

FIGURE 31.10 The full equivalent circuit of a three-phase synchronous generator.

generated voltage for each of the phases is shown in series with the synchronous reactance X_S and the stator winding resistance R_A. The three phases are identical except that the voltages and currents are 120° apart in angle.

Figure 31.11 illustrates that the phases can be either Y- or Δ-connected. When they are Y-connected, the terminal voltage V_T is related to the phase voltage V_ϕ by

$$V_T = \sqrt{3}\, V_\phi$$

When they are Δ-connected, then

$$V_T = V_\phi$$

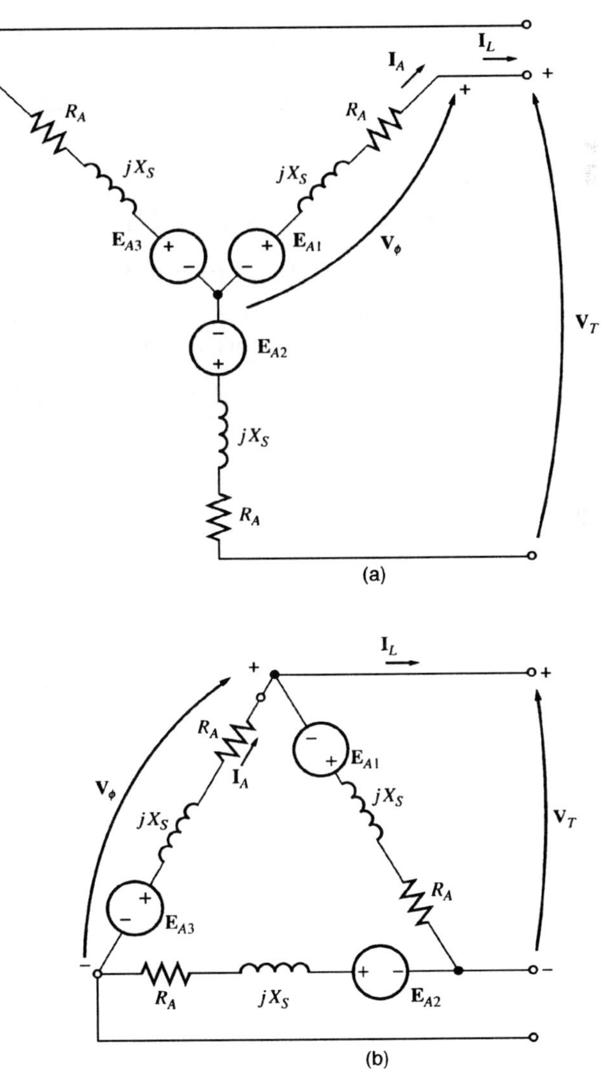

FIGURE 31.11 The generator equivalent circuit connected in Y (*a*) and in Δ (*b*).

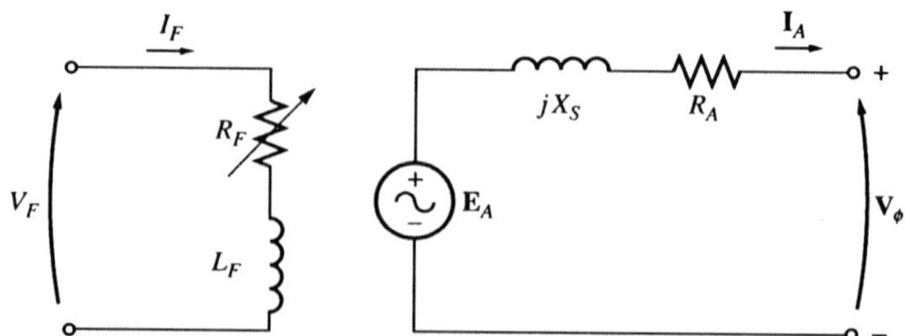

FIGURE 31.12 The per-phase equivalent circuit of a synchronous generator. The internal field circuit resistance and the external variable resistance have been combined into a single resistor R_F.

Since the three phases are identical except that their phase angles are different, the *per-phase equivalent circuit* is used (Fig. 31.12).

THE PHASOR DIAGRAM OF A SYNCHRONOUS GENERATOR

Phasors are used to describe the relationships between AC voltages. Figure 31.13 illustrates these relationships when the generator is supplying a purely resistive load (at unity power factor). The total voltage E_A differs from the terminal voltage V_ϕ by the resistive and inductive voltage drops. All voltages and currents are referenced to V_ϕ, which is assumed arbitrarily to be at angle 0°.

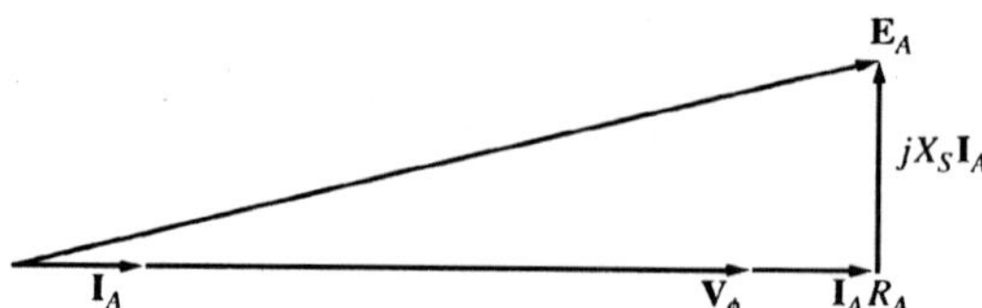

FIGURE 31.13 The phasor diagram of a synchronous generator at unity power factor.

Figure 31.14 illustrates the phasor diagrams of generators operating at lagging and leading power factors. Notice that for a given phase voltage and armature current, lagging loads require larger internal generated voltage EA than leading loads. Therefore, a larger field current is required for lagging loads to get the same terminal voltage, because:

$$E_A = K\phi\omega$$

where ω must remain constant to maintain constant frequency. Thus, for a given field current and magnitude of load current, the terminal voltage for lagging loads is lower than the one for leading loads. In real synchronous generators, the winding resistance is much smaller than the synchronous reactance. Therefore, R_A is often neglected in qualitative studies of voltage variations.

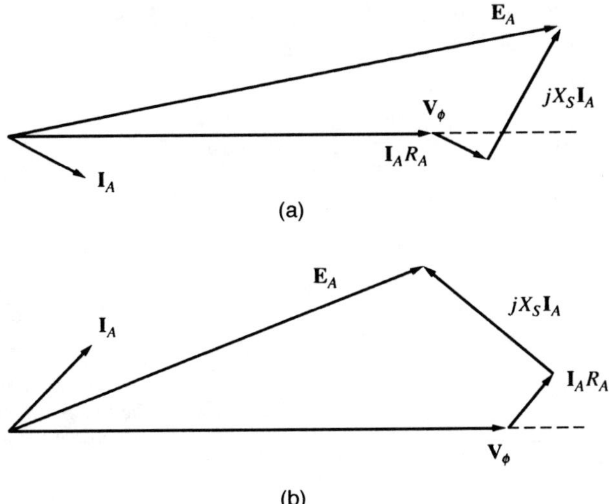

FIGURE 31.14 The phasor diagram of a synchronous generator at lagging (*a*) and leading (*b*) power factor.

POWER AND TORQUE IN SYNCHRONOUS GENERATORS

A synchronous generator is a machine that converts mechanical power to three-phase electrical power. The mechanical power is usually given by a turbine. However, the rotational speed must remain constant to maintain a steady frequency.

Figure 31.15 illustrates the power flow in a synchronous generator. The input mechanical power is $P_{\text{in}} = \tau_{\text{app}}\omega_m$, while the power converted from mechanical to electrical energy is

$$P_{\text{conv}} = \tau_{\text{ind}}\omega_m$$

$$P_{\text{conv}} = 3E_A I_A \cos \gamma$$

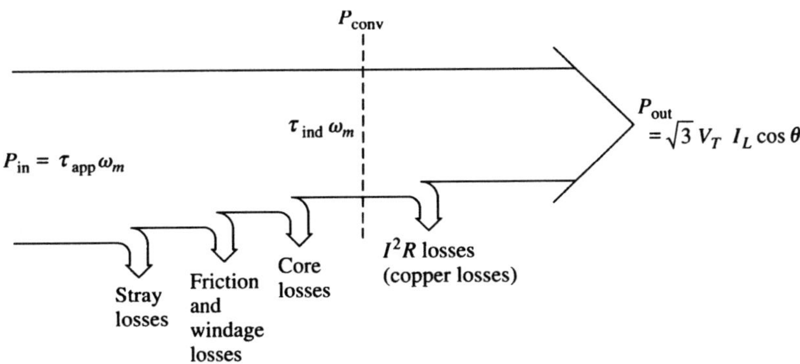

FIGURE 31.15 The power flow diagram of a synchronous generator.

where γ is the angle between E_A and I_A. The real electric output power of the machine is:

$$P_{\text{out}} = \sqrt{3} V_T I_L \cos \theta$$

or in phase quantities as

$$P_{\text{out}} = 3 V_\phi I_A \cos \theta$$

The reactive power is

$$Q_{\text{out}} = \sqrt{3}\, V_T I_L \sin \theta$$

or in phase quantities as

$$Q_{\text{out}} = 3 V_\phi I_A \sin \theta$$

A very useful expression for the output power can be derived if the armature resistance R_A is ignored (since $X_s >> R_A$). Figure 31.16 illustrates a simplified phasor diagram of a synchronous generator when the stator resistance is ignored. The vertical segment bc can be expressed as either $E_A \sin \delta$ or $X_S I_A \cos \theta$. Therefore,

$$I_A \cos \theta = \frac{E_A \sin \delta}{X_S}$$

and substituting into the output power equation

$$\boxed{P = \frac{3 V_\phi E_A \sin \delta}{X_S}}$$

There are no electrical losses in this generator, because the resistances are assumed to be zero, and $P_{\text{conv}} = P_{\text{out}}$.

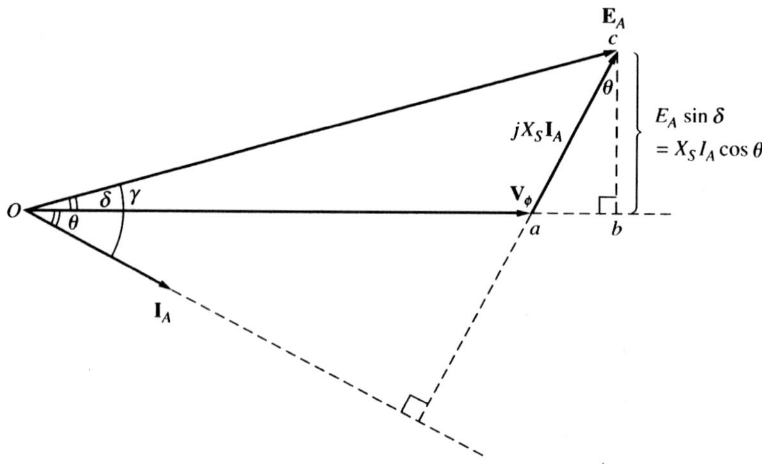

FIGURE 31.16 Simplified phasor diagram with armature resistance ignored.

The output power equation shows that the power produced depends on the angle δ (torque angle) between V_ϕ and E_A. Normally, real generators have a full load torque angle of between 15 and 20°.

The induced torque in the generator can be expressed as

$$\tau_{\text{ind}} = \text{k}\, \mathbf{B}_R \times \mathbf{B}_S$$

or as

$$\tau_{\text{ind}} = \text{k}\, \mathbf{B}_R \times \mathbf{B}_{\text{net}}$$

The magnitude of the expressed torque is

$$\tau_{\text{ind}} = k\, \text{B}_R\, \text{B}_{\text{net}} \sin \delta$$

where δ (the torque angle) is the angle between the rotor and net magnetic fields. An alternative expression for the induced torque in terms of electrical quantities is

$$\boxed{\tau_{\text{ind}} = \frac{3V_\phi E_A \sin \delta}{\omega_m X_S}}$$

THE SYNCHRONOUS GENERATOR OPERATING ALONE

When a synchronous generator is operating under load, its behavior varies greatly depending on the power factor of the load and if the generator is operating alone or in parallel with other synchronous generators. Throughout the upcoming sections, the effect of R_A is ignored, and the speed of the generators and the rotor flux will be assumed constant.

THE EFFECT OF LOAD CHANGES ON A SYNCHRONOUS GENERATOR OPERATING ALONE

Figure 31.17 illustrates a generator supplying a load. What are the effects of load increase on the generator? When the load increases, the real and/or reactive power drawn from the

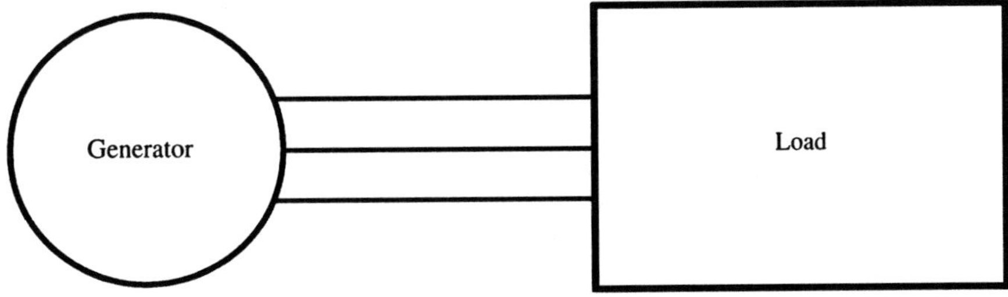

FIGURE 31.17 A single generator supplying a load.

generator increases. The load increase increases the load current drawn from the generator.

The flux ϕ is constant because the field resistor did not change, and the field current is constant. Since the prime mover governing system maintains the mechanical speed ω constant, *the magnitude of the internal generator voltage* $E_A = K\phi\omega$ *is constant.*

Since $\mathbf{E_A}$ is constant, which parameter is varying with the changing load? If the generator is operating at a lagging power factor and an additional load is added at the *same power factor,* then the magnitude of $\mathbf{I_A}$ increases, but angle θ between $\mathbf{I_A}$ and $\mathbf{V_\phi}$ remains constant. Therefore, the armature reaction voltage $jX_S\mathbf{I_A}$ has increased while keeping the same angle. Since

$$E_A = V_\phi + jX_S\mathbf{I}_A$$

$jX_S\mathbf{I_A}$ must increase while the magnitude of E_A remains constant [Fig. 31.18 (*a*)]. Therefore, when the load increases, the voltage V_ϕ decreases sharply. Figure 31.18 (*b*) illustrates the effect when the generator is loaded with a unity power factor. It can be seen that $\mathbf{V_\phi}$ decreases slightly. Figure 31.18 (*c*) illustrates the effect when the generator is loaded with leading-power-factor loads. It can be seen that $\mathbf{V_\phi}$ increases.

The *voltage regulation* is a convenient way to compare the behavior of two generators. The generator voltage regulation (VR) is given by

$$\text{VR} = \frac{V_{\text{nl}} - V_{\text{fl}}}{V_{\text{fl}}} \times 100\%$$

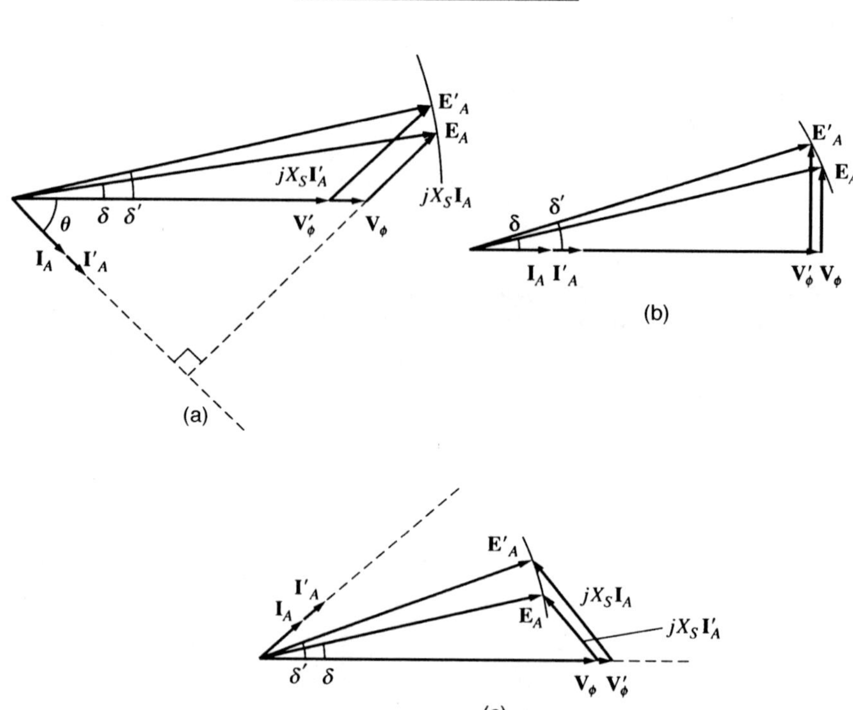

FIGURE 31.18 The effect of an increase in generator loads at constant-power factor upon its terminal voltage. (*a*) Lagging power factor; (*b*) unity power factor; (*c*) leading power factor.

where V_{nl} and V_{fl} are the no-load and full-load voltages of the generator. When a synchronous generator is operating at a lagging power factor, it has a large positive voltage regulation. When a synchronous generator is operating at a unity power factor, it has a small positive voltage regulation, and a synchronous generator operating at a leading power factor has a negative voltage regulation.

During normal operation, it is desirable to maintain constant the voltage that is supplied to the load even when the load varies. The terminal voltage variations can be corrected by varying the magnitude of $\mathbf{E}_A$ to compensate for changes in the load. Since $E_A = K\phi\omega$ and ω remains constant, E_A can be controlled by varying the flux in the generator. For example, when a lagging load is added to the generator, the terminal voltage will fall. The field resistor R_F is decreased to restore the terminal voltage to its previous level. When R_F decreases, the field current I_F increases. This causes the flux to increase, which results in increasing E_A and, therefore, the phase and terminal voltage. This process is reversed to decrease the terminal voltage.

PARALLEL OPERATION OF AC GENERATORS

In most generator applications, there is more than one generator operating in parallel to supply power to various loads. The North American grid is an extreme example of a situation where thousands of generators share the load on the system.

Three major advantages for operating synchronous generators in parallel are

1. The reliability of the power system increases when many generators are operating in parallel, because the failure of any one of them does not cause a total power loss to the loads.
2. When many generators operate in parallel, one or more of them can be taken out when failures occur in power plants or for preventive maintenance.
3. If one generator is used, it cannot operate near full load (because the loads are changing), then it will be inefficient. When several machines are operating in parallel, it is possible to operate only a fraction of them. The ones that are operating will be more efficient because they are near full load.

THE CONDITIONS REQUIRED FOR PARALLELING

Figure 31.19 illustrates a synchronous generator (G_1) supplying power to a load with another generator (G_2) that is about to be paralleled with G_1 by closing the switch (S_1). If

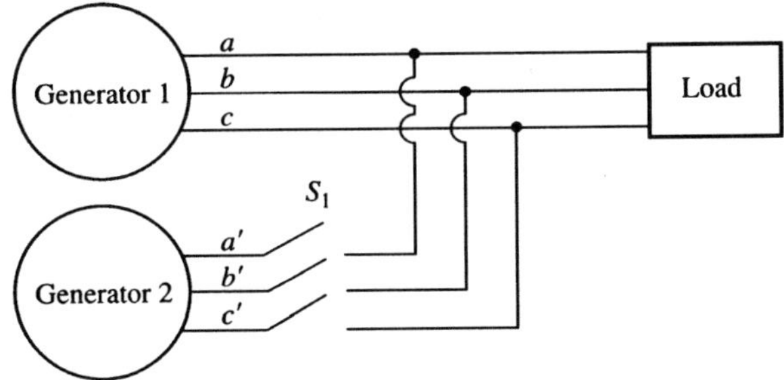

FIGURE 31.19 A generator being paralleled with a running power system.

the switch is closed at some arbitrary moment, the generators could be severely damaged and the load may lose power. If the voltages are different in the conductor being tied together, there will be *very* large current flow when the switch is closed.

This problem can be avoided by ensuring that each of the three phases has the *same voltage magnitude and phase angle* as the conductor to which it is connected. To ensure this match, these four *paralleling conditions* must be met:

1. The two generators must have the same rms line voltages.
2. The *phase sequence* must be the same in the two generators.
3. The two *a* phases must have the same phase angles.
4. The frequency of the *oncoming generator* must be slightly higher than the frequency of the running system.

If the sequence in which the phase voltages peak in the two generators is different [Fig. 31.20 (*a*)], then two pairs of voltages are 120° out of phase, and only one pair of

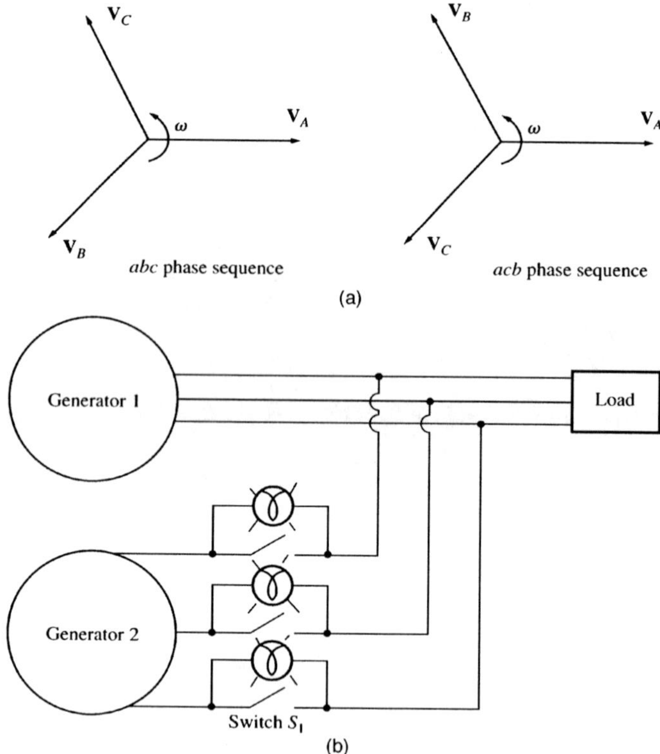

FIGURE 31.20 (*a*) The two possible phase sequences of a three-phase system. (*b*) The three-lightbulb method for checking phase sequence.

voltages (the *a* phases) are in phase. If the generators are connected in this manner, large currents would flow in phases *b* and *c,* causing damage to both machines.

The phase sequence problem can be corrected by swapping the connections on any two of the three phases on one of the generators. If the frequencies of the power supplied by the two generators are not almost equal when they are connected together, large power transients will occur until the generators stabilize at a common frequency. The frequencies of the two generators must differ by a small amount so that the phase angles of the oncoming generator will change slowly, relative to the phase angles of the running system. The angles between the voltages can be observed and switch S_1 can be closed when the systems are exactly in phase.

THE GENERAL PROCEDURE FOR PARALLELING GENERATORS

If generator G_2 is to be connected to the running system (Fig. 31.20), the following two steps should be taken to accomplish paralleling:

1. The terminal voltage of the oncoming generator should be adjusted by changing the field current until it is equal to the line voltage of the running system.
2. The phase sequence of the oncoming generator and the running system should be the same. The phase sequence can be checked by using the following two methods:
   a. A small induction motor can be connected alternately to the terminals of each of the two generators. If the motor rotates in the same direction each time, then the phase sequence of both generators is the same. If the phase sequences are different, the motor would rotate in opposite directions. In this case, two of the conductors on the incoming generator must be reversed.
   b. Figure 31.20 (*b*) illustrates three lightbulbs connected across the terminals of the switch connecting the generator to the system. When the phase changes between the two systems, the lightbulbs become bright when the phase difference is large, and they become dim when the phase difference is small. *When the systems have the same phase sequence, all three bulbs become bright and dim simultaneously.* If the systems have opposite phase sequence, the bulbs would get bright in succession.

The frequency of the oncoming generator should be slightly higher than the frequency of the running system. A frequency meter is used until the frequencies are close, then changes in phase between the system are observed. The frequency of the oncoming generator is adjusted to a slightly higher frequency to ensure that when it is connected, it will come on-line supplying power as a generator, instead of consuming it as a motor.

Once the frequencies are almost equal, the voltages in the two systems will change phase relative to each other very slowly. This change in phase is observed, and the switch connecting the two systems together is closed when the phase angles are equal (Fig. 31.21). A confirmation that the two systems are in phase can be done by watching the three lightbulbs. The systems are in phase when the three lightbulbs all go out (because the voltage difference across them is zero). This simple scheme is useful, but it is not very accurate. A synchroscope is more accurate. It is a meter that measures the difference in phase angle between the *a* phases of the two systems (Fig. 31.22).

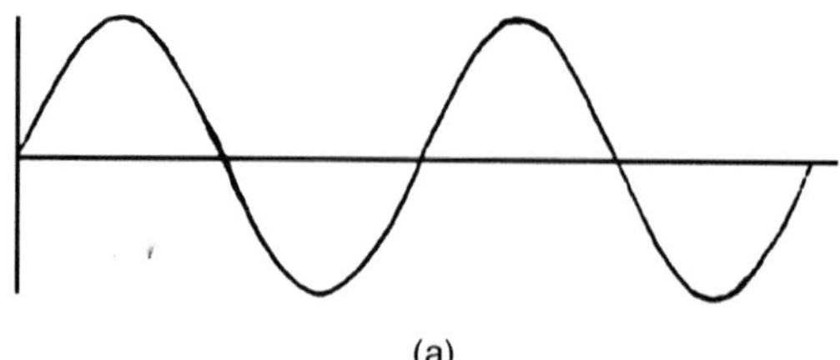

(a)

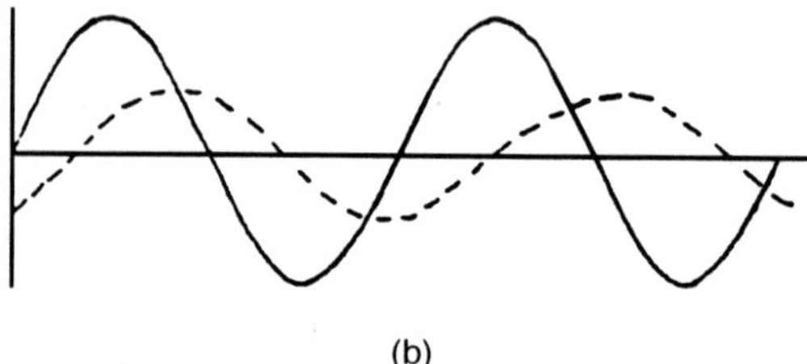

(b)

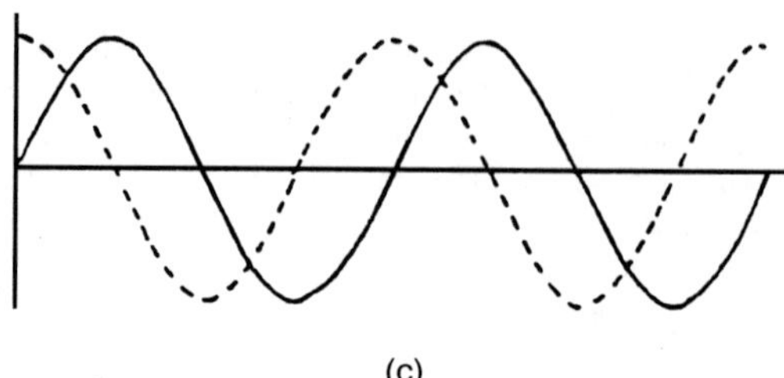

(c)

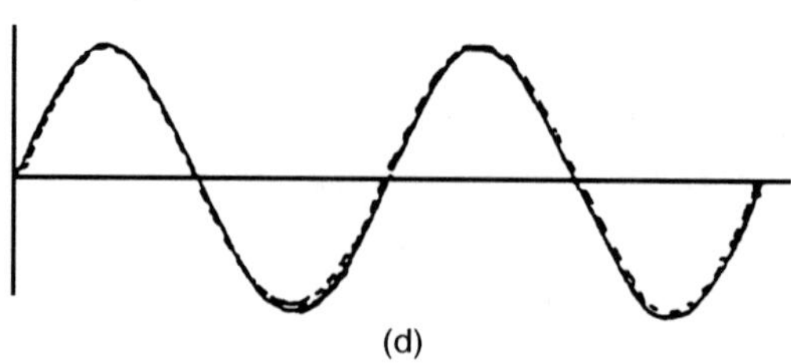

(d)

FIGURE 31.21 Steps taken to synchronize an incoming AC generator to the supply system. (*a*) Existing system voltage wave (one phase only shown). (*b*) Machine voltage wave shown dotted. Out of phase and frequency. Being built up to equal the system max. volts by adjustment of field rheostat. (*c*) Machine voltage now equal to system. Voltage waves out of phase, but frequency being increased by increasing speed of prime mover. (*d*) Machine voltage now equal to system, in phase, and with equal frequency. Synchroscope shows 12 o'clock. Switch can now be closed.

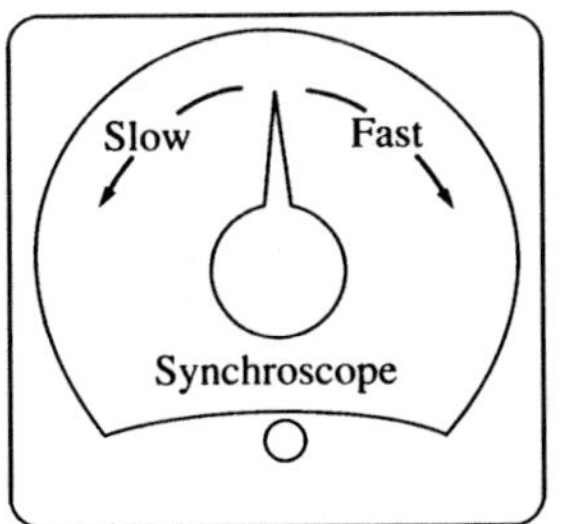

FIGURE 31.22 A synchroscope.

The phase difference between the two *a* phases is shown by the dial. When the systems are in phase (0° phase difference), the dial would be at the top. When they are 180° out of phase, the dial would be at the bottom.

The phase angle on the meter changes slowly because the frequencies of the two systems are slightly different. Since the oncoming generator frequency is slightly higher than the system frequency, the synchroscope needle rotates clockwise because the phase angle advances.

If the oncoming generator frequency is lower than the system frequency, the needle would rotate counterclockwise. When the needle of the synchroscope stops in the vertical position, the voltages are in phase and the switch can be closed to connect the systems.

However, the synchroscope provides the relationship for only one phase. It does not provide information about the phase sequence.

The whole process of paralleling large generators to the line is done by a computer. For small generators, the operator performs the paralleling steps.

FREQUENCY-POWER AND VOLTAGE-REACTIVE POWER CHARACTERISTICS OF A SYNCHRONOUS GENERATOR

The mechanical source of power for the generator is a *prime mover,* such as diesel engines or steam, gas, water, and wind turbines. All prime movers behave in a similar fashion. As the power drawn from them increases, the rotational speed decreases. In general, this decrease in speed is nonlinear. However, the governor makes this decrease in speed linear with increasing power demand.

Thus, the governing system has a slight speed-drooping characteristic with increasing load. The speed droop (SD) of a prime mover is defined by

$$\boxed{\mathrm{SD} = \frac{n_{\mathrm{nl}} - n_{\mathrm{fl}}}{n_{\mathrm{fl}}} \times 100\%}$$

where n_{nl} is the no-load speed of the prime mover, and n_{fl} is the full-load speed of the prime mover.

The speed droop of most generators is usually 2 to 4 percent. In addition, most governors have a setpoint adjustment to allow the no-load speed of the turbine to be varied. A typical speed-power curve is shown in Fig. 31.23. Since the electrical frequency is related to the shaft speed and the number of poles by

$$f_e = \frac{n_{\mathrm{nl}}P}{120}$$

the power output is related to the electrical frequency.

Figure 31.23 (*b*) illustrates a frequency-versus-power graph. The power output is related to the frequency by

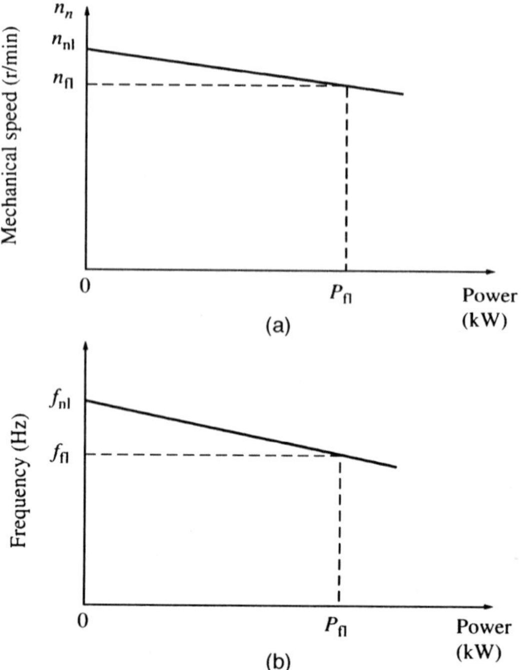

FIGURE 31.23 (*a*) The speed-versus-power curve for a typical prime mover. (*b*) The resulting frequency-versus-power curve for the generator.

$$P = S_P (f_{nl} - f_{sys})$$

where P = power output of generator
f_{nl} = no-load frequency of generator
f_{sys} = operating frequency of system
S_P = slope of curve, kW/Hz or MW/Hz

The reactive power Q has a similar relationship with the terminal voltage V_T. As previously described, the terminal voltage drops when a lagging load is added to a synchronous generator. The terminal voltage increases when a leading load is added to a synchronous generator. Figure 31.24 illustrates a plot of terminal voltage versus reactive power. This plot has a drooping characteristic that is not generally linear, but most generator voltage regulators have a feature to make this characteristic linear. When the no-load terminal voltage setpoint on the voltage regulator is changed, the curve can slide up and down. The frequency-power and terminal voltage-reactive power characteristics play important roles in parallel operation of synchronous generators.

When a single generator is operating alone, the real power P and reactive power Q are equal to the amounts demanded by the loads. The generator's controls cannot control the real and reactive power supplied. Therefore, for a given real power, the generator's operating frequency f_e is controlled by the governor setpoints. For a given reactive power, the generator's terminal voltage V_T is controlled by the field current.

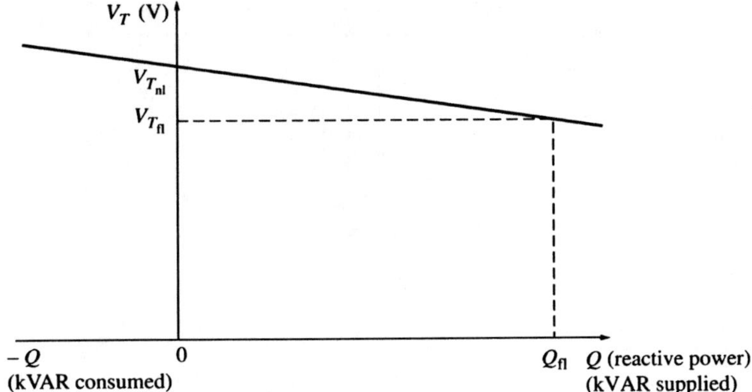

FIGURE 31.24 The terminal voltage (V_T)-versus-reactive power (Q) curve for a synchronous generator.

OPERATION OF GENERATORS IN PARALLEL WITH LARGE POWER SYSTEMS

The power system is usually so large that *nothing* the operator of a synchronous generator connected to it does will have any effect on the power system. An example of this is the North American power grid, which is so large that any action taken by one generator cannot have an observable change on the overall grid frequency.

This principle is idealized by the concept of an infinite bus, which is a very large power system, such that its voltage and frequency do not change regardless of the amounts of real and reactive power supplied to or drawn from it. Figure 31.25 illustrates the power-frequency and reactive power-terminal voltage characteristics of such a system.

The behavior of a generator connected to an infinite bus is easier to explain when the automatic field current regulator is not considered. Thus, the following discussion will ignore the slight differences caused by the field regulator (Fig. 31.26).

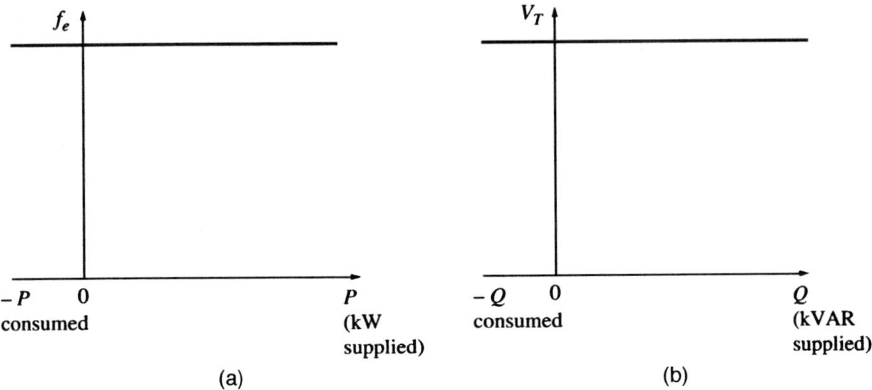

FIGURE 31.25 The frequency-versus-power (*a*) and terminal-voltage-versus-reactive-power (*b*) curves for an infinite bus.

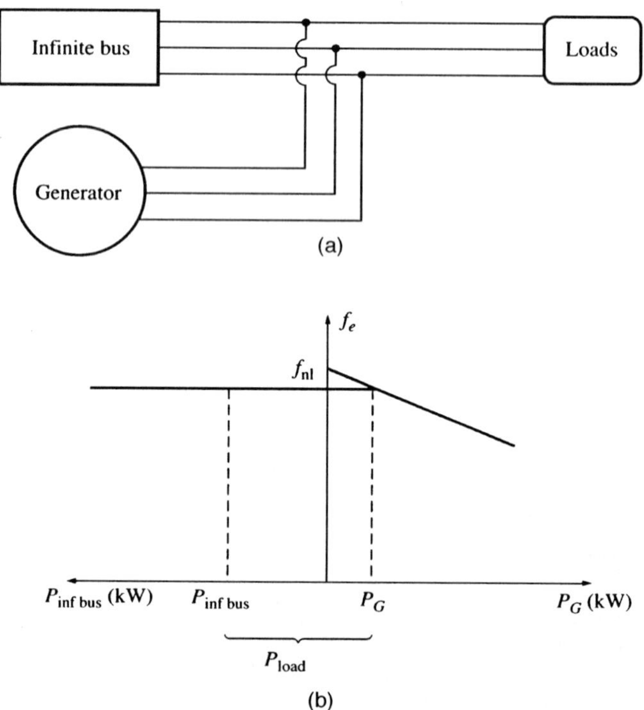

FIGURE 31.26 (*a*) A synchronous generator operating in parallel with an infinite bus. (*b*) The frequency-versus-power diagram (or *house diagram*) for a synchronous generator in parallel with an infinite bus.

When a generator is connected in parallel with another generator or a large system, *the frequency and terminal voltage of all the generators must be the same because their output conductors are tied together.* Therefore, a common vertical axis can be used to plot the real power-frequency and reactive power-voltage characteristics back-to-back.

If a generator has been paralleled with the infinite bus, it will be essentially "floating" on-line. It supplies a small amount of real power and little or no reactive power (Fig. 31.27).

If the generator that has been paralleled to line has a slightly lower frequency than the running system (Fig. 31.28), the no-load frequency of the generator would be less than the operating frequency. In this case, the power supplied by the generator is negative (it consumes electric energy because it is running as a motor). The oncoming generator frequency should be adjusted to be slightly higher than the frequency of the running system to ensure that the generator comes on-line supplying power instead of consuming it.

In reality, most generators have a reverse-power trip connected to them. They must be paralleled when their frequency is higher than that of the running system. If such a generator starts to "motor" (consume power), it will be automatically disconnected from the line.

Once the generator is connected, the governor setpoint is increased to shift the no-load frequency of the generator upward. Since the frequency of the system remains constant (the frequency of the infinite bus cannot change), the generator output power increases. The house diagram and the phasor diagram are illustrated in Fig. 31.29 (*a, b*).

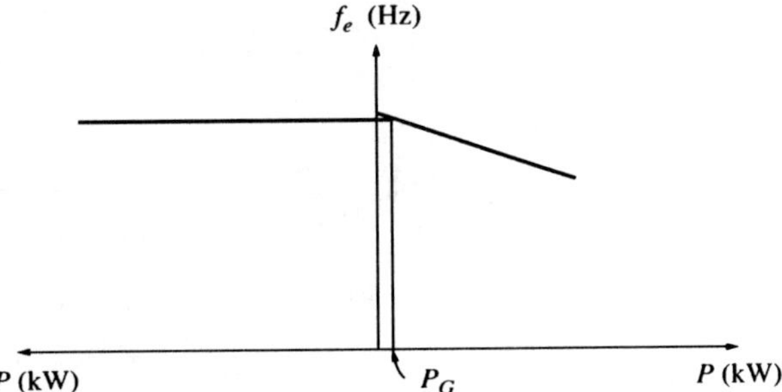

FIGURE 31.27 The frequency-versus-power diagram at the moment just after paralleling.

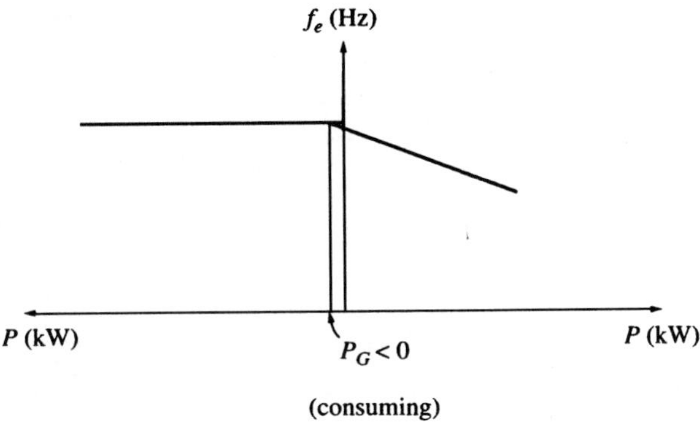

FIGURE 31.28 The frequency-versus-power diagram if the no-load frequency of the generator were slightly *less* than system frequency before paralleling.

Notice in the phasor diagram that the magnitude of $\mathbf{E}_A$ ($= K\phi\omega$) remains constant because I_F and ω remained unchanged, while $E_A \sin \delta$ (which is proportional to the output power as long as V_T remains constant) has increased.

When the governor setpoint is increased, the no-load frequency and the output power of the generator increase. As the power increases, the magnitude of E_A remains constant while $E_A \sin \delta$ is increased further.

If the output power of the generator is increased until it exceeds the power consumed by the load, the additional power generated flows back into the system (infinite bus). By definition, the infinite bus can consume or supply any amount of power while the frequency remains constant. Therefore, the additional power is consumed.

Figure 31.29 (*b*) illustrates the phasor diagram of the generator when the real power has been adjusted to the desired value. Notice that at this time, the generator has a slightly leading power factor. It is acting as a capacitor, consuming reactive power. The field current can be adjusted so the generator can supply reactive power. However, there are some constraints on the operation of the generator under these circumstances.

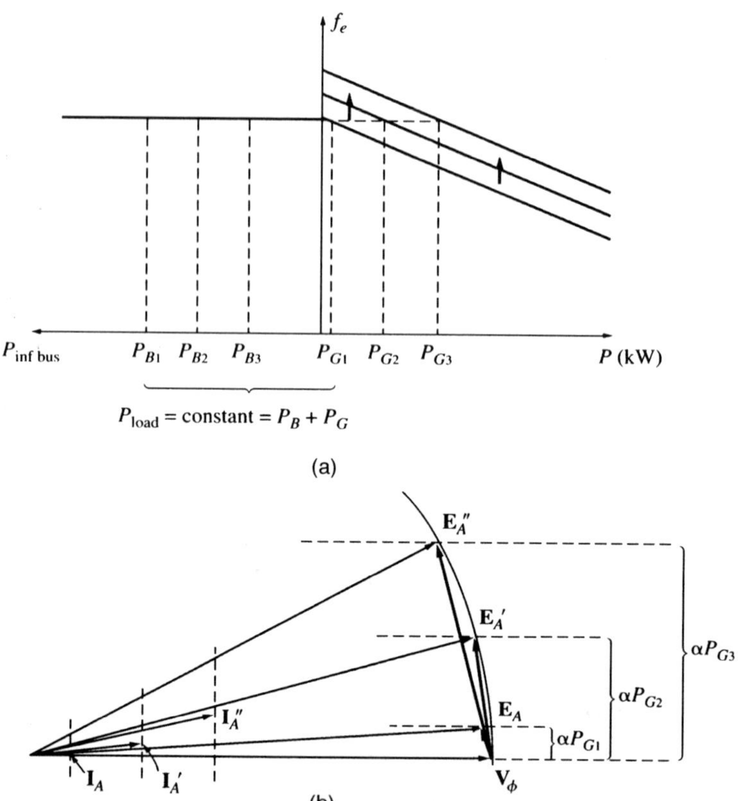

FIGURE 31.29 The effect of increasing the governor's setpoints on (*a*) the house diagram and (*b*) the phasor diagram.

- When I_F is changing, *the power must remain constant.* The power given to the generator is $P_{\text{in}} = \tau_{\text{app}}\omega_m$.
- For a given governor setting, the prime mover of the generator has a fixed-torque-speed characteristic. When the governor setpoint is changed, the curve moves.
- Since the generator is tied to the system (infinite bus), its speed *cannot* change. Therefore, since the governor setpoint and the generator's speed have not changed, the power supplied by the generator must remain constant.
- Since the power supplied does not change when the field current is changing, then $I_A \cos\theta$ and $E_A \sin\delta$ (the distance proportional to the power in the phasor diagram) cannot change.

The flux ϕ increases when the field current is increased. Therefore, E_A ($= K\phi\omega$) must increase. If E_A increases, while $E_A \sin\delta$ remains constant, then phasor $\mathbf{E_A}$ must slide along the constant-power line shown in Fig. 31.30. Since $\mathbf{V}_\phi$ is constant, the angle of $jX_S\mathbf{I_A}$ changes as shown. Therefore, the angle and magnitude of $\mathbf{I_A}$ change.

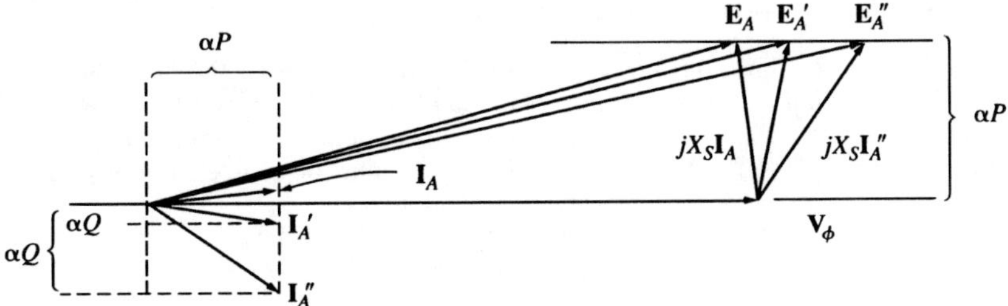

FIGURE 31.30 The effect of increasing the generator's field current on the phasor diagram of the machine.

Notice that the distance proportional to Q ($\mathbf{I}_A \sin \theta$) increases. This means that *increasing the field current in a synchronous generator operating in parallel with a power system (infinite bus) increases the reactive power output of the generator.*

In summary, when a generator is operating in parallel with a power system (infinite bus):

- The power system connected to the generator controls the frequency and the terminal voltage.
- The real power supplied by the generator to the system is controlled by the governor setpoint.
- The reactive power supplied by the generator to the system is controlled by the field current.

SYNCHRONOUS GENERATOR RATINGS

There are limits to the output power of a synchronous generator. These limits are known as *ratings* of the generator. Their purpose is to protect the generator from damage caused by improper operation. The synchronous generator ratings are: voltage, frequency, speed, apparent power (kilovoltamperes), power factor, field current, and service factor.

The Voltage, Speed, and Frequency Ratings

The common system frequencies used today are 50 Hz (in Europe, Asia, etc.), and 60 Hz (in the Americas). Once the frequency and the number of poles are known, there is only one possible rotational speed.

One of the most important ratings for the generator is the voltage at which it operates. Since the generator's voltage depends on the flux, the higher the design voltage, the higher the flux. However, the flux cannot increase indefinitely, because the field current has a maximum value.

The main consideration in determining the rated voltage of the generator is the breakdown value of the winding insulation. The voltage at which the generator operates must not approach the breakdown value. A generator rated for a given frequency (e.g., 60 Hz) can be operated at 50 Hz as long as some conditions are met. Since there is a maximum flux achievable in a given generator, and since $E_A = K\phi\omega$, the maximum allowable E_A must change when the speed is changed. For example, a generator rated for 60 Hz can be operated at 50 Hz if the voltage is derated to 50/60, or 83.3 percent of its design value. The opposite effect would happen when a generator rated for 50 Hz is operated at 60 Hz.

Apparent Power and Power-Factor Ratings

The factors that determine the power limits of electric machines are the shaft torque and the heating of the windings. In general, the shaft can handle more power than that for which the machine is rated. Therefore, the steady-state power limits are determined by the heating in the windings of the machine. The windings that must be protected in a synchronous generator are the armature windings and the field windings.

The maximum allowable current in the armature determines the maximum apparent power for the generator. Since the apparent power S is given by

$$S = 3V_\phi I_A$$

if the rated voltage is known, the maximum allowable current in the armature determines the rated apparent power of the generator. *The power factor of the armature current does not affect the heating of the armature windings.* The stator copper losses heating effect is

$$P_{SCL} = 3I_A^2 R_A$$

These effects are independent of the angle between the I_A and V_ϕ. These generators are not rated in megawatts (MW), but in megavoltamperes (MVA).

The field windings copper losses are

$$P_{RCL} = I_F^2 R_F$$

Therefore, the maximum allowable heating determines the maximum field current for the machine. Since $E_A = K\phi\omega$, this also determines the maximum acceptable E_A. Since there is a maximum value for I_F and E_A, there is a minimum acceptable power factor of the generator when it is operating at the rated MVA.

Figure 31.31 illustrates the phasor diagram of a synchronous generator with the rated voltage and armature current. The current angle can vary, as shown. Since $\mathbf{E_A}$ is the sum of $\mathbf{V}_\phi$ and $jX_S\mathbf{I_A}$, there are some current angles for which the required E_A exceeds $E_{A\max}$. If

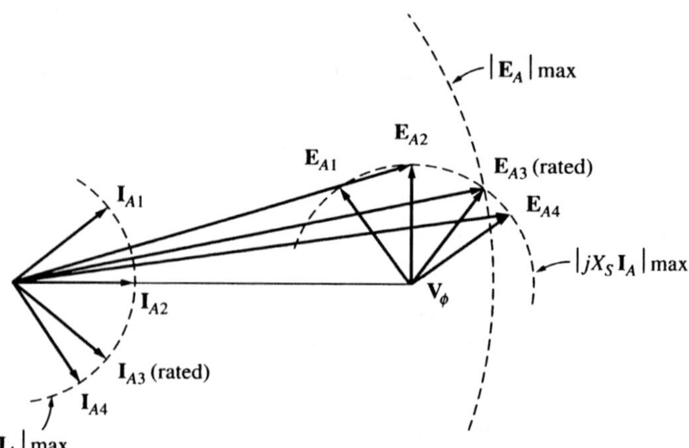

FIGURE 31.31 How the rotor field current limit sets the rated power factor of a generator.

the generator is operated at these power factors and the rated armature current, the field windings will burn.

The angle of $\mathbf{I_A}$ that results in the maximum allowable $\mathbf{E_A}$ while $\mathbf{V_\phi}$ is at the rated value determines the generator-rated power factor. The generator can be operated at a lower power factor (more lagging) than the rated value, but only by reducing the MVA output of the generator.

SYNCHRONOUS GENERATOR CAPABILITY CURVES

The generator *capability diagram* expresses the stator and rotor heat limits and any external limits on the generator. The capability diagram illustrates the complex power $S = P + jQ$. It is derived from the generator's phasor diagram, assuming that $\mathbf{V_\phi}$ is constant at the generator's rated voltage.

Figure 31.32 illustrates the phasor diagram of a synchronous generator operating at its rated-voltage and lagging-power factor. The orthogonal axes are drawn with units of volts. The length of the vertical segment AB is $X_S I_A \cos\theta$, and horizontal segment $0A$ is $X_s I_A \sin\theta$. The generator's real power output is

$$P = 3V_\phi I_A \cos\theta$$

The reactive power output is

$$Q = 3V_\phi I_A \sin\theta$$

The apparent power output is

$$S = 3V_\phi I_A$$

Figure 31.32 (*b*) illustrates how the axes can be recalibrated in terms of real and reactive power. The conversion factor used to change the scale of the axis from volts (V) to voltamperes (VA) is $3V_\phi/X_S$:

$$P = 3V_\phi I_\phi \cos\theta = \frac{3V_\phi}{X_S}(X_S I_A \cos\theta)$$

$$Q = 3V_\phi I_\phi \sin\theta = \frac{3V_\phi}{X_S}(X_S I_A \sin\theta)$$

On the voltage axes, the origin of the phasor diagram is located at $-V_\phi$. Therefore, the origin on the power diagram is located at

$$Q = \frac{3V_\phi}{X_S}(-V_\phi) = \frac{-3V_\phi^2}{X_S}$$

On the power diagram, the length corresponding to E_A is

$$D_E = \frac{3E_A V_\phi}{X_S}$$

The length that corresponds to $X_S I_A$ on the power diagram is $3V_\phi I_A$.

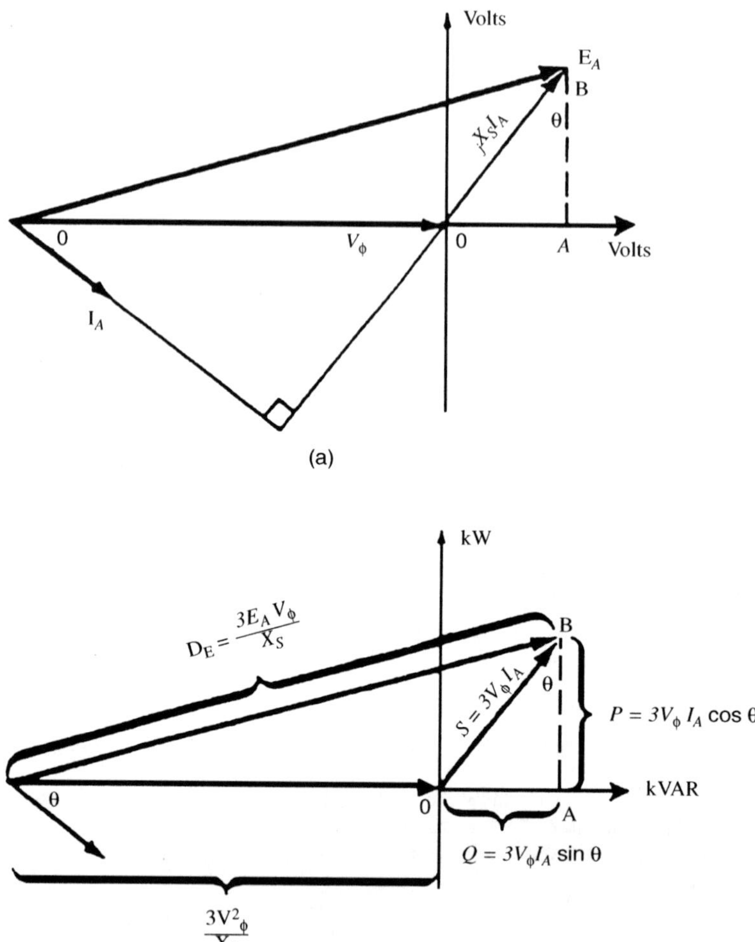

FIGURE 31.32 Derivation of a synchronous generator capability curve. (*a*) The generator phase diagram; (*b*) the corresponding power units.

Figure 31.33 illustrates the final capability curve of a synchronous generator. It illustrates a plot of real power P versus reactive power Q. The lines representing constant armature current I_A are shown as lines of constant apparent power $S - 3V_\phi I_A$, which are represented by concentric circles around the origin. The lines representing constant field current corresponds to lines of constant E_A. These are illustrated by circles of magnitude $3E_AV_\phi/X_S$ centered at:

$$Q = \frac{-3V_\phi^2}{X_S}$$

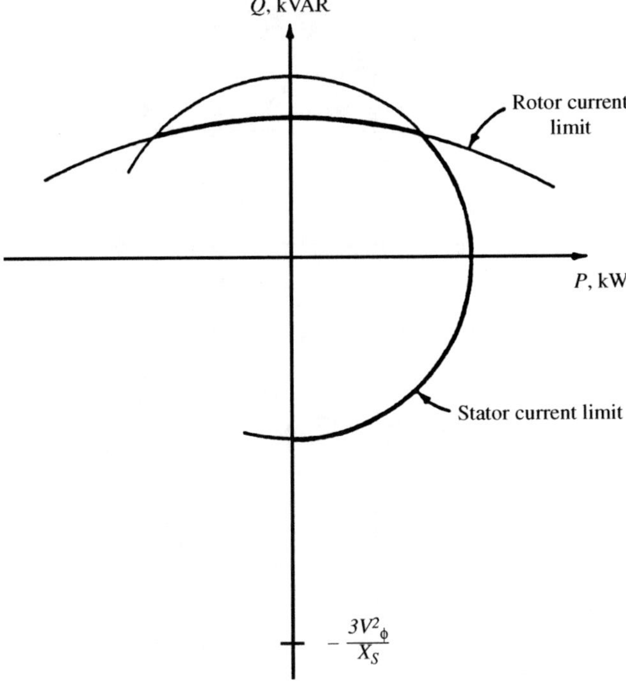

FIGURE 31.33 The resulting generator capability curve.

The armature current limit is illustrated by the circle corresponding to the rated I_A or MVA. The field current limit is illustrated by the circle corresponding to the rated I_F or E_A. *Any point located within both circles is a safe operating point for the generator.* Additional constraints, such as the maximum prime-mover power, can also be shown on the diagram (Fig. 31.34).

SHORT-TIME OPERATION AND SERVICE FACTOR

The heating of the armature and field windings of a synchronous generator is the most important limit in steady-state operation. The power level at which the heating limit usually occurs is much lower than the maximum power that the generator is mechanically and magnetically able to supply.

In general, a typical synchronous generator can supply up to 300 percent of its rated power until its windings burn up. This ability to supply more power than the rated amount is used for momentary power surges, which occur during motor starting and other load transients.

A synchronous generator can supply more power than the rated value for longer periods of time, as long as the windings do not heat up excessively before the load is removed. For example, a generator rated for 1 MW is able to supply 1.5 MW for 1 min without causing serious damage to the windings. This generator can operate for longer periods at lower power levels.

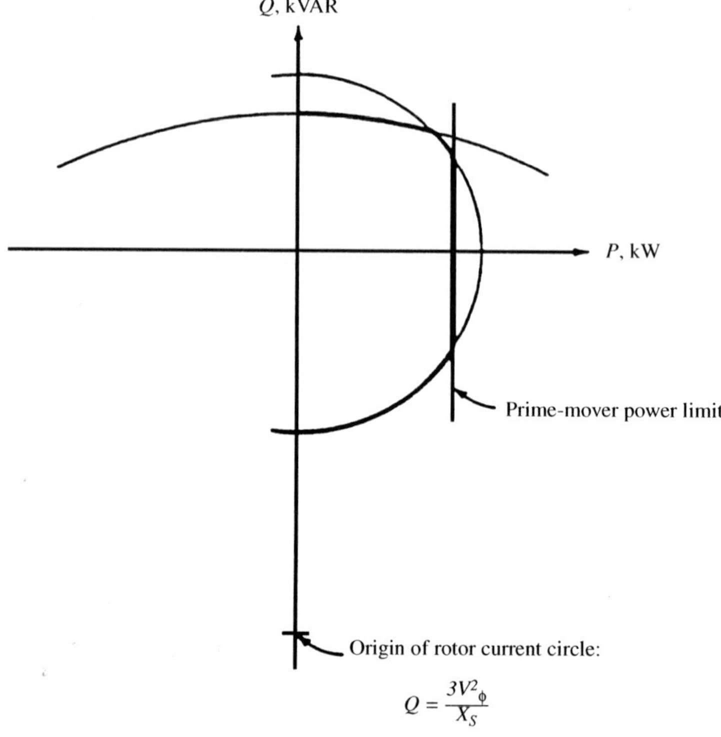

FIGURE 31.34 A capability diagram showing the prime-mover power limit.

The *insulation class* of the windings determines the maximum temperature rise in the generator. The standard insulation classes are A, B, F, and H. In general, these classes correspond to temperature rises above ambient of 60, 80, 105, and 125°C, respectively. The power supplied by a generator increases with the insulation class without overheating the windings.

In motors and generators, overheating the windings is a *serious problem.* In general, when the temperature of the windings increases by 10°C above the rated value, the average lifetime of the machine is reduced by half. Since the increase in the temperature of the windings above the rated value drastically reduces the lifetime of the machine, a synchronous generator should not be overloaded unless it is absolutely necessary.

The *service factor* is the ratio of the actual maximum power of the machine to its nameplate rating. A 1.15 service factor of a generator indicates that it can operate indefinitely at 115 percent of the rated load without harm. The service factor of a motor or a generator provides a margin for error in case the rated loads were improperly estimated.

REFERENCE

1. Chapman, S. J., *Electric Machinery Fundamentals,* 2d ed., McGraw-Hill, New York, 1991.

CHAPTER 32
GENERATOR COMPONENTS, AUXILIARIES, AND EXCITATION

Figure 32.1 illustrates a sectional view of a large generator.[1] Hydrogen is used to cool most generators having a rating larger than 50 MW.

THE ROTOR

The *rotor* is made from a single steel forging. The steel is vacuum-degassed to minimize the possibility of hydrogen-initiated cracking. Reheating and quenching also hardens the forging. Stress-relieving heat treatment is done following rough machining. Ultrasonic examination is performed at various stages of the rotor. Figure 32.2 illustrates the winding slots in the rotor. Figure 32.3 illustrates a rotor cross section and the gas flow.

The generator countertorque increases to 4 to 5 times the full-load torque when a short circuit occurs at the generator terminals. The rotor and turbine-end coupling must be able to withstand this peak torque.

ROTOR WINDING

Each winding turn is assembled separately in half-turns or in more pieces. The joints are at the centers of the end turns or at the corners. They are brazed together after assembling each turn, to form a series-connected coil. The coils are made of high-conductivity copper with a small amount of silver to improve the creep properties. The gas exits through radially aligned slots.

Slot liners of molded glass fiber insulate the coils. These separators of glass fiber are used between each turn. They insulate against almost 10 V between adjacent turns (Fig. 32.4). The end rings and end discs are separated from the end windings by thick layers of insulation. Insulation blocks are placed in the spaces between the end windings to ensure the coils do not distort. The winding slots are cut in diametrically opposite pairs. They are equally pitched over two-thirds of the rotor periphery, leaving the pole faces without winding slots. This results in a difference between the stiffness in the two perpendicular axes. This difference leads to vibration at twice the speed. Equalizing slots are cut in the pole faces (Fig. 32.5) to prevent this problem from occurring. The slots are wider and shallower than the winding slots. They are filled with steel blocks to restore the magnetic properties. The blocks contain holes to allow the ventilating gas to flow.

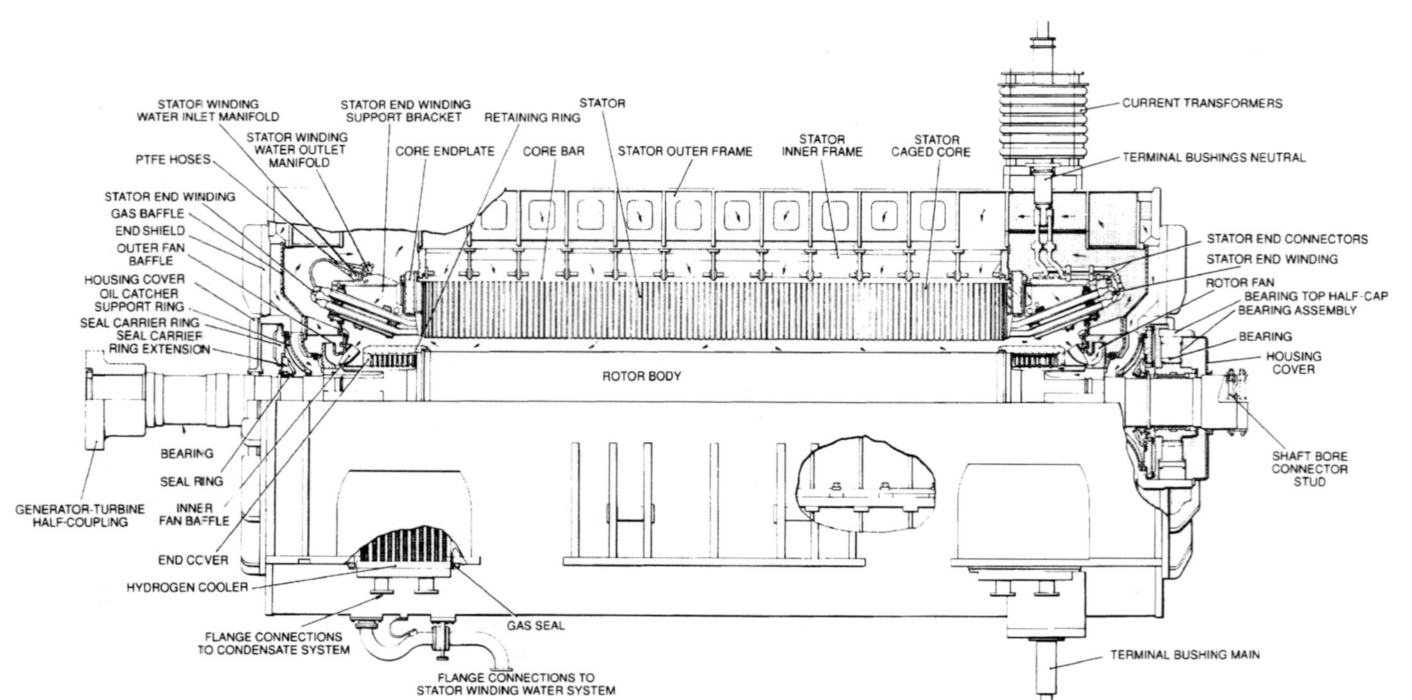
STATOR WINDING WATER INLET MANIFOLD
STATOR END WINDING SUPPORT BRACKET
RETAINING RING
STATOR
STATOR WINDING WATER OUTLET MANIFOLD
CORE ENDPLATE
CORE BAR
STATOR OUTER FRAME
STATOR INNER FRAME
STATOR CAGED CORE
CURRENT TRANSFORMERS
TERMINAL BUSHINGS NEUTRAL
PTFE HOSES
STATOR END WINDING
GAS BAFFLE
END SHIELD
OUTER FAN BAFFLE
HOUSING COVER
OIL CATCHER SUPPORT RING
SEAL CARRIER RING
SEAL CARRIER RING EXTENSION
STATOR END CONNECTORS
STATOR END WINDING
ROTOR FAN
BEARING TOP HALF-CAP
BEARING ASSEMBLY
BEARING
HOUSING COVER
ROTOR BODY
BEARING
SEAL RING
GENERATOR-TURBINE HALF-COUPLING
INNER FAN BAFFLE
END COVER
HYDROGEN COOLER
SHAFT BORE CONNECTOR STUD
GAS SEAL
FLANGE CONNECTIONS TO CONDENSATE SYSTEM
FLANGE CONNECTIONS TO STATOR WINDING WATER SYSTEM
TERMINAL BUSHING MAIN

FIGURE 32.1 Sectional view of a 660-MW generator.

FIGURE 32.2 Cutting winding slots in a rotor.

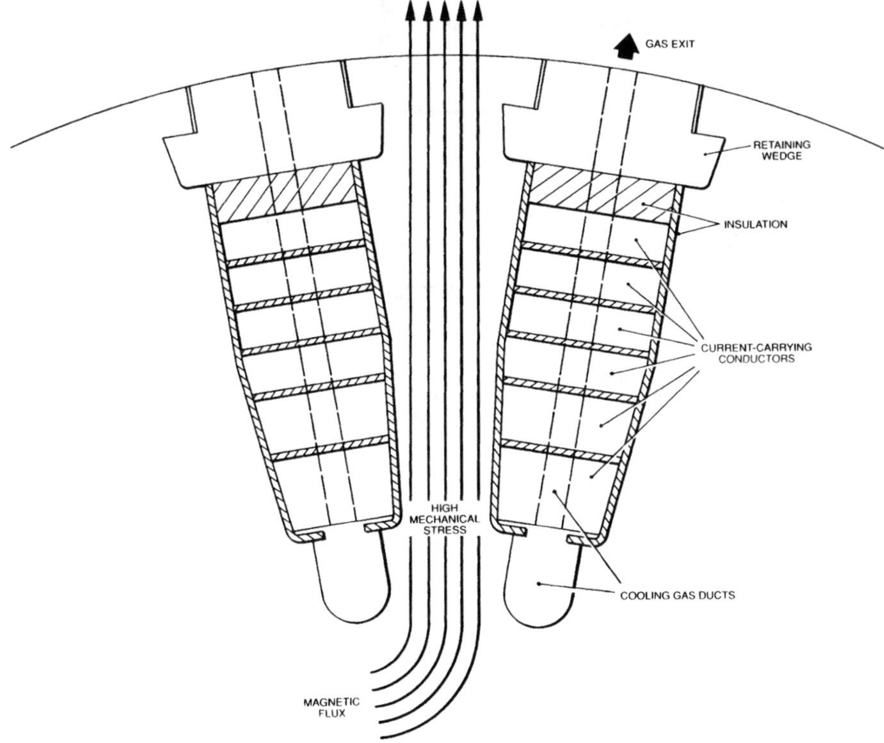

FIGURE 32.3 A section of a rotor.

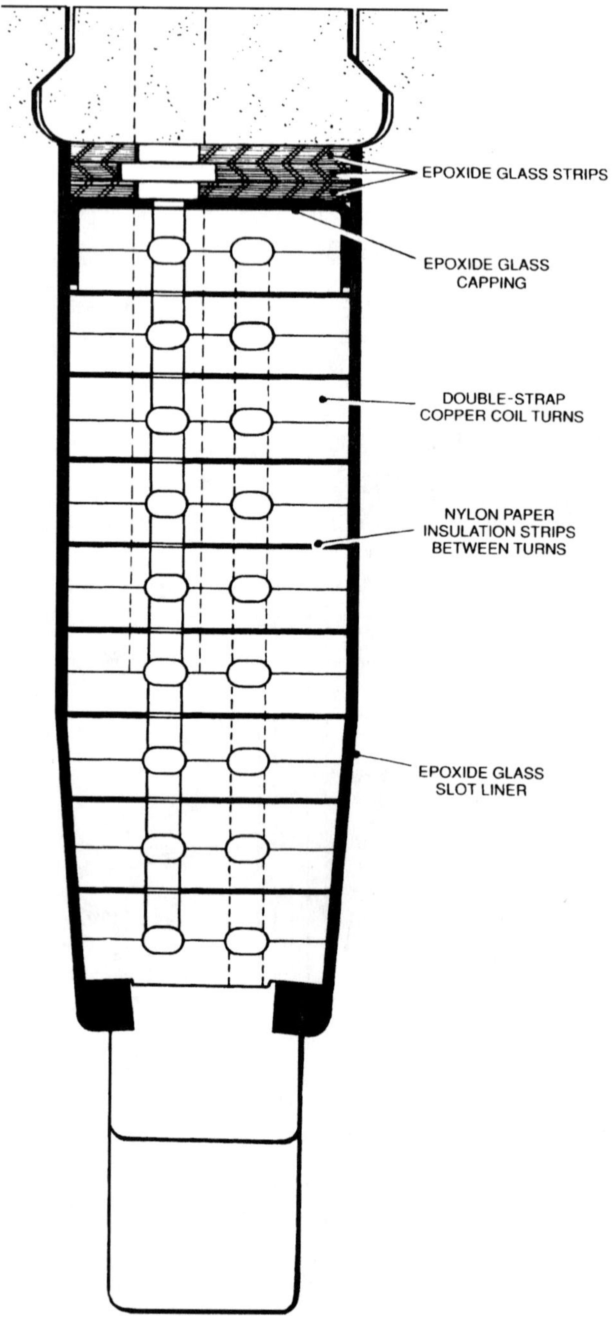

FIGURE 32.4 Rotor slot.

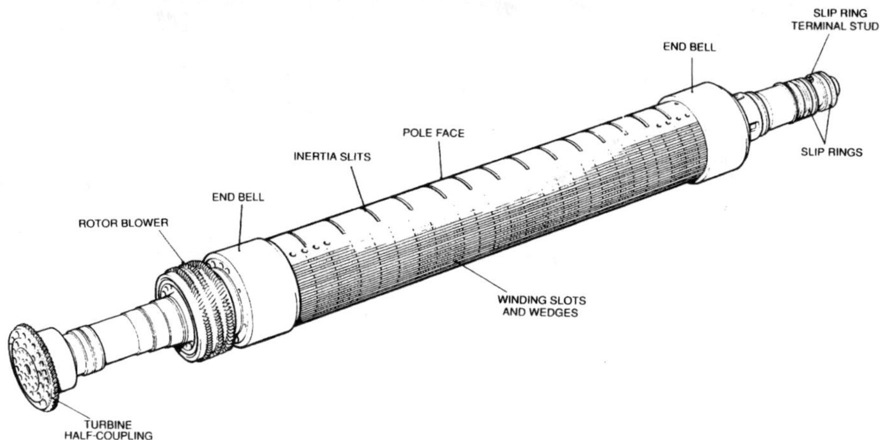

FIGURE 32.5 Stiffness compensation.

The average winding temperature should not exceed 115°C. The hydrogen enters the rotor from both ends under the end windings and emerges radially from the wedges. Fig. 32.6 illustrates the fans used to drive the hydrogen through the stator.

Flexible leads made of thin copper strips are connected to the ends of the winding. These leads are placed in two shallow slots in the shaft. Wedges retain them. The leads are connected to radial copper studs, which are connected to D-shaped copper bars placed in the shaft bore. Hydrogen seals are provided on the radial studs. The D-leads are connected to the slip rings by radial connection bolts (Fig. 32.7).

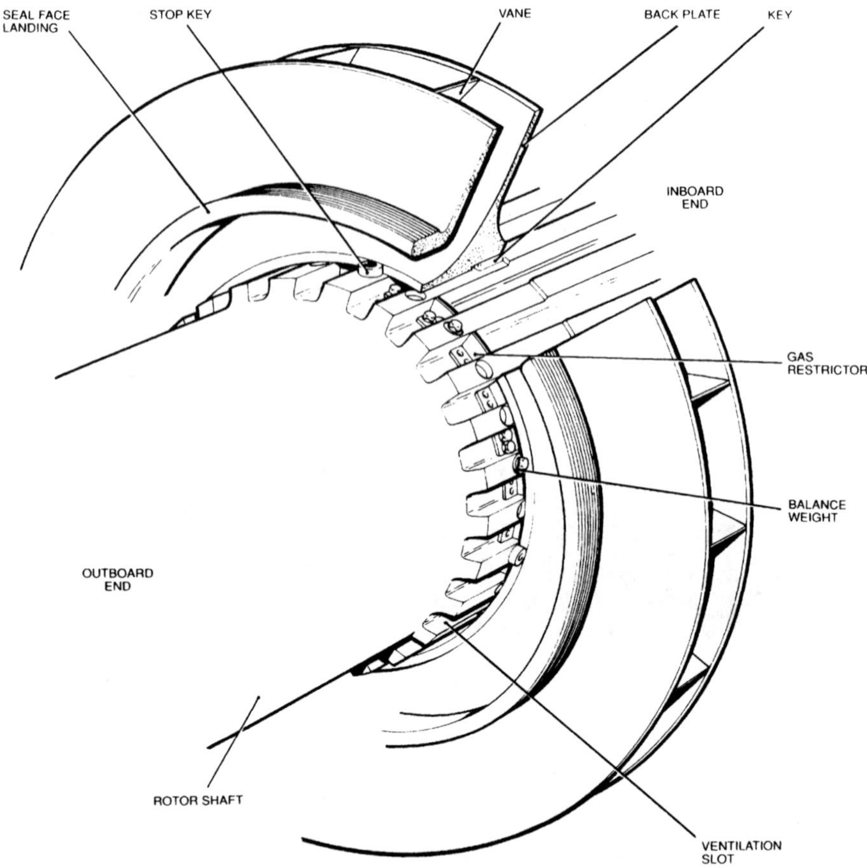

FIGURE 32.6 Rotor fan.

ROTOR END RINGS

The *end rings* (Fig. 32.8) are used to restrain the rotor end windings from flying out under centrifugal forces. These rings have traditionally been made from nonmagnetic austenitic steel, typically 18 percent Mn, 4 percent Cr. A ring is machined from a single forging. It is shrunk-fit at the end of the rotor body. The material of the end rings was proven to be susceptible to stress-corrosion cracking. A protective finish is given to all the surfaces except the shrink-fit to ensure that hydrogen, water vapor, and so forth do not contact the metal. The rings should be removed during long maintenance outage (every 8 to 10 years) and inspected for detailed surface cracking using a fluorescent dye. Ultrasonic scanning is not sufficient due to the coarse grain structure. A recent development has proven that austenitic steel containing 18 percent Mn and 18 percent Cr is immune to stress-corrosion cracking. New machines use this alloy. It is also used for replacement rings. This eliminates the need for periodic inspection. It is important to mention that a fracture of an end ring can result in serious damage to the machine and at least a few months' outage. It is highly recommended to replace the traditional material with the new material.

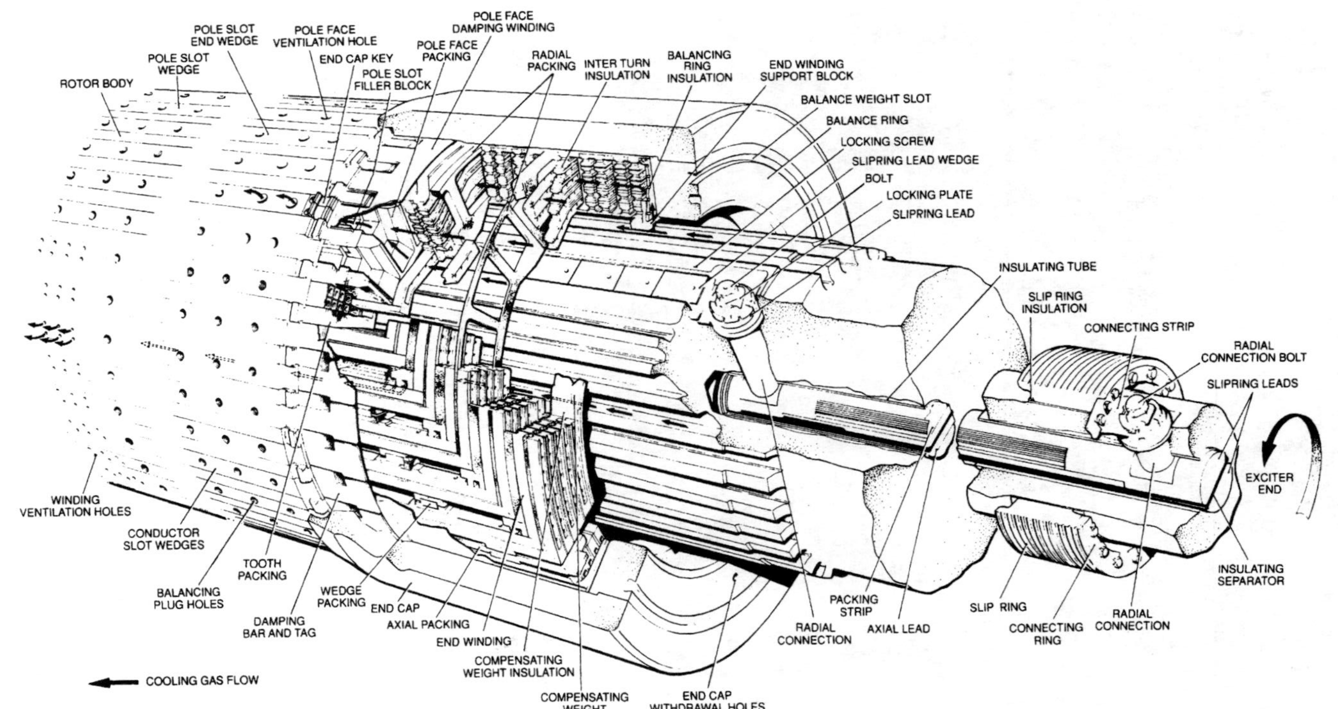

FIGURE 32.7 Rotor winding.

FIGURE 32.8 Rotor end ring.

The rings must be heated to 300°C to expand sufficiently for the shrink surface. Induction heating is preferred to direct heating to prevent possible damage to the rings. The end ring is insulated from the end winding with a molded-in glass-based liner or a loose cylinder sleeve. Hydrogen enters the rotor in the clearance between the end winding and the shaft. The outboard end of the ring is not permitted to contact the shaft to prevent the shaft flexure from promoting fatigue and fretting damage at the interfaces. A balancing ring is also included in the end disc for balancing the rotor.

WEDGES AND DAMPERS

Wedges are used to retain the winding slot contents. They are designed to withstand stresses from the windings while allowing the hydrogen to pass through holes. They must also be nonmagnetic to minimize the flux leakage around the circumference of the rotor. They are normally made of aluminum. One continuous wedge is used for each slot.

During system faults, or during unbalanced electrical loading, negative phase sequence currents and fluxes occur, leading to induced currents in the surface of the rotor. These currents will flow in the wedges, which act as a "damper winding" similar to the bars in the rotor of an induction motor. The end rings act as shorting rings in the motor. Arcing and localized pitting may occur between the end rings and the wedges.

SLIP RINGS, BRUSH GEAR, AND SHAFT GROUNDING

The D-leads in the bore are connected through radial copper connectors (which normally have backup hydrogen seals) and flexible connections to the slip rings (Fig. 32.9). The excitation current is around 5000 A DC for a 660-MW generator. The surface area of the slip rings must be large to run cool while transferring the current. Figure 32.10 illustrates the brush gear, including brushes and holders of a removable bracket. The holders can be replaced on-power. Constant-pressure springs are used to maintain brush pressure. A brush life should be at least 6 months. A separate compartment houses the brush gear. A shaft-mounted fan provides separate ventilation so that brush dust is not spread on other excitation components. Small amounts of hydrogen may pass through the connection seals. They may accumulate in the brush gear compartments during extended outages. The fan dilutes them safely during start-up before applying excitation current. The brush gear can be easily inspected through windows in the cover. Figure 32.11 illustrates brushless rotor connections.

A large generator produces normally an on-load voltage of between 10 and 50 V between its shaft ends due to magnetic dissymmetry. This voltage drives an axial current through the rotor body. The current returns through bearings and journals. It causes damage to their surfaces. Insulation barriers are installed to prevent such current from circulating. The insulation is installed at all locations where the shaft could contact earthed metal (e.g., bearings, seals, oil scrapers, oil pipes, and gear-driven pumps).

Some designs have two layers with a "floating" metallic component between them. The integrity of insulation is confirmed by a simple resistance measurement between the floating component and earth.

If the insulation remains clean and intact, a difference in voltage will exist between the shaft at the exciter end and ground. This provides another method to confirm the integrity of the insulation. The shaft voltage is monitored by a shaft-riding brush. An alarm is initiated when the shaft voltage drops below a predetermined value.

It is important to maintain the shaft at the turbine end of the generator at ground level. A pair of shaft-riding brushes ground the shaft through a resistor. Since carbon brushes develop a high-resistance glaze when operated for extended periods of time without current flow, a special circuit introduces a *wetting current* into and out of the shaft through the brushes. This circuit also detects loss of contact between the brush and the shaft.

FANS

Fans drive the hydrogen through the stator and the coolers. Two identical fans are mounted at each end of the shaft. Centrifugal or axial-type fans are used (Fig. 32.12).

ROTOR THREADING AND ALIGNMENT

The stator bore is about 25 cm larger than the rotor diameter. The rotor is inserted into the stator by supporting the inserted end of the rotor on a thick steel skid plate that slides into the stator, while the outboard end is supported by a crane.

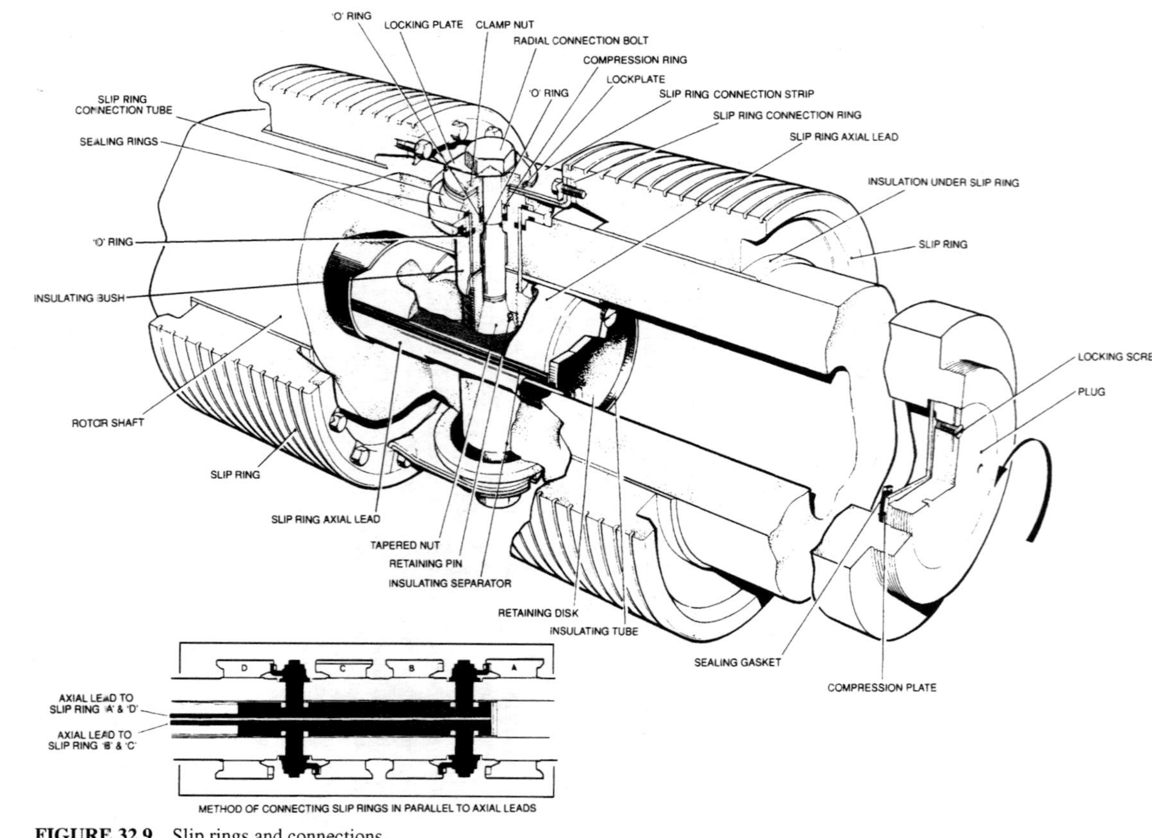
'O' RING
LOCKING PLATE
CLAMP NUT
RADIAL CONNECTION BOLT
COMPRESSION RING
LOCKPLATE
'O' RING
SLIP RING CONNECTION STRIP
SLIP RING CONNECTION RING
SLIP RING AXIAL LEAD
INSULATION UNDER SLIP RING
SLIP RING
SLIP RING CONNECTION TUBE
SEALING RINGS
'O' RING
INSULATING BUSH
ROTOR SHAFT
SLIP RING
SLIP RING AXIAL LEAD
TAPERED NUT
RETAINING PIN
INSULATING SEPARATOR
RETAINING DISK
INSULATING TUBE
SEALING GASKET
COMPRESSION PLATE
LOCKING SCREW
PLUG
D
C
B
A
AXIAL LEAD TO SLIP RING 'A' & 'D'
AXIAL LEAD TO SLIP RING 'B' & 'C'
METHOD OF CONNECTING SLIP RINGS IN PARALLEL TO AXIAL LEADS

FIGURE 32.9 Slip rings and connections.

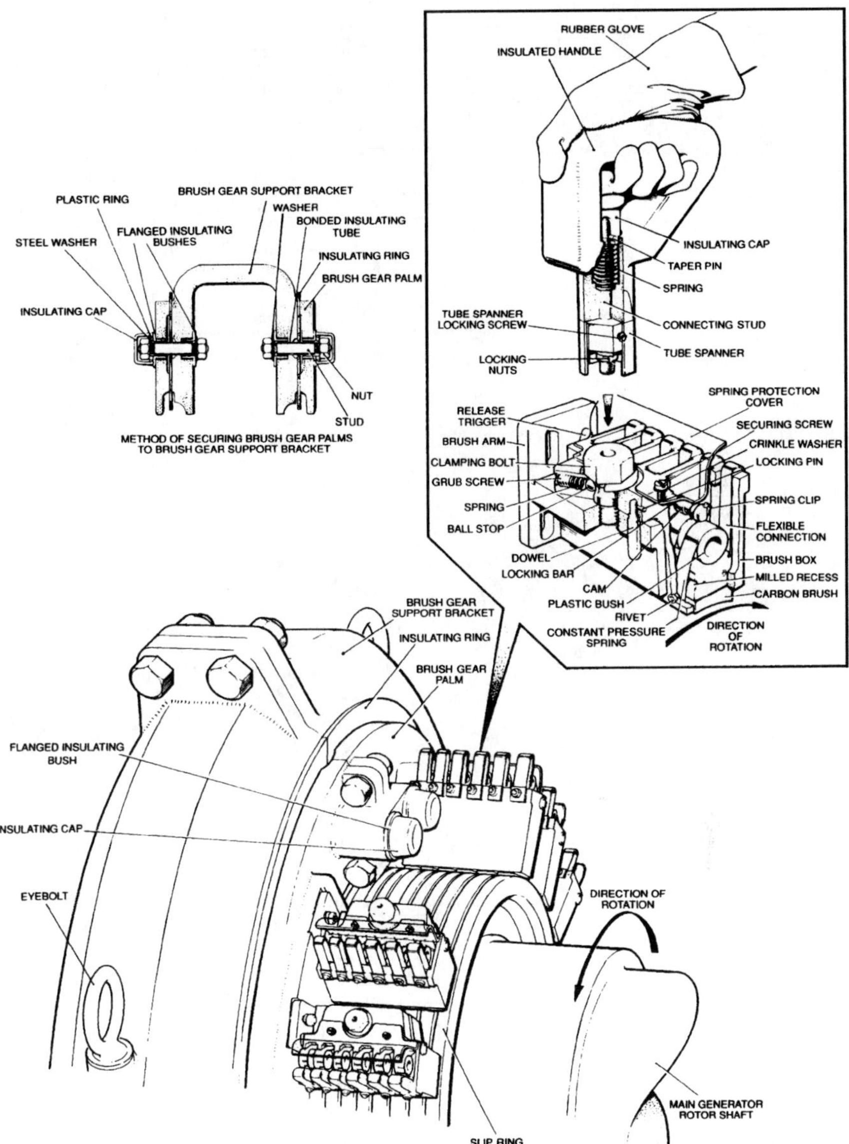

FIGURE 32.10 Slip ring brush gear and brushes.

VIBRATION

Generator rotors rated at between 500 and 600 MW have two main critical speeds (natural resonance in bending). Simple two-plane balancing techniques are not adequate to obtain the high degree of balance that is required and to ensure low vibration levels during run-up and rundown. Therefore, balancing facilities are provided along the rotor in the form of taped holes in cylindrical surfaces. The manufacturer balances the rotor at operating

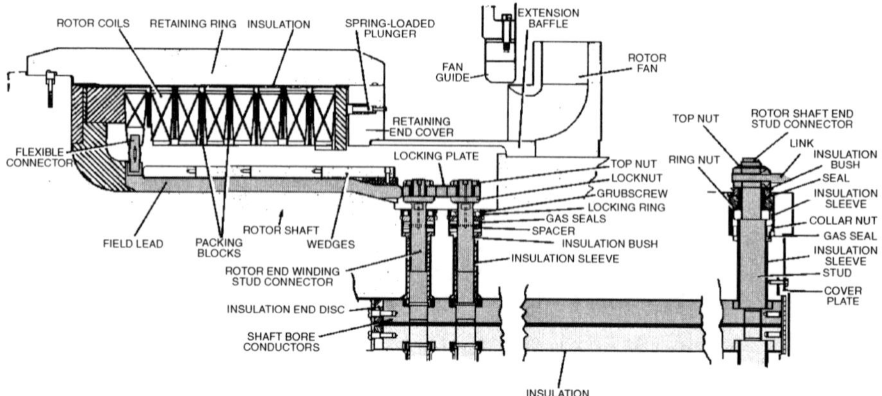

FIGURE 32.11 Brushless rotor connections.

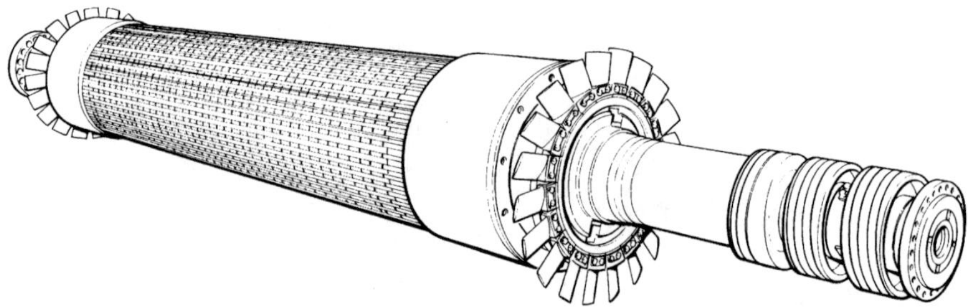

FIGURE 32.12 Axial flow fans on rotor.

speed. The winding is then heated and the rotor is operated at 20 percent overspeed. This allows the rotor to be subjected to stresses higher than the ones experienced in service. Trim balancing is then conducted, if required. There is a relationship between vibration amplitude and temperature in some rotors. For example, uneven ventilation can create a few degrees of difference in temperature between two adjacent poles. This effect can be partially offset by balancing to optimize the conditions at operating temperature (Fig. 32.13).

Uneven equalization of stiffness will cause vibration having a frequency of twice the operating speed. It is important to distinguish between the vibration caused by unbalance (occurring at 1 × operating speed) and equalization of stiffness. A large crack in the rotor will have a relatively larger effect on the double-frequency vibration component. Vibration signals during rundown are analyzed and compared with the ones obtained in previous rundowns. Oil whirl in bearings can cause vibration at half the speed. The amplitude and phase of vibration are recorded at the bearings of the generator and exciter using accelerometers mounted on the bearing supports and by proximity probes, which detect shaft movements.

BEARINGS AND SEALS

The generator bearings are spherically seated to facilitate alignment. They are pressure-lubricated, have jacking oil taps, and are insulated from the pedestals. Seals (Fig. 32.14) are

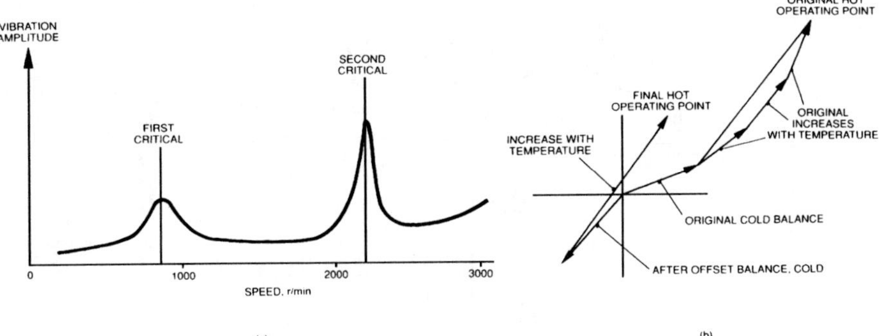

FIGURE 32.13 Rotor vibration.

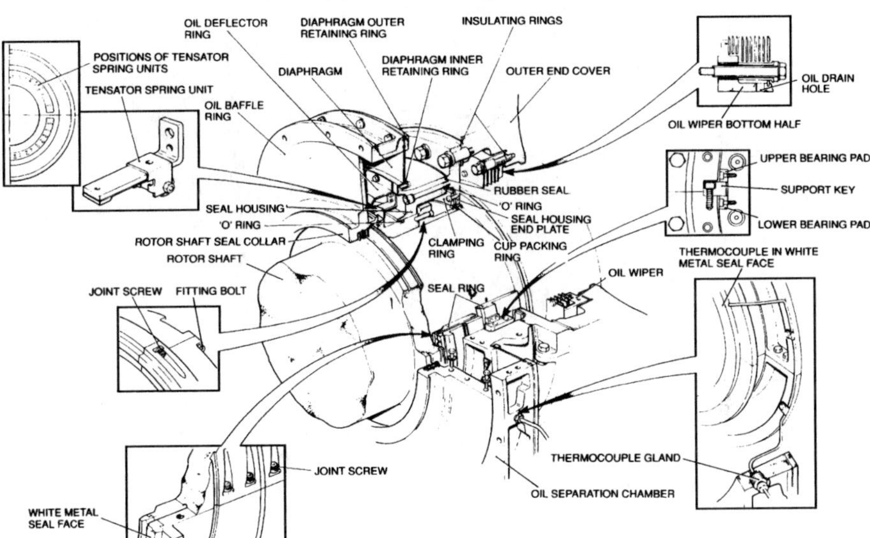

FIGURE 32.14 Thrust-type shaft seal.

provided in the end shields to prevent hydrogen from escaping along the shaft. Most seals have a nonrotating white-metalled ring bearing against a collar on the shaft. Oil is fed to an annular groove in the ring. It flows radially inward across the face into a collection space and radially outward into an atmospheric air compartment. The seal ring must be maintained against the rotating collar. Therefore, it must be able to move axially to accommodate the thermal expansion of the shaft. Figure 32.15 illustrates a seal that resembles small journal bearings (radial seal). The oil is applied centrally. It flows axially inward to face the hydrogen pressure. It also flows axially outboard into an atmospheric compartment. The seal does not have to move axially, because the shaft can move freely inside it. This is a major advantage over the seal design illustrated in Fig. 32.14. Most generators use radial seals.

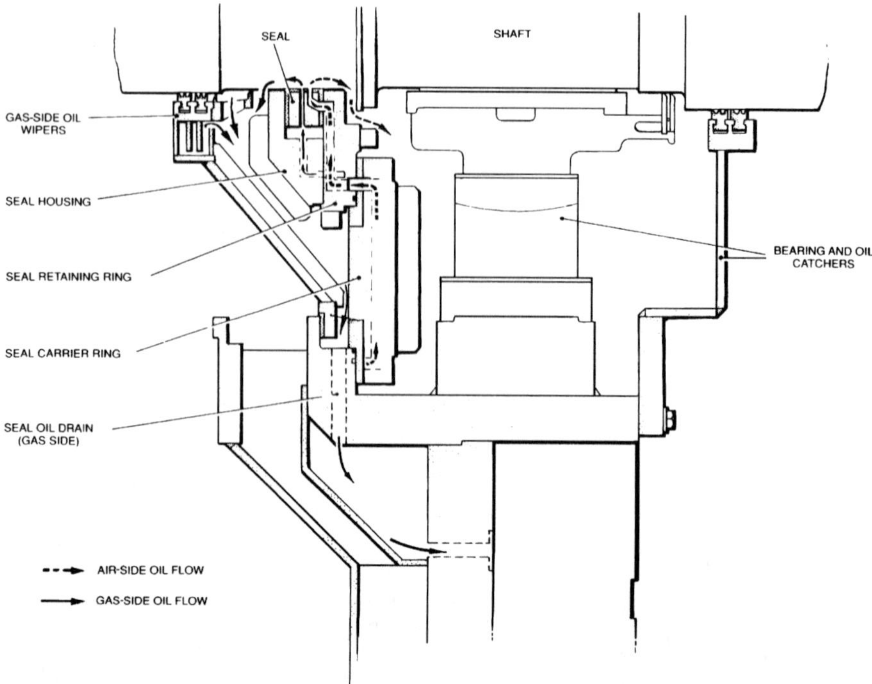

FIGURE 32.15 Double-flow ring seal (radial seal).

SIZE AND WEIGHT

The rotor of a 660-MW generator is up to 16.5 m long and weighs up to 75 tonnes (t). The rotor must never be supported on its end rings. The weight must be supported by the body surface. The rotor must also be protected from water contamination, while in transient or storage. A weatherproof container with an effective moisture absorbent must be used. If the rotor is left inside an open stator, dry air must be circulated.

TURBINE-GENERATOR COMPONENTS—THE STATOR

Stator Core

The core laminations are normally 0.35 or 0.5 mm thick. They are coated with thin layers of backed-on insulating varnish. Core flux tests are done on the complete core with a flux density of between 90 and 100 percent of the rated value. If there is contact between two adjacent plates, local hot spots will develop. The stator bore is scanned using an infrared camera to identify areas of higher-than-normal temperature during such a test. A bonding agent is used in some designs to ensure that individual plates, and particularly the teeth, do not vibrate independently. Packing material is used to correct any waviness in core buildup.

Some designs use grain-oriented sheets of steel. They have deliberately different magnetic properties in the two perpendicular axes (Fig. 32.16). The low-loss orientation is arranged for the flux in the circumferential direction. This allows higher flux density in the back of the core compared with nonoriented steel, for the same specific loss. The core plates of grain-oriented steel are specially annealed after punching.

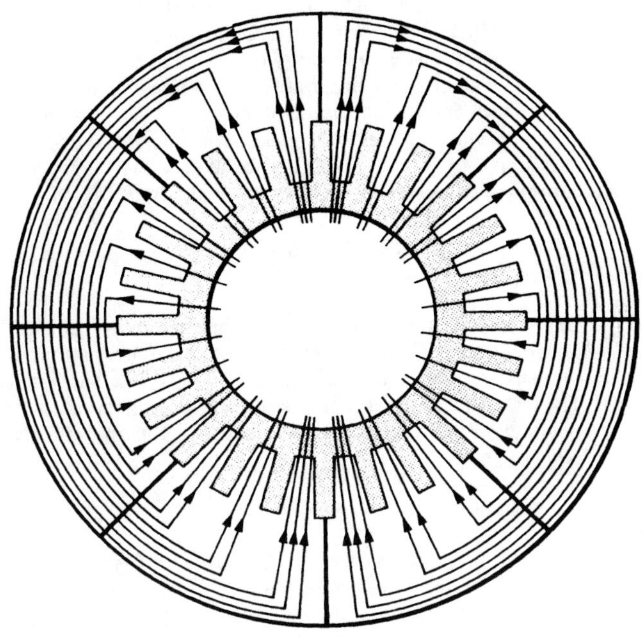

DIAGRAMMATIC REPRESENTATION OF MAGNETIC FLUX
IN STATOR CORE, OPEN-CIRCUIT CONDITIONS

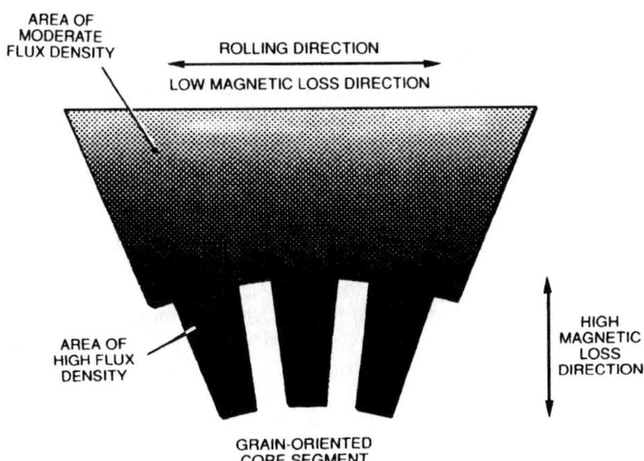

FIGURE 32.16 Flux in stator core.

The net axial length of magnetic steel that the flux can use is less than the measured stacked length by a factor of 0.9 to 0.95. This is known as the *stacking factor*. This is caused by the varnish layers and air spaces between the laminations due to uneven plate thickness and imperfect consolidation.

Hysteresis and eddy current losses in the core constitute a significant portion of the total losses. In some designs, the heat produced by these losses is removed by hydrogen circulating radially through the ducts and axially through holes (Fig. 32.17).

Thermocouples are installed in the hottest areas of the core. If a hot spot develops in service, it will not normally be detected by existing thermocouples. A flux test is the way to detect a hot spot. If accidental contacts occur at the tooth tips or damage the slot surfaces, circulating currents could occur. The magnitude of the current depends on the contact resistances between the back of the core plates and the core frame bars on which the plates are assembled. In most designs, all these bars (except for the one, which grounds the core) are insulated from the frame to reduce the possibility of circulating currents.

Core Frame

Figure 32.18 illustrates the core frame. The core end plate assembly is normally made from a thick disc of nonmagnetic steel. Conducting screens of copper or aluminum, about 10 mm thick, cover the outer surfaces of the core end plates (Fig. 32.19). They are called the *end plate flux shield.* The leakage flux creates circulating currents in these screens. These currents prevent the penetration of an unacceptable amount of flux into the core end plate or the ends of the core.

Stator Winding

In large two-pole generators, the winding of each phase is arranged in two identical parallel circuits, located diametrically opposite each other (Fig. 32.20). If the conductor is made of an assembly of separate strips, the leakage flux (the lines of induction that do not engage the rotor) density of each strip increases linearly with distance from the bottom strip (Fig. 32.21). This alternating leakage flux induces an alternating voltage along the lengths of the strips that varies with the square of the distance of the strip from the bottom of the slot. If a solid conductor were used, or if the strips were parallel to each other and connected together at the core ends, currents would circulate around the bar due to the unequal voltages. This will cause unacceptable eddy current losses and heating. This effect is minimized by dividing the conductor into lightly insulated strips. These strips are arranged in two or four stacks in the bar width. They are transposed along the length of the bar by the Roebel method (Fig. 32.22). Each strip occupies every position in the stack for an equal axial distance. This arrangement equalizes the eddy current voltages, and the eddy currents will not circulate between the strips. Demineralized water circulates in the rectangular section tubes to remove the heat from the strips (Fig. 32.23).

The conductors are made of hard-drawn copper having a high conductivity. Each strip has a thin coating of glass-fiber insulation. The insulation is wound along the length of the bar, consisting of a tape of mica powder loaded with a synthetic resin, with a glass-fiber backing. Electrical tests are performed to confirm the integrity of the insulation. A semiconducting material is used to treat the slot length of each bar to ensure that bar-to-slot electrical discharges do not occur. The surface discharge at the ends of the slots is limited by applying a high-resistance stress grading finish.

The bars experience large forces because they carry large currents and they are placed in a high-flux density. These forces are directed radially outward toward the bottom (closed

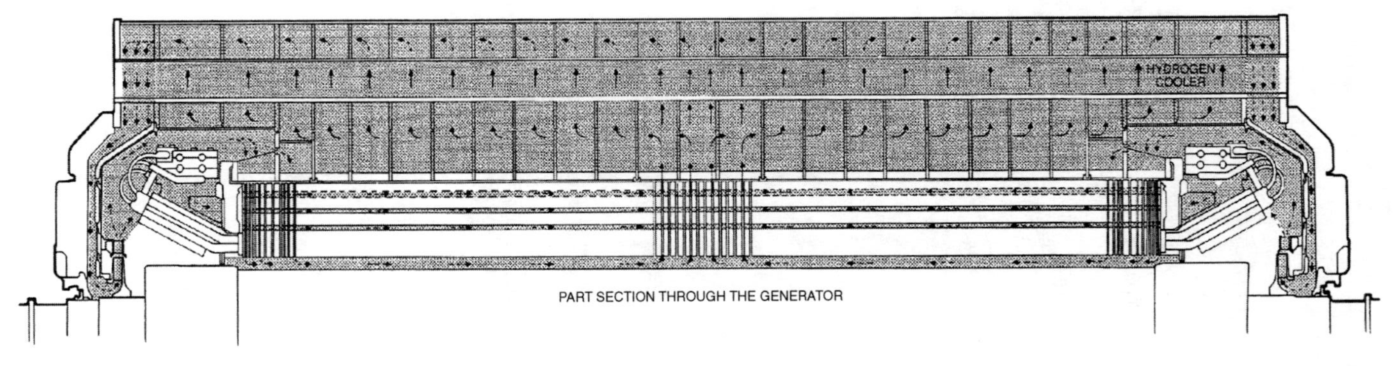

FIGURE 32.17 Stator ventilation.

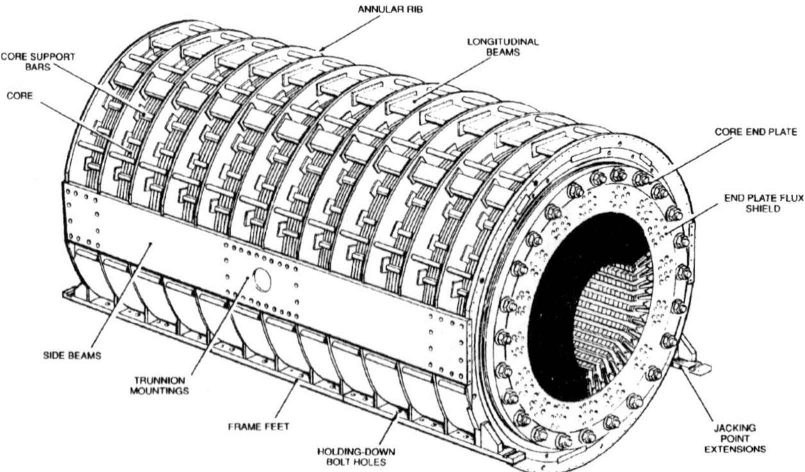

FIGURE 32.18 Core frame.

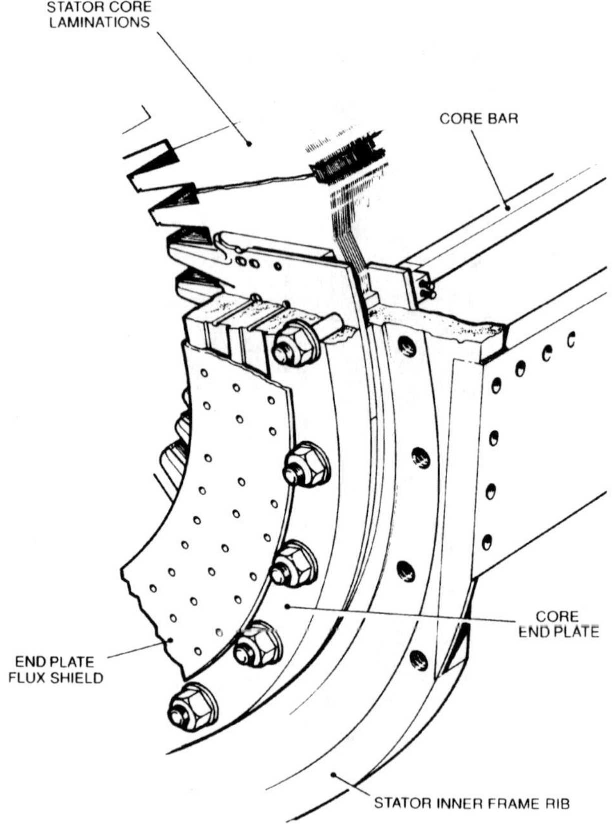

FIGURE 32.19 Core end plate and screen.

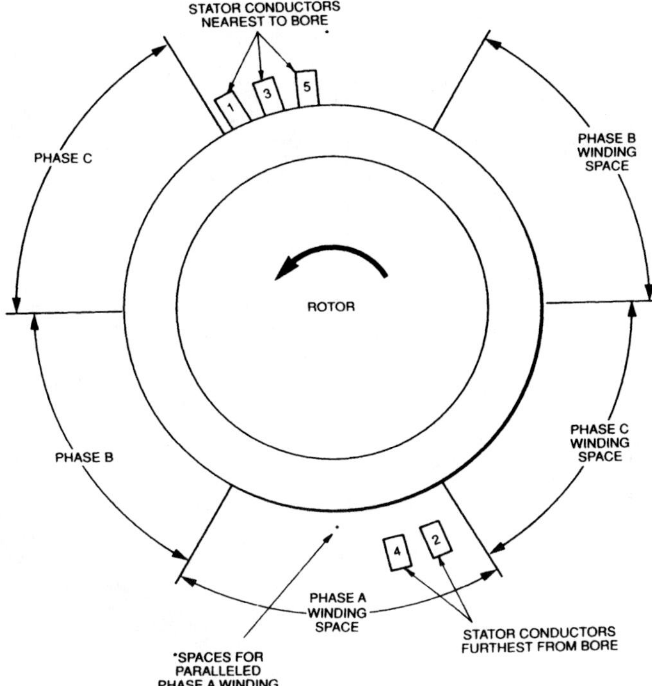

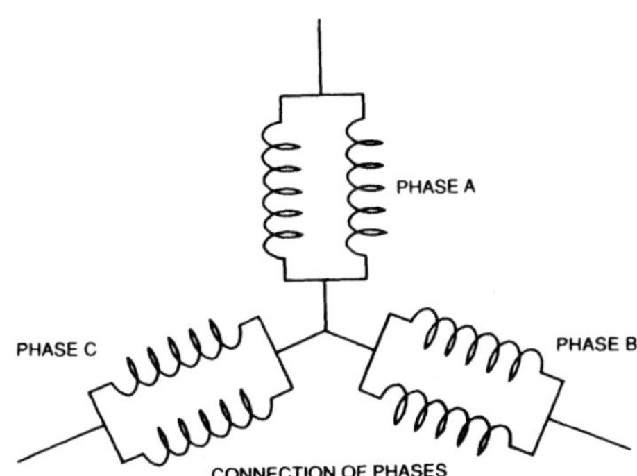

FIGURE 32.20 Arrangement of stator conductors.

end) of the slot. They alternate at 120 Hz. The closing wedges are not therefore needed to restrain these bars against these forces. However, the bars should not vibrate. The wedges are designed to exert a radial force by tapered packers or by a corrugated glass-spring member. Some designs have a sideway restraint by a corrugated glass-spring packer in the slot side. Insulation material consisting of packers, separators, and drive strips are also used in the slot (Fig. 32.23).

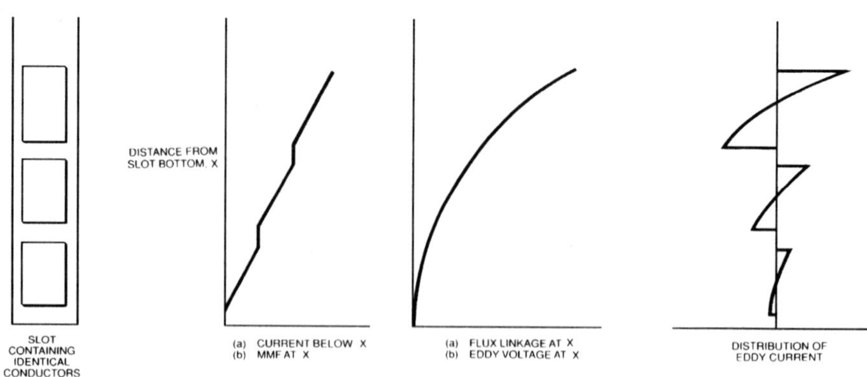

FIGURE 32.21 Variations of eddy currents in stator conductors.

FIGURE 32.22 Roebel transpositions.

The stator winding electrical loss consists of I^2R heating (R is measured using DC resistance of the winding phases at operating temperature) and "stray" losses, which include:

- AC resistance is larger than DC resistance (skin effect).
- Eddy currents (explained earlier).
- Currents induced in core end plates, screens, and end teeth.
- Harmonic currents induced in the rotor and end ring surfaces.
- Currents induced in the frame, casings, end shields, fan baffles, and so forth. Appropriate cooling methods are needed for these losses in order to avoid localized hot spots.

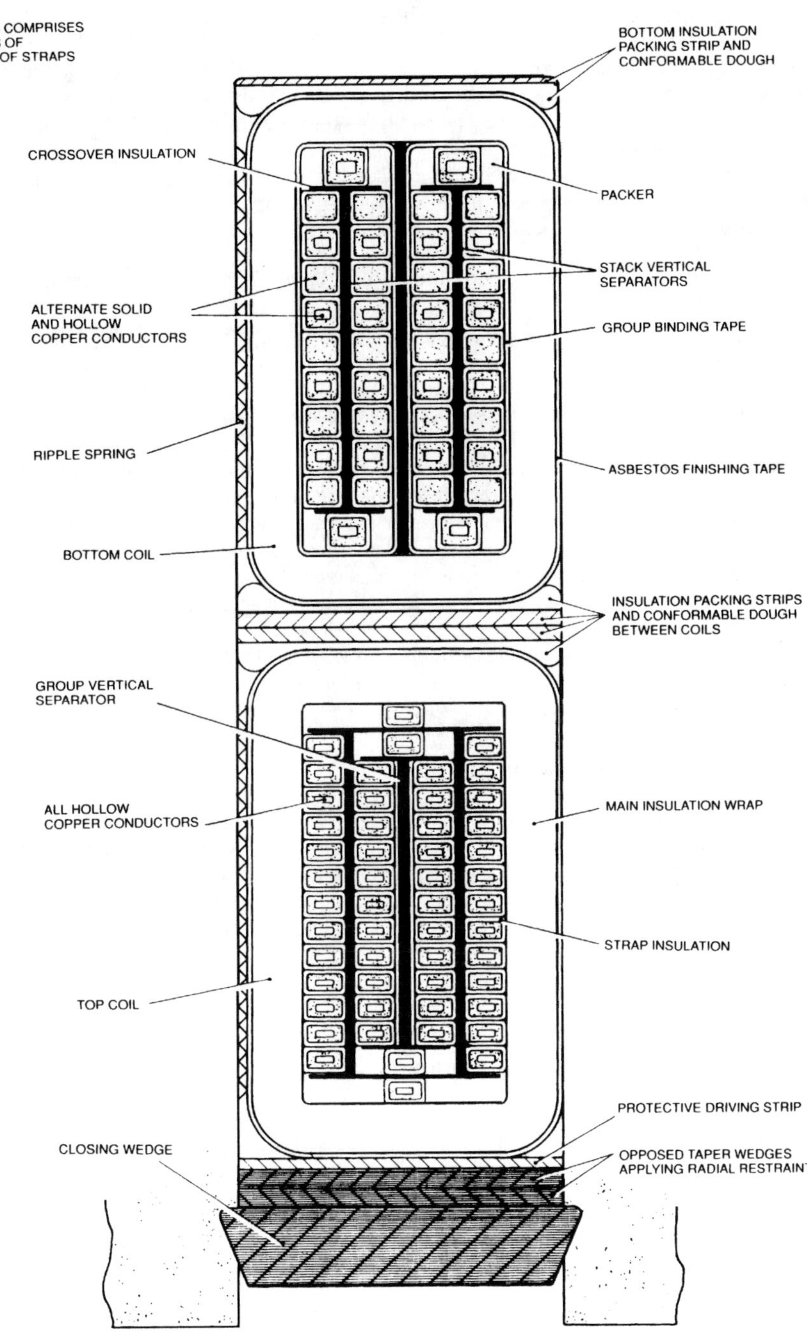

FIGURE 32.23 Stator slot.

End Winding Support

Bands of conductors are arranged side by side in the end windings. They all carry the same currents (some in-phase with each other and some are not). Large electromagnetic forces are produced in the end windings during normal operation, and especially during fault conditions when large current peaks occur. The end turns must be strongly braced to withstand these peak forces and minimize the 120-Hz vibrations.

A large magnetic flux is produced in the end regions by the magnetomotive force (mmf) in the end windings of the stator and rotor. Metallic components cannot be used to fasten the end winding because of the following reasons:

- They would have Eddy currents induced in them. This will cause additional loss and possibly hot spots.
- Metallic components also vibrate and tend to become loose, or wear away their surrounding medium.

Therefore, nonmetallic components such as molded glass fiber are normally used. Large support brackets are bolted to the core end plate. They provide a support for a large glass-fiber conical support ring (Fig. 32.24). The vibration of the end windings must be limited because it can create fatigue cracking in the winding copper. This can have particularly serious consequences if it occurs in a water-carrying conductor because hydrogen will leak into the water system. Resonance near 120 Hz must be avoided because the core ovalizing and the winding exciting force occur at this frequency. Vibration increase in the end windings due to slackening of the support is monitored by accelerometers. The amplitude of vibration depends highly on the current. Any looseness developed after a period of operation is corrected by tightening the bolts, inserting or tightening wedges, and/or by pumping a thermosetting resin into rubber bags located between conductor bars.

Electrical Connections and Terminals

The high-end (line end) conductor bars and the low-voltage end (neutral end) of a phase band are electrically connected to tubular connectors. These connectors run circumferentially behind the end windings at the exciter end to the outgoing terminals. The connectors have internal water cooling. However, they must be insulated from the line voltage. Figure 32.25 illustrates a terminal bushing. It is a paper-insulated item, cooled internally from the stator winding water system. The insulation is capable of withstanding the hydrogen pressure in the casing without having any leakage.

Stator Winding Cooling Components

Demineralized water is used for cooling the stator windings. It must be pure enough to be electrically nonconducting. The water is degassed and treated continuously in an ion exchanger. The target values are as follows.

Conductivity	100 μS/m
Dissolved oxygen:	200 μg/L max (in some systems, >2000 μ/L is acceptable)
Total copper:	150 μg/L maximum
pH value	9 maximum

FIGURE 32.24 View of a 660-MW generator stator end windings.

These levels have proven to have no aggressive attack on the winding copper after many years of service. Water enters one or more manifolds made of copper or stainless-steel pipes. The manifolds run circumferentially around the core end plate. Flexible polytetrafluoroethylene (PTFE) hoses connect the manifolds to all water inlet ports on the stator conductor joints. In a two-pass design, water flows through both bars in parallel. It is then transferred to the two connected bars at the other end. The water returns through similar hoses to the outlet manifold (Fig. 32.26).

The hydrogen is maintained at a higher pressure than the water. If a leak develops, hydrogen enters the water. The winding insulation would be damaged if the water were to enter the

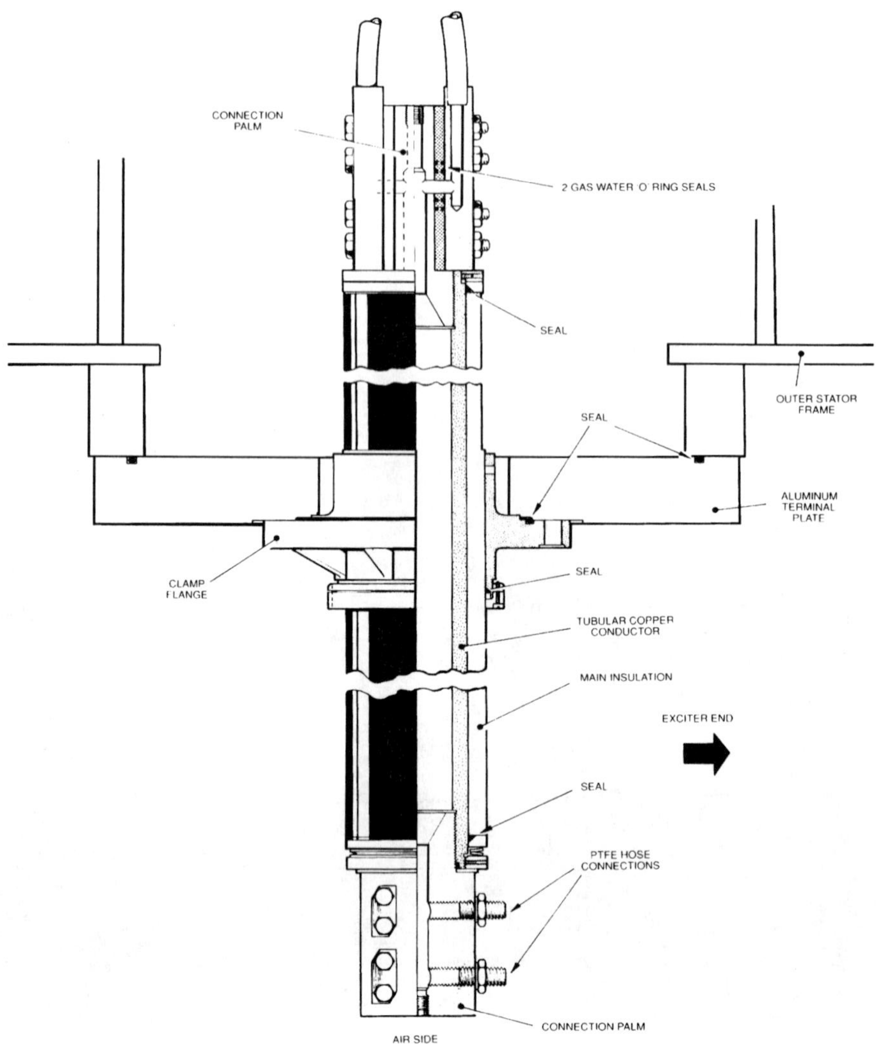

FIGURE 32.25 Generator terminals.

hydrogen system. The water temperature increases by less than 30°C. The inlet temperature of the water is 40°C. There is a significant margin before boiling occurs at between 115 and 120°C (at the working pressure). The water temperature of each bar is monitored by thermocouples in the slots or in the water outlets. This allows detection of reduced water flow.

Hydrogen Cooling Components

Hydrogen is brought into the casing by an axially oriented distribution pipe at the top. Carbon dioxide is used to scavenge the hydrogen (air cannot be used for this function

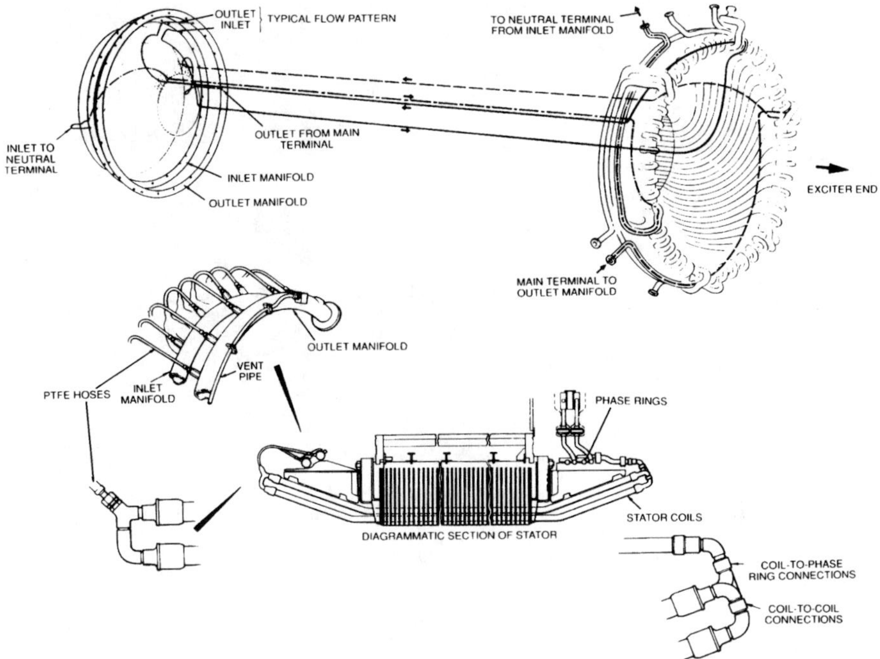

FIGURE 32.26 Stator winding water cooling system components.

because an explosive mixture of hydrogen and oxygen will form when the volumetric concentration is between 4 and 76 percent). The carbon dioxide is admitted through a similar pipe at the bottom. The rotor fans drive hydrogen over the end windings and through the cores of the stator and rotor. During normal operation, the hydrogen temperature increases by about 25°C during the few seconds required to complete the circuit. Two or four coolers are mounted inside the casing. They consist of banks of finned or wire-wound tubes. The water flows into the tubes while hydrogen flows over them (Fig. 32.27).

The headers of the coolers are accessible. The tubes can be cleaned without degassing the casing. The supports of the tubes and the cooler frame are designed to avoid resonance near the principle exciting frequencies of 60 and 120 Hz. It is important to prevent moisture condensation on the stator end windings (electrical breakdown can occur). The dew point of the hydrogen emerging from the coolers is monitored by hygrometers. This dew point must be at least 20°C lower than the temperature of the cooled hydrogen emerging from the coolers. During normal operation, the stator winding temperature is above 40°C. Thus, if condensation occurred, it will be on the hydrogen coolers first. During start-up, the cooling water of the stator windings is cold. It is preheated electrically, or circulated for a period of time to increase the winding temperature before exciting the generator. This prevents the possibility of having condensation on the windings.

Stator Casing

The stator core and core frame are mounted inside the casing. The casing must withstand the load and fault torques. It must also provide a pressure-tight enclosure for the hydrogen.

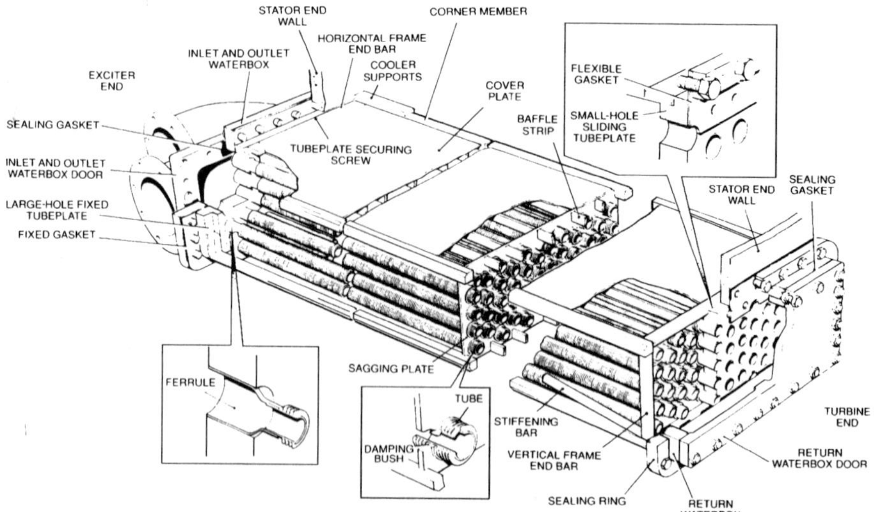

FIGURE 32.27 Hydrogen cooler.

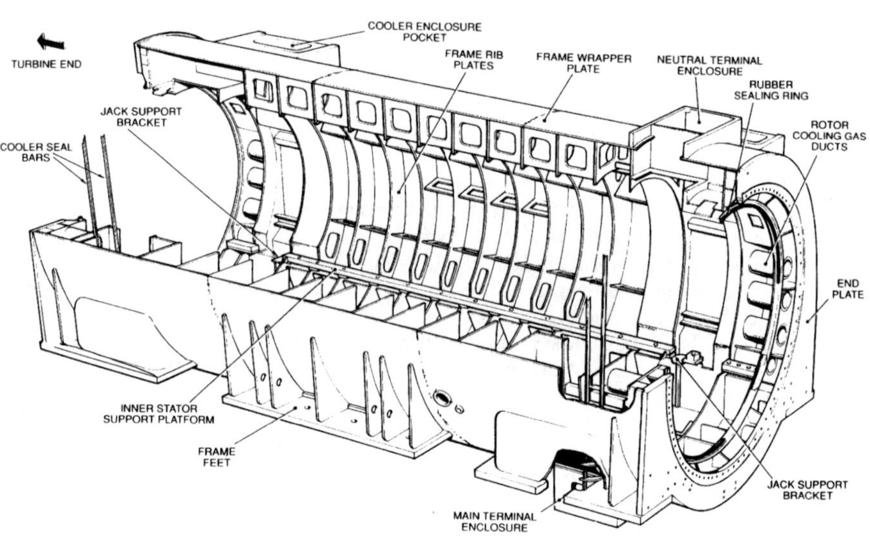

FIGURE 32.28 Outer stator casing.

Annular rings and axial members are mounted inside the casings to strengthen them and allow the hydrogen to flow (Figs. 32.28 and 32.29).

The end shields are made of thick circular steel plates. They are reinforced by ribs to withstand the casing pressure with minimal axial deflection. The stationary components of the shaft seal are housed in the end shields. The outboard bearing is also housed inside the end shields in some designs. The sealing of the end shield and casing joints must be leak-free against hydrogen pressure.

FIGURE 32.29 Core frame being inserted into casing.

A hydrostatic pressure test is conducted on the whole casing. The casing must also be leak-tight when the hydrogen pressure drops from 4 to 0.035 bar in 24 h. Any leaks of oil or water are drained from the bottom of the casing to liquid-leakage detectors. These detectors initiate an alarm. A temperature sensor is installed at the carbon dioxide (CO_2) inlet. It initiates an alarm if the incoming CO_2 has not been heated sufficiently. Cool gas can create unacceptably high localized thermal stresses. Electrical heaters are mounted in the bottom half of the casing. They prevent condensation during outages.

COOLING SYSTEMS

The efficiency of a large generator is about 98.5 percent. In some designs, the losses are transferred to the boiler feedwater system.

Hydrogen Cooling

Hydrogen has four advantages over air for heat removal from the generator:

1. The density of hydrogen is one-fourteenth that of air. The windage losses (caused by churning the gas around the rotor) are much less with hydrogen.
2. The heat removal capability of hydrogen (at operating pressure) is about 10 times higher than that for air.
3. The degradation by oxidation processes cannot occur, because hydrogen is free from oxygen.
4. Hydrogen does not support fire, which can start by arcing.

The main disadvantage of hydrogen is that it forms an explosive mixture when it combines with air within a volumetric concentration in the range from 4 to 76 percent. Sophisticated sealing arrangements are required to ensure leak-tight casing.

Hydrogen Cooling System

It is essential to prevent air and hydrogen mixture inside the generator. Carbon dioxide is used as a buffer gas between air and hydrogen. The process is called *scavenging* or *gassing-up* and *degassing*. Carbon dioxide is normally stored as a liquid. It is expanded to a low pressure above atmospheric. It is also heated to prevent it from freezing due to the expansion process. CO_2 is fed into the bottom of the casing through a long perforated pipe. It displaces the air from the top via the hydrogen inlet distribution pipe to atmosphere outside the station. The proportion of CO_2 in the gas passing to atmosphere is being monitored by a gas analyzer. When the CO_2 concentration becomes sufficiently high, the flow of CO_2 is interrupted (Fig. 32.30).

High-purity hydrogen is fed to the casing from a central storage tank or electrolytic process. The hydrogen reaches the gas control panel at about 10 bar. Its pressure is reduced before it flows through the top admission pipe into the casing. Since hydrogen is much lighter than CO_2, it displaces the CO_2 from the bottom of the casings through the CO_2 pipe to the atmosphere. The reverse of this procedure is followed to remove hydrogen from the generator for long outages.

Separate procedures are used to scavenge tanks to prevent dangerous mixtures. The reverse of the listed procedure is done using CO_2 and dry compressed air to remove hydrogen from the generator. The hydrogen purity is normally high because air cannot enter a pressurized system.

A sample of casing hydrogen is circulated continuously through a Katharometer-type purity monitor (thc sample is driven by the differential pressure developed across the rotor fans). The monitor initiates an alarm if the purity falls below 97 percent. Pure gases from the piped supplies are used to calibrate the purity monitor (and the gas analyzer).

Hydrogen is admitted by a pressure-sensitive valve when the casing pressure drops. A relief valve releases hydrogen to the atmosphere if the pressure becomes excessive. The hydrogen makeup is normally monitored.

Several thermocouples are used to monitor the hydrogen temperature. Hydrogen is flowing at 30 m^3/s typically (in a 500-MW generator). The heat absorbed by the hydrogen

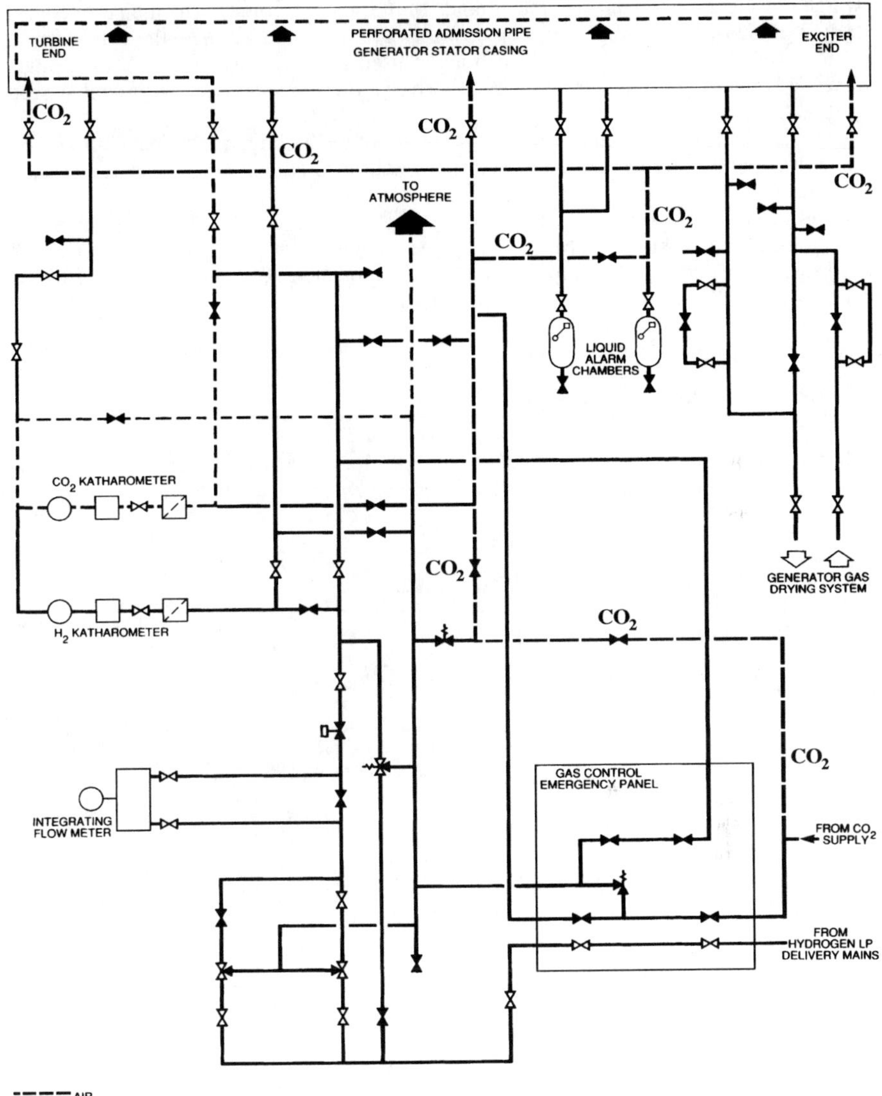

FIGURE 32.30 Generator gas system—displacing air with CO_2.

is about 5 MW. The increase in temperature of the hydrogen is about 30°C. The cooled gas should not be at a temperature higher than 40°C. Thus, the hydrogen entering the coolers should not be hotter than 70°C.

The water pressure in the stator windings and hydrogen coolers is lower than the hydrogen pressure. Therefore, water cannot leak into the hydrogen system from the stator windings or hydrogen cooler. However, water can be released from the oil used for shaft sealing. The water concentration will increase if the oil is untreated turbine lubricating oil, which has picked up water from the glands of the steam turbines. The moisture concentration in the hydrogen should be kept low to prevent condensation on the windings. The differential pressure across the rotor fans is used to send a hydrogen flow through a dryer. When the rotor is not turning, a motor-driven blower maintains a flow through the rotor (Fig. 32.31).

Hygrometers are used to monitor the humidity of the hydrogen. The maximum permissible dew point is more than 20°C below the cold gas temperature (measured at casing pressure).

In the event of a serious seal failure, hydrogen will escape rapidly. If it encounters an ignition source such as the shaft rubbing, it will burn intensely. In this case, the hydrogen in the casing should be vented to the atmosphere. CO_2 should be admitted into the casing.

SHAFT SEALS AND SEAL OIL SYSTEM

The seals are located in the end shields. They seal the hydrogen in the machine where the rotor shaft emerges from the casing and shields. The main type of seals are thrust and journal seal.

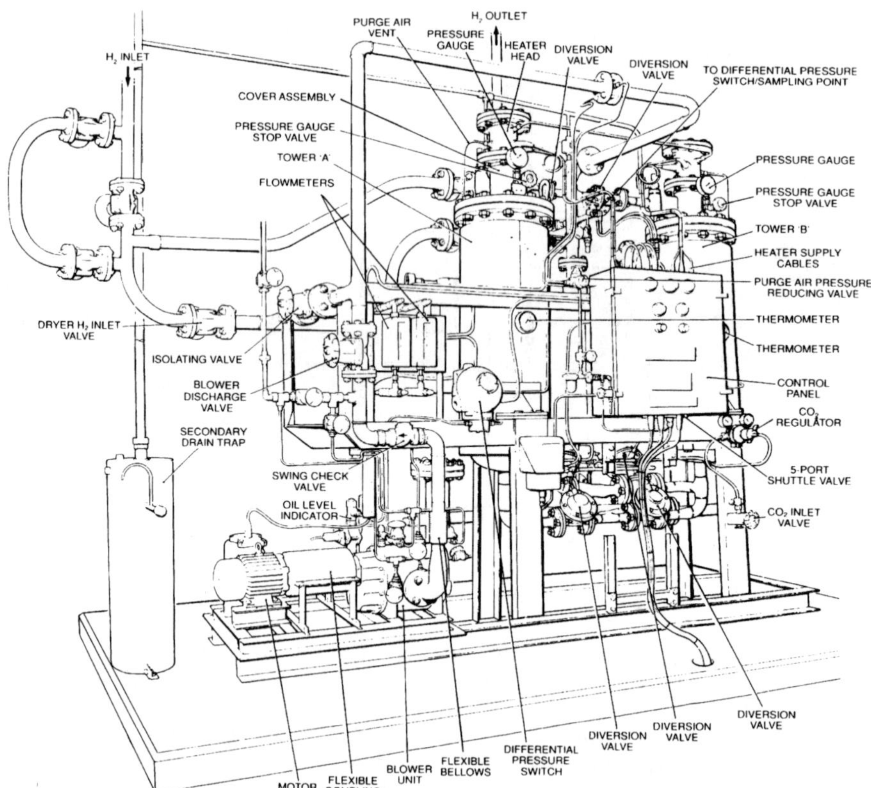

FIGURE 32.31 Gas dryer and blower.

Thrust-Type Seal

Figure 32.14 illustrates a thrust-type seal. The seal ring acts like a thrust face acting on a shaft collar. Oil is supplied to a central circumferential groove in the white-metalled face of the seal ring. The oil pressure is higher than the casing hydrogen. Most of the oil flows outward due to centrifugal forces over the thrust face. It then drains into a well. A small oil flow moves inward against centrifugal forces. This flow is driven by the difference between the oil and the hydrogen into a drainage compartment, which is at hydrogen pressure. Entrained air and water can be released from this oil, resulting in contamination of the hydrogen. Therefore, it is important to minimize this oil flow.

The housing of the seal ring must be able to move axially about 30 mm to accommodate the thermal expansion of all the coupled rotors. The housing is designed to move inside a stationary member. It uses rubber sealing rings to contain the oil and exert axial pressure at the seal face.

Some seal designs have an additional chamber between the fixed and sliding components. It is fed with oil at varying pressures to control the overall pressure at the seal face. Other seal designs have additional pressure provided by springs.

Journal-Type Seal

This seal design is similar to a journal bearing floating on the shaft. This design allows the shaft to move axially through the seal. Thus, it does not need to accommodate the thermal expansion of the shaft. Again, oil is supplied to an annular groove in the white-metal ring. It flows in the clearances between the shaft and the bore of the seal. The flow is outward to a drain and inward to the space pressurized by hydrogen. The inward flow rate is much larger than the inward flow rate in the thrust-type seal because it is not inhibited by centrifugal forces. Thus, this flow is capable of contaminating the hydrogen significantly. The oil fed to the seals is subjected to vacuum treatment to reduce the contamination level of the hydrogen. The treatment involves the removal of air and water from the oil. Despite this disadvantage, the journal-type seal is considered better able to handle the axial movement of the shaft.

A more sophisticated design of the journal-type seal involves two separate oil supplies (Fig. 32.15). They are for the inward and outward flows. This design eliminates the need for vacuum treatment. The oil supplied is different from the turbine lubricating oil supply, which is the main source of entrained water.

Seal Oil System

In conventional design (Fig. 32.32), the shaft-driven lubricating oil pump supplies the oil for the main seal. The oil pressure is controlled by a diaphragm valve, which maintains a constant differential pressure above the hydrogen pressure at the seals. A water-cooled heat exchanger is used to cool the oil. The oil is sent through a fine filter to prevent metallic particles from reaching the tight clearances in the seal. When the unit is shut down, motor-driven pumps are used to supply the seals with oil. They are used as emergency backup. They are initiated by dropping the pressure of the seal oil. They are normally vertically submerged pumps mounted on top of the lubricating oil tank. A DC pump is also provided in case of emergencies (loss of AC power). This pump is expected to operate for a few hours only while the hydrogen is scavenged. There is a possibility that hydrogen enters the drain tank. Low-level alarms are normally installed. A blower is used to exhaust the gas above the oil in the tank to the atmosphere. The blower reduces the pressure in the bearing housings by creating a vacuum in the tank to reduce the egress of oil vapor at the bearings.

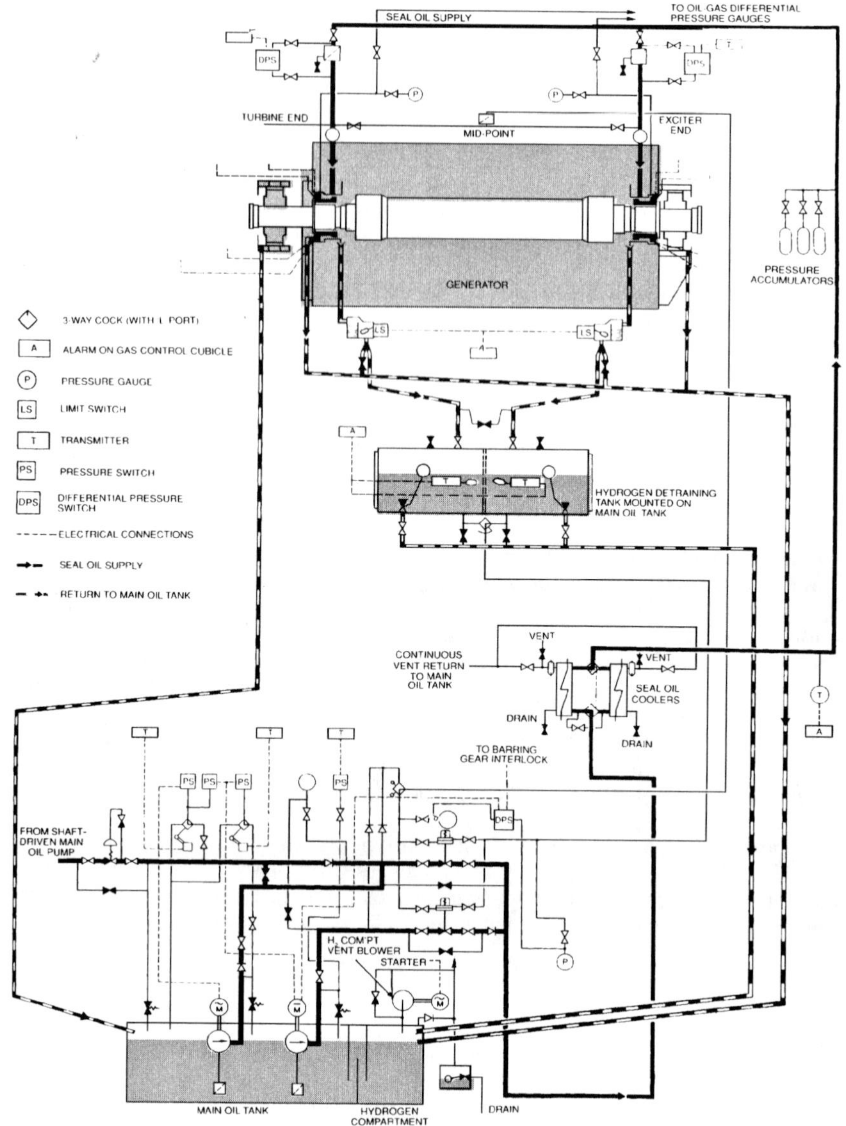

FIGURE 32.32 Seal oil system.

STATOR WINDING WATER COOLING SYSTEM

Figure 32.33 illustrates the demineralized water system used to remove the heat from the stator bars. The main criteria are as follows:

- Very low conductivity to prevent current flow and electrical flashover.
- High-integrity insulation is used to transfer water into the conductors.

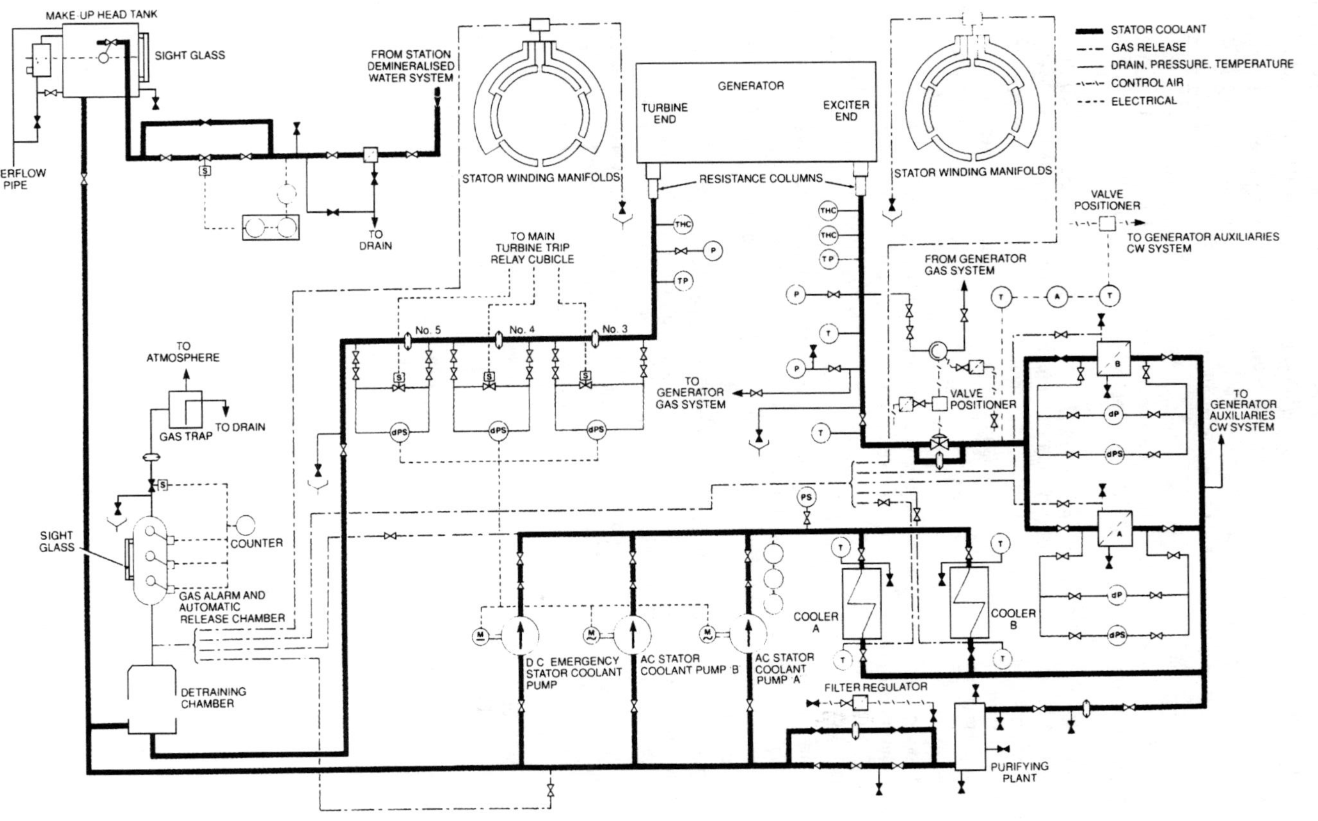

FIGURE 32.33 Stator winding water cooling system.

- Low water velocity to prevent erosion. Corrosion must also be prevented. Erosion or corrosion could result in a buildup of conducting material, leading to an electrical flashover.
- The maximum water pressure must be lower than the hydrogen pressure. If a leakage occurs, the hydrogen enters the water circuit. If water is allowed to enter the hydrogen, the winding insulation could become damaged.
- The maximum water temperature should be well below saturation (boiling occurs at 115°C at system pressure) to ensure adequate heat removal capability. The normal inlet and outlet temperatures are around 40 and 67°C, respectively.

A portion of the water is circulated through a demineraliser (Fig. 32.34). All the metals in contact with the water are nonferrous or stainless steel. If the metals had even a small amount of ferrous materials, magnetite will form. They will be held by electromagnetic forces. The water flows in flexible translucent hoses made of PTFE into and out of the conductors (Fig. 32.35). In the double-pass design, the water supply enters a circular manifold. The manifold is supported from the stator core end plate. The PTFE hoses are used to connect the manifold to the bars and between the top and bottom bars. The water flows in parallel channels in these bars. At the exciter end, the water is transferred through another PTFE hose to the outlet manifold. The inlet and outlet manifolds are located alongside each other. The terminal bushings and phase connections are cooled by a small flow. A higher pressure is required for the double-pass design compared with the single-pass design. However, only half the number of hoses is needed. This reduces the chance of leakage. In the single-pass arrangement, the manifolds are at opposite ends. The water flows through the bars in-parallel.

The water temperature rises rapidly if the flow is reduced. The differential pressure across an orifice plate or the stator windings is used to detect a reduction in flow. In this case, the standby pump should be started immediately, or the unit should be tripped.

An initial test is done on the water circuit to confirm it has a very low leak rate. However, a small quantity of hydrogen still enters the water. It is detected in a settling tank installed on the outlet side of the generator. Most of the gas is largely detrained in a header tank. The gas is collected in a chamber that is equipped with timed release valves. An alarm is initiated if the release rate exceeds a predetermined level (Fig. 32.36).

Thermocouples are installed in each of the winding slots. They detect low-flow conditions. Modern machines have a thermocouple in each outlet hose. They provide a direct indication of low flow. As noted earlier, condensation should not occur on the windings. Some generators have an electric heating element. Other designs have an automatic cooler bypassing system. It prevents cold water from circulating in the windings during start-up and low-load conditions.

OTHER COOLING SYSTEMS

The hydrogen is cooled by passing it through a water-cooled heat exchanger mounted in the casing. The heat exchanger has nonferrous tubes. The heat exchangers have a double-pass water circulation to the inlet and outlet water connections at the same end. Demineralized water is used for these coolers.

Lake water is not used for these coolers due to the danger of corrosion. The hydrogen is maintained at a higher pressure than the cooling water in the heat exchanger. In the event of a leak, hydrogen will leak into the water (water ingress into the hydrogen can have serious consequences). In modern design, the water circuit has hydrogen detectors (Fig. 32.37). The hydrogen coolers have some redundancy. It is possible to operate with one hydrogen cooler isolated. The loss of cooling water is detected by increase in cooling temperature.

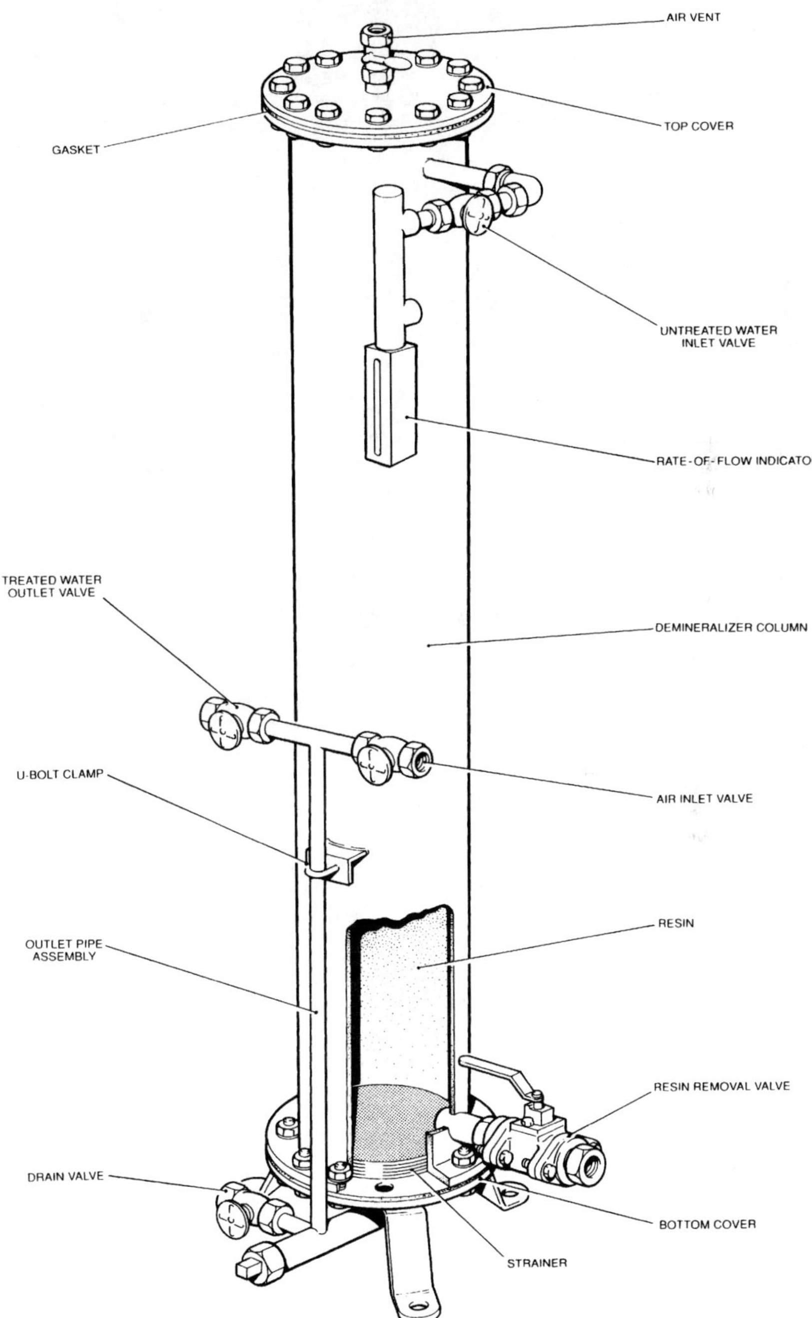

FIGURE 32.34 Demineralizer.

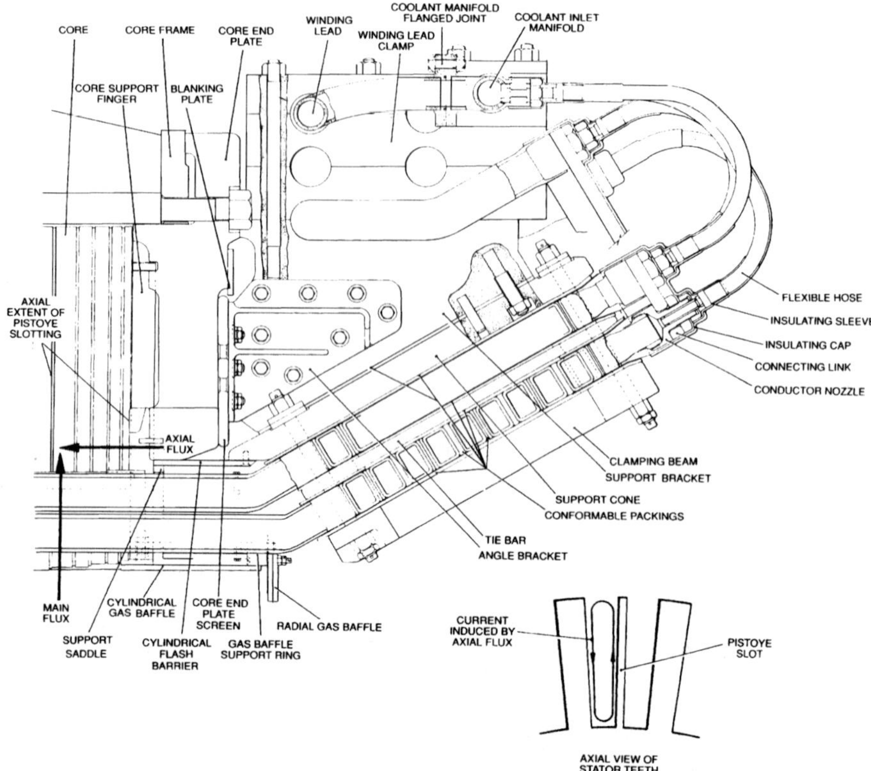

FIGURE 32.35 Water flow in the conductors.

The rapid increase in hydrogen temperature will cause the unit to trip. The rotating exciters, and slip ring/brush gear or rotating rectifier chambers, have air-cooling systems. A closed-air circuit with a water-cooled heat exchanger is used for the rotating exciter. Open-air ventilation is normally used for the slip rings.

EXCITATION

AC Excitation Systems

Figure 32.38 illustrates a typical AC excitation scheme. It shows the shaft-mounted main and pilot exciters together with their brush gear. Permanent-magnet pilot exciters are used to minimize dependency on external power supplies. The pilot exciter provides the excitation power for the automatic voltage regulator (AVR) control equipment. A 660-MW plant has a salient-pole pilot exciter with ratings near 100 kW. The main and pilot exciters are cooled by air. Shaft-mounted fans are used to provide the cooling. The performance is monitored by measuring the temperature at the inlet and outlet of the cooling system.

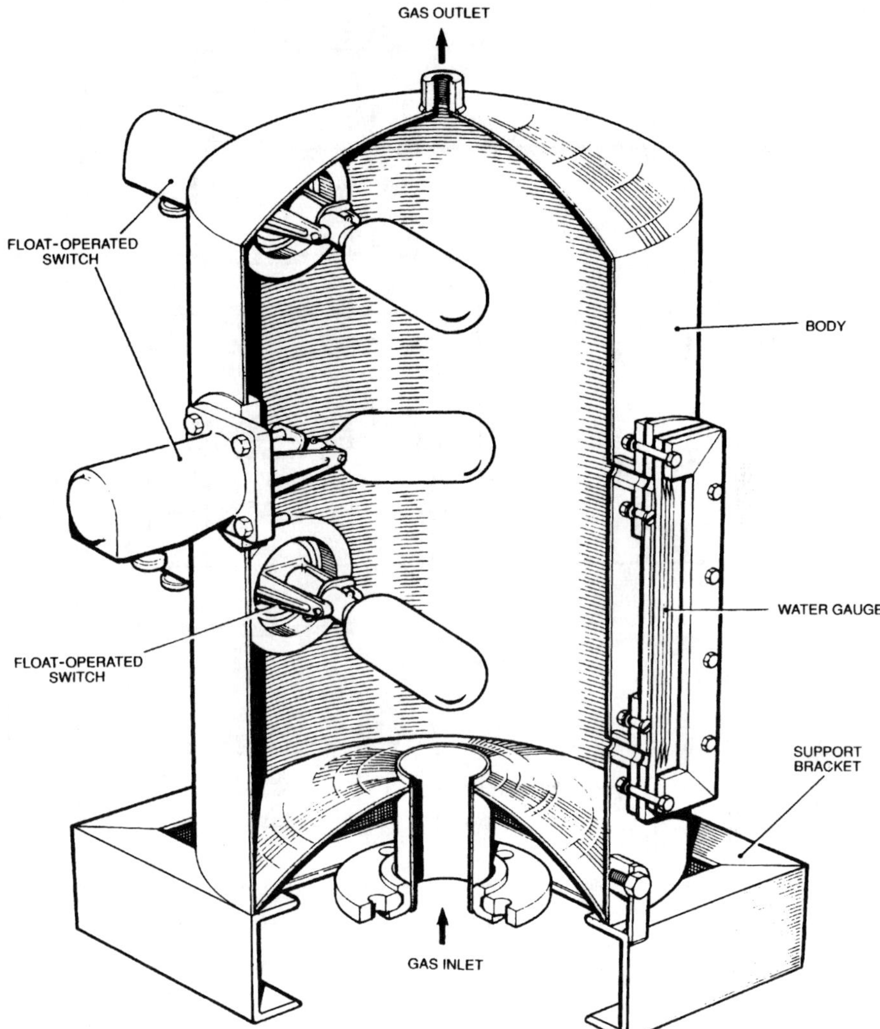

FIGURE 32.36 Gas in water detection chamber.

Exciter Transient Performance

The ceiling requirements for exciters are considerably higher than rated full-load conditions. The transient performance of an exciter is given by

$$\text{Exciter response ratio} = \frac{\text{average rate of increase in excitation open-circuit voltage (V/s)}}{\text{nominal excitation voltage}}$$

In a typical exciter, the output voltage needs to be increased from 100 to 200 percent within 3.5 s. Figure 32.39 illustrates the average rate of increase of excitation open circuit voltage.

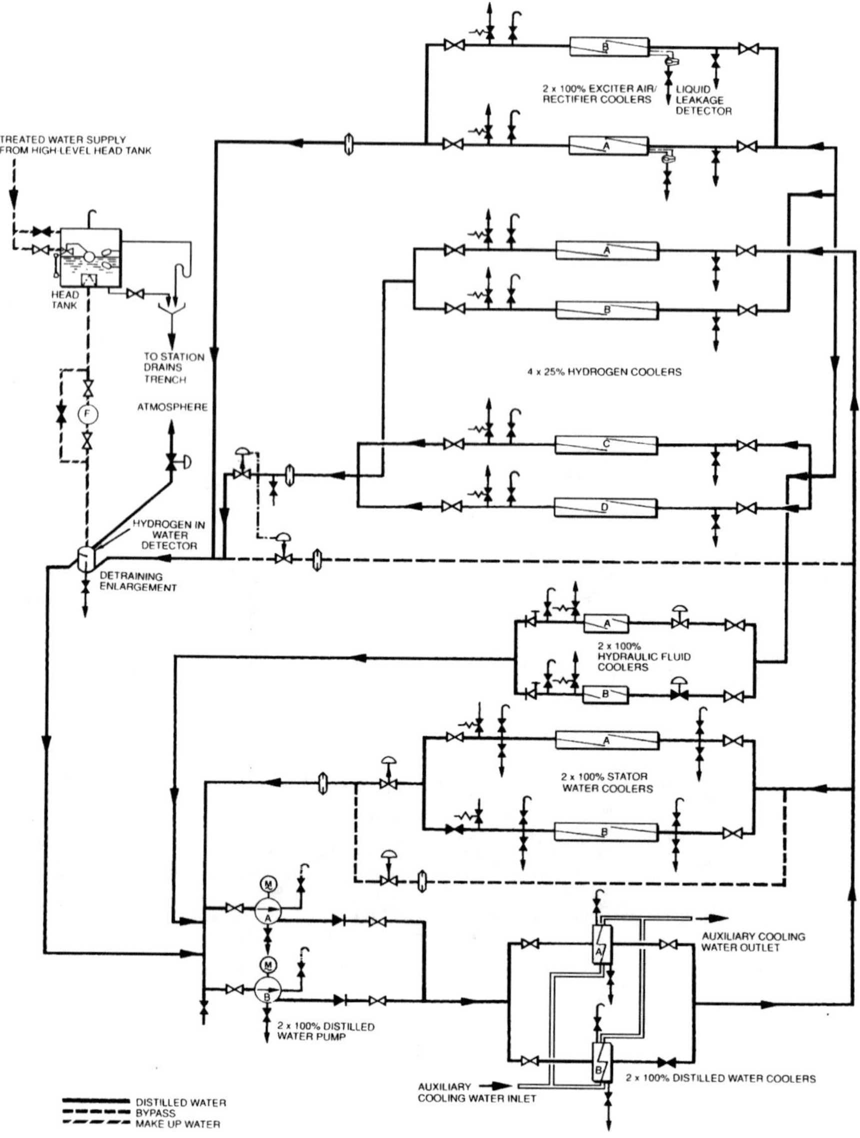

FIGURE 32.37 Distilled water cooling system.

The Pilot Exciter

The permanent-magnet generator (PMG) pilot exciters used for 660-MW units are salient-pole design (Fig. 32.40). This design provides a constant voltage supply to the thyristor converter and AVR control circuits. A high-energy material like Alcomax is used for the permanent-magnet poles. The poles are bolted to a steel hub and held in place by pole shoes. A nonmagnetic steel is used for the bolts to prevent the formation of a magnetic

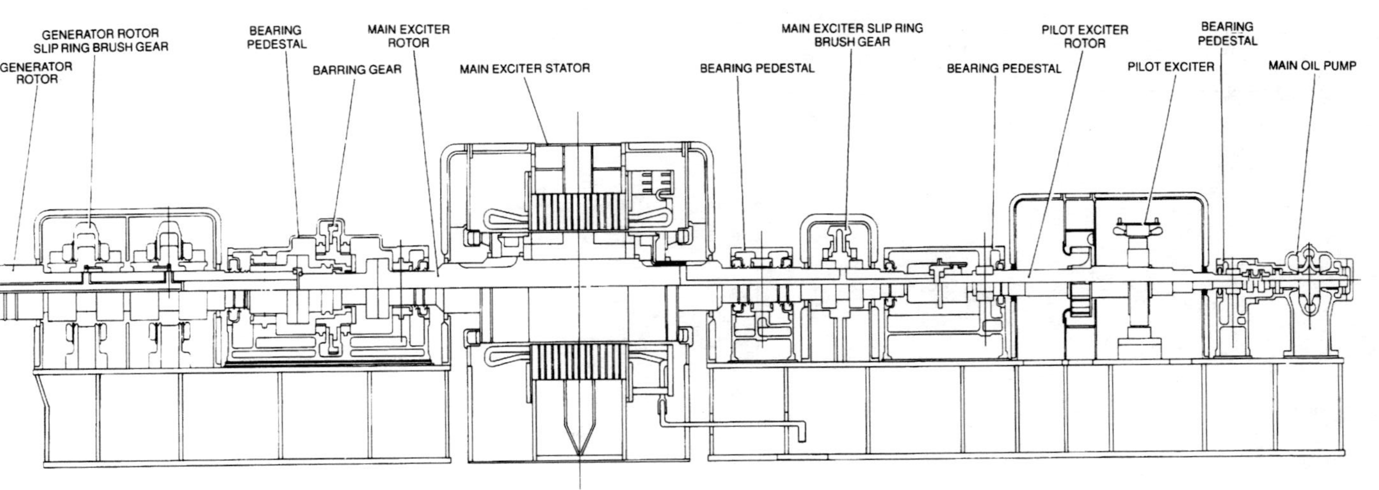

FIGURE 32.38 Section through main and pilot exciters.

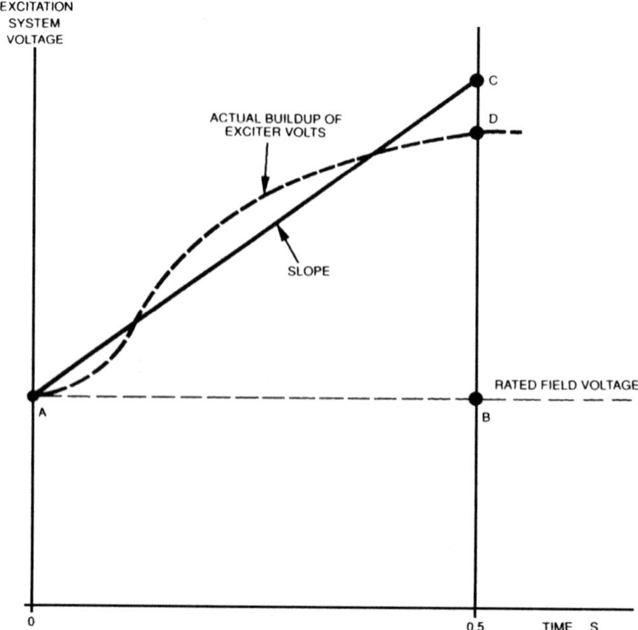

FIGURE 32.39 Concept of the exciter response ratio.

shunt. The pole shoes are skewed in some designs to improve the waveform of the output voltage and reduce electrical noise. The stator windings are arranged in a two-layer design. The stator conductors are insulated with polyester enamel. The coil insulation is a class F epoxy glass material.

The Main Exciter

The main AC exciter normally has four or six poles (Fig. 32.41).

Exciter Performance Testing

The manufacturer of the exciters is required to perform these tests: open- and short-circuit, overspeed balancing, and high voltage.

Pilot Exciter Protection

The pilot exciter delivers its full current during field forcing. Modern AVRs have a time/current limiter. It allows the pilot exciter to deliver maximum current during a determined interval. The current is brought back to a normal value following this interval. The main exciter, like the pilot exciter, has a considerably higher margin than required. It has a 3.3-kV winding insulation despite having a working voltage of 500 V. The voltage ceiling of the main exciter is 1000 V. Its rated current is much lower than the maximum current.

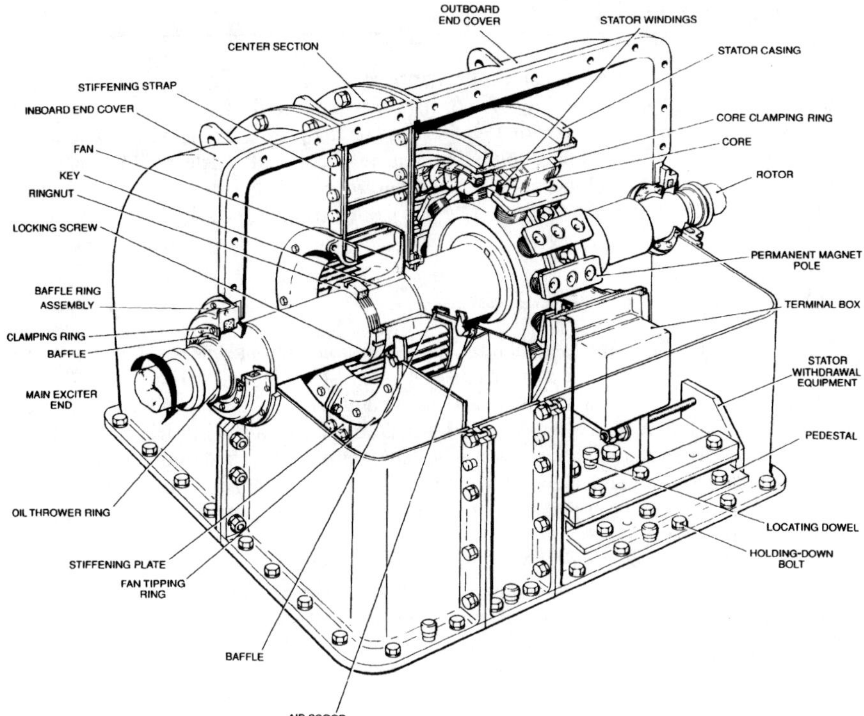

FIGURE 32.40 Salient-pole permanent-magnet generator.

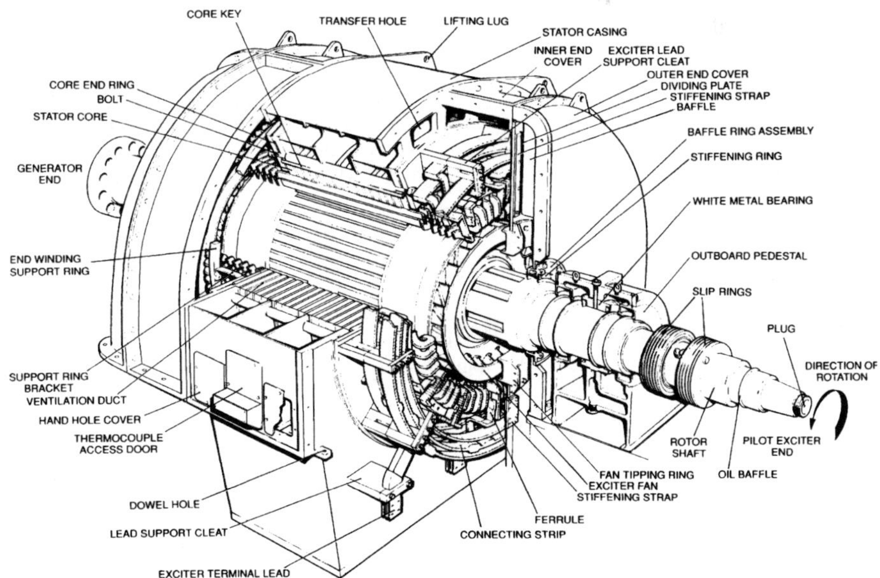

FIGURE 32.41 Main exciter.

BRUSHLESS EXCITATION SYSTEMS

Most modern gas turbines use brushless excitation systems. The rotating diodes are arranged as a three-phase bridge. The bridge arm consists of two diodes in series. If one of them fails (due to a short circuit), the second diode will continue to operate. Thus, the bridge continues to operate normally. If both diodes fail in the same arm, the fault is detected by a monitoring circuit, which trips the machine. Essential measurements, such as ground-fault indication, field current, and voltage, are taken by telemetry or instrument slip rings.

The Rotating Armature Main Exciter

Brushless machines require less maintenance than conventional ones. They also do not have sliding or rubbing electrical contacts that cause sparking and carbon dust. The main exciter is a three-phase rotating armature AC generator. The DC field is in the stator, and the AC winding is on the rotor. A typical rotating armature main exciter is illustrated in Fig. 32.42.

The exciter armature is made of low-loss steel laminations. The laminations are shrunk onto a shaft forged from annealed-carbon steel. Cooling air enters axial slots along the rotor body. The rotor conductors are made of braided strips in parallel. They are radially transposed to reduce eddy current losses.

The rotating rectifier of a 660-MW generator is illustrated in Fig. 32.43. It is mounted on the outboard of the main AC exciter. The three-phase AC power is supplied from the main exciter to the silicon diode rectifier by axial conductors taken along the surface of the shaft. A steel retaining ring contains the components of the rectifier against centrifugal forces. The retaining ring is shrunk on the outside of the hub.

THE VOLTAGE REGULATOR

Background

Early voltage regulators used mechanical components. They had a large deadband, long response time, and required regulator maintenance. Modern AVRs use integrated circuits or digital microprocessor techniques. Figure 32.44 illustrates a modern dual-channel arrangement.

System Description

The main function of the AVR is to maintain constant generator terminal voltage while the load conditions are changing. A dual-channel AVR with manual backup is normally used. The reliability of this design is high because the loss of one channel does not affect operational performance. The faulty channel can be repaired during operation.

The Regulator

The AVR is a closed-loop controller. It compares a signal proportional to the terminal voltage of the generator with a steady voltage reference. The difference (error) is used to control the exciter output.

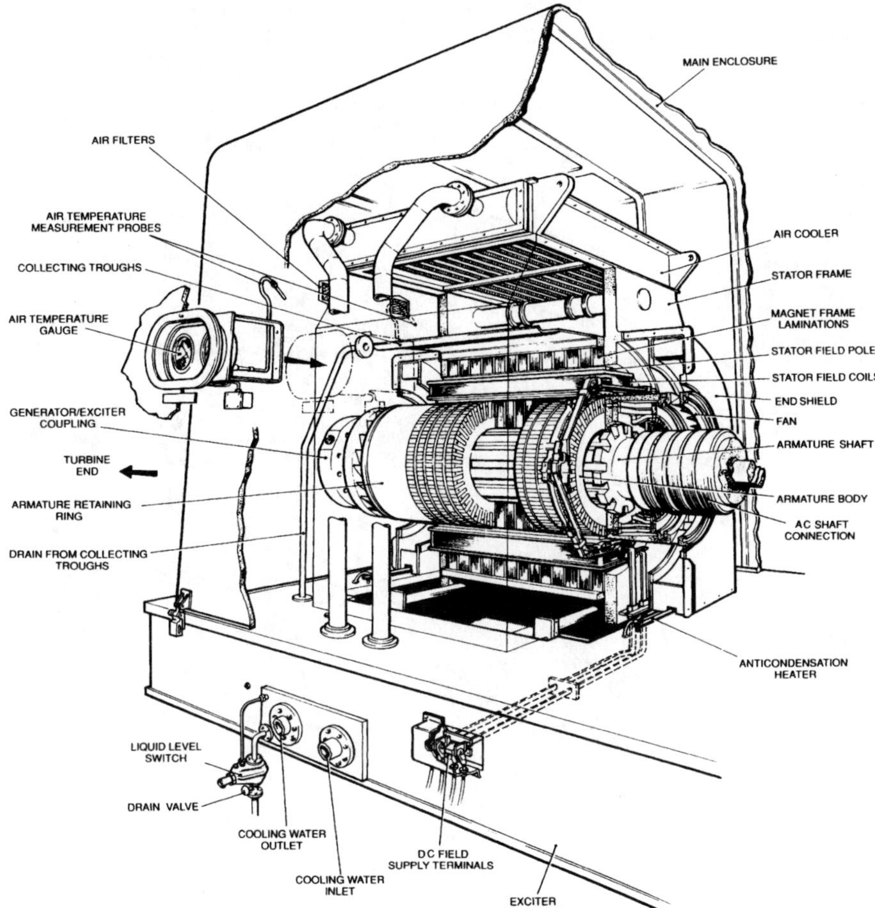

FIGURE 32.42 Rotating armature main exciter.

When the load changes, the error increases. The channel A AVR applies a proportional-integral-derivative (PID) algorithm to the error and provides a corrective signal. This signal is amplified by the channel A converter. It is then sent to vary a field resistance. The excitation current will change, and the terminal voltage will change accordingly. It is critical to have a fast, stable response from the AVR. Special signal conditioning networks are introduced in the PID control to prevent instability. Accurate tuning (selection of PID coefficients) of the voltage response is achieved by having adjustable time constants.

The AVR receives the generator terminal voltage signal through its own interposing voltage transformer. The voltage signal is rectified and filtered before comparing it with the reference voltage.

Auto Follow-Up Circuit

In a dual-channel AVR, both channels can be active simultaneously. Each channel provides half the excitation requirements. An alternative design allows one channel to be active

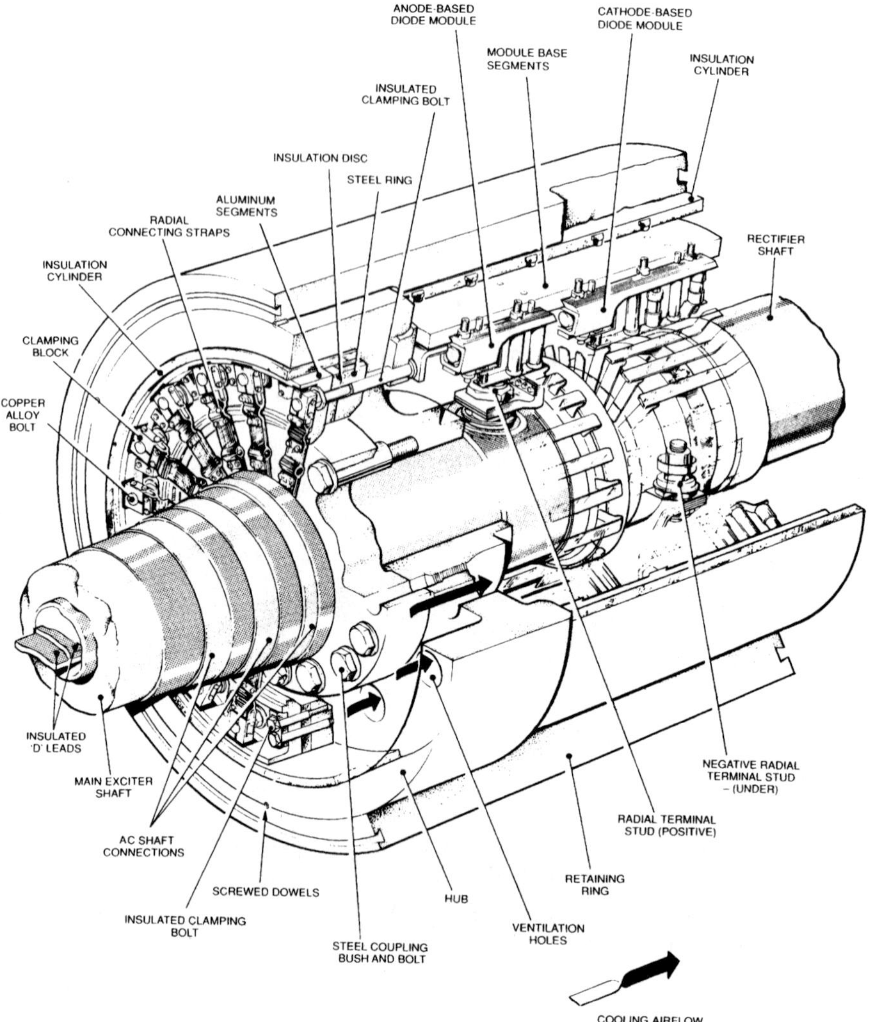

FIGURE 32.43 Rotating rectifier.

while the other follows passively. If a channel trips, the other picks up the full excitation requirement in a "bumpless" manner. A follow-up circuit is used to achieve this function. It tracks the primary (or active) channel and drives the output of the standby channel to match the output of the primary channel.

Manual Follow-Up

This is a manual follow-up system similar to the auto follow-up system. When the AVR fails, the manual control takes over in a bumpless manner.

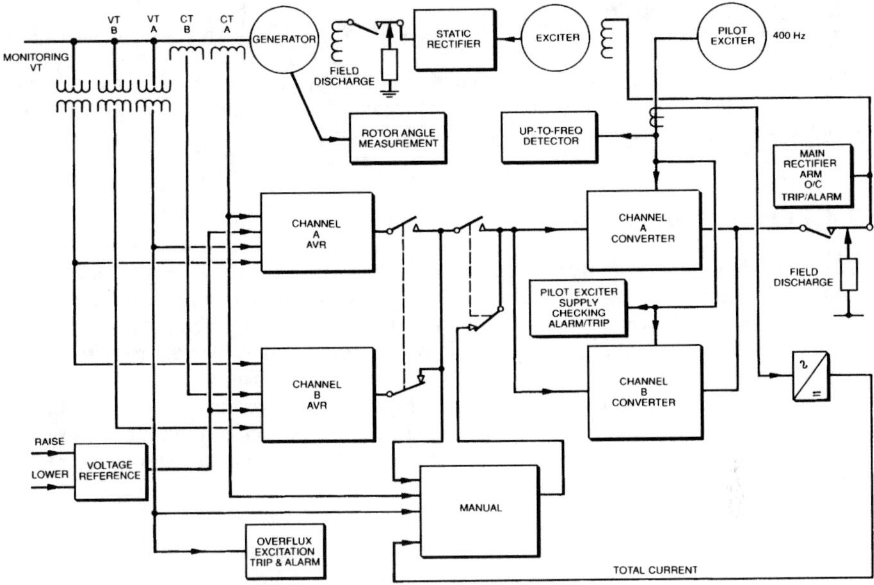

FIGURE 32.44 Dual-channel AVR.

AVR Protection

The AVR plays a critical role in the overall protection scheme of the generator because it controls the suppression of the field after faults. The generator should also be protected against AVR component failure, which could jeopardize its operation. An overvoltage relay monitors the terminal voltage of the generator. If the voltage exceeds a safe level, the field current is reduced in minimum time. This relay is only active when the generator is not synchronized.

An overfluxing relay is also active only during unsynchronized operation. If the safe voltage-frequency ratio is exceeded, the generator transformer could be overfluxed. A special relay detects this condition and initiates an alarm. The AVR controls reduce excitation to a safe level. If this condition persists, the excitation is tripped. A component failure within the AVR results in over- or underexcitation. The active channel output is compared with the minimum and maximum field current. When a limit is exceeded for a few seconds, the channel is tripped.

The Digital AVR

The use of microprocessors in AVRs has many advantages. The reliability will increase due to the reduction of the number of components. Most of the control logic in solid-state AVRs is done by electromechanical relays. These relays will be replaced by a specified microprocessor software. The cost of microprocessor-based AVRs is lower than conventional solid-state AVRs. This is due to the replacement of the customized printed circuit boards by standard memory circuits. However, the main advantage of microprocessor-based AVRs is in the wide range of sophisticated control features. One type of controller, called the *adaptive regulator,* is capable of adjusting its structure to accommodate the changing plant conditions.

EXCITATION CONTROL

Modern excitation equipment includes a number of limiter circuits. These limiters operate like parallel controllers. Their signals replace the generator voltage, which is the controlled variable when the input signals exceed predefined limits.

Rotor Current Limiter

All exciters have the capability of supplying a field current significantly higher than the one required during normal operation. This field-forcing capability or margin is needed during a fault to increase the reactive power. However, the duration of the increase in current must be limited to prevent overheating of the rotor, which would lead to degradation of the insulation system. During a system fault, the AVR boosts excitation. This situation lasts normally milliseconds before the circuit breaker clears the fault. However, the backup protection is allowed to last up to 5 s (or more). After this delay, the rotor current limit circuit sends a signal that overrides the one from the AVR, causing a reduction in excitation current.

Overfluxing Limit

Modern AVRs have overfluxing limiter circuits in addition to the overfluxing protection circuit. The overfluxing limiter circuit is a closed-loop controller. It monitors the voltage-frequency ratio when the generator is not synchronized. When a predefined ratio is exceeded, the limiter reduces excitation.

THE POWER SYSTEM STABILIZER

When a generator is synchronized with the grid, it is magnetically coupled to hundreds of other generators. This coupling is not rigid like a mechanical coupling. It is a flexible coupling similar to a connection with rubber bands. During normal operation, the generator oscillates slightly with respect to the grid. These oscillations are similar to vibrations of a mass attached to a rigid surface by a spring. These electromechanical oscillations normally have a frequency of between 0.2 and 2.0 Hz. This frequency depends on the load and location of the generator with respect to other large generators. Each machine can have different modes of oscillations. The frequency of these oscillations can be 0.3 Hz or 1 to 2 Hz normally. Therefore, the electrical power that is produced by the generator is not matching the mechanical power produced by the turbine at every instant. However, the average mechanical power produced matches the electrical power that is generated by the unit.

In some cases, groups of generators at one end of a transmission line oscillate with respect to those at the other end. For example, in a four-unit generating plant, the four generators tend to be coherent. They tend to oscillate as a group. An oscillation of between 10 and 50 MW (above and below the 600-MW rating) is expected. These oscillations are called *power system oscillations.* They depend on the load. They must be prevented. Otherwise, they can severely limit the megawatt transfer across the transmission system. Following a system fault, an accelerating torque will be applied to the generator as a result of changes in the electrical transmission system. The generator must produce a breaking torque in this situation to counter the accelerating torque. The *damper winding* will produce a counter (breaking or damping) torque.

Note: The damper windings are bars normally made of copper or brass. They are inserted in the pole face slots and connected at the ends. They form closed circuits as in a squirrel-cage winding. During normal operation, the generator is operating at synchronous speed. The damper winding also moves at the same speed. Thus, it is inactive. During a transient, the generator speed changes. The damper winding is now moving at a different speed than the synchronous speed. The currents induced in the damper winding generate an opposing torque to the relative motion. This action helps return the rotor to its normal speed.

The losses (e.g., windage and bearing friction) are speed-dependent. They also produce a countertorque that will help to reduce the overspeed. (Windage losses increase with the cube of the speed. The journal bearing losses increase with the square of the speed. The axial thrust bearing loss increases with the speed.)

The power system stabilizer (PSS) is added when there is insufficient countertorque (damping). All units over 10 MW must be reviewed for need of PSS. Most of them require a PSS. The PSS measures the shaft speed and real power generated. It determines the difference between the mechanical power and the electrical power. It produces a signal based on this difference that changes the speed of the machine (it produces a component of generator torque in phase with the speed changes). *The objective of the PSS is to keep the power leaving the machine constant.* It changes the excitation current at the same frequency as the electromechanical oscillations. This action changes the generator voltage with respect to the voltage in the grid. Power will flow from the grid to the unit to provide the countertorque required when the speed of the shaft exceeds the synchronous speed. It is important to mention that an improperly tuned PSS can lead to disastrous consequences. This is due to the voltage variations that it creates during operation. If the voltage variations are incorrect, excessive torque changes can occur leading to significant damage.

In summary, the salient features about PSS are the following:

1. The PSS acts as a shock absorber to dampen the power swings.
2. The AVR cannot handle power swings, because it is monitoring the voltage only.
3. A fault on the line can excite a unit severely if the damping is poor.
4. The PSS monitors the change in power and change in speed.
5. During steady-state operation, the PSS will not interfere.
6. When a fault occurs, the voltage drops. The field current must be increased to push as much active power out to increase the synchronizing torque. However, this increase in synchronizing torque (active power out) lasts for a few seconds only due to these reasons:
   a. Active power flow between the generator and the load is proportional to:

$$\frac{V_{\text{generator}} \times V_{\text{load}}}{(\text{Reactance between generator and load}) \times \sin\alpha}$$

   where, α is the angle between the phasors of $V_{\text{generator}}$ and V_{load}, and the reactance includes the step-up transformer only.
   If excitation is increased, $V_{\text{generator}}$ increases but α changes within a few seconds so that the active power flow remains unchanged.
   b. The active power flow is determined by the turbine.

It is also important to mention that the reactive power flow is proportional to:

$$\frac{V_{\text{generator}} - V_{\text{load}}}{\text{Reactance between the generator and the load}}$$

Any change in $V_{\text{generator}}$ will result in significant change in the reactive power sent to the grid. Therefore, when the excitation changes, $V_{\text{generator}}$ will change resulting in significant transfer of reactive power.

CHARACTERISTICS OF GENERATOR EXCITER POWER SYSTEM (GEP)

The characteristics of a GEP are established by extensive system investigations. All plant operating modes must be examined to identify the conditions of marginal stability. In general, the periods of low system demand (at night) are the most critical. The generator operates at a leading power factor during these times. In pumped-storage plants (where the turbine is used to pump the water upstream during the night. This is done because the price of electricity is very low at night. The same water is allowed down through the turbine during the day because the price of electricity is higher) the situation is more critical. This is because of the large rotor angle (angle between the rotor flux and stator flux. This angle normally increases with the load when the generator operates) in comparison with the remaining machines on the system during the night. The generator is operating as a motor in this situation.

A number of simulations are done on the unit (including AVR and PSS). The PSS settings are adjusted for optimum performance of excitation under all critical operating conditions. These settings are then used during plant commissioning. This is done to reduce on-site testing, which can be expensive.

EXCITATION SYSTEM ANALYSIS

The generator excitation system has the primary responsibility for power system dynamic and transient stability. *Dynamic stability* refers to the performance of the system following small load changes. This can result in sustained oscillations around 0.5 Hz when large power is transferred over long distances. These oscillations must be rapidly attenuated. Otherwise, the transmission system will be severely limited. *Transient stability* refers to the ability of a generator or group of generators to maintain synchronous operation following system faults.

Following a fault, a boost of synchronous torque is required to maintain the generator in synchronism. (*Note:* The synchronous torque is the torque used to maintain the generator in synchronism. It is created by active power sent to the grid. This is done by increasing the field current.)

In this situation, the AVR bucks (resists, opposes) and/or boosts the field current to develop the additional synchronizing torque. Therefore, the AVR must be properly tuned to play an essential role in maintaining stable system operation under all operating conditions.

GENERATOR OPERATION

Running Up to Speed

Before running up to speed, air will have been scavenged from the generator casing. Hydrogen will fill the casing to almost-rated pressure. The hydrogen pressure increases with temperature. Rated pressure is achieved on steady load. The stator windings should remain warmer than the hydrogen to prevent condensation.

It is recommended to go through the first and second critical (around 900 and 2200 r/min) of the rotor quickly to avoid high vibrations (Fig. 32.13).

As the rated speed is approached, excitation is applied automatically by the voltage regulator (or manually) by closing the switches of the exciter and the main field. The voltage-frequency control device prevents the voltage from exceeding the rated voltage-frequency. This is done to prevent overfluxing of the generator transformer. The rated voltage should be established at rated speed with the machine on open circuit.

Open-Circuit Conditions and Synchronizing

Generators are generally operated near their rated voltage. If the grid requires a different voltage, the transformer tap changers will accommodate this request. A voltage range of ±5 percent is normally specified. The open-circuit characteristic is normally determined by the manufacturer. Several measurements of rotor currents and stator voltage are taken and plotted (Fig. 32.45). The relationship is linear (the air gap line) up to about 75 percent rated voltage.

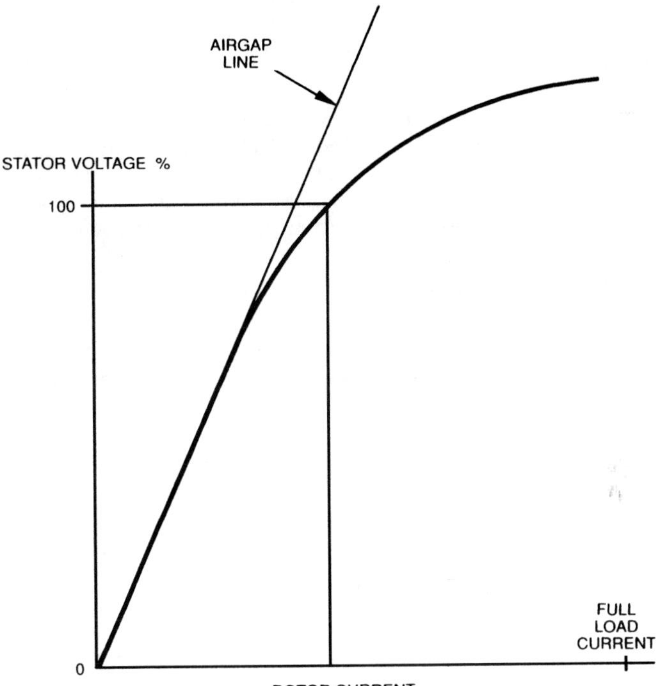

FIGURE 32.45 Open-circuit characteristics.

Note: The MMF is applied across the reluctance of the air gap and the reluctance of the core. The reluctance of the air gap dominates because it is much larger than the one of the core. When saturation is reached, the reluctance of the iron starts to change. This occurs at the knee of the curve (Fig. 32.45).

During a long outage, the open-circuit characteristic should be checked by measuring the parameters at a few points along the curve. Improper synchronization can have serious consequences. If the magnitude or angular position of the voltage phasors were significantly different when the circuit breaker is closed, large current would circulate from the system through the stator windings due to the voltage difference. This causes high forces in the windings.

If there is a significant difference in frequency, a large torque would be imposed on the rotor due to the sudden pulling into synchronism. A backup device confirms adequate synchronization conditions before allowing the circuit breaker to close.

The Application of a Load

If the generator voltage phasors (magnitude and angular position) match exactly, there will be no current flow nor an electrical torque. An imbalance in phasors must be created in order to generate a load. The steam turbine governing valves are opened gradually. The rotor starts to accelerate due to the additional torque. It moves forward relative to its no-load position while still remaining in synchronism with the grid. The difference in voltage phasor created by this angular change generates current in the stator windings. An electrical torque is generated, which balances the increased mechanical torque.

Capability Chart

Figure 32.46 illustrates the capability chart of a generator. It is an MW-MVAR diagram. A constant megawatt limit is drawn at the rated power output of the turbine. The rated stator current locus cuts the rated megawatt line at the rated megavoltampere and power factor point. The rated rotor current imposes a limit on megawatt and lagging power factor. The capability chart shows the limits of generated megawatt and MVAR.

Neutral Grounding

The neutral ends of the three stator winding phases are connected together outside the casing. The star point is connected to ground through a neutral grounding device. It is designed to

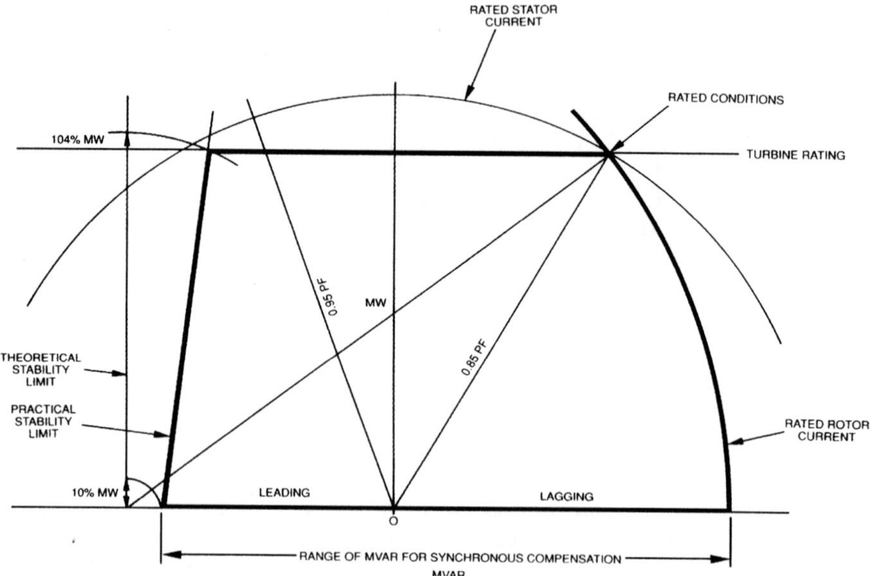

FIGURE 32.46 Capability chart.

limit the fault current upon a ground fault in the stator winding. The neutral grounding device consists of a single-phase transformer. Its primary is connected between the generator star point and ground. Its secondary is connected to a resistor. This arrangement is chosen because the apparent impedance of the resistor appears on the primary side as a^2Z, where $a = N_p/N_s$, and Z is the impedance of the resistor. This creates a very high impedance that limits the fault current to 15 A.

Rotor Torque

During electrical faults, the stator currents are many times larger than the rated value. The associated electromagnetic torques have similar magnitudes. The shaft and coupling must be designed to withstand stipulated fault conditions without failure. However, the coupling bolts exhibit distortion in some cases after a severe electrical fault.

REFERENCE

1. British Electricity International, *Modern Power Station Practice*, 3d ed., Pergamon Press, Oxford, United Kingdom, 1991.

CHAPTER 33

GENERATOR TESTING, INSPECTION, AND MAINTENANCE

GENERATOR OPERATIONAL CHECKS (SURVEILLANCE AND MONITORING)

Regular monitoring of the following six parameters is required:

1. Temperature of stator windings
2. Core temperature
3. Temperature of slip rings
4. Vibration levels at the bearings
5. Brush gear inspection (monthly or bimonthly)

   Remove the brush holder. Clean the carbon brushes by compressed air. Inspect the brushes for uneven wear (do not touch the brushes with bare hands). Replace worn brushes. Use a stroboscope to inspect the slip rings. Vary the frequency of the stroboscope to check for uneven wear of the slip rings. The temperature of the slip rings should be measured using an infrared detector. If the slip ring temperature is high, the brushes would overheat and wear quickly. Generator derating is required if the slip ring temperature is high.
6. On-line partial discharge activity

MAJOR OVERHAUL (EVERY 8 TO 10 YEARS)

The electrical and mechanical tests that are required are described in Appendixes A and B, respectively. In summary, the work includes the following:

1. Perform insulation resistance and polarization index tests.
2. Investigate causes of partial discharge.
3. Check the tightness of the stator wedges by tapping them with a hammer. The wedges must be tight to minimize the movement of the stator conductor bars during operation. Rewedging and adding packing may be required.
4. Perform EL-CID test to determine if there is any loosening in the core laminations or deterioration in the core insulation. Apply penetrating epoxy if insulation is degrading.
5. Perform casing pressure, and stator pressure and vacuum decay tests.

6. Refurbish rotor, including inspection of radial pin and end caps (including ultrasonic and dye penetrant testing), vacuum test, slip ring refurbishment, and checking for copper dusting.

   Note: Copper dusting occurs due to fretting of the rotor copper windings as they move in the slots when the machine is on turning gear. This problem does not occur during normal operation because centrifugal forces push the windings against the wedges. Copper dusting can cause shorts in the machine.

7. Calibrate protection equipment.

APPENDIX A: GENERATOR DIAGNOSTIC TESTING

The following factors affect the insulation systems in generators:

- High temperature
- Environment
- Mechanical effects (e.g., thermal expansion and contraction, vibration, electromagnetic bar forces, and motor start-up forces in the end turns)
- Voltage stresses during operating and transient conditions

All of these factors contribute to loss of insulation integrity and reliability. These aging factors interact frequently to reinforce each other's effects. For example, high-temperature operation could deteriorate the insulation of a stator winding, loosen the winding bracing system, increase vibration, and cause erosion. At some point, high-temperature operation could lead to delamination of the core and internal discharge. This accelerates the rate of electrical aging and could lead to a winding failure.

Nondestructive diagnostic tests are used to determine the condition of the insulation and the rate of electrical aging. The description of the recommended diagnostic tests for the insulation system of motors, along with the conditions they are designed to detect, will be presented later.

Stator Insulation Tests

An electrical test is best suited to determine the condition of electrical insulation. The tests on insulation systems in electrical equipment can be divided into two categories:

1. High-potential (hipot), or voltage-withstand, tests
2. Tests that measure some specific insulation property (e.g, resistance or dissipation factor)

Tests in the first category are performed at some elevated alternating current (AC) or direct current (DC) voltage to confirm that the equipment is not in imminent danger of failure if operated at its rated voltage. Various standards give the test voltages that are appropriate to various types and classes of equipment. They confirm that the insulation has not deteriorated below a predetermined level and that the equipment will most likely survive in service for a few more years. However, they do not give a clear indication about the condition of the insulation.

The second category of electrical tests indicates the moisture content, presence of dirt, development of flaws (voids), cracks and delamination, and other damage to the insulation. A third category of tests includes the use of electrical or ultrasonic probes that can determine the specific location of damage in a stator winding. These tests require access to the air gap and energization of the winding from an external source. These tests are considered an aid to visual inspection.

Direct Current Tests for Stator and Rotor Windings

These tests are sensitive indicators to the presence of dirt, moisture, and cracks. They must be performed off-line with the winding isolated from ground, as shown in Fig. 33.1.

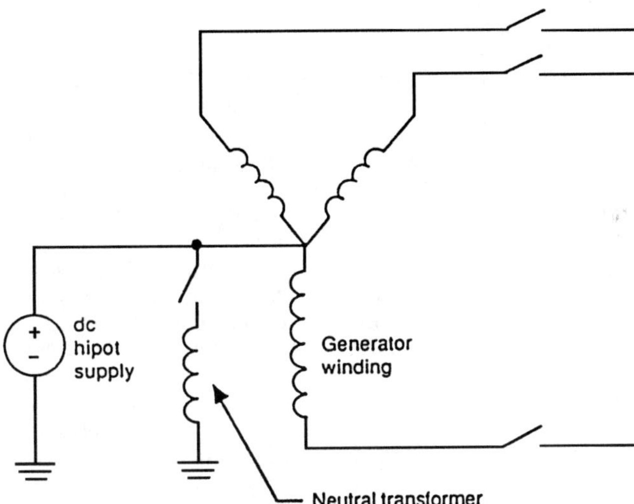

FIGURE 33.1 Direct current testing of a generator winding.

Suitable safety precautions should be taken when performing all high-potential tests. When high-voltage DC tests are performed on water-cooled windings, the tubes or manifolds should be dried thoroughly to remove current leakage paths to the ground, and to avoid the possibility of damage by arcing between moist patches inside the insulating water tubes. For greater sensitivity, these tests can be performed on parts of the windings (phases) isolated from one another.

The charge will be retained in the insulation system for up to several hours after the application of high DC voltages. Hence, the windings should be kept grounded for several hours after a high-voltage DC test to protect personnel from a shock.

Tests using DC voltages have been preferred over the ones using AC voltages for routine evaluation of large machines for two reasons:

1. The high DC voltage applied to the insulation during a test is far less damaging than high AC voltages due to the absence of partial discharges.
2. The size and weight of the DC test equipment is far less than the AC test equipment needed to supply the reactive power of a large winding.

Insulation Resistance and Polarization Index. The polarization index (PI) and insulation resistance tests indicate the presence of cracks, contamination, and moisture in the insulation. They are commonly performed on any motor and generator winding. They are suitable for stator and insulated rotor windings.

The *insulation resistance* is the ratio of the DC voltage applied between the winding and ground to the resultant current. When the DC voltage is applied, the following three current components flow:

1. The charging current into the capacitance of the windings.
2. A polarization or absorption current due to the various molecular mechanisms in the insulation.
3. A "leakage" current between the conductors and ground (the creepage path). This component is highly dependent on the dryness of the windings.

The first two components of the current decay with time. The third component is mainly determined by the presence of moisture or a ground fault. However, it is relatively constant. Moisture is usually absorbed in the insulation and/or condensed on the end winding surfaces. If the leakage current is larger than the first two current components, then the total charging current (or insulation resistance) will not vary significantly with time.

Therefore, the dryness and cleanliness of the insulation can be determined by measuring the insulation resistance after 1 min and after 10 min. The PI is the ratio of the 10-min to the 1-min reading.

Test Setup and Performance. Several suppliers, such as Biddle Instruments and Genrad, offer insulation resistance meters that can determine the insulation resistance accurately by providing test voltages of 500 to 5000 V direct current. For motors and generators rated 4 kV and higher, 1000 V is usually used for testing the windings of a rotor, and 5000 V is used for testing the stator windings.

To perform the test on a stator winding, the phase leads and the neutral lead (if accessible) must be isolated. The water must be drained from any water-cooled winding, and any hoses must be removed or dried thoroughly by establishing a vacuum (it is preferable to remove the hoses because vacuum-drying is usually impossible).

The test instrument is connected between the neutral lead or one of the phase leads and the machine frame (Fig. 33.1). To test a rotor winding, the instrument should be connected between a lead from a rotor winding and the rotor steel. During the test, the test leads should be lean and dry.

Interpretation. If there is a fault, or if the insulation is punctured, the resistance of the insulation will approach zero. The Institute of Electrical and Electronics Engineers (IEEE) standard recommends a resistance in excess of ($V_{L\text{-}L}$ + 1) megohm (MΩ). If the winding is 13.8 kV, the minimum acceptable insulation resistance is 15 MΩ. This value must be considered the absolute minimum since modern machine insulation is in the order of 100 to 1000 MΩ. If the air around the machine had high humidity, the insulation resistance would be in the order 10 MΩ.

The insulation resistance depends highly on the temperature and humidity of the winding. To monitor the changes of insulation resistance over time, it is essential to perform the test under the same humidity and temperature conditions. The insulation resistance can be corrected for changes in winding temperature. If the corrected values of the insulation resistance are decreasing over time, then there is deterioration in the insulation.

It is more likely, however, that the changes in insulation resistance are caused by changes in humidity. If the windings were moist and dirty, the leakage component of the current (which is relatively constant), will predominate over the time-varying components. Hence, the total current will reach a steady value rapidly. Therefore, the PI is a direct measure of the dryness and cleanliness of the insulation. The PI is high (>2) for a clean and dry winding. However, it approaches unity for a wet and dirty winding.

The insulation resistance test is a very popular diagnostics test due to its simplicity and low cost. It should be done to confirm that the winding is not wet and dirty enough to cause a failure that could have been averted by a cleaning and drying-out procedure.

The resistance testing has a pass-fail criterion. It cannot be relied upon to predict the insulation condition, except when there is a fault in the insulation.

The high-potential tests, whether direct current or alternating current, are destructive testing. They are not generally recommended as maintenance-type tests. For stator windings rated 5 kV or higher, a *partial discharge* (pd) test, which in the past has been referred to as *corona,* should be done. The level of pd should be determined because it can erode the insulation and lead to insulation aging.

Direct Current High-Potential Test. A high-DC voltage withstand test is performed on a stator or rotor winding to ensure that the groundwall insulation can be stressed to normal operating voltage. The outcome of the test is simply pass or fail. Thus, it is not classified as a diagnostic test. The DC hipot test is done sometimes following maintenance on the winding, to confirm that the winding has not been damaged. It is important to consider the consequences of a hipot failure. Spare parts and outage time should be available before proceeding with this test.

The DC hipot test is based on the principle that weakened insulation will puncture if exposed to a high enough voltage. The test voltage is selected such that damaged insulation will fail during the test and good insulation will survive. Insulation that fails during a hipot test is expected to fail within a short period of time if placed in service. The distribution of electrical stresses within the insulation during a DC test is different from normal AC operation because the DC electric field is determined by resistances rather than capacitances. Figure 33.1 illustrates how the test is done. The winding is isolated and a high voltage connected between the winding and ground. If the stator windings are water-cooled, they must be drained and the system dried thoroughly to avoid electrical tracking of the coolant hoses. The hoses should be removed to ensure that they are not damaged by the test. The stator frame and all temperature sensors must be grounded. All accessories such as current and potential transformers must be disconnected or shorted. The suggested voltage test for a new winding is 1.7 times the root-mean-square (rms) ac voltage. A typical routine voltage used during maintenance is ($2 \times V_{L\text{-}L}$) kV direct current. However, the test voltages used by the manufacturer and during commissioning are significantly higher than the maintenance test voltage level. The rotor windings do not have a standard test voltage level.

If a hipot test is successful, it confirms that there are no serious cracks in the groundwall and the insulation system. The insulation will most likely withstand normal operating stresses until the next scheduled maintenance test.

High-Voltage Step and Ramp Tests. The variation of current (or insulation resistance) should be monitored as the DC hipot test is performed. If there is a weakness in the groundwall, a sudden nonlinear increase in current (or decrease in insulation resistance) will precede a breakdown as the voltage is increasing. An experienced operator can interrupt the test when the first indication of warning occurs. If the voltage achieved is considered sufficient, the machine can be returned to service until the repairs can be planned. Following identification of a suspect phase, the location of the weakness must be found. The variations of voltage with current obtained during the test can be used in future comparisons on the same winding if the same conditions exist.

The winding must be completely isolated (Fig. 33.1). A special ramp or conventional high-voltage DC test set is used for this test. The leakage current must be calculated at the end of each voltage step. The test operator must make a judgment based on the increase in leakage current before increasing the voltage further. The test voltage can alternatively be increased slowly with a recorder plotting the variations of leakage current against voltage [Fig. 33.2 (*a, b*)].

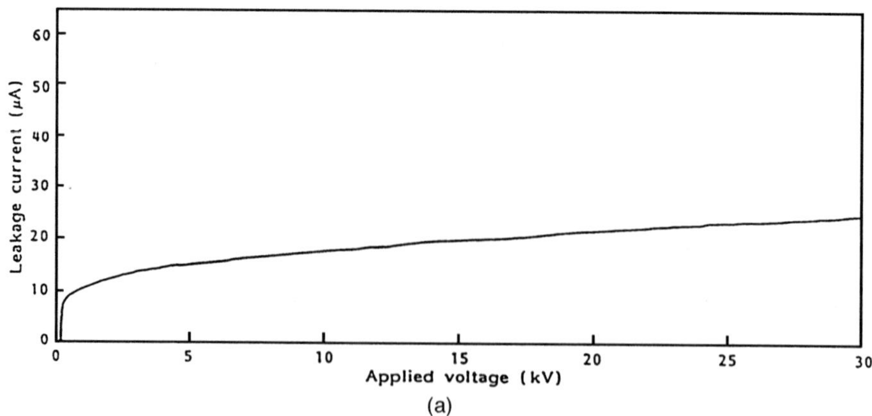

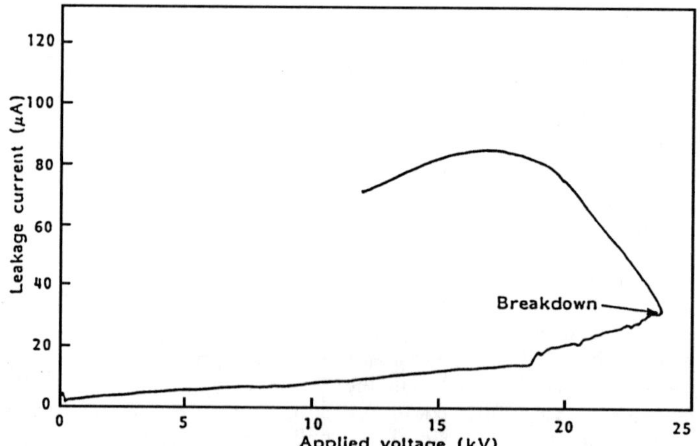

FIGURE 33.2 Ramp test characteristic output. (*a*) Voltage-current plot for a good winding, (*b*) voltage-current plot showing instabilities prior to insulation puncture.

A weakness in the groundwall can be detected by a sudden increase in leakage current. If the condition of the groundwall is questionable, the machine can be returned to service if the achieved voltage is considered sufficient. Further investigations can be scheduled at a more convenient time.

Alternating Current Tests for Stator Windings

The DC tests are only capable of measuring the conductivity of the insulation system. The AC tests are usually more revealing of the insulation condition. However, they are more onerous than DC tests. The AC tests are also capable of being sensitive to the mechanical condition of the system. For example, if delamination (air-filled layers) is present in the groundwall, the capacitance between the conductors and the core will decrease. However, if the winding is wet, the capacitance will increase.

Partial Discharge Tests. Partial discharges or pd's (known in the past as corona), are spark charges that occur in voids within high-voltage insulation (>5 kV). They occur between the windings and core, or in the end winding region. These are "partial" discharges because there is some remaining insulation. The pd can erode the insulation and therefore contributes to its aging. However, a pd is a symptom of insulation aging caused by thermal or mechanical stresses. The measurement of a pd activity in a stator winding is an indication of the health of the insulation. Partial discharge tests provide the best means for assessing the condition of the insulation without a visual inspection. These tests should be done on stator windings in motors and generators rated higher than 5 kV.

Off-Line Conventional Partial Discharge Test. The conventional pd test involves energizing the winding to normal line-to-ground AC voltage with an external supply. A pd detector is used to measure the pd activity in the winding. The sparks caused by pd are fast-current pulses that travel through the stator windings. These pulses and the accompanying voltage pulses increase with the pd pulse. Figure 33.3 illustrates a high-voltage capacitor that can block the power frequency voltage and allow the high-frequency pulse signals to reach

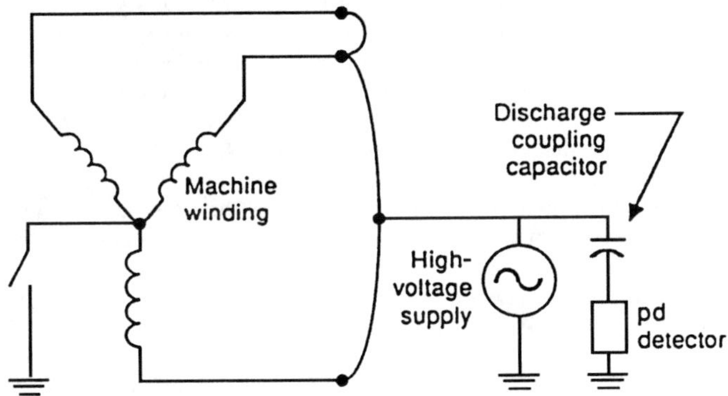

FIGURE 33.3 Test arrangement for conventional pd test.

the pd detector. An oscilloscope is used to display the pulse signals after further filtering.

The pulse magnitudes are calibrated in picocoulombs (pC), even though the actual measurements are in millivolts (mV). The conventional test is done off-line. A separate voltage supply is used to energize the windings to normal voltage. The interference from high-frequency electrical noise in this test is a minimum.

Test Setup and Performance. The conventional test involves isolating the winding from the ground and energizing one phase of the winding by a 60-Hz power supply cable to rated line-to-ground voltage. This test is normally done on each phase separately while the remaining two are grounded. The phases are disconnected from one another at the neutral. Draining of the water-cooled winding is not required.

The test equipment includes a power separation filter (high-voltage) capacitor and a high-pass filter to block the power frequency and its harmonics—Fig. 33.3. The oscilloscope displays the pd pulses (Fig. 33.4). A pulse height analyzer is used to process the pulse data. It gives the pulse counts, pulse magnitudes, and comparisons between positive and negative pulses.

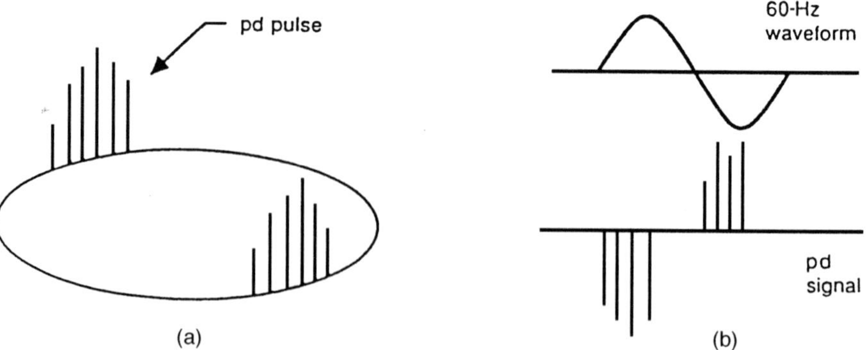

FIGURE 33.4 Typical outputs of pd detectors. The higher the pulses, the more deteriorated the winding. (*a*) Shows the elliptical trace from many types of commercial detectors, where the pulse position on the ellipse indicates the phase position. (*b*) Shows the display on a conventional dual-channel oscilloscope.

The AC voltage is raised gradually until pd pulses are observed on the oscilloscope. The voltage at which pd starts is called the *discharge inception voltage* (DIV). When the test voltage reaches the normal voltage, the magnitude of the pulses is read from the screen. The analysis of the pulse height is normally recorded. As the AC voltage is decreased, the voltage at which the pd pulses disappear is recorded. This is called the *discharge extinction voltage* (DEV). It is usually lower than the DIV. The actual test takes about 30 min, normally. However, the setup and disassembly can take up to a day.

Interpretation. There is no general agreement on the acceptable magnitudes of pd, DIV, and DEV. The inductive nature of the windings makes the calibration of the measured pd magnitudes (conversion from millivolts on the screen of the oscilloscope into picocoulombs) difficult. Thus, the measurement of the pulses may not provide an accurate value of the pd activity. These measurements cannot be calibrated from machine to machine or among the different types of commercial detectors.

The most useful method for interpreting the pd test results is by performing the test at regular intervals and monitoring for trends. The recommended interval for air-cooled machines is once or twice per year and every 2 years for hydrogen-cooled generators. As the condition of the insulation worsens, the magnitude of the pd will increase and those of the DIV and DEV will decrease. An increasing trend of pd activity indicates that the insulation is aging. Visual inspection of the winding condition may be required. Partial discharge results should only be compared if the same equipment and procedures are used during testing. This is due to the calibration problems mentioned earlier. Comparison of results can also be misleading if there are differences between the types of rating of the windings. Comparison of pd results are valid if the windings and test methods are identical.

A pd magnitude of less than 1000 pC indicates that the winding should not fail during the next few years. A visual inspection is recommended if the pd magnitude is more than 10,000 pC, especially if other identical machines have a pd less than 1000, and if the insulation is made of epoxy-mica. The DIV in modern epoxy or polyester windings should be greater than half the operating line-to-ground voltage. The test indicates that slot discharge is occurring if the DIV value is very low in epoxy-mica windings. However, older asphaltic and micafolium windings may not be in danger even if the magnitude of the discharge is high and the DIVs are low. This is in contrast with newer machines that have synthetic insulation, especially Mylar. Their condition deteriorates quickly in the presence of pd. However, older windings should be inspected if there is an increasing trend of pd activity.

There are many disadvantages for off-line conventional pd tests. Since the entire winding, including the neutral end, is fully energized, sites that are not normally analyzed can generate pulses. Large discharges can occur in sites that are not normally subjected to high voltages. This is misleading because the operator may believe that the winding is deteriorating.

On-Line Conventional pd Test. This test is similar to the off-line test except that an external power supply is not used to energize the winding. The generator is driven at normal speed by the turbine, and sufficient field excitation is applied. Therefore, the stator is at the normal operating voltage. The test can be performed with the generator synchronized to the grid or not. When the test is done on a motor, the winding is energized by the normal power supply. Extreme caution is required when the test is performed due to the considerable risk to personnel and the machine if the capacitor fails.

The test is more realistic than the off-line one because the voltage distribution in the windings is normal. Also, slot discharges that are caused from bar or coil movement are present.

The equipment used in the off-line test can be used in this test. The blocking capacitors are connected to the phase terminals during an outage. *Dangerous events can occur if the capacitor fails during the test.* An experienced operator can distinguish true pd from electrical interference from brushes, thyristor excitation systems, and background. If the generator is not synchronized, some generators can handle variations in the field current. In these cases, the DIV and DEV can be measured.

Some utilities leave the test equipment connected during normal operation. The pd activity can then be measured at low and full power. Deterioration in the condition of the insulation is detected by an increasing trend of pd. Since the test is done during normal operation, it gives the most accurate indication of the true condition of the insulation. External interference (from a power line carrier, radio station, etc.) can be severe during the test, especially in large generators. The interference can be misleading. The operator may believe that high pd activity is occurring while the winding is perfectly good.

Dissipation Factor and Tip-up Tests. The condition of the insulation system in a high-voltage winding can be evaluated by treating it as a dielectric in a capacitor. The capacitance and the dissipation factor (or power factor, or tan δ) of a winding can be measured during an outage.* These measurements are normally made over a voltage range. Since pd's are initiated when there are voids in the groundwall insulation, the change in dissipation factor with voltage is a measure of the initiation of additional internal losses in a winding.

Machine manufacturers use dissipation factor and tip-up (change in tan δ as the voltage is increased or Δ tan δ) as quality control tests for new stator bars and coils. A general weakness in the bulk insulation normally caused by incorrect composition or insulation that is not fully cured is indicated by an abnormally high dissipation factor. Excessive voids within the insulation will discharge at high voltage. They are indicated by a higher-than-normal increase in dissipation factor when the voltage is increased (tip-up).

The winding must be isolated into coils or coil groups to obtain a sensitive measurement during this test. This consumes a significant amount of time. Thus, this test is not widely used for testing motors and generators in utilities.

Tip-up Test. A half-day outage is normally required for a dissipation factor test. It can be performed on motors and generators of all sizes. A single measurement of dissipation factor on a complete winding has limited use. However, trends of measurements on coils or coil groups over years provide useful information. This test is most useful when done on low and high voltage. As the voltage is increased from a low to a high value, the dissipation factor will increase (i.e., tip-up). The pd activity within the insulation will increase with the voltage level. Dissipation factor is a measure of electrical losses in the insulation system. It

**Note:* Angle δ is defined as $\delta + \theta = 90°$, where θ is the phase angle between the current and the voltage.

is a property of the insulation. It is desirable to have a low dissipation factor. However, a high dielectric loss does not confirm that the insulation is poor. A capacitance bridge is normally used to measure the dissipation factor. For example, the dissipation factor of a good epoxy-mica and asphaltic insulation is 0.5 and 3 percent, respectively.

The dissipation factor will not increase with the voltage in a perfect insulation. However, if air-filled voids are present in the insulation, pd will occur at a high-enough voltage. The electrical losses in the winding will increase due to energy consumption by heat and light generated by the discharges. The dissipation factor will increase with the voltage. As the pd activity increases, the tip-up will increase, and the condition of the winding will worsen. Therefore, the pd activity is measured indirectly by a tip-up test. A bridge is used to measure the dissipation factor. It effectively measures the ratio of the in-phase current in the sample to the capacitive (or quadrature) current. This ratio is determined over the total current in the sample. Thus, it represents the average loss over the entire winding being tested.

Stator Turn Insulation Surge Test. The surge tests are hipot tests used to check the integrity of the interturn, as well as the capability of the groundwall insulation, to withstand steep transients that are likely to be encountered in normal service. These surge tests are normally done on new windings in the factory to detect faults. A voltage is applied for a very short time to the turn insulation during the test, causing weak insulation to fail. Thus, the surge test is not a diagnostic test but a hipot test for the turn insulation. The impedances of two matching sections of the winding are compared by commercial surge testers. A voltage surge having around 0.2 μs risetime and adjustable magnitude is applied simultaneously to the two winding sections, L_1 and L_2 (Fig. 33.5). The shape of the surges is superimposed on an oscilloscope. A high-voltage transient is developed across the winding turns due to the short risetime. The two waveforms will be identical if both windings are free from faults (because the impedances are the same). Any discrepancy in the two waveforms may indicate a shorted turn in one of the windings. An experienced operator can identify the nature of the fault (Fig. 33.6) by comparing the magnitude and type of the discrepancy between the two waveforms.

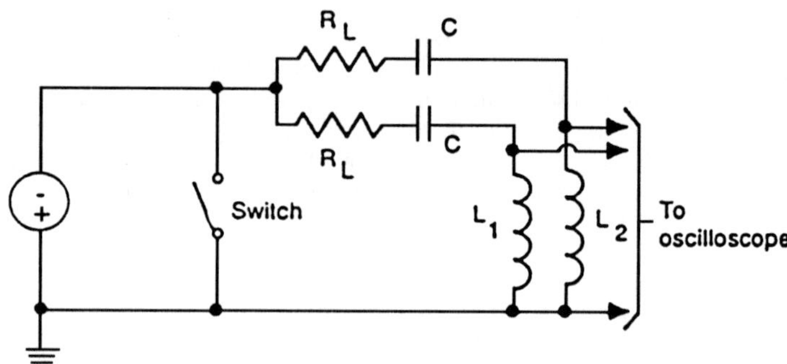

FIGURE 33.5 Simplified schematic for a turn insulation surge tester. L_1 and L_2 are either coils or phases in a winding.

In some cases, the surge voltage is applied to an exciter coil, which is placed over the stator coil to be tested (direct connection of the surge tester to a stator coil is not required). This allows testing of coils in complete windings without disconnecting each coil from the other. The voltage is induced into the stator coil by transformer action when the surge is applied. This produces the turn-to-turn stress in the stator coil. However, interpretation of

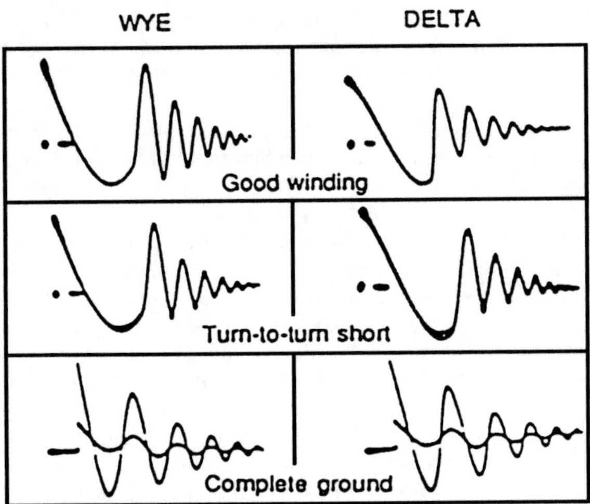

FIGURE 33.6 Typical waveforms from a surge tester. For good coils, both traces will be the same.

the result is even more difficult. This induced surge test should be done carefully because high voltages may also be induced into coils other than the coil being tested. The test is normally performed by connecting the high-voltage output of the surge tester to two of the phases. The third phase is grounded to the surge tester. The voltage is applied and increased to specified limits, which should not exceed the groundwall DC hipot voltage. If the surge waveforms are identical, the turn insulation is presumed sound.

This test is based on comparing the shapes of surges applied with two winding sections. The two surge shapes may not be identical if the two winding sections being tested have slightly different impedances due to having different dimensions of coils. This will suggest a fault even when the insulation system is in good condition. It is also difficult to detect a turn fault in a coil tested in a circuit parallel with more than 10 coils because a shorted turn will have a minor change in the total impedance of the winding. As the number of coils being tested increases, it becomes more difficult to determine if a defective coil is present. This test does not indicate the relative condition of the turn insulation in different coils. It only indicates if shorts exist. It is a go/no-go proof test like the AC and DC hipot test for the stator groundwall insulation.

Synchronous Machine Rotor Windings

The presence of faults in rotor winding insulation can sometimes be indicated by a change in machine performance rather than by the operation of a protective relay. For example, if a coil develops a short circuit, a thermal bend may develop due to an asymmetric heat input into the rotor. This could lead to an increase in shaft vibration with increasing excitation current. This change can be used in some cases to determine if the interturn fault is significant. The location and severity of a fault cannot always be found easily even when the rotor is removed. This is especially true in large turbine generator rotors whose concentric field windings are embedded in slots in the rotor body and covered by retaining rings at the ends. Many ground and interturn failures disappear at reduced speed or at a standstill. This makes their detection very difficult and emphasizes the need for an on-line detection technique. The following tests are used to determine if faults exist in the rotor winding, and/or they indicate their location. Solid-state devices used in exciters should be shorted out before conducting any test involving the induction or application of external voltages to the rotor winding.

Open-Circuit Test for Shorted Turns. An open-circuit test can be used to confirm if shorted turns in rotor field windings exist when there are indirect symptoms such as a change in vibration levels with excitation. The machine should be taken out of service for a short while but does not need to be disassembled.

Figure 33.7 illustrates the open-circuit characteristic of a synchronous machine. It relates the terminal voltage to field current while the machine is running at synchronous speed with its terminals disconnected from the grid. The open-circuit curve can be used to verify shorted turns if an open-circuit test characteristic with healthy turn insulation was done previously. A higher field current will be required to generate the same open-circuit voltage if there are shorted turns in a rotor field winding. If the difference between the two curves is more than 2 percent, the possibility of a turn insulation fault will be confirmed. The difference in characteristics to indicate a shorted turn depends on the number of turns in the field winding and the number of shorted turns. For example, a single shorted turn cannot be detected by this test if the connected field winding has a large number of turns. This test is done while the machine is running at synchronous speed with its stator winding terminal open-circuited and the field winding is energized. Generators can easily be driven at synchronous speed because their drivers are designed to operate at synchronous speed. Motors may

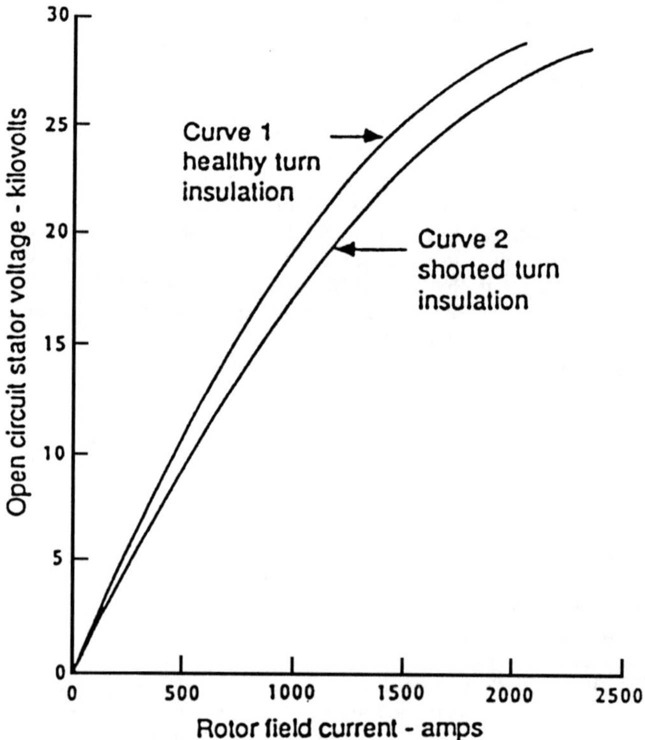

FIGURE 33.7 Detecting shorted rotor winding turns.

need to be driven by AC or DC drive at synchronous speed. If the test indicates the possibility of shorted turns, further confirmation should be obtained by performing additional tests. This test has the following two limitations:

1. It may not detect shorted turns, if the machine has a large number of turns and/or if there are parallel circuits in the field winding.
2. Differences in the open-circuit curve will also be created when the machine's magnetic characteristics change (e.g., when the rotor wedges are replaced with a different material).

Air Gap Search Coil for Detecting Shorted Turns. Interturn faults in rotors are detected by an air gap search coil. Methods have been developed for on-line and off-line testing. This technique is especially useful for detecting faults present at operating speed, which disappear on shutdown. The coils and slots having shorted turns, as well as the number of turns shorted, can be identified by this method. Permanent flux probes have already been installed on some machines. Each rotor slot has local fields around it. This leakage flux is related to the current in the rotor. The magnetic field associated with a coil will be affected if the coil is shorted. The search coil records the high-frequency waveform (known as *slot ripple*) generated in the air gap. Each rotor slot generates a peak of the waveform in proportion to the leakage flux around it. If an interturn fault occurs, the peaks associated with the two slots containing the faulted coil will be reduced. The recorded data are analyzed to identify the faulted coil and the number of faults. Shorted turns also generate significant levels of even harmonics (multiples of the frequency), while a fault-free rotor generates only odd harmonics.

The search coil is normally mounted on a stator wedge. A gas-tight gland is required for the leads of the probe. Shorted rotor turns should not be a cause of grave concern if the rotor vibration is not excessive and the required excitation is maintained. A generator can operate adequately for a period of time under this condition. However, these shorted turns are normally caused by serious local degradation of the interturn insulation and possibly major distortion of the conductors. In some cases, where static exciters are used, arcing damage and local welding have been found.

It is difficult to interpret the on-load test results from the search coil due to the effects of saturations and magnetic anomalies in the rotor body. More complex and time-consuming detection techniques are required. However, modern on-line monitors have overcome these difficulties. They are designed for use with turbine generators equipped with an air gap search coil. The output from the search coil is continuously being processed. An alarm is initiated when a current-carrying shorted turn occurs in the rotor winding.

Impedance Test with Rotor Installed. Shorted turns in a field winding can also be detected by periodic measurement of rotor impedance using an AC power supply. These tests should ideally be performed while the machine is operating at synchronous speed because shorted turns may only exist when centrifugal forces are acting on the turn conductors. When the machine is shut down, there may not be any contact, or the fault resistance may be high. Shorted turns can be detected more accurately by impedance rather than resistance measurements. This is due to the induced backward current in a single shorted turn, which opposes the magnetomotive force (mmf) of the entire coil, resulting in a significant reduction in reactance. This technique is particularly effective in salient pole rotors, where one short-circuited turn eliminates the reactance of the complete pole. There is a sudden change in impedance when a turn is shorted during run-up or rundown (Fig. 33.8). A sudden change of more than 5 percent is needed to verify shorted turns.

The highest field current used for this test should be significantly lower than the normal current required for rated stator voltage at open circuit. The voltage applied should not exceed the rated no-load stator voltage. A normal winding will exhibit a reduction in

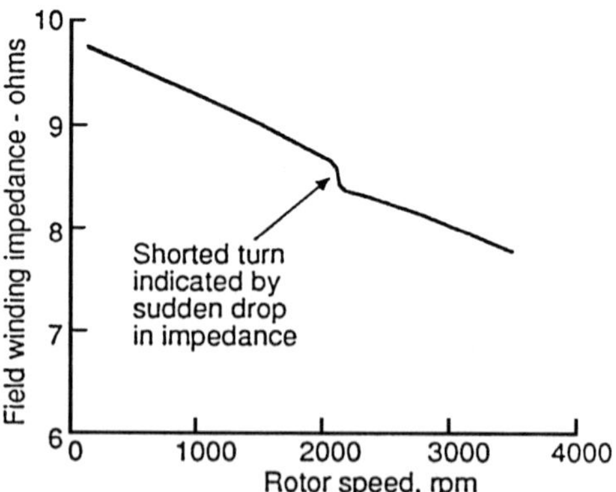

FIGURE 33.8 Detecting shorted rotor turns by impedance measurements.

impedance up to 10 percent between standstill and operating conditions due to the effects of eddy currents on the rotor.

This test can only be performed if the field winding is accessible through collector rings because the low-voltage AC power should be applied while the machine is running. A 120-V, 1-ph, 60-Hz AC power is applied. The voltage, current, and shaft speed are measured. The power supply should be ungrounded because the rotor could get damaged if the field winding has a ground fault. The test includes the following five steps:

1. Perform an insulation resistance test on the field winding of the machine to be tested to check for ground faults. The impedance test should not be performed if a ground fault is found. The ground fault should be located using a different procedure.
2. Connect an instrumented and ungrounded power supply to the field winding (Fig. 33.9). The instruments used should be properly calibrated.
3. Take the reading from the local speed indicator to determine the relationship between impedance and speed.
4. Adjust the field winding voltage to give a maximum permissible current of 75 percent of the current required to achieve the rated open-circuit stator voltage.
5. Increase and decrease the speed of the machine while the stator windings are disconnected from the power supply. Measure the current, voltage, and speed, starting at 0 and increasing the speed at 100-r/min intervals until the rated speed is reached. Continuous measurements can also be recorded simultaneously on a multichannel strip chart recorder.

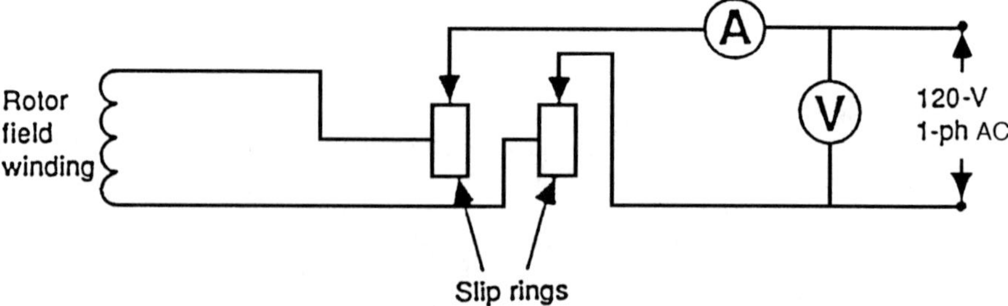

FIGURE 33.9 Test setup for impedance measurement with rotor installed.

The values of the impedance ($Z = V/I$) should be plotted against the speed (Fig. 38.8). A sudden change in impedance of 5 percent or more or a gradual change of more than 10 percent will indicate a strong possibility of shorted turns in the winding. This test is not as sensitive as the previous two described earlier. It is also important to note that solidly shorted turns will not produce an abrupt change in impedance.

Detecting the Location of Shorted Turns with Rotor Removed

The exact location of a shorted turn should be found to minimize the disturbance to the winding when making repairs. One or a combination of the following four procedures should be used:

1. *Low-voltage AC test.* When the field winding of a synchronous machine rotor having shorted turns is connected to a low AC voltage (typically, 120 V), the tips of the teeth on either side of the slot(s) having the shorted turns will have significantly different flux induced in them. Figure 33.10 illustrates how the relative magnitudes of tooth fluxes can be measured. The teeth are bridged by a flux survey using a laminated-steel or air-core search coil, which is connected to a voltmeter and wattmeter. The voltage is measured by the voltmeter, and the direction of the induced flux is given by the wattmeter. The search coil is moved across all the teeth of the rotor and voltage and watts readings are taken. The search coil readings depend on its axial location along the rotor. Therefore, all the readings should be taken with the coil located at the same axial distance from the end of the rotor. Since the readings vary significantly near the end of the rotor, the coil should not be placed near the end of the rotor. It is important to note that core saturation may occur when a 60-Hz power supply is used. A higher frequency should be used if possible to reduce this problem.

The equipment that is used for the EL-CID test, described later, can be used to detect the shorted field winding turns. This test can be done without removing the end winding

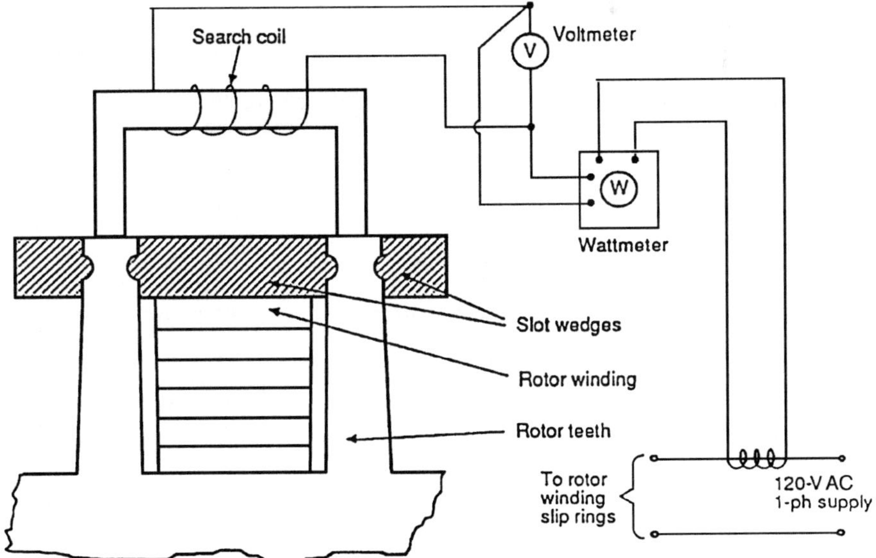

FIGURE 33.10 Setup for AC flux survey test with rotor removed.

retaining rings if the rotor has steel wedges and no damper winding. If the rotor has a separate damper winding or aluminum-alloy slot wedges (shorted at the ends) used as a damper winding, they must be open-circuited at the ends before the test can be done. In this case, the retaining rings should be removed. Since many shorts are created by the action of centrifugal forces, they may not appear at standstill.

Figure 33.11 illustrates the flux distribution for a rotor with and without shorted turns. The sharp change in direction of the induced flux indicates the slot containing the shorted turns.

2. *Low-voltage DC test (voltage-drop test).* This method is used to locate the shorts based on a DC voltage drop between turns. The end rings should be removed to provide access to the turns. In some cases, the shorts should be induced by applying a radial force to the coils. This is normally done by tapping the wedges with a wooden block or clamping the coils at the corner.

The test is done by applying a DC voltage to the field winding and measuring the drop in voltage across the turns. If a short occurs, the voltage drop across the turn would be lower than normal.

3. *Field winding ground fault detectors.* A large generator rotor operates at 500 V DC and 4000 A DC normally. If the insulation between the winding and the body is damaged or bridged by conducting materials, there will be a shift of the DC potential of the winding and exciter. The part of the winding where the fault occurred becomes the new zero-potential point. In most cases, this will not cause an immediate problem if there is no additional ground fault. A second ground fault in the rotor will be catastrophic.

A rotor ground-fault detector is used to enunciate when a fault occurs. Some units are tripped automatically due to possible extensive damage to the rotor body by a DC arc across a separate copper connection. Ground-fault detectors have various configurations. The rotor winding is grounded in simple DC schemes on one end through a high ohmic resistance. However, these schemes become insensitive if the fault occurs close to this end. Ohm's law determines the magnitude of leakage current from the rotor winding to the ground-fault relay. The shaft should also be grounded.

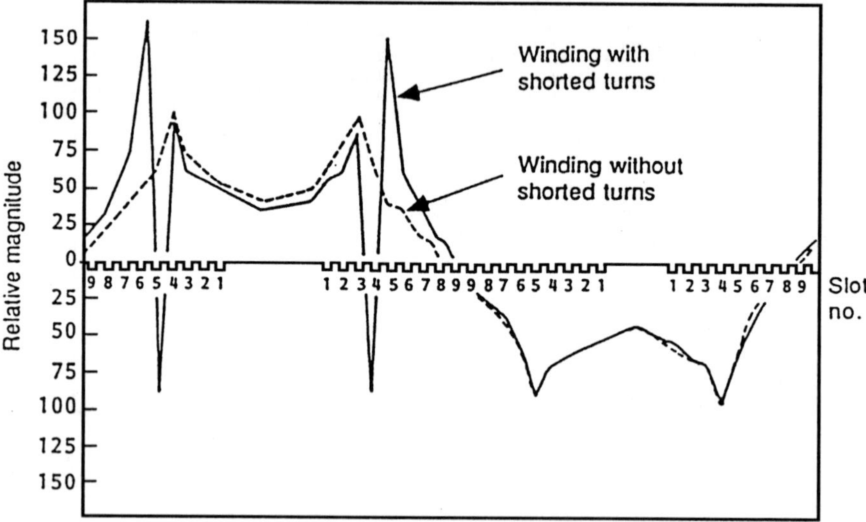

FIGURE 33.11 Flux distribution survey for two-pole turbine generator.

A sophisticated technique was developed to continue operation of a generator having a known ground fault (second ground-fault detector). It uses a microprocessor and measuring resistors to determine whether the power that is dissipated by the leakage current exceeds a value that would cause a failure if there are two or more ground faults from the winding. A search coil mounted in the air gap has been used to detect interturn faults and a second ground fault.

If a fault is identified, measurements of the slip ring–to–shaft voltages will give an indication of the location of the fault (is the fault at the middle or end of the winding). After disconnecting the ground-fault detector and while the generator is still on-line, the voltage readings between the brush holders and the shaft are taken. If one ground fault is present, the approximate location of the fault in percent of winding resistance is

$$\frac{\text{Lower ring-to-shaft voltage}}{\text{Sum of two ring-to-shaft voltages}} \times 100\%$$

During rundown of the unit (when it is unloaded and tripped), an insulation resistance tester is used to test the fault resistance. The brushes are raised or the field circuit breaker is opened to determine if the fault is in the generator rotor, external bus, or the exciter. The fault is also monitored as the speed drops. If the fault disappears, it will be impossible to find its location. The operator may decide to put the machine back in service. If the fault reappears when the unit is returned to service, the process should repeated. If the fault is sustained, a low voltage is applied across the slip rings while the rotor is at standstill. It is usually provided from a 12-V car battery or from a 120-V AC variac. The voltage between the rotor body and each slip ring is measured. If the readings are full voltage with one and zero with the other, there is likely a low-resistance path at the slip rings. It could be caused by carbon dust or insulation failure. It may easily be corrected with a good cleanup. The rotor should be withdrawn if the fault is within the winding. When the rotor is removed, the low-voltage source is reapplied to the slip rings, and a voltmeter is installed between the rotor body and a long insulated wire. The insulation is removed off the last 5 mm of the wire, and it is used as a probe to contact the rotor winding metal through ventilation holes and under the retaining rings. This technique will identify the slot, bar, or ventilation hole having the closest voltage to the rotor body. The fault is usually located under the wedge near this location. The problem is rectified sometimes by cleaning the ventilation ducts. Otherwise, additional dismantling may be required

If the ground fault is transient and needs to be found, a failure is forced with a moderate hipot test, and the same technique is used. The hipot test should be used as a last option.

4. *Surge testing for rotor shorted turns and ground faults.* This off-line method is used to detect rotor winding faults on stationary and rotating shafts. The location of the fault is identified. This method is very effective in finding ground faults and shorted turns. There is electrical symmetry in a healthy rotor winding. The travel time of an identical electrical pulse injected at both slip rings through the winding should be identical. The reflection of the pulse back to the slip rings would also be identical. If there is a short or ground fault, some of the pulse energy will be reflected back to the slip ring due to the drop in impedance at the fault. The reflections will change the input pulse waveform, depending on the distance to the fault. Therefore, a fault will generate different waveforms at each slip ring unless it is located exactly halfway in the winding.

The *recurrent surge oscillography* (RSO) is a technique based on the aforementioned principle. This test cannot be done on-line, because the winding should be isolated from the exciter. Two identical, fast-rising voltage pulses are injected simultaneously at the slip rings. The potential at each injection point is plotted versus time. Identical records should be obtained if there is no fault due to the symmetry in the winding. Differences between the traces are indicative of the winding fault. The fault is located from the time at which irregularity occurred. Ground faults having a resistance of less than 500 Ω will be detected by the RSO method. These faults are also normally detected by the generator protection systems. The RSO technique is used to confirm ground faults. Interturn faults having a resistance of less than 10 Ω will also be detected by RSO. Faults that have a resistance of more than 10 Ω are more significant during operation and less severe off-load. These faults cannot be detected by RSO.

Low-Core Flux Test (EL-CID)

The conventional method for testing for imperfections in the core insulation of motors and generators has been the *rated-flux test.* This test requires high power levels of the excitation winding to induce rated flux in the core area behind the winding slots. The alternative low-flux test described in this section has been performed successfully across the world. Its main advantage is that is requires a much smaller power supply for the excitation winding. Only 3 to 4 percent of rated flux is induced in the core. In reality, the power supply can be obtained from a 120-V AC wall socket source. Also, the time required to perform this test is much shorter.

The *Electromagnetic Core Imperfection Detector* (EL-CID) identifies faulty core insulation. It is based on the fact that eddy currents will flow through failed or significantly aged core insulation, even if the flux is a few percent of the rated flux. A *Chattock coil* (or *Maxwell's worm*) is used to obtain a voltage signal proportional to the eddy current flowing between the laminations. The solenoid coil is wound in a U shape.

Figure 33.12 illustrates how the coil is placed to bridge the two core teeth. The fault current I_F is approximately proportional to the line integral of alternating magnetic field along its length l (Ampere's law). Thus, if the effects of the field in the core are ignored, the voltage output in the Chattock coil is proportional to the eddy current flowing in the area encompassed by the coil (the two teeth and the core behind them).

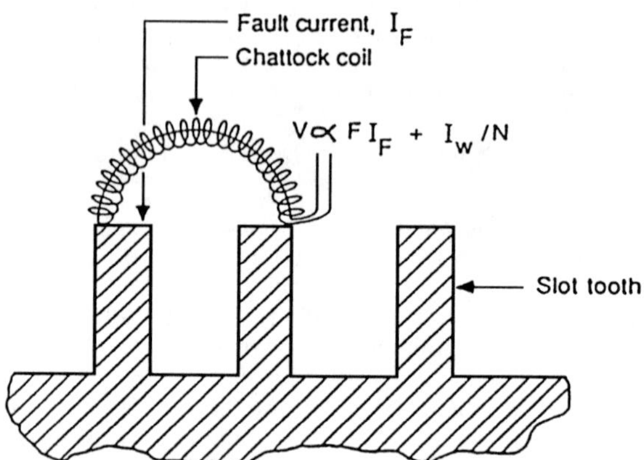

FIGURE 33.12 Chattock coil mounting configuration and output voltage.

The excitation winding that generates the test flux in the core induces an additional voltage across the coil due to the circumferential magnetic field. A signal processor receives the output voltage from the Chattock coil. It eliminates the portion that is generated by the excitation winding and gives a voltage proportional to the eddy current (Fig. 33.13).

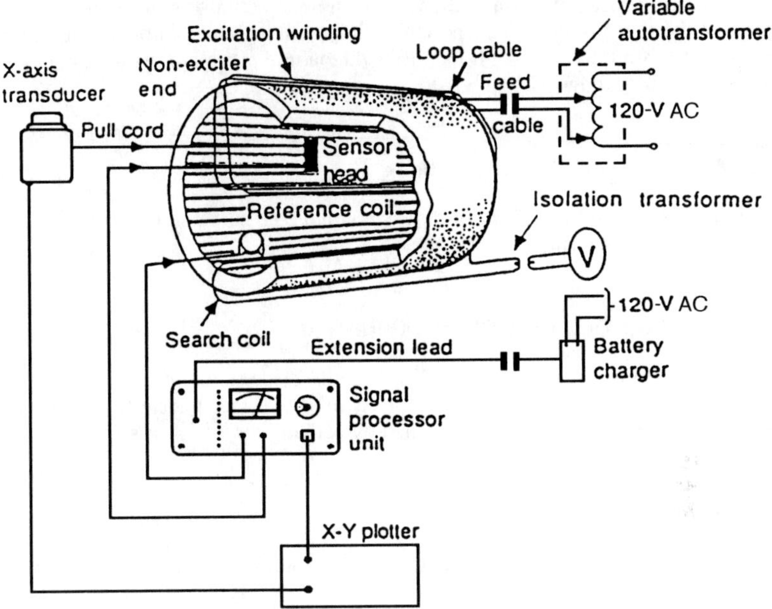

FIGURE 33.13 EL-CID test setup for large generator.

The output milliamperes of the signal-processing unit is proportional to the voltage in the Chattock coil generated by axial eddy currents. High milliampere readings are normally caused by faulty insulation in the core or interlamination shorts at the core surfaces. A reading higher than 100 mA indicates significant core plate shorting.

The Chattock coil is moved along the teeth of the core and the current readings are recorded. Areas where the readings exceed 100 mA should be marked with a nonconductive substance and examined for defects.

APPENDIX B: MECHANICAL TESTS

These tests will help to determine the integrity of the windings. Loose stator windings can cause mechanical and electrical damage to the groundwall insulation. Large machines are more susceptible due to the increased forces and slot discharges. Following are the tests that should be done during outages.

Stator Winding Tightness Check

The tightness of the stator wedges in the slot should be checked on a regular basis. The effective methods are wedge tapping and ultrasonic detection.

The stator wedge is struck by a blunt object. The tightness of the wedge in the slot will determine the type of sound ring. A tight wedge will give a dull sound, and a slack wedge a hollow sound. A ring between these extremes indicates that the wedge will become loose in the future.

A measuring instrument using ultrasonic technique can also be used to determine the tightness of the stator wedges. This portable equipment uses a vibrator, accelerometer, and force gauge to excite the wedge. It identifies the natural vibration resonance and assesses the tightness of the wedge assembly.

Stator Winding Side Clearance Check

This test is done to ensure a tight fit between conductor bars and the slot sides. A feeler gauge is inserted to determine the tightness.

Core Lamination Tightness Check (Knife Test)

This test involves inserting a standard winder's knife blade (maximum thickness, 0.25 mm) between laminations at several locations in the core. If the blade penetrates more than 6 mm, then the core is soft. It should be retightened by packing.

Visual Techniques

If there is indication of insulation aging or a fault, the machine should be visually inspected. Flashlights and magnifying glasses are normally used. Small mirrors can be used for examining the inside edges of retaining rings. Boroscopes are used sometimes to gain access to stator core laminations or conductors. Magnetic strips are swept along the internal surfaces to pick up small magnetic fragments.

Groundwall Insulation. Early detection of deterioration of insulation can help in extending the life of the machine. Dusting or powdering of the insulation along the slot wedges or in the ventilation ducts may indicate damage to the insulation by mechanical abrasion. This powder should not be confused with the reddish powder that is caused by core problems, or copper dusting (which occurs due to fretting of the rotor winding when the machine is on turning gear). Another white or grey powder is caused by pd. This powder is only found in bars and coils near the line ends of the winding. This powder should be confused with the one caused by abrasion, which is found throughout the winding.

Other signs of mechanical distress are debris at the slot exit, stretch marks and cracks in surface paint in the slot area, or in the mechanical supports in the end winding area. Thermal aging is indicated normally by discoloration or undue darkening of the insulation surface. Electrical effects are normally indicated by carbonized tracking paths to grounded components. External pd, which normally occurs in line end coils, is confirmed by a grey or white powder. Chemical analysis of the dust will show a high percentage of salts.

Rotor Winding. Mirrors and boroscopes are used to perform rotor inspection without disassembly. In some cases, it may be necessary to disassemble the rotor partially by removing the retaining rings and some wedges.

Turn Insulation. The location of the turn faults in the rotor cannot usually be determined by visual means without some disassembly. Turn faults in the end windings become visible after removing the end caps. Those in the slot become visible by removing the wedges and lifting the turns. Faults caused by copper dusting can be verified by small copper particles in the slots and vent ducts.

Slot Wedges and Bracing. The movement of slot packing under wedges in gas-cooled rotors can be detected without disassembly. This problem can be identified by examining the gas exhaust holes in the wedges to see if packing has been moved to block the flow of cooling gas out through them. The problem is also indicated by rotor thermal unbalance. The rotor should be disassembled if there is evidence of early signs of deterioration in slot wedges.

Stator and Rotor Cores. Severe overheating and melting would occur at the surfaces of laminated cores due to insulation faults. These can easily be detected by a visual examination. Faults that occur in the slot region are normally hidden by the winding and slot wedges. These are normally indicated by signs of burning in the vicinity of the insulation and wedges.

FREQUENTLY ASKED QUESTIONS

REVIEW OF THERMODYNAMICS PRINCIPLES (CHAP. 1)

1. Why does the power generated by some steam power plants drop in the summer?

ANSWER: The power delivered by a steam turbine is given by

$$\text{power} = \dot{m}(h_1 - h_2)$$

where $\dot{m}$ is the steam flow, h_1 is the inlet enthalpy to the turbine, and h_2 is the outlet enthalpy of the turbine.

During the hot summer months, the lake temperature increases. The temperature of steam being condensed on the shell side of the condenser increases due to an increase in the cooling water temperature coming from the lake. The pressure of the steam being condensed also increases due to an increase in temperature. The process of condensation occurs at saturation. The temperature and pressure are tied together at saturation. An increase in temperature will result in an increase in pressure. The enthalpy of the steam being condensed (h_2), which depends on the temperature and pressure, increases. Thus, the power generated will decrease due to an increase in h_2. A typical decrease in power output is around 0.5 percent.

Some modern power plants take condenser-cooling water through a duct immersed more than 25 m below the surface of the lake. The changes in the temperature of the water at this elevation are minimal during the year. Thus, the reduction in power generated in the hot summer months is negligible.

2. What are the steam conditions at the inlet to the high-pressure turbine in a steam power plant?

ANSWER: These are the steam conditions at the inlet to the high-pressure turbine in a steam power plant:

- *Coal-fired steam power plants.* From 10 to 17 MPa (1470 to 2500 psi) and from 427 to 566°C (800 to 1050°F)
- *Cogeneration and combined-cycle plants.* From 4 to 10 MPa (600 to 1470 psi) and from 343 to 566°C (650 to 1050°F)
- *Supercritical power plants.* From 23.8 to 27 MPa (3500 to 3969 psi) and from 566 to 580°C (1050 to 1076°F)

3. What are the advantages of supercritical power plants?

ANSWER: Supercritical power plants have higher efficiency than conventional power plants. Their efficiency is around 38 to 44 percent, while the efficiency of a conventional power plant is around 32 to 35 percent.

Note: The efficiency of a power plant is defined as the ratio of the net power output from the plant to the heat supplied to the plant (fuel consumption). The heat rate is the inverse of the efficiency (1/efficiency).

4. How does the second law of thermodynamics apply to power plants?

ANSWER: The second law of thermodynamics is focused on the value of energy. Since the efficiency of a typical steam power plant is around 33 percent, only one-third of the energy delivered to the plant in the form of heat is converted to electricity. The remaining two-thirds is discharged into the environment. Thus, the value of electricity is much higher than the value of steam (heat). Consider these two cogeneration plants:

- Plant A, with an efficiency of 84 percent: 10 percent of its output is electrical, and the rest is steam.
- Plant B, with an efficiency of 70 percent: 30 percent of its output is electrical, the rest is steam.

The revenues generated by plant B will normally be higher than those of plant A if both plants consume the same amount of fuel. This is because electricity is a more precious commodity than steam. This concept can be extended further to a combined cycle, generating electrical power only at an efficiency of 60 percent (plant C). The revenues generated by plant C will probably be higher than the revenues generated by plant B if both plants consume the same amount of fuel. The increase in revenue generated by plant C will be more significant in the hot summer months due to the significant increase in the price of electricity compared with the spring (the price of electricity in the hot summer months can be 70 times higher than the price of electricity in the spring). Thus, energy can exist in the form of electricity or heat. They are both measured in megawatts (MW). Electricity is measured $MW_{electrical}$ and steam in $MW_{thermal}$. However, the value of 1 $MW_{electrical}$ is much higher than 1 $MW_{thermal}$.

Note: The efficiency of a cogeneration plant is given by

$$\eta_{co} = \frac{E + \Delta H}{Q}$$

where E is the electrical output of the plant. ΔH is the difference in enthalpy between steam leaving the plant to the host and the enthalpy of the condensate returning from the host, Q is the heat delivered to the plant (fuel consumption).

5. How does the Carnot cycle apply to power plants?

ANSWER: The Carnot cycle states that any power plant (e.g., steam power plant, gas turbine, etc.) operates between two temperatures. T_H is the highest temperature in the plant, and T_L is the lowest temperature in the plant. For example, the highest temperature in a steam power plant occurs at the output of the steam generators. The lowest temperature in a steam power plant occurs in the shell side of the condenser [normally around 35°C

(95°F)]. In a gas turbine, the highest temperature occurs in the combustors and the lowest temperature is the ambient (air is discharged from the gas turbine to the ambient). Carnot proved that the efficiency of any power plant is given by

$$\eta_{\text{Carnot}} = \frac{T_H - T_L}{T_H}$$

[It should be noted that this is the Carnot cycle efficiency, which is based on isentropic (ideal) compression and expansion processes.]

Therefore, the Carnot cycle efficiency is proportioned to the difference between T_H and T_L. The gas turbines that were designed and manufactured in the 1960s had a firing temperature around 800 to 900°C (1470 to 1652°F). Their efficiency was around 24 to 26 percent. Modern gas turbines have a firing temperature around 1371 to 1427°C (2500 to 2600°F). Their efficiency is around 43 to 44 percent. Thus, the increase in firing temperature improves the efficiency.

It should be noted that there are other factors that contribute to the increase in efficiency of modern gas turbines. They include increase in pressure across the compressor and improvement in the aerodynamics of the turbine and compressor blades. However, the preceding example was provided to show that the Carnot cycle principle is valid. The following is a second example that proves the validity of the Carnot cycle principle. If we consider the performance of two identical gas turbines operating at different ambient temperatures, the temperature of the ambient air around the first gas turbine is +35°C (95°F) and the second −35°C (−31°F). We find that the second gas turbine has a 40 percent higher output than the first. Its efficiency is also higher than the first gas turbine by around 10 percent. This proves that lowering the lowest temperature (T_L) in the cycle improves the efficiency. Therefore, the Carnot cycle provides a basic understanding about the variation of efficiency with temperature in a power plant.

6. What is the maximum allowable concentration of water in the steam leaving the low-pressure turbine in a power plant?

ANSWER: The steam entering the low-pressure turbine is normally superheated. Its temperature and pressure drop while it expands across the turbine. When the temperature and pressure reach the saturation conditions, condensation starts to occur. The amount of condensed water (in the form of droplets entrained with the steam) continues to increase as the temperature and pressure drop. The maximum allowable concentration of water in the steam leaving the low-pressure turbine is around 12 to 13 percent in mass. In other words, the steam quality is between 87 and 88 percent.

Note: The steam quality is defined as

$$x = \frac{\dot{m}_g}{\dot{m}_g + \dot{m}_L}$$

where x is the steam quality, $\dot{m}_g$ is the mass flow of the steam, $\dot{m}_L$ is the mass flow of water.

7. Are feedwater heaters required for all steam power plants?

ANSWER: Feedwater heaters are normally shell-and-tube heat exchangers installed between the condenser and the steam generators. Steam is extracted from the turbines to the shell side of the feedwater heater. The condensate (water leaving the condenser) flowing in the tubes of the feedwater heater is heated by the steam being condensed on the shell side of the feedwater heater. Thus, the temperature of the condensate increases gradually across the feedwater heaters. It leaves the condenser at 35°C (95°F) and enters the steam generators within 30°C (86°F) of the temperature of the tubes in the economizer (first section in the steam generators). If the condensate temperature were much cooler than the temperature of the tubes in the economizer, the tubes would crack due to a "thermal shock." In other words, the tubes in the economizer would fracture due to significant thermal stresses created by the cool condensate flowing on them. Thus, the feedwater heaters are needed to prevent thermal shock in the steam generators. Every steam power plant has from three to seven feedwater heaters.

The feedwater heaters have a second advantage: improvement of plant efficiency due to reduction in heat losses. The heat losses (known also as external irreversibilities) that occur in the any heat exchange equipment (e.g., steam generator, heat exchanger, etc.) are proportional to the temperature difference between the heating medium (e.g., combustion gases in a steam generator) and the heated medium. In other words, if the temperature of the heating fluid is much higher than the temperature of the fluid being heated, the heat losses to the ambient will be high. This is due to a higher temperature difference between the heating fluid and the ambient. If feedwater heaters are not used, the heating fluid in the steam generator must be used to heat the condensate coming from the condenser. The temperature difference between the heating fluid and the condensate would be 800 − 35 = 765°C (1409°F). The losses from the heating medium to the ambient (external heat losses) would be excessive. Thus, the efficiency of the plant will be low. In a feedwater heater, the steam that enters the shell side (extracted from the turbine) of the feedwater heater is at a slightly higher temperature than the condensate flowing inside the tubes. The heat that is given to the condensate is mainly a result of the condensation of the steam (latent heat). Therefore, the external heat losses to the ambient in this case are minimal, resulting in an increase in plant efficiency.

FUNDAMENTALS OF ELECTRIC SYSTEMS (CHAP. 26)

1. Why does the current lead the voltage in a capacitor?

ANSWER: A capacitor is an energy storage device. It stores energy in an electric field. The current goes through the capacitor before the voltage can be established across it. Thus, the voltage must lag the current. The relationship between the current and the voltage in the capacitor is given by:

$$i = C\,\frac{dV}{dt}$$

where i is the current, V is the voltage, and C is the capacitor.
The voltage is normally given by

$$V = V_m \sin \omega t$$

where V_m is the maximum value of the voltage, and $\omega = 2\pi f$ [f is the frequency, measured in hertz (Hz)]:

$$i = C\,\frac{dV}{dt} = C\,\frac{d}{dt}\,(V_m \sin \omega t) = I_m \cos \omega t$$

Thus,

$$i = I_m \cos \omega t = I_m \sin (\omega t + 90°)$$

cos ωt is 90° ahead (leading) sin ωt. Therefore, the current in the capacitor leads the voltage by 90°.

2. What are the right-hand rules that are associated with the magnetic field?

ANSWER: There are two right-hand rules associated with the magnetic fields. The first deals with the force exerted on a charge moving through a magnetic field. The force is given by

$$\mathbf{F} = q_0 \mathbf{V} \times \mathbf{B}$$

where **F** is the force, q_0 is a positive charge, **V** is the velocity of the charge, and **B** is the magnetic field.

The force **F** will always be at a right angle to the plane formed by **V** and **B.** The right-hand rule will specify the orientation of the force with respect to the plane. The right-hand rule states that if the index finger is held in the direction of the velocity (**V**) and the middle finger in the direction of the flux (**B**), the thumb will indicate the direction of the force (**F**).

The second right-hand rule is associated with the magnetic field surrounding a current-carrying conductor. The right-hand rule is: *If the current is grasped by the right hand and the thumb points in the direction of the current, the fingers will curl around the wire in the direction of the magnetic field **B**.*

3. Explain Faraday's law.

ANSWER: Faraday provided the most important law in electromagnetism. It is given by

$$V = \frac{d\Phi_B}{dt}$$

where V is the voltage, N is the number of turns in the coil, and $\frac{d\Phi_B}{dt}$ is the rate of change of the flux. If the flux is changing at a high rate inside the coil, the induced voltage in the coil will be large.

Note: Faraday's law also has another explanation. If the voltage applied across the coil is varying with time [this is always the case in alternating current (AC) circuits], it will induce a flux inside it according to the same equation.

4. Explain the power factor (PF).

ANSWER: The PF is defined as

$$\text{PF} = \cos \theta$$

where θ is the angle between the total current and the voltage. The value of the PF represents the ratio of the real current to the total current. In other words, the PF indicates the nature of the load. The ratio of the magnitude of the resistance to the magnitude of the inductance can be found from the angle θ. The penalties imposed by the utilities are also based on the PF.

INTRODUCTION TO MACHINERY PRINCIPLES (CHAP. 27)

1. How can a generator act as a motor?

ANSWER: A generator is exactly the same machine as a motor. The only difference between them is that the flow of energy in the machine is reversed. A generator converts mechanical energy (in the form of torque and speed) delivered by a prime mover (e.g., a turbine) to electrical energy. A motor converts electrical energy to mechanical energy. While a generator is synchronized to a grid (i.e., it is operating in parallel with hundreds of other generators), if the torque delivered by the prime mover is interrupted (e.g., if the steam valves to the turbine fail shut), the generator will continue to rotate at the same speed in the same direction. In this mode of operation, it is taking power from the grid to continue to rotate at the same speed. This is called *motoring*. The generator is taking enough power from the grid to overcome the friction and windage losses. The friction losses are caused by the resistance at the bearings. The windage losses are caused by the resistance that the air imposes on the rotor (the drag). The sum of the friction and windage losses for a generator is around 1 to 2 percent of the normal power rating of the machine.

Another example of a generator motoring is provided by the *power reserves application.* In today's society, power reserves must be available to control the frequency on the grid. If a large load is added suddenly to a grid that does not have power reserves, the frequency of the grid would drop. Power reserves are used to prevent the decrease in frequency on the grid. They consist of a hydraulic turbine coupled to a generator. The gate of the penstock (pipe used to supply water to the turbine) is closed to prevent water from reaching the turbine and delivering power to the grid. The generator is synchronized to the grid. It is motoring, by taking power from the grid to continue to rotate at the normal speed. At this stage, the generator is driving the turbine. When a large load is added suddenly to the grid, the frequency starts to drop. At this moment, the gate of the penstock is opened. The water starts to flow in the penstock and hits the buckets of the hydraulic turbine. This generates a torque on the shaft. The flow of energy reverses direction. Power now is delivered to the grid rather than consumed from the grid. This method is used around the world to provide the 3-min power reserve.

2. What is the sum of the torques on the shaft of a turbine generator or a pump motor assembly during normal operation?

ANSWER: The sum of the torques on a shaft is given by Newton's law of rotation:

$$T = J\alpha$$

where T is the sum of the torques on the shaft, J is the moment of inertia of the shaft, and α is the angular acceleration of the shaft (the rate of variation of the shaft speed). During normal operation, the speed of rotation is constant. Thus, $\alpha = 0$. Therefore, $T = 0$.

This indicates that the sum of the torques on a shaft of a machine operating normally is nil. This means that during normal operation, the generator is providing a countertorque on the shaft of equal magnitude to the torque delivered by the prime movers (e.g., turbines). The pump is also providing a countertorque of equal magnitude to the torque delivered by the motor.

3. What will happen when a generator is suddenly disconnected from the grid?

ANSWER: As is explained in question 2 of this section, during normal operation, the generator provides a countertorque of equal magnitude to the torque delivered by the prime movers. However, this torque is in the opposite direction to the torque delivered by the turbine. In other words, the sum of the generator torque and the turbine torque is nil. When a full-load rejection occurs, the circuit breaker connecting the generator to the grid opens suddenly. The countertorque that the generator was exerting on the shaft is eliminated immediately. However, the torque applied by the prime movers is still acting on the shaft. This generates significant acceleration that increases the speed of the shaft very quickly. A mechanism must be used to interrupt the torque delivered by the prime mover as soon as the circuit breaker opens to prevent an overspeed situation that could have serious consequences. A turbine generator assembly relies on the governing system to interrupt the flow of steam to a steam turbine or fuel to a gas turbine when a full-load rejection occurs. The overspeed is normally limited to less than 8 percent. The governing system eliminates the overspeed after a short period of time.

4. Why are the cores used in transformers, generators, and motors made from steel?

ANSWER: Steel has a relative permeability of between 2000 and 7000. Therefore, for a given current, the flux established in a steel core is from 2000 to 7000 times stronger than in a corresponding volume of air. All of the cores in transformers and in the stators and rotors of generators and motors are made from steel to have a higher flux and a higher power rating in the machine.

5. Are all cores laminated?

ANSWER: All the cores in transformers and in the stators and rotors of generators and motors are laminated to reduce eddy currents. The only exception to this rule is large generator rotors. They are made of a single forging. The reason for this is the large electrical, mechanical, and thermal stresses that these rotors experience during normal operation. These rotors are normally more than 30 m long and weigh more than 200 ton. If they were laminated, they will not be able to withstand the significant stresses imposed on them.

TRANSFORMERS (CHAP. 28)

1. Does a transformer have an inrush current?

ANSWER: A transformer has an inrush (starting) current around 12 times greater than the normal current through the transformer. This inrush normally lasts for about 15 cycles of the AC current. This means that one-quarter of a second (15 cycles last one-quarter of a second) after the transformer is started, the current will reach its normal value.

2. What is the arrangement of the windings in a transformer?

ANSWER: The insulation is installed around the core. The low-voltage winding is installed on the core insulation. This is done to reduce the voltage stress on the insulation. The high-voltage winding is installed around the low-voltage winding with spacers in between them. In other words, the low-voltage winding is installed inside the high-voltage winding. This is done to minimize the flux leakage in the transformer.

3. Does the main output transformer of a power plant have an effect on the size of the conductors used in the transmission lines?

ANSWER: The main output transformer of a power plant is normally a step-up transformer. It increases the voltage by at least 10 times. The corresponding decrease in transmission losses is about 100-fold. This significant advantage is still not the main advantage of the main output transformer. The main advantage of this transformer is the ability to reduce the size of the conductors in the transmission lines. When the voltage is increased by 10 times across the transformer, the output current decreases by 10-fold. This allows the use of much thinner conductors in the transmission lines. Therefore, the main output transformer has reduced the copper requirement in the transmission lines significantly and allowed the transmission towers to be located far apart.

4. What are the relationships between the input and output current and voltage of a transformer?

ANSWER: The relationships between the input and output current and voltage of a transformer are

$$\frac{\mathbf{V}_P}{\mathbf{V}_S} = a \quad \text{and} \quad \frac{\mathbf{I}_P}{\mathbf{I}_S} = \frac{1}{a}$$

where, $\mathbf{V}_P$ is the primary voltage, $\mathbf{V}_S$ is the secondary voltage, $\mathbf{I}_P$ is the primary current, and $\mathbf{I}_S$ is the secondary current.

$$a = \frac{N_P}{N_S}$$

where N_P is the number of turns in the primary circuit, and N_S is the number of turns in the secondary circuit. For example, an increase in voltage by 10-fold across the transformer will result in a reduction in current by 10-fold. It is also important to mention that the phasor of the primary voltage $\mathbf{V}_P$ is related to the phasor of the secondary voltage $\mathbf{V}_S$ by a constant ($\mathbf{V}_P = a\mathbf{V}_s$). Therefore, the primary voltage is in-phase with the secondary voltage. Similarly, the primary current is in-phase with the secondary current.

5. Explain the apparent impedance and provide an application for it.

ANSWER: The apparent impedance of the primary is

$$Z'_L = a^2 Z_L$$

where Z_L is the impedance of the load on the secondary side, a is the turns ratio of the transformer [$a = (N_P/N_S)$] and Z'_L is the apparent impedance on the primary side of a load that is located on the secondary side of the transformer. In other words, this is the equivalent impedance of a load that is located on the secondary side of the transformer if it is placed on the primary side of the transformer. For example, a load having an impedance Z_L on the secondary side of the transformer will be equivalent to a load having an impedance Z'_L on the primary side of the transformer.

The concept of apparent impedance is very useful. Without this concept, analysis of systems containing a transformer cannot be done. The impedances should be in one circuit without transformers in between them to allow an analysis to be performed on the system. An application of apparent impedance exists in large generators. The stator core is normally grounded through a single-phase transformer having a high resistance on the secondary side of the transformer. This resistance will have a very large apparent impedance on the primary side of the transformer because the turns ratio a is high ($Z'_L = a^2 Z_L$). Thus, if a ground fault (insulation failure allowing the current in the stator windings to reach the stator core through the failed insulation) occurs, the current going to ground would be small due to the high apparent impedance. In the absence of this impedance, the current going to ground will be very large, leading to a meltdown of the stator core.

6. Does the reactive power have an effect on transmission losses?

ANSWER: The reactive power is supplied to an inductive load to create the magnetic field in it. This power is not consumed in the load. It is only stored in the load in the form of a magnetic field. The reactive power moves back and forth between the load and the power plant every half cycle. Despite the fact that reactive power is not consumed in the load, it does contribute to transmission losses. The reason for this is that the total current flowing in the transmission line between the plant and load is given by

$$\mathbf{I}_T = \mathbf{I}_R + \mathbf{I}_L$$

$\mathbf{I}_R$ is the resistive current; $\mathbf{I}_L$ is the inductive current; and $\mathbf{I}_T$ is the total current. The transmission losses are given by:

$$P_{\text{losses}} = I_T^2 R_{\text{transmission}}$$

where $R_{\text{transmission}}$ is the resistance of the transmission system. Thus, the inductive current increases the transmission losses because it increases the total current.

7. What are the characteristics of reactive power?

ANSWER: Reactive power has the following characteristics:

- It contributes to transmission losses.
- It creates a voltage dip at an industry requiring reactive power. This can only be adjusted by adding capacitor banks at the industry or using synchronous motors in conjunction with induction motors to correct the PF.
- It is difficult to deliver reactive power for long distances because the transmission system itself is inductive.
- It is generated by increasing the excitation current (DC current) of the synchronous generator in the power plant.

8. What are the losses in a transformer?

ANSWER: The losses in a transformer are as follows:

- *Copper losses:* These are the resistive losses in the primary and secondary windings of the transformer. In a three-phase transformer, they are given by

$$\text{Copper losses} = 3\, I_P^2 R_P + 3 I_S^2 R_S$$

where I_P is the primary current
R_P is the resistance in one phase of the primary winding
I_S is the secondary current
R_S is the resistance on one phase of the secondary winding

- *Eddy current losses:* These are resistive losses in the core of the transformer. They appear in the form of heat. They are proportional to the square of the voltage applied to the transformer. All transformer cores are laminated to reduce eddy current losses.
- *Hysteresis losses:* These are caused by the rearrangement of the magnetic domains in the core every half cycle. They appear in the core in the form of heat.

Note: The sum of eddy current losses and hysteresis losses are called *core losses.*

- *Leakage flux.* The leakage fluxes in the primary and secondary windings are ϕ_{LP} and ϕ_{LS}. They are fluxes that pass through one winding only. They are not a part of the mutual flux that links both windings. There is a self-inductance in the primary and secondary windings associated with these leakage fluxes.

TRANSFORMER COMPONENTS AND MAINTENANCE (CHAP. 29)

1. Why is the dew point of nitrogen in a transformer less than −50°C?

ANSWER: Nitrogen is used in a transformer as a buffer gas between the oil and air. It separates outside air (containing water vapor) from the oil. Water vapor has devastating effects on the dielectric (insulation) strength of the oil. For example, one spoonful of water can reduce the dielectric strength of the oil in a large transformer by half. The dew point is the temperature at which the water vapor in the air starts to condense. It varies with the concentration of water vapor in the gas. For example, if the gas is very dry, its dew point will be around −70°C. As the concentration of water vapor in the gas increases, its dew point will increase as well. Thus, the dew point is a measure of the dryness of the gas. In the transformer, we need a very dry gas to prevent contamination of the oil with water vapor. The maximum acceptable dew point is −50°C. In industry, most transformers use nitrogen having a dew point of −70°C.

2. How would electrical faults occur?

ANSWER: The insulation in electrical equipment deteriorates due to the following factors:

- Heat
- Contamination such as dirt, moisture, or oxygen
- Electrical stress
- Mechanical stress and strain

The insulation loses its strength when it deteriorates. As it weakens, it loses flexibility and becomes brittle. It would not be able to resist the mechanical stresses resulting from the magnetic forces, differential temperature expansion, and vibration. The insulation disintegrates causing electrical faults.

3. Why would the forces between the windings increase during a short circuit?

ANSWER: The force acting on a current-carrying conductor placed in a magnetic field **B** is given by

$$F = ILB \sin \theta$$

where I is the current in the conductor; L the length of the conductor in the magnetic field; B is the magnetic field; and θ is the angle between **L** and **B.**

During a short circuit (failure of the insulation between the windings and the core), the current increases significantly (e.g., more than 10-fold) because the impedance exposed to the voltage drops dramatically. The voltage was applied across a high-impedance circuit before the short circuit occurred. Following the short circuit, the voltage becomes applied across the impedance located between the voltage source and ground. This is minimal impedance compared with the circuit impedance. Therefore, the current will increase significantly because it is given by

$$I = \frac{V}{Z}$$

where V is the voltage and Z is the impedance.

When Z decreases, the current will increase. The forces between the windings will increase as a result of increase in current. The bracing of the windings must be able to withstand the forces that occur during a short circuit.

4. How would a transformer fail?

ANSWER: The insulation between the windings and the core is made of Kraft paper. It is one of the best dielectrics known in industry when it is impregnable with good, clean, dry oil. Water has devastating effects on Kraft paper. Most transformers fail due to the presence of water. The water acts as a solvent to dissolve and weaken the paper by destroying its fiber. This results in loosening the windings, and the constant movement of the windings will abrade the paper insulation. A total transformer failure occurs by having a failure in an extremely small amount of the paper in the transformer. Adequate measures must be taken early and promptly to prevent transformer failure. The best solution for this problem involves continuous dehydration of the transformer during normal operation. A less expensive solution involves servicing the transformer every 3 to 5 years.

5. What is the upper moisture limit that should be specified when selecting a transformer?

ANSWER: The aging factor of a transformer is controlled by controlling the amount of moisture in the paper. It is expressed as percent of moisture by dry weight (%M/dw). The upper limit of 0.5%M/dw should be specified when a transformer is selected. If this limit is not specified, the moisture content could be as high as 1.5 to 2.0%M/dw.

6. What are the most important tests for oil in a transformer?

ANSWER: The most important tests for oil in a transformer are

- *Dielectric breakdown strength.* Gives an indication about the water content in the oil.
- *Neutralization (or acid) number (NN).* Detects the concentration of acids present in the oil. The NN increases with time and temperature. Minute amounts of water will enhance the oxidation process and the formation of acids.
- *Interfacial tension (IFT).* Detects the presence of sludge in the oil.
- *Color of the oil.* The change in the oil color provides good indication of the oil condition.

7. When would preventive maintenance be required for oil in a transformer?

ANSWER: Preventive maintenance would be required for an oil having a Meyers Index Number (MIN) lower than 600. For example, the NN is in the range 0.05 to 0.10, and the IFT is in the range 27.1 to 29.9. Deferral of transformer maintenance will lead to inadequate cooling of the windings and possible tripping or explosion of the transformer.

8. What are the methods of dealing with bad oil in a transformer?

ANSWER: There are two options to deal with oil having an MIN lower than 600: replacement or reclamation of the oil. The reclamation process involves these three steps:

1. Dissolving the sludge that was formed on the internals of the transformer
2. Purging the sludge from the transformer
3. Filtering the sludge from the oil to restore it to like-new condition

The sludge deposited on the internal components of the transformer will not be removed when the oil is replaced. Simple replacement will only put new oil in a contaminated container.

There are also problems associated with the handling and disposal of the used oil. The reclamation process is the same regardless of the degree of oil deterioration. The reclamation process is performed in a "closed loop." The oil is heated continuously, filtered through absorbent beds, and recirculated in the transformer. The oil is heated to around 82°C during the process. The hot oil acts as a strong solvent for decay products. The sludge is removed usually by 6 to 10 recirculation cycles. Twenty recirculation cycles may be required to desludge the transformer if it is badly sludged (oil with NN > 0.3 and IFT < 18).

If the transformer is in an extremely sludged condition (NN > 1.5), many separate reclamation/desludging treatments are needed. Replacement of the transformer should be considered at this stage. The reclamation/desludging should be performed before NN exceeds 1.5 and IFT drops below 24.0 to minimize the deterioration of the insulation. The transformer oil can be reclaimed/desludged while the transformer is on-line (energized and in-service).

9. What are the causes of gas formation in the oil of a transformer?

ANSWER: The two main causes of gas formation in the oil of an operating transformer are thermal and electrical disturbances. Heat losses from the conductors and core losses produce gases from decomposition of the oil and solid insulation. Gases are also generated from the decomposition of oil and insulation exposed to arc temperatures. The detection of certain gases generated in the oil is the first indication of a malfunction that may eventually lead to failure if not corrected. Arcing, corona discharge, sparking, overloading, and overheating in the insulation system can result in decomposition of the insulating materials and the formation of gases. The generated gases in the transformer can be found in the oil, in the gas blanket above the oil, or in gas-collecting devices.

10. What is the purpose of the gas detector relay?

ANSWER: Gases are generated by the chemical and electrical phenomena associated with the development of faults in oil-filled transformers. A significant amount of gas is normally formed in the early stage of the fault. The gases that are generated and the air that is expelled from the oil by the fault rises to the top of the transformer and gets collected in a gas relay, which is mounted on the transformer. The gas detector relay gives an early indication of faults in oil-filled transformers. The two types of faults are

1. *Minor faults that result in a slow evolution of gases.* These faults result from the following: local overheating, defective insulation structures, ground faults, and short circuit turns.
2. *Major faults that result in a sudden increase in pressure.* These faults are normally caused by flashover between parts.

The relay will detect both types of faults.

11. How does the gas relay operate?

ANSWER: The gas relay has two sections:

1. *A gas accumulation chamber located at the top of the relay.* It consists of an oil chamber with a gas bleeder needle valve. A float in the oil chamber operates a magnetic oil gauge with an alarm switch.
2. *A pressure chamber at the bottom of the relay.* It has two parts. (a) An oil chamber at the rear of the relay, which is connected to the transformer by a pipe entering the back of the relay; and (b) a test valve located at the base, which is used for making operation checks. Sensitive brass bellows separate the first section from the second.

There is an air chamber in the front of the relay. It contains stops for the bellows to prevent overtravel, a flexible diaphragm, and a microswitch. When the bellows move, they compress the air behind the diaphragm. This action activates the microswitch, which is fastened to the diaphragm. When arcing occurs in the transformer, it causes a rapid evolution of gas in the oil. A pressure wave is generated through the oil. The wave will reach the relay through the pipe. It will compress the flexible bellows. The air in the chamber is compressed by the displacement of the bellows. Since the air cannot pass quickly through the bypass valve, it forces the flexible diaphragm to close the contact of the trip switch. This action disconnects the transformer.

It is essential to find the fault when the pressure contact trips the transformer. The fault should be corrected before putting the transformer back in service.

12. What is the purpose of the unit service transformer (UST)?

ANSWER: The loads inside the unit (e.g., pumps, compressors, lighting, heating, etc.) are supplied through the UST. Its rating is about 6 to 7 percent of the rating of the main output transformer. The gross power of the unit is the total power delivered by the generator. The net power of the unit is given by

Net power of unit = gross power of unit − (power consumed by the auxiliary loads inside the power plant through the UST) .

13. What is the purpose of the station service transformer (SST)?

ANSWER: Power is supplied from the grid to the station through the SST. This power is used for these purposes:

- For certain auxiliary loads inside the station (available in some stations only)
- For all the loads required to restart the units when all the generators are shut down

14. Why are half the auxiliary loads inside some power plants supplied through the SST and the remaining half through the UST?

ANSWER: Some power plants supply half their auxiliary loads through the SST and the remaining half through the UST. This arrangement was considered to be more reliable than supplying all the loads through the SST or UST separately. The reason for this is that if the tie breaker (normally open) connecting the two 4-kV buses in the unit (the one supplied from the SST and the one supplied from the UST) failed to close following an impairment of the power supply to one of these buses, half the auxiliary loads within the unit will still be supplied with power. Since essential loads inside the unit use fully redundant equipment (e.g., two 100 percent pumps, each is capable of meeting the requirements of the system) where each equipment is supplied from a different bus, the impairment of one of the buses supplied through the SST or UST will not result in impairment of any of the essential loads inside the unit. However, if all the loads inside the unit were supplied through one transformer (e.g., through the UST), the failure of this power supply could impair all the essential loads if the tie breaker providing backup supply through the second transformer (e.g., the SST) failed to close.

Despite the enhanced reliability in power supply obtained by supplying half the auxiliary loads through the SST and the remaining half through the UST, modern power plants have opted to supply all the power required for their auxiliary loads through the UST. The incoming power through the SST is used as a backup. The reason for this change is the desire to prevent the effects of the disturbances (such as voltage or frequency fluctuations) that occur normally on some grids from reaching the plant auxiliary loads.

15. How would the unit auxiliary loads be affected if the power supply through the SST and the UST were impaired?

ANSWER: When the power supplied through the SST and the UST becomes impaired, some stations rely on standby generators (gas turbines) that start within 3 min to supply the auxiliary loads inside the station. However, some loads, such as the following, cannot be interrupted for 3 min:

- The computer systems that control the station
- The lubricating oil flow to the bearings of the turbines and generator
- The oil flow to the hydrogen seals of the generator
- The cooling water flow inside the generator stators bars

These loads are normally supplied from a large battery bank if they require DC power (e.g., the emergency lubricating oil pumps, emergency hydrogen seal oil pumps, and emergency generator stator cooling pumps). However, for loads requiring AC power (e.g., the computer systems), the power is provided from an uninterruptible power system (UPS). It consists of a large battery bank feeding the loads through an inverter, which converts DC power to AC power.

16. Would the breaker connecting the power plant to the grid open immediately following a turbine trip?

ANSWER: A turbine trip is defined as an internal problem to the plant (e.g., high vibration that leads to shutting the unit by closing the steam valves in a steam turbine or the fuel valve in a gas turbine). A turbine trip is different from a load rejection, which occurs when the breaker connecting the unit to the grid opens due to a disturbance in the grid. There are two types of turbine trip. The first type includes trips on high vibration and low oil pressure in the bearings. Following this type of a turbine trip, the breaker connecting the unit to the grid remains closed. This is done to prevent the turbine generator shaft from overspeeding. When this breaker is closed, the shaft speed cannot increase beyond the operating speed. This is due to the fact that the frequency in the three phases of the generator stator is maintained at 60 Hz by the grid. Thus, when the breaker is closed, the generator is coupled magnetically to the grid, and the speed of the shaft cannot change. This feature is advantageous in this type of a turbine trip because the shaft is prevented from overspeeding and causing possible damage to the machine.

However, the breaker remains closed for a short period of time following the closure of the steam valves (in a steam turbine) or fuel valves (in a gas turbine). The reason for this is that following the closure of the steam valves or fuel valves, the torque developed by the turbine drops significantly. Below a specified value of the torque (e.g., 2 percent of the torque developed during full-load operation in a steam power plant), the generator starts motoring. At this stage, the generator acts as a motor by consuming power from the grid to continue rotating at the some speed. As soon as reversed power (power flow from the grid to the unit) is detected, the breaker opens.

In summary, the breaker connecting the unit to the grid remains closed following a turbine trip on some parameters (e.g., high vibration or low bearing oil pressure). This is done to prevent overspeed of the shaft that would occur if the breaker opened as soon as the steam valves (in a steam turbine) or the fuel valve (in a gas turbine) closed. When reverse power occurs shortly after, the breaker opens. However, the breaker connecting the unit to the grid opens immediately following a turbine trip on other parameters (e.g., a short circuit in the generator). This is done to prevent further damage to the generator that would occur if the breaker remained closed.

17. Would the breaker connecting the power plant to the grid open if the grid voltage drops below its normal value?

ANSWER: The breaker connecting the power plant to the grid does not open if the grid voltage drops below its normal value. The power plant will continue to operate despite a reduction in the grid voltage. If a power plant were allowed to trip when the grid voltage drops slightly below its normal value, the grid voltage will drop further due to elimination of the reactive power delivered by the power plant. This will have a cascading effect on all power plants, leading to collapse of the grid voltage. However, a drop in grid voltage below the normal value can have serious effects on the power plant. If the grid voltage drops by 10 percent below the normal value, the voltage in the generator stator will drop by the same percentage. Thus, the voltage supplied by the UST will also drop by the same amount.

Therefore, all the auxiliary loads inside the power plant will be supplied by power having a 10 percent lower voltage than normal. The motors driving the pumps, compressors, and other components inside the power plant will start to pull higher current to make up for the reduction in voltage. This will result in tripping the motors on overload. Thus, a reduction of grid voltage beyond 10 percent of the normal value will result in impairment of some auxiliary systems inside the power plant. This will lead to a plant trip. Most grids establish a scheme of load shedding when the grid voltage starts to fall. The scheme includes shedding of loads in areas away from the power plant as soon as the grid voltage starts to fall. This is done to help maintain the grid voltage around its normal value near the power plant to avoid losing the power generated by the power plant due to a reduction in grid voltage.

18. Does the power plant trip on underfrequency in the grid?

ANSWER: The generator in the power plant trips on underfrequency in the grid. Normally, the trip is set around 57.5 Hz in locations where the grid frequency is 60 Hz.

AC MACHINE FUNDAMENTALS (CHAP. 30)

1. What is the difference between a motor and a generator?

ANSWER: Motors are identical to generators. The only difference between them is the flow of energy. A motor converts electrical energy to mechanical. A generator converts mechanical energy to electrical.

2. Why is the conversion of energy in motors and generators occurring between mechanical energy and real power only?

ANSWER: The conversion of energy in motors and generators occurs between mechanical energy and real power only because the reactive power is not consumed. It is only stored in the machine to magnetize it. The real energy is consumed in a motor. It is converted to mechanical energy (torque × speed) and heat losses. Reactive energy is generated in a generator by increasing the field current (DC) in the rotor of the generator. It does not require mechanical energy to generate it.

3. What is the main principle of operation of an AC induction motor?

ANSWER: The main principle of operation of an AC induction motor is that a three-phase set of currents, each of equal magnitude and differing in phase by 120°, is supplied to the stator (armature) of the induction motor. The three currents produce a rotating magnetic field of constant magnitude ($\mathbf{B}_S$) that rotates inside the stator at a speed ω, where ω equals

3600 r/min for a two-pole motor. ω is called the synchronous speed of the motor. The rotating magnetic field crosses the bars of the rotor. It induces currents in the rotor bars that produce a magnetic field ($\mathbf{B}_R$) that rotates inside the stator. The interaction between the magnetic field produced by the three currents in the stator ($\mathbf{B}_S$) and the magnetic field produced by the currents flowing in the rotor ($\mathbf{B}_R$) generates the torque that drives the rotor.

4. What is the main principle of operation of an AC synchronous generator?

ANSWER: The main principle of operation of an AC synchronous generator is described as a constant-magnitude DC current, known as the *field of the generator,* is supplied to the rotor. It creates a magnetic field ($\mathbf{B}_R$) of constant magnitude that rotates at the same speed as the rotor. For a two-pole generator, the speed of rotation of the rotor is 3600 r/min. The rotating magnetic field crosses the bars of the stator. It induces a three-phase set of currents, each of equal magnitude and differing in phase by 120°. The three currents flowing in the stator produce a magnetic field of constant magnitude ($\mathbf{B}_S$) that rotates inside the stator at the same speed as the rotor. The interaction between the two magnetic fields $\mathbf{B}_S$ and $\mathbf{B}_R$ generates a countertorque on the shaft that is equal to the driving torque generated by the prime mover (e.g., turbine). In other words, the countertorque developed by the generator is in the opposite direction to the torque developed by the prime mover. Thus, during normal operation, the sum of the torque developed by the prime mover and the countertorque developed by the generator is nil. The generator operates at constant speed. If there were a mismatch between the torque that is developed by the prime mover and the countertorque that is developed by the generator, the shaft would accelerate or decelerate.

SYNCHRONOUS GENERATORS (CHAP. 31)

1. Are the cores in the stator and rotor of all generators laminated?

ANSWER: The cores in the stator and rotor of small generators are laminated. However, the rotor of large generators is not. It is made of a single forging. The reason for this is that large rotors are more than 20 m long and weigh more than 150 ton. They are subjected to significant electrical, mechanical, and thermal stresses during normal operation. They cannot be laminated. The stator of a large generator is laminated.

2. What are the advantages and disadvantages of each excitation method?

ANSWER:

1. *Slip rings and brushes (static excitation).* The DC current is normally rectified from a stationary AC power. It is fed to a slip ring on the generator shaft through carbon brushes. The main advantage of this method is that the time required to change the terminal voltage by varying the excitation (magnitude of DC current entering the rotor) is very short. The response time to change the terminal voltage using this method is around 0.2 s. This feature is essential for stabilizing the power delivered by the generator. This type of excitation is required for most generators having a rating larger than 50 MW. The main disadvantage of this method is the high maintenance requirement of the slip rings and brushes. The brush holders are replaced on power. This is a cumbersome process for the maintainers having electrical hazard.
2. *Brushless excitation.* This method involves the use of an exciter, which is a small generator mounted along the same shaft as the main generator. Its rating is around 7 percent

of the main generator. The DC current is supplied to the stator of the exciter through a stationary three-phase rectifier. The magnetic field of the DC current supplied to the stator of the exciter creates three-phase AC currents in the rotor (armature) of the exciter. The three-phase AC currents in the rotor of the exciter are rectified by rotating the three-phase rectifier to produce the DC current to the rotor of the main generator. The main advantage of this method is the elimination of the slip rings and brushes. Thus, the maintenance requirements for this method are much lower than the slip-rings-and-brushes method. However, the response time required to change the terminal voltage of the main generator is around 0.5 to 1.0 s. This is much larger than the response time required by the slip-rings-and-brushes method. Thus, this method is not recommended for most generators having a rating larger than 50 MW if they are used to supply power to a grid. However, this method can be used for a large generator operating alone (islanding method).

3. *Brushless excitation including a pilot exciter—permanent magnet (PMG).* This method uses an exciter and a pilot exciter mounted along the same shaft as the main generator. The pilot exciter is a very small generator having PMGs mounted on its rotor. When the shaft rotates, the magnets induce a three-phase AC voltage in the stator of the pilot exciter. A three-phase rectifier is used to rectify the three-phase alternating current to a DC current that is fed to the stator of the exciter. A variable resistance is installed in the stator of the exciter. It is used to vary the DC current entering the stator of the exciter to vary the voltage at the terminals of the main generator. The DC current flowing in the stator of the exciter induces three-phase ac voltages in the rotor of the exciter. A three-phase rotating rectifier mounted on the shaft rectifies the three-phase AC currents generated at the rotor of the exciter to provide the DC current required by the rotor of the main generator. The advantages of this method are the following:

   - *The elimination of the requirement of an outside power supply to provide excitation.* Thus, this method is used commonly in applications where it is difficult to provide an independent power supply to deliver excitation current.
   - *The elimination of slip rings and brushes.* Thus, the maintenance requirements of this method are much lower than the slip-rings-and-brushes method.

   However, the response time required to change the terminal voltage of the main generator is around 0.5 to 1.0 s. This is much larger than the response time required by the slip-rings-and-brushes method. Thus, this method is not recommended for generators having a rating of 50 MW if they are used to supply power to a grid. However, this method can be used for large generators operating alone (islanding method).

4. *Field-flashing excitation.* It consists of a DC current supplied from a battery bank through slip rings and brushes to the rotor of the main generator. It has all the features of the slip-rings-and-brushes method. However, the duration of this excitation method is very short. It is used until the voltage is established at the terminals of the generator. At this time, the field current (excitation) is obtained by rectifying AC power from the terminals of the generator. This method is used in applications where it is difficult to provide excitation from an outside source. It is also used sometimes with PMG excitation. In these applications, it provides excitation when the PMG fails.

3. What is the mechanical speed of rotation of a synchronous generator?

ANSWER: The mechanical speed of rotation of a synchronous generator or motor is the same as the synchronous speed (speed of rotation of the magnetic fields inside the stator). In other words, a synchronous machine does not have a slip (difference between synchronous speed and mechanical speed) like an induction machine (generator or motor). Thus, the mechanical speed of rotation or synchronous speed is related to the number of poles and stator electrical frequency by

$$f_e = \frac{n_m P}{120}$$

where f_e = electrical frequency, Hz
n_m = rotational speed of rotor for synchronous machines (rotational speed of the magnetic field) , r/s
P = number of poles

A synchronous generator rotor, for example, must rotate at the following speeds to generate electricity at 60 Hz:

Number of poles	Mechanical speed of rotation (synchronous speed), revolutions per minute (r/min)
2	3600
4	1800
6	1200
8	900

4. What are the applications of low-speed generators?

ANSWER: Low-speed generators are normally used with hydraulic turbines. This is due to the fact that hydraulic turbines operate more efficiently at low speed. For example, the rotational speed of a hydraulic turbine generator is 240 r/min when it has 30 poles.

5. What are the parameters that affect the magnitude of the generator voltage?

ANSWER: The magnitude of the voltage induced in one phase of the generator stator is given by

$$E_A = K\phi\omega$$

where E_A = the open-circuit voltage (the voltage induced in the stator when the generator breaker is open)
K = constant that depends on the generator size and design
ϕ = is the flux in the machine [it is mainly a function of the DC current flowing in the rotor (excitation)]
ω = the rotational speed in rad/s.

It is clear that the induced voltage increases with increasing excitation. It is also important to mention that E_A has a maximum value. It corresponds to the value of the flux reached when the core is saturated (the domains have all lined up). A further increase in current beyond the value that has produced saturation in the core will not increase the flux or the voltage.

6. Does the mechanical power delivered by the turbine (torque × speed) generate the reactive power in the generator?

ANSWER: The mechanical power delivered by the turbine generates only the real power that is delivered by the generator. It does not contribute toward generating reactive power. The reactive power is generated by increasing the excitation (DC current) in the rotor.

7. What are stray losses?

ANSWER: Stray losses are caused by induced currents in areas of the generator where they cannot be used in a useful manner. Stray losses appear in the generator in the form of heat. Flux screens are installed at both sides of the stator to reflect the flux back to the core to reduce stray losses.

8. What is the efficiency of a typical large generator?

ANSWER: The efficiency of a typical large generator is around 98.5 to 99 percent. It normally uses hydrogen as a coolant to reduce the windage losses (rubbing of hydrogen against the rotor).

9. Why are large generators cooled by hydrogen?

ANSWER: All generators having a rating lower than 20 MW are cooled by air. Generators having a rating of between 20 and 100 MW are cooled by air or hydrogen. Most generators having a rating higher than 100 MW are cooled by hydrogen. However, there are a small number of generators having a rating up to 250 MW, cooled by air.

- *Hydrogen is 14 times lighter than air.* Thus, the windage losses (i.e., the friction that the gas exerts on the rotor while it is rotating) of hydrogen are significantly lower than air.
- *Hydrogen's thermal properties are significantly better than those of air.* Hydrogen removes more heat from the rotor and stator than air. Thus, generators cooled by hydrogen operate cooler than the ones cooled by air. They have a longer lifetime and significantly fewer problems during normal operation than the generators cooled by air. Serious problems (e.g., winding overheating and short-circuit faults) have occurred in generators having a rating larger than 100 MW when they are cooled by air.
- *Hydrogen is an inert gas.* It does not oxidize or corrode the metals inside the generator.
- *Hydrogen extinguishes sparks and fire created by arcing.* Air is a fire hazard when used as a coolant inside generators.

However, a volumetric mixture of hydrogen and oxygen in the range of 4 to 76 percent can be explosive. Numerous explosions such as the Hindenburg and the shuttle Challenger have occurred because of this mixture. Oil seals normally seal hydrogen at both ends of the generator. Failure of these seals can lead to an explosion inside the power plant.

10. What are the modes of operation of a generator?

ANSWER: The generator can operate in two different modes: *islanding* and *synchronized.* In the islanding mode, the generator operates independently from the grid. This mode of operation is used commonly on ships, in remote locations, islands, or inside industries that do not rely on power from the grid. In this mode of operation, the governing system (controlling the steam flow to the turbine or the fuel flow to a gas turbine) controls the speed of the shaft (i.e., the frequency of the power generated). The power developed by the generator is controlled by virtue of controlling the speed. In other words, an increase in load will increase the countertorque developed by the generator on the shaft. The governing system detects the decrease in the speed of the turbine generator shaft. It opens the steam valves further (for a steam turbine) or fuel valve (for a gas turbine) to restore the speed (and hence the frequency) to its normal value.

In a synchronized mode of operation, the generator operates in parallel with hundreds of other generators. The system supplied by these generators is called the *grid.* The voltage and frequency across the grid are uniform.

This mode of operation has the following advantages:

- The power supplied from the grid has higher reliability than power supplied from one generator.
- The generator will be able to operate at its 100 percent rating most of the time. This is a more efficient mode of operation than islanding, which requires cyclic operation.

In islanding mode, the load at 2:00 A.M. could be around 20 percent of the load at 6:00 P.M. The load also varies with the season and ambient temperature.

The synchronized mode of operation, however, has the following disadvantages:

- Any transient occurring on the grid will affect all generators.
- The power delivered to the grid experiences some oscillations. Power system stabilizers are required on generators larger than 10 MW to stabilize the power that is generated.

11. What is the effect of a load increase on a synchronous generator operating alone (islanding mode)?

ANSWER: As explained in question 10, an increase in load supplied by a synchronous generator requires an increase in the mechanical power (torque × speed) delivered by the turbine to the generator. The governing system will increase the steam flow to a steam turbine or fuel flow to a gas turbine to restore the speed and hence, the frequency of the power delivered by the generator. However, the increase in load has additional effects on the generator. The following is a summary of these effects:

- The terminal voltage of the generator will drop slightly if the load is resistive.
- The terminal voltage of the generator will experience a greater drop if the load is inductive.
- The terminal voltage of the generator will increase if the load is capacitive.

Since most loads are either resistive or inductive, the terminal voltage of the generator will decrease. The automatic voltage regulator (AVR) is used to restore the terminal voltage of the generator.

12. What is the AVR of a synchronous generator?

ANSWER: The AVR is a system used to maintain the terminal voltage of a synchronous generator at the required value. It consists of a closed feedback control system that monitors the variation in terminal voltage of the generator. When the terminal voltage drops, it increases the field current entering the rotor (excitation) to restore the voltage to its desired value. The AVR varies the DC field current by varying a resistor in the circuit. The AVR includes a controller having a proportional-integral-derivative (PID) algorithm. It provides the required adjustment in excitation to restore the terminal voltage to the desired value without causing oscillations or instabilities in the voltage. The AVR normally has two automatic channels and one manual channel. If one automatic channel fails, the second automatic channel picks up the control of the AVR in a bumpless manner. If both automatic channels fail, the operator can adjust the excitation manually and continue operation.

13. What are the conditions required to synchronize a generator to a grid?

ANSWER: The conditions required to synchronize a generator to a grid are as follows:

- The generator must have the same voltage as the grid.

- The frequency of the generator must be slightly higher (e.g., 0.05 Hz) than the frequency in the grid.
- The A phase of the generator must have the same phase angle as the A phase in the grid. In other words, both A phases must be in-phase with each other.
- The phase sequence of the generator must be the same as the grid. In other words, the A, B, and C phases of the generator must be connected to the corresponding phases in the grid. Serious problems have occurred when a B phase of the generator was connected inadvertently to a C phase in the grid. The phase sequence confirmation is required during commissioning of the generator.

14. What is the speed droop of a turbine generator governing system?

ANSWER: The governing system is a closed feedback control system. It relies on a measurement of shaft speed to make adjustments in the opening of the steam valves in a steam power plant or fuel valve for a gas turbine to match the operating speed of the turbine generator with the desired setpoint. During turbine run-up, the no-load speed setpoint of the governing system, which represents the desired speed, is increased to a higher value than the actual speed of the turbine generator. The governing system calculates the difference between the no-load speed setpoint and the actual speed of the turbine generator. This difference is called the *error*. The governing system increases the opening of the steam valves in a steam power plant or the fuel valve in a gas turbine to eliminate the error. When the error is eliminated, the no-load speed setpoint is increased further. This sequence of events continues until the operating speed is reached. At this stage, the no-load speed setpoint matches the actual speed of the turbine generator. The unit is synchronized to the grid at the operating speed. There is no load delivered by the unit immediately following synchronization. The no-load speed setpoint corresponds to 100 percent of its value, which is the operating speed.

In a steam power plant, the steam flow required to reach the full operating speed of the turbine generator is around 2 percent of the steam flow required when the unit is at 100 percent load. This steam flow is required to overcome the friction at the bearings and windage losses (rubbing of hydrogen gas against the rotor of the generator). In a gas turbine, the fuel flow required to reach the full operating speed is around 60 to 67 percent of the fuel flow required at 100 percent load. This fuel flow is required to rotate the compressor at the operating speed and overcome the friction at the bearings and windage losses. The load can be increased following synchronization by increasing the no-load speed setpoint beyond 100 percent. Since the generator is synchronized to the grid, its speed cannot increase. The grid determines the frequency in the three phases of the generator stator (60 Hz in North America). This ensures that the rotor continues to rotate at the operating speed as long as the unit is synchronized to the grid (i.e., the breaker connecting the unit to the grid is closed). The no-load speed setpoint is typically increased to 104 percent. This corresponds to 100 percent load in a steam power plant or a gas turbine. The 4 percent above 100 percent is known as the *speed-drooping characteristic* of the turbine generator governing system. It should be noted that in a steam power plant, the governing valves controlling the steam flow to the turbine open from 2 to 100 percent when the no-load speed setpoint increases from 100 to 104 percent. In a gas turbine, the fuel valve opens from 67 to 100 percent when the no-load speed setpoint increases from 100 to 104 percent. In both cases, the load delivered to the grid increases from 0 to 100 percent. It is also important to note that there is normally a linear variation between the speed-drooping characteristic and the load delivered by the unit. Following are the loads delivered at the various no-load speed setpoints:

No-load speed setpoint	Load delivered to the grid
100%	0
101%	25%
102%	50%
103%	75%
104%	100%

15. What is the voltage-reactive power-drooping characteristic of a synchronous generator?

ANSWER: The terminal voltage of the generator drops when an inductive load is added to it. Thus, the terminal voltage of the generator decreases with increasing reactive power delivered by the generator. The AVR increases the excitation (DC currents into the rotor) to deliver the reactive power required and restore the terminal voltage to its setpoint. The magnitude of decrease in terminal voltage as the reactive power delivered by the generator increases is known as the *voltage-reactive droop characteristic.*

16. What are the consequences of synchronizing a generator to a grid when the frequency of the generator is slightly less than the grid frequency?

ANSWER: When a generator having a slightly lower frequency than the grid (i.e., the rotating speed of the turbine generator is slightly lower than the normal operating speed) is synchronized to the grid, it will operate as a motor rather than a generator. It consumes real power to continue rotating at the same speed. Most generators trip on reverse power (i.e., when the generator is operating as a motor). This situation can be avoided by synchronizing the generator to the grid when its frequency is slightly higher than the frequency in the grid. This ensures that the generator comes on-line delivering rather than consuming power. A block load of around 5 percent of the total load is normally applied to the generator as soon as it is synchronized to ensure that it does not act as a motor.

17. What is the capability diagram of a synchronous generator?

ANSWER: The capability diagram of a synchronous generator outlines the limits on real and reactive power that a generator can deliver. The real and reactive power limits of the generator are determined by the heat limits in the stator and rotor, respectively. Thus, the generator should always be operated within the limits specified on the capability diagram to prevent any damage from occurring.

GENERATOR COMPONENTS, AUXILIARIES, AND EXCITATION (CHAP. 32)

1. What is copper dusting?

ANSWER: Copper dusting occurs in the rotor of a synchronous generator when it is operated for extended periods of time at low speed (between 6 and 30 r/min). The turbine generator is normally operated at low speed following a shutdown by a turning gear to prevent *sagging* and *hogging* of the turbine generator shaft. Sagging occurs when the hot metal of the turbine generator shaft sags when it is left stationary for many hours. Hogging occurs when the hot gases in the upper half of the turbine cause the upper half of the turbine generator shaft to expand more than the lower half. Each of these phenomena creates an unbalance in the turbine generator shaft leading to vibration in the machine.

The main cause of copper dusting is abrasion between the copper windings in the rotor and insulation inside the slots of the rotor. This abrasion normally occurs when the contents (copper winding and insulation) of the rotor slots move inside the slots while the machine is being operated on turning gear. This abrasion does not occur during normal operation. This is due to the fact that the copper windings expand axially and radially when their temperature increases during normal operation. The content of the slots is also pushed against the wedges by centrifugal forces during normal operation. Thus, the content of the slots does not move during normal operation. However, when the machine is cold following a shutdown, the copper windings contract. The contents of the slots move inside the slots when the machine is operated on turning gear (at low speed), causing abrasion of the windings and resulting in copper dusting.

Copper dusting can have serious detrimental effects on the rotor, causing short circuits and overheating inside the rotor. Copper dusting can be minimized by limiting the duration of operating the turbine generator on turning gear.

2. How does an interturn fault in the rotor windings manifest itself?

ANSWER: An interturn fault in the rotor windings will cause the current in the rotor windings to bypass the turn where the fault exists. This will create an uneven temperature distribution in the rotor due to variations in current in different sections of the windings. The uneven temperature distribution in the rotor will cause unbalance in the rotor leading to high vibrations.

3. What is the critical speed of a turbogenerator?

ANSWER: Every component has a natural frequency. The component will vibrate at this frequency when struck by an object. For example, the string of a guitar will vibrate at a specific frequency when struck. This is called the *natural frequency* of the string. Turbine generators, pump motor assemblies, and so on also have a natural frequency. If the forcing frequency (the speed of the shaft) coincides with the natural frequency of the assembly, resonance (significant vibrations) will occur. Serious damage (due to rubbing of the moving blades with the stationary blades) can occur to a turbogenerator during resonance. The critical speed of an assembly is the rotational speed at which resonance occurs. Some turbogenerators have more than one critical speed below the operating speed. All turbogenerators have critical speeds above the operating speed. During start-up of a turbogenerator, the rotor is accelerated at a higher rate across the critical speeds to avoid having resonance and damage to the turbine generator.

4. What are the differences between axial- (thrust-) type and radial-type hydrogen seals?

ANSWER: The axial-type (also known as thrust-type) hydrogen seal has a rotating ring, mounted on the shaft, rubbing against a stationary ring. There is an oil flow between the rings, which are mounted concentrically with the shaft. The seal is established in a perpendicular plane to the shaft. This design has a significant disadvantage due to the fact that it must accommodate the axial growth of the shaft. The axial growth (between cold and hot state) of the shaft from the thrust bearing to the inboard bearing (the bearing facing the turbine) is around 3.2 to 3.6 cm (1.25 to 1.4 in), while the axial growth of the shaft from the thrust bearing to the outboard bearing (the bearing located on the other side of the turbine) is from 3.6 to 3.8 cm (1.4 to 1.5 in). The seal relies on springs to accommodate the growth in the shaft. This makes the seal prone to failure and leakage.

The radial-type seal relies on two rings mounted around the shaft. The seal is established in this design between the rings and the shaft (along the shaft). The growth of the shaft is not accommodated by springs. This makes the seal more reliable. More than 90 percent of generators use radial-type seals.

5. Are there any problems encountered with the cooling water system of the generator stator bars?

ANSWER: Large generators rely on demineralized cooling water to remove the heat from the stator bars. The current flowing in the bars of a large generator exceeds 15,000 A. The water flows through thin channels inside the bars. An oxide layer can build up inside the channels due to poor water chemistry. This reduces the flow, resulting in a higher temperature at the outlet. This problem can be rectified by flushing the channels with a mild acid. This technique can be implemented on-line and off-line (during an outage).

6. Why is carbon dioxide used in a generator?

ANSWER: Generators that use hydrogen as a coolant rely on carbon dioxide (CO_2) as a buffer gas. Air cannot be used to purge the hydrogen out of the generator because hydrogen and oxygen form an explosive mixture when the volumetric concentration of hydrogen is between 4 and 76 percent of the mixture. Carbon dioxide is used to purge the hydrogen, and air is used to purge the CO_2 to prevent an explosion inside the generator.

INDEX

ABOUT THE AUTHOR

Philip Kiameh, M.A.Sc., B.Eng., P.Eng., D.Eng., teaches at the University of Toronto. During the past twelve years, he taught certified courses in power generation, electrical equipment, power plant engineering, industrial instrumentation, and modern control systems. In May 1996, Mr. Kiameh was awarded the first "Excellence in Teaching" award by the University of Toronto. He received his engineering degree from Dal-Tech (formerly, Technical University of Nova Scotia) "with distinction" and completed his graduate studies at the University of Ottawa. He performed research on power generation equipment with Atomic Energy of Canada Limited (AECL) at their Chalk River and Whiteshell Laboratories. Mr. Kiameh also worked in the power plants of Ontario Power Generation (formerly, Ontario Hydro) for over eighteen years where he was responsible for the operation and maintenance of different power plant systems.